Battle Angel Alita Paperback volume 2 is a work of fiction. Names, characters, places, and incidents are the products of the author's imagination or are used fictitiously. Any resemblance to actual events, locales, or persons, living or dead, is entirely coincidental.

A Kodansha Comics Trade Paperback Original
Battle Angel Alita Paperback volume 2 copyright © 2016 Yukito Kishiro
English translation copyright © 2021 Yukito Kishiro

Published in the United States by Kodansha Comics, an imprint of
Kodansha USA Publishing, LLC, New York.

Publication rights for this English edition arranged through
Kodansha Ltd., Tokyo.

First published in Japan in 2016 by Kodansha Ltd., Tokyo,
as *Battle Angel Alita* volume 1-2.

ISBN 978-1-64651-258-4

Printed in the United States of America.

www.kodansha.us

9 8 7 6 5 4 3 2 1
Translation: Stephen Paul
Lettering: Scott O. Brown, Evan Hayden
Editing: Ajani Oloye, Alejandro Arbona
Kodansha Comics edition cover design by Phil Balsman

Publisher: Kiichiro Sugawara

Director of publishing services: Ben Applegate
Associate director of operations: Stephen Pakula
Publishing services managing editors: Alanna Ruse, Madison Salters
Production managers: Emi Lotto, Angela Zurlo
Logo © Kodansha USA Publishing, LLC

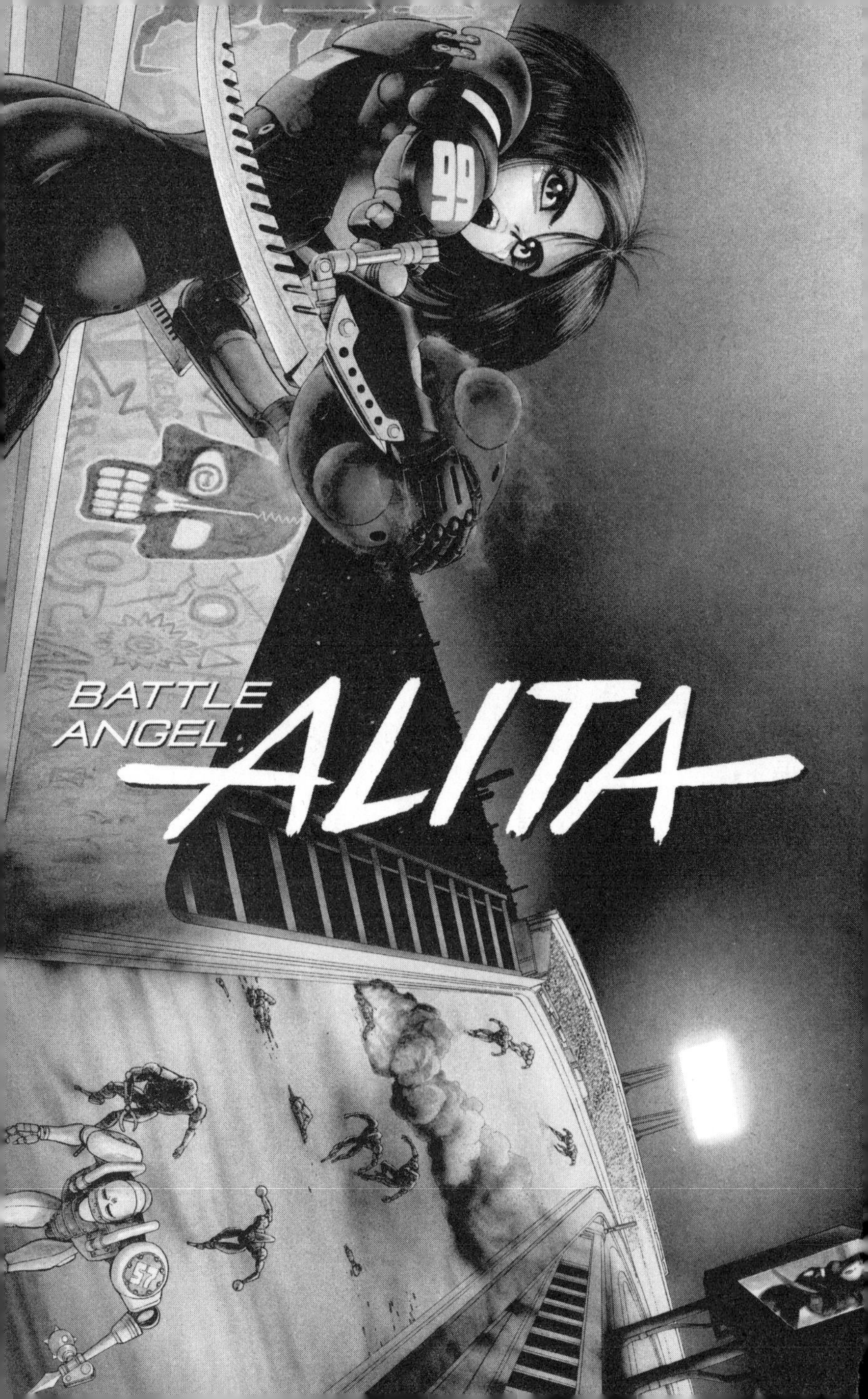
BATTLE
ANGEL
ALITA
99
57

C O N T E N T S

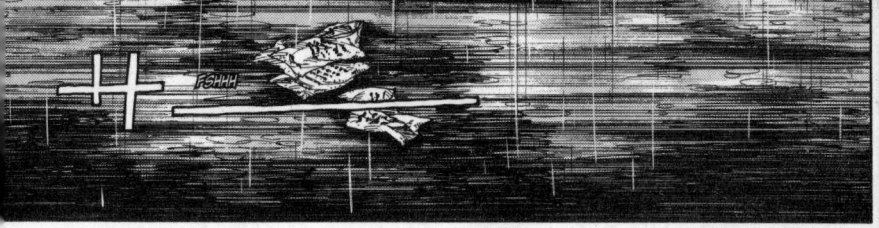

TODAY'S LATEST BOUNTY UPDATES

ZZT

Bounty info is available here…

ZZT
ZZZT

ZZT

PRINT
NUMBER
7

INSERT
CHIP
1 0

PRINT
OUT
DATA

DNA.CODE

CRIMINAL NUMBER:3491625C7
NAME: YUGO
CRIMINALITY:VERTEBRAL COLUMN ROBBER
AND
BRAIN MURDER
ARMS: FIRE BOTTLE
BODY: NON CYBORG
DRUG USAGE: NONE

NOTE: WOUNDED IN THE LEFT SHOULDER

PRICE: ₵ 80'000.
INFORMANT ₵ 5000

…where Hunter-Warriors can print out the relevant details.

3

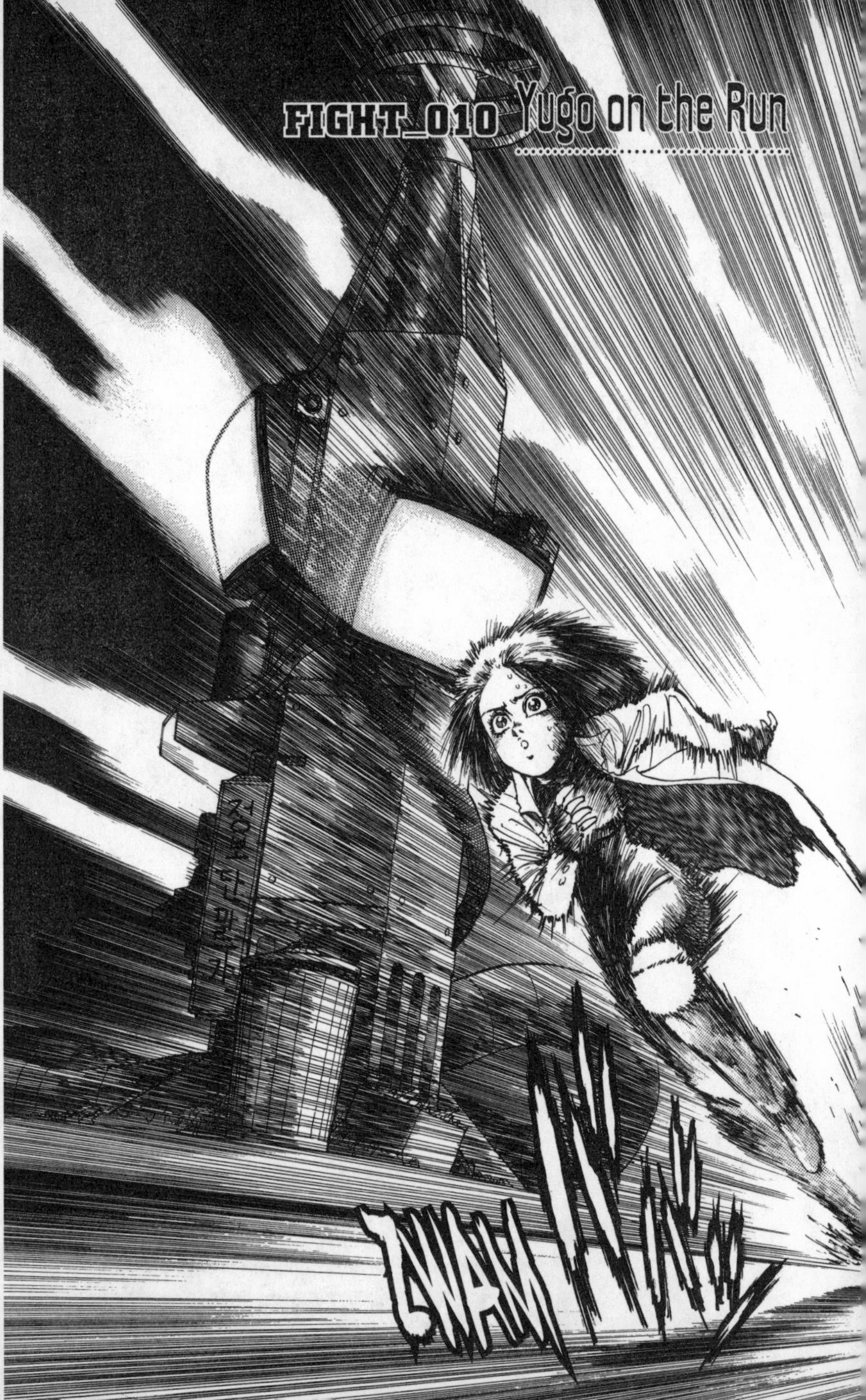
FIGHT_010 Yugo on the Run

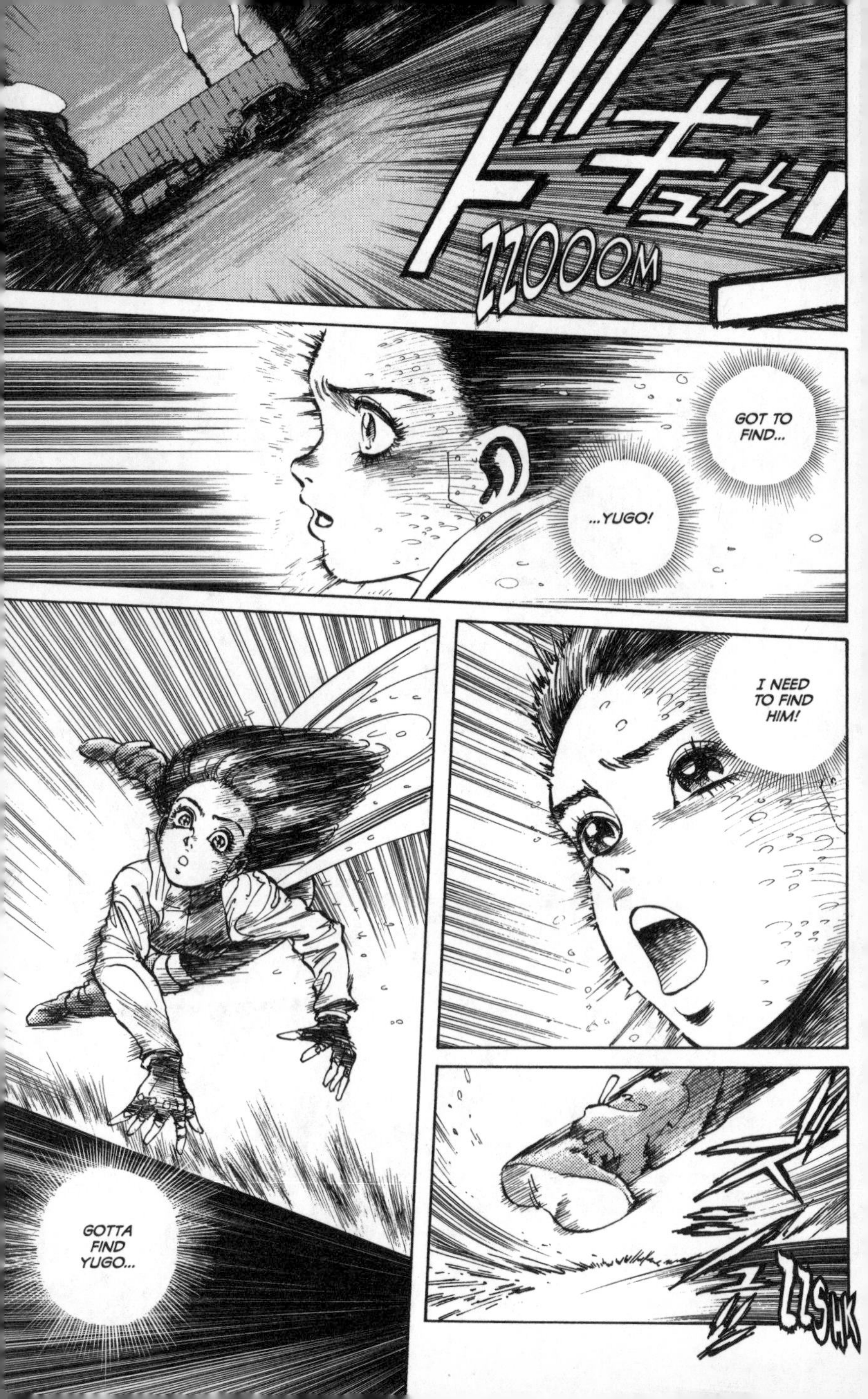
ZZOOOM
GOT TO FIND...
...YUGO!
I NEED TO FIND HIM!
ZZSHK
GOTTA FIND YUGO...

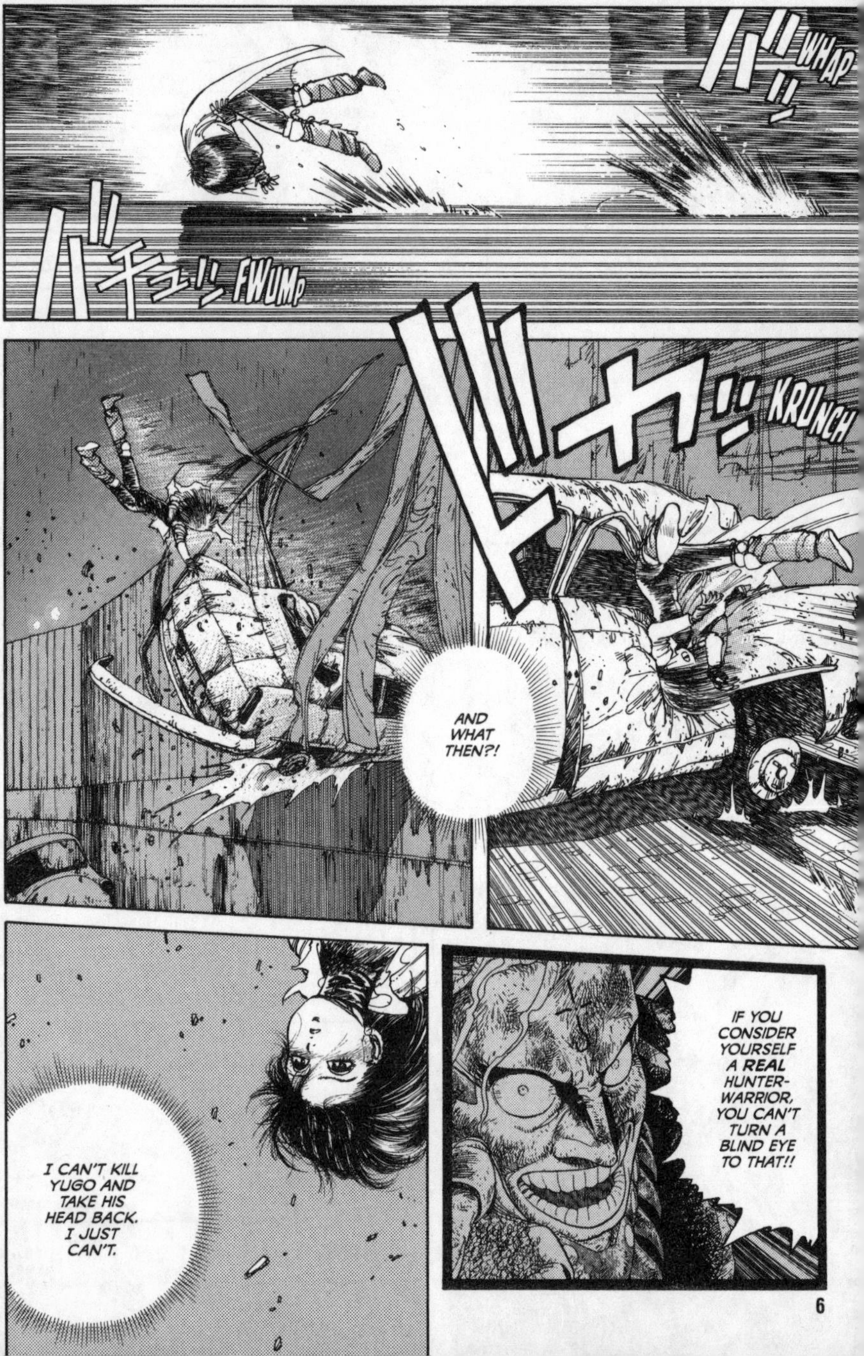
WHAP
FWUMP
KRUNCH
AND WHAT THEN?!
IF YOU CONSIDER YOURSELF A REAL HUNTER-WARRIOR, YOU CAN'T TURN A BLIND EYE TO THAT!!
I CAN'T KILL YUGO AND TAKE HIS HEAD BACK. I JUST CAN'T.

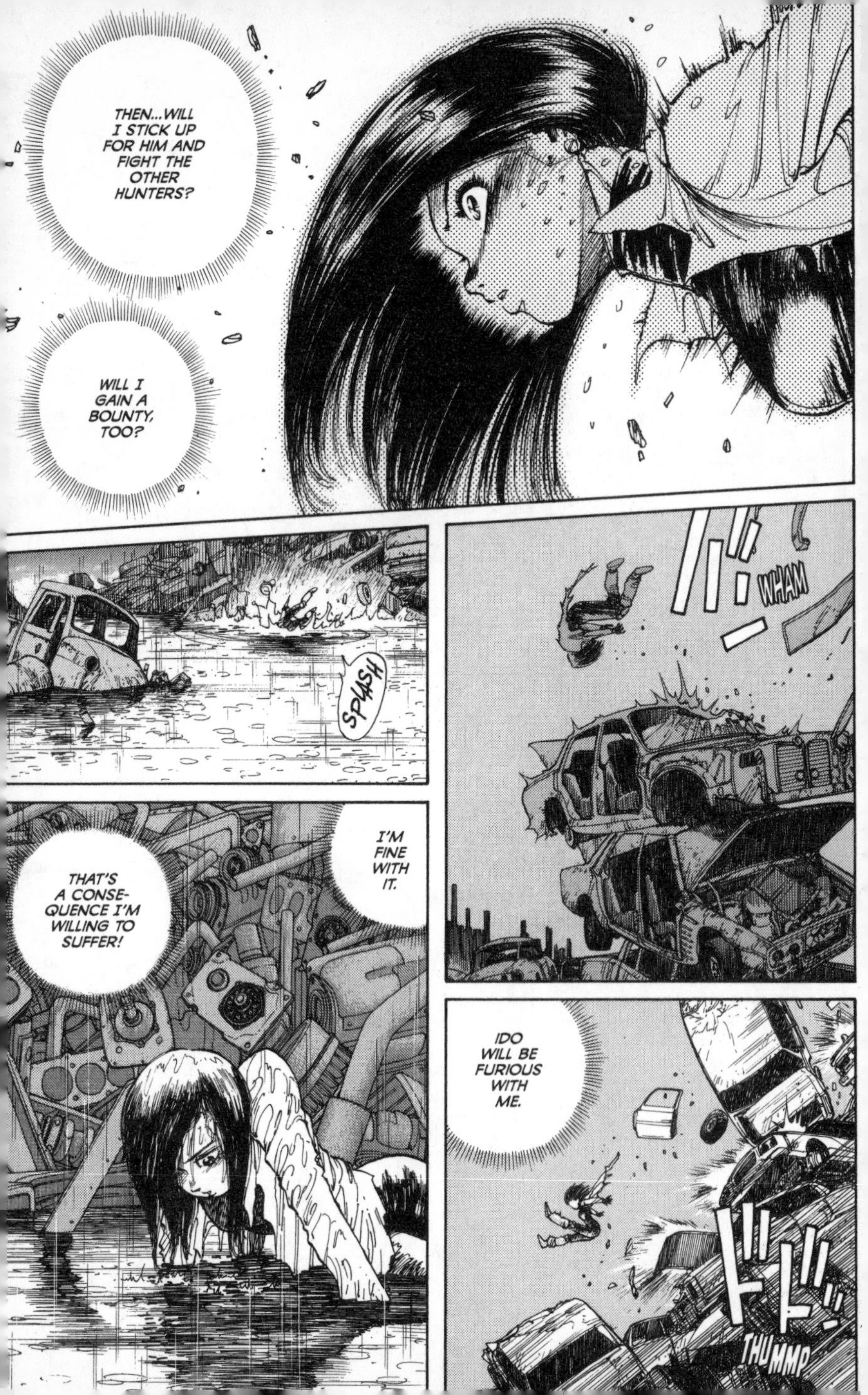
THEN...WILL I STICK UP FOR HIM AND FIGHT THE OTHER HUNTERS?
WILL I GAIN A BOUNTY, TOO?
WHAM
IDO WILL BE FURIOUS WITH ME.
THUMMP
SPLASH
I'M FINE WITH IT.
THAT'S A CONSEQUENCE I'M WILLING TO SUFFER!

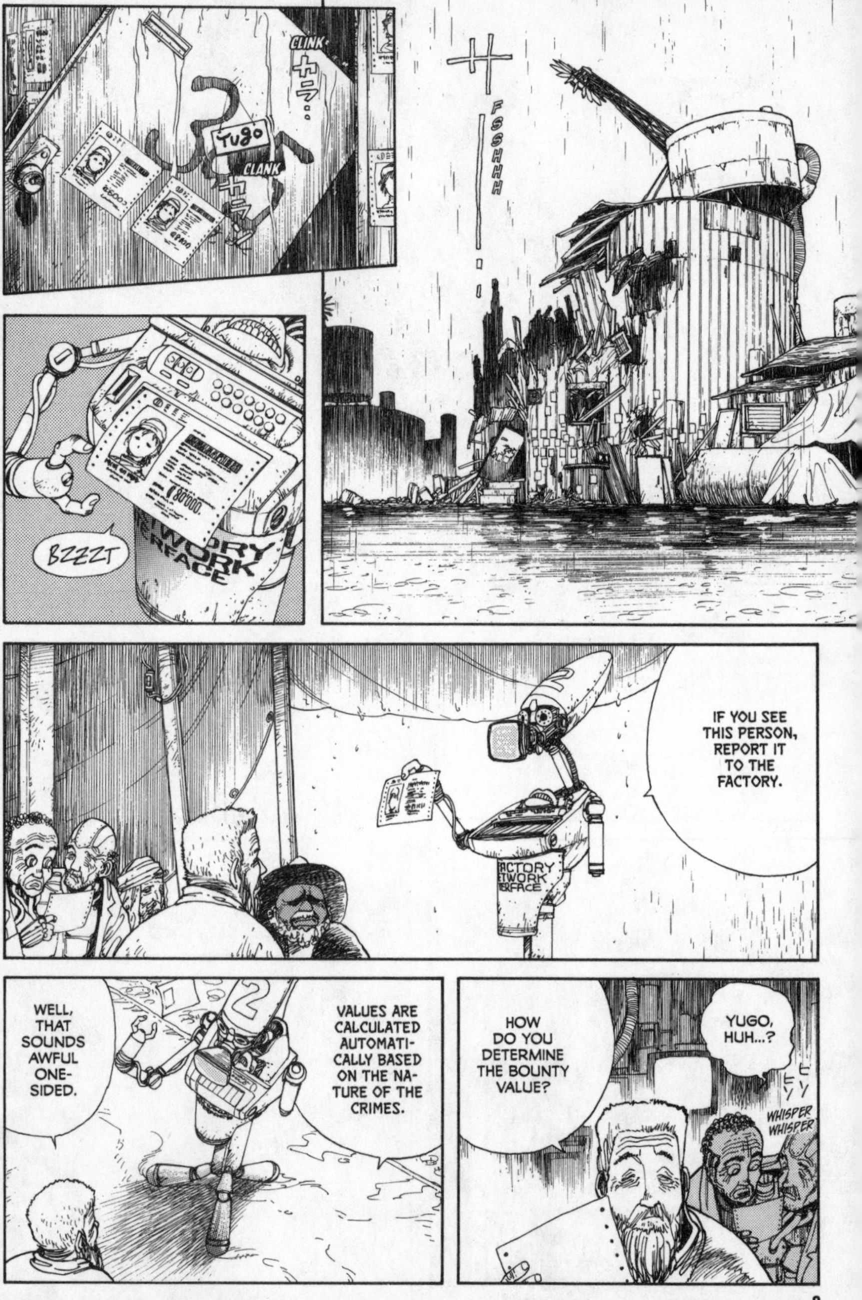
FSSHHH
CLINK
カラ
Tugo
CLANK
カラ
BZZZT
IF YOU SEE THIS PERSON, REPORT IT TO THE FACTORY.
HOW DO YOU DETERMINE THE BOUNTY VALUE?
YUGO, HUH...?
ヒソヒソ
WHISPER WHISPER
VALUES ARE CALCULATED AUTOMATI-CALLY BASED ON THE NA-TURE OF THE CRIMES.
WELL, THAT SOUNDS AWFUL ONE-SIDED.

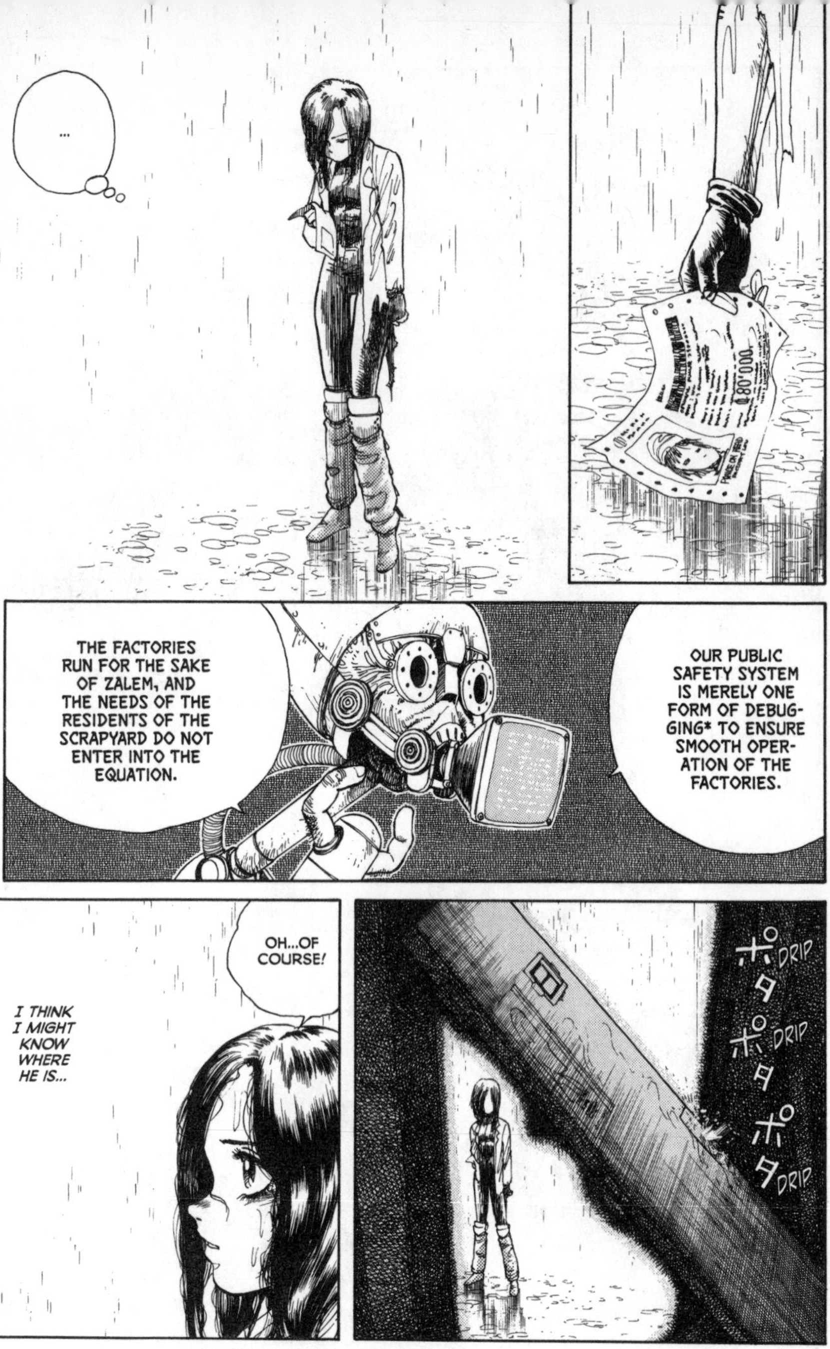
...
OUR PUBLIC SAFETY SYSTEM IS MERELY ONE FORM OF DEBUG-GING* TO ENSURE SMOOTH OPER-ATION OF THE FACTORIES.
THE FACTORIES RUN FOR THE SAKE OF ZALEM, AND THE NEEDS OF THE RESIDENTS OF THE SCRAPYARD DO NOT ENTER INTO THE EQUATION.
DRIP DRIP DRIP
OH...OF COURSE!
I THINK I MIGHT KNOW WHERE HE IS...

***Debugging:** The process of finding and correcting errors (bugs) in computer programs. In this case, he likens criminals to bugs in the system.

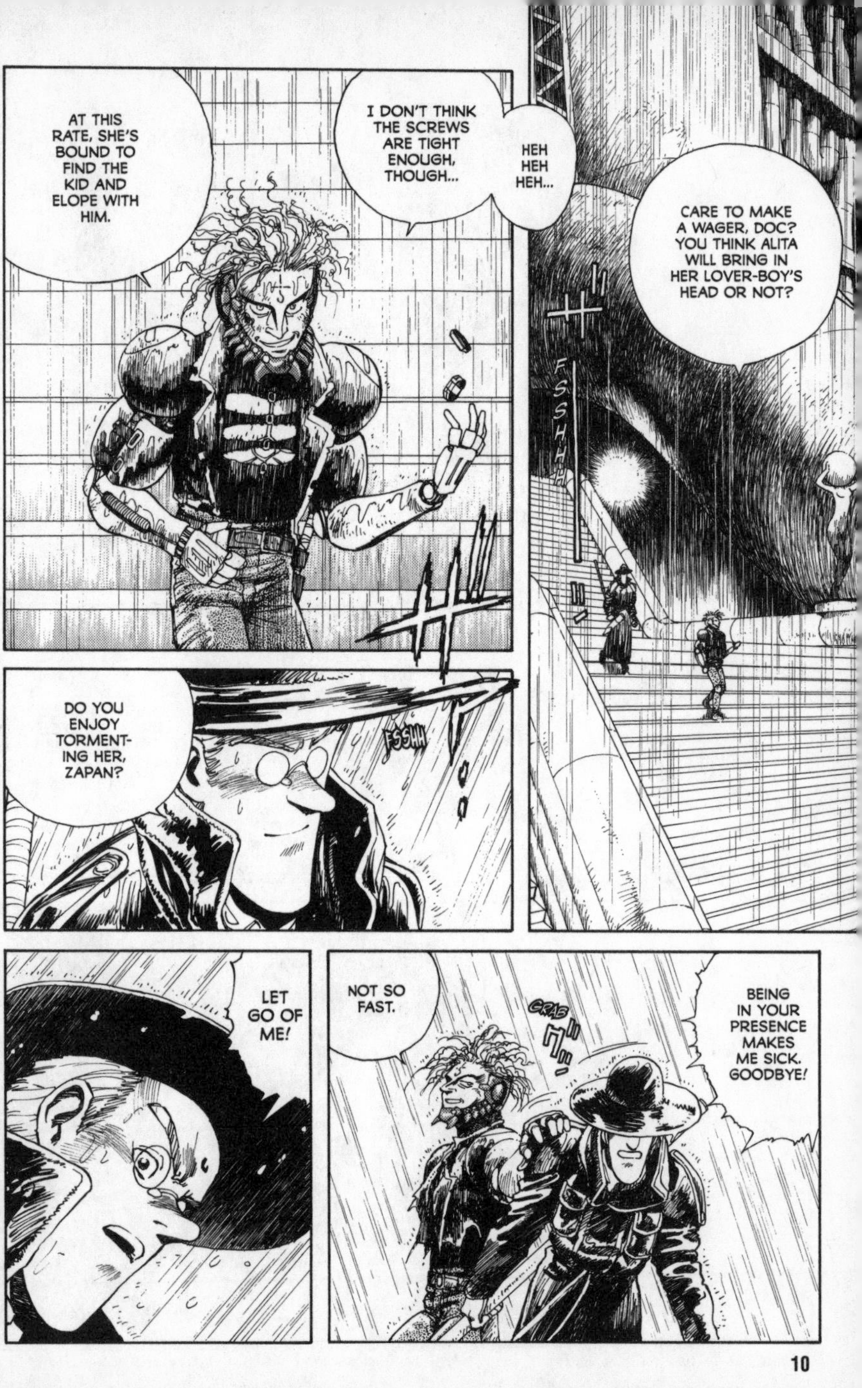
CARE TO MAKE A WAGER, DOC? YOU THINK ALITA WILL BRING IN HER LOVER-BOY'S HEAD OR NOT?
FSSHHH
AT THIS RATE, SHE'S BOUND TO FIND THE KID AND ELOPE WITH HIM.
I DON'T THINK THE SCREWS ARE TIGHT ENOUGH, THOUGH...
HEH HEH HEH...
DO YOU ENJOY TORMENT-ING HER, ZAPAN?
FSSHH
BEING IN YOUR PRESENCE MAKES ME SICK. GOODBYE!
GRAB
NOT SO FAST.
LET GO OF ME!

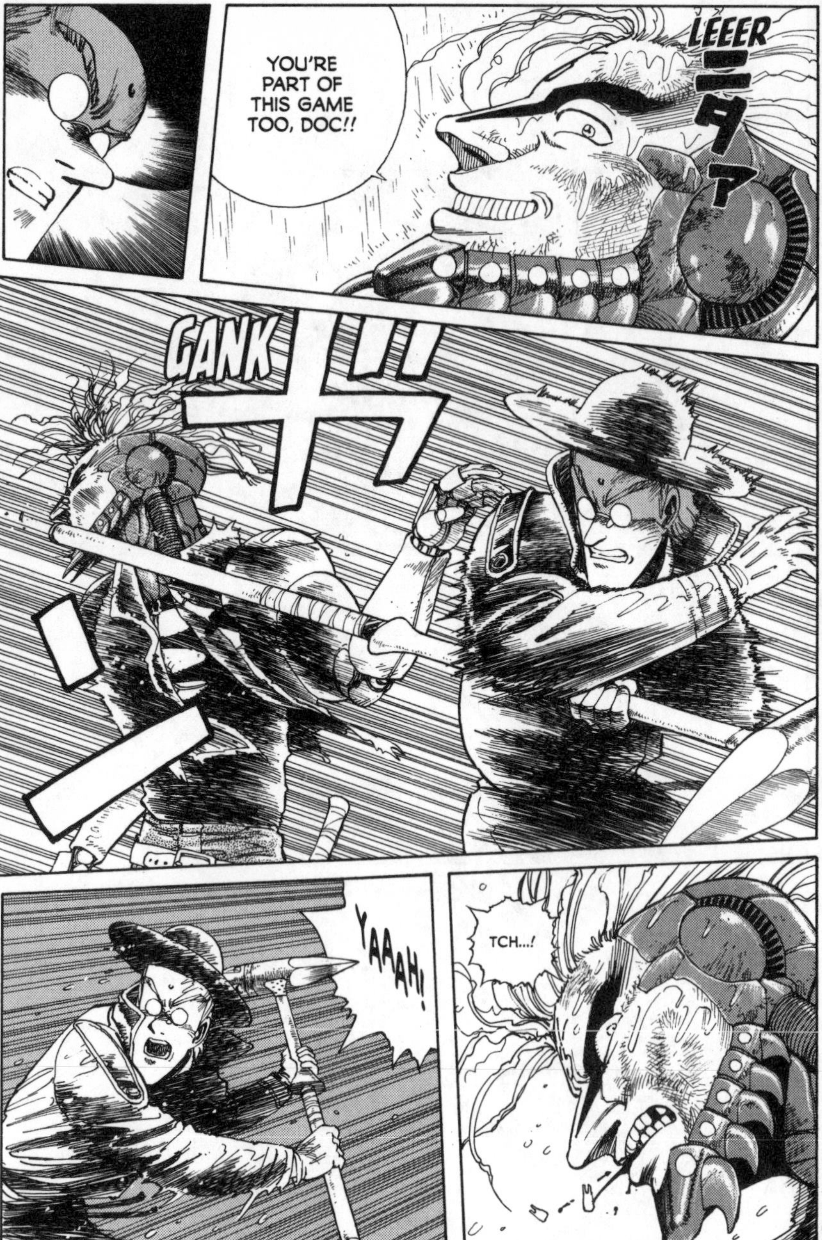
LEEER
ニタァ
YOU'RE PART OF THIS GAME TOO, DOC!!
GANK
TCH...!
YAAAH!

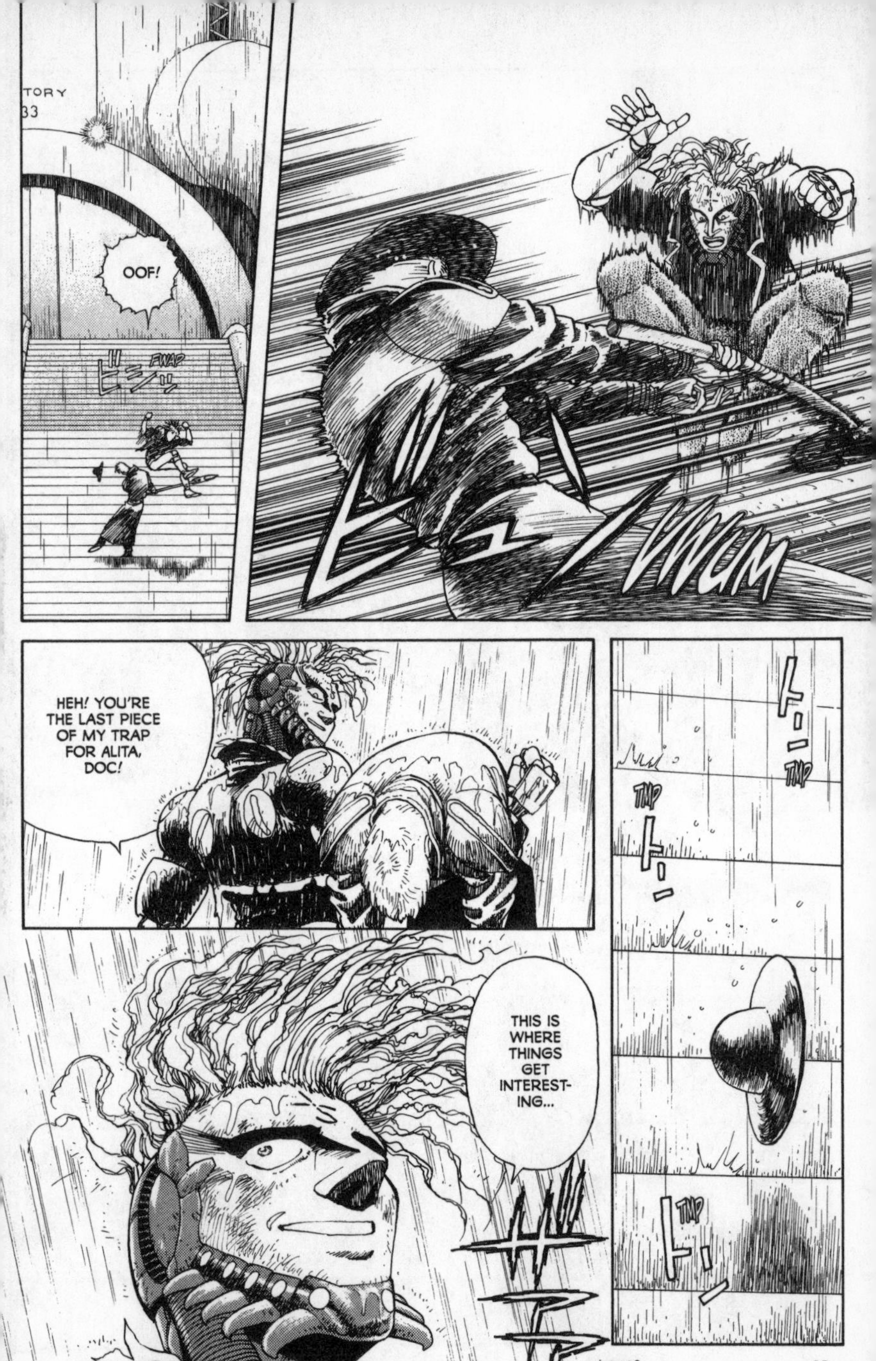
VVUUM
TORY
33
OOF!
FWAP
TMP
TMP
TMP
HEH! YOU'RE THE LAST PIECE OF MY TRAP FOR ALITA, DOC!
THIS IS WHERE THINGS GET INTEREST-ING...
FSHHAAA

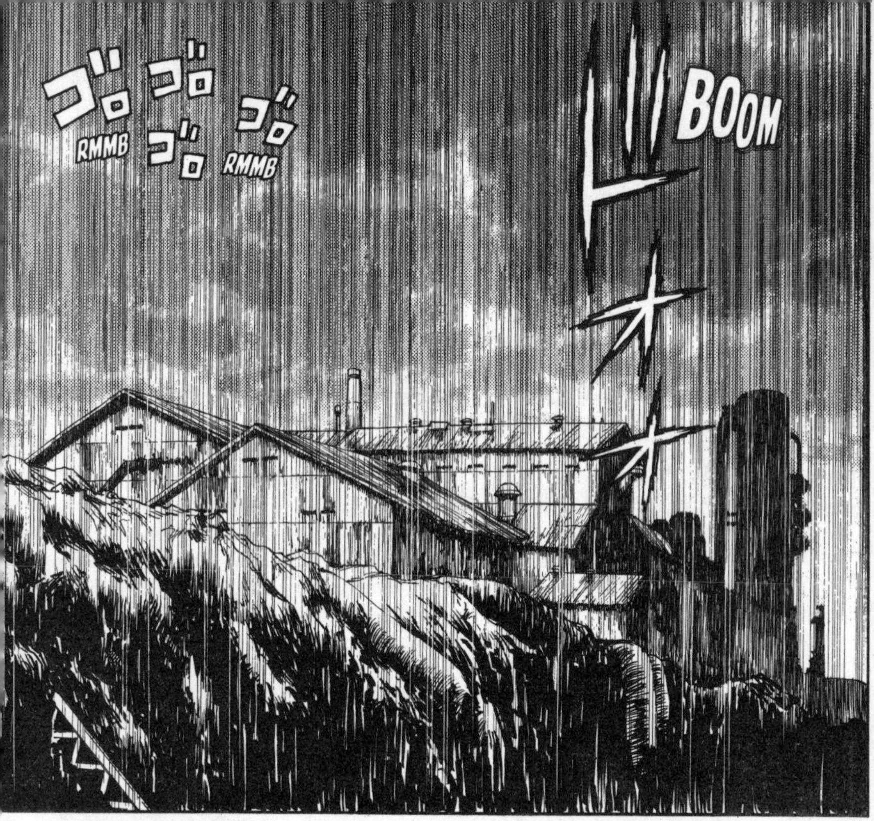
BOOM
RMMB
RMMB
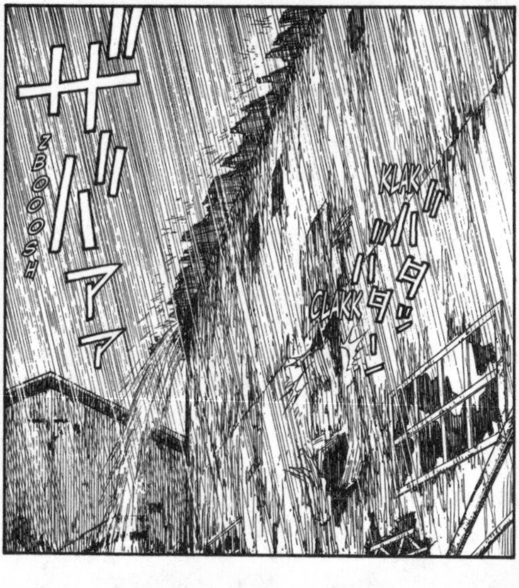
ZBOOOOSH
KLAK
CLAKK
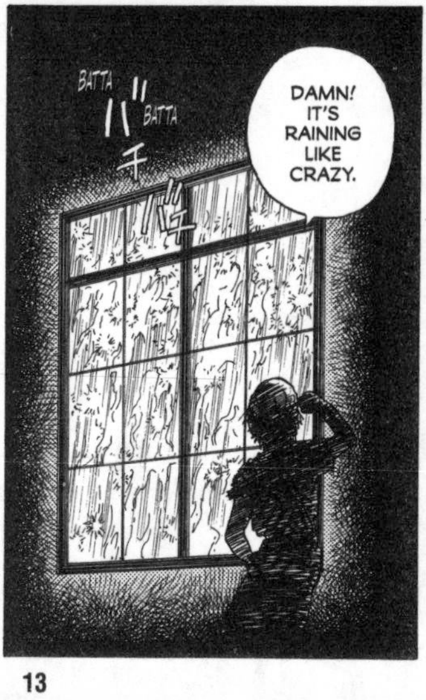
BATTA
BATTA
DAMN! IT'S RAINING LIKE CRAZY.

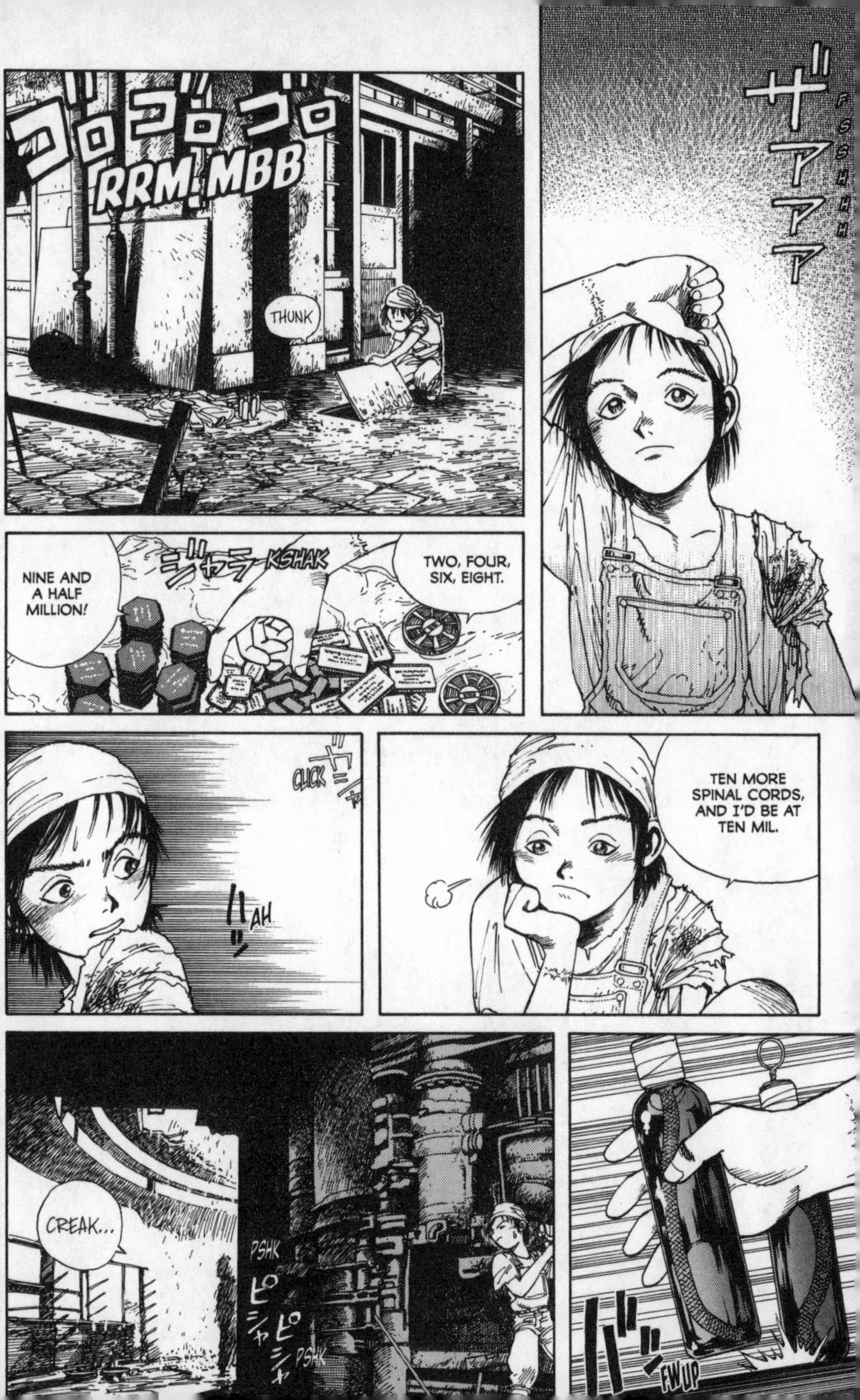
ザァァ
FSHHH
ゴロゴロゴロ
RRM MBB
THUNK
TWO, FOUR, SIX, EIGHT.
ジャラ KSHAK
NINE AND A HALF MILLION!
TEN MORE SPINAL CORDS, AND I'D BE AT TEN MIL.
カチャ CLICK
AH
FWUP
CREAK...
PSHK ピシャ
ピシャ PSHK

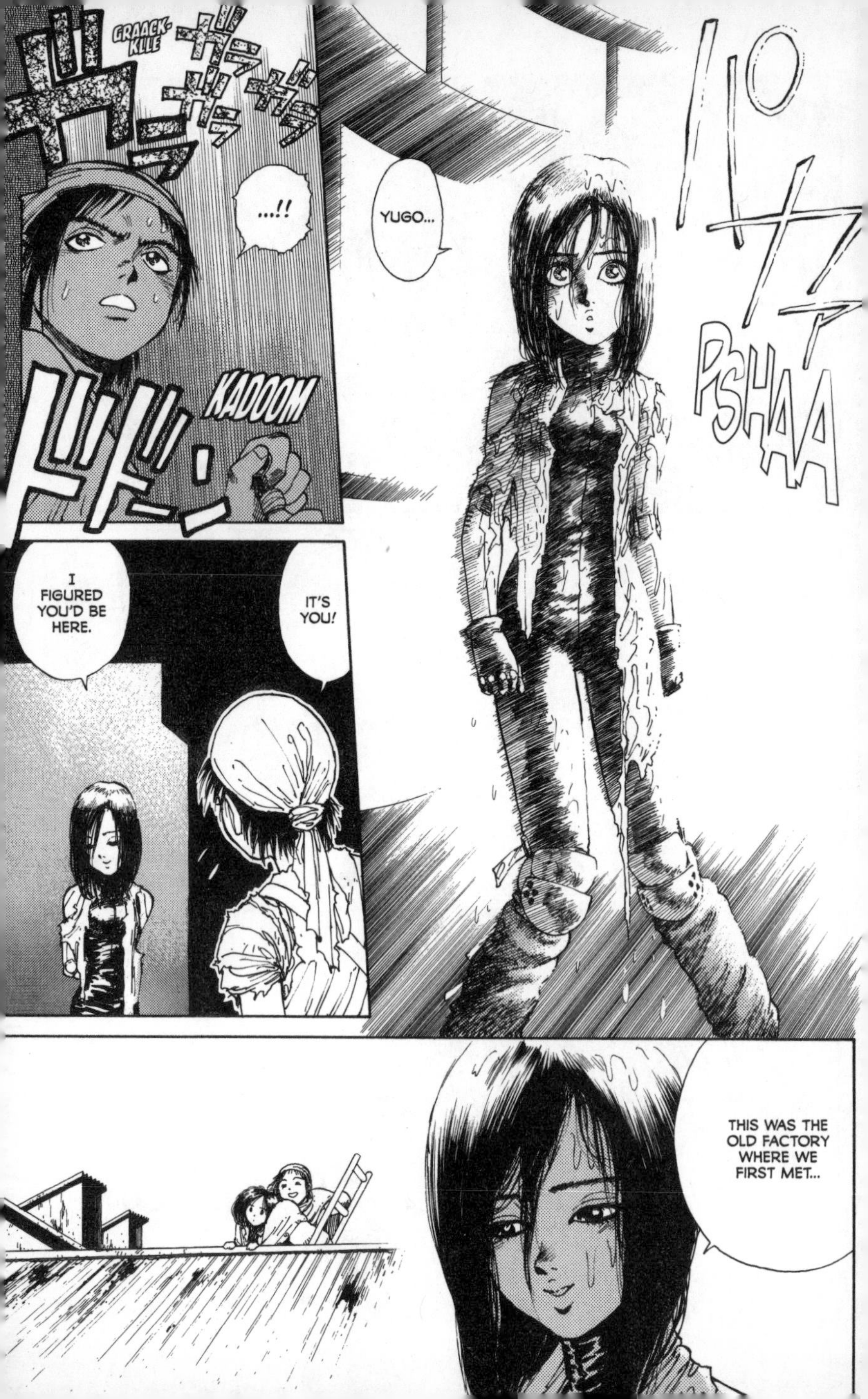

パシャァ
PSHAA
YUGO...
GRAACK-KLLE
...!!
KADOOM
IT'S YOU!
I FIGURED YOU'D BE HERE.
THIS WAS THE OLD FACTORY WHERE WE FIRST MET...

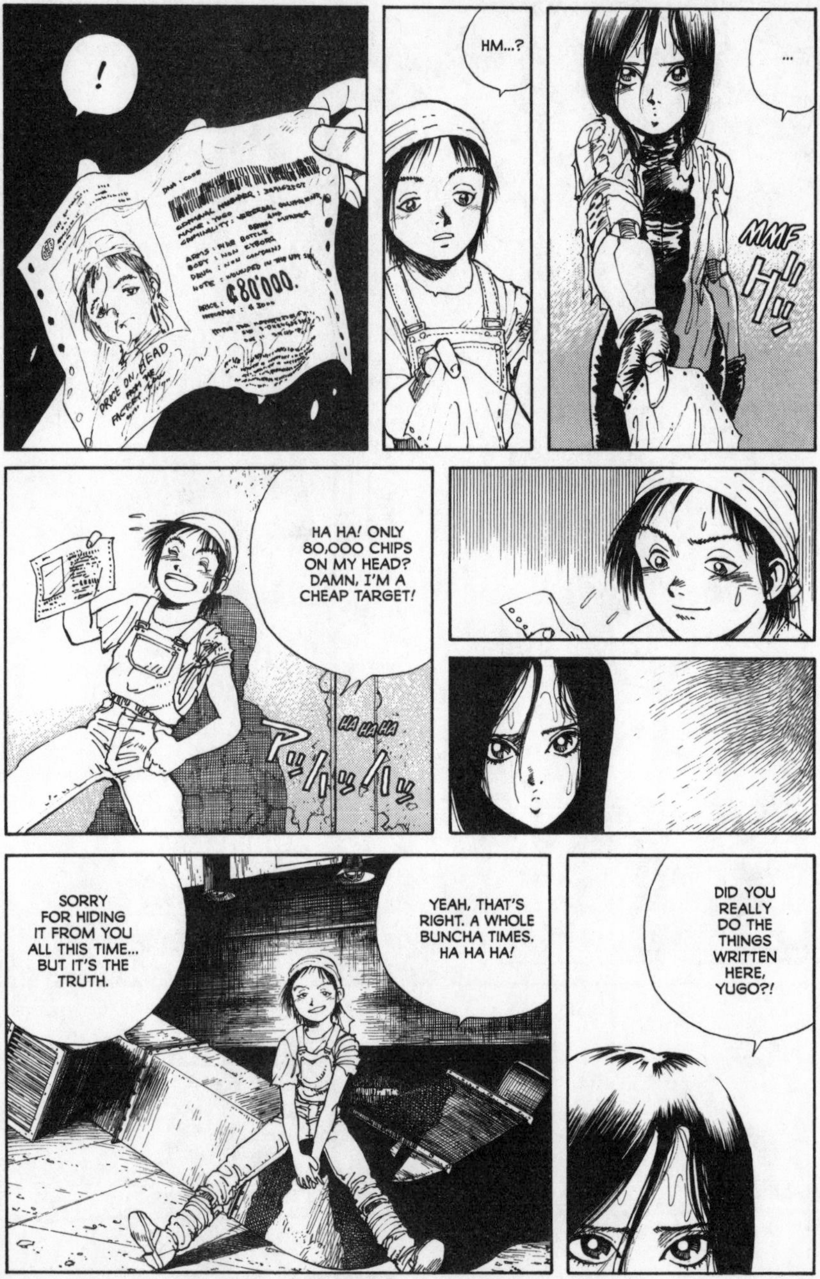
...
MMF
HM...?
!
PRICE ON HEAD
FROM THE FACTORY
₵80'000.
HA HA! ONLY 80,000 CHIPS ON MY HEAD? DAMN, I'M A CHEAP TARGET!
HA HA HA
DID YOU REALLY DO THE THINGS WRITTEN HERE, YUGO?!
YEAH, THAT'S RIGHT. A WHOLE BUNCHA TIMES. HA HA HA!
SORRY FOR HIDING IT FROM YOU ALL THIS TIME... BUT IT'S THE TRUTH.

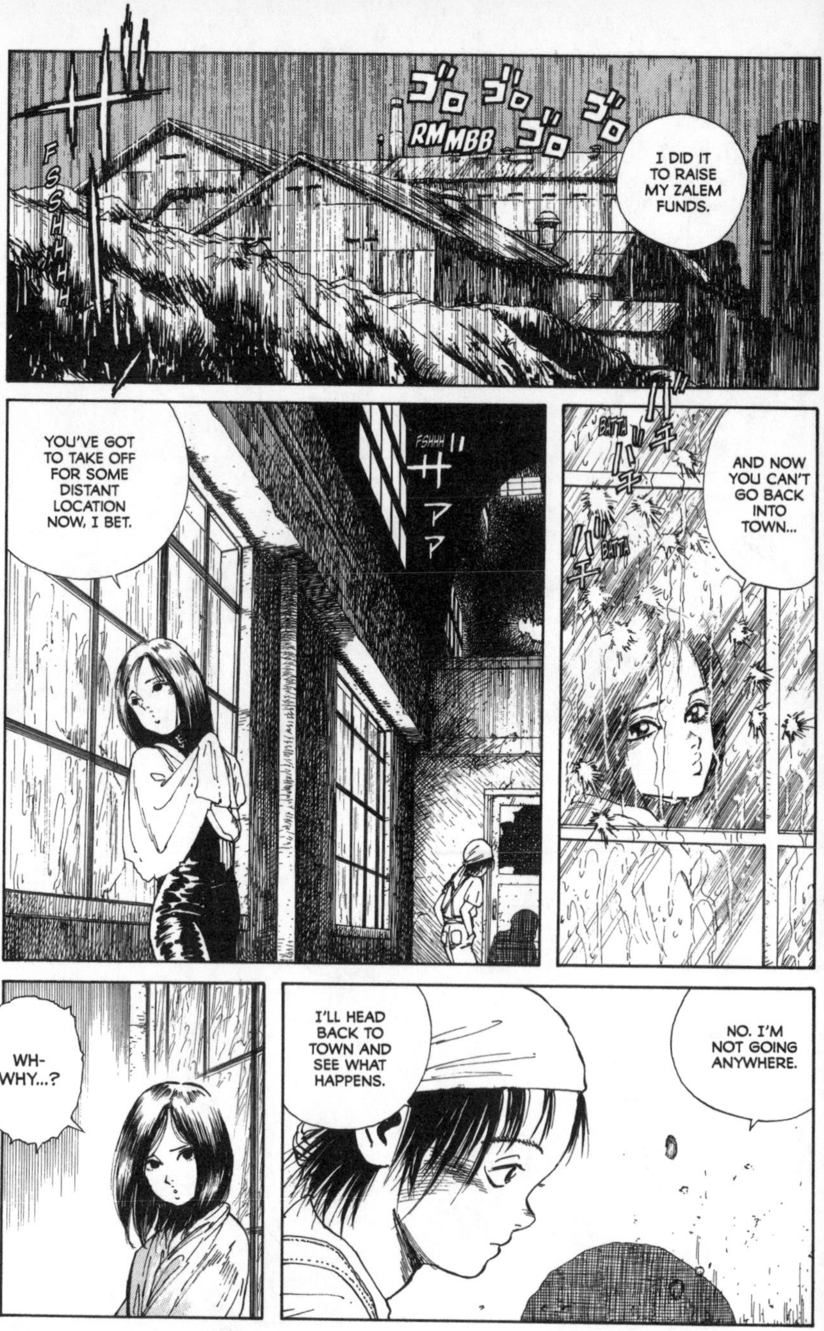
ゴロ ゴロ ゴロ ゴロ
RMMBB
FSSHHHH
I DID IT TO RAISE MY ZALEM FUNDS.
BATTA
BATTA
AND NOW YOU CAN'T GO BACK INTO TOWN...
FSHHH
ザァァ
YOU'VE GOT TO TAKE OFF FOR SOME DISTANT LOCATION NOW, I BET.
NO. I'M NOT GOING ANYWHERE.
I'LL HEAD BACK TO TOWN AND SEE WHAT HAPPENS.
WH- WHY...?

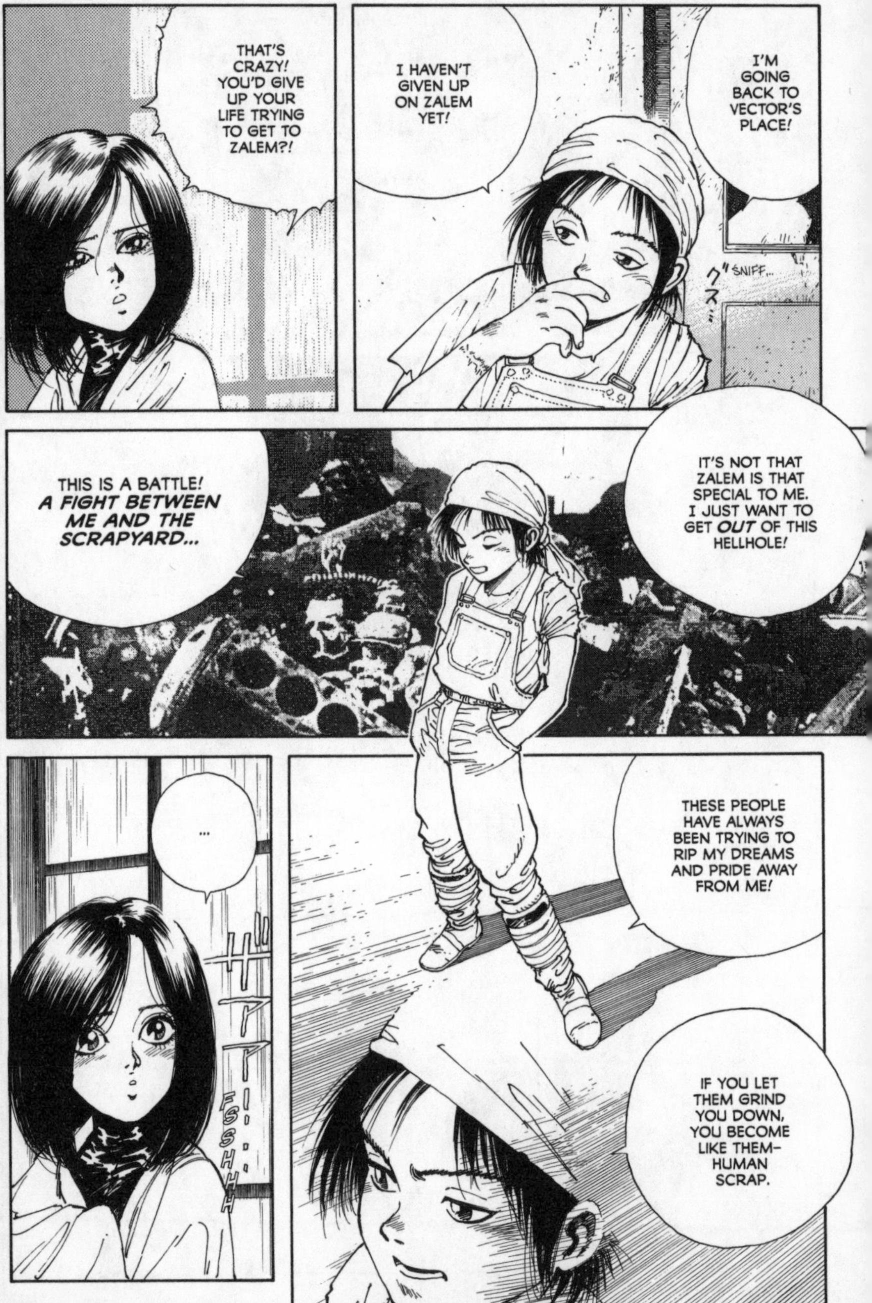
I'M GOING BACK TO VECTOR'S PLACE!
SNIFF...
I HAVEN'T GIVEN UP ON ZALEM YET!
THAT'S CRAZY! YOU'D GIVE UP YOUR LIFE TRYING TO GET TO ZALEM?!
IT'S NOT THAT ZALEM IS THAT SPECIAL TO ME. I JUST WANT TO GET *OUT* OF THIS HELLHOLE!
THIS IS A BATTLE! ***A FIGHT BETWEEN ME AND THE SCRAPYARD...***
THESE PEOPLE HAVE ALWAYS BEEN TRYING TO RIP MY DREAMS AND PRIDE AWAY FROM ME!
IF YOU LET THEM GRIND YOU DOWN, YOU BECOME LIKE THEM– HUMAN SCRAP.
...
FSSHHH

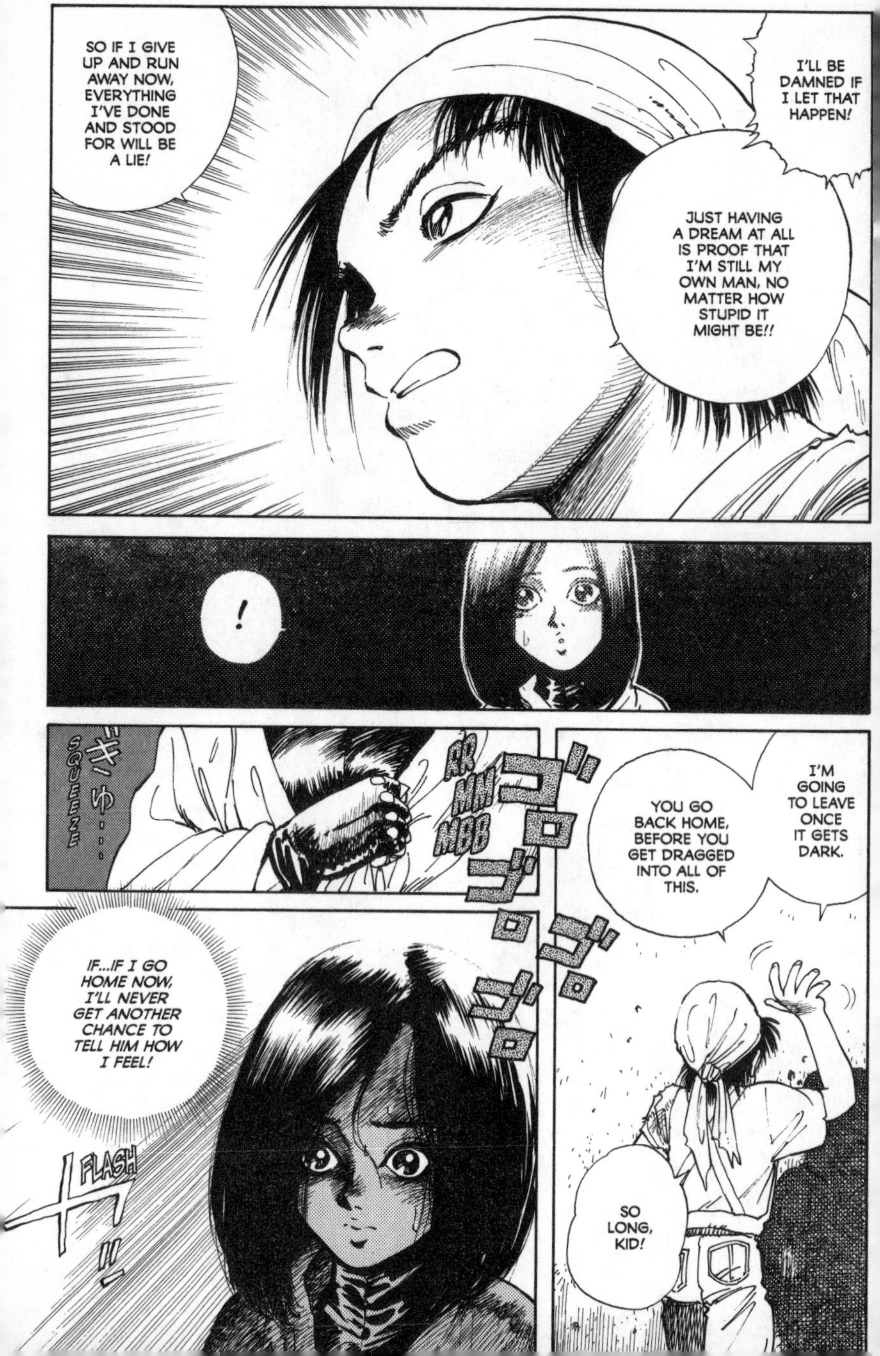
JUST HAVING A DREAM AT ALL IS PROOF THAT I'M STILL MY OWN MAN, NO MATTER HOW STUPID IT MIGHT BE!!
SO IF I GIVE UP AND RUN AWAY NOW, EVERYTHING I'VE DONE AND STOOD FOR WILL BE A LIE!
I'LL BE DAMNED IF I LET THAT HAPPEN!
!
I'M GOING TO LEAVE ONCE IT GETS DARK.
YOU GO BACK HOME, BEFORE YOU GET DRAGGED INTO ALL OF THIS.
ゴロゴロゴロ
AR MM MBB
SO LONG, KID!
ぎゅ…
SQUEEZE
IF...IF I GO HOME NOW, I'LL NEVER GET ANOTHER CHANCE TO TELL HIM HOW I FEEL!
FLASH

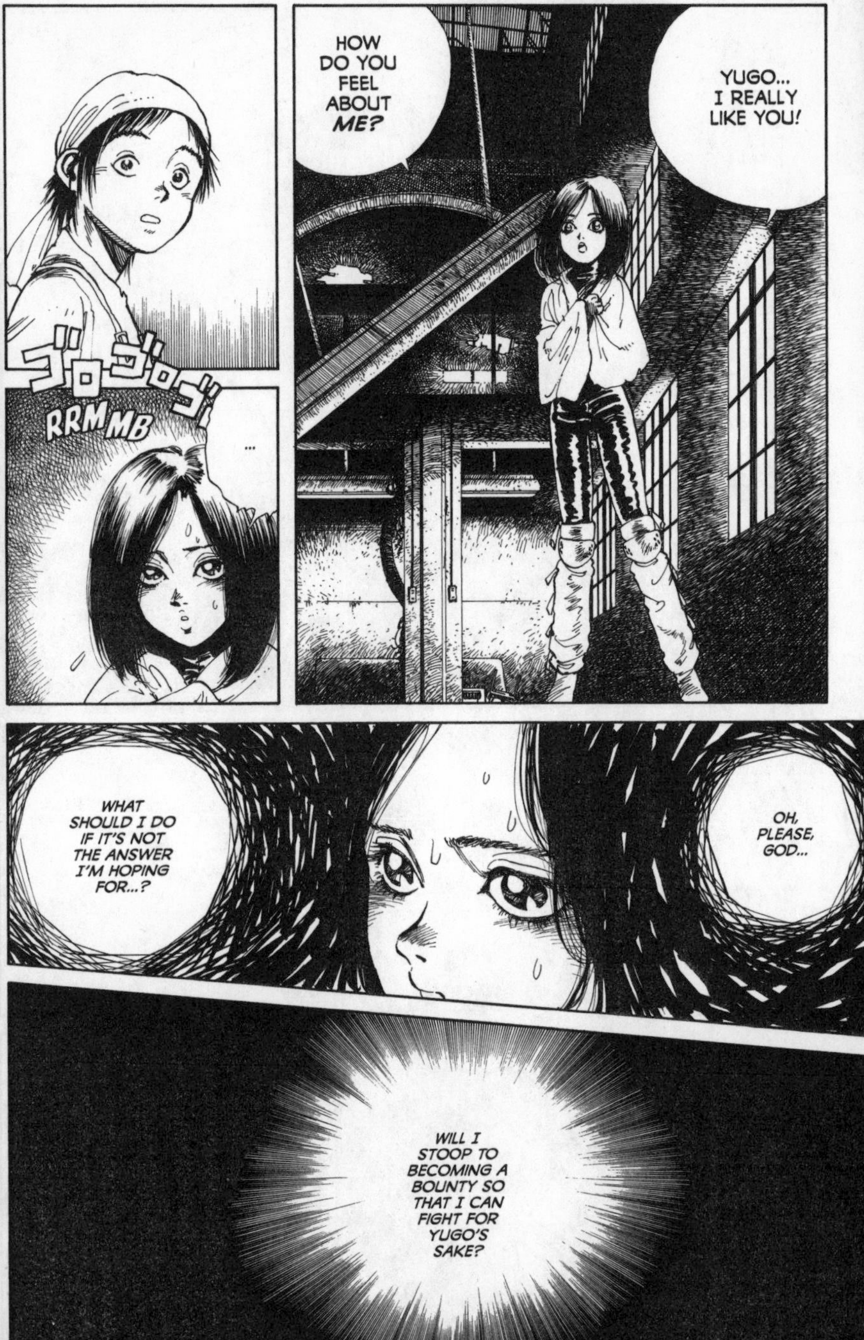
YUGO... I REALLY LIKE YOU!
HOW DO YOU FEEL ABOUT ME?
ゴロゴロゴ
RRMMB
...
OH, PLEASE, GOD...
WHAT SHOULD I DO IF IT'S NOT THE ANSWER I'M HOPING FOR...?
WILL I STOOP TO BECOMING A BOUNTY SO THAT I CAN FIGHT FOR YUGO'S SAKE?

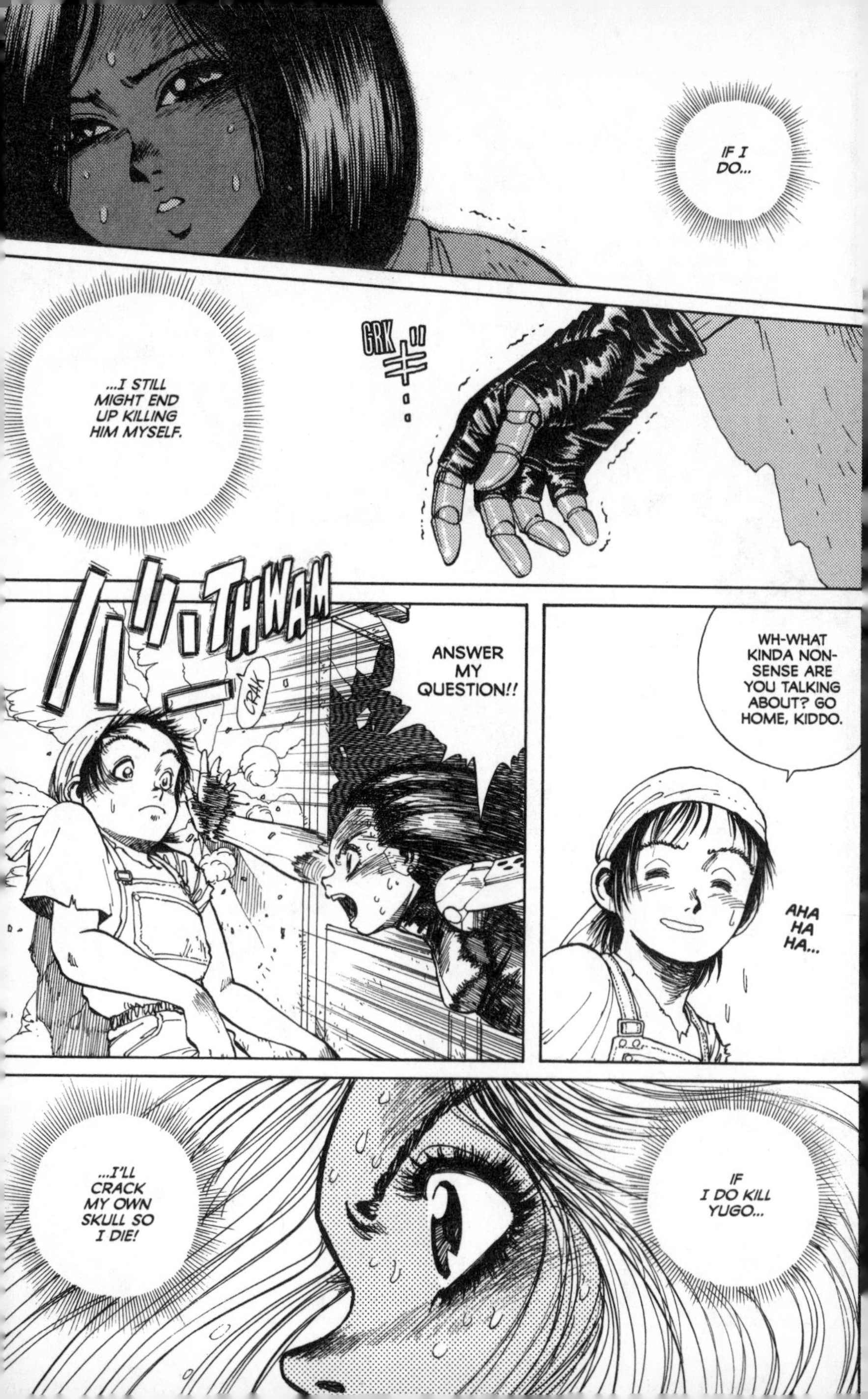
IF I DO...
GRK
...I STILL MIGHT END UP KILLING HIM MYSELF.
WH-WHAT KINDA NON-SENSE ARE YOU TALKING ABOUT? GO HOME, KIDDO.
AHA HA HA...
ANSWER MY QUESTION!!
THWAM
CRAK
IF I DO KILL YUGO...
...I'LL CRACK MY OWN SKULL SO I DIE!

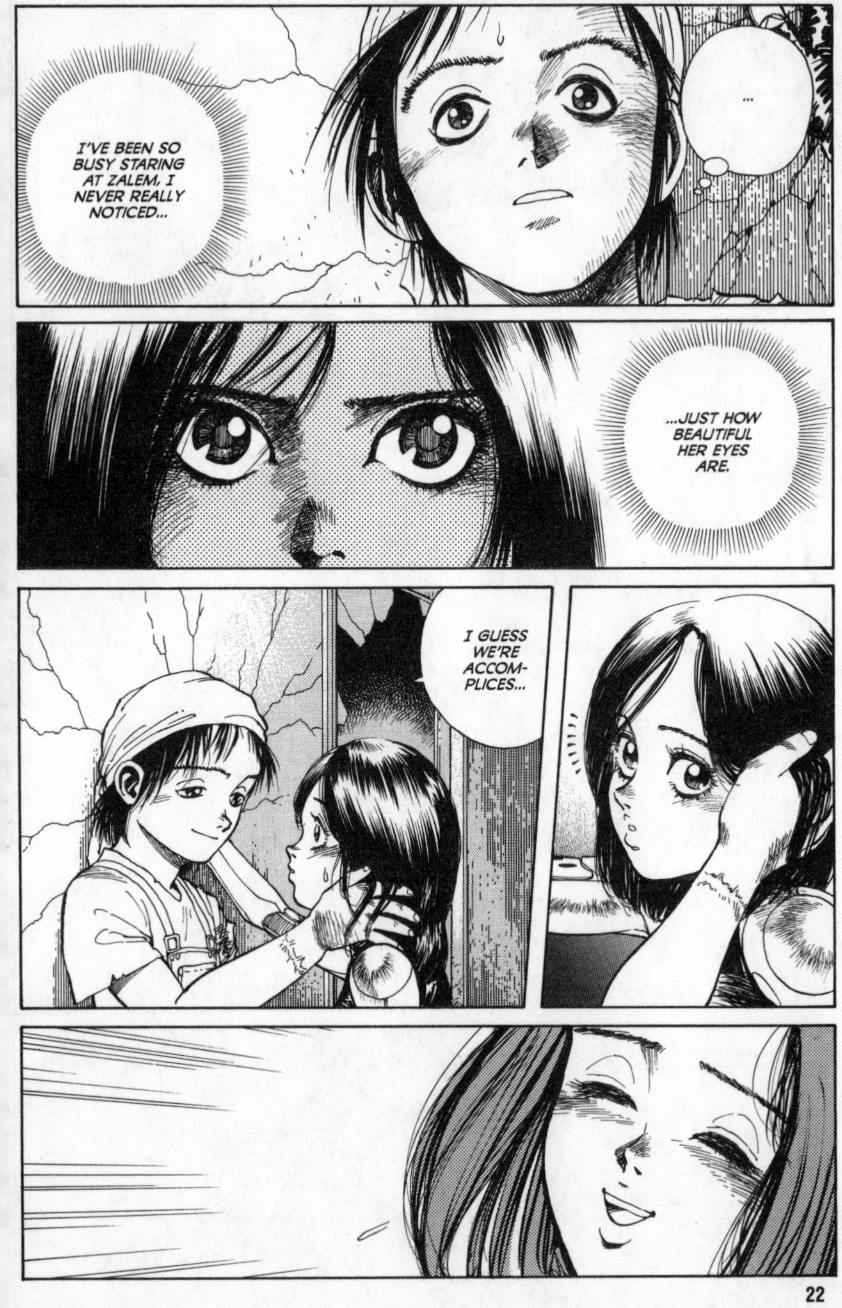
...
I'VE BEEN SO BUSY STARING AT ZALEM, I NEVER REALLY NOTICED...
...JUST HOW BEAUTIFUL HER EYES ARE.
I GUESS WE'RE ACCOMPLICES...

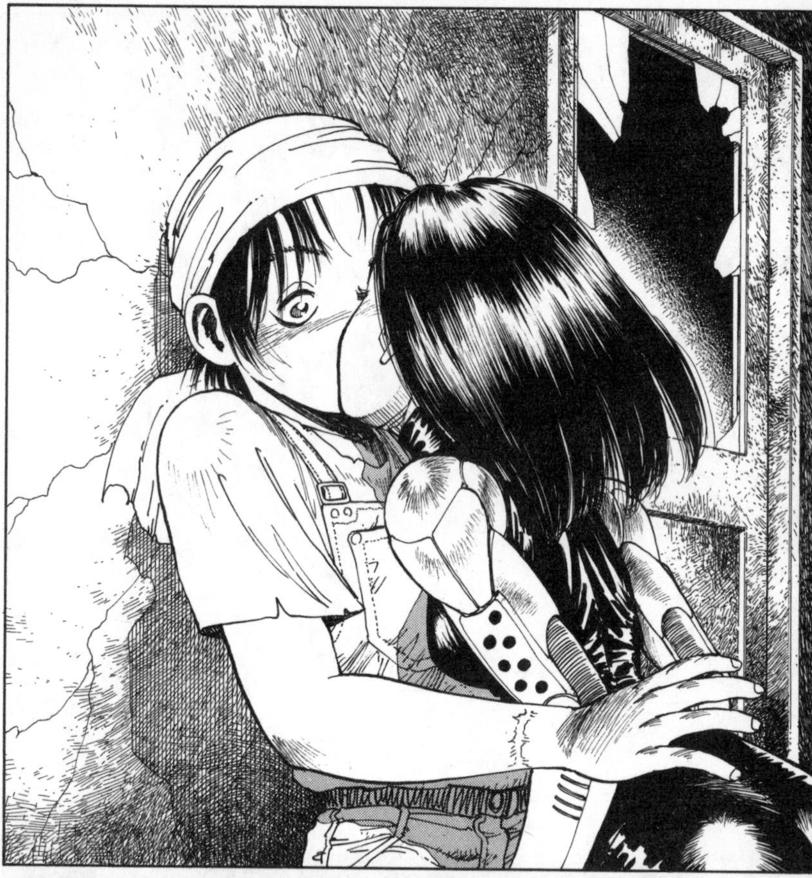
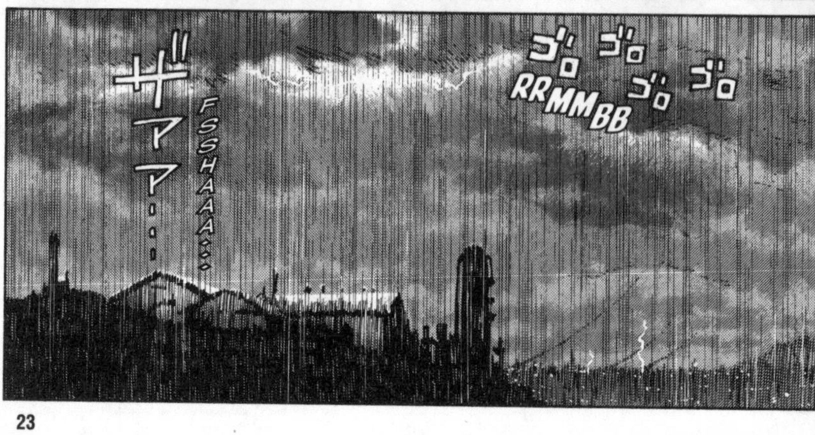
ゴロ ゴロ ゴロ ゴロ
RRMMBB
ザアア…
FSSHAAA…

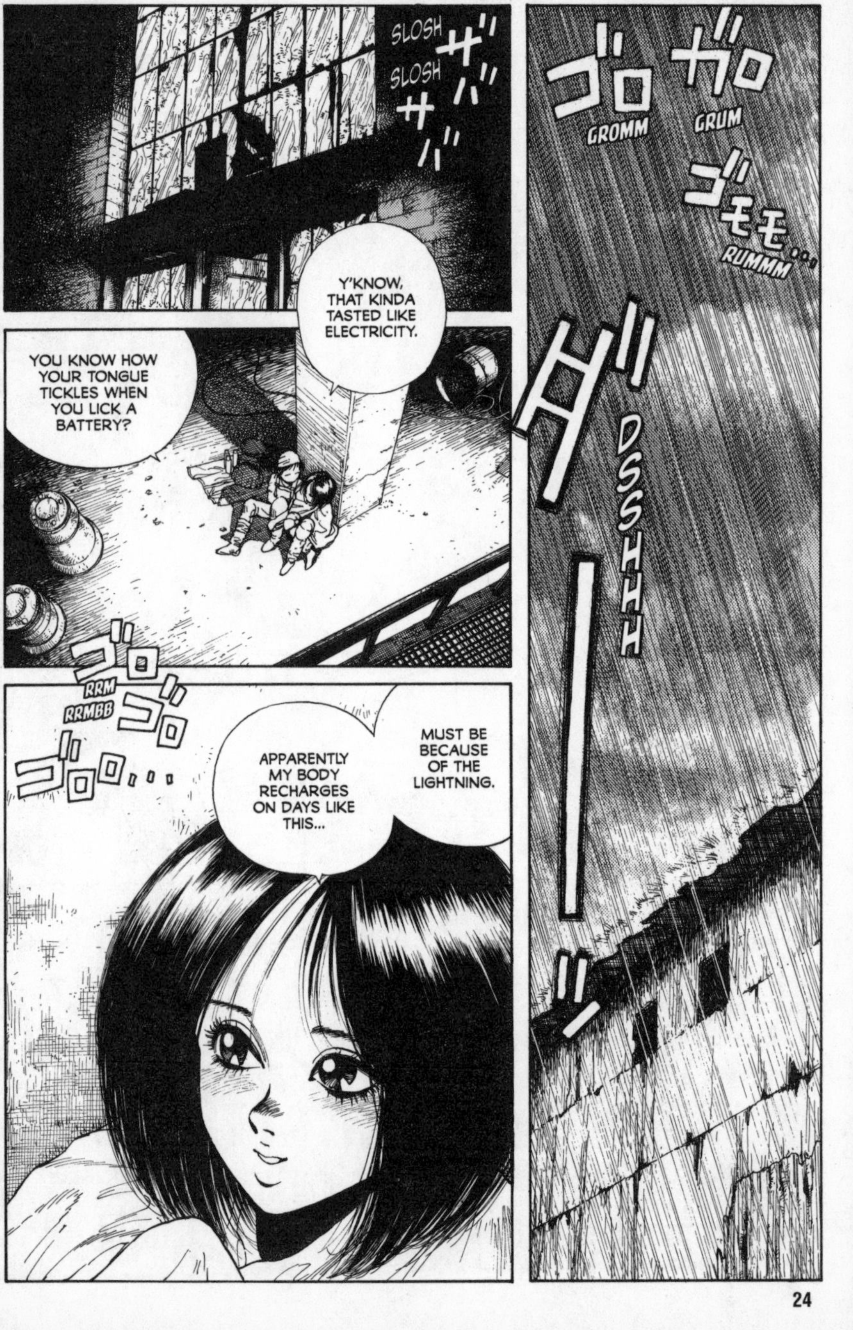
GROMM
GRUM
RUMMM
DSSHHH
SLOSH
SLOSH
Y'KNOW, THAT KINDA TASTED LIKE ELECTRICITY.
YOU KNOW HOW YOUR TONGUE TICKLES WHEN YOU LICK A BATTERY?
RRM
RRMBB
MUST BE BECAUSE OF THE LIGHTNING.
APPARENTLY MY BODY RECHARGES ON DAYS LIKE THIS...

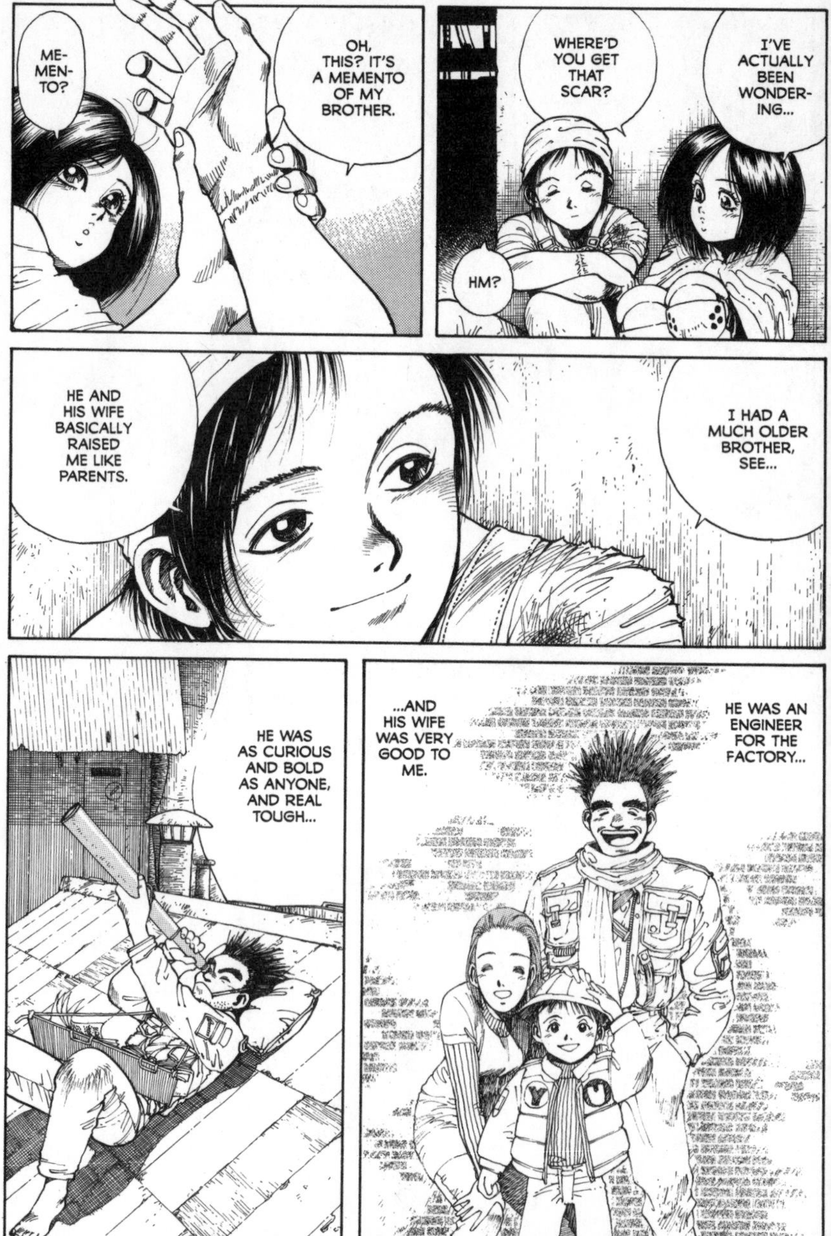
I'VE ACTUALLY BEEN WONDER-ING...
WHERE'D YOU GET THAT SCAR?
HM?
OH, THIS? IT'S A MEMENTO OF MY BROTHER.
ME-MEN-TO?
I HAD A MUCH OLDER BROTHER, SEE...
HE AND HIS WIFE BASICALLY RAISED ME LIKE PARENTS.
HE WAS AN ENGINEER FOR THE FACTORY...
...AND HIS WIFE WAS VERY GOOD TO ME.
HE WAS AS CURIOUS AND BOLD AS ANYONE, AND REAL TOUGH...

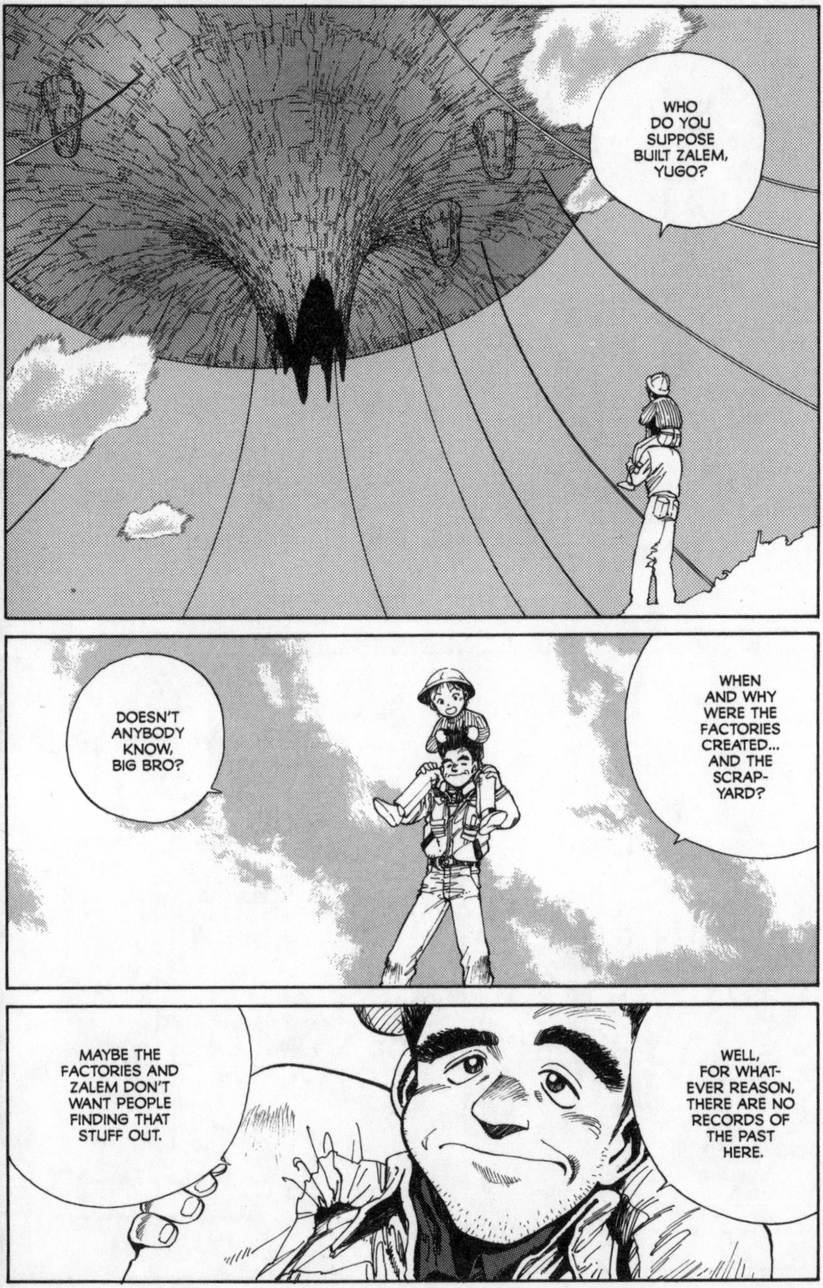
WHO DO YOU SUPPOSE BUILT ZALEM, YUGO?
WHEN AND WHY WERE THE FACTORIES CREATED... AND THE SCRAP-YARD?
DOESN'T ANYBODY KNOW, BIG BRO?
WELL, FOR WHAT-EVER REASON, THERE ARE NO RECORDS OF THE PAST HERE.
MAYBE THE FACTORIES AND ZALEM DON'T WANT PEOPLE FINDING THAT STUFF OUT.

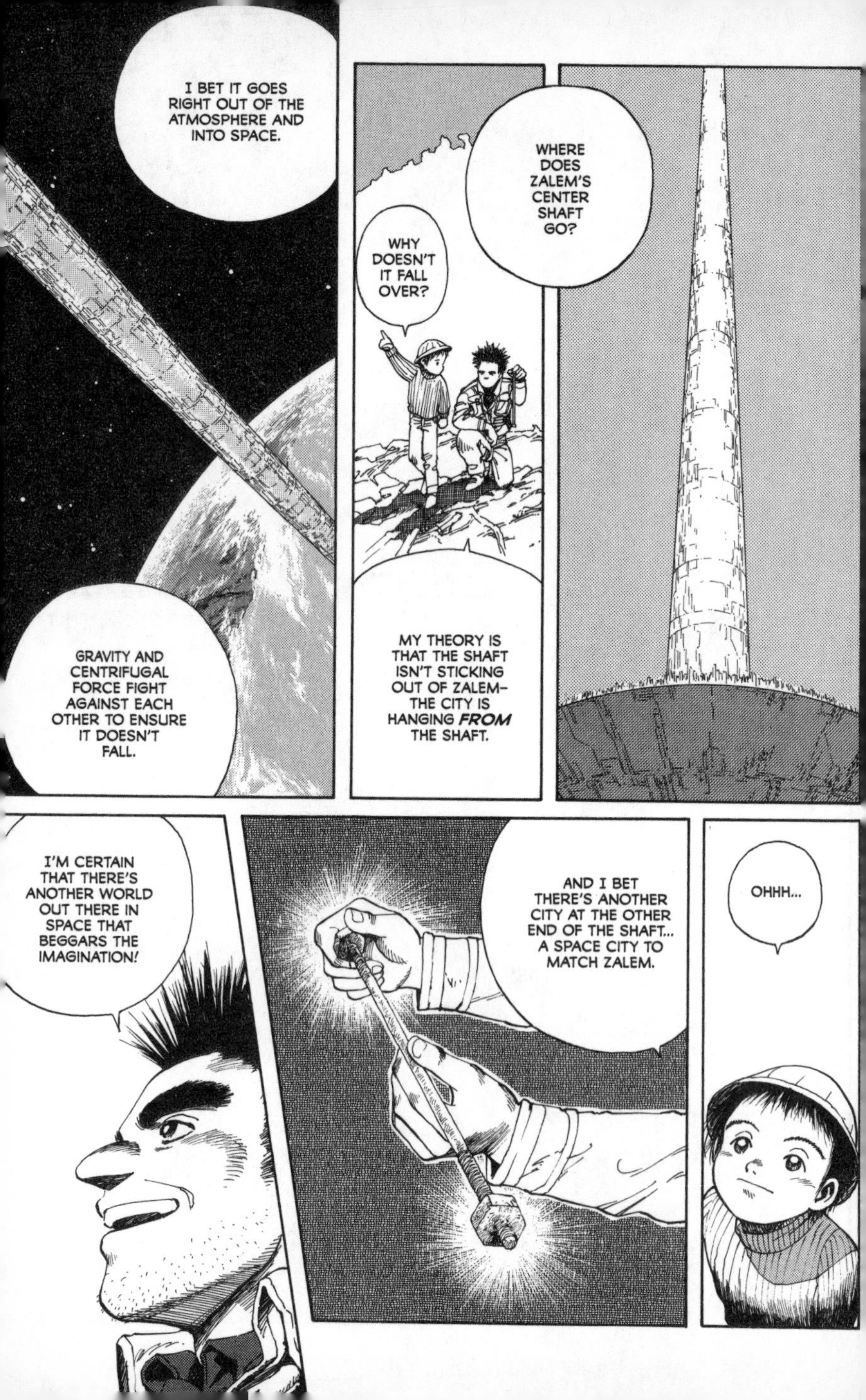
WHERE DOES ZALEM'S CENTER SHAFT GO?
WHY DOESN'T IT FALL OVER?
MY THEORY IS THAT THE SHAFT ISN'T STICKING OUT OF ZALEM– THE CITY IS HANGING *FROM* THE SHAFT.
I BET IT GOES RIGHT OUT OF THE ATMOSPHERE AND INTO SPACE.
GRAVITY AND CENTRIFUGAL FORCE FIGHT AGAINST EACH OTHER TO ENSURE IT DOESN'T FALL.
I'M CERTAIN THAT THERE'S ANOTHER WORLD OUT THERE IN SPACE THAT BEGGARS THE IMAGINATION!
AND I BET THERE'S ANOTHER CITY AT THE OTHER END OF THE SHAFT... A SPACE CITY TO MATCH ZALEM.
OHHH...

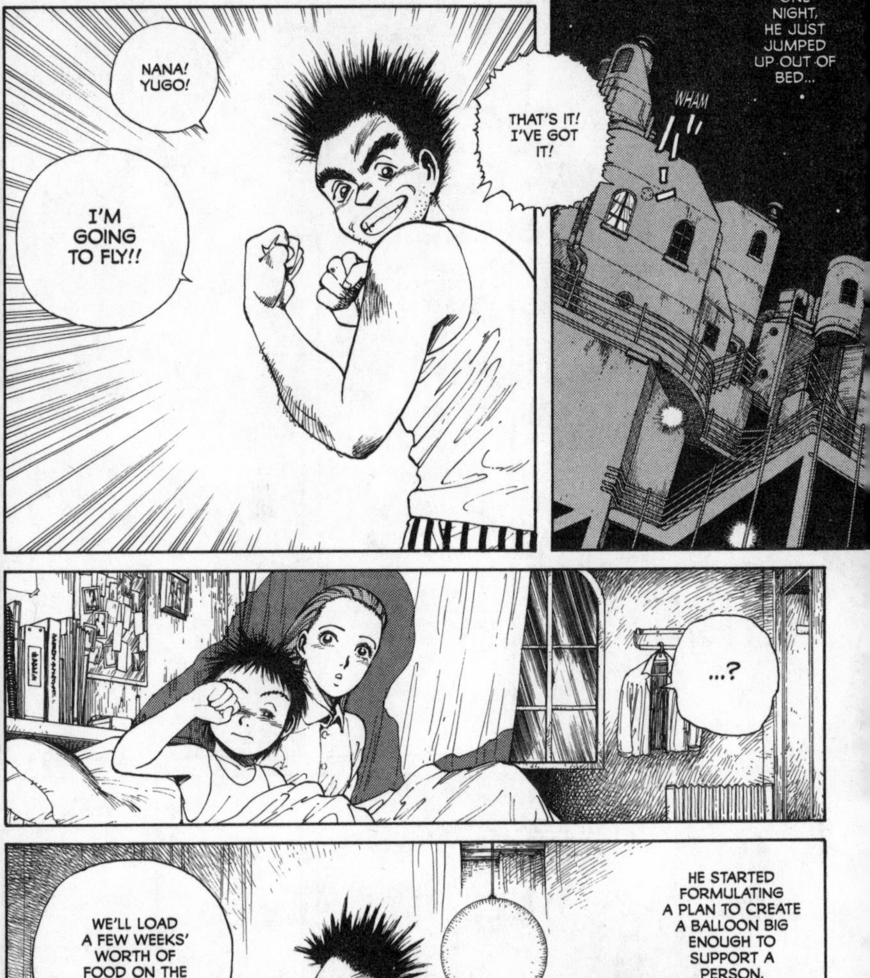
ONE NIGHT, HE JUST JUMPED UP OUT OF BED...
WHAM
THAT'S IT! I'VE GOT IT!
NANA! YUGO!
I'M GOING TO FLY!!
...?
HE STARTED FORMULATING A PLAN TO CREATE A BALLOON BIG ENOUGH TO SUPPORT A PERSON.
WE'LL LOAD A FEW WEEKS' WORTH OF FOOD ON THE GONDOLA, SEE...

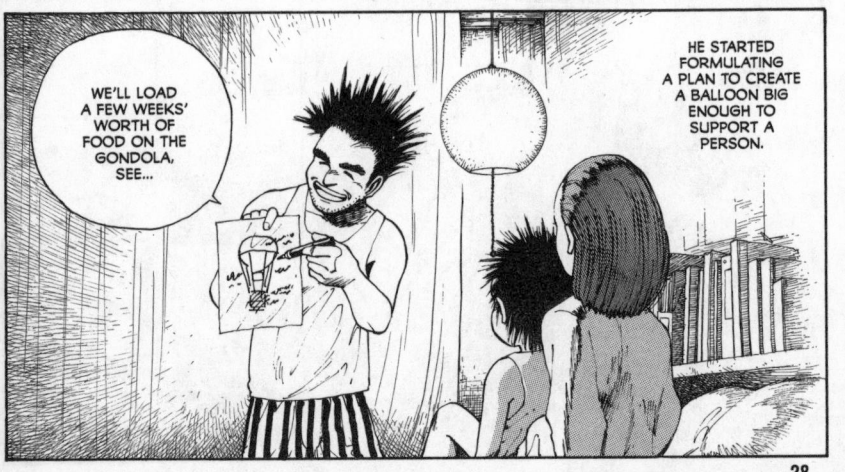

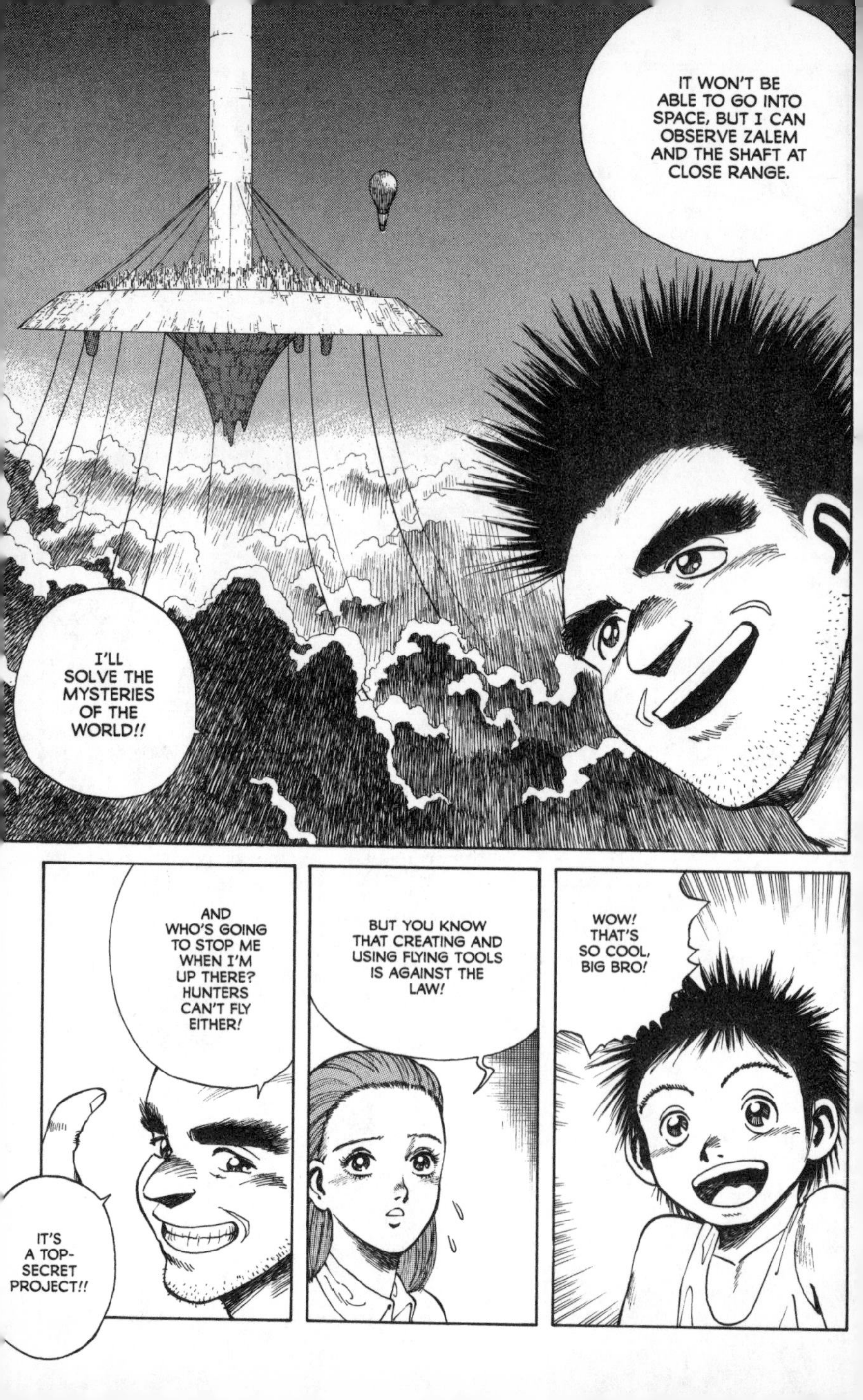
IT WON'T BE ABLE TO GO INTO SPACE, BUT I CAN OBSERVE ZALEM AND THE SHAFT AT CLOSE RANGE.
I'LL SOLVE THE MYSTERIES OF THE WORLD!!
WOW! THAT'S SO COOL, BIG BRO!
BUT YOU KNOW THAT CREATING AND USING FLYING TOOLS IS AGAINST THE LAW!
AND WHO'S GOING TO STOP ME WHEN I'M UP THERE? HUNTERS CAN'T FLY EITHER!
IT'S A TOP-SECRET PROJECT!!

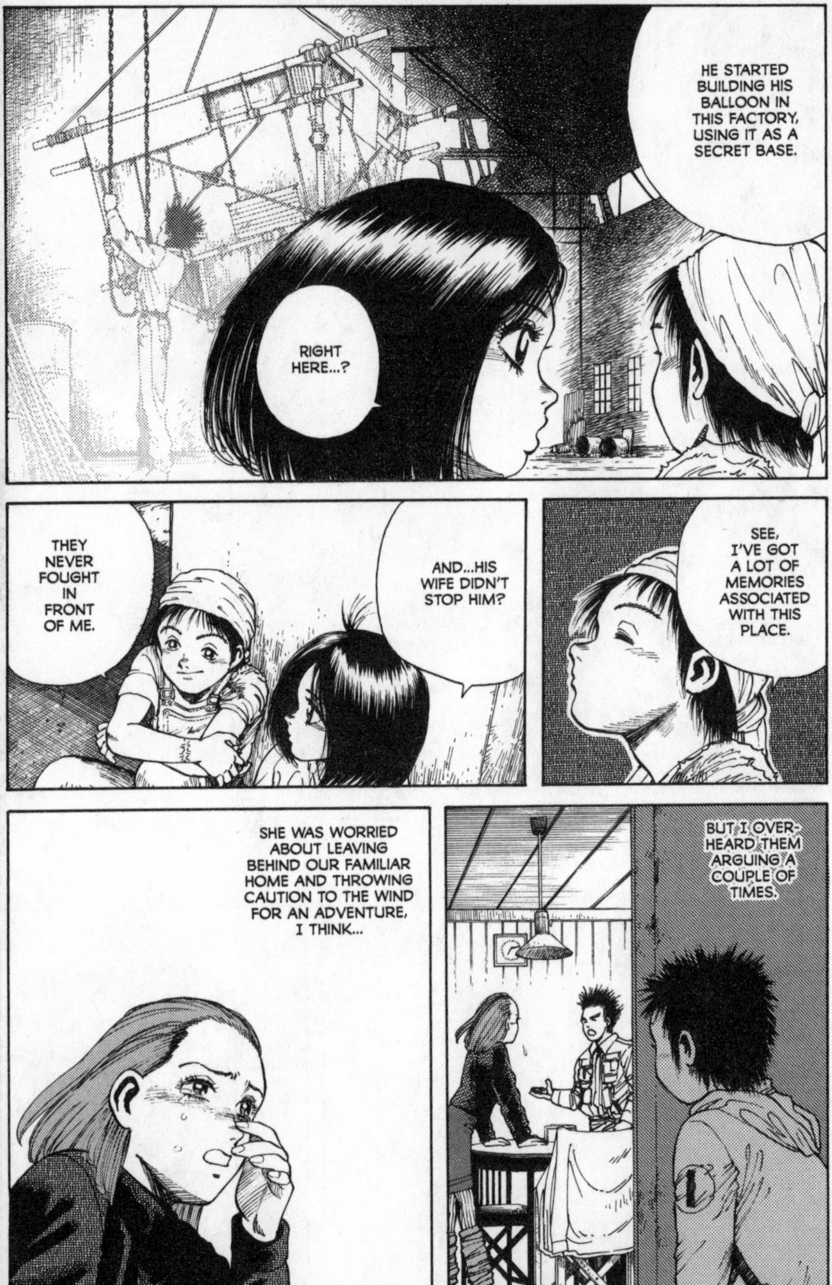
HE STARTED BUILDING HIS BALLOON IN THIS FACTORY, USING IT AS A SECRET BASE.
RIGHT HERE...?
SEE, I'VE GOT A LOT OF MEMORIES ASSOCIATED WITH THIS PLACE.
AND...HIS WIFE DIDN'T STOP HIM?
THEY NEVER FOUGHT IN FRONT OF ME.
BUT I OVERHEARD THEM ARGUING A COUPLE OF TIMES.
SHE WAS WORRIED ABOUT LEAVING BEHIND OUR FAMILIAR HOME AND THROWING CAUTION TO THE WIND FOR AN ADVENTURE, I THINK...

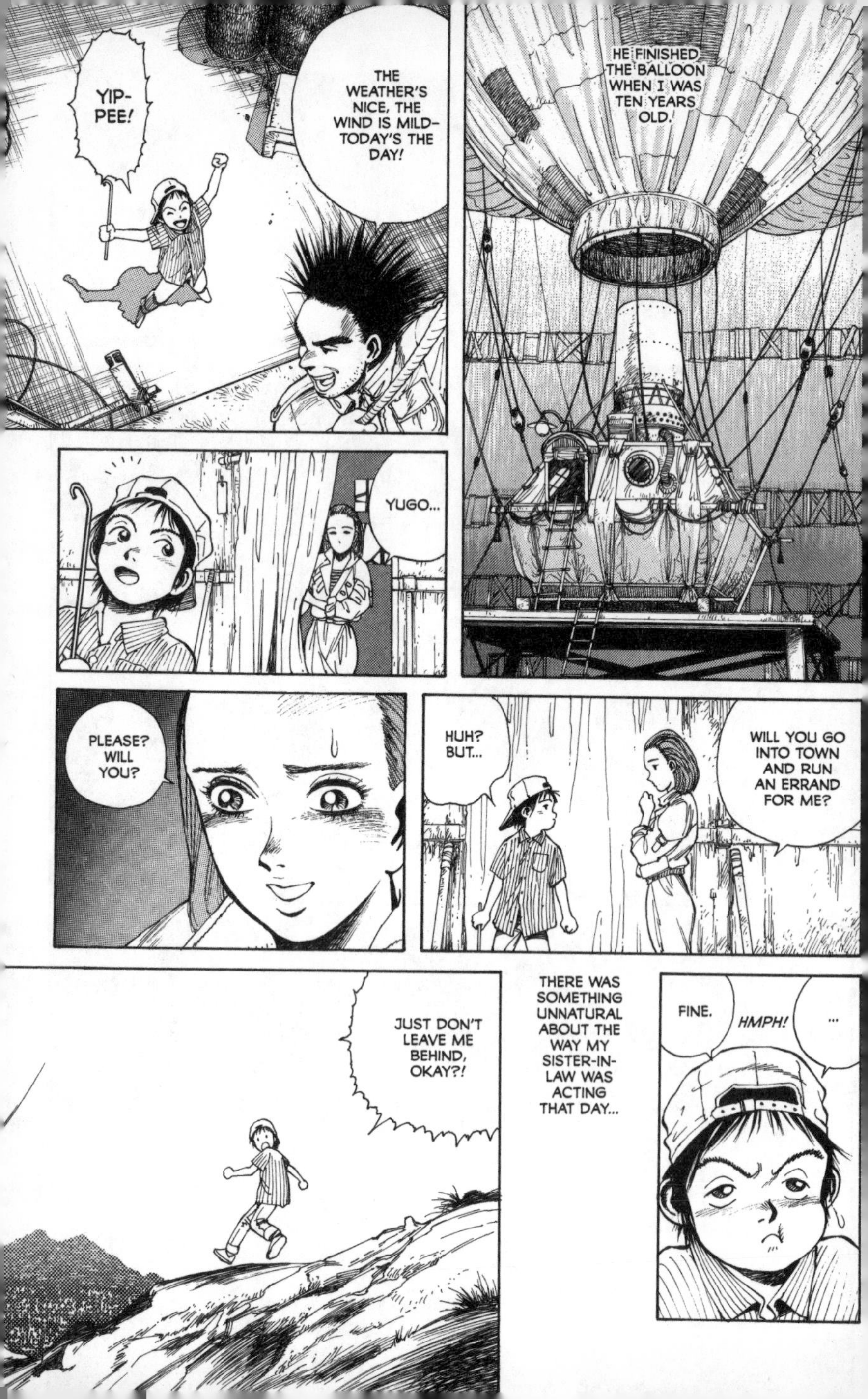
HE FINISHED THE BALLOON WHEN I WAS TEN YEARS OLD.
THE WEATHER'S NICE, THE WIND IS MILD-TODAY'S THE DAY!
YIP-PEE!
YUGO...
WILL YOU GO INTO TOWN AND RUN AN ERRAND FOR ME?
HUH? BUT...
PLEASE? WILL YOU?
...
HMPH!
FINE.
THERE WAS SOMETHING UNNATURAL ABOUT THE WAY MY SISTER-IN-LAW WAS ACTING THAT DAY...
JUST DON'T LEAVE ME BEHIND, OKAY?!

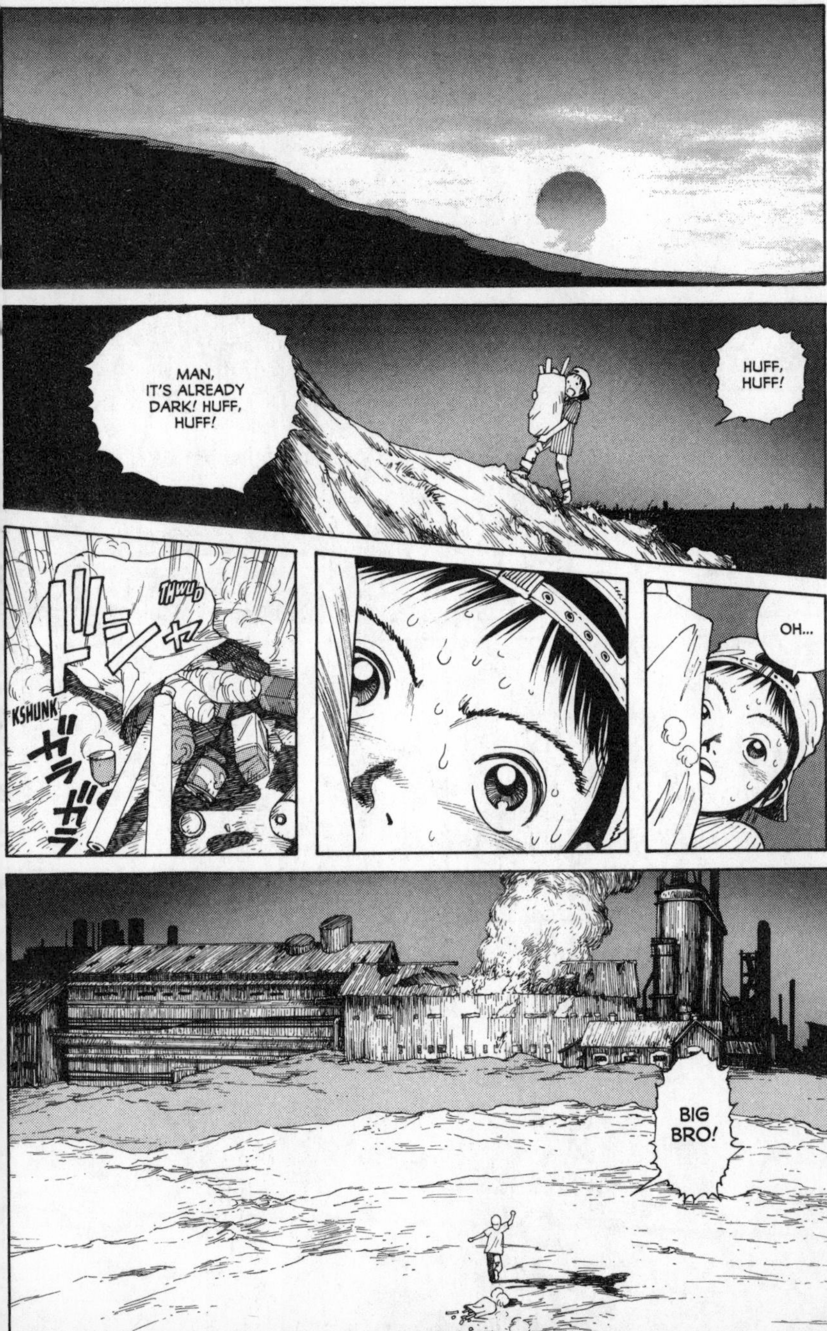
HUFF, HUFF!
MAN, IT'S ALREADY DARK! HUFF, HUFF!
OH...
THWUD
ドシャ
KSHUNK
BIG BRO!

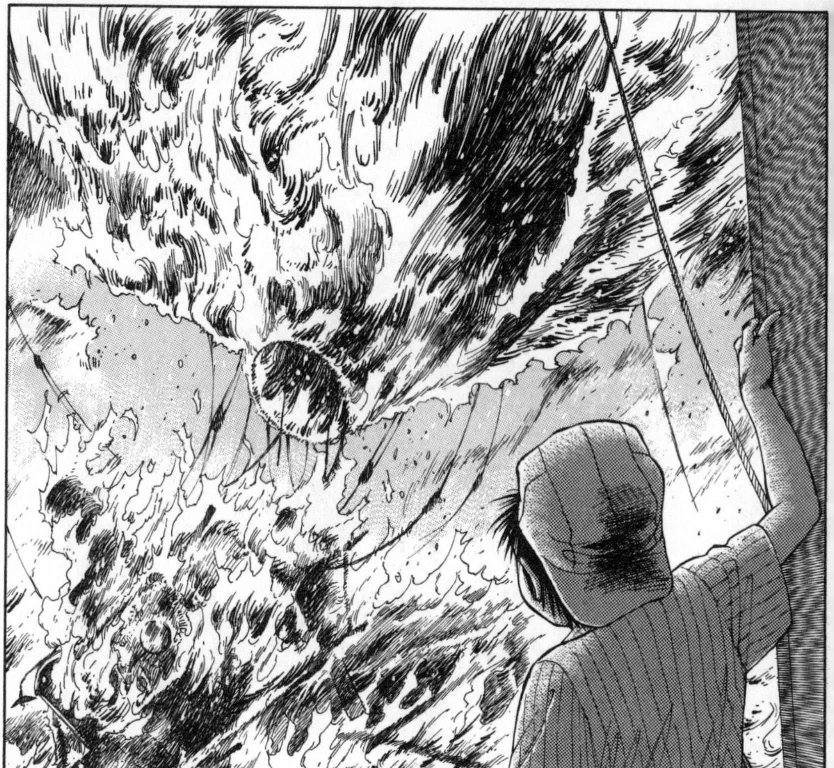
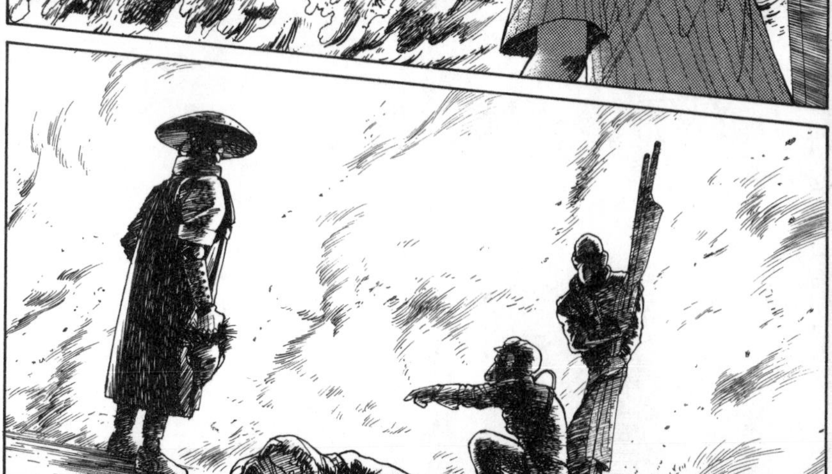

PLEASE...
PLEASE
JUST TAKE
IT AND
GO!!

B...BIG
BRO...

NO, YUGO!
DON'T
WATCH!!

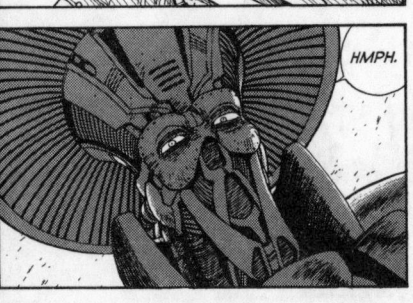

HMPH.

WHUD

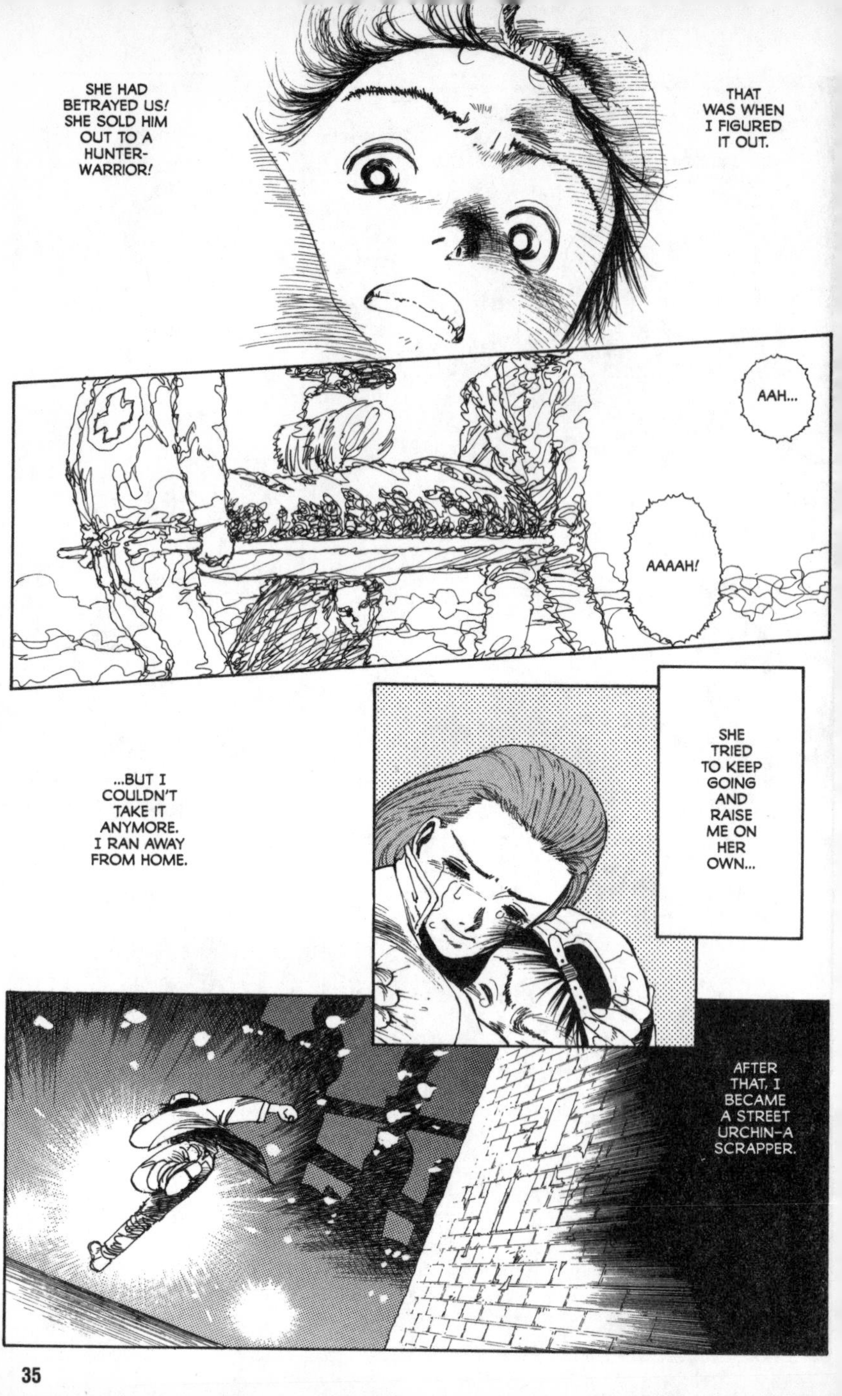
THAT WAS WHEN I FIGURED IT OUT.
SHE HAD BETRAYED US! SHE SOLD HIM OUT TO A HUNTER-WARRIOR!
AAH...
AAAAH!
SHE TRIED TO KEEP GOING AND RAISE ME ON HER OWN...
...BUT I COULDN'T TAKE IT ANYMORE. I RAN AWAY FROM HOME.
AFTER THAT, I BECAME A STREET URCHIN–A SCRAPPER.

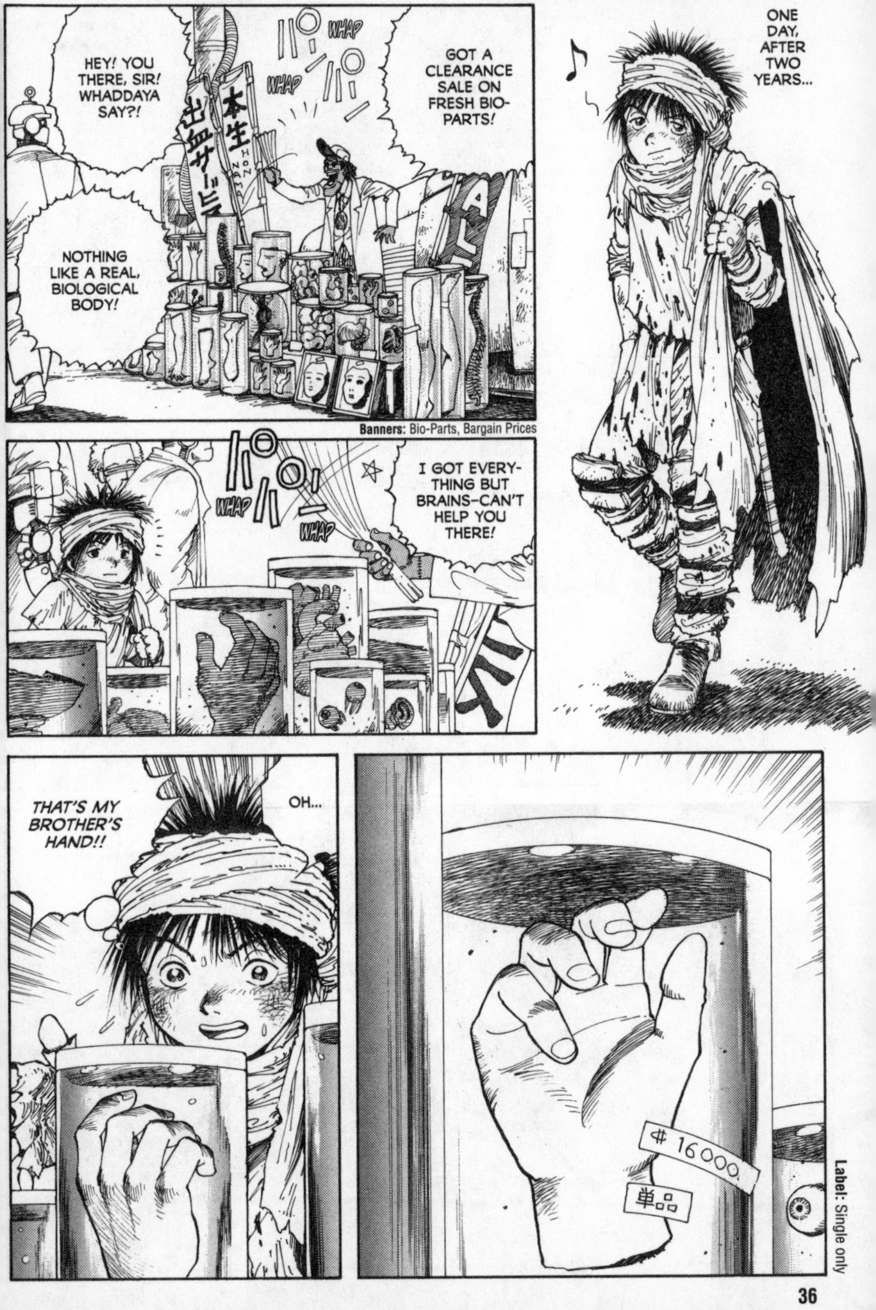
ONE DAY, AFTER TWO YEARS...
GOT A CLEARANCE SALE ON FRESH BIO-PARTS!
WHAP
WHAP
HEY! YOU THERE, SIR! WHADDAYA SAY?!
NOTHING LIKE A REAL, BIOLOGICAL BODY!
本生
出血サービス
Banners: Bio-Parts, Bargain Prices
I GOT EVERY-THING BUT BRAINS–CAN'T HELP YOU THERE!
WHAP
WHAP
16000
単品
Label: Single only
OH...
THAT'S MY BROTHER'S HAND!!

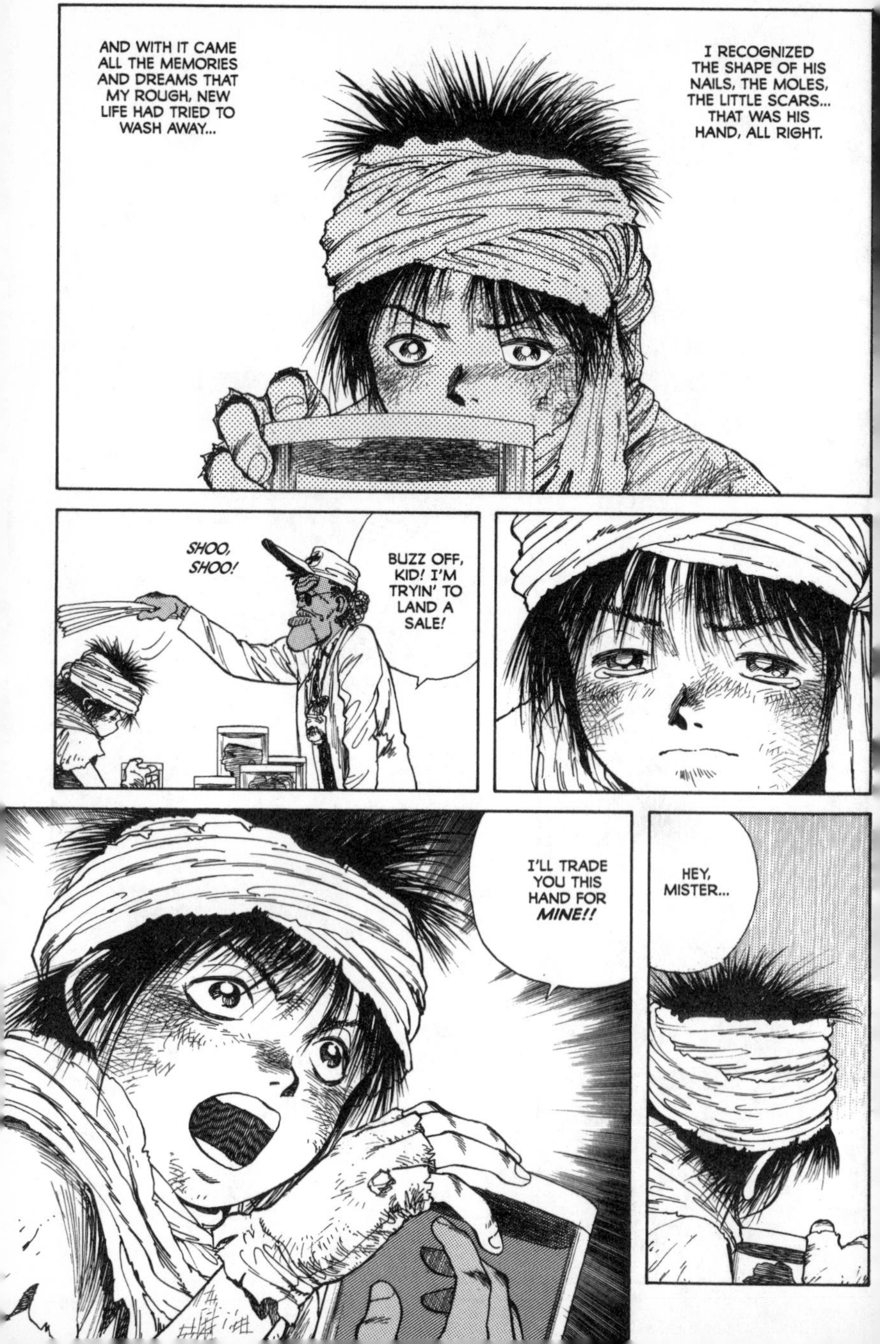
I RECOGNIZED THE SHAPE OF HIS NAILS, THE MOLES, THE LITTLE SCARS... THAT WAS HIS HAND, ALL RIGHT.
AND WITH IT CAME ALL THE MEMORIES AND DREAMS THAT MY ROUGH, NEW LIFE HAD TRIED TO WASH AWAY...
BUZZ OFF, KID! I'M TRYIN' TO LAND A SALE!
SHOO, SHOO!
HEY, MISTER...
I'LL TRADE YOU THIS HAND FOR MINE!!

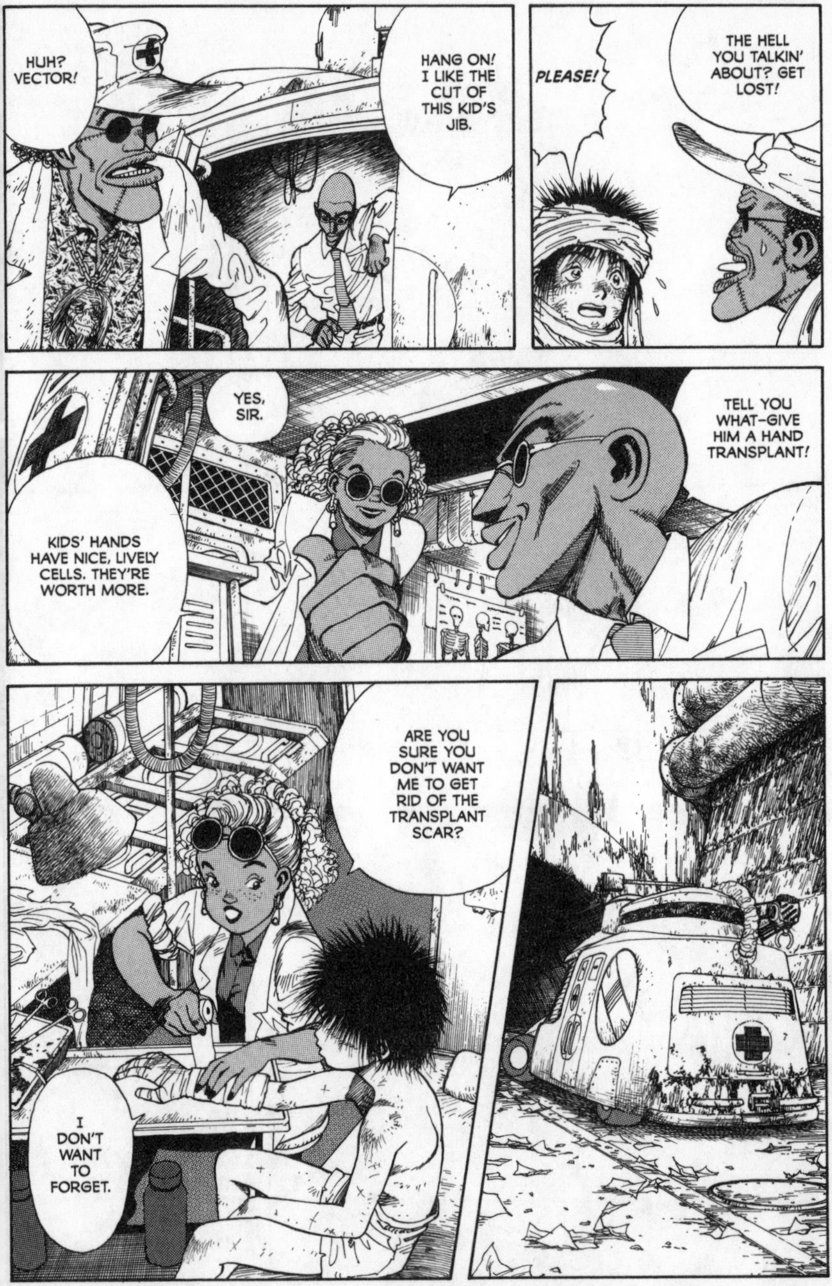
THE HELL YOU TALKIN' ABOUT? GET LOST!
PLEASE!
HANG ON! I LIKE THE CUT OF THIS KID'S JIB.
HUH? VECTOR!
TELL YOU WHAT–GIVE HIM A HAND TRANSPLANT!
YES, SIR.
KIDS' HANDS HAVE NICE, LIVELY CELLS. THEY'RE WORTH MORE.
ARE YOU SURE YOU DON'T WANT ME TO GET RID OF THE TRANSPLANT SCAR?
I DON'T WANT TO FORGET.

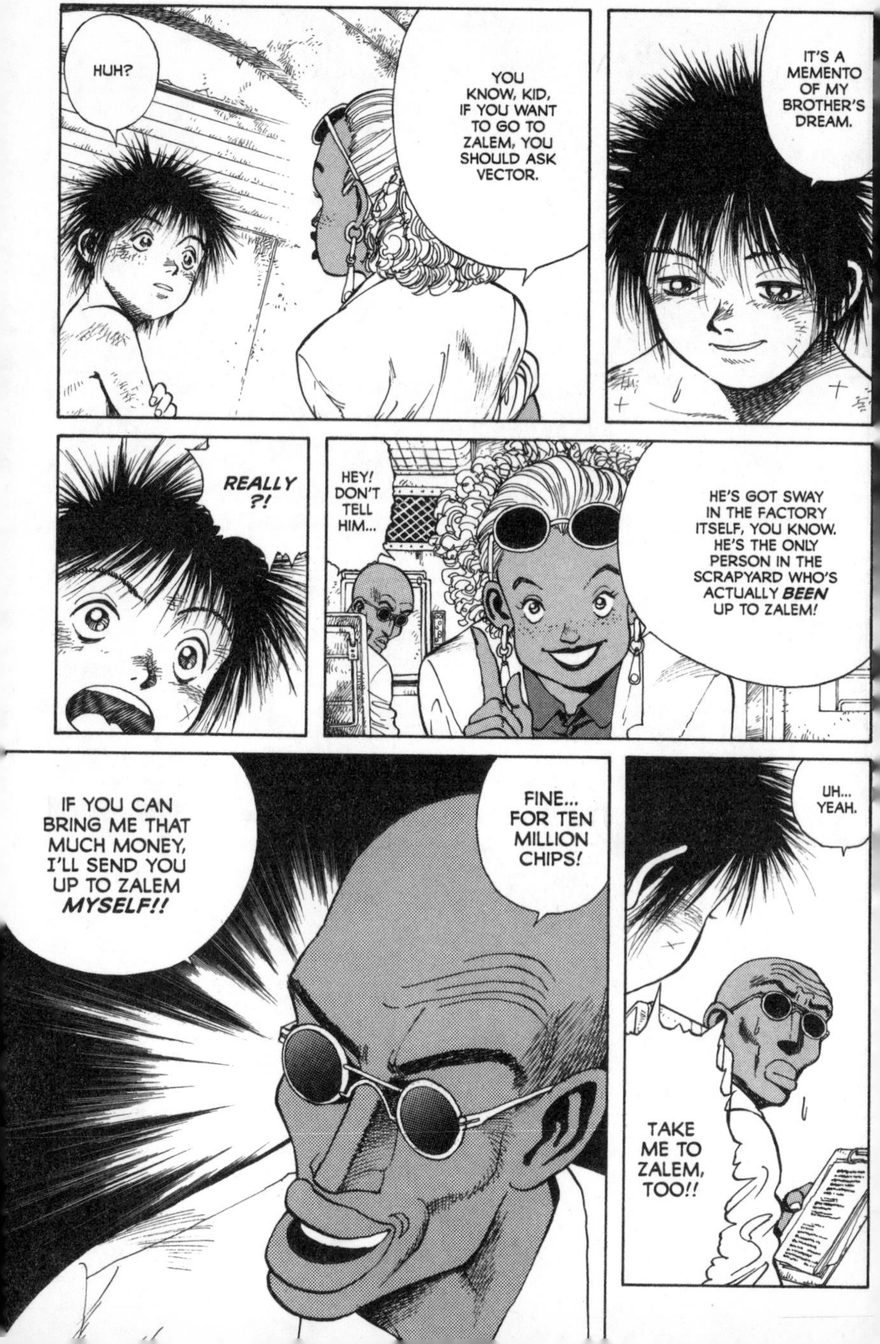
IT'S A MEMENTO OF MY BROTHER'S DREAM.
YOU KNOW, KID, IF YOU WANT TO GO TO ZALEM, YOU SHOULD ASK VECTOR.
HUH?
HE'S GOT SWAY IN THE FACTORY ITSELF, YOU KNOW. HE'S THE ONLY PERSON IN THE SCRAPYARD WHO'S ACTUALLY ***BEEN*** UP TO ZALEM!
HEY! DON'T TELL HIM...
REALLY ?!
UH... YEAH.
TAKE ME TO ZALEM, TOO!!
FINE... FOR TEN MILLION CHIPS!
IF YOU CAN BRING ME THAT MUCH MONEY, I'LL SEND YOU UP TO ZALEM ***MYSELF!!***

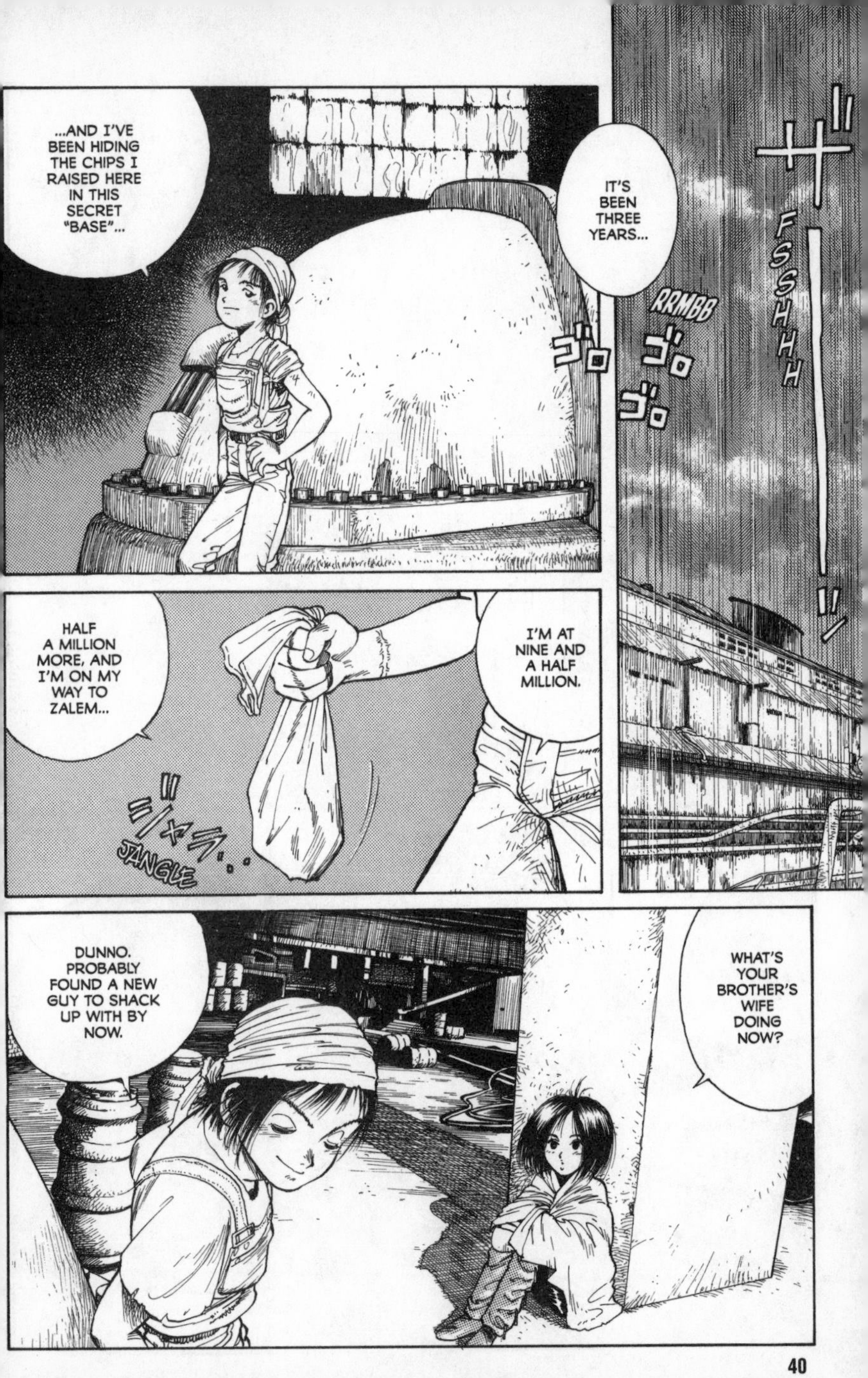
ザーッ
FSSHHH
ゴロゴロゴロ
RRMBB
IT'S BEEN THREE YEARS...
...AND I'VE BEEN HIDING THE CHIPS I RAISED HERE IN THIS SECRET "BASE"...
I'M AT NINE AND A HALF MILLION.
HALF A MILLION MORE, AND I'M ON MY WAY TO ZALEM...
ジャラ..
JANGLE
WHAT'S YOUR BROTHER'S WIFE DOING NOW?
DUNNO. PROBABLY FOUND A NEW GUY TO SHACK UP WITH BY NOW.

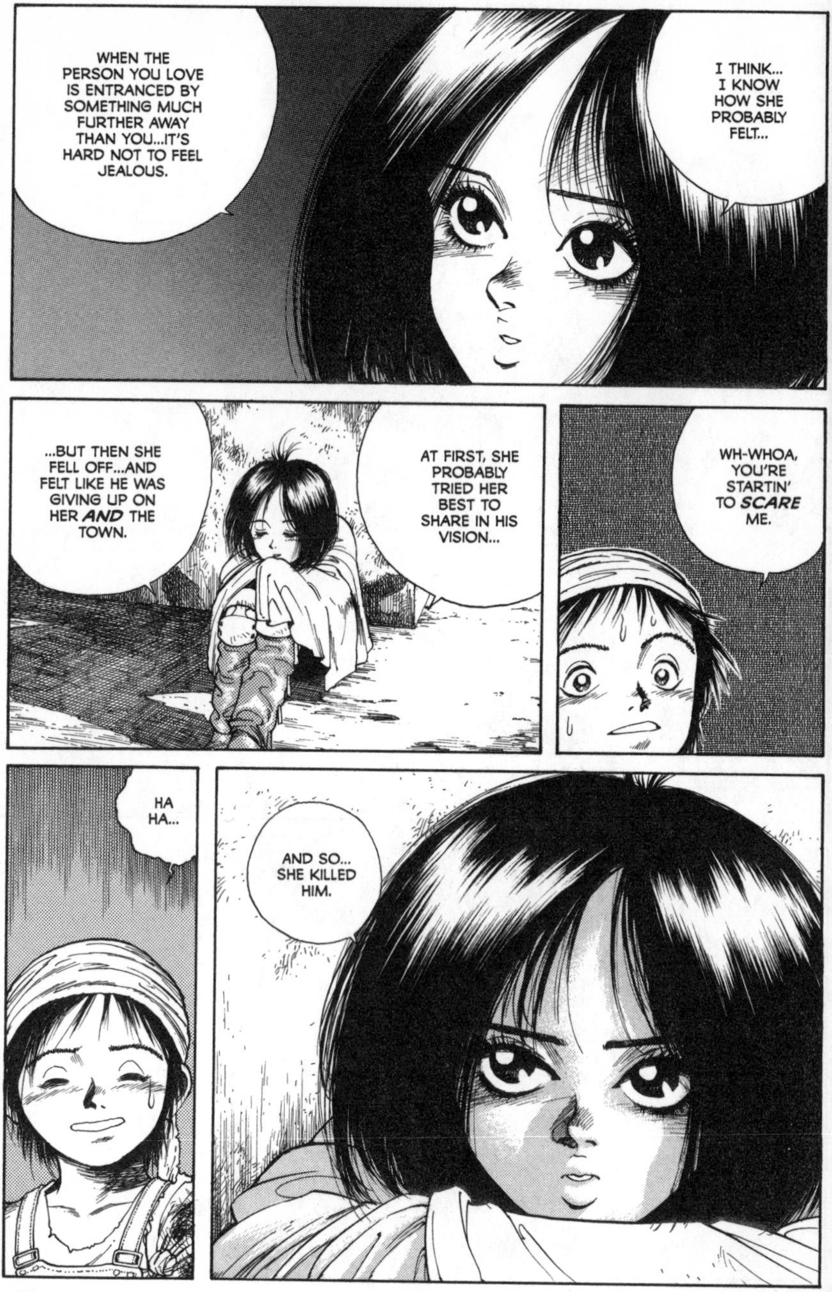
I THINK... I KNOW HOW SHE PROBABLY FELT...
WHEN THE PERSON YOU LOVE IS ENTRANCED BY SOMETHING MUCH FURTHER AWAY THAN YOU...IT'S HARD NOT TO FEEL JEALOUS.
WH-WHOA, YOU'RE STARTIN' TO ***SCARE*** ME.
AT FIRST, SHE PROBABLY TRIED HER BEST TO SHARE IN HIS VISION...
...BUT THEN SHE FELL OFF...AND FELT LIKE HE WAS GIVING UP ON HER ***AND*** THE TOWN.
AND SO... SHE KILLED HIM.
HA HA...

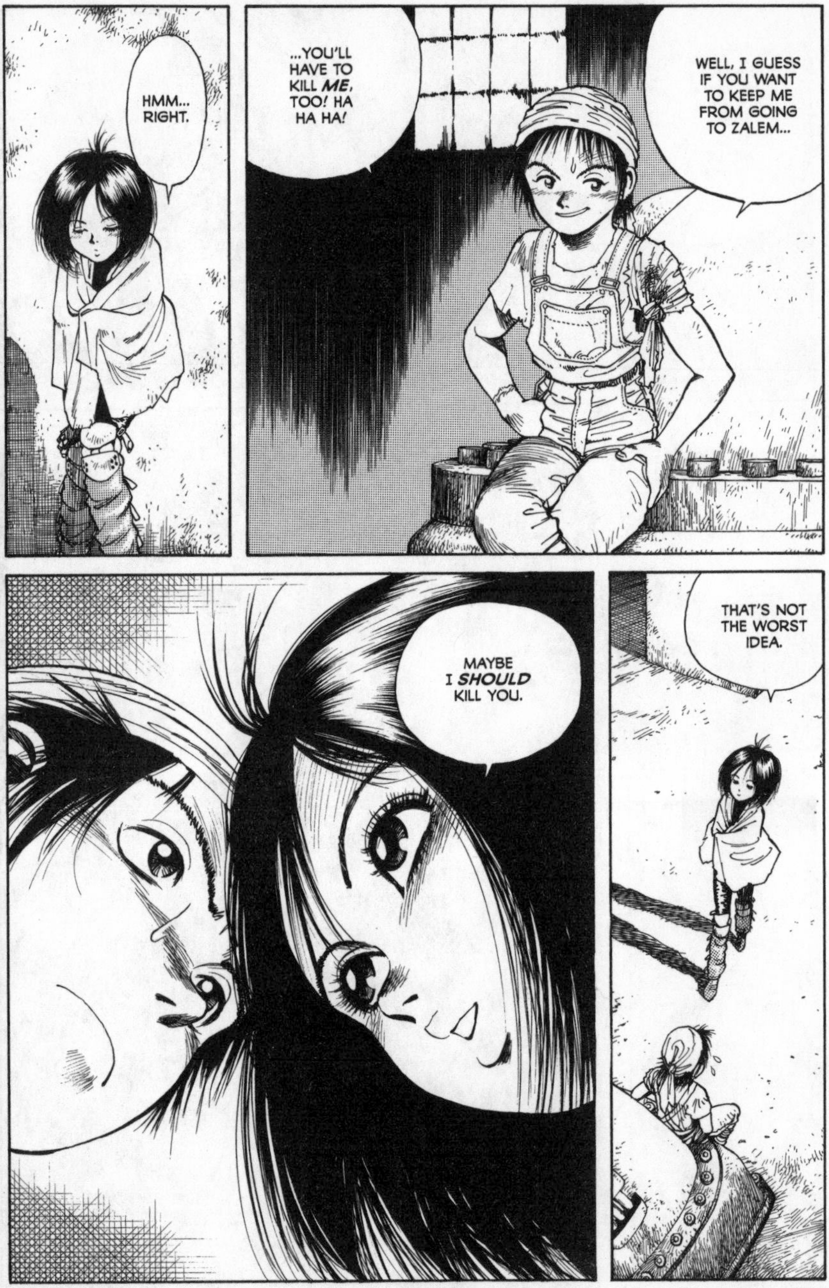
WELL, I GUESS IF YOU WANT TO KEEP ME FROM GOING TO ZALEM...
...YOU'LL HAVE TO KILL *ME*, TOO! HA HA HA!
HMM... RIGHT.
THAT'S NOT THE WORST IDEA.
MAYBE I *SHOULD* KILL YOU.

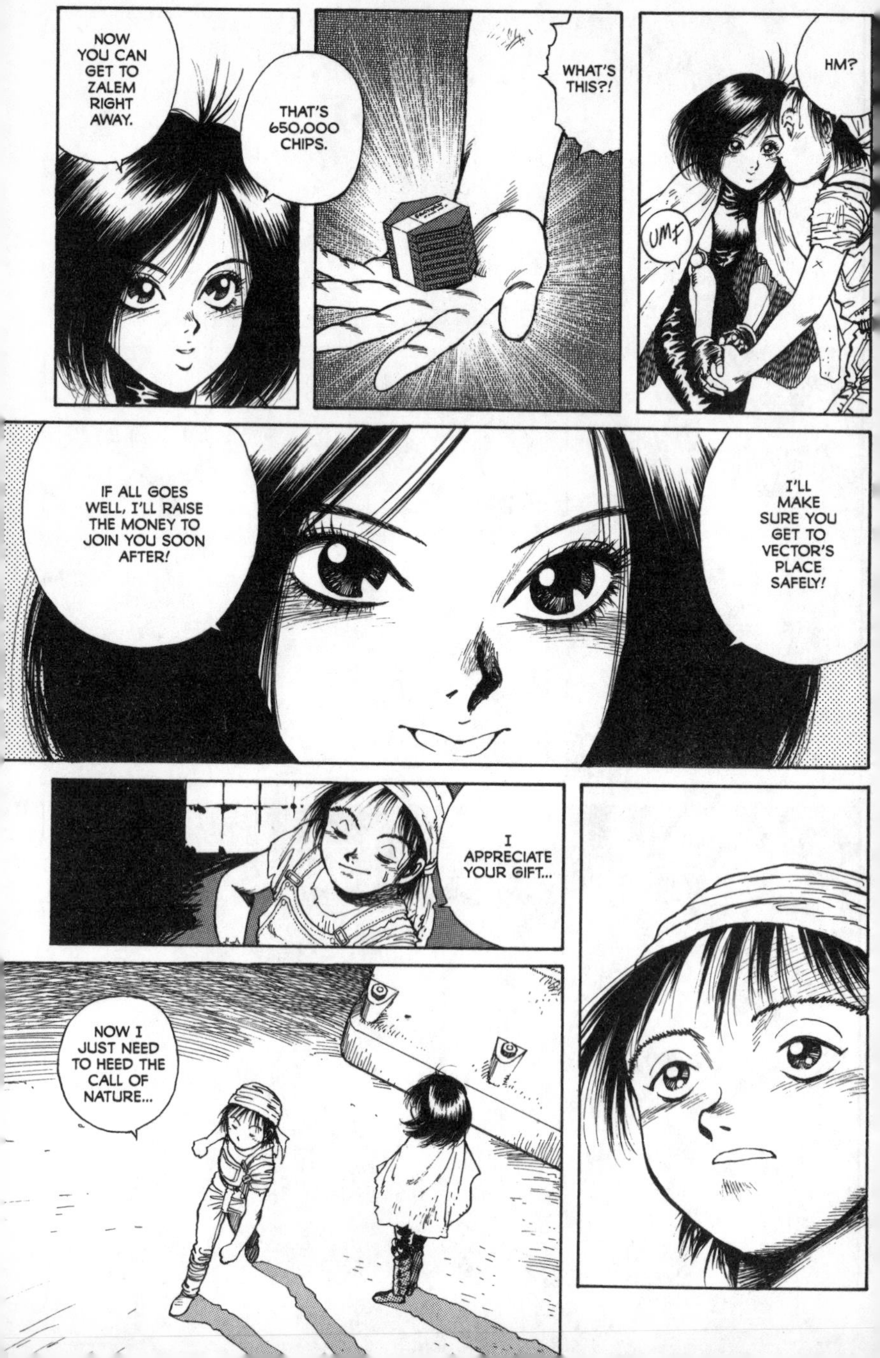
HM?
UMF
WHAT'S THIS?!
NOW YOU CAN GET TO ZALEM RIGHT AWAY.
THAT'S 650,000 CHIPS.
I'LL MAKE SURE YOU GET TO VECTOR'S PLACE SAFELY!
IF ALL GOES WELL, I'LL RAISE THE MONEY TO JOIN YOU SOON AFTER!
I APPRECIATE YOUR GIFT...
NOW I JUST NEED TO HEED THE CALL OF NATURE...

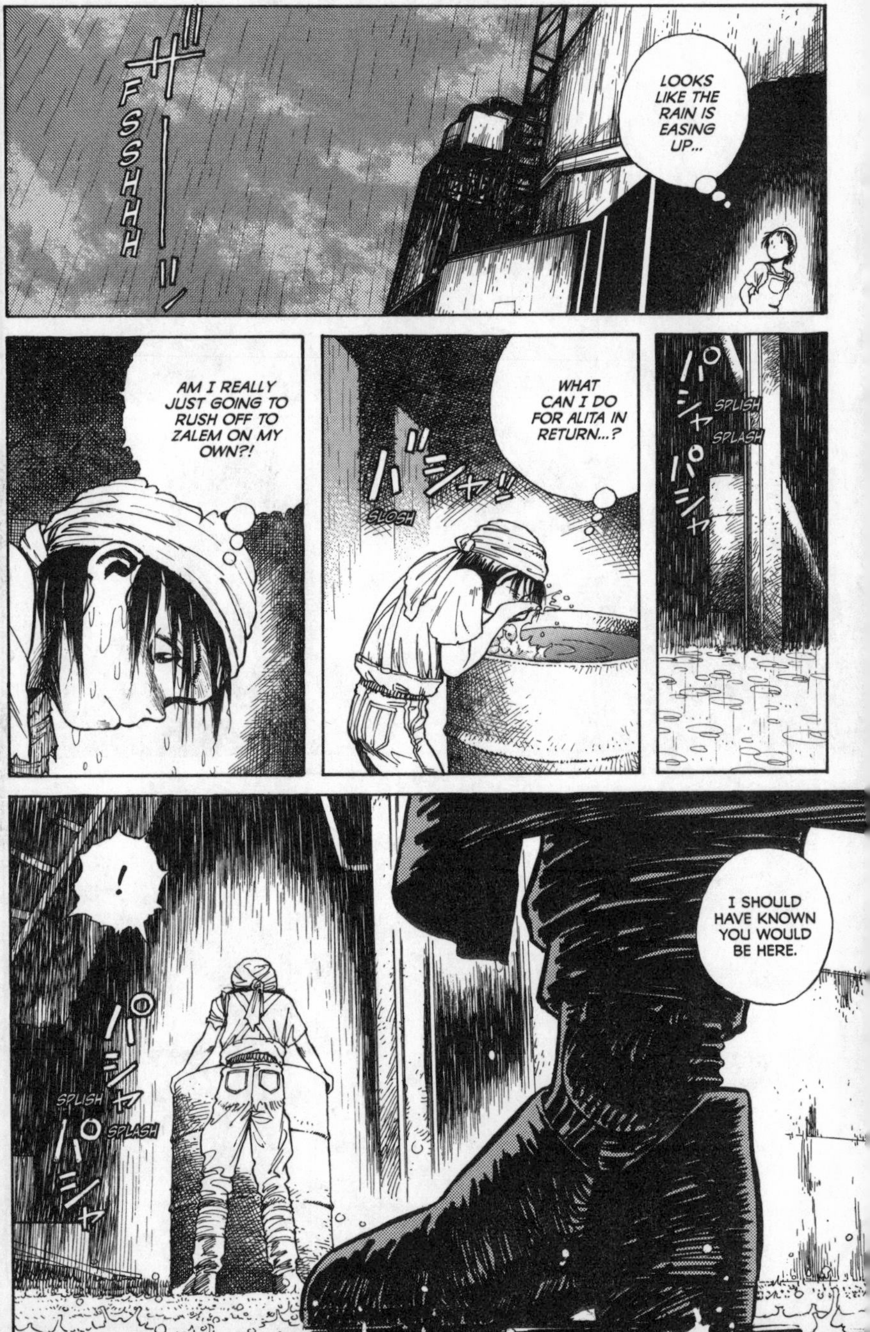
FSSHHH
LOOKS LIKE THE RAIN IS EASING UP...
SPLISH
SPLASH
WHAT CAN I DO FOR ALITA IN RETURN...?
SLOSH
AM I REALLY JUST GOING TO RUSH OFF TO ZALEM ON MY OWN?!
I SHOULD HAVE KNOWN YOU WOULD BE HERE.
!
SPLISH
SPLASH

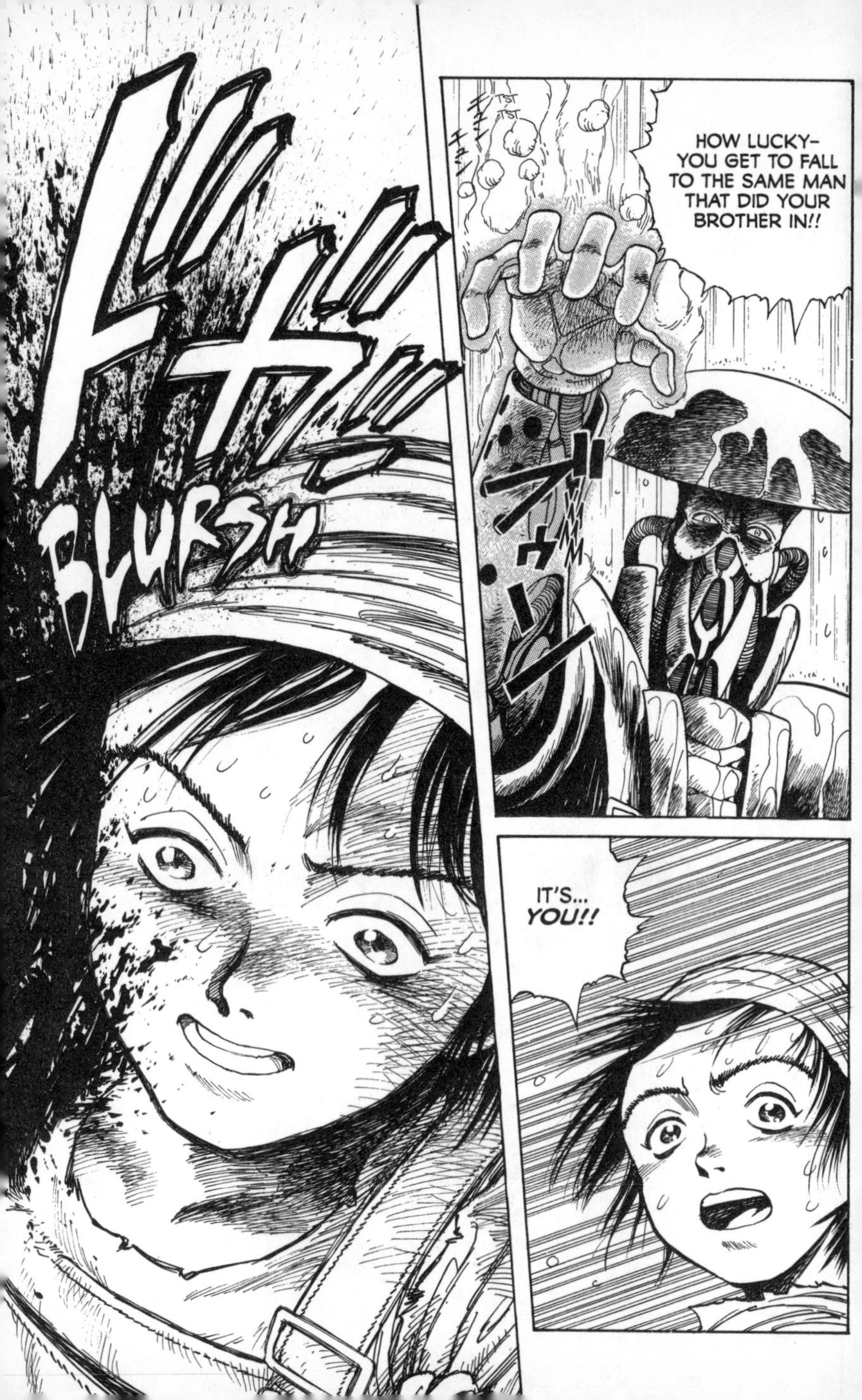
TST TST
HOW LUCKY–
YOU GET TO FALL
TO THE SAME MAN
THAT DID YOUR
BROTHER IN!!
IT'S...
YOU!!
BLURSH

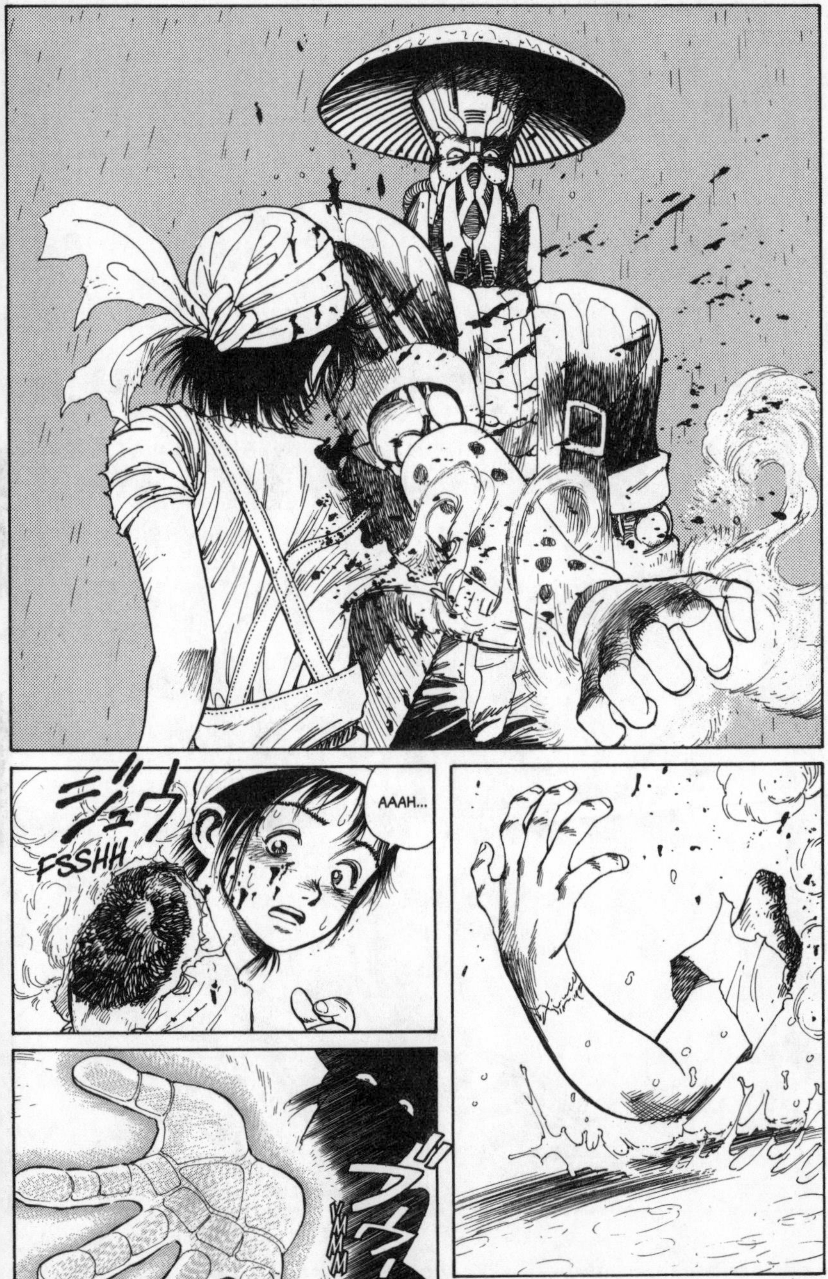
AAAH...
ジュウ
FSSHH
ブウーー
VMMM

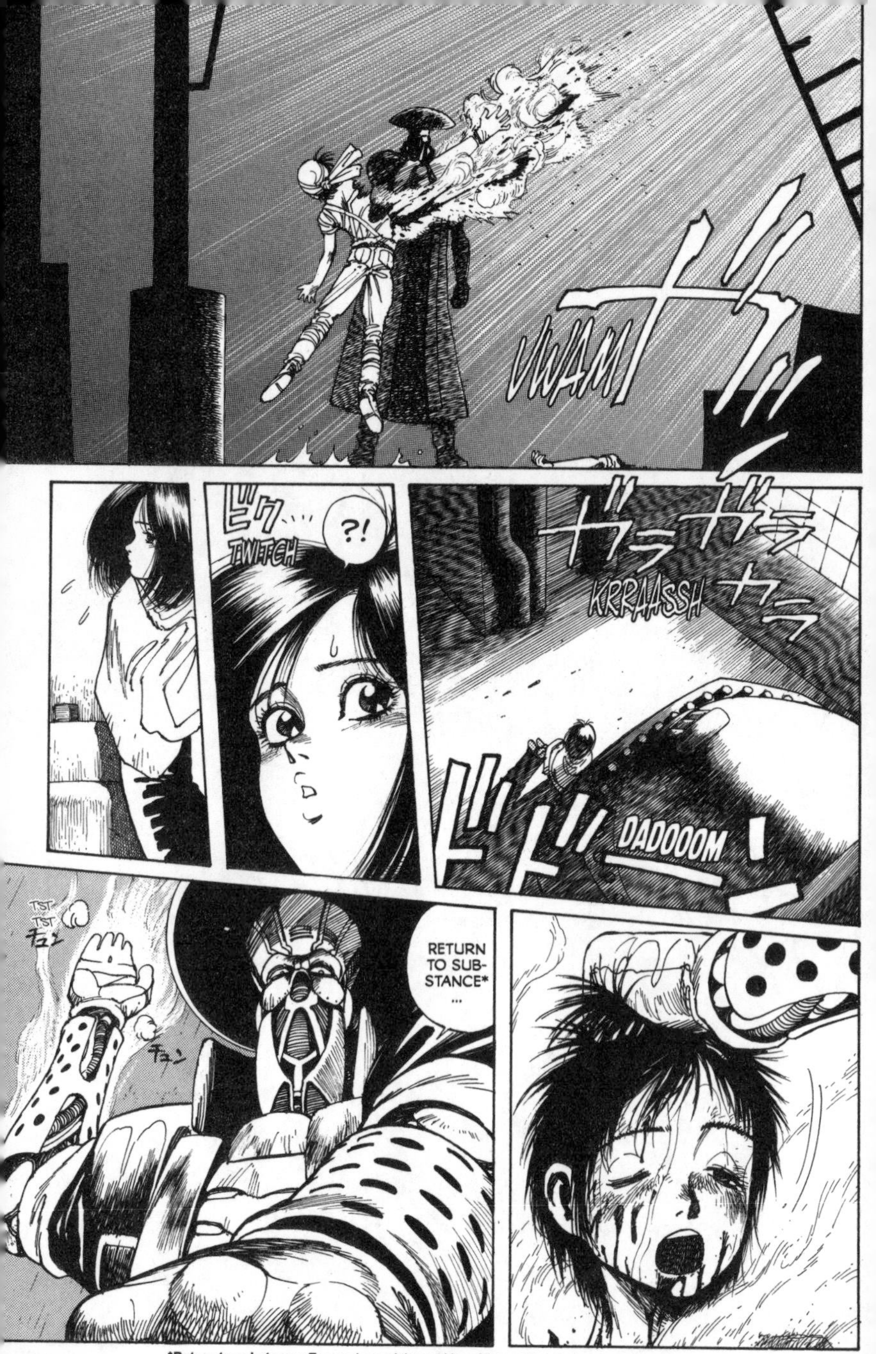
ザシュ
WAM
ガラガラ
KRRAASSH
カラ
ドドーン
DADOOOM
ビク
TWITCH
?!
RETURN TO SUB-STANCE* ...
チュン
TST TST
チュン

*Return to substance:** To pass beyond the troubles of the world and return to matter. A phrase from "Substantist Thought," an offshoot of Cartesian dualism.

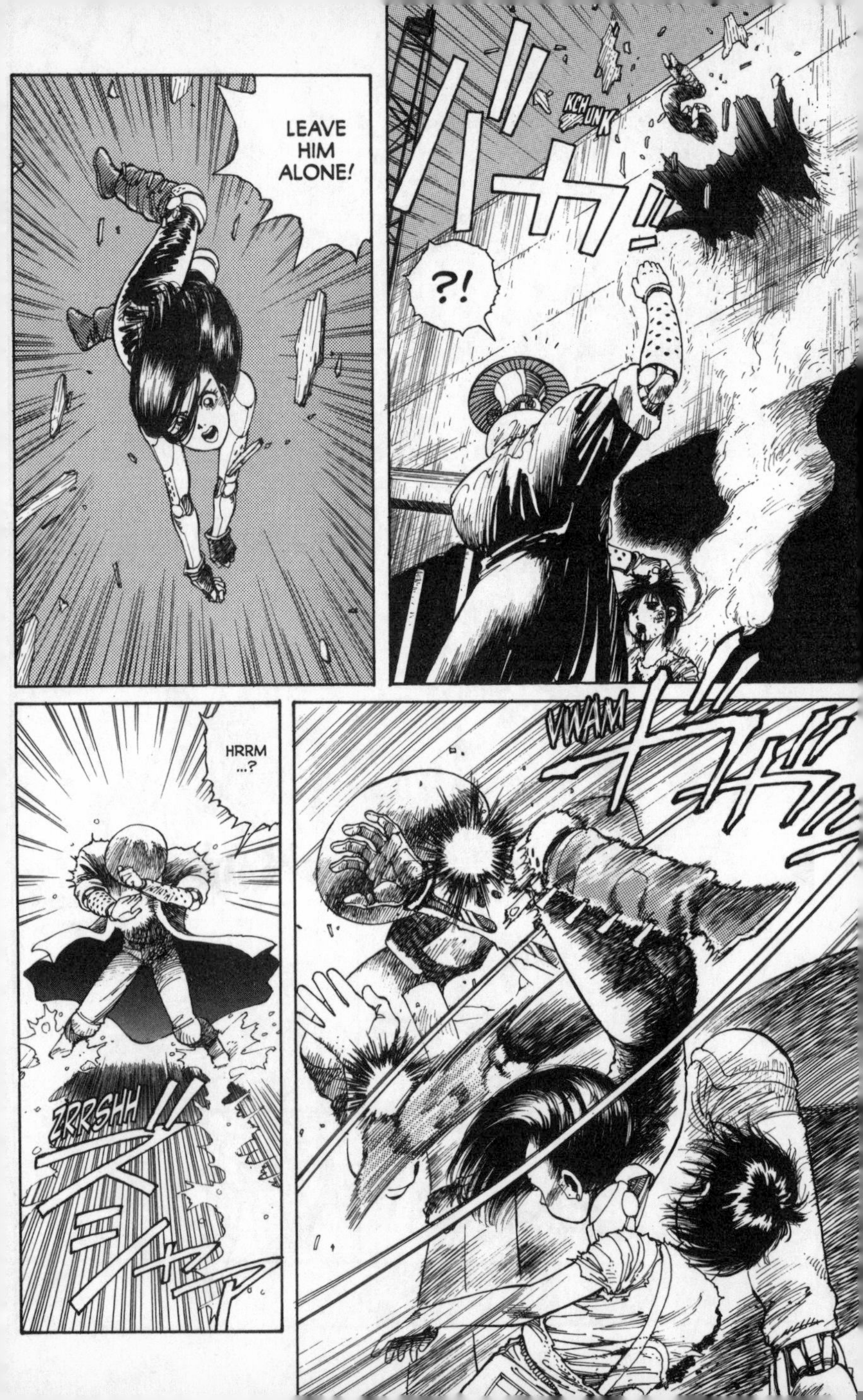
KCHUNK
?!
LEAVE HIM ALONE!
VWAM
HRRM ...?
ZRRSHH!!

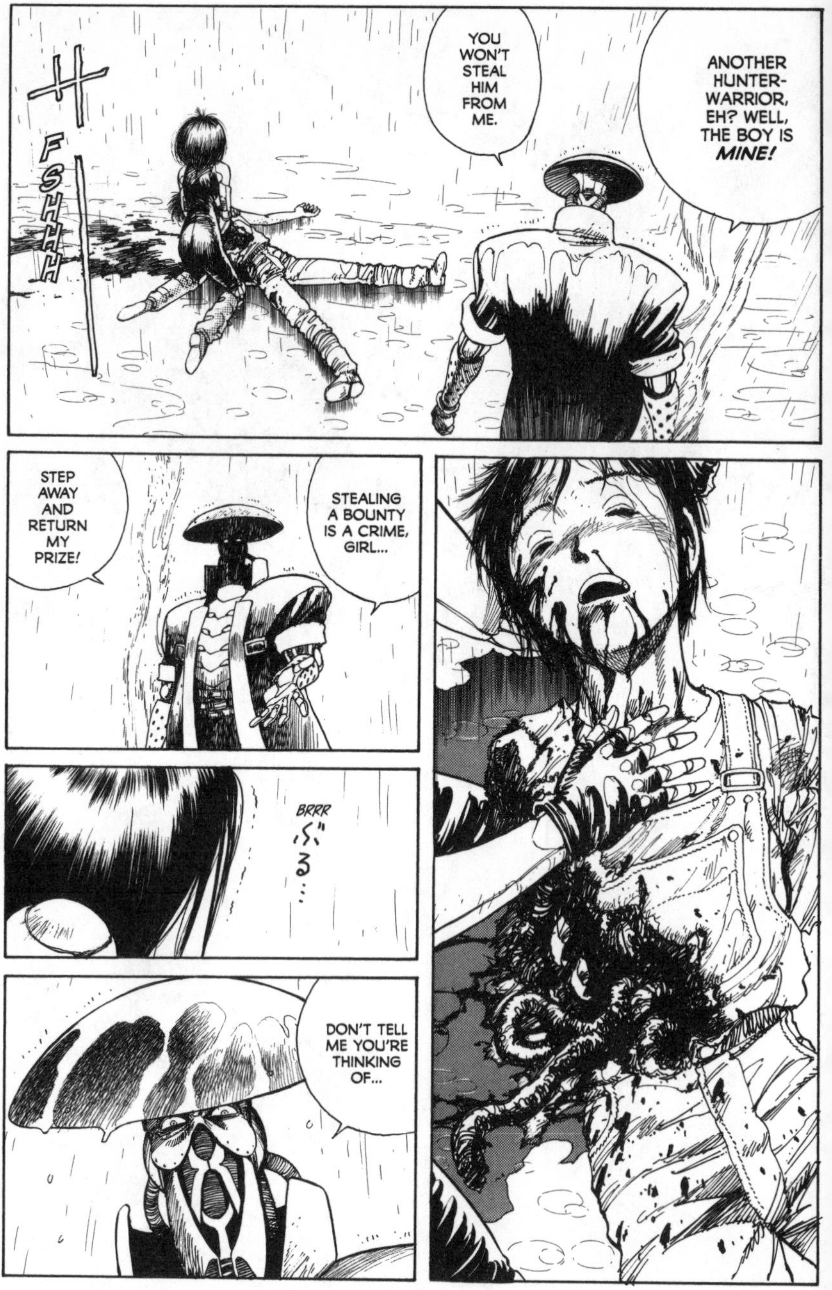
ANOTHER HUNTER-WARRIOR, EH? WELL, THE BOY IS MINE!
YOU WON'T STEAL HIM FROM ME.
FSHHH
STEALING A BOUNTY IS A CRIME, GIRL...
STEP AWAY AND RETURN MY PRIZE!
BRRR
ぶる…
DON'T TELL ME YOU'RE THINKING OF...

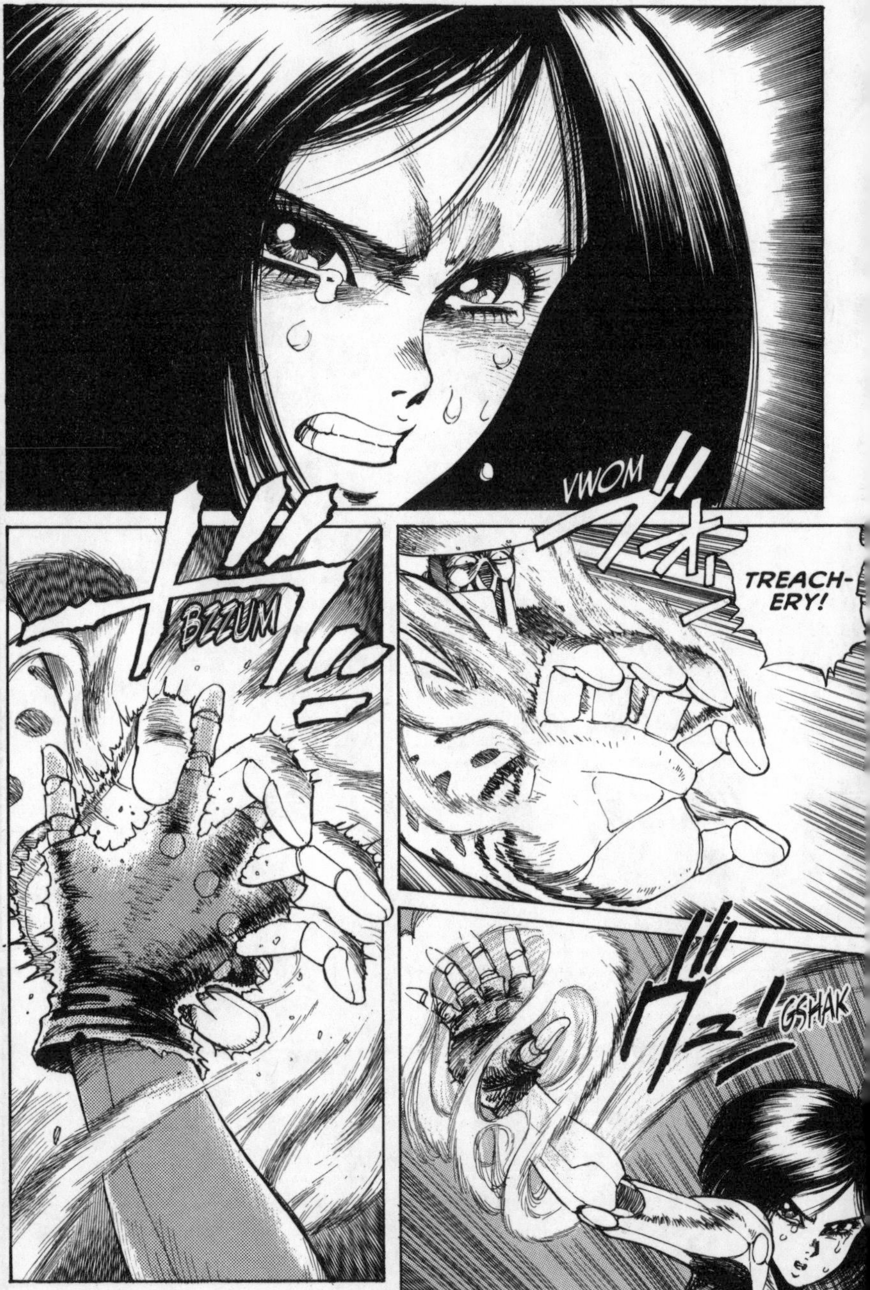
VWOM
TREACH-
ERY!
GSHAK
BZZUM

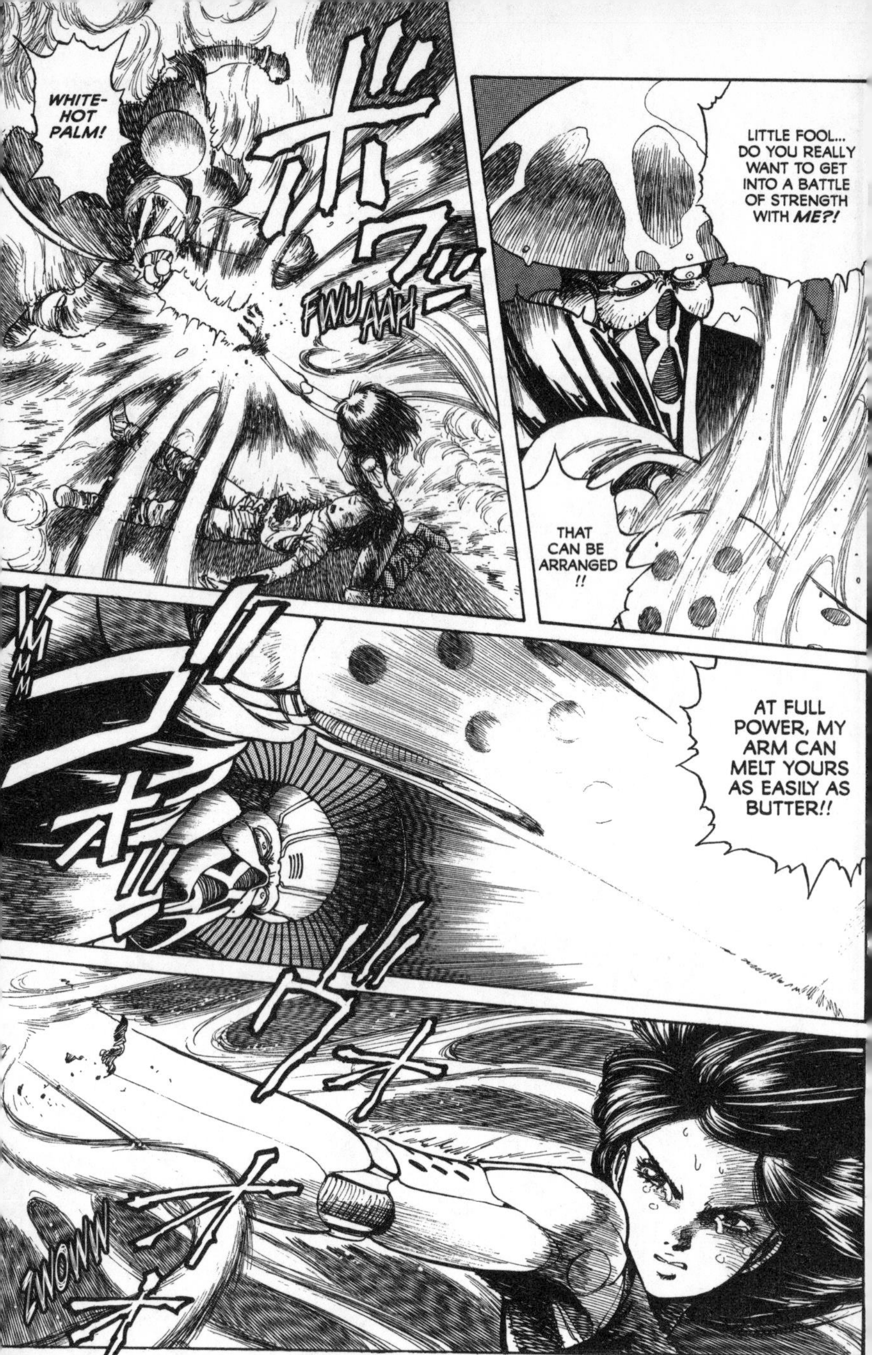
LITTLE FOOL... DO YOU REALLY WANT TO GET INTO A BATTLE OF STRENGTH WITH *ME?!*
THAT CAN BE ARRANGED !!
WHITE-HOT PALM!
FWUAAH
AT FULL POWER, MY ARM CAN MELT YOURS AS EASILY AS BUTTER!!
MMM
ZWOWW

KSSSHT

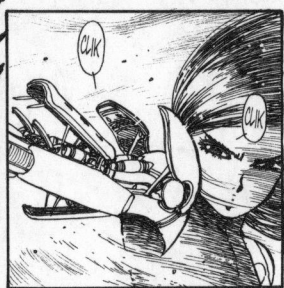

CLIK

CLIK

CLIK

?!

ZZAP

ZAP

ZAP

ZAP

CRAKK

TSSST

?!

HRM
...?

HA HA HA...
DO YOU REALLY
THINK THIS WEAK
LITTLE EXCUSE FOR
A CURRENT CAN
STOP ME?!

BZZT

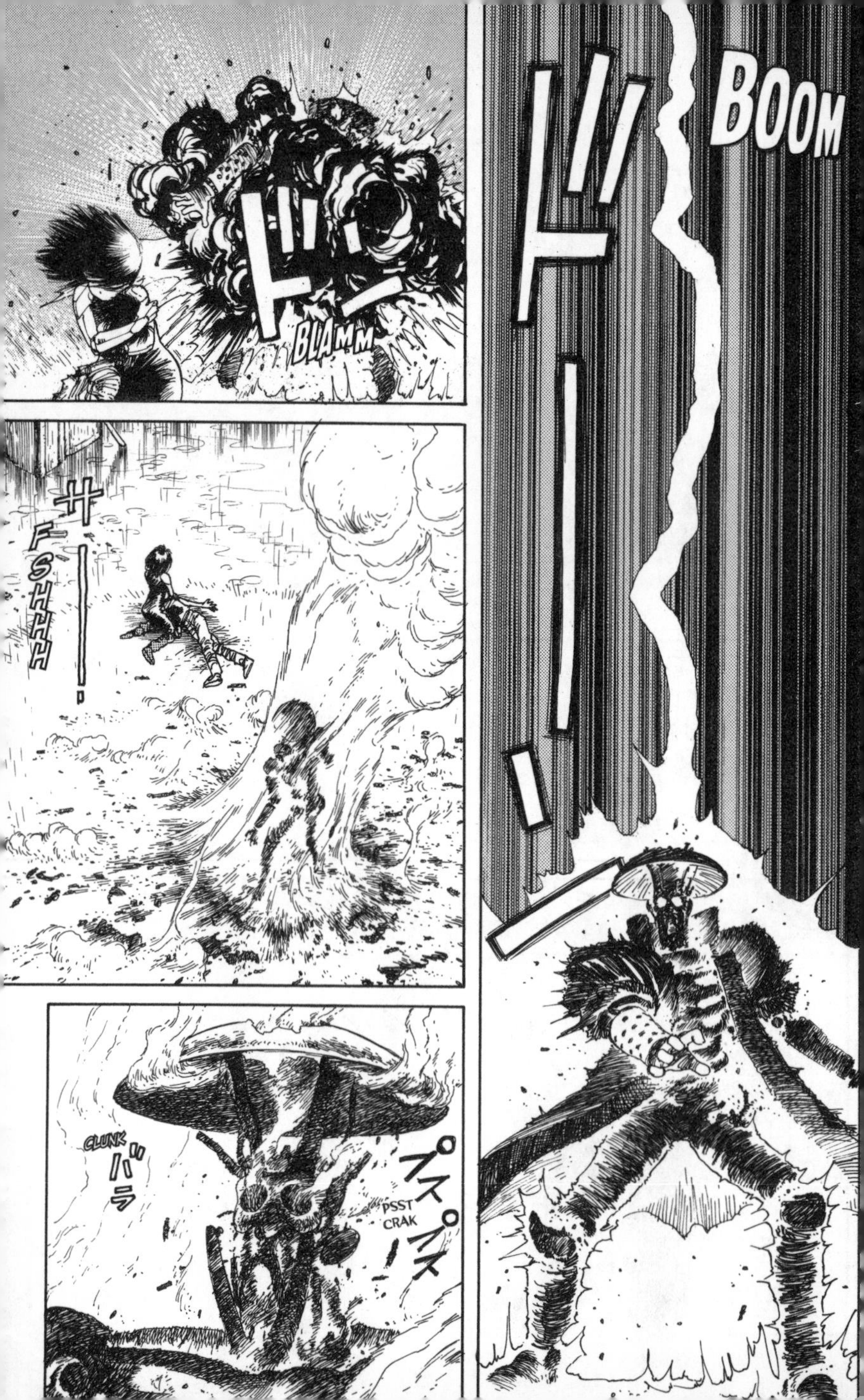
BOOM
BLAMM
サー
FSHHHH
バラ
CLUNK
パスパス
PSST
CRAK

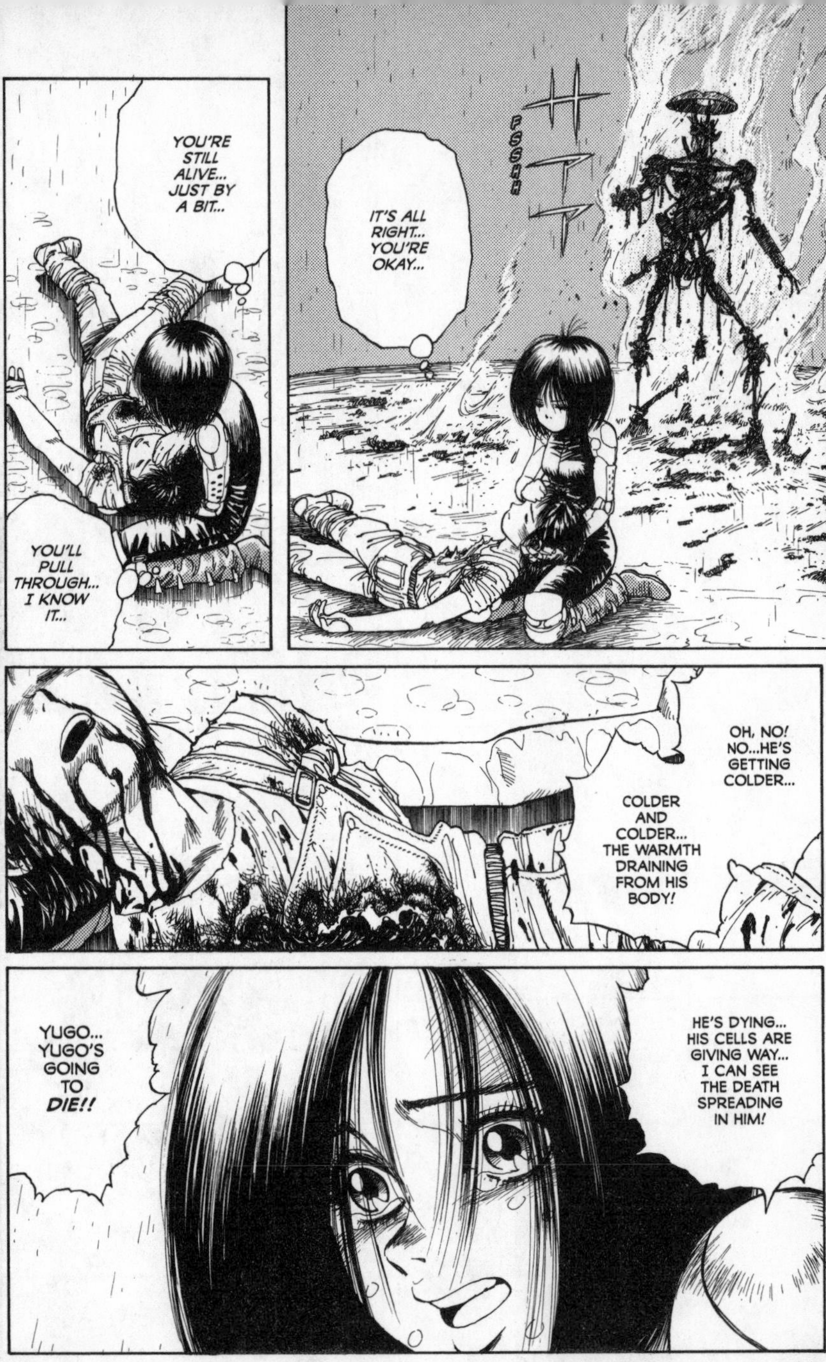
FSSHH
IT'S ALL RIGHT... YOU'RE OKAY...
YOU'RE STILL ALIVE... JUST BY A BIT...
YOU'LL PULL THROUGH... I KNOW IT...
OH, NO! NO...HE'S GETTING COLDER...
COLDER AND COLDER... THE WARMTH DRAINING FROM HIS BODY!
HE'S DYING... HIS CELLS ARE GIVING WAY... I CAN SEE THE DEATH SPREADING IN HIM!
YUGO... YUGO'S GOING TO DIE!!

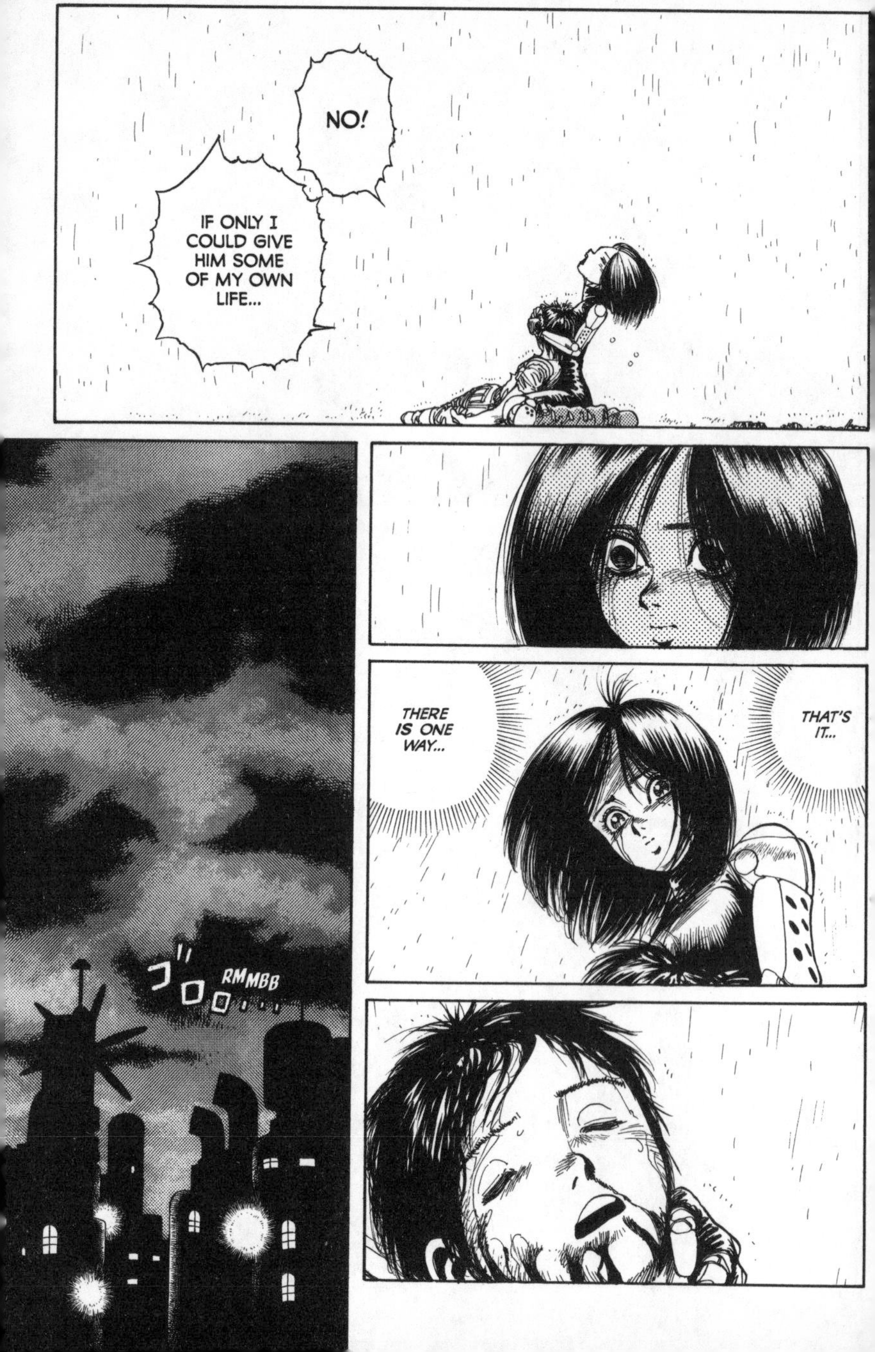
NO!
IF ONLY I COULD GIVE HIM SOME OF MY OWN LIFE...
THAT'S IT...
THERE IS ONE WAY...
RMMBB

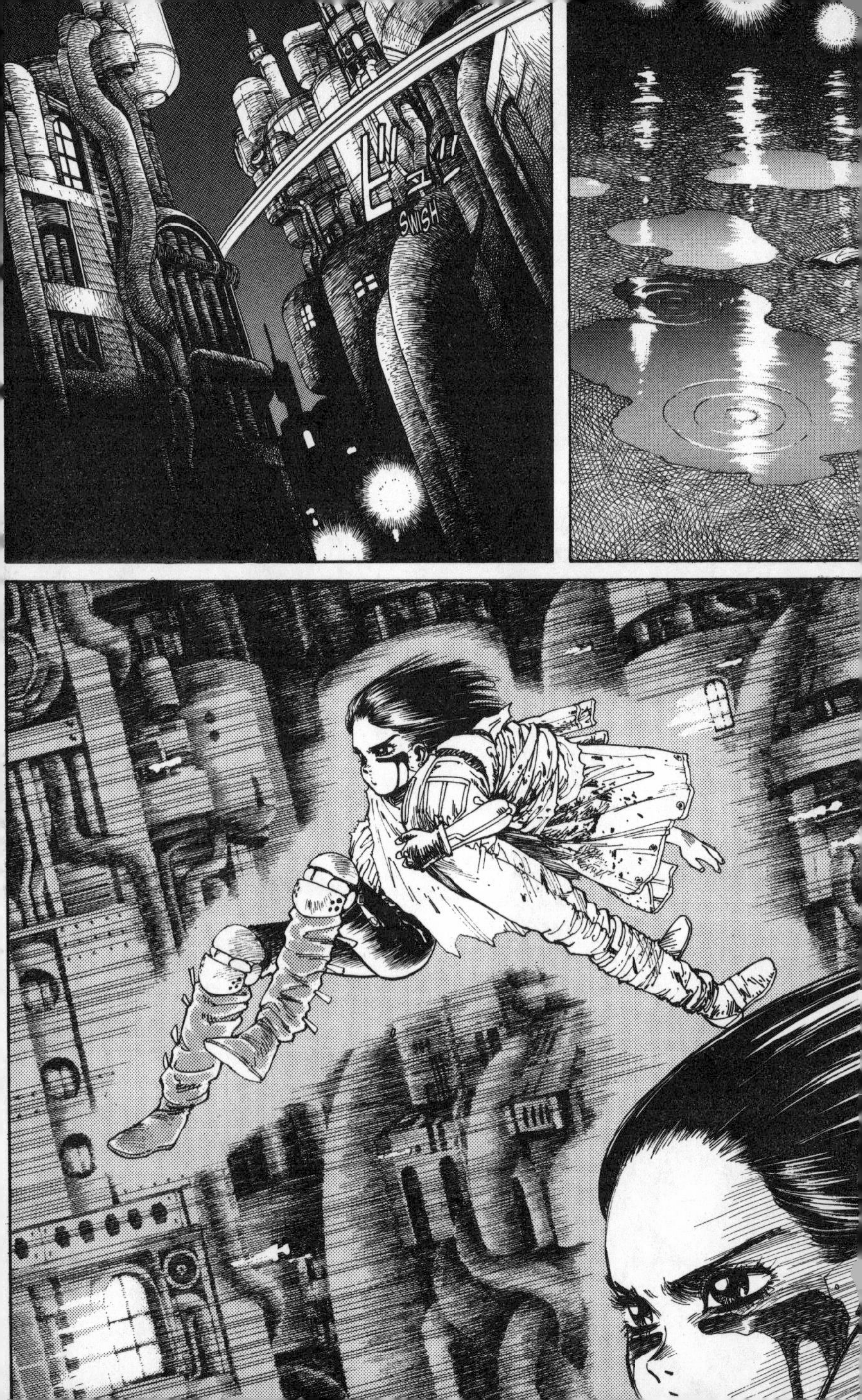
SWISH

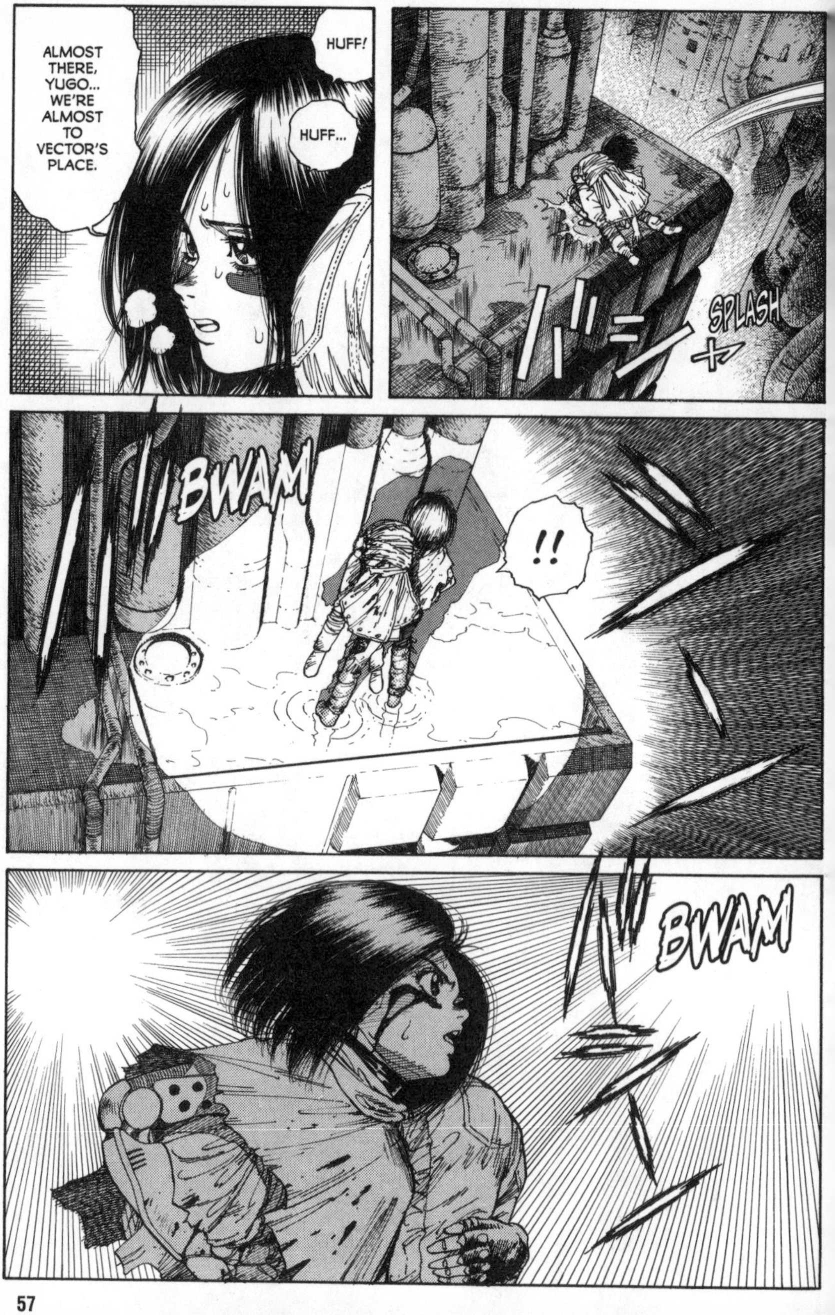
SPLASH
HUFF!
ALMOST THERE, YUGO... WE'RE ALMOST TO VECTOR'S PLACE.
HUFF...
!!
BWAM
BWAM

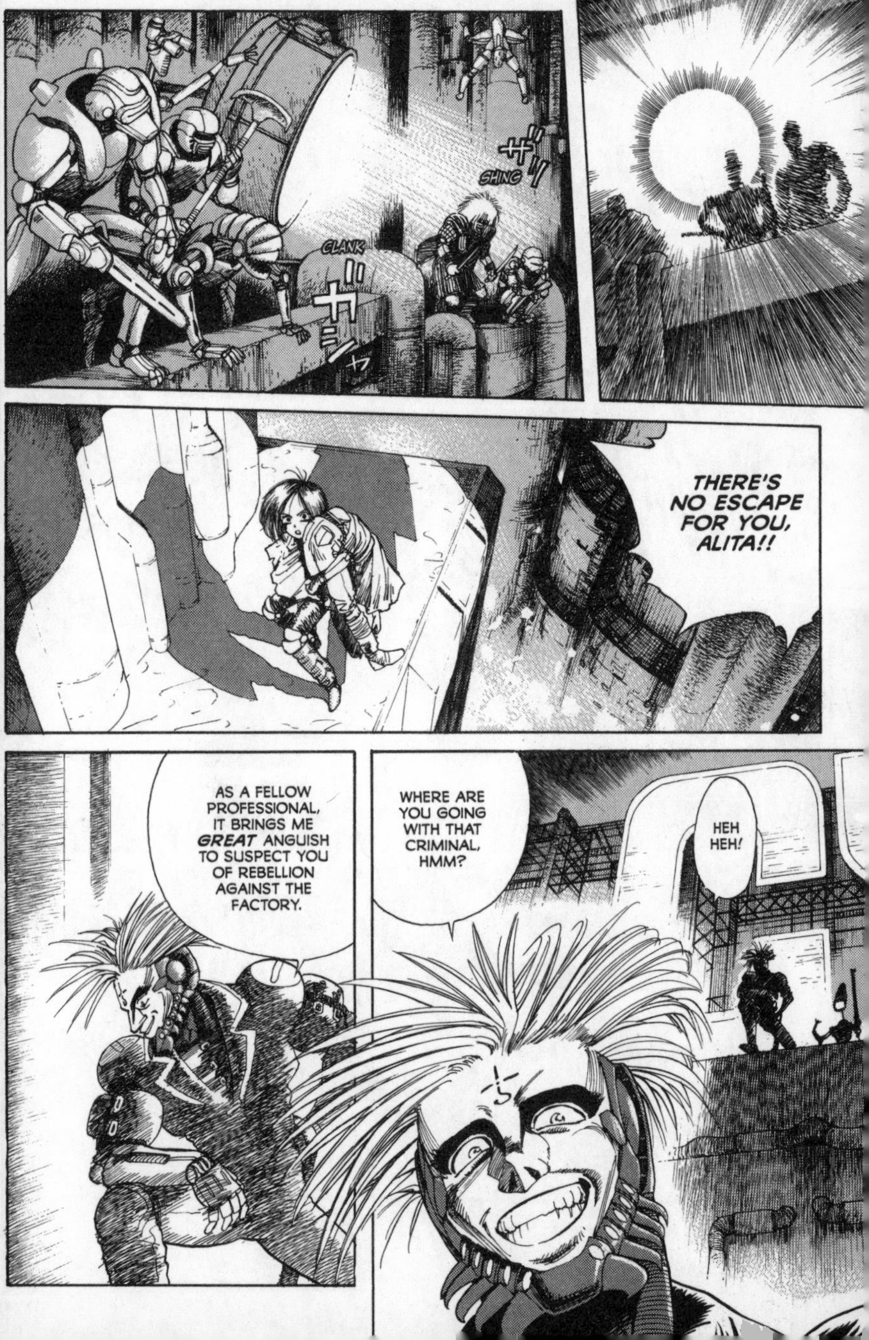
SHING
CLANK
THERE'S NO ESCAPE FOR YOU, ALITA!!
HEH HEH!
WHERE ARE YOU GOING WITH THAT CRIMINAL, HMM?
AS A FELLOW PROFESSIONAL, IT BRINGS ME **GREAT** ANGUISH TO SUSPECT YOU OF REBELLION AGAINST THE FACTORY.

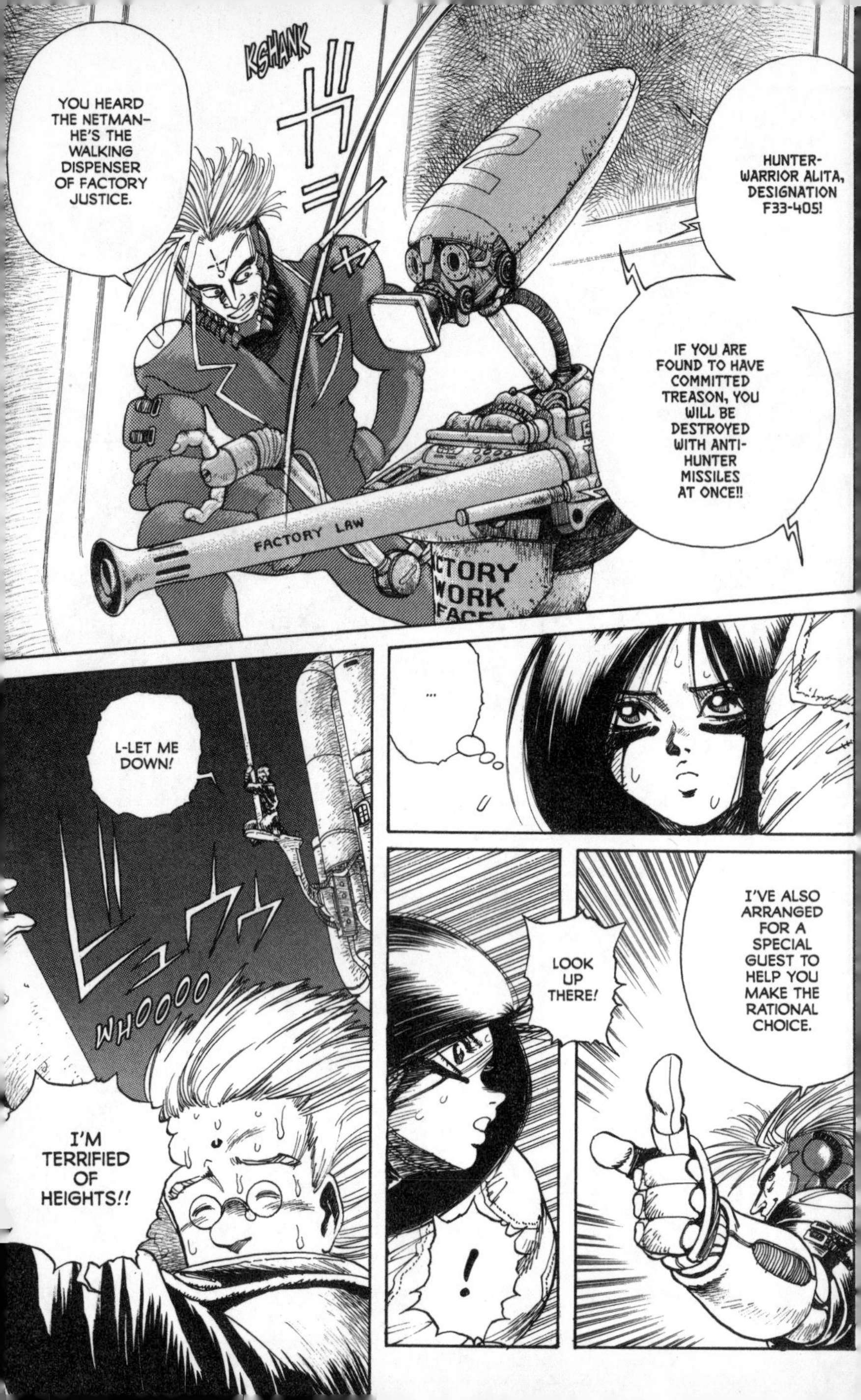
HUNTER-WARRIOR ALITA, DESIGNATION F33-405!
IF YOU ARE FOUND TO HAVE COMMITTED TREASON, YOU WILL BE DESTROYED WITH ANTI-HUNTER MISSILES AT ONCE!!
YOU HEARD THE NETMAN-HE'S THE WALKING DISPENSER OF FACTORY JUSTICE.
KSHANK
FACTORY LAW
...
I'VE ALSO ARRANGED FOR A SPECIAL GUEST TO HELP YOU MAKE THE RATIONAL CHOICE.
LOOK UP THERE!
!
L-LET ME DOWN!
WHOOOO
I'M TERRIFIED OF HEIGHTS!!

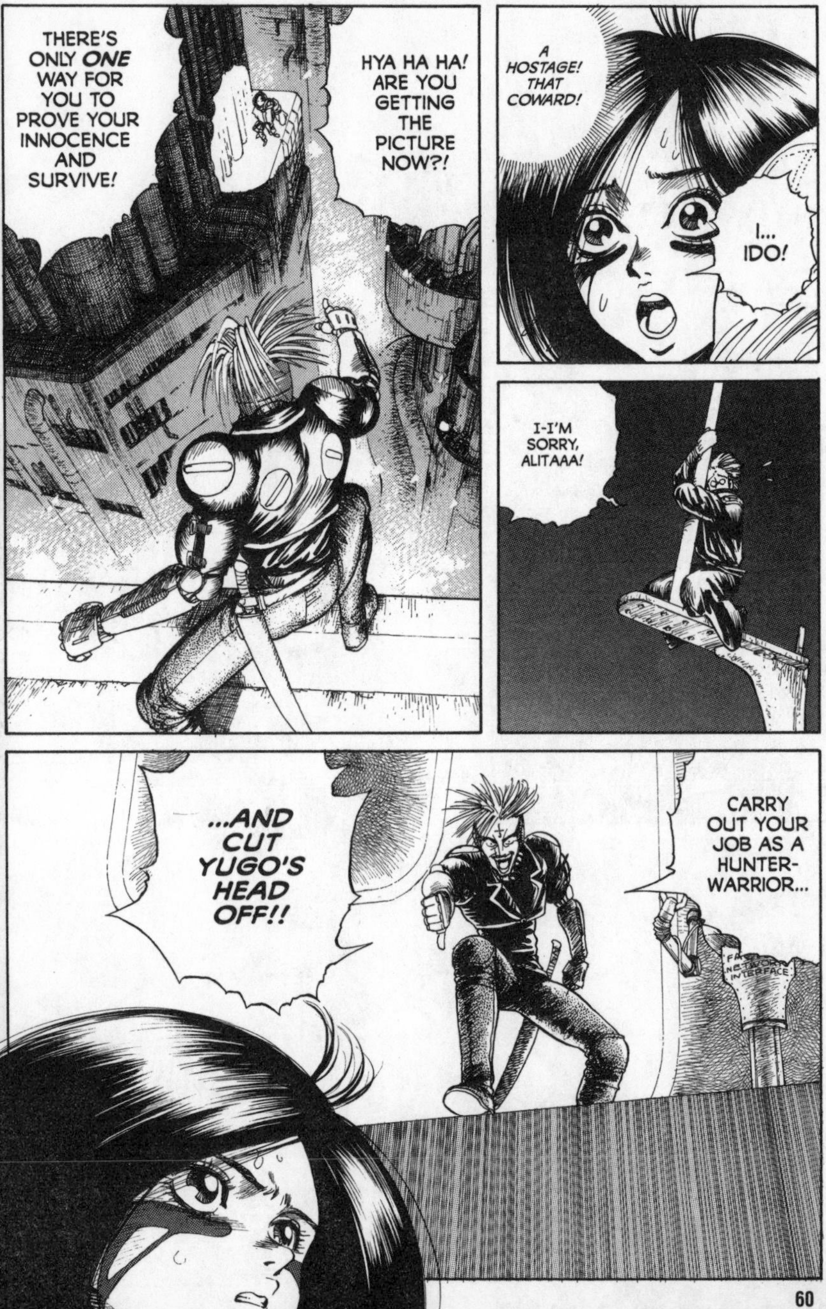
A HOSTAGE! THAT COWARD!
I... IDO!
I-I'M SORRY, ALITAAA!
HYA HA HA! ARE YOU GETTING THE PICTURE NOW?!
THERE'S ONLY ONE WAY FOR YOU TO PROVE YOUR INNOCENCE AND SURVIVE!
CARRY OUT YOUR JOB AS A HUNTER-WARRIOR...
...AND CUT YUGO'S HEAD OFF!!

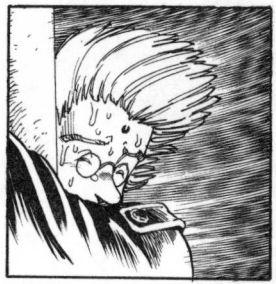

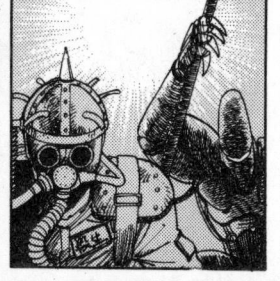

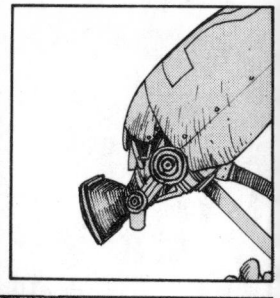

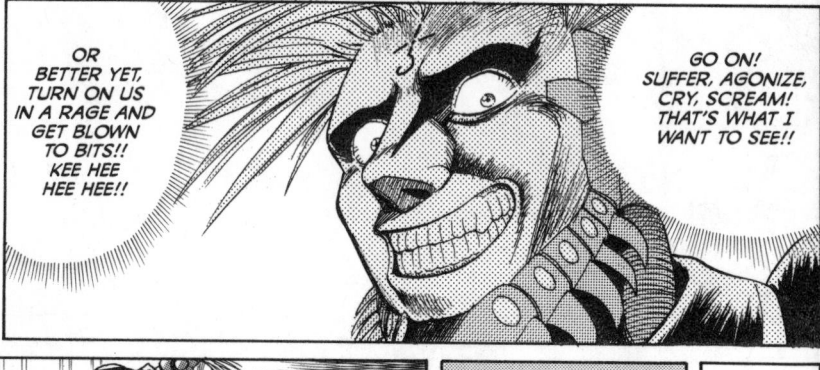

GO ON! SUFFER, AGONIZE, CRY, SCREAM! THAT'S WHAT I WANT TO SEE!!
OR BETTER YET, TURN ON US IN A RAGE AND GET BLOWN TO BITS!! KEE HEE HEE HEE!!
?!
SHP

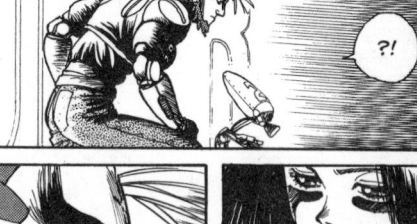

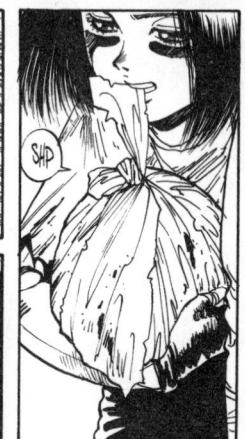

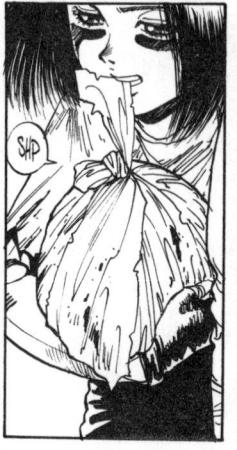

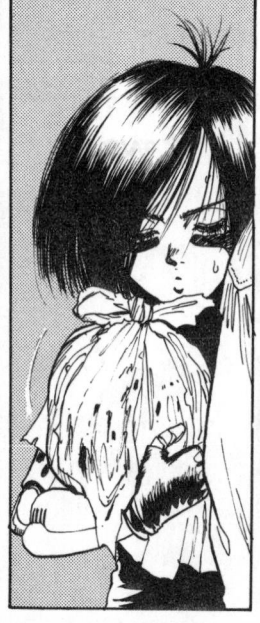

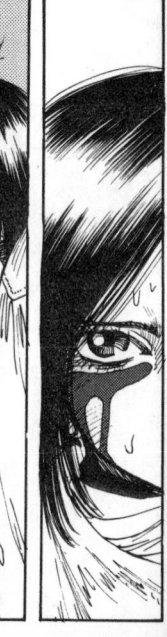

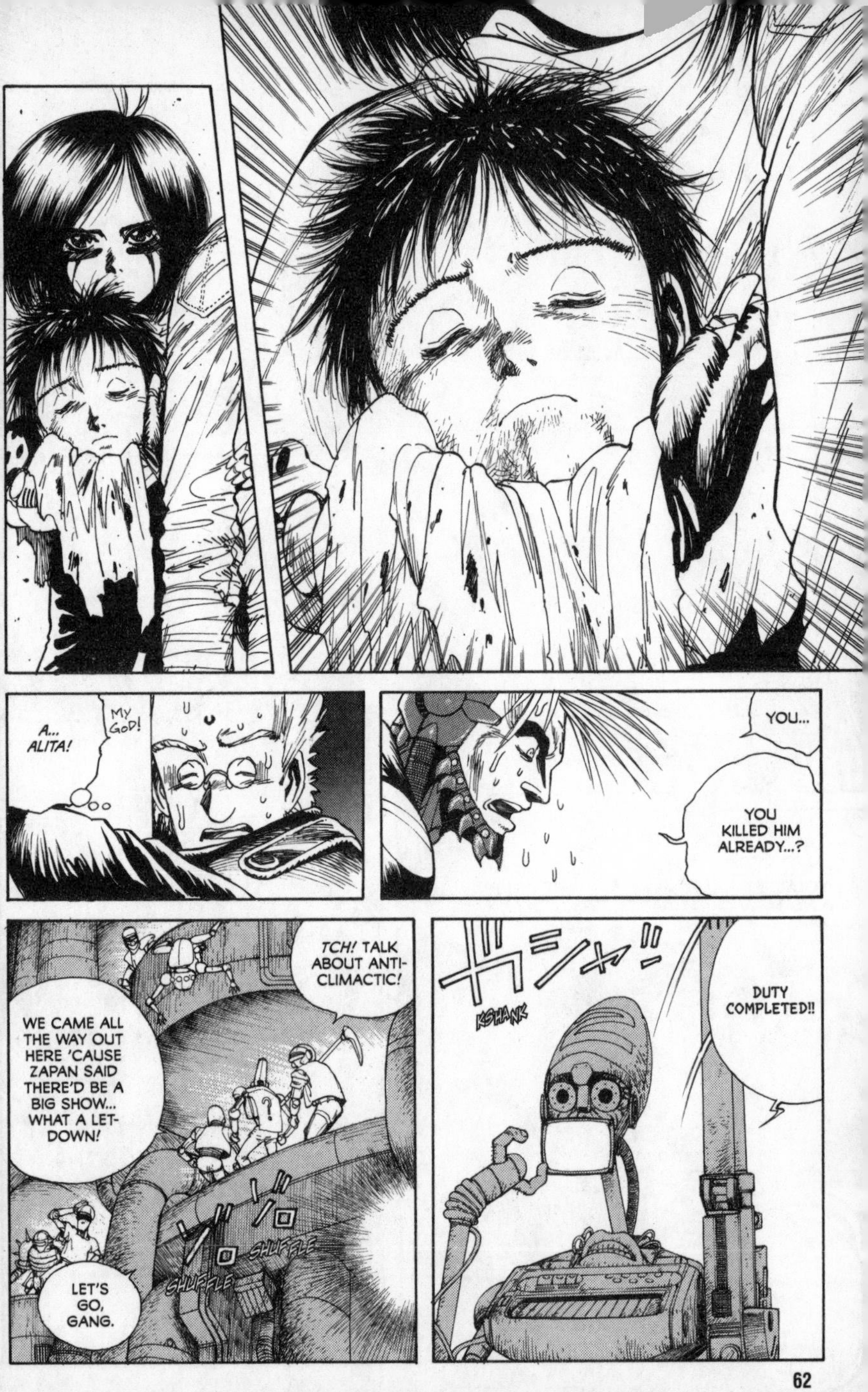
YOU...
YOU KILLED HIM ALREADY...?
A... ALITA!
MY GOD!
DUTY COMPLETED!!
KSHANK
TCH! TALK ABOUT ANTI-CLIMACTIC!
WE CAME ALL THE WAY OUT HERE 'CAUSE ZAPAN SAID THERE'D BE A BIG SHOW... WHAT A LET-DOWN!
SHUFFLE SHUFFLE
LET'S GO, GANG.

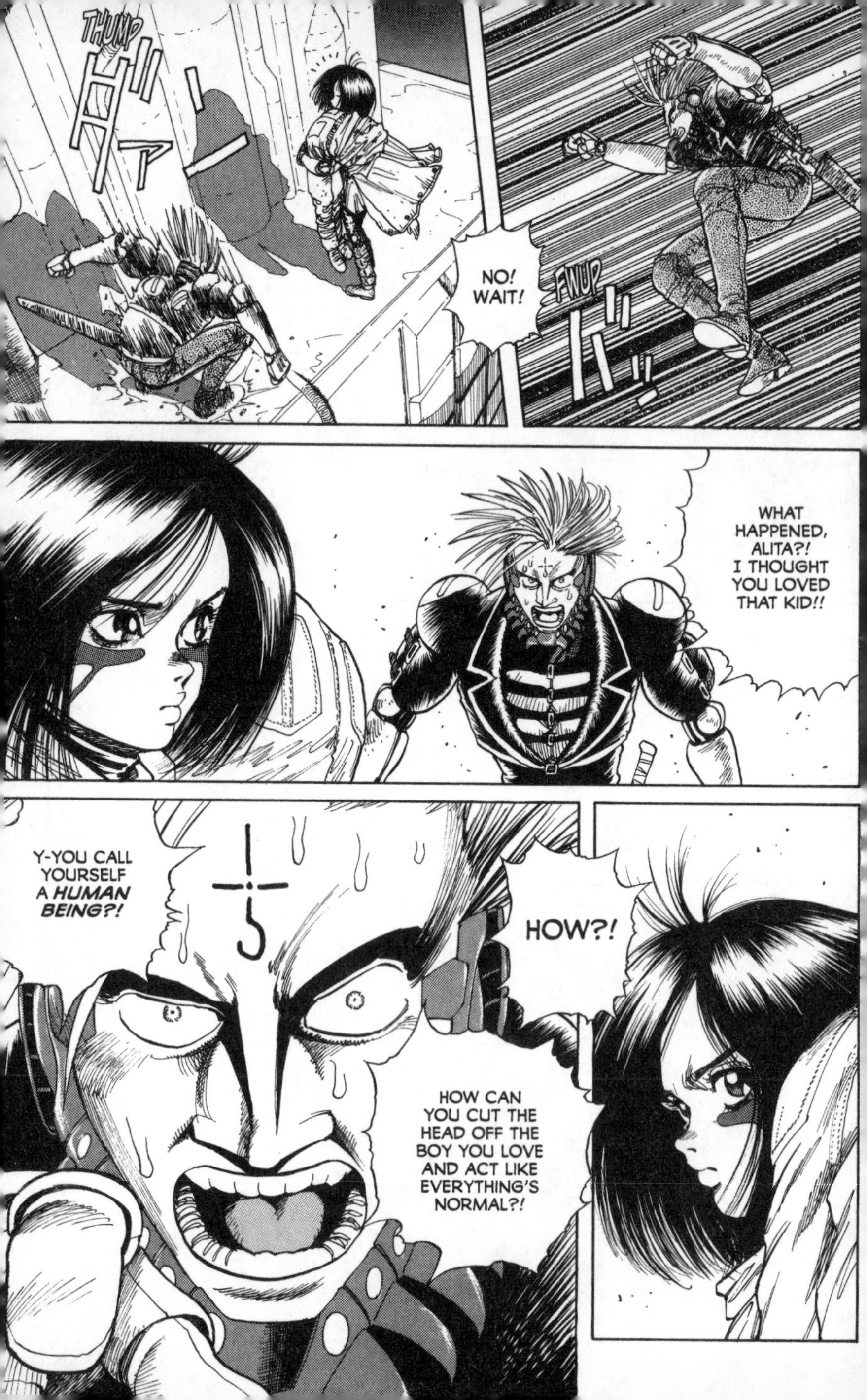
FWUP
NO! WAIT!
THUMP
WHAT HAPPENED, ALITA?! I THOUGHT YOU LOVED THAT KID!!
HOW?!
HOW CAN YOU CUT THE HEAD OFF THE BOY YOU LOVE AND ACT LIKE EVERYTHING'S NORMAL?!
Y-YOU CALL YOURSELF A *HUMAN BEING?!*

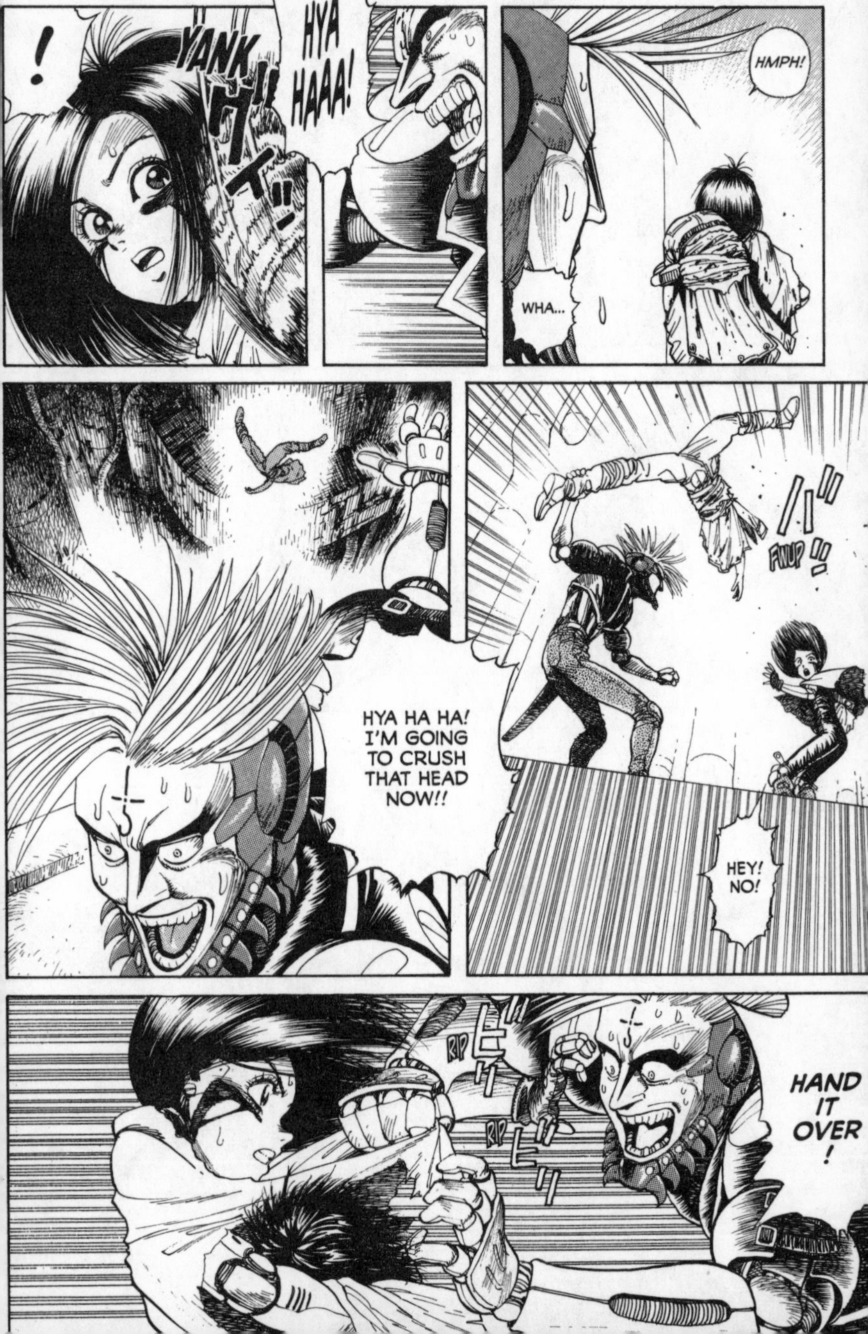
HMPH!
WHA...
HYA HAAA!
YANK!!
!
FWUP!!
HEY! NO!
HYA HA HA! I'M GOING TO CRUSH THAT HEAD NOW!!
RIP
RIP
HAND IT OVER!

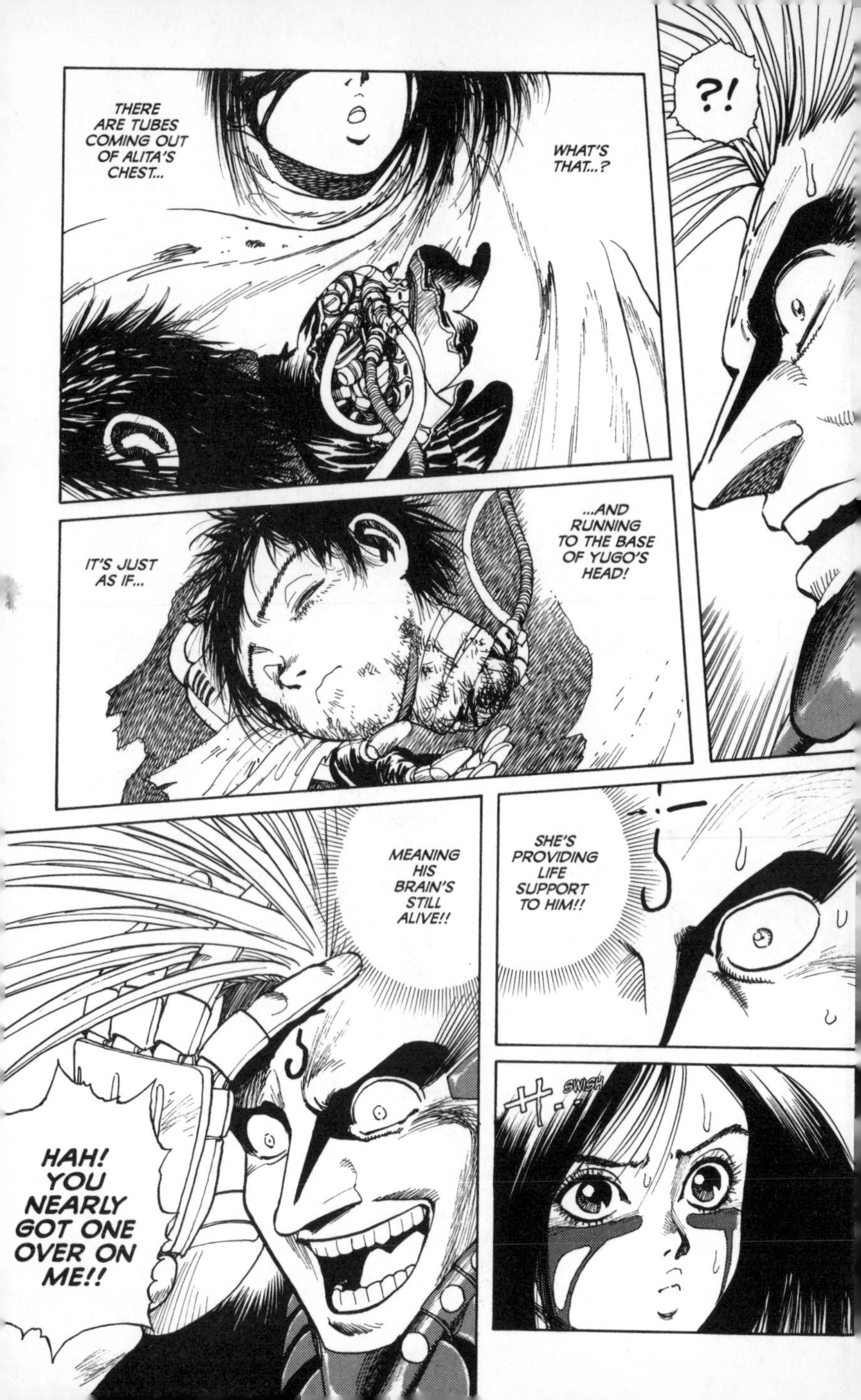
?!
WHAT'S THAT...?
THERE ARE TUBES COMING OUT OF ALITA'S CHEST...
...AND RUNNING TO THE BASE OF YUGO'S HEAD!
IT'S JUST AS IF...
SHE'S PROVIDING LIFE SUPPORT TO HIM!!
SWISH
MEANING HIS BRAIN'S STILL ALIVE!!
HAH! YOU NEARLY GOT ONE OVER ON ME!!

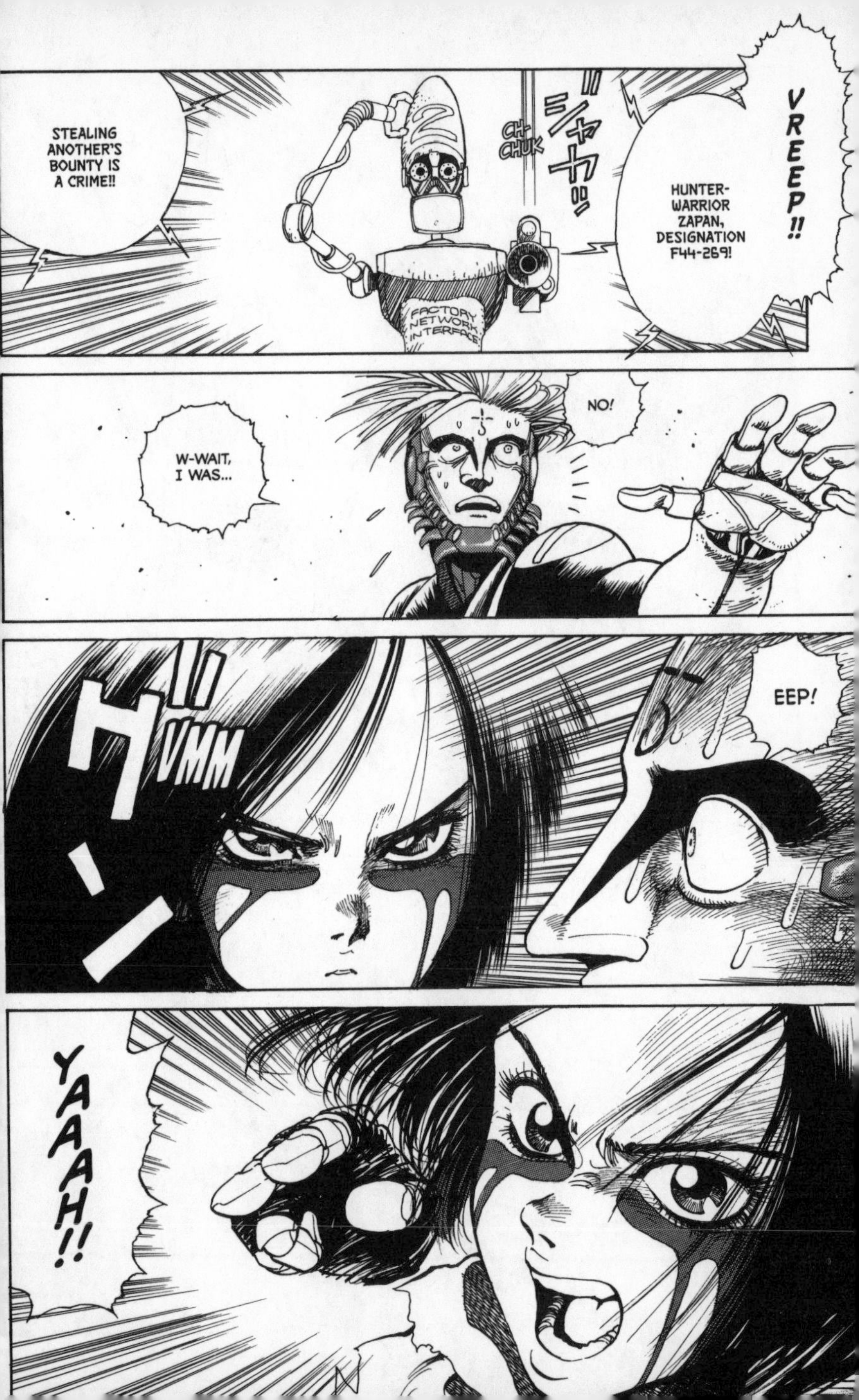
VREEP!!
HUNTER-WARRIOR ZAPAN, DESIGNATION F44-269!
CH-CHUK
FACTORY NETWORK INTERFACE
STEALING ANOTHER'S BOUNTY IS A CRIME!!
NO!
W-WAIT, I WAS...
EEP!
VMM
YAAAH!!

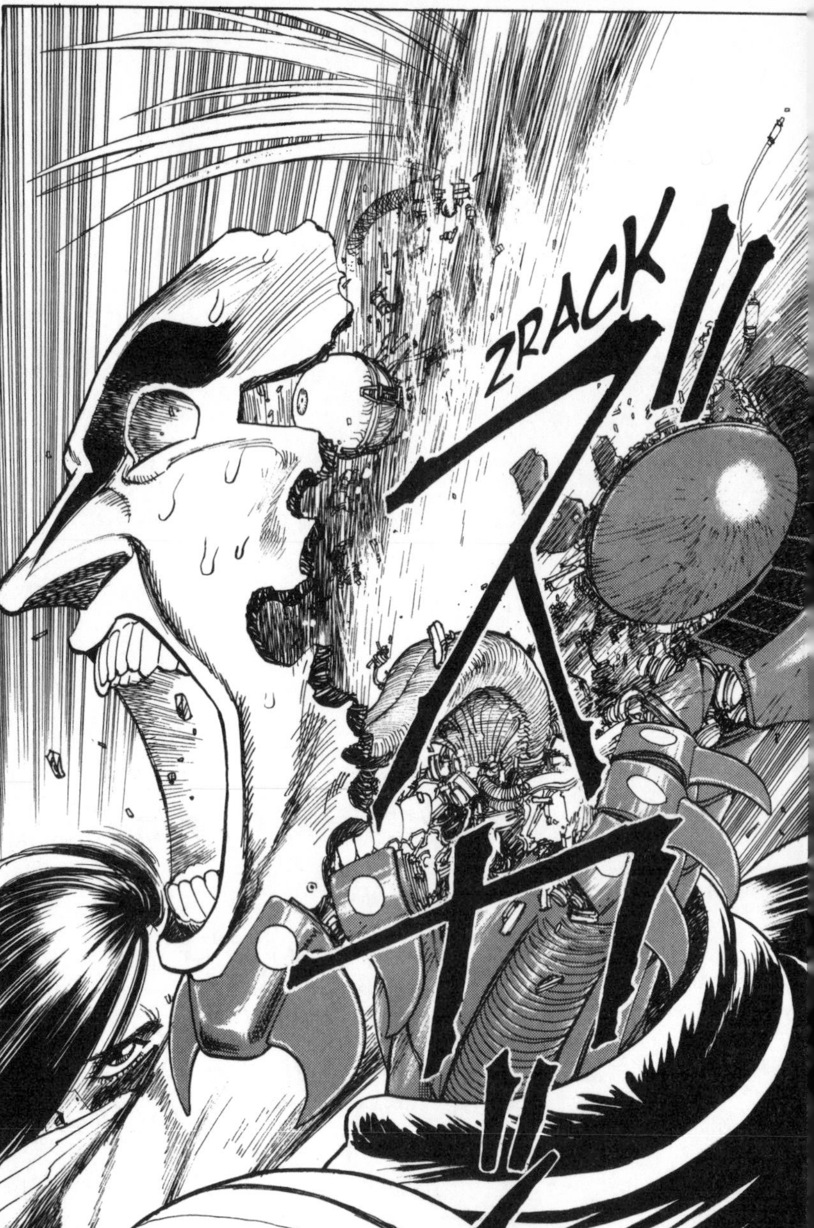
ZRACK

FIGHT 011 Guilty Dreams

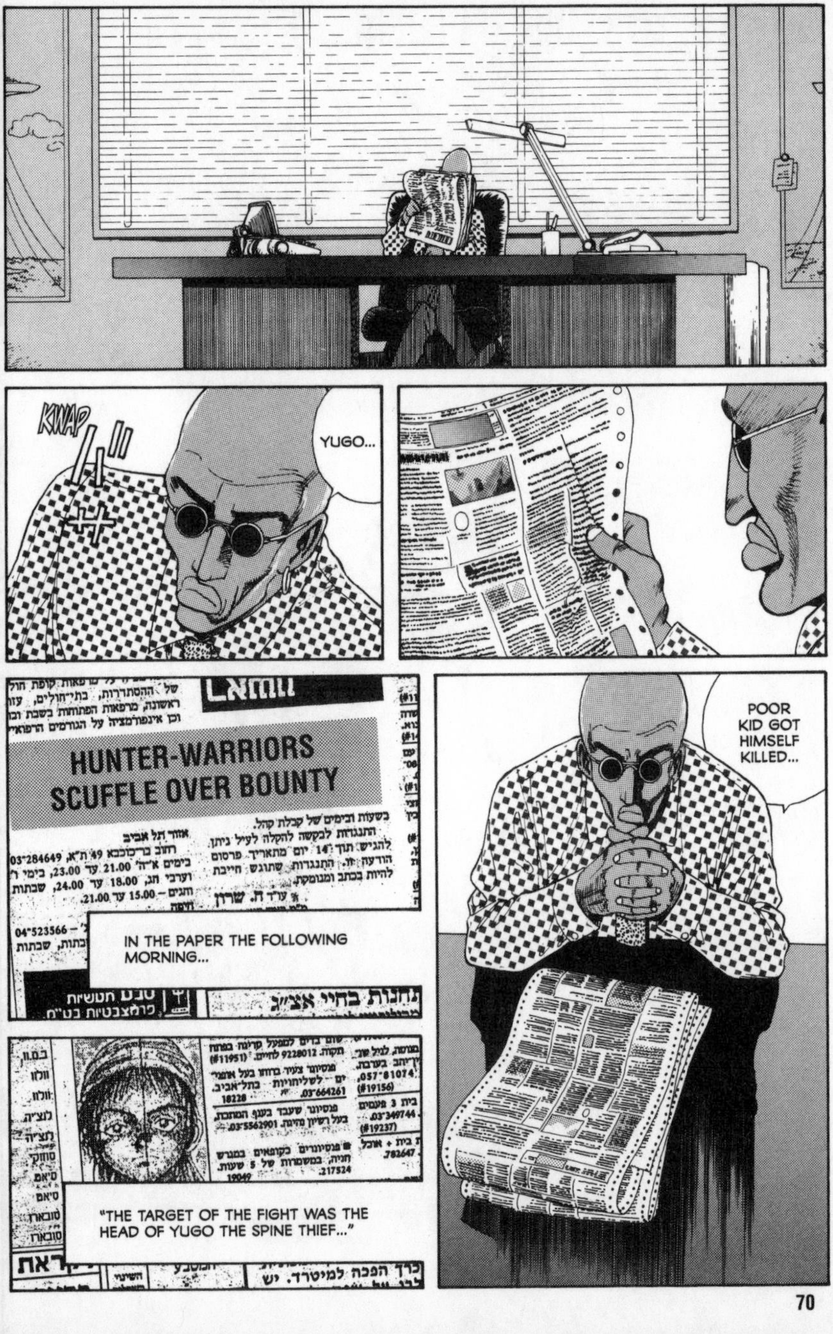
YUGO...
KWAP
POOR KID GOT HIMSELF KILLED...
HUNTER-WARRIORS SCUFFLE OVER BOUNTY
IN THE PAPER THE FOLLOWING MORNING...
"THE TARGET OF THE FIGHT WAS THE HEAD OF YUGO THE SPINE THIEF..."

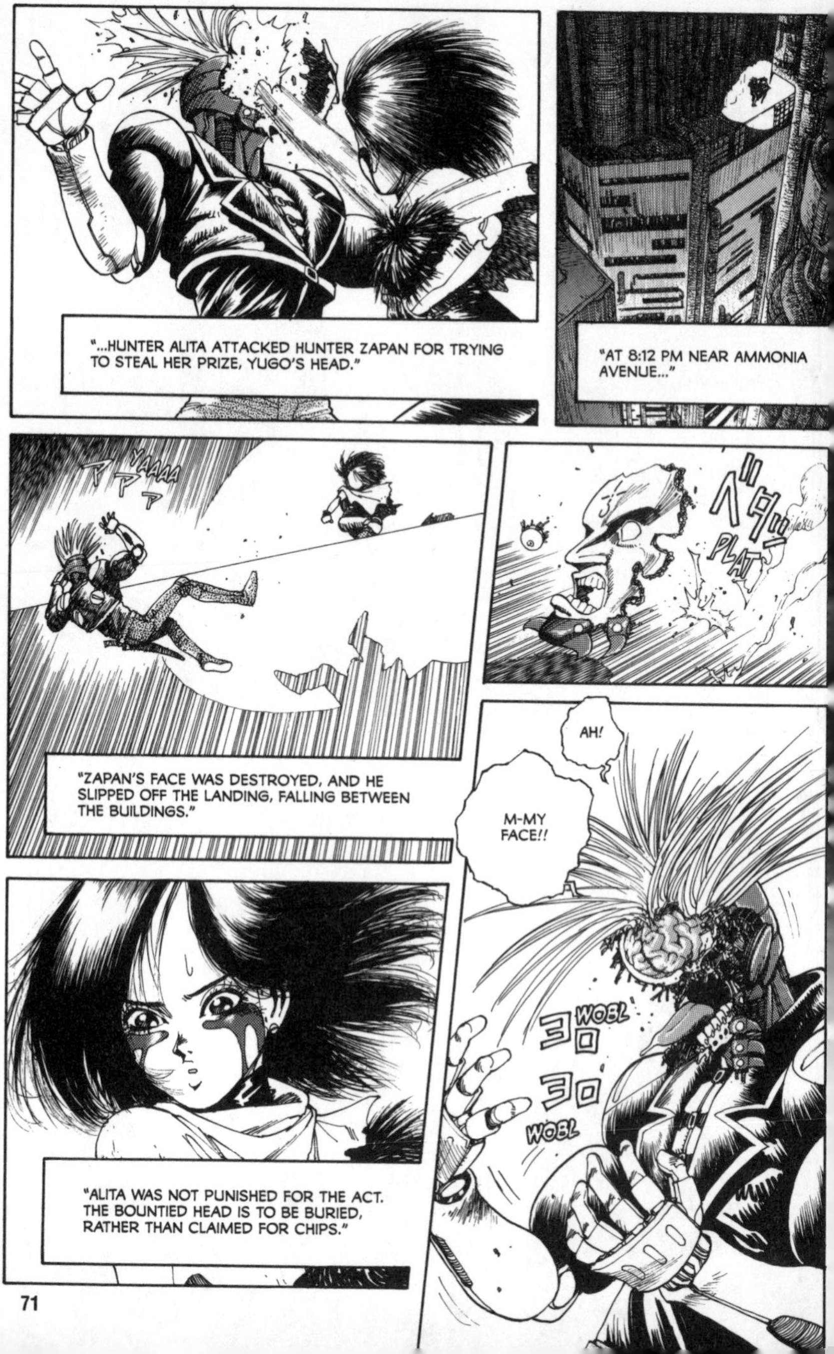
"AT 8:12 PM NEAR AMMONIA AVENUE..."
"...HUNTER ALITA ATTACKED HUNTER ZAPAN FOR TRYING TO STEAL HER PRIZE, YUGO'S HEAD."
PLAT
YAAAA
"ZAPAN'S FACE WAS DESTROYED, AND HE SLIPPED OFF THE LANDING, FALLING BETWEEN THE BUILDINGS."
AH!
M-MY FACE!!
WOBL
WOBL
"ALITA WAS NOT PUNISHED FOR THE ACT. THE BOUNTIED HEAD IS TO BE BURIED, RATHER THAN CLAIMED FOR CHIPS."

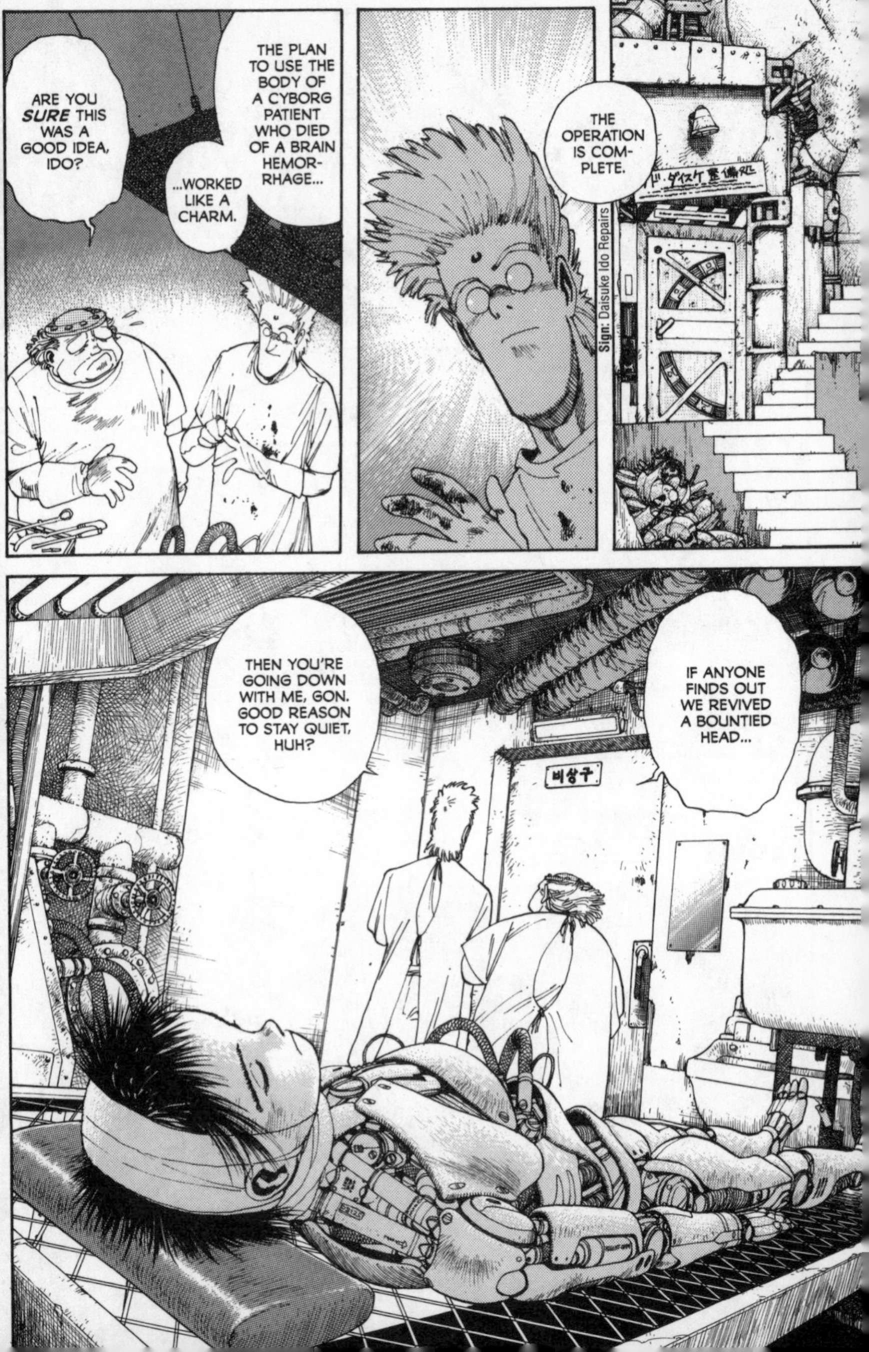
Sign: Daisuke Ido Repairs
THE OPERATION IS COMPLETE.
ARE YOU *SURE* THIS WAS A GOOD IDEA, IDO?
THE PLAN TO USE THE BODY OF A CYBORG PATIENT WHO DIED OF A BRAIN HEMORRHAGE...
...WORKED LIKE A CHARM.
IF ANYONE FINDS OUT WE REVIVED A BOUNTIED HEAD...
비상구
THEN YOU'RE GOING DOWN WITH ME, GON. GOOD REASON TO STAY QUIET, HUH?

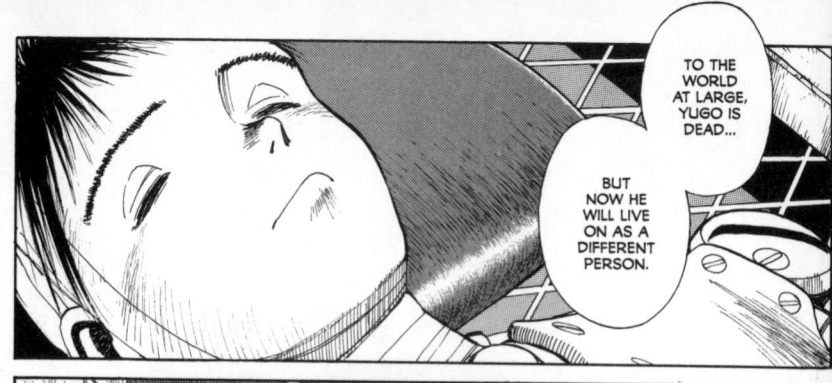

TO THE WORLD AT LARGE, YUGO IS DEAD...

BUT NOW HE WILL LIVE ON AS A DIFFERENT PERSON.

YOU CAN STOP WORRYING, ALITA.

EVERYTHING WENT OFF WITHOUT A HITCH.

WELL, HE CERTAINLY WOULDN'T BE ALIVE NOW IF IT WEREN'T FOR YOUR LIFE-SAVING MEASURES.

TH-THANKS, IDO...

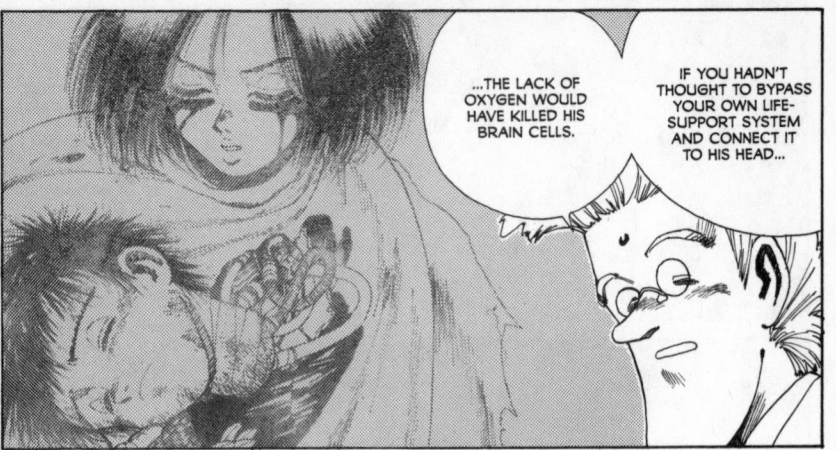

IF YOU HADN'T THOUGHT TO BYPASS YOUR OWN LIFE-SUPPORT SYSTEM AND CONNECT IT TO HIS HEAD...
...THE LACK OF OXYGEN WOULD HAVE KILLED HIS BRAIN CELLS.
BUT IF I'D BEEN SMARTER, IT NEVER WOULD HAVE COME TO THAT IN THE FIRST PLACE...
HE TOOK A WRONG TURN WHEN HE BELIEVED HE COULD GET TO ZALEM.
HE WAS TAKEN ADVANTAGE OF.
WHAT DO YOU MEAN?

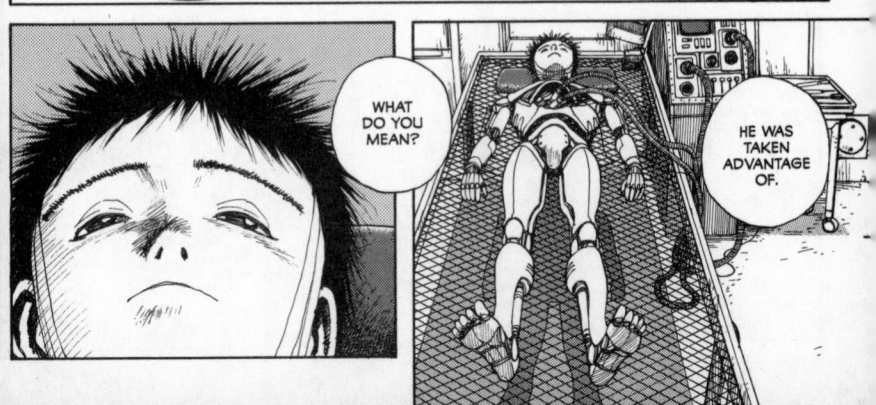

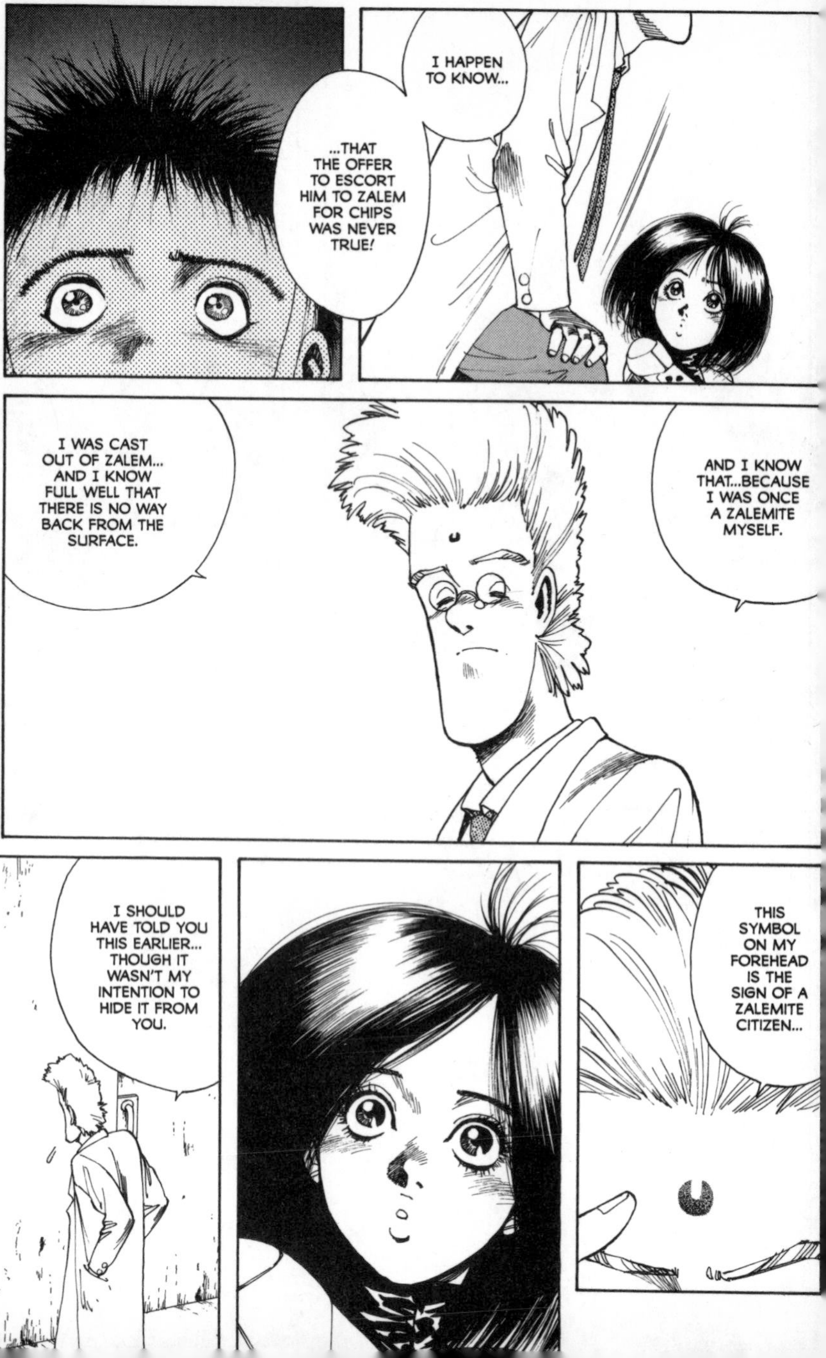
I HAPPEN TO KNOW...
...THAT THE OFFER TO ESCORT HIM TO ZALEM FOR CHIPS WAS NEVER TRUE!
AND I KNOW THAT...BECAUSE I WAS ONCE A ZALEMITE MYSELF.
I WAS CAST OUT OF ZALEM... AND I KNOW FULL WELL THAT THERE IS NO WAY BACK FROM THE SURFACE.
THIS SYMBOL ON MY FOREHEAD IS THE SIGN OF A ZALEMITE CITIZEN...
I SHOULD HAVE TOLD YOU THIS EARLIER... THOUGH IT WASN'T MY INTENTION TO HIDE IT FROM YOU.

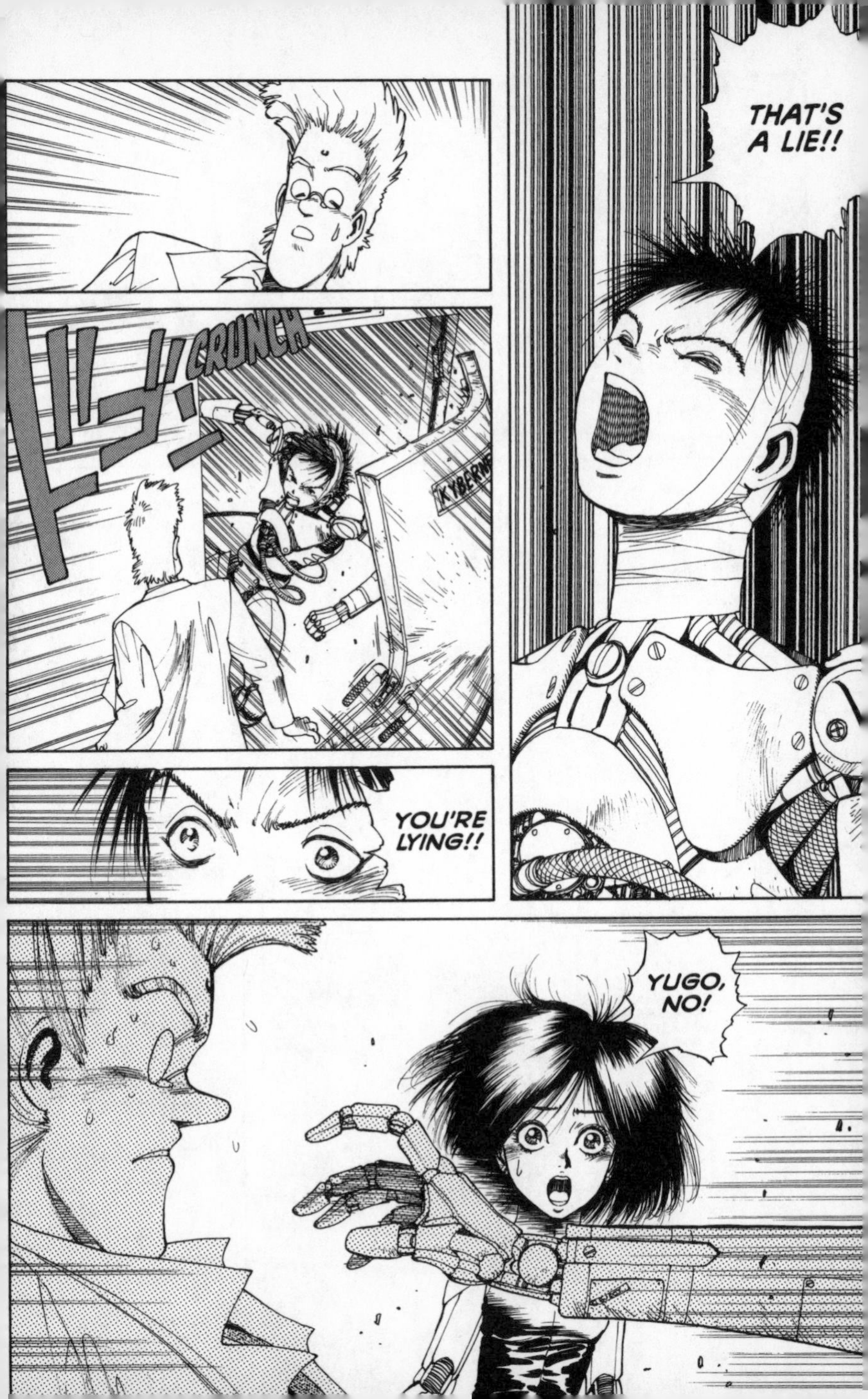
THAT'S A LIE!!
CRUNCH
KYBERNE
YOU'RE LYING!!
YUGO, NO!

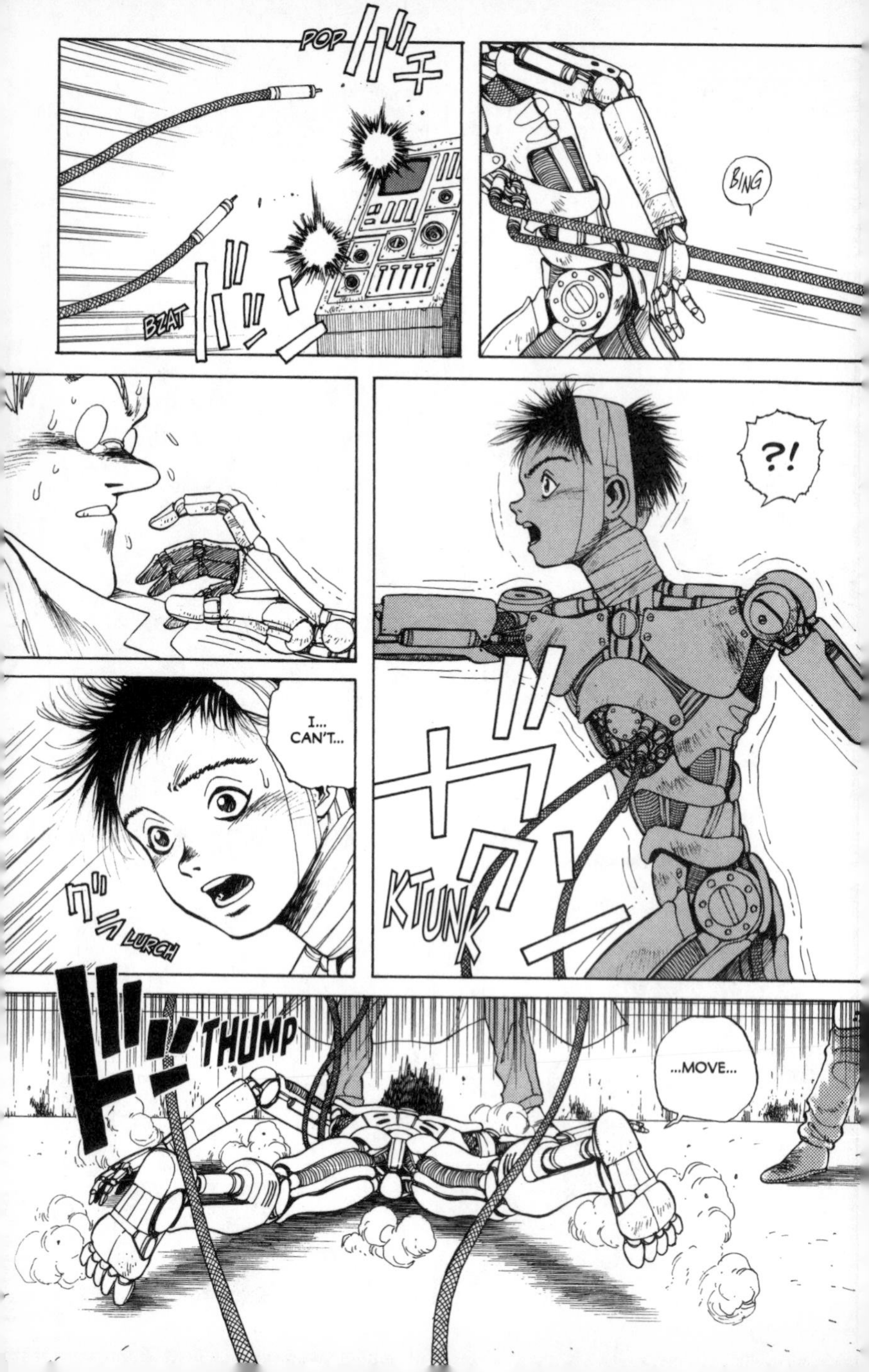
BING
POP
BZAT
?!
KTUNK
I... CAN'T...
LURCH
THUMP
...MOVE...

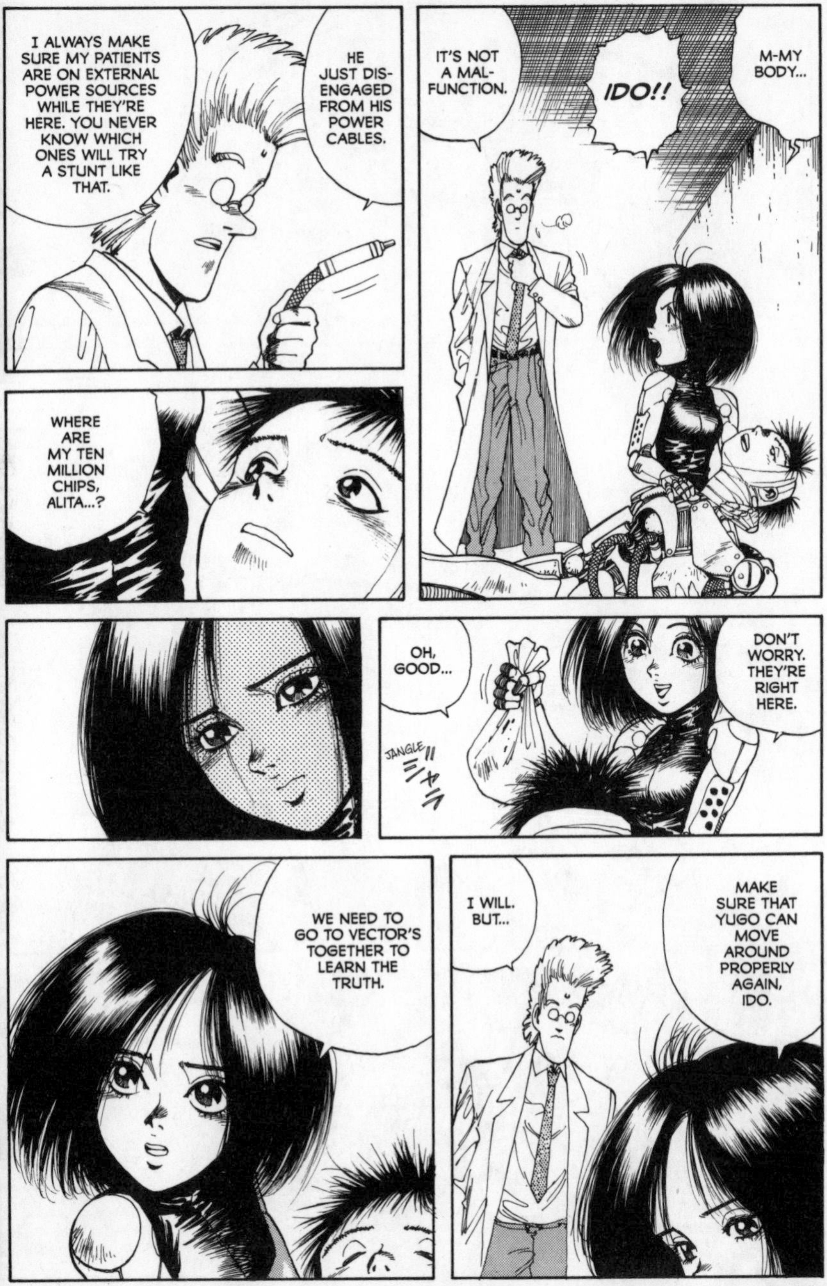
M-MY BODY...
IDO!!
IT'S NOT A MAL-FUNCTION.
HE JUST DIS-ENGAGED FROM HIS POWER CABLES.
I ALWAYS MAKE SURE MY PATIENTS ARE ON EXTERNAL POWER SOURCES WHILE THEY'RE HERE. YOU NEVER KNOW WHICH ONES WILL TRY A STUNT LIKE THAT.
WHERE ARE MY TEN MILLION CHIPS, ALITA...?
DON'T WORRY. THEY'RE RIGHT HERE.
OH, GOOD...
JANGLE
MAKE SURE THAT YUGO CAN MOVE AROUND PROPERLY AGAIN, IDO.
I WILL. BUT...
WE NEED TO GO TO VECTOR'S TOGETHER TO LEARN THE TRUTH.

AND IF IT TURNS OUT THAT VECTOR WAS LYING TO HIM...

HEY, MR. VECTOR! WE GOT TWO WEIRDOS SHOVIN' THEIR WAY INSIDE!!

I'M BUSY. KICK THEM OUT...

?!

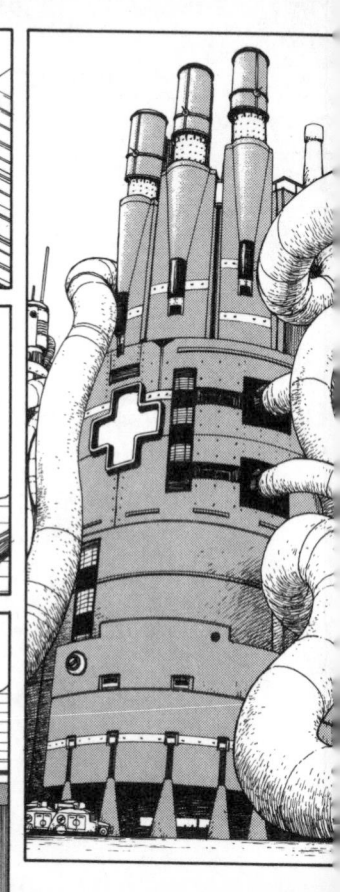

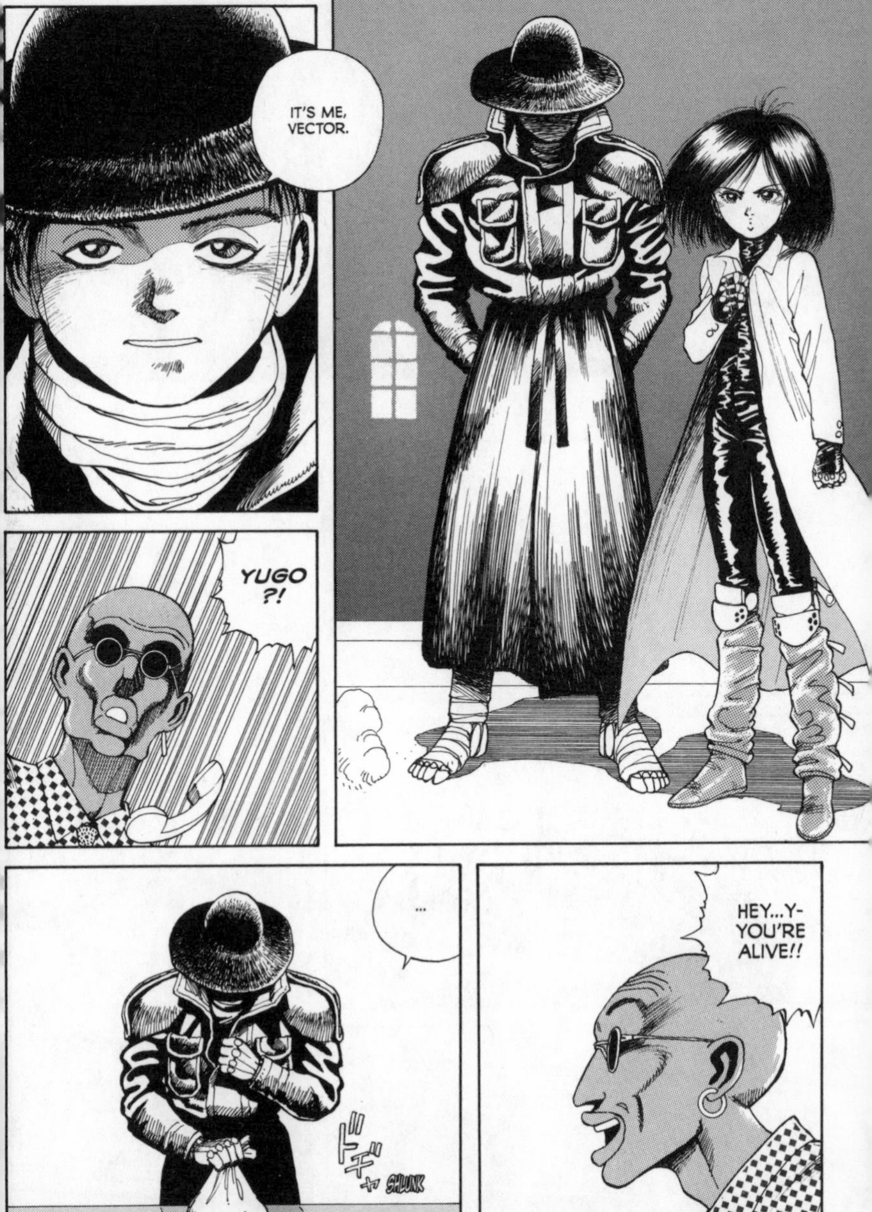

IT'S ME, VECTOR.
YUGO ?!
HEY...Y- YOU'RE ALIVE!!
...
ドギャ
SHUNK

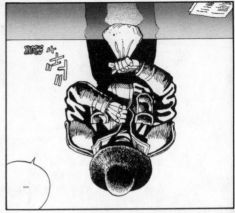

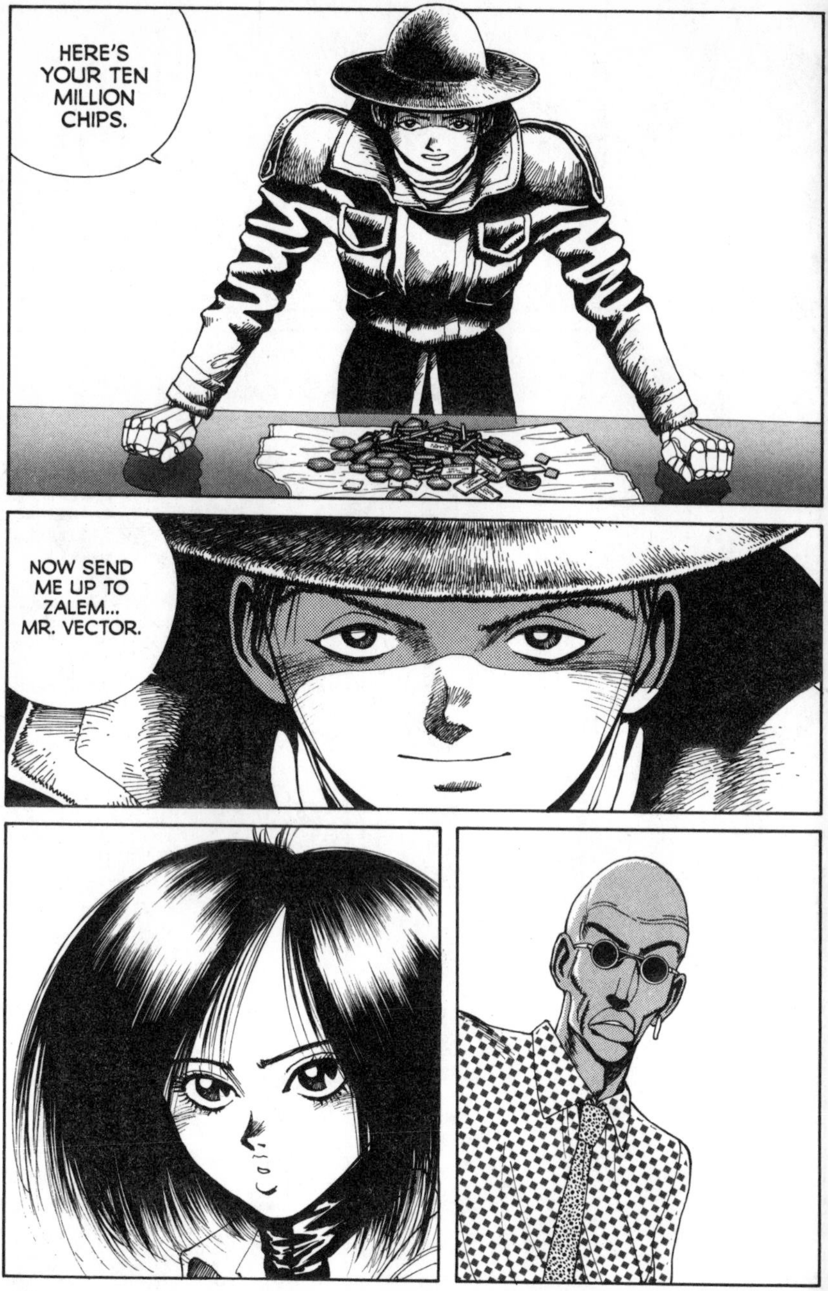
HERE'S YOUR TEN MILLION CHIPS.
NOW SEND ME UP TO ZALEM... MR. VECTOR.

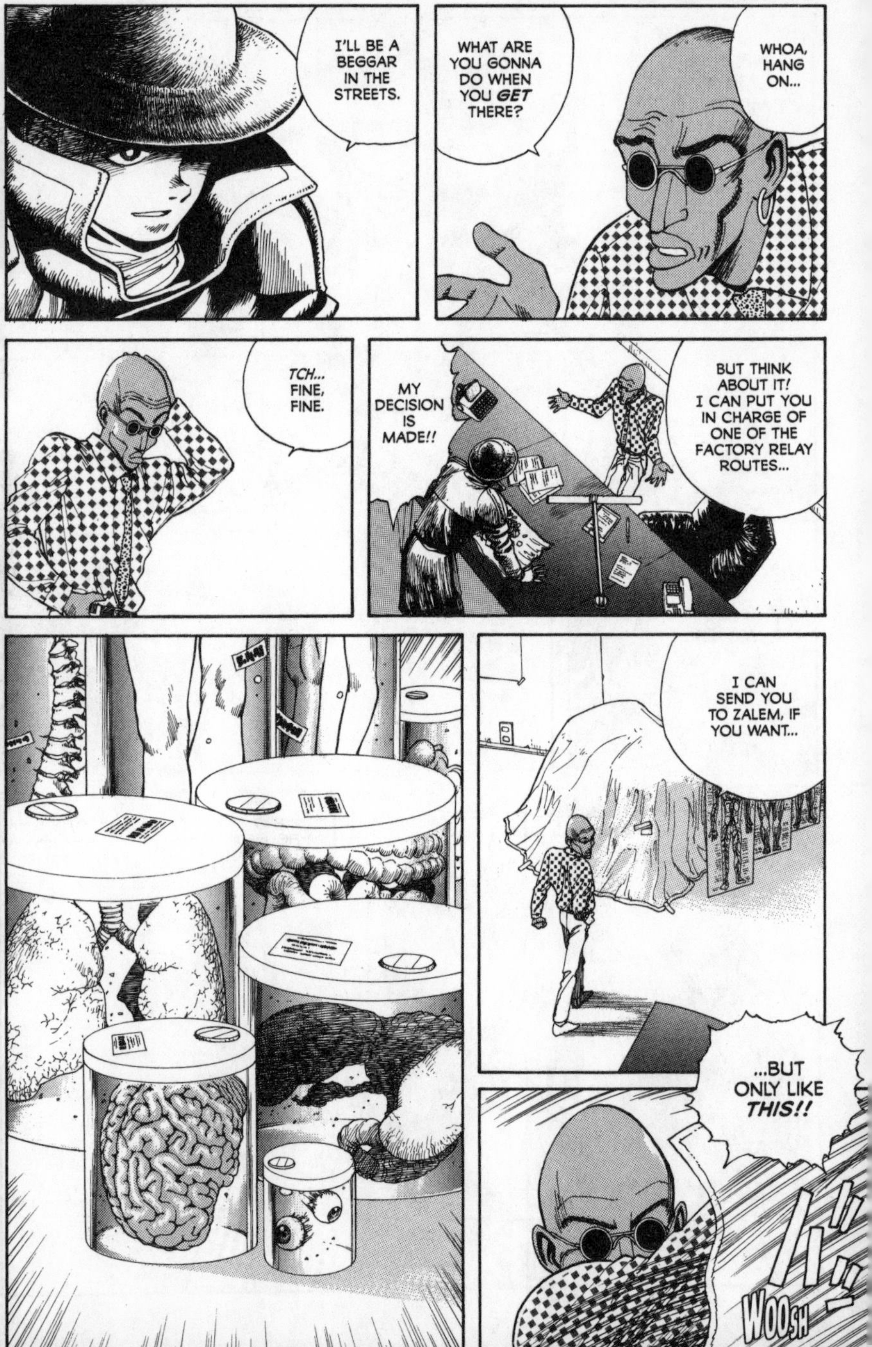
WHOA, HANG ON...
WHAT ARE YOU GONNA DO WHEN YOU *GET* THERE?
I'LL BE A BEGGAR IN THE STREETS.
BUT THINK ABOUT IT! I CAN PUT YOU IN CHARGE OF ONE OF THE FACTORY RELAY ROUTES...
MY DECISION IS MADE!!
TCH... FINE, FINE.
I CAN SEND YOU TO ZALEM, IF YOU WANT...
...BUT ONLY LIKE *THIS!!*
WOOSH

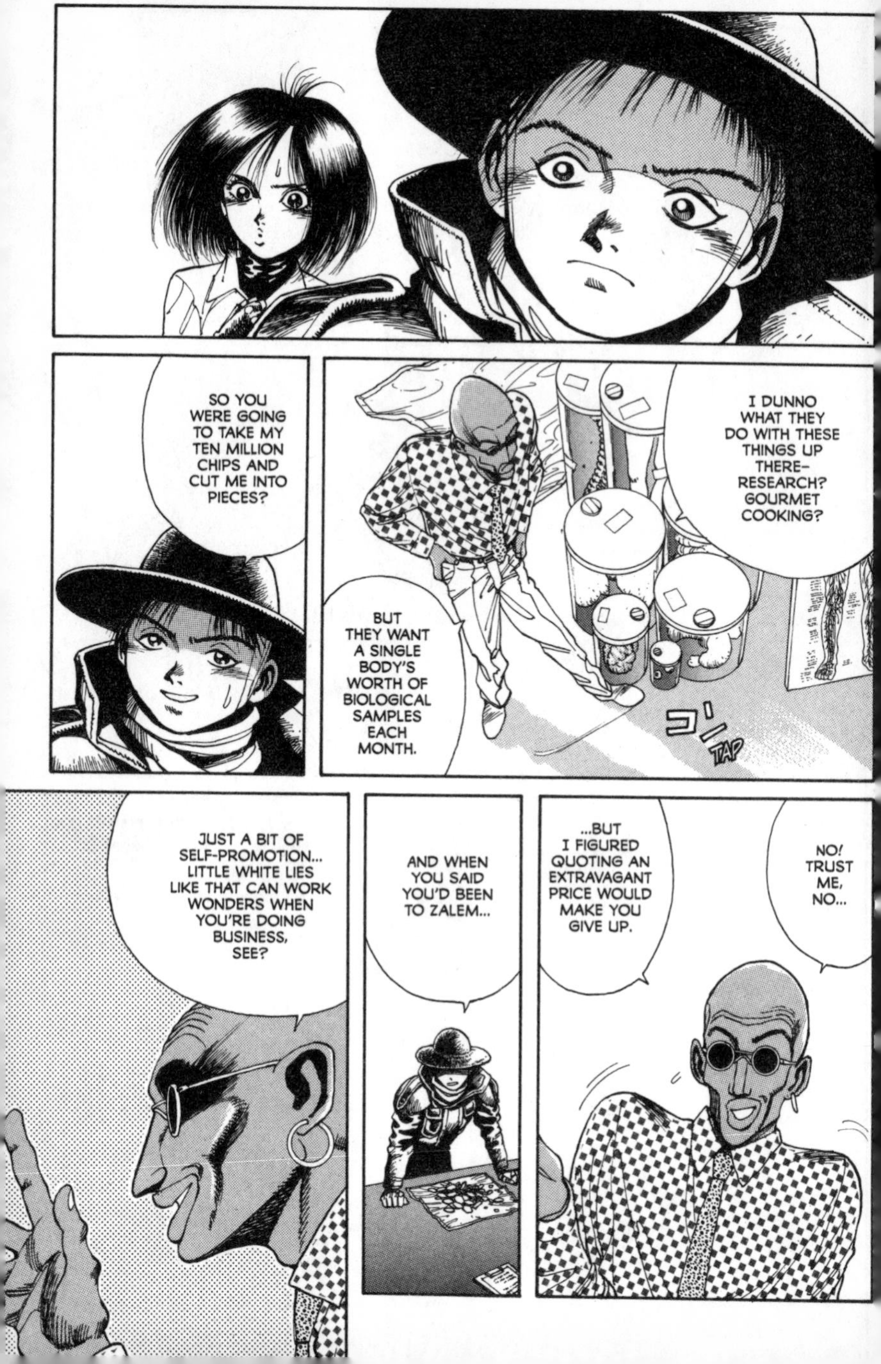
I DUNNO WHAT THEY DO WITH THESE THINGS UP THERE– RESEARCH? GOURMET COOKING?
BUT THEY WANT A SINGLE BODY'S WORTH OF BIOLOGICAL SAMPLES EACH MONTH.
TAP
SO YOU WERE GOING TO TAKE MY TEN MILLION CHIPS AND CUT ME INTO PIECES?
NO! TRUST ME, NO...
...BUT I FIGURED QUOTING AN EXTRAVAGANT PRICE WOULD MAKE YOU GIVE UP.
AND WHEN YOU SAID YOU'D BEEN TO ZALEM...
JUST A BIT OF SELF-PROMOTION... LITTLE WHITE LIES LIKE THAT CAN WORK WONDERS WHEN YOU'RE DOING BUSINESS, SEE?

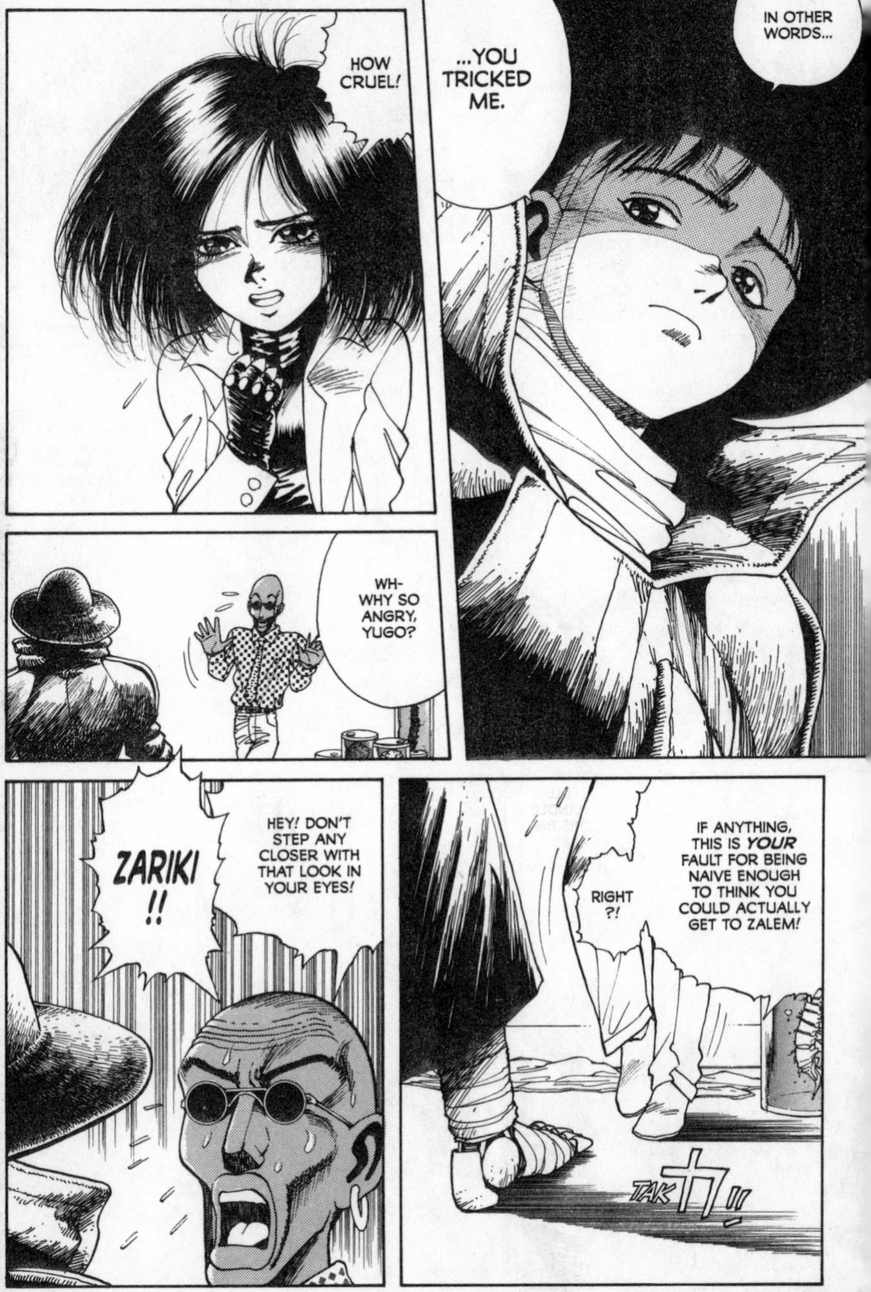
IN OTHER WORDS...
...YOU TRICKED ME.
HOW CRUEL!
WH- WHY SO ANGRY, YUGO?
IF ANYTHING, THIS IS *YOUR* FAULT FOR BEING NAIVE ENOUGH TO THINK YOU COULD ACTUALLY GET TO ZALEM!
RIGHT ?!
TAK!!
HEY! DON'T STEP ANY CLOSER WITH THAT LOOK IN YOUR EYES!
ZARIKI !!

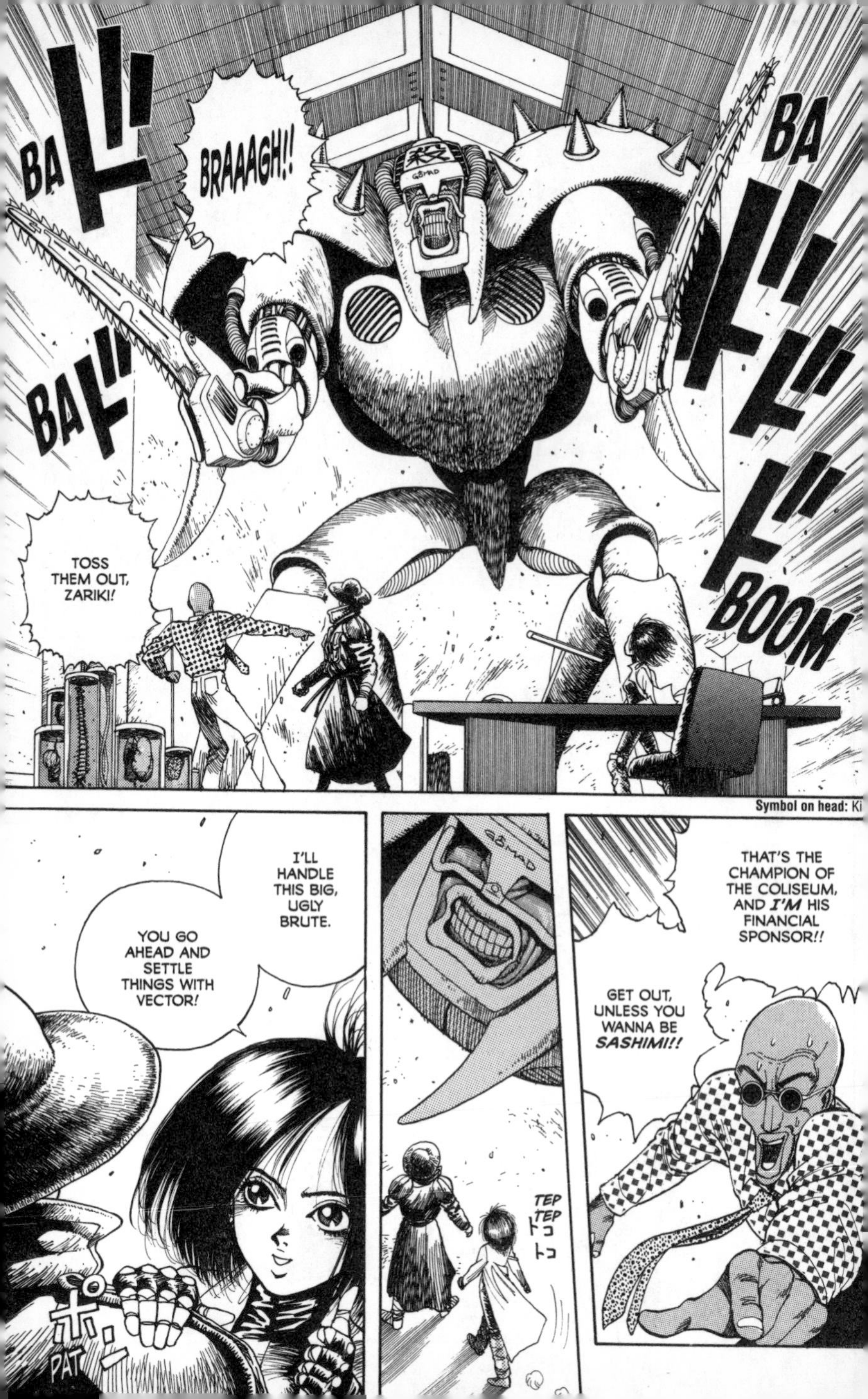
BA-BA-BA
BOOM
BRAAAGH!!
BA
BA
TOSS THEM OUT, ZARIKI!
GŌMAD
Symbol on head: Ki
THAT'S THE CHAMPION OF THE COLISEUM, AND *I'M* HIS FINANCIAL SPONSOR!!
GET OUT, UNLESS YOU WANNA BE ***SASHIMI!!***
TEP TEP トコトコ
I'LL HANDLE THIS BIG, UGLY BRUTE.
YOU GO AHEAD AND SETTLE THINGS WITH VECTOR!
PAT ポン

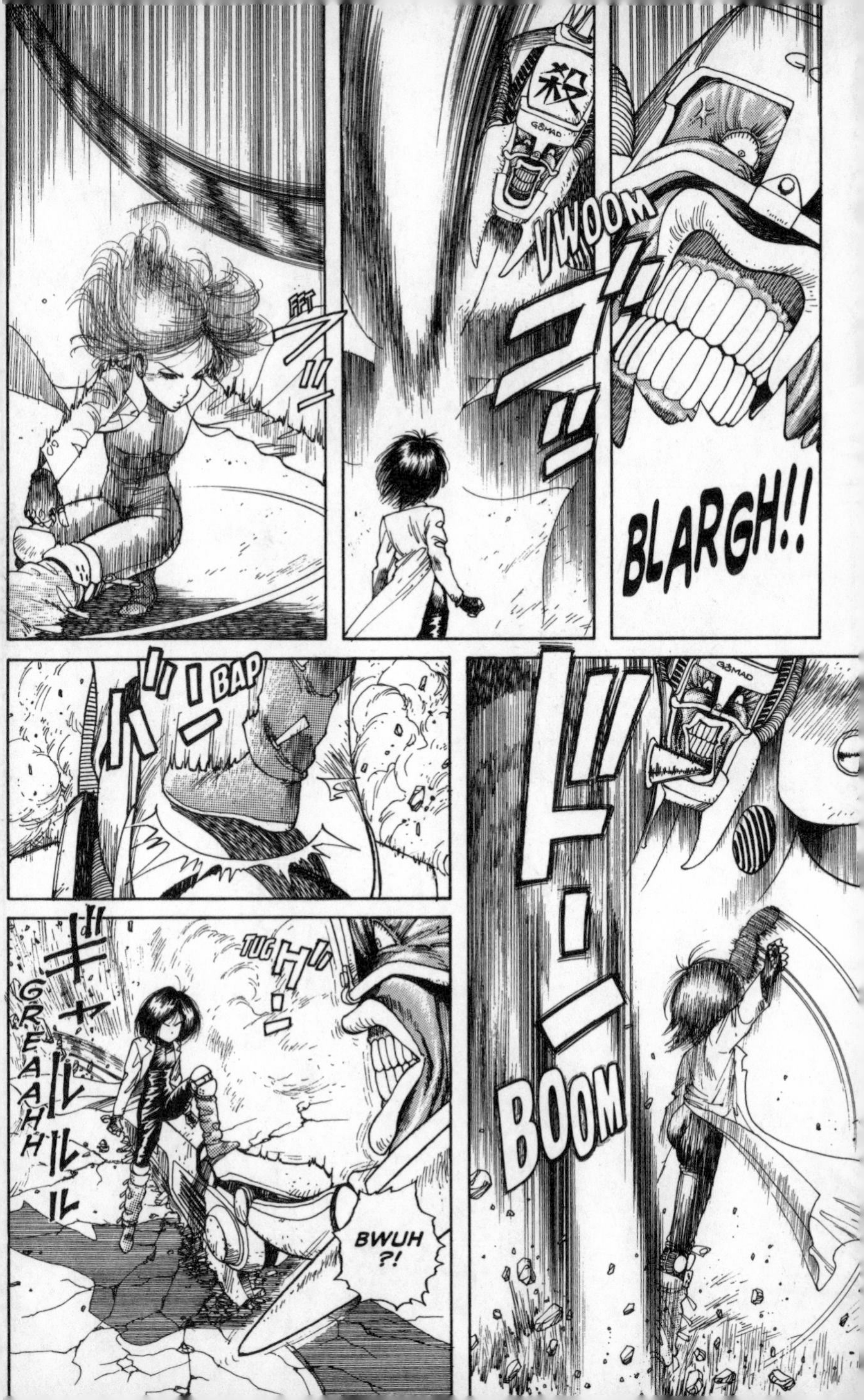
BLARGH!!
殺
GŌMAD
VWOOM
FFT
GŌMAD
BOOM
BAP
GREAAHH
TUG
BWUH ?!

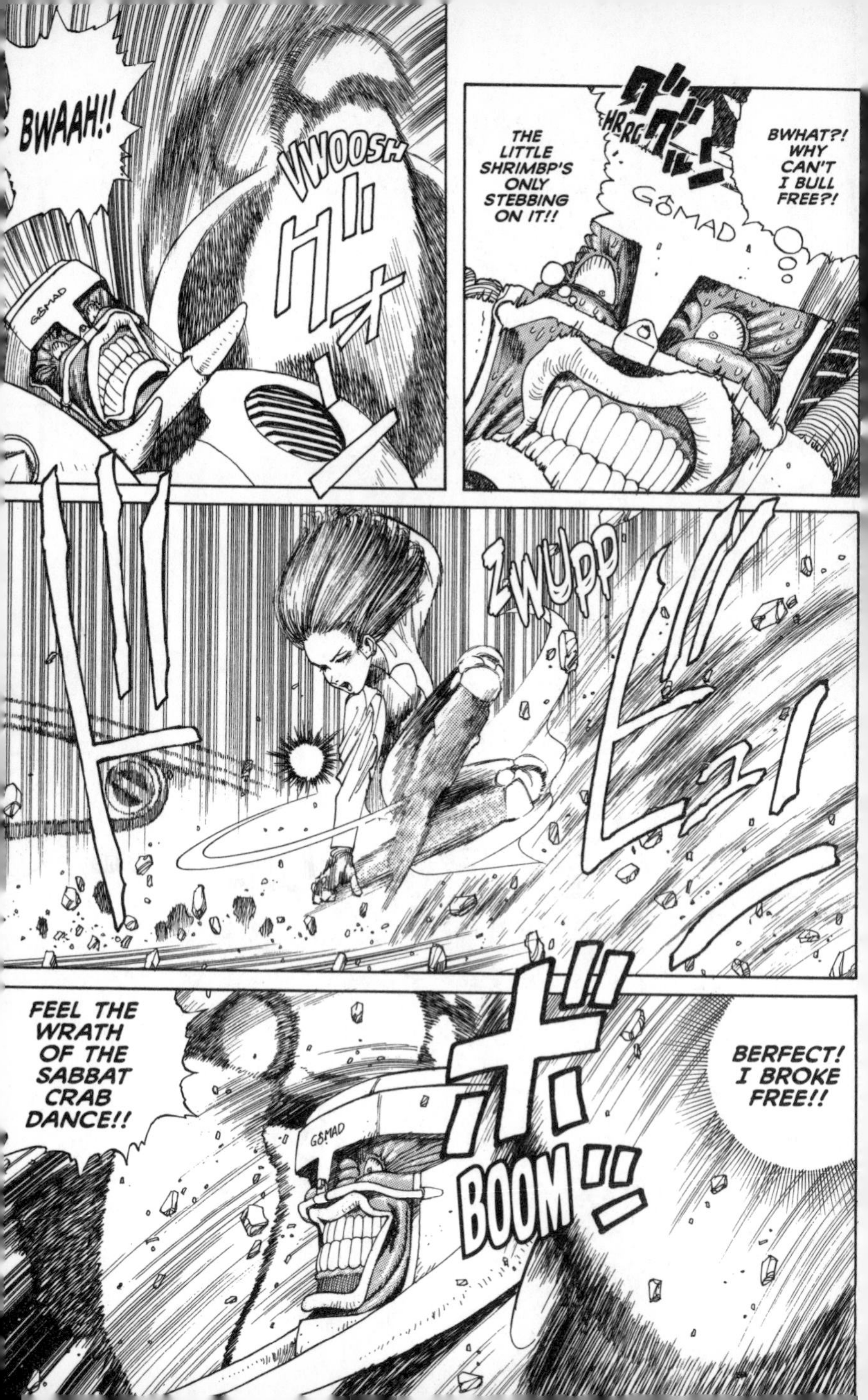
BWHAT?! WHY CAN'T I BULL FREE?!
HRRG
GÔMAD
THE LITTLE SHRIMBP'S ONLY STEBBING ON IT!!
BWAAH!!
VWOOSH
ZWUPP
BERFECT! I BROKE FREE!!
BOOM!!
FEEL THE WRATH OF THE SABBAT CRAB DANCE!!
GÔMAD

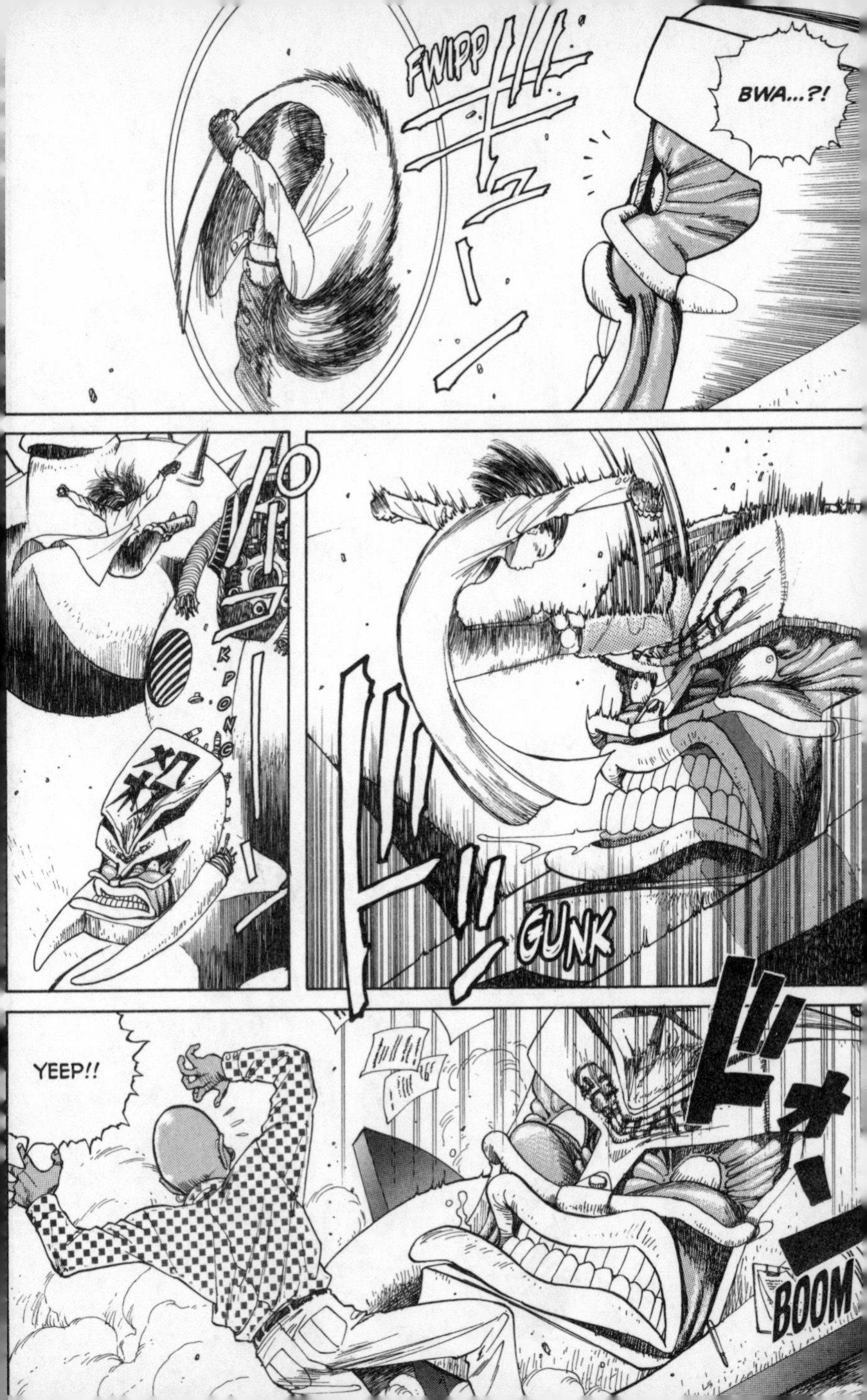
BWA...?!
FWIPP
GUNK
KPONG
BOOM
YEEP!!

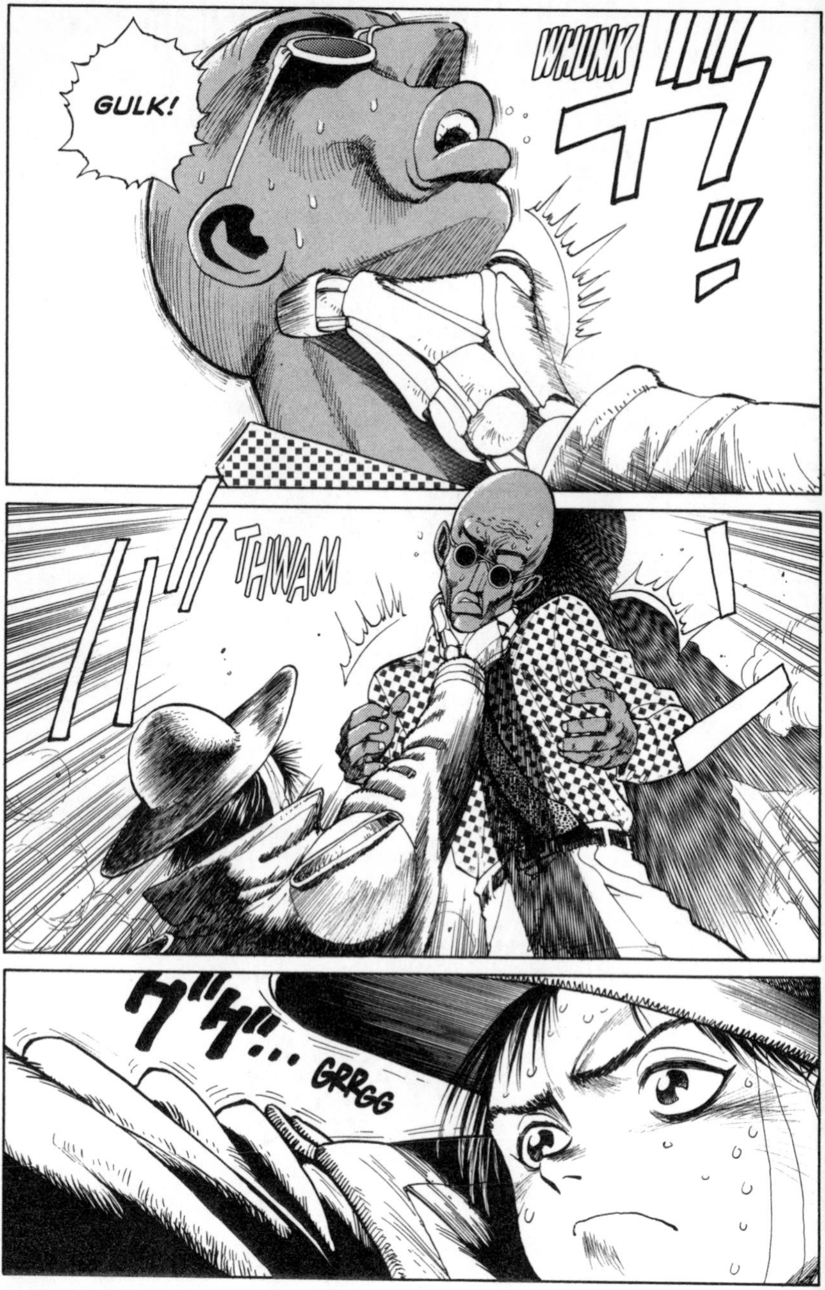
WHUNK
GULK!
THWAM
GRRGG

Netmen and the Public Safety System

EXPLAINED!

FACTORY LAW

AS A SUBORDINATE ORGAN OF ZALEM, THE FACTORIES OPERATE UNDER WHAT IS CALLED "FACTORY LAW" WITHIN THEIR TERRITORY. THIS IS DESIGNED TO ENSURE THAT THE PRODUCTION PROCESS RUNS SMOOTHLY AND TO MAINTAIN THE SAFETY OF THE FACILITIES AND THEIR WORKERS. IT IS NOT MEANT TO PROTECT THE RIGHTS OF THE PEOPLE LIVING IN THE SCRAPYARD.

FACTORY LAW RANKS CRIMES IN TWO MAIN CATEGORIES.

	CLASS-A CRIMES	CLASS-B CRIMES
TYPES OF CRIMES	∘DESTRUCTION OF FACTORY PROPERTY ∘THEFT OF FACTORY GOODS ∘HACKING INTO FACTORY/ZALEM ∘PRODUCING/POSSESSING MEANS OF FLIGHT ∘PRODUCING/POSSESSING FIREARMS ∘HUNTER-WARRIOR TREASON	∘BRAIN MURDER ⎱ EXCEPT DURING ∘BRAIN ASSAULT ⎰ COMPETITIVE EVENTS ∘PURCHASE/SALE OF BIOLOGICAL BRAINS ∘STEALING BODY PARTS FROM THE LIVING

NETMEN

EXTERNAL FACTORY UNITS CALLED "NETMEN" ARE USED TO ENFORCE ORDER WITHIN THE SCRAPYARD.

ORDINARILY, A NETMAN IS STATIONED AT THE CORNER OF A STREET LIKE A MAILBOX, AND ACTS AS A KIND OF MICRO POLICE STATION, TAKING REPORTS FROM CITIZENS AND CRIME VICTIMS, GATHERING EYEWITNESS ACCOUNTS AND CRIMINAL DNA SAMPLES, AND DOING SIMPLE CRIMINAL ID AND INVESTIGATION. IF A CRIMINAL CAN BE CONFIRMED, HE IS ADDED TO THE BOUNTY LIST. IF A CRIMINAL IS NOT CONFIRMED, NO FURTHER INVESTIGATION IS CONDUCTED INTO NON-CLASS-A CRIMES.

THE NETMEN THEMSELVES DO NOT APPREHEND CRIMINALS, EXCEPT IN THE CASE OF CLASS-A CRIMES, WHERE THEY WILL ARM THEMSELVES, SUMMON HUNTER-WARRIORS, AND TAKE AN ACTIVE ROLE IN MAKING COMMANDS AND TRACKING DOWN THE TARGET.

THE FATE OF A CRIMINAL

THERE ARE NO COURTS OR PRISONS IN THE FACTORIES, ONLY BODY BANKS AND FURNACES. A FACTORY WILL RUN A DNA SCAN ON SAMPLES AND ACCEPT THE HEADS OF BOUNTIED CRIMINALS. THE BRAINS ARE EITHER CREMATED OR SENT TO PROCESSING FACTORIES AS RAW MATERIALS.

A CLOSER LOOK AT NETMAN #2

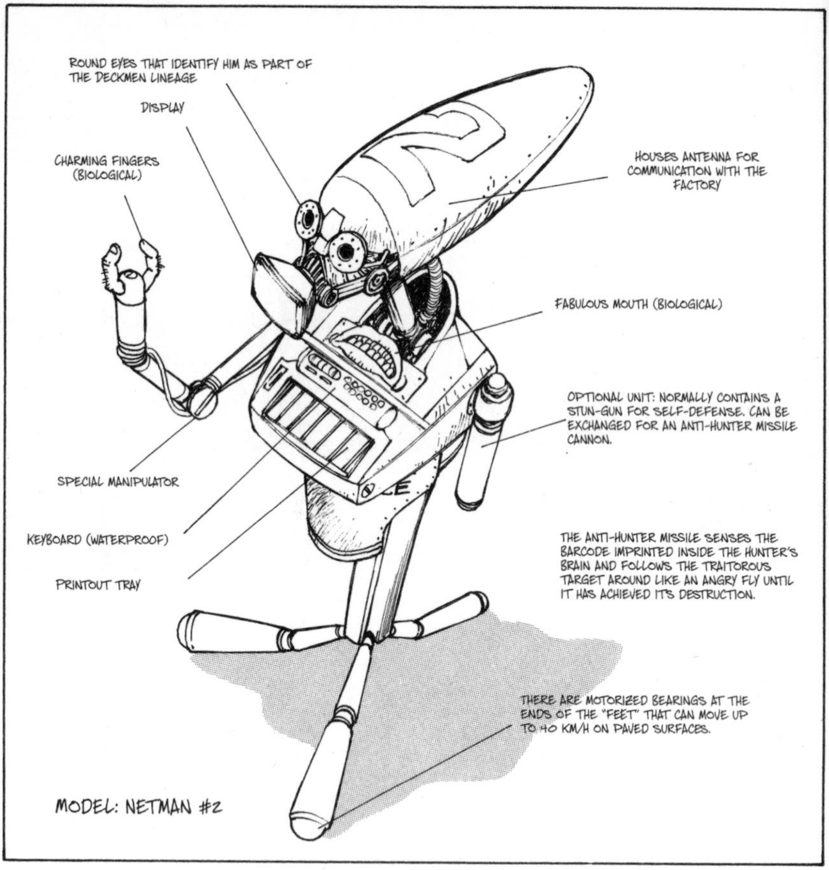

ROUND EYES THAT IDENTIFY HIM AS PART OF THE DECKMEN LINEAGE
DISPLAY
CHARMING FINGERS (BIOLOGICAL)
HOUSES ANTENNA FOR COMMUNICATION WITH THE FACTORY
FABULOUS MOUTH (BIOLOGICAL)
OPTIONAL UNIT: NORMALLY CONTAINS A STUN-GUN FOR SELF-DEFENSE. CAN BE EXCHANGED FOR AN ANTI-HUNTER MISSILE CANNON.
SPECIAL MANIPULATOR
KEYBOARD (WATERPROOF)
PRINTOUT TRAY
THE ANTI-HUNTER MISSILE SENSES THE BARCODE IMPRINTED INSIDE THE HUNTER'S BRAIN AND FOLLOWS THE TRAITOROUS TARGET AROUND LIKE AN ANGRY FLY UNTIL IT HAS ACHIEVED ITS DESTRUCTION.
THERE ARE MOTORIZED BEARINGS AT THE ENDS OF THE "FEET" THAT CAN MOVE UP TO 40 KM/H ON PAVED SURFACES.
MODEL: NETMAN #2

AS YOU CAN SEE, THE FATE OF A CRIMINAL IS BRUTALLY UNYIELDING, BUT WITH THEIR LACK OF PROPER ORGANIZATION AND TEAMWORK, THE HUNTER-WARRIORS AS A GROUP ONLY CATCH A SMALL PERCENTAGE OF THE CRIMINALS IN TOTAL. THE SCRAPYARD REMAINS A HOTBED OF CRIME.

YUKITO.
1992.1.8.

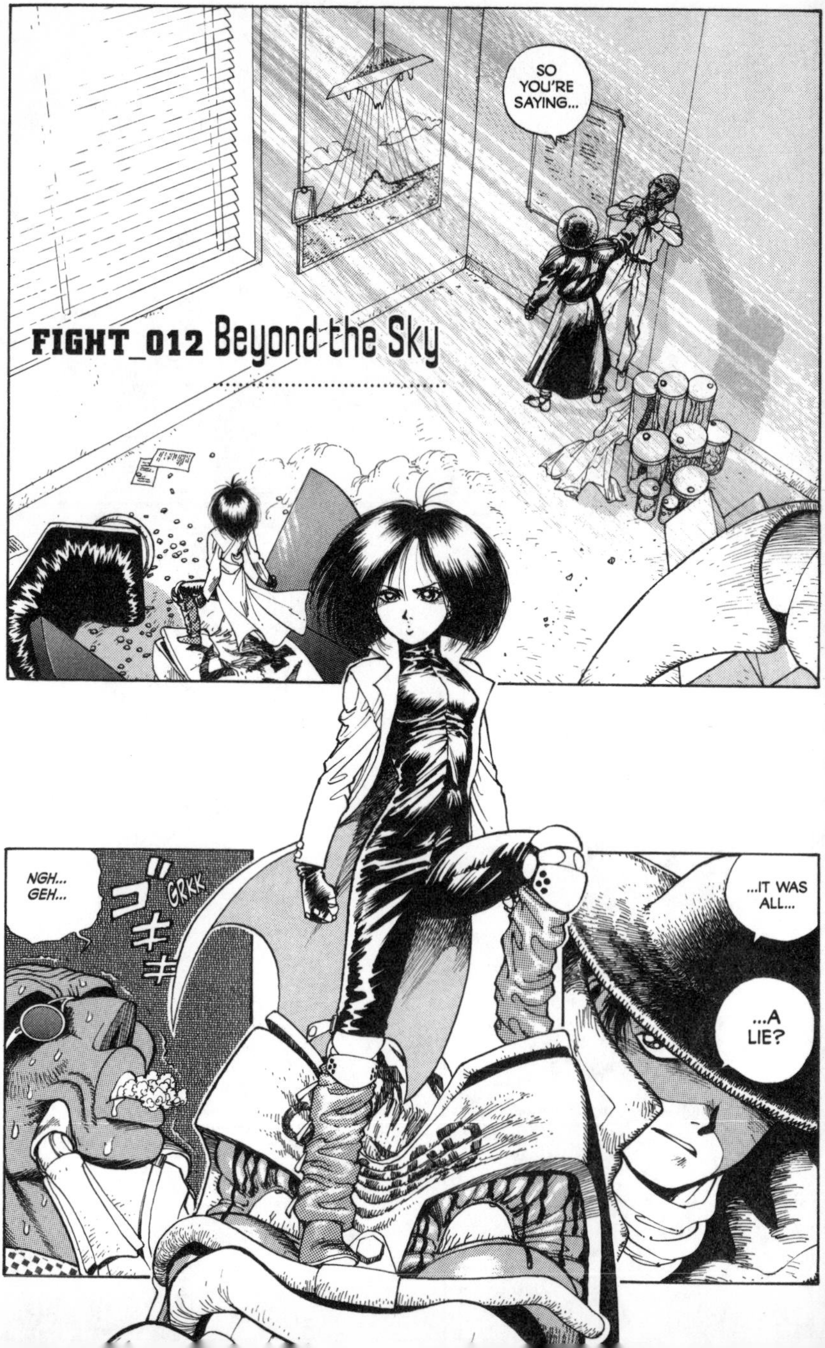
FIGHT_012 Beyond the Sky
SO YOU'RE SAYING...
...IT WAS ALL...
...A LIE?
NGH... GEH...
ゴキキ
GRKK

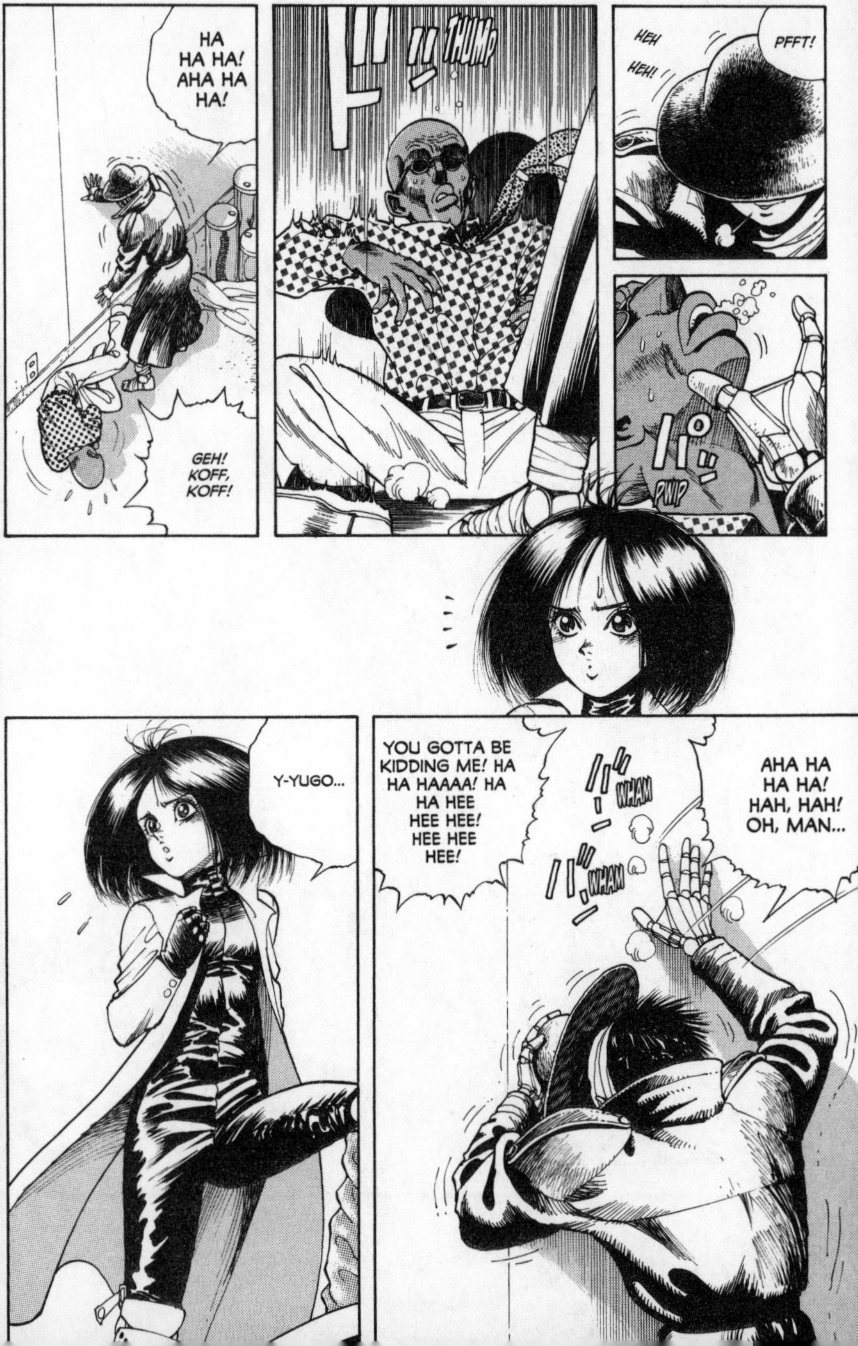
PFFT!
HEH HEH!
PWIP
THUMP
HA HA HA! AHA HA HA!
GEH! KOFF, KOFF!
AHA HA HA HA! HAH, HAH! OH, MAN...
WHAM
WHAM
YOU GOTTA BE KIDDING ME! HA HA HAAAA! HA HA HEE HEE HEE! HEE HEE HEE!
Y-YUGO...

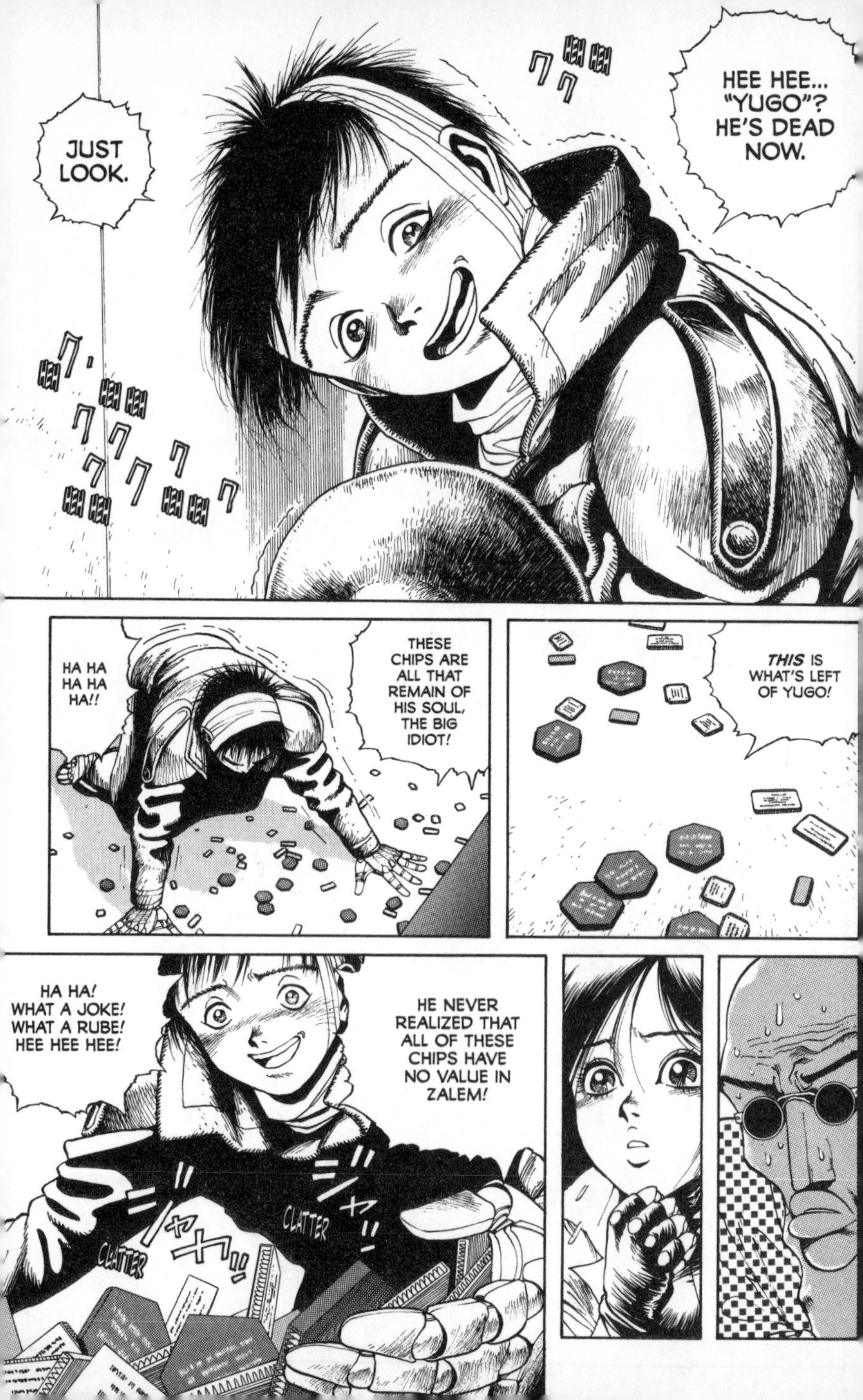
HEE HEE... "YUGO"? HE'S DEAD NOW.
HEH HEH
JUST LOOK.
HEH HEH HEH HEH HEH HEH HEH
THIS IS WHAT'S LEFT OF YUGO!
THESE CHIPS ARE ALL THAT REMAIN OF HIS SOUL, THE BIG IDIOT!
HA HA HA HA HA!!
HE NEVER REALIZED THAT ALL OF THESE CHIPS HAVE NO VALUE IN ZALEM!
HA HA! WHAT A JOKE! WHAT A RUBE! HEE HEE HEE!
CLATTER
CLATTER

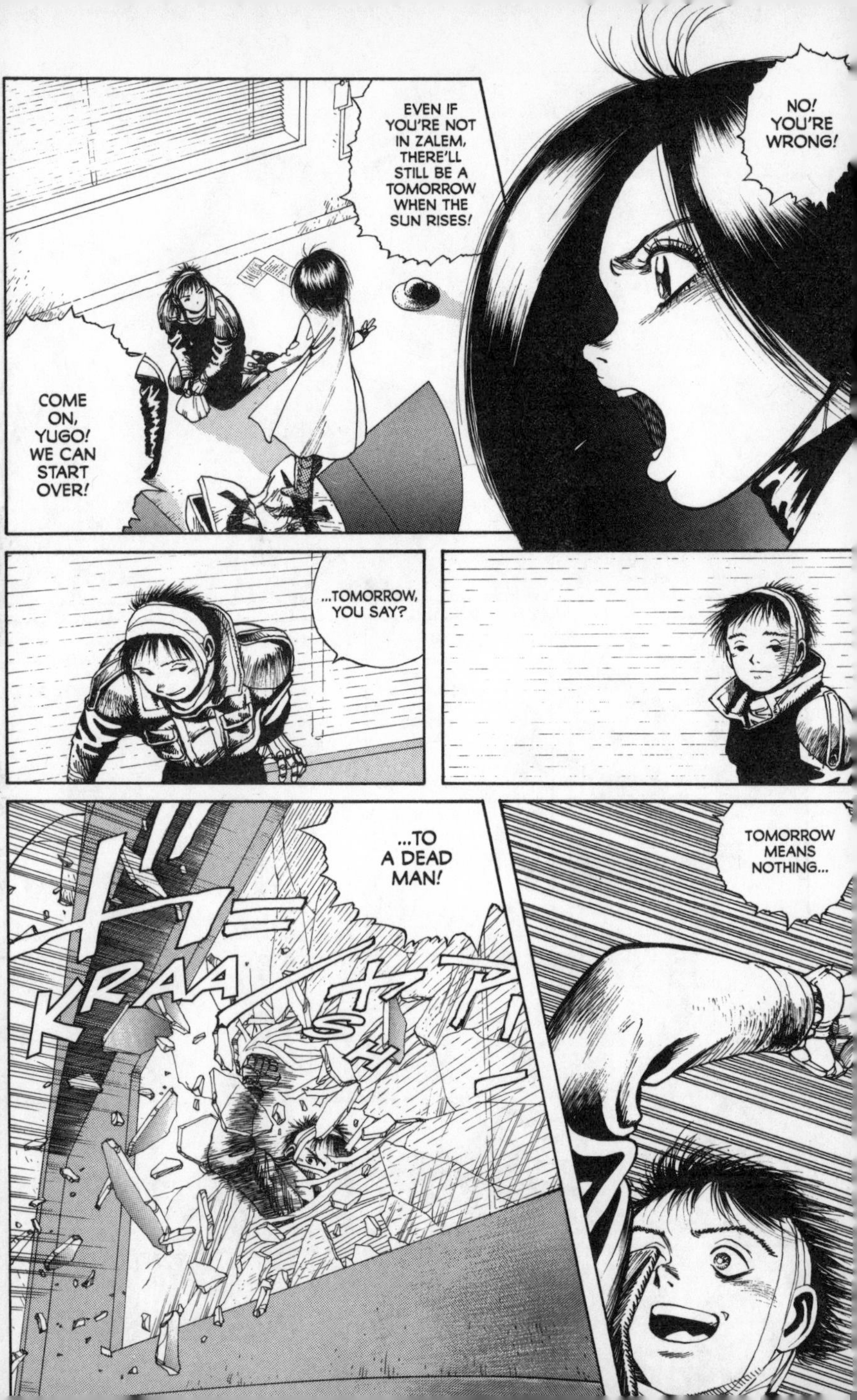
NO! YOU'RE WRONG!
EVEN IF YOU'RE NOT IN ZALEM, THERE'LL STILL BE A TOMORROW WHEN THE SUN RISES!
COME ON, YUGO! WE CAN START OVER!
...TOMORROW, YOU SAY?
TOMORROW MEANS NOTHING...
...TO A DEAD MAN!
KRAASHHH

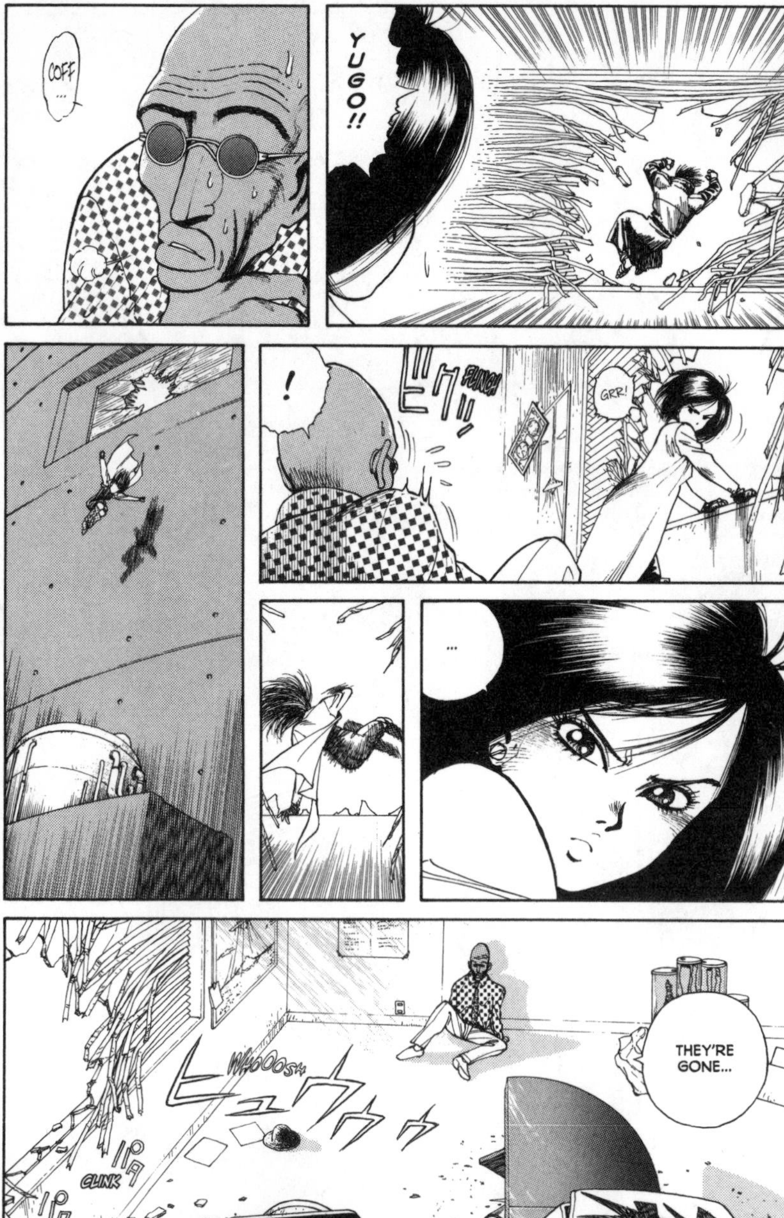
YUGO!!
COFF ...
GRR!
PUNCH
!
...
WHOOOSH
CLINK
CLANK
THEY'RE GONE...

Sign: Daisuke Ido Repairs

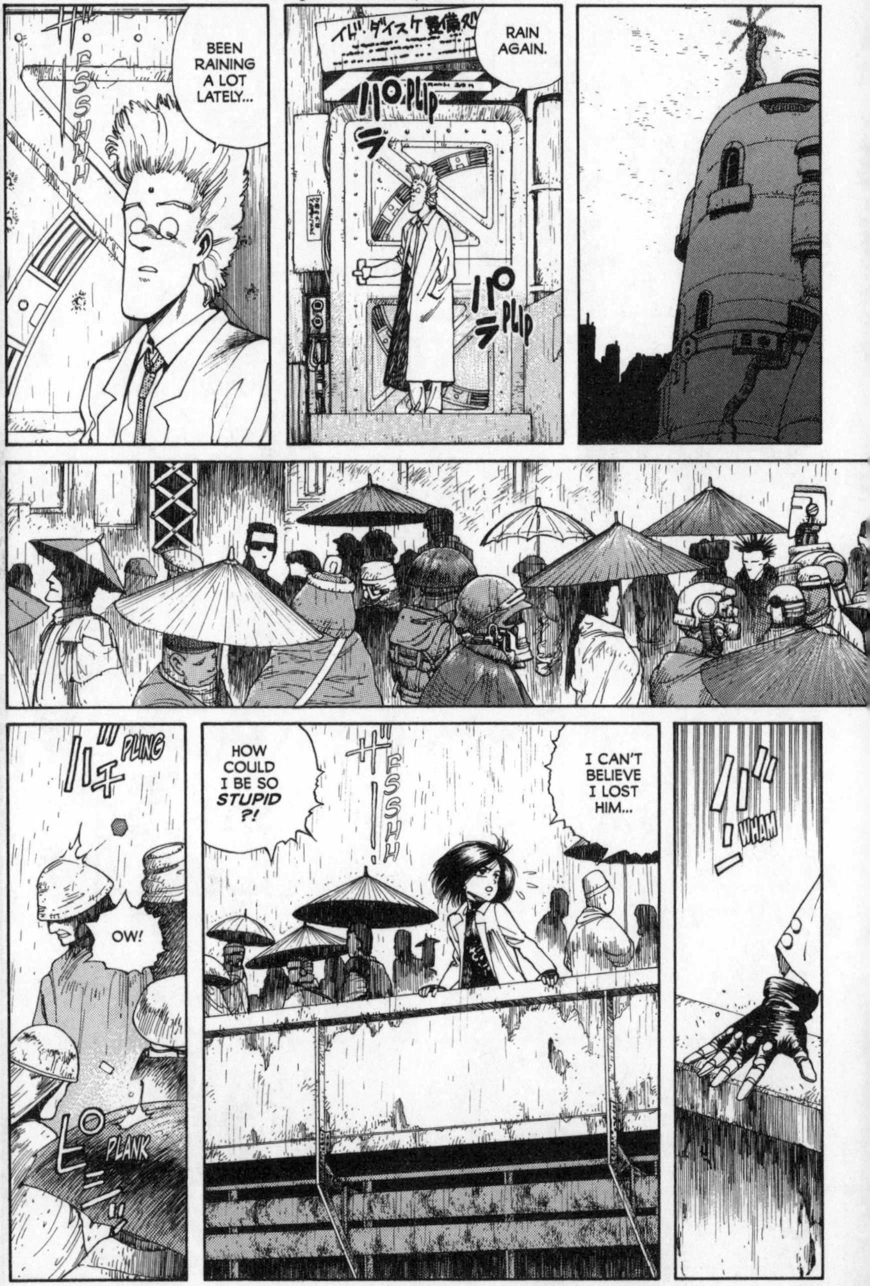
イド・ダイスケ整備所
RAIN AGAIN.
PLIP
PLIP
BEEN RAINING A LOT LATELY...
FSSHHH
WHAM
I CAN'T BELIEVE I LOST HIM...
FSSHH
HOW COULD I BE SO *STUPID* ?!
PLING
OW!
PLANK

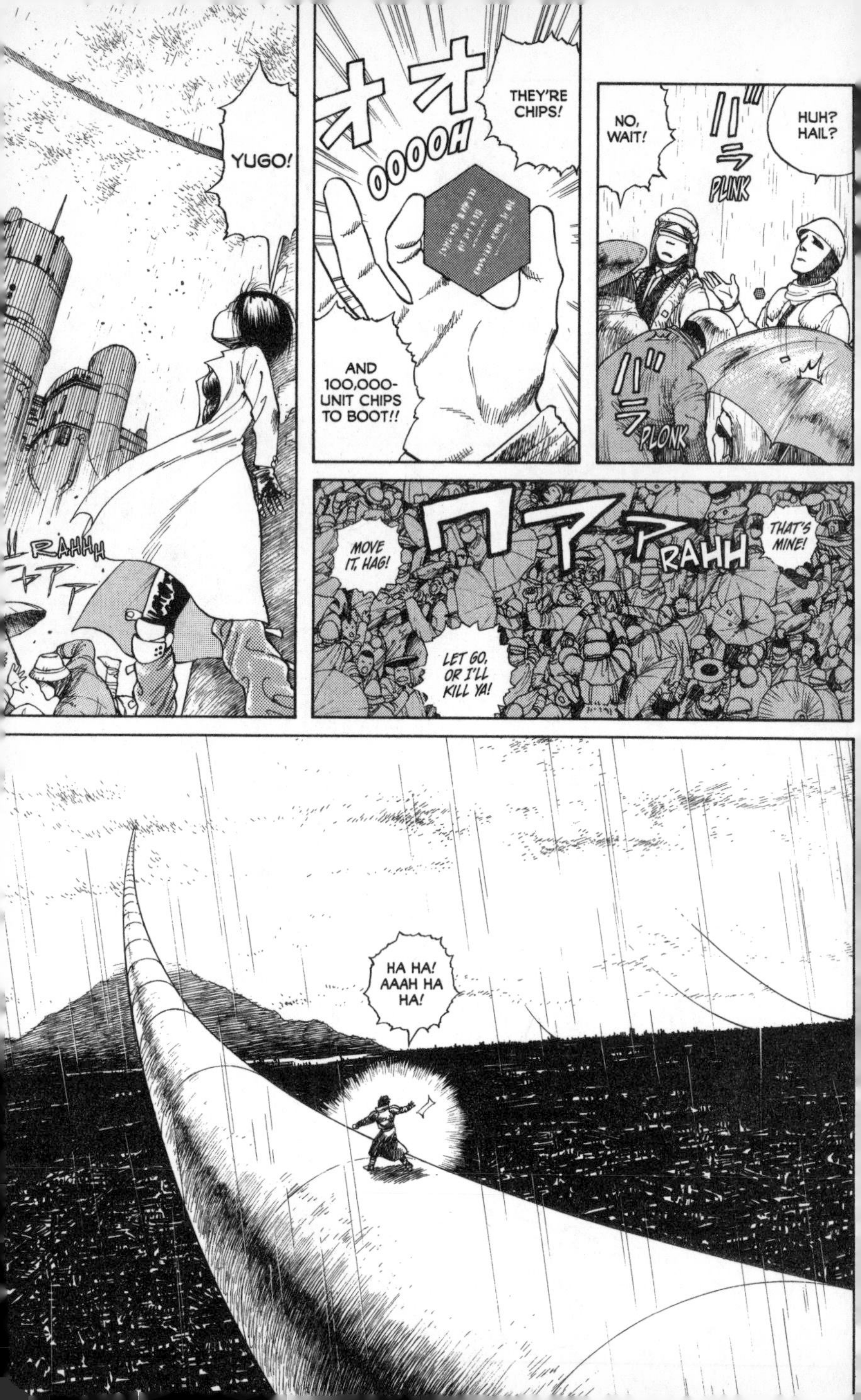
HUH? HAIL?
バラ PLINK
NO, WAIT!
バラ PLONK
THEY'RE CHIPS!
オオ OOOOH
AND 100,000-UNIT CHIPS TO BOOT!!
YUGO!
ワァァ RAHHH
THAT'S MINE!
ワァ RAHH
MOVE IT, HAG!
LET GO, OR I'LL KILL YA!
HA HA! AAAH HA HA!

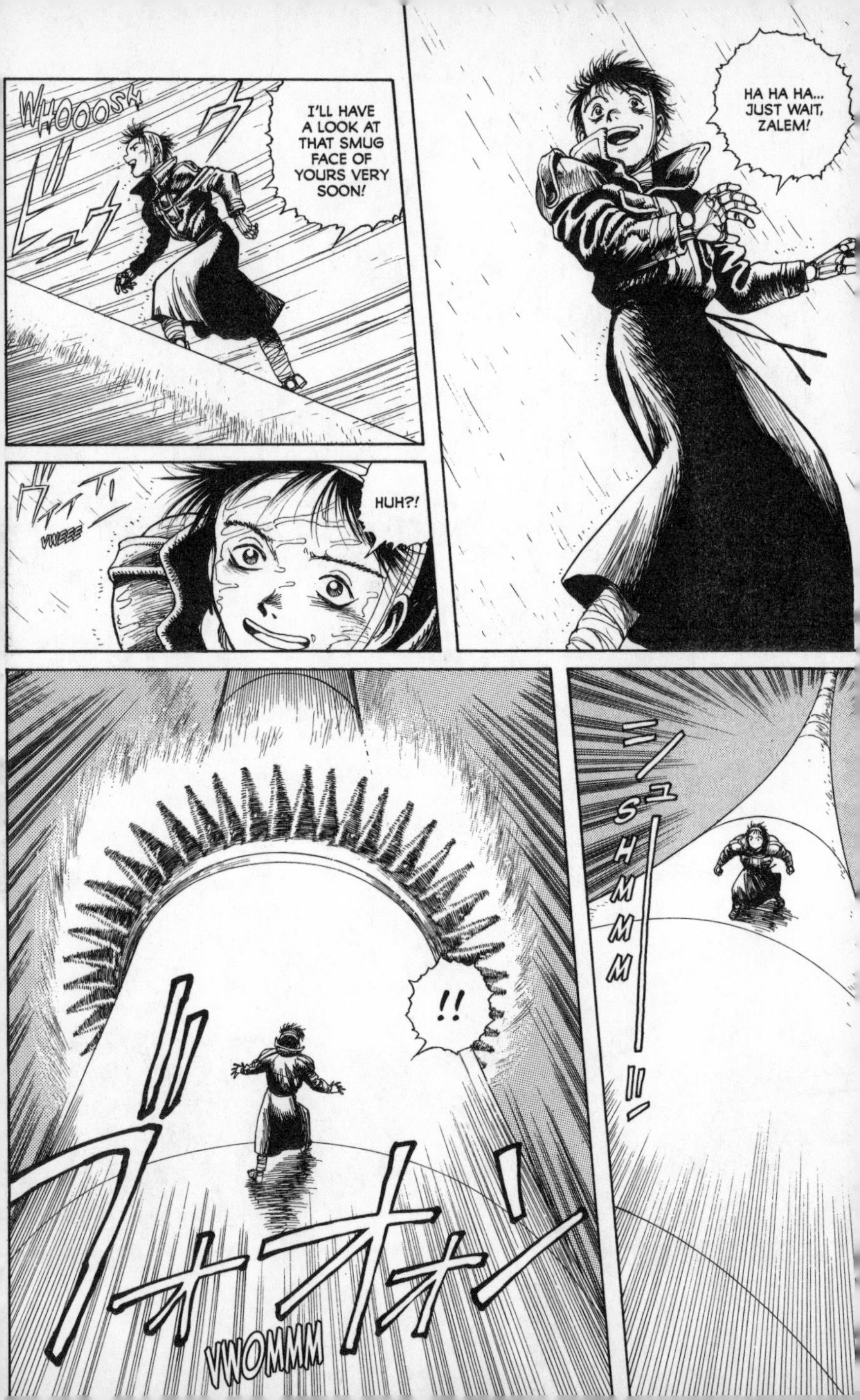
HA HA HA... JUST WAIT, ZALEM!
WHOOOSH
I'LL HAVE A LOOK AT THAT SMUG FACE OF YOURS VERY SOON!
HUH?!
VWEEE
SHMMMM
!!
VWOMMM

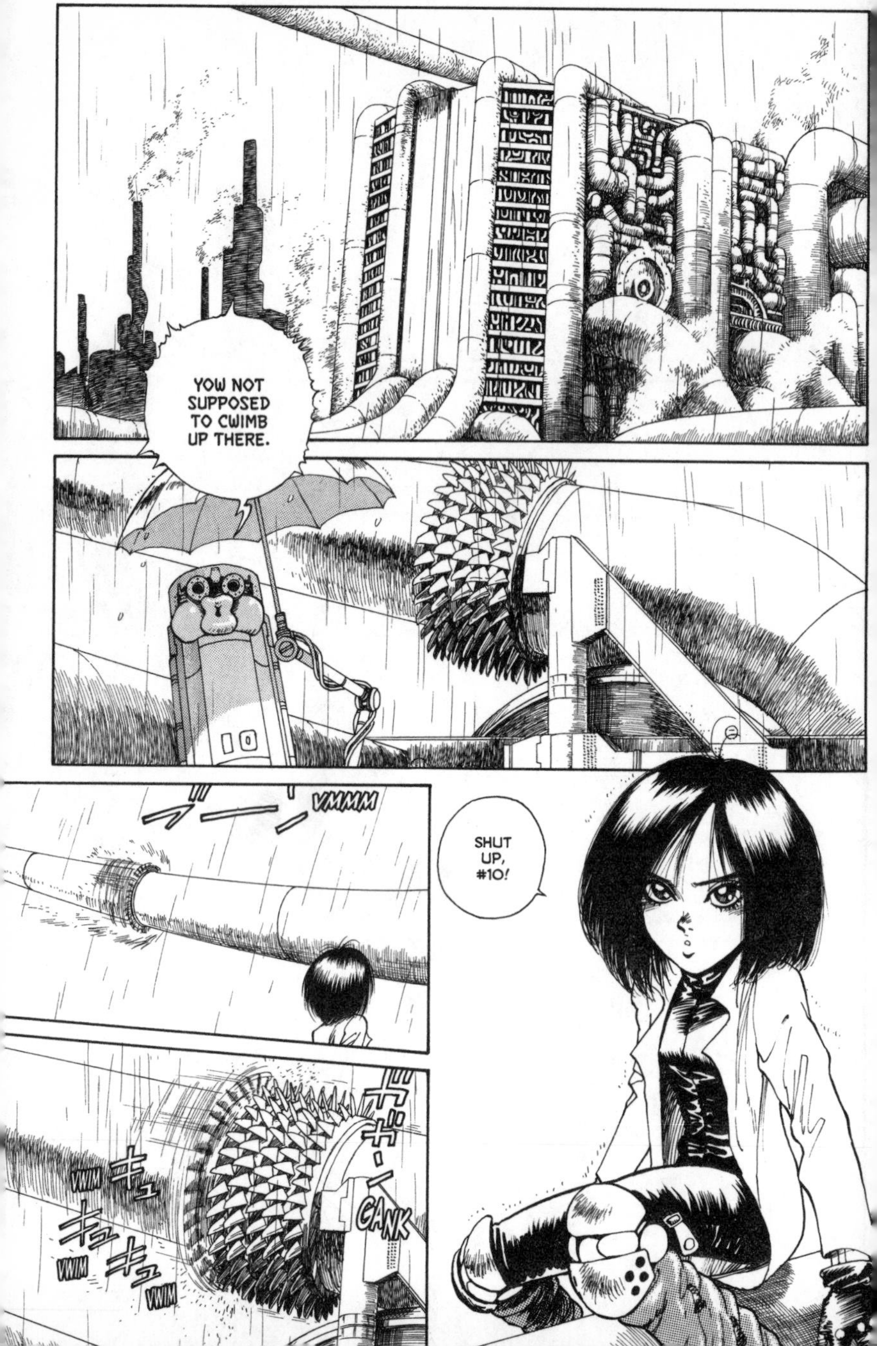
YOW NOT SUPPOSED TO CWIMB UP THERE.
SHUT UP, #10!
VMMMM
GANK
VWIM
VWIM
VWIM

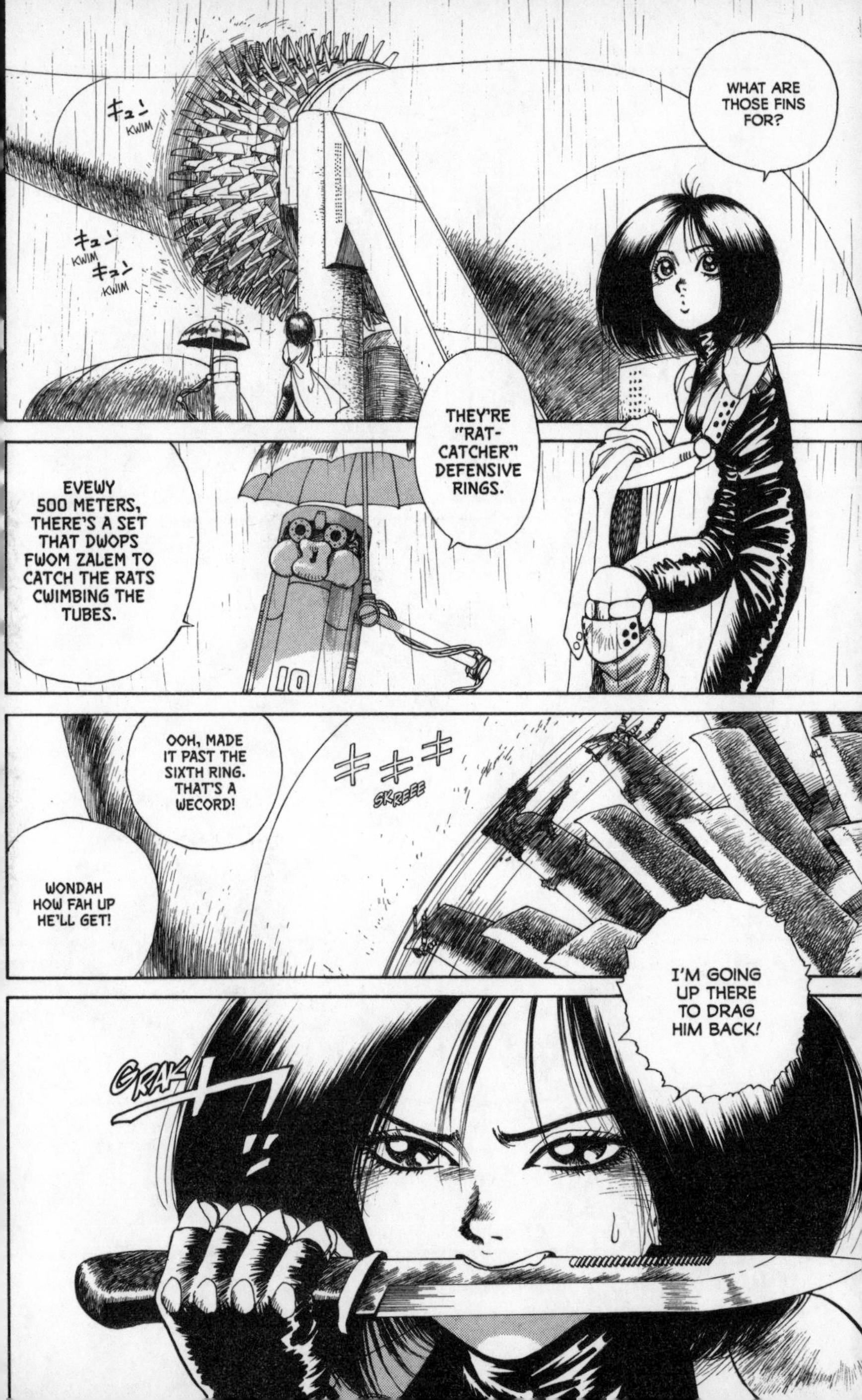
WHAT ARE THOSE FINS FOR?
キュン
KWIM
キュン
KWIM
キュン
KWIM
THEY'RE "RAT-CATCHER" DEFENSIVE RINGS.
EVEWY 500 METERS, THERE'S A SET THAT DWOPS FWOM ZALEM TO CATCH THE RATS CWIMBING THE TUBES.
OOH, MADE IT PAST THE SIXTH RING. THAT'S A WECORD!
キキキ
SKREEE
WONDAH HOW FAH UP HE'LL GET!
I'M GOING UP THERE TO DRAG HIM BACK!
GRAK

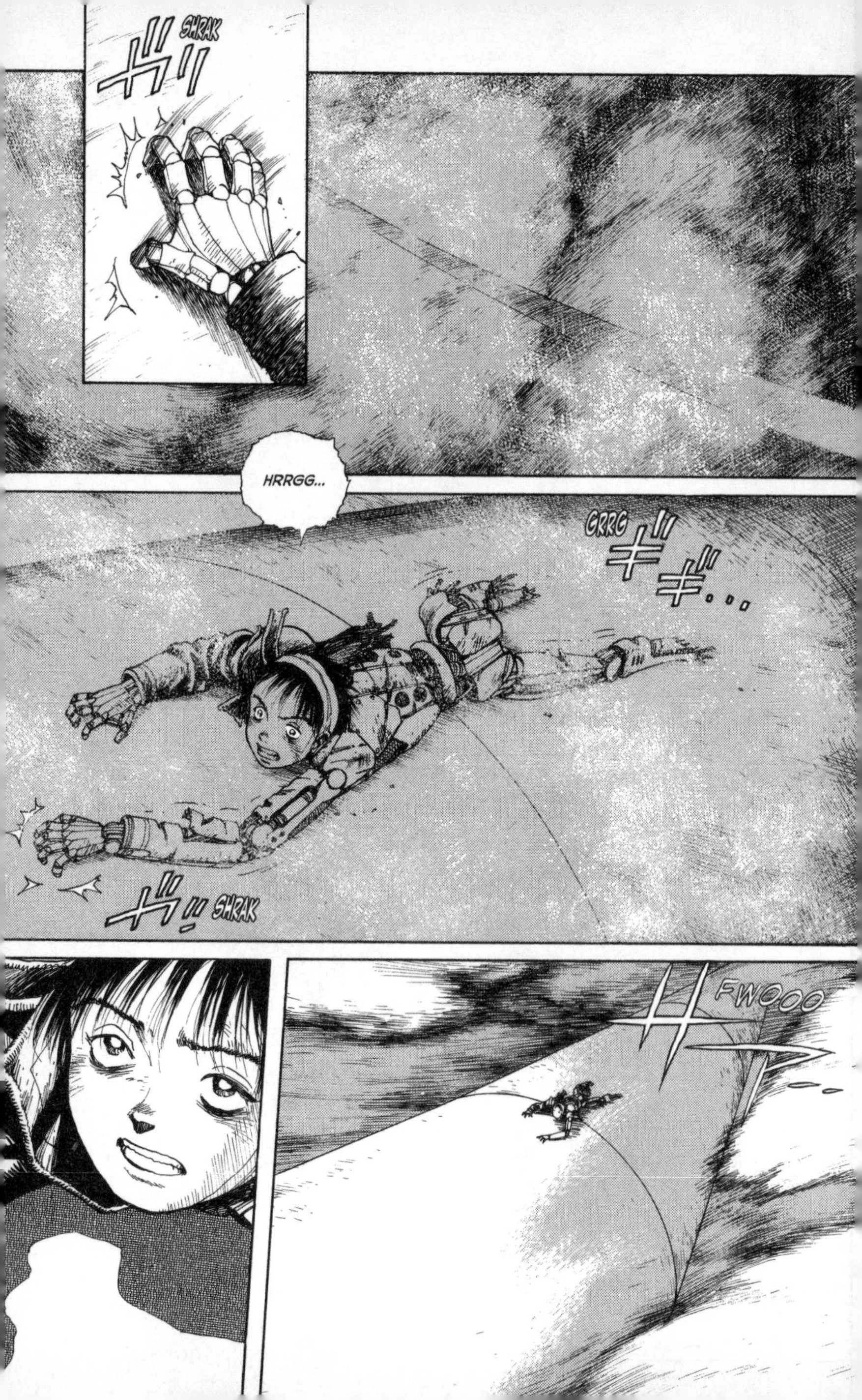
SHRAK
HRRGG...
GRRG
SHRAK
FWOOO

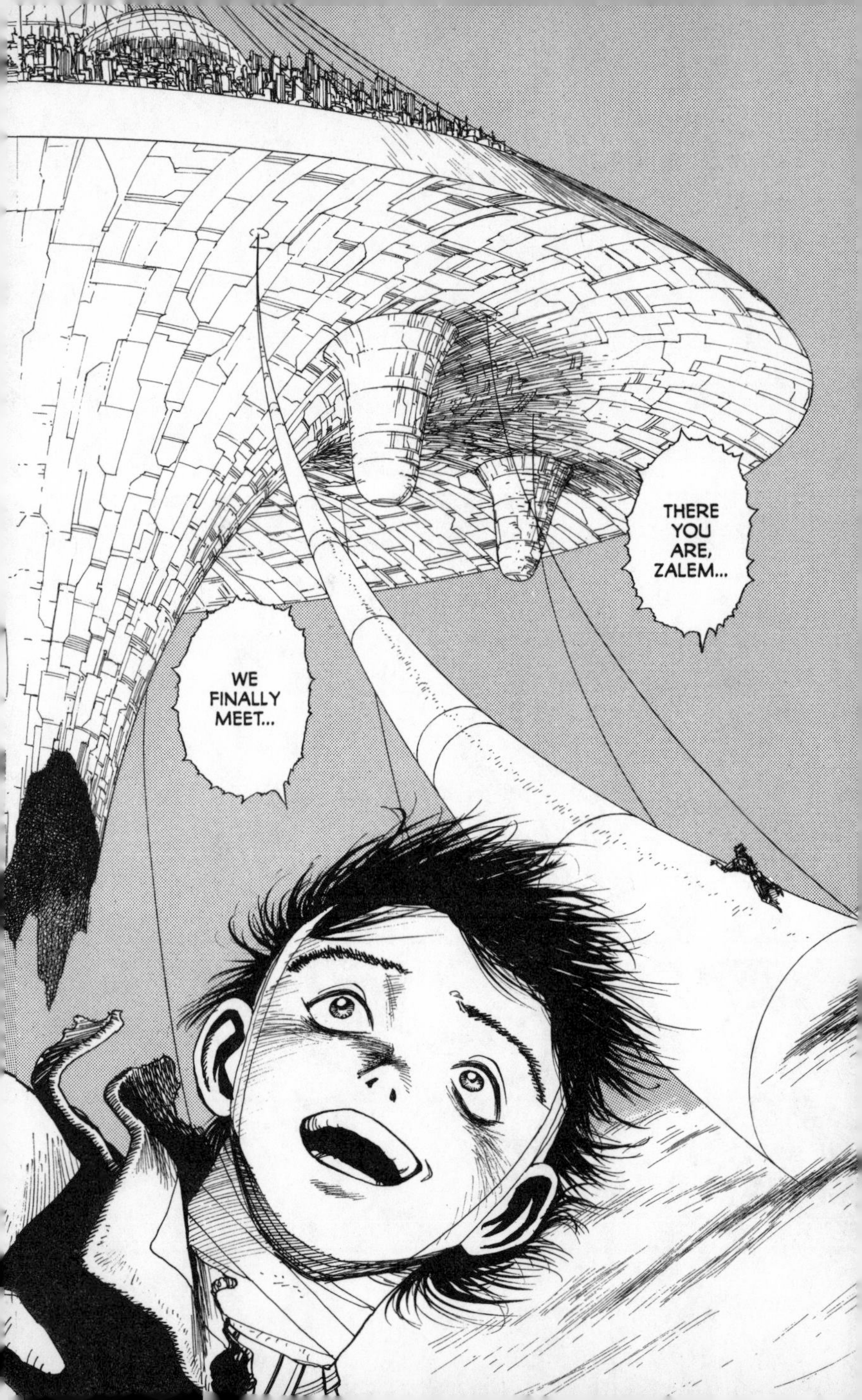
THERE YOU ARE, ZALEM...
WE FINALLY MEET...

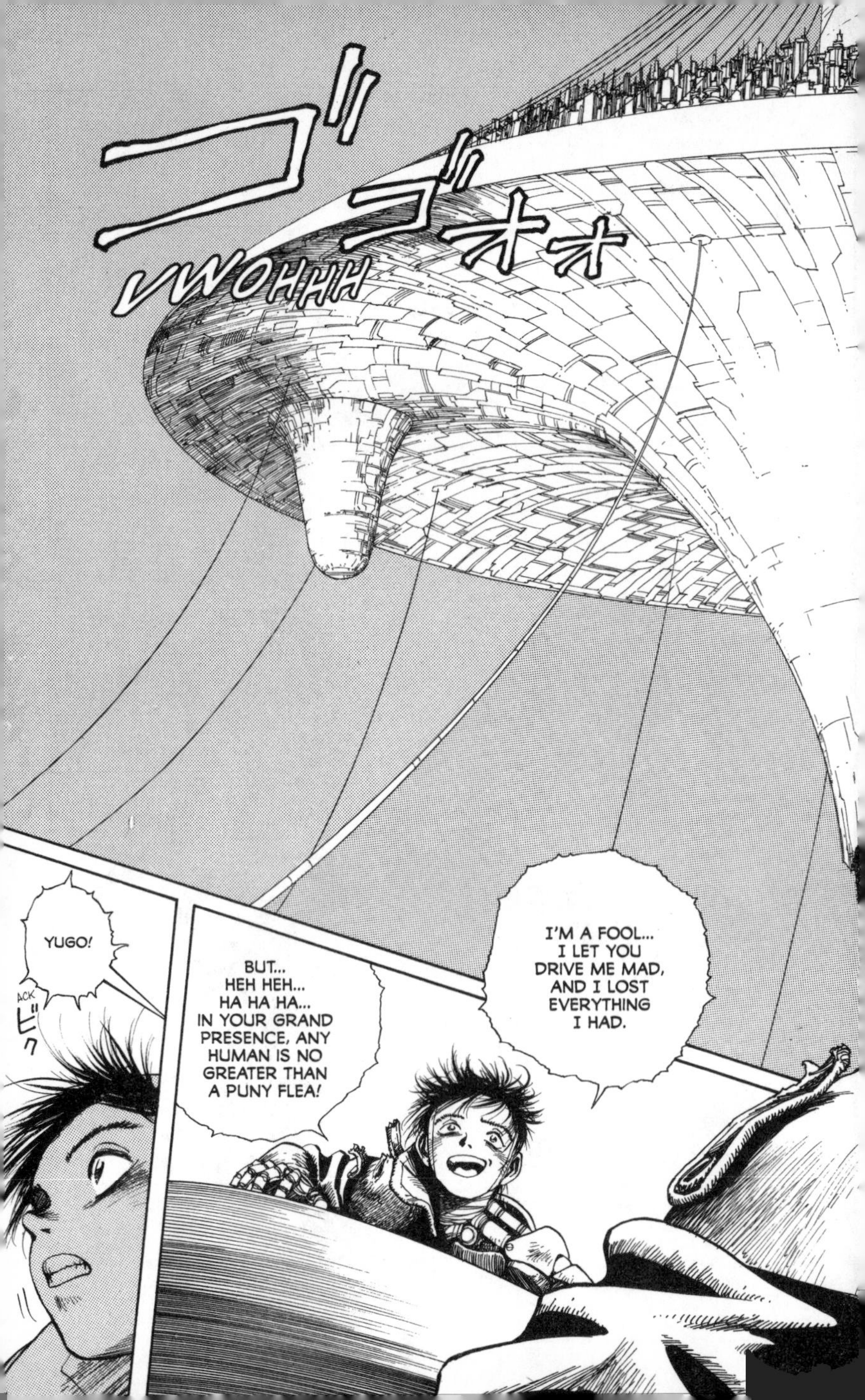
ゴゴオオ
VWOHHH
I'M A FOOL... I LET YOU DRIVE ME MAD, AND I LOST EVERYTHING I HAD.
BUT... HEH HEH... HA HA HA... IN YOUR GRAND PRESENCE, ANY HUMAN IS NO GREATER THAN A PUNY FLEA!
YUGO!
ビク
ACK

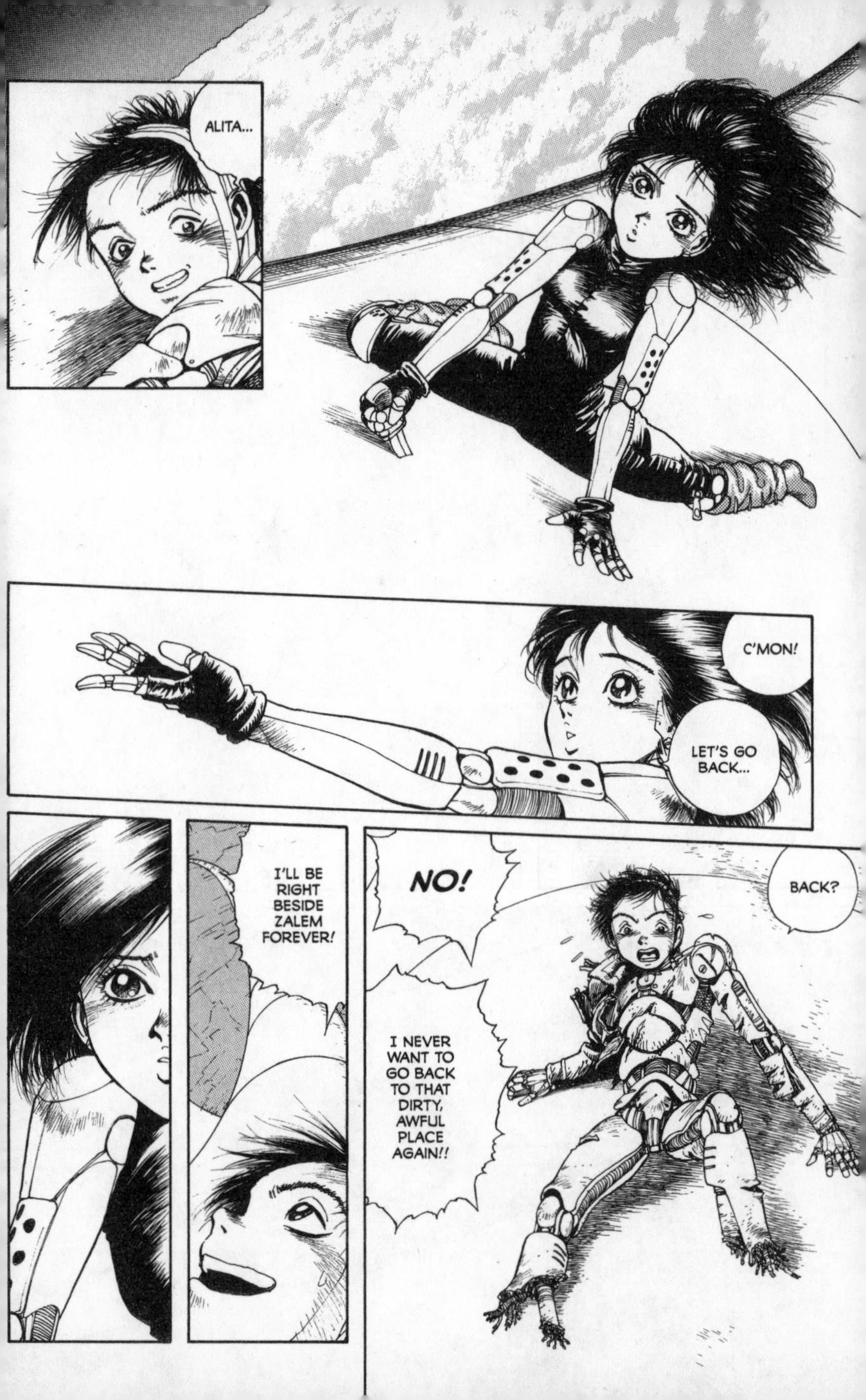
ALITA...
C'MON!
LET'S GO BACK...
BACK?
NO!
I NEVER WANT TO GO BACK TO THAT DIRTY, AWFUL PLACE AGAIN!!
I'LL BE RIGHT BESIDE ZALEM FOREVER!

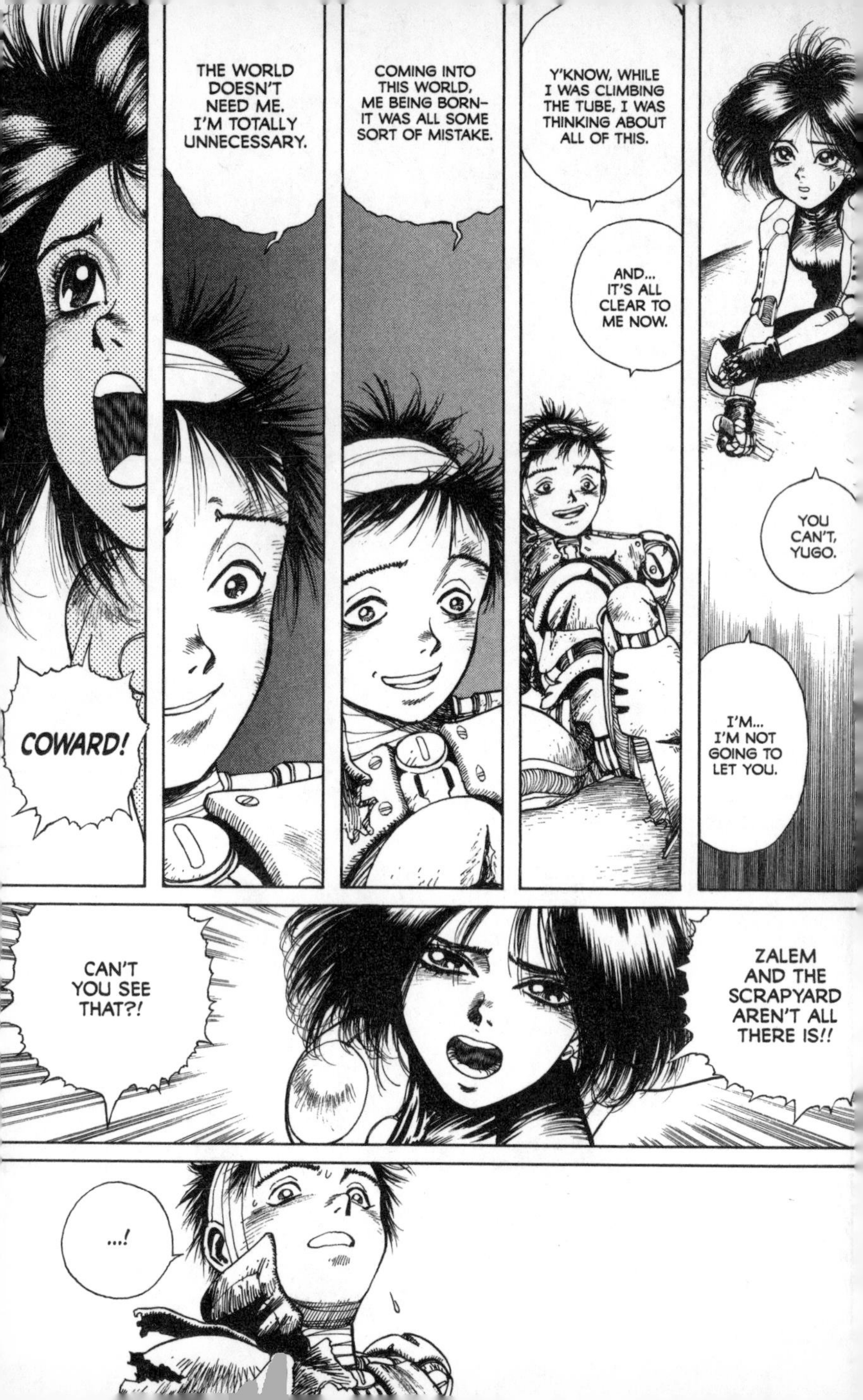
YOU CAN'T, YUGO.
I'M... I'M NOT GOING TO LET YOU.
Y'KNOW, WHILE I WAS CLIMBING THE TUBE, I WAS THINKING ABOUT ALL OF THIS.
AND... IT'S ALL CLEAR TO ME NOW.
COMING INTO THIS WORLD, ME BEING BORN– IT WAS ALL SOME SORT OF MISTAKE.
THE WORLD DOESN'T NEED ME. I'M TOTALLY UNNECESSARY.
COWARD!
ZALEM AND THE SCRAPYARD AREN'T ALL THERE IS!!
CAN'T YOU SEE THAT?!
...!

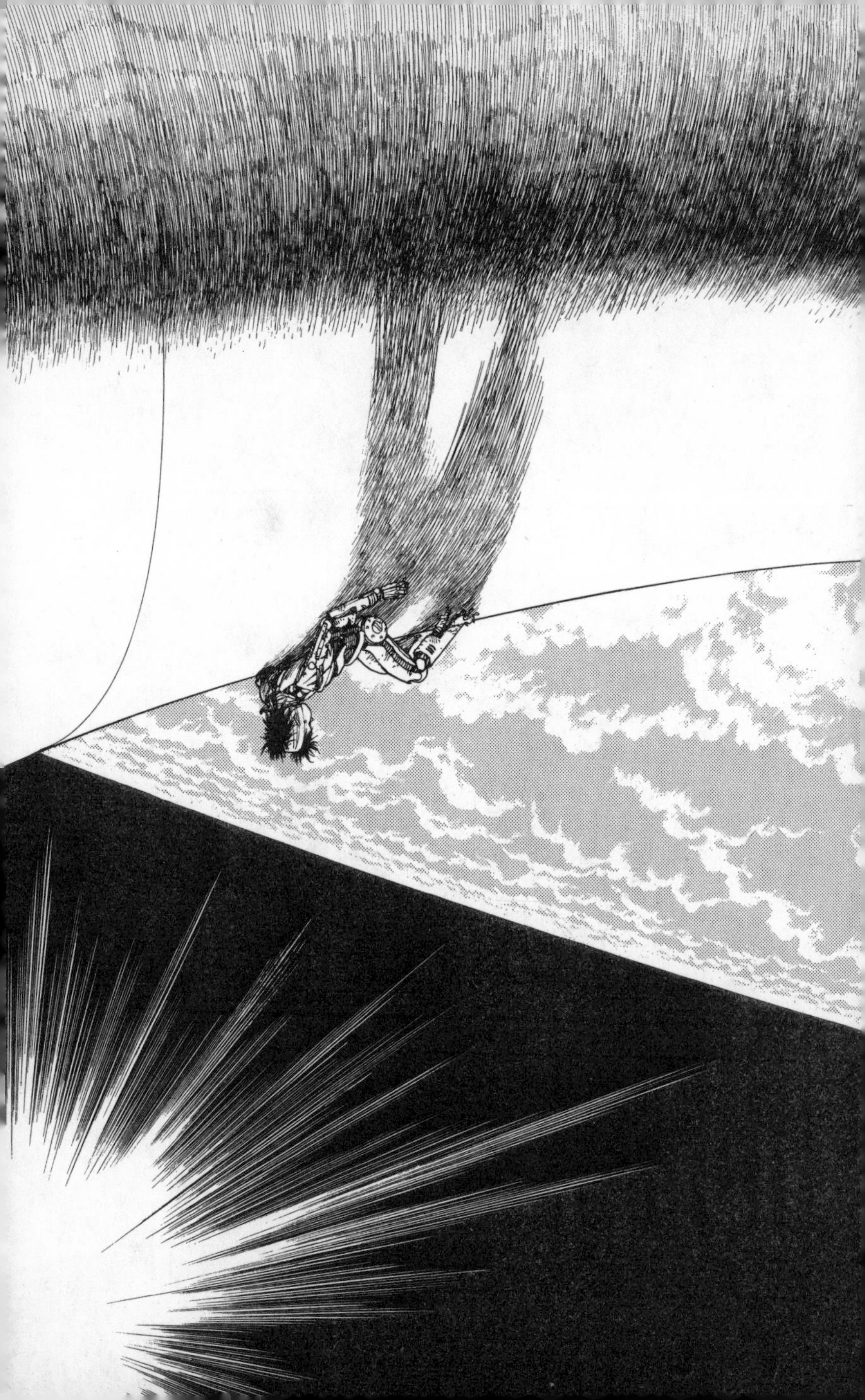

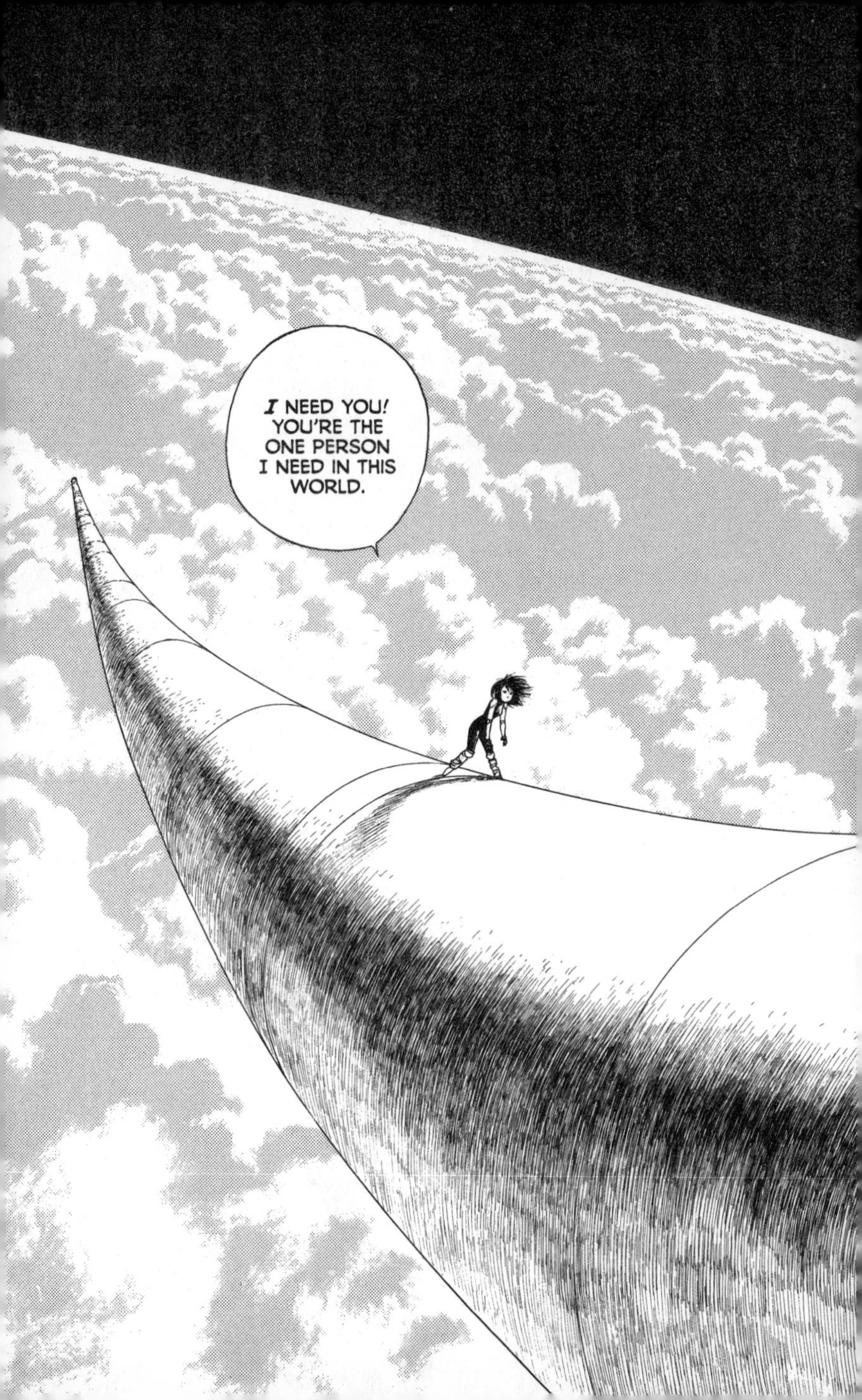
I NEED YOU! YOU'RE THE ONE PERSON I NEED IN THIS WORLD.

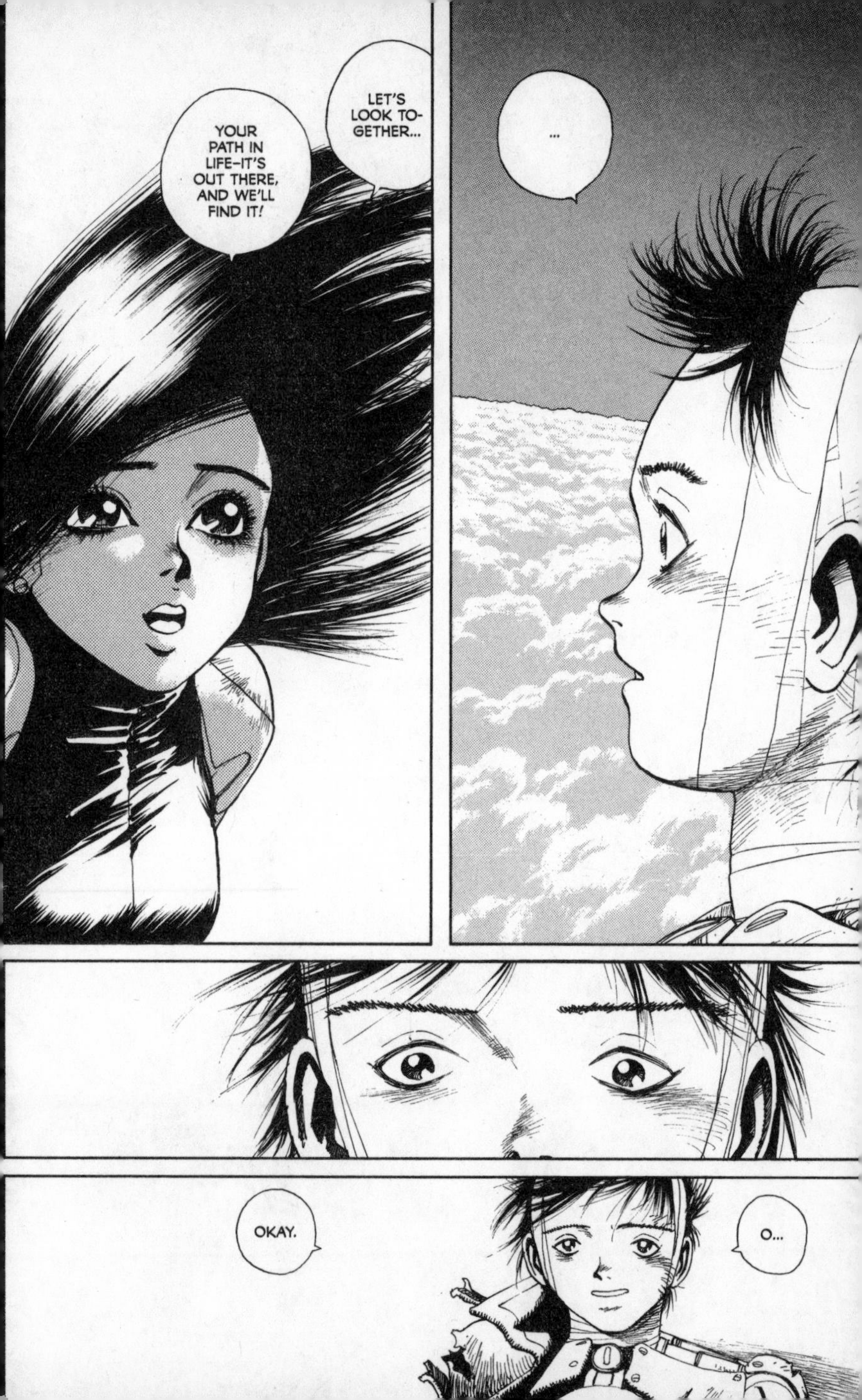
...
LET'S LOOK TO-GETHER...
YOUR PATH IN LIFE—IT'S OUT THERE, AND WE'LL FIND IT!
O...
OKAY.

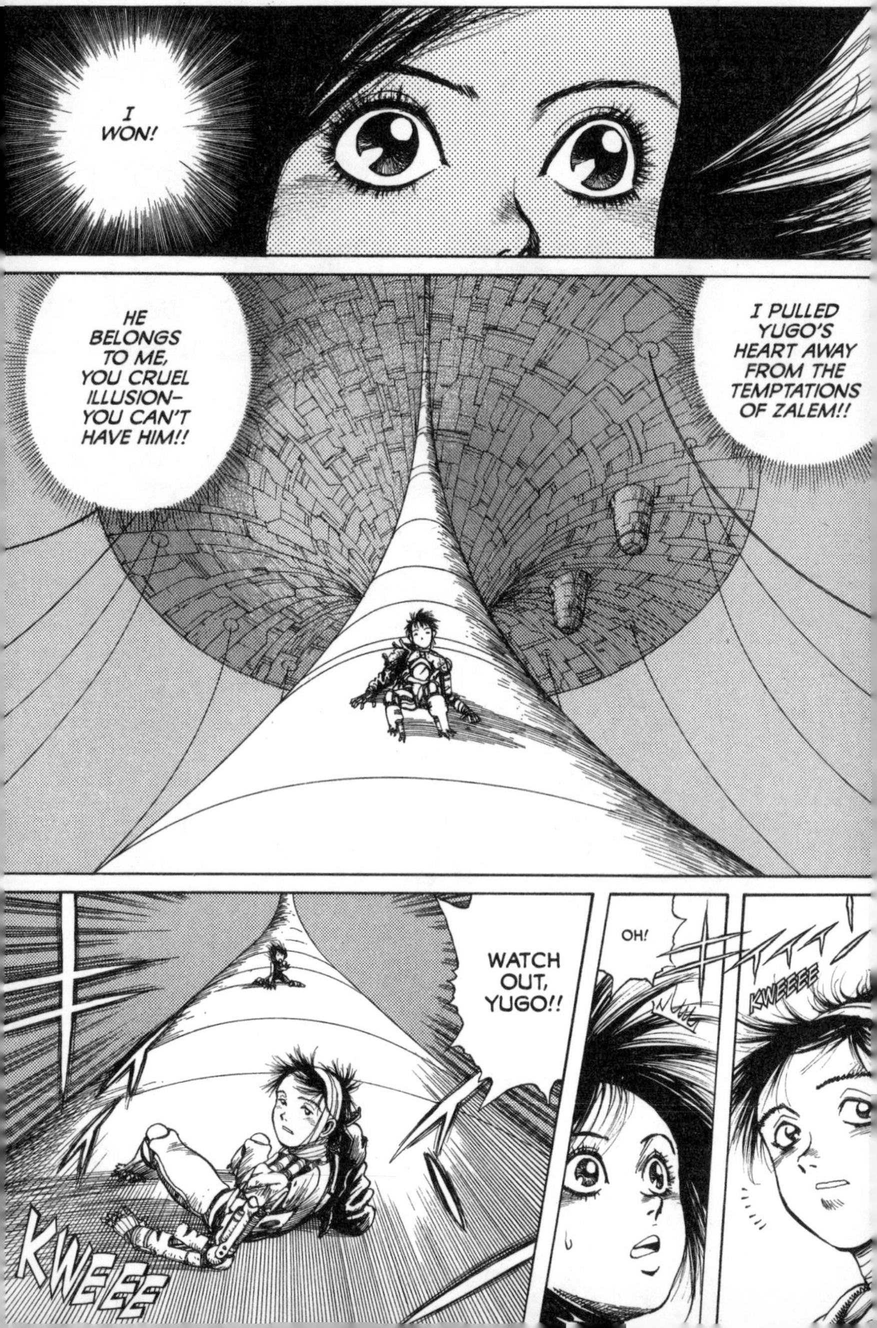
I WON!
I PULLED YUGO'S HEART AWAY FROM THE TEMPTATIONS OF ZALEM!!
HE BELONGS TO ME, YOU CRUEL ILLUSION– YOU CAN'T HAVE HIM!!
KWEEEE
OH!
WATCH OUT, YUGO!!
KWEEEE

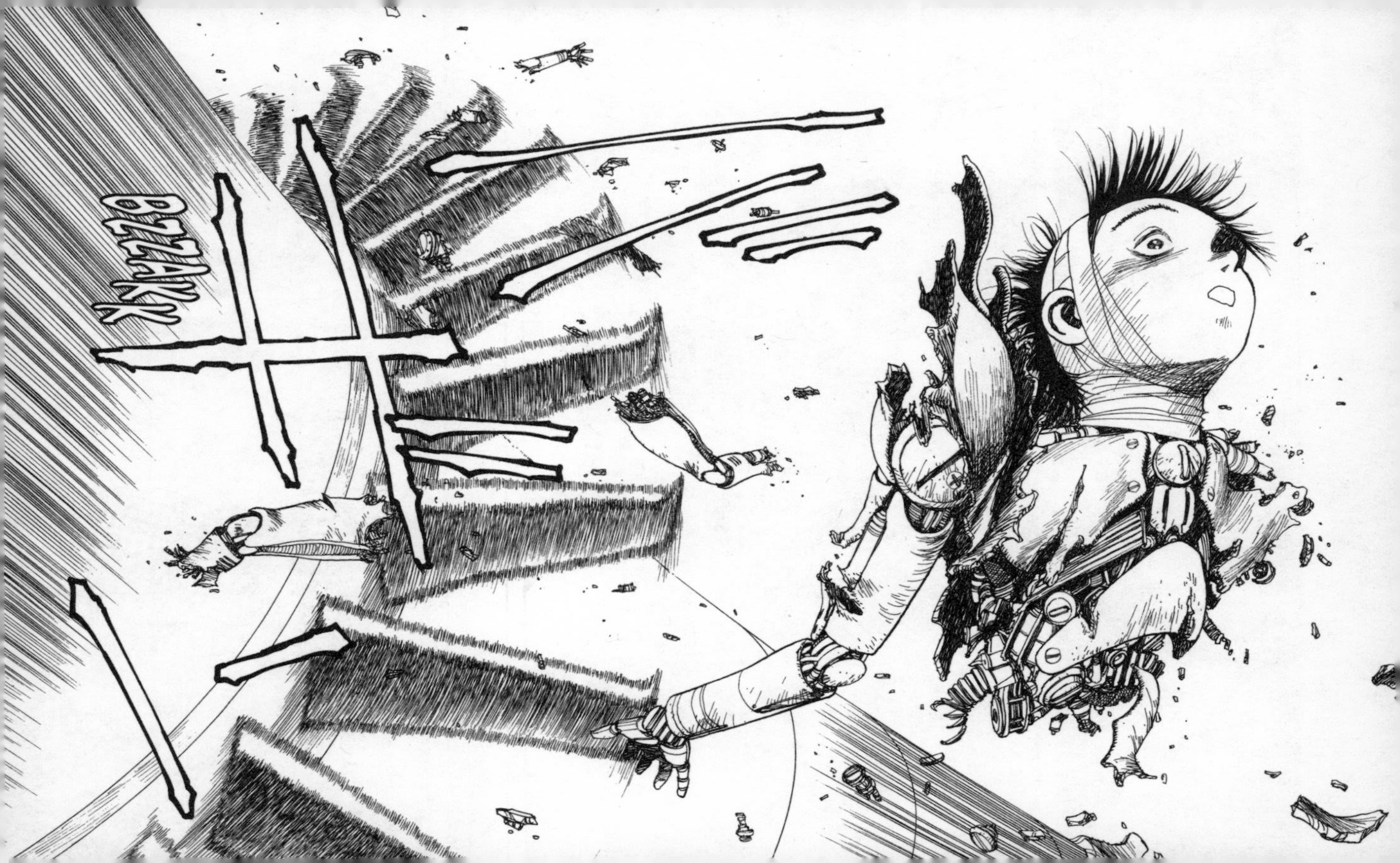
BZZAKK

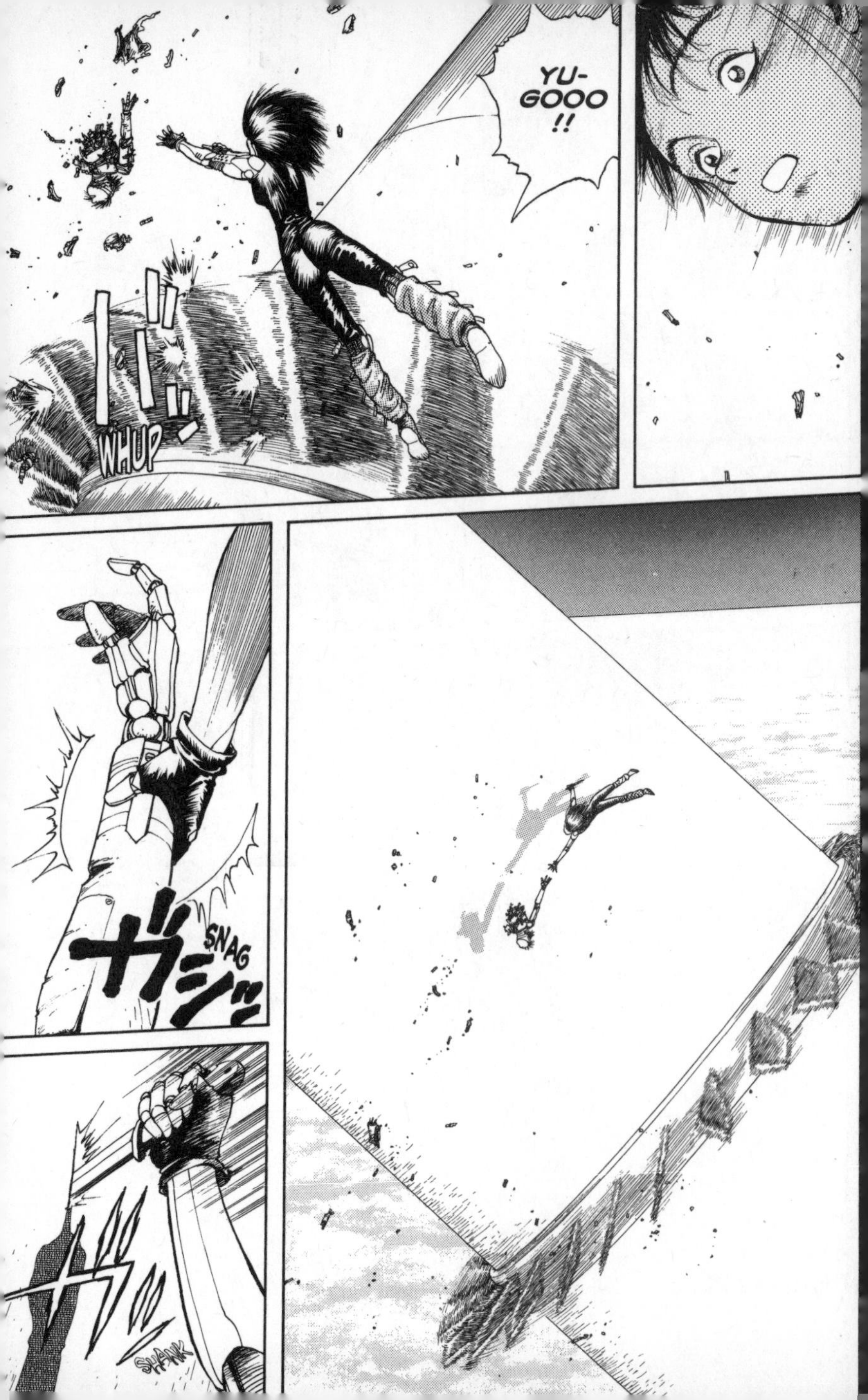
YU-GOOO !!
WHUP
SNAG
SHANK

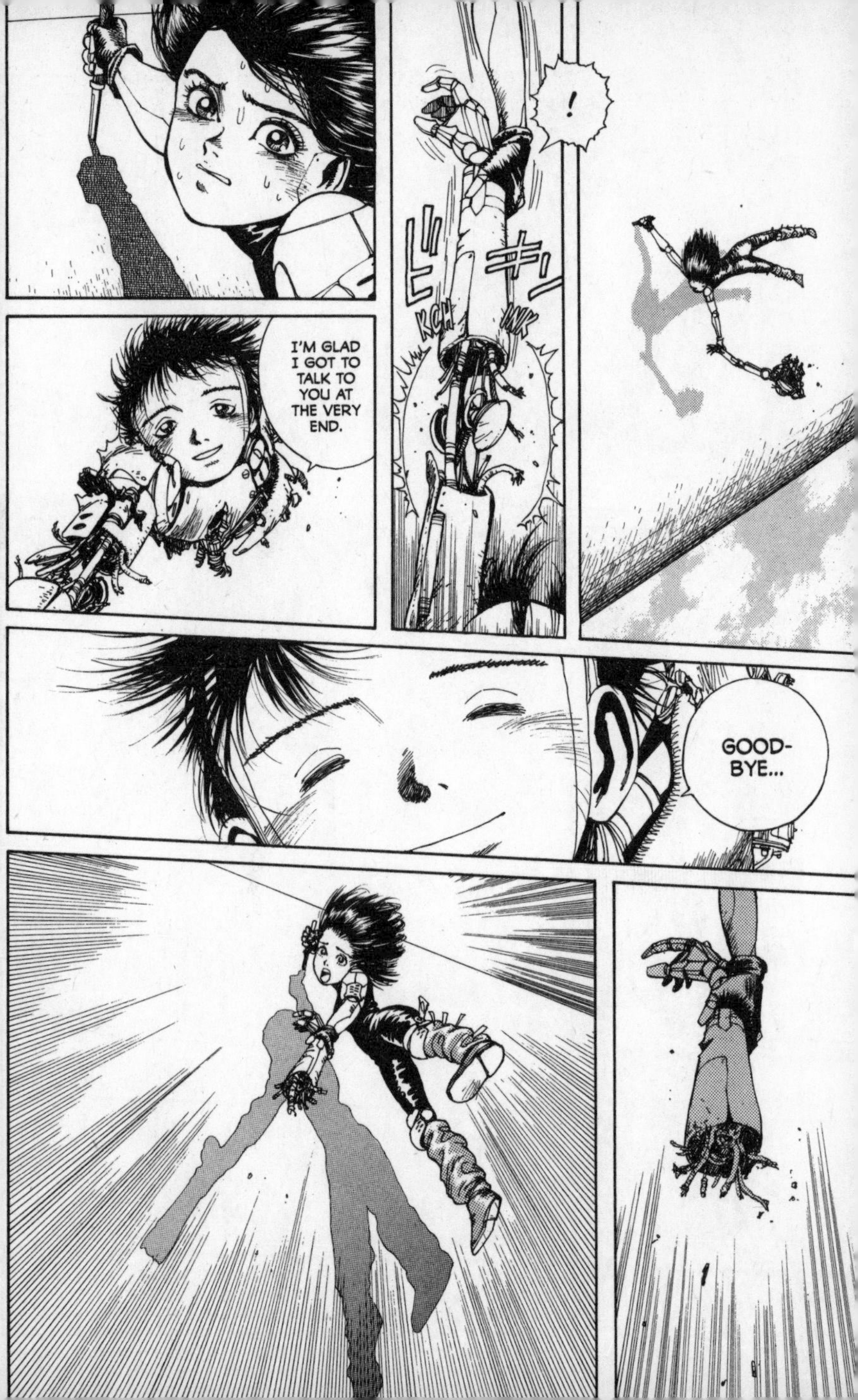
!
ビキン
KCH
INK
I'M GLAD I GOT TO TALK TO YOU AT THE VERY END.
GOOD-BYE...

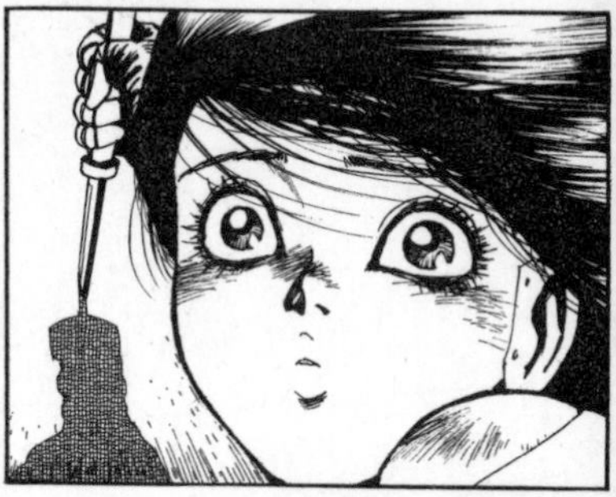
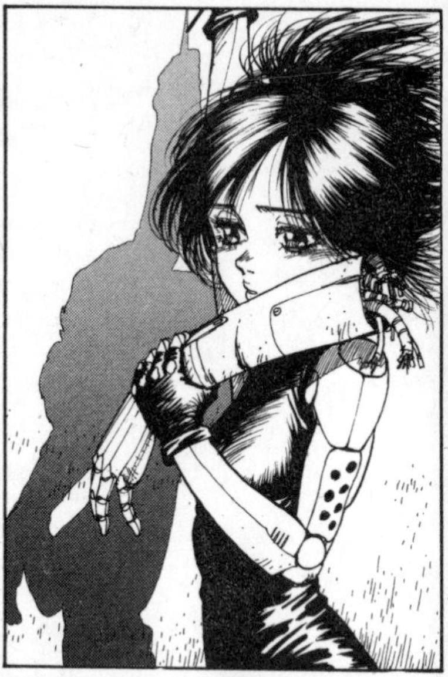
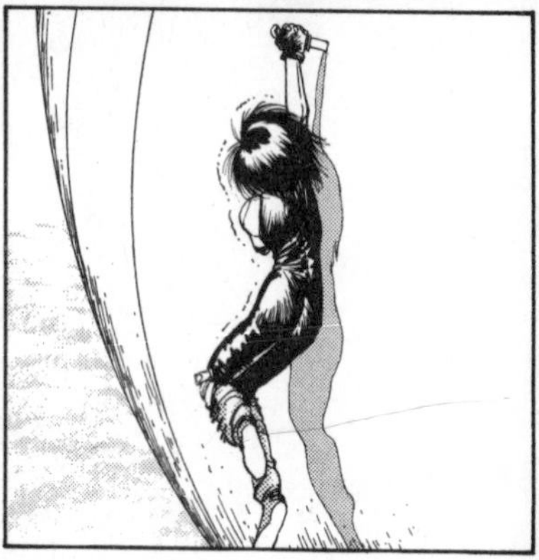
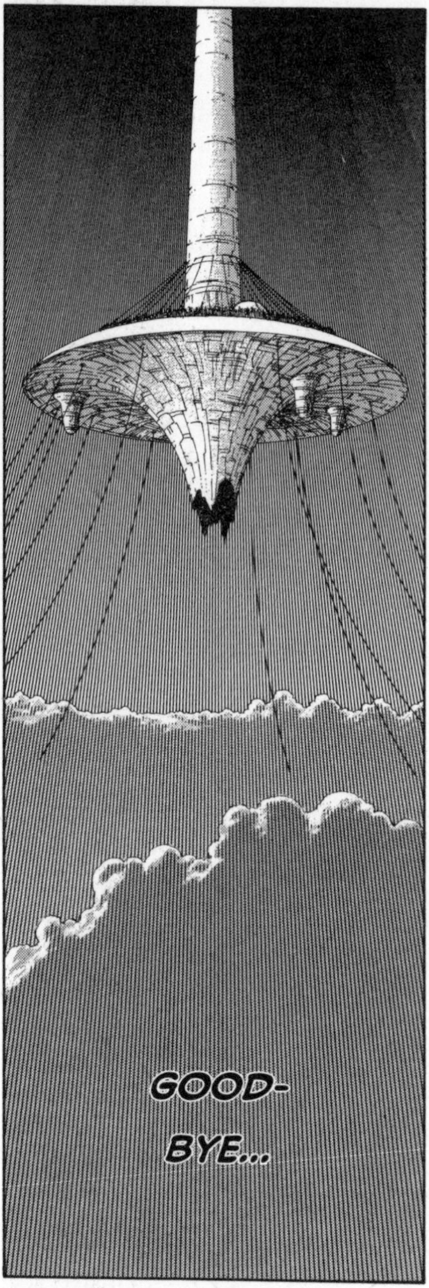
GOOD-
BYE...

FIGHT_013 Killing Angel

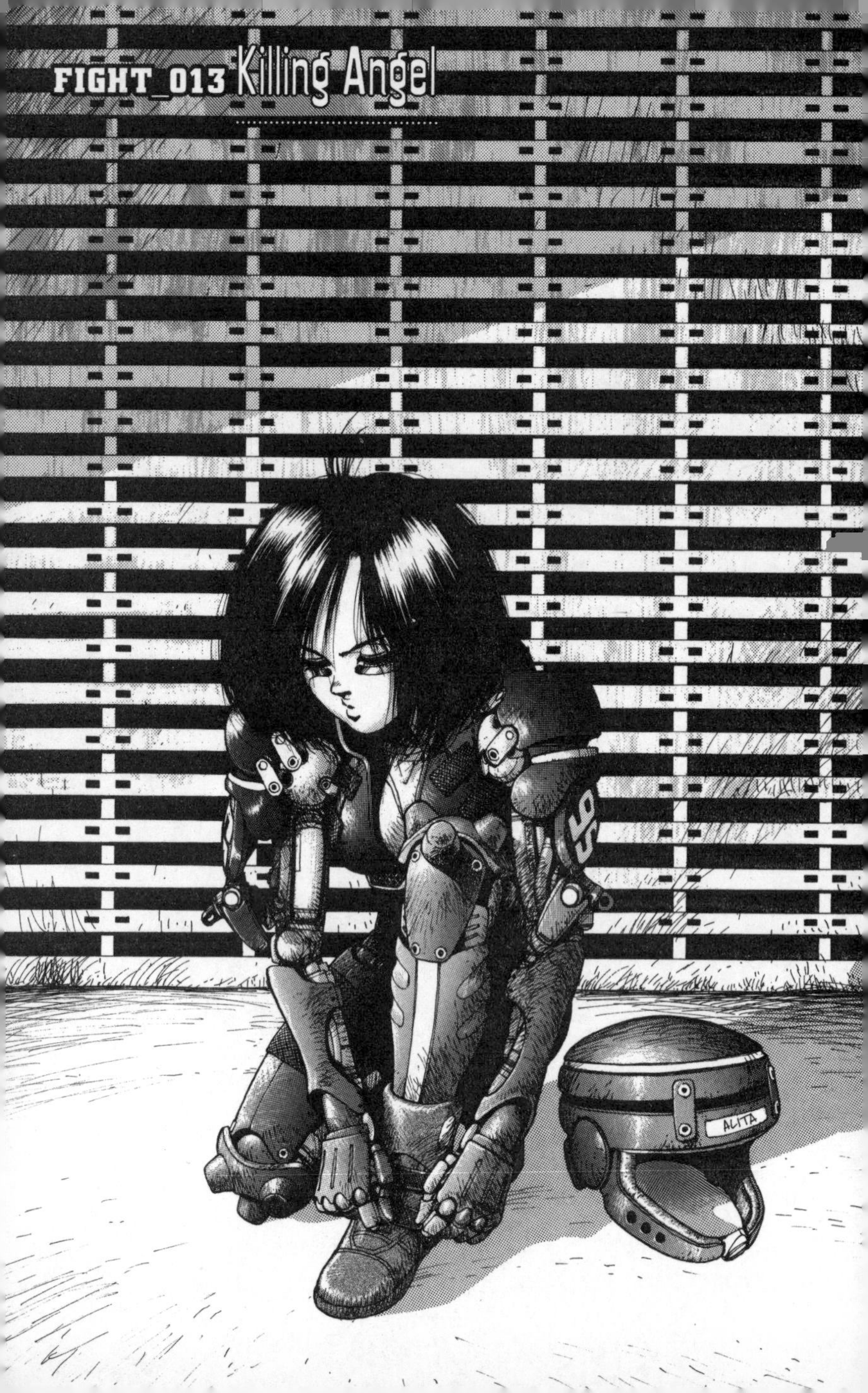
95
ALITA

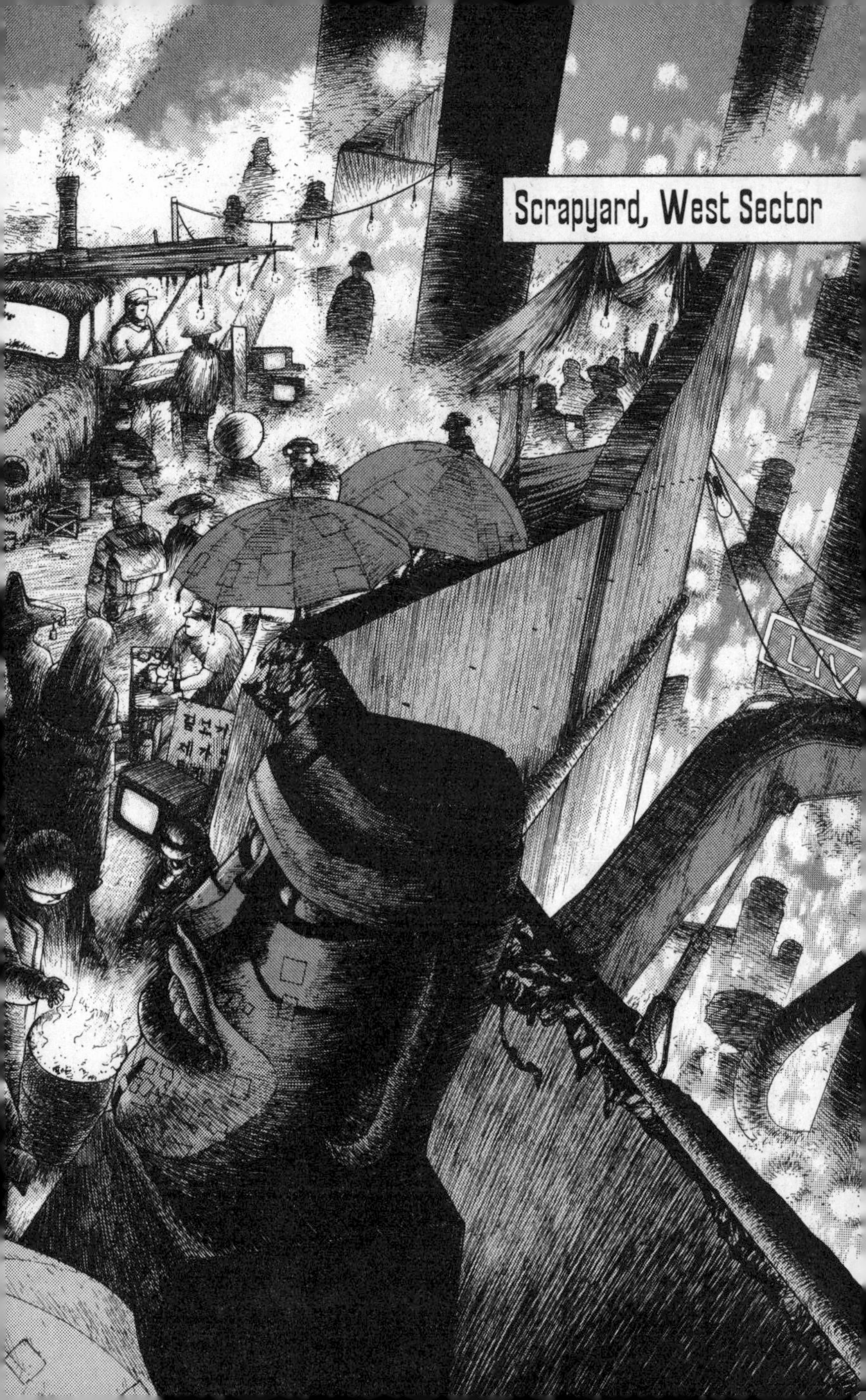
Scrapyard, West Sector

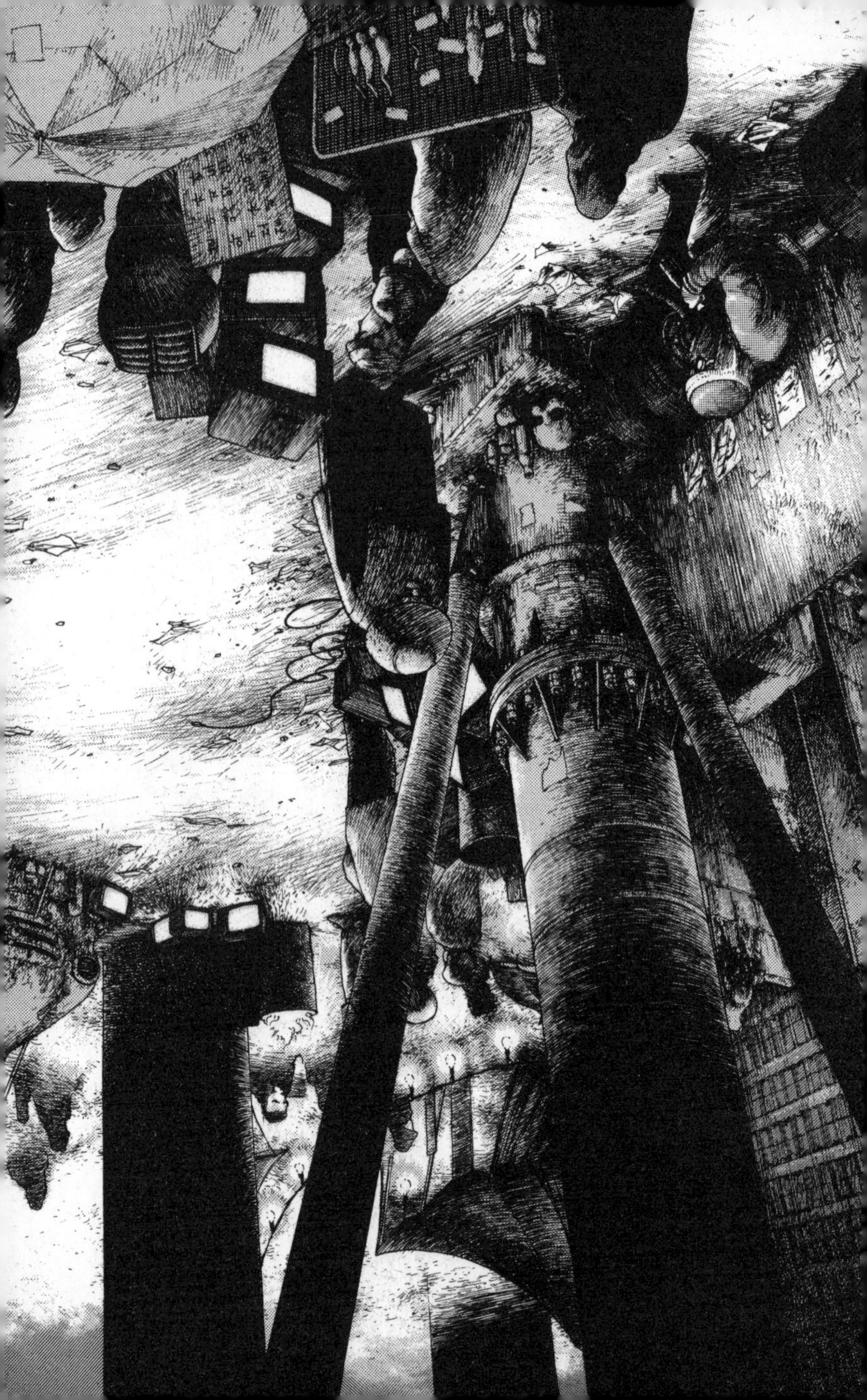

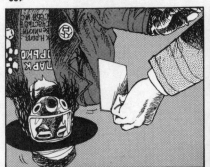

IT'S BEEN ONE MONTH SINCE ALL OF THAT...

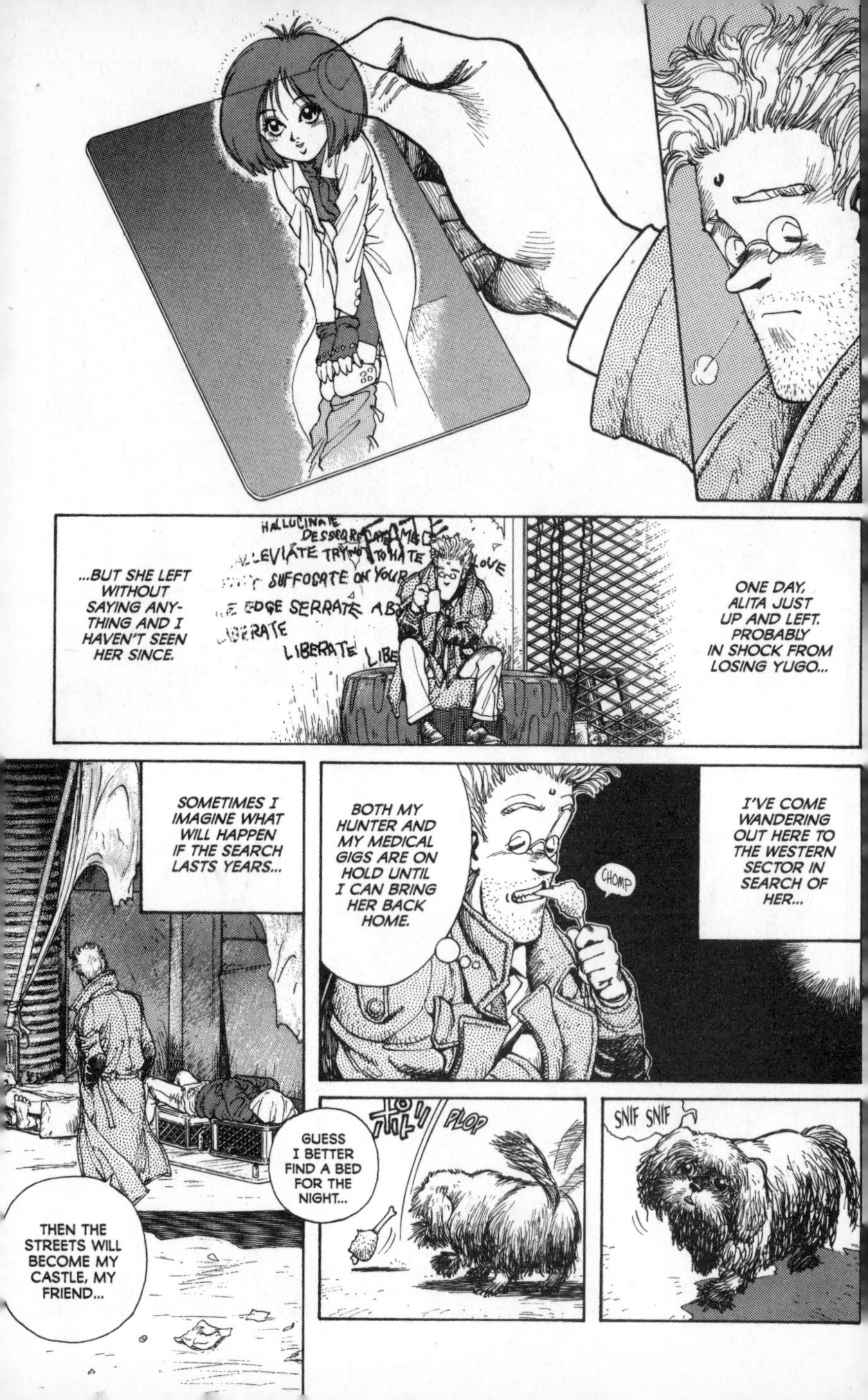
ONE DAY, ALITA JUST UP AND LEFT. PROBABLY IN SHOCK FROM LOSING YUGO...
...BUT SHE LEFT WITHOUT SAYING ANY-THING AND I HAVEN'T SEEN HER SINCE.
LIBERATE
I'VE COME WANDERING OUT HERE TO THE WESTERN SECTOR IN SEARCH OF HER...
BOTH MY HUNTER AND MY MEDICAL GIGS ARE ON HOLD UNTIL I CAN BRING HER BACK HOME.
CHOMP
SNIF SNIF
PLOP
SOMETIMES I IMAGINE WHAT WILL HAPPEN IF THE SEARCH LASTS YEARS...
GUESS I BETTER FIND A BED FOR THE NIGHT...
THEN THE STREETS WILL BECOME MY CASTLE, MY FRIEND...

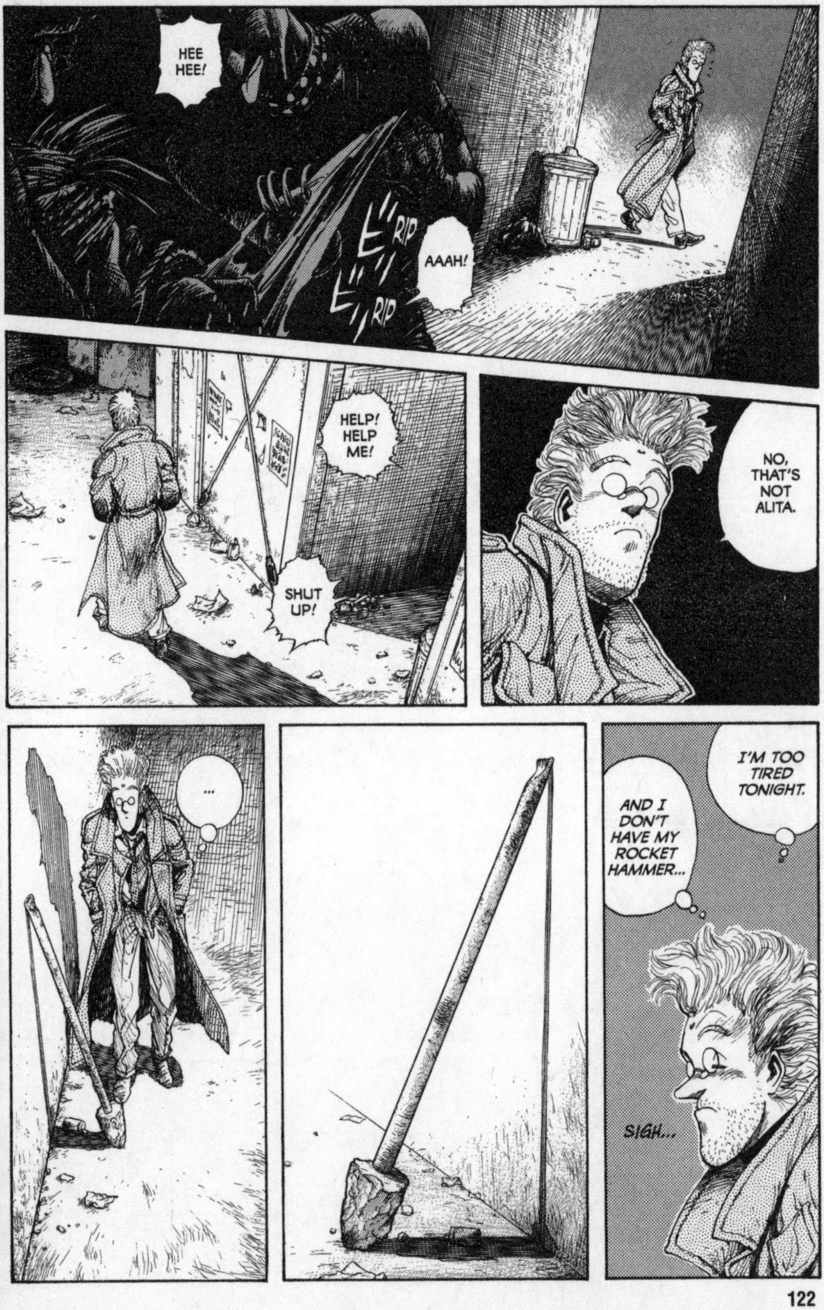
AAAH!
RIP
RIP
HEE HEE!
NO, THAT'S NOT ALITA.
HELP! HELP ME!
SHUT UP!
I'M TOO TIRED TONIGHT.
AND I DON'T HAVE MY ROCKET HAMMER...
SIGH...
...

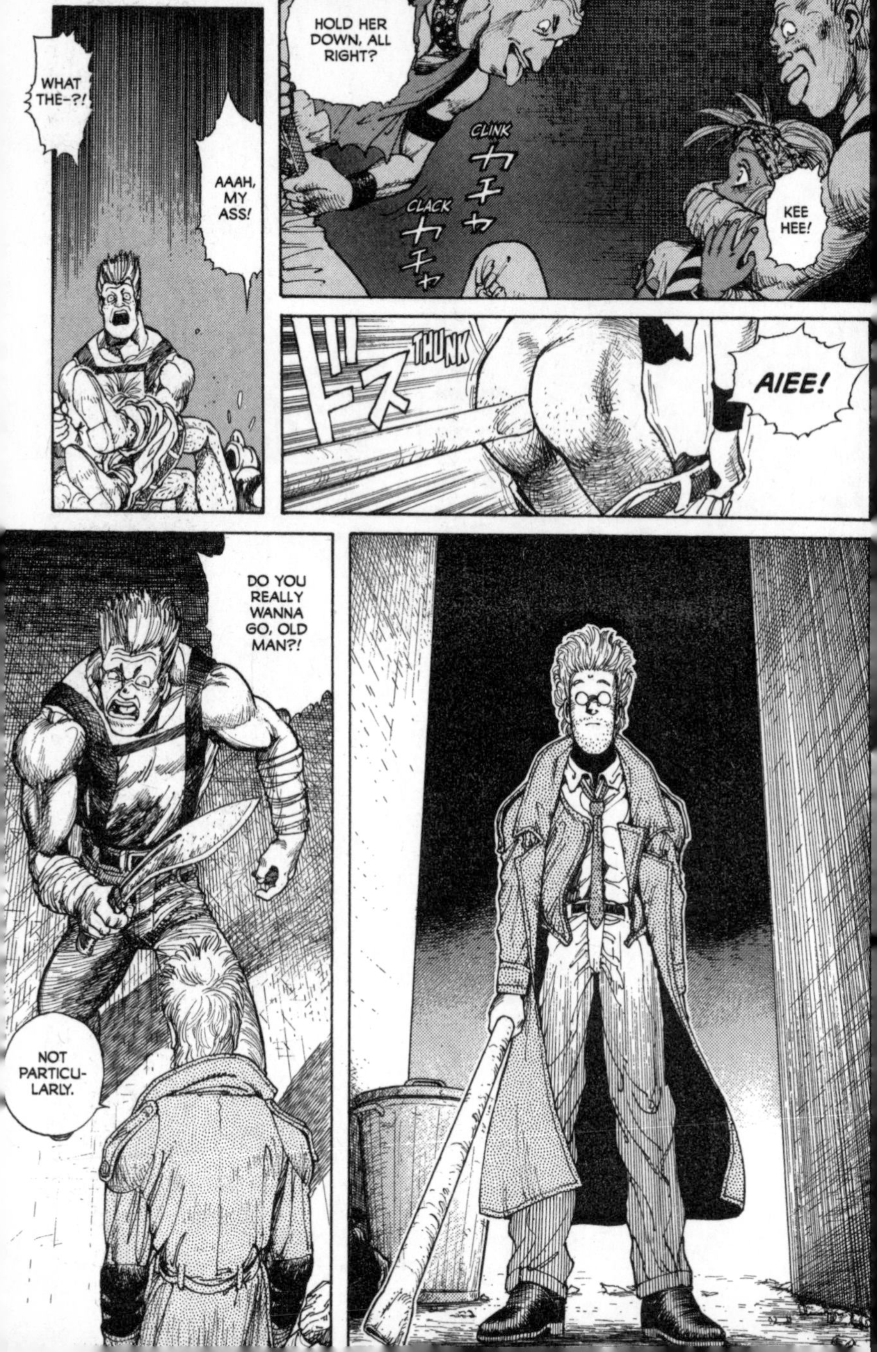
KEE HEE!
HOLD HER DOWN, ALL RIGHT?
CLINK
CLACK
AIEE!
THUNK
WHAT THE-?!
AAAH, MY ASS!
DO YOU REALLY WANNA GO, OLD MAN?!
NOT PARTICU- LARLY.

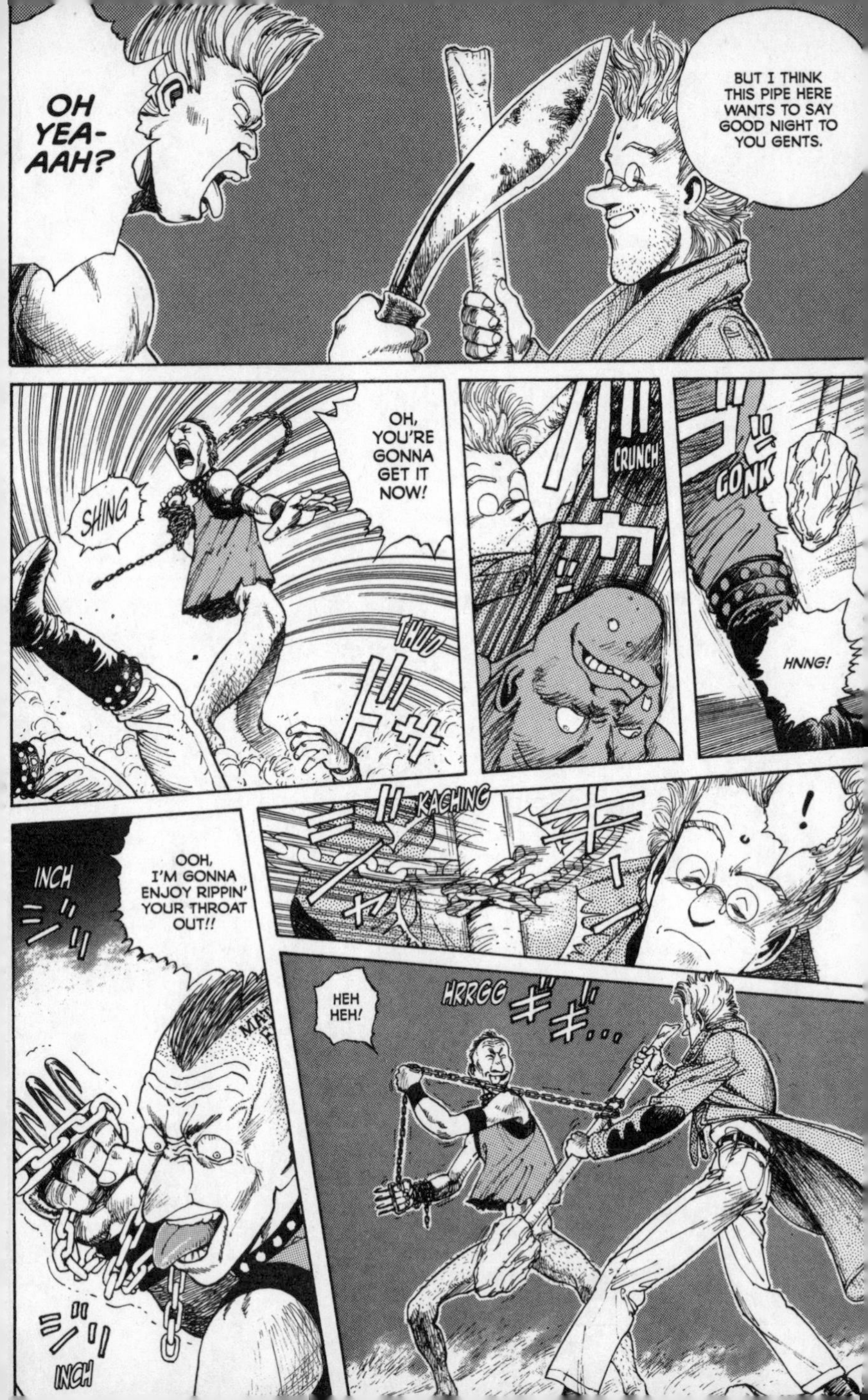
BUT I THINK THIS PIPE HERE WANTS TO SAY GOOD NIGHT TO YOU GENTS.
OH YEA-AAH?
HNNG!
GONK
CRUNCH
OH, YOU'RE GONNA GET IT NOW!
SHING
THUD
!
KACHING
HEH HEH!
HRRGG
OOH, I'M GONNA ENJOY RIPPIN' YOUR THROAT OUT!!
INCH
INCH

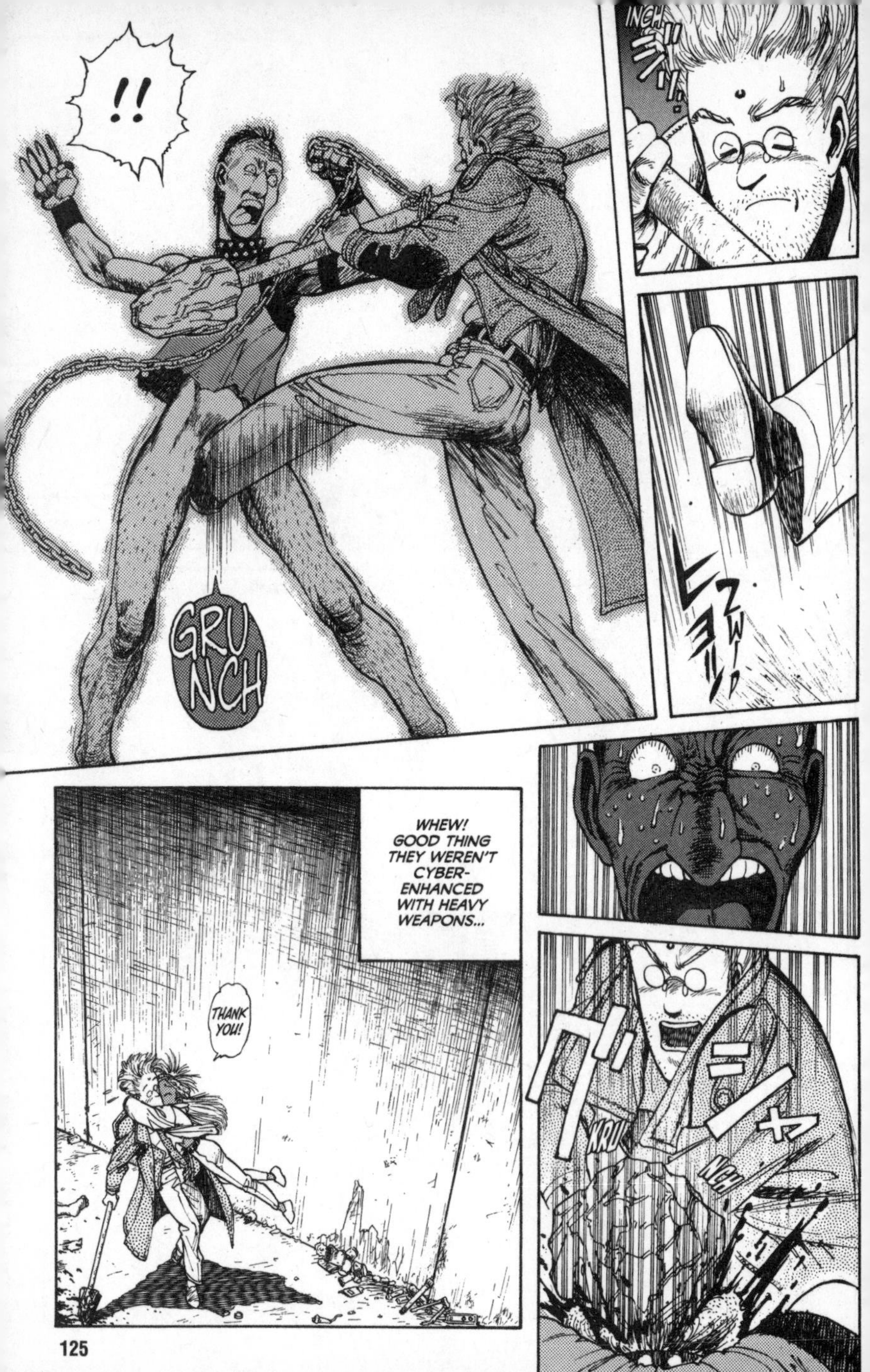
INCH
ZWIP
!!
GRUNCH
KRUNCH
WHEW! GOOD THING THEY WEREN'T CYBER-ENHANCED WITH HEAVY WEAPONS...
THANK YOU!

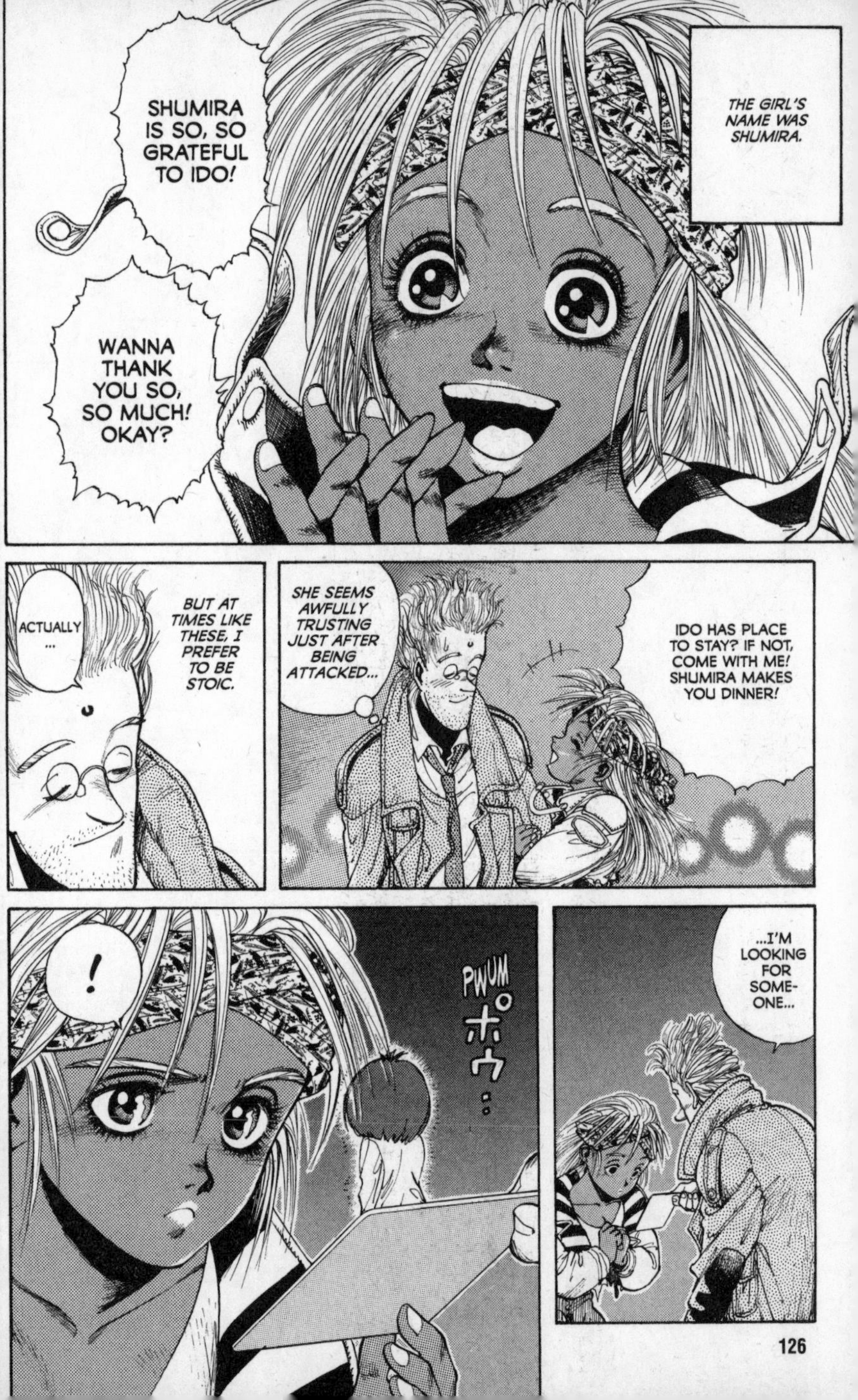
THE GIRL'S NAME WAS SHUMIRA.
SHUMIRA IS SO, SO GRATEFUL TO IDO!
WANNA THANK YOU SO, SO MUCH! OKAY?
IDO HAS PLACE TO STAY? IF NOT, COME WITH ME! SHUMIRA MAKES YOU DINNER!
SHE SEEMS AWFULLY TRUSTING JUST AFTER BEING ATTACKED...
BUT AT TIMES LIKE THESE, I PREFER TO BE STOIC.
ACTUALLY ...
...I'M LOOKING FOR SOME-ONE...
PWUM ポホウ
!

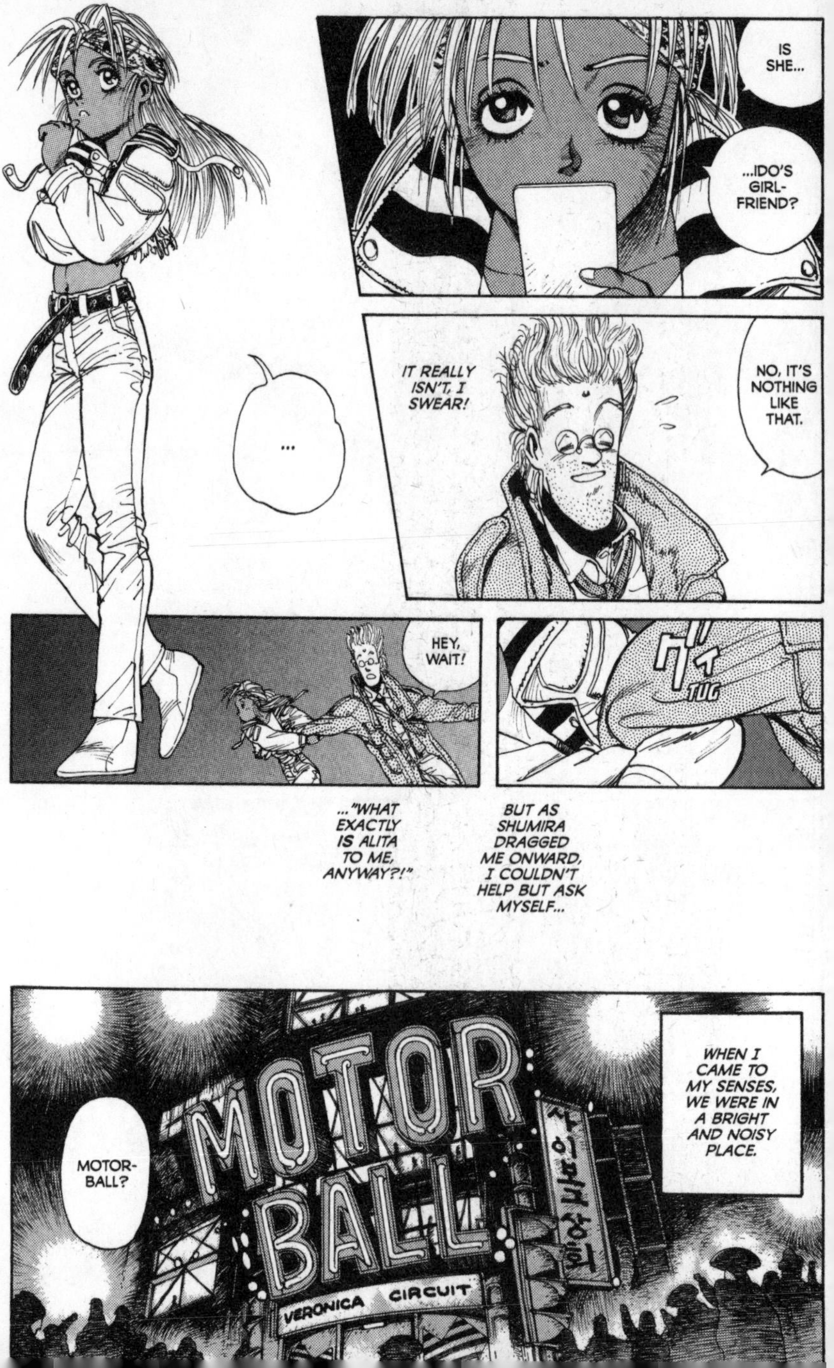
IS SHE...
...IDO'S GIRL-FRIEND?
NO, IT'S NOTHING LIKE THAT.
IT REALLY ISN'T, I SWEAR!
...
TUG
HEY, WAIT!
BUT AS SHUMIRA DRAGGED ME ONWARD, I COULDN'T HELP BUT ASK MYSELF...
..."WHAT EXACTLY IS ALITA TO ME, ANYWAY?!"
WHEN I CAME TO MY SENSES, WE WERE IN A BRIGHT AND NOISY PLACE.
MOTOR BALL
VERONICA CIRCUIT
MOTOR-BALL?

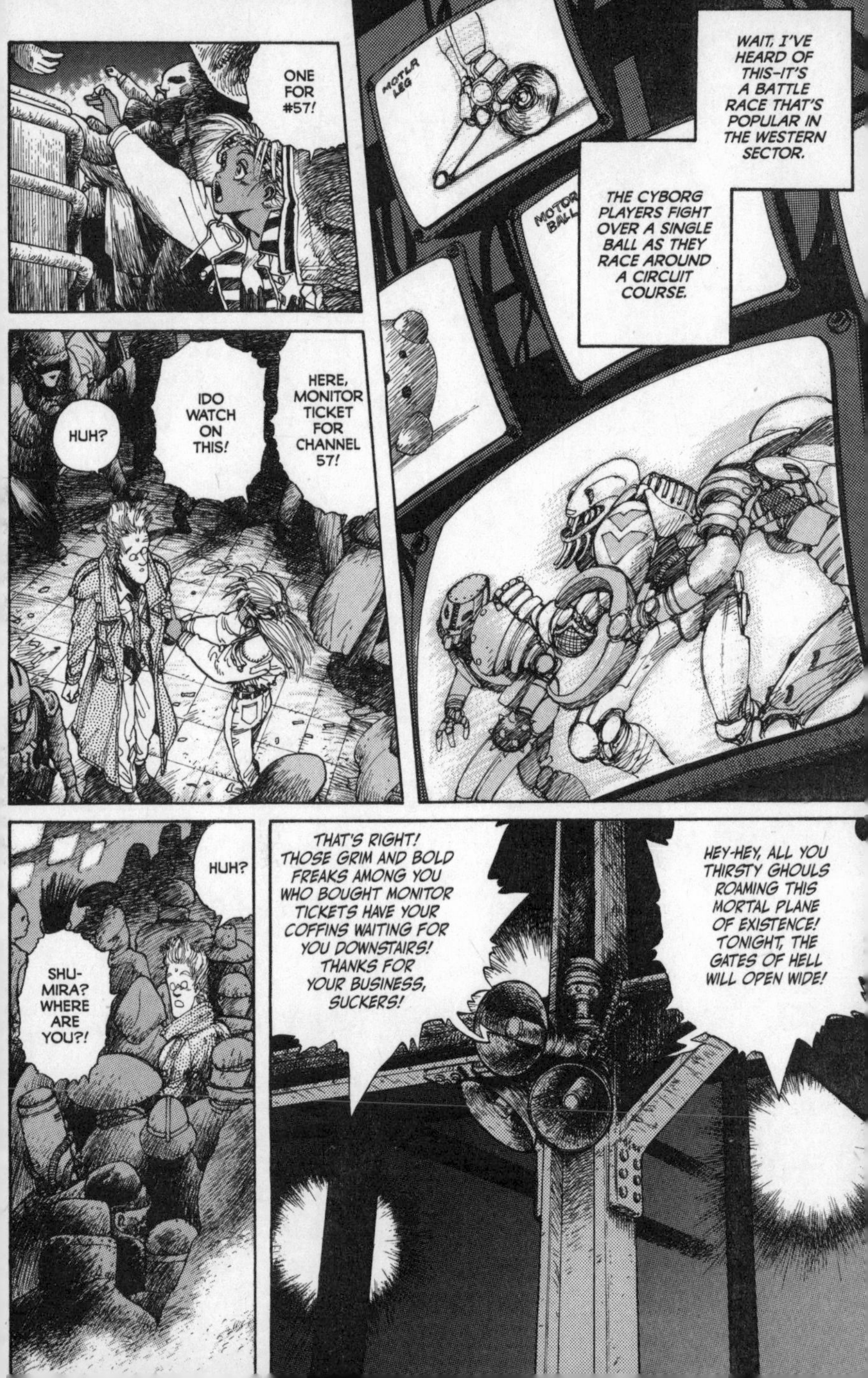
WAIT, I'VE HEARD OF THIS–IT'S A BATTLE RACE THAT'S POPULAR IN THE WESTERN SECTOR.
THE CYBORG PLAYERS FIGHT OVER A SINGLE BALL AS THEY RACE AROUND A CIRCUIT COURSE.
MOTOR BALL
MOTLR LEG
ONE FOR #57!
HERE, MONITOR TICKET FOR CHANNEL 57!
IDO WATCH ON THIS!
HUH?
HEY-HEY, ALL YOU THIRSTY GHOULS ROAMING THIS MORTAL PLANE OF EXISTENCE! TONIGHT, THE GATES OF HELL WILL OPEN WIDE!
THAT'S RIGHT! THOSE GRIM AND BOLD FREAKS AMONG YOU WHO BOUGHT MONITOR TICKETS HAVE YOUR COFFINS WAITING FOR YOU DOWNSTAIRS! THANKS FOR YOUR BUSINESS, SUCKERS!
HUH?
SHU-MIRA? WHERE ARE YOU?!

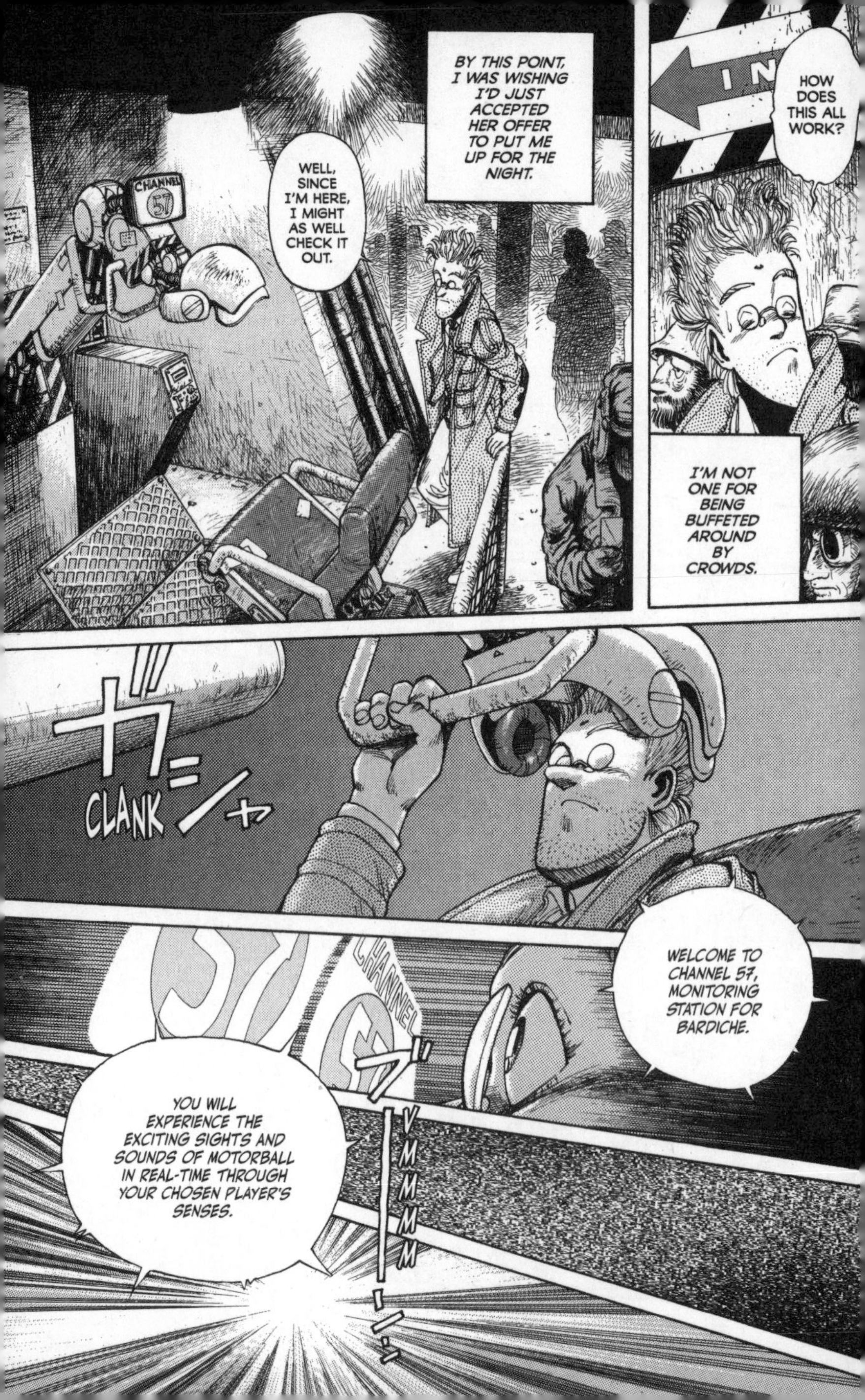
HOW DOES THIS ALL WORK?
I'M NOT ONE FOR BEING BUFFETED AROUND BY CROWDS.
BY THIS POINT, I WAS WISHING I'D JUST ACCEPTED HER OFFER TO PUT ME UP FOR THE NIGHT.
WELL, SINCE I'M HERE, I MIGHT AS WELL CHECK IT OUT.
CHANNEL 57
CLANK
WELCOME TO CHANNEL 57, MONITORING STATION FOR BARDICHE.
CHANNEL 57
YOU WILL EXPERIENCE THE EXCITING SIGHTS AND SOUNDS OF MOTORBALL IN REAL-TIME THROUGH YOUR CHOSEN PLAYER'S SENSES.
VMMMMM

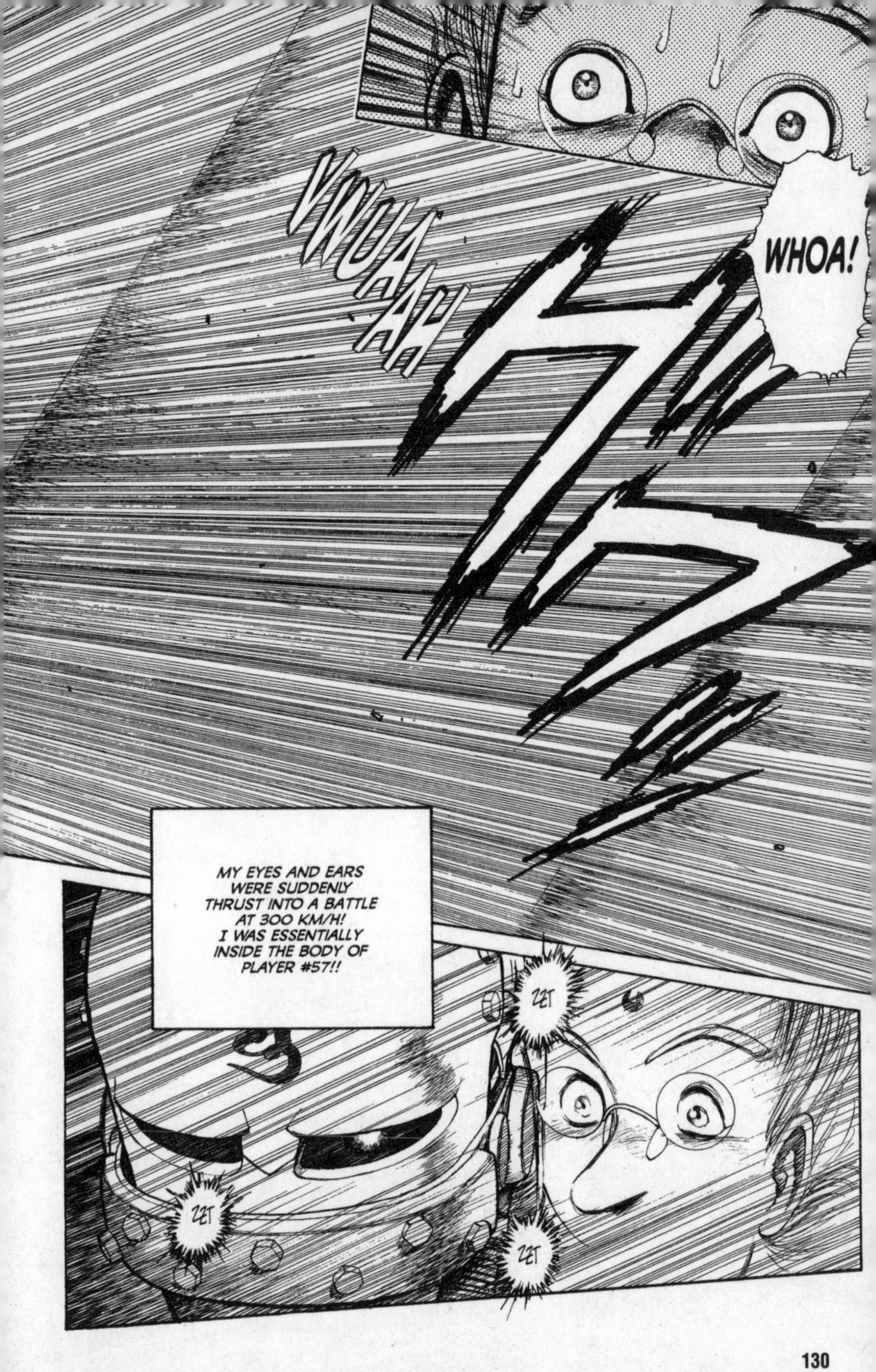
WHOA!
VWUAAH
MY EYES AND EARS WERE SUDDENLY THRUST INTO A BATTLE AT 300 KM/H! I WAS ESSENTIALLY INSIDE THE BODY OF PLAYER #57!!
ZZT
ZZT
ZZT

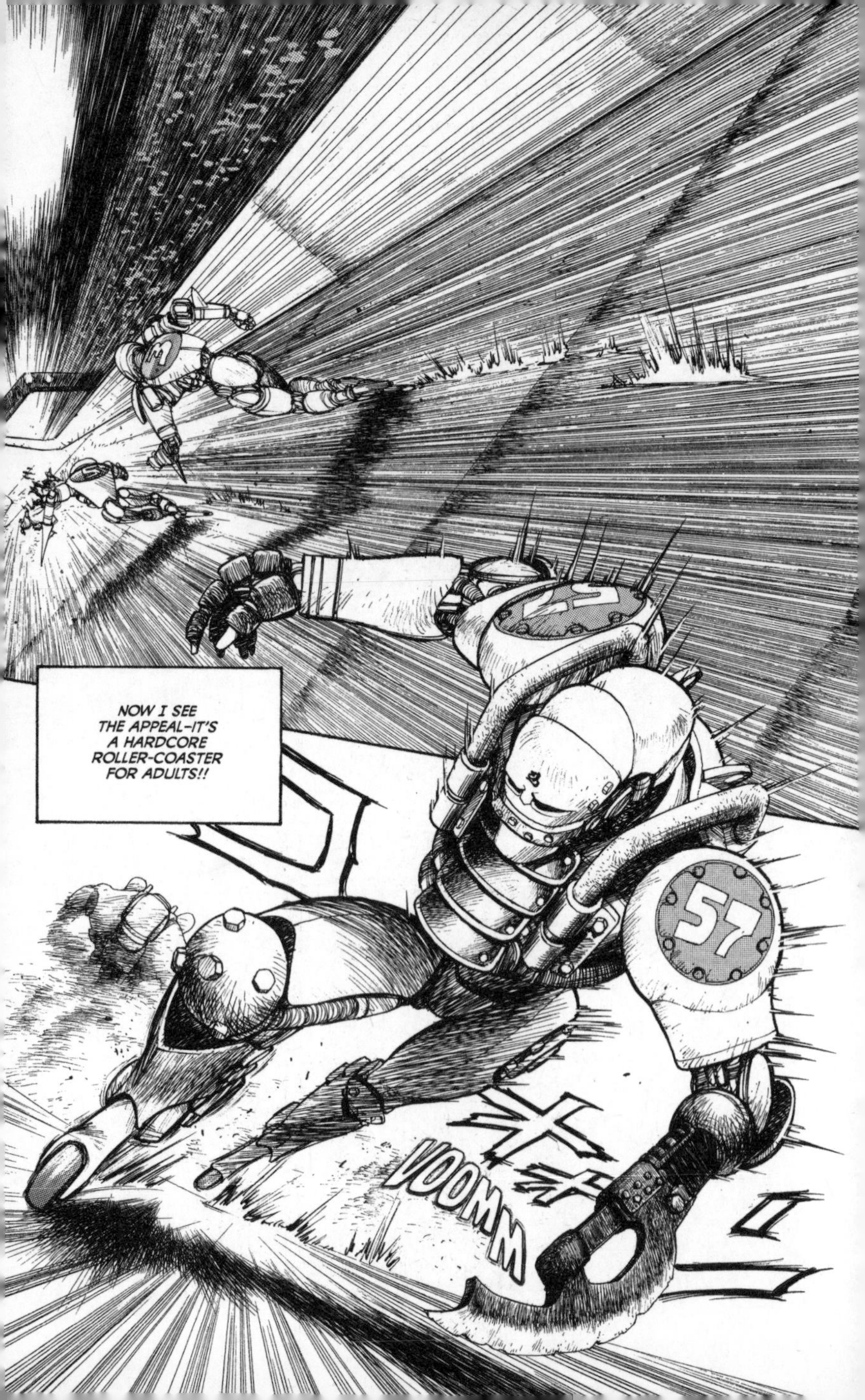
NOW I SEE THE APPEAL–IT'S A HARDCORE ROLLER-COASTER FOR ADULTS!!
VOOMM
57

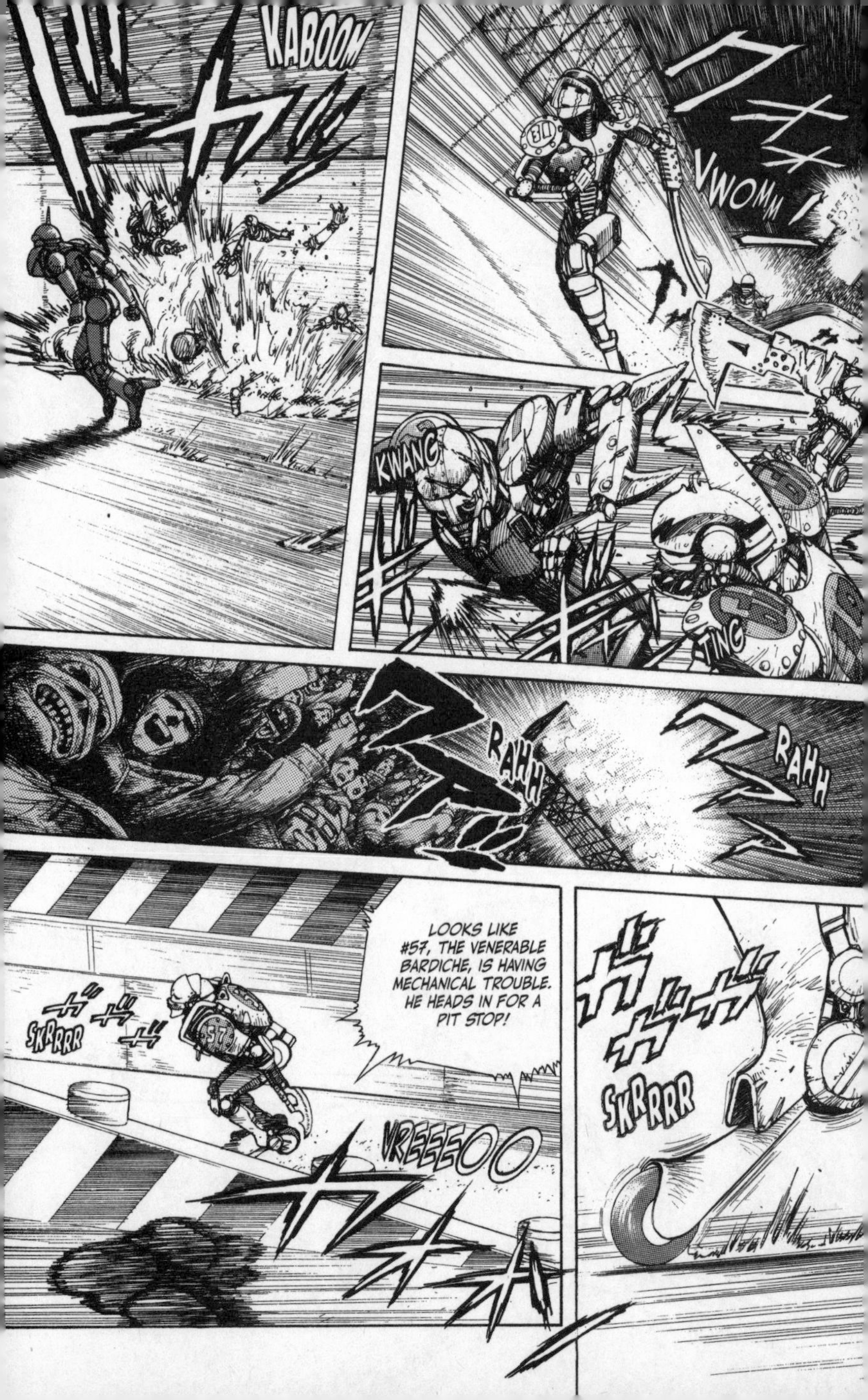
VWOMM
KWANG
TING
KABOOM
RAHH
RAHH
SKRRRR
LOOKS LIKE #57, THE VENERABLE BARDICHE, IS HAVING MECHANICAL TROUBLE. HE HEADS IN FOR A PIT STOP!
VREEEOO
SKRRRR

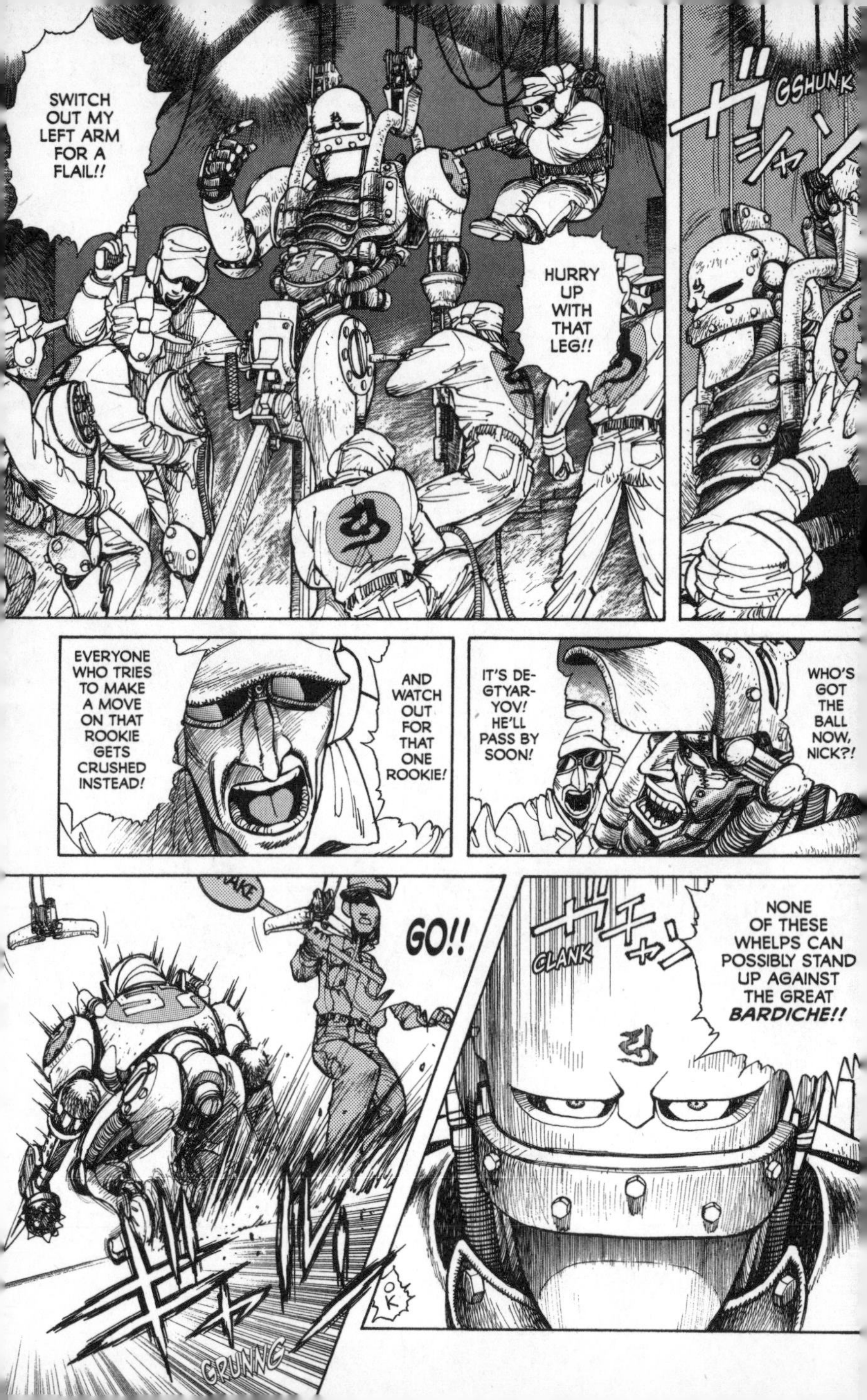
GSHUNK
HURRY UP WITH THAT LEG!!
SWITCH OUT MY LEFT ARM FOR A FLAIL!!
WHO'S GOT THE BALL NOW, NICK?!
IT'S DEGTYARYOV! HE'LL PASS BY SOON!
AND WATCH OUT FOR THAT ONE ROOKIE!
EVERYONE WHO TRIES TO MAKE A MOVE ON THAT ROOKIE GETS CRUSHED INSTEAD!
NONE OF THESE WHELPS CAN POSSIBLY STAND UP AGAINST THE GREAT *BARDICHE!!*
CLANK
GO!!
OK
CRUNNG

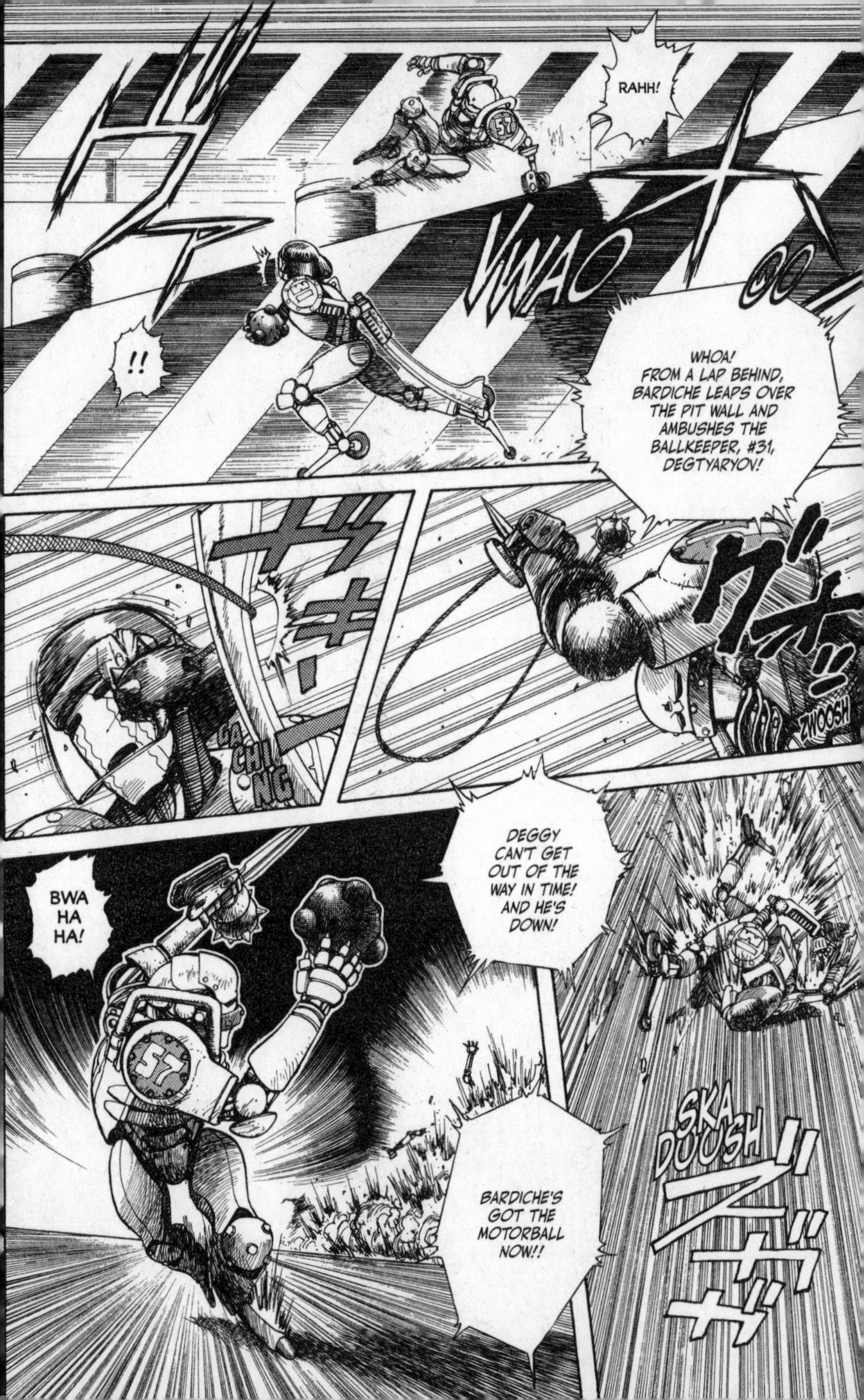
RAHH!
VWAO
WHOA! FROM A LAP BEHIND, BARDICHE LEAPS OVER THE PIT WALL AND AMBUSHES THE BALLKEEPER, #31, DEGTYARYOV!
!!
ZWOOSH
GACHING
DEGGY CAN'T GET OUT OF THE WAY IN TIME! AND HE'S DOWN!
SKADOUSH
BARDICHE'S GOT THE MOTORBALL NOW!!
BWA HA HA!

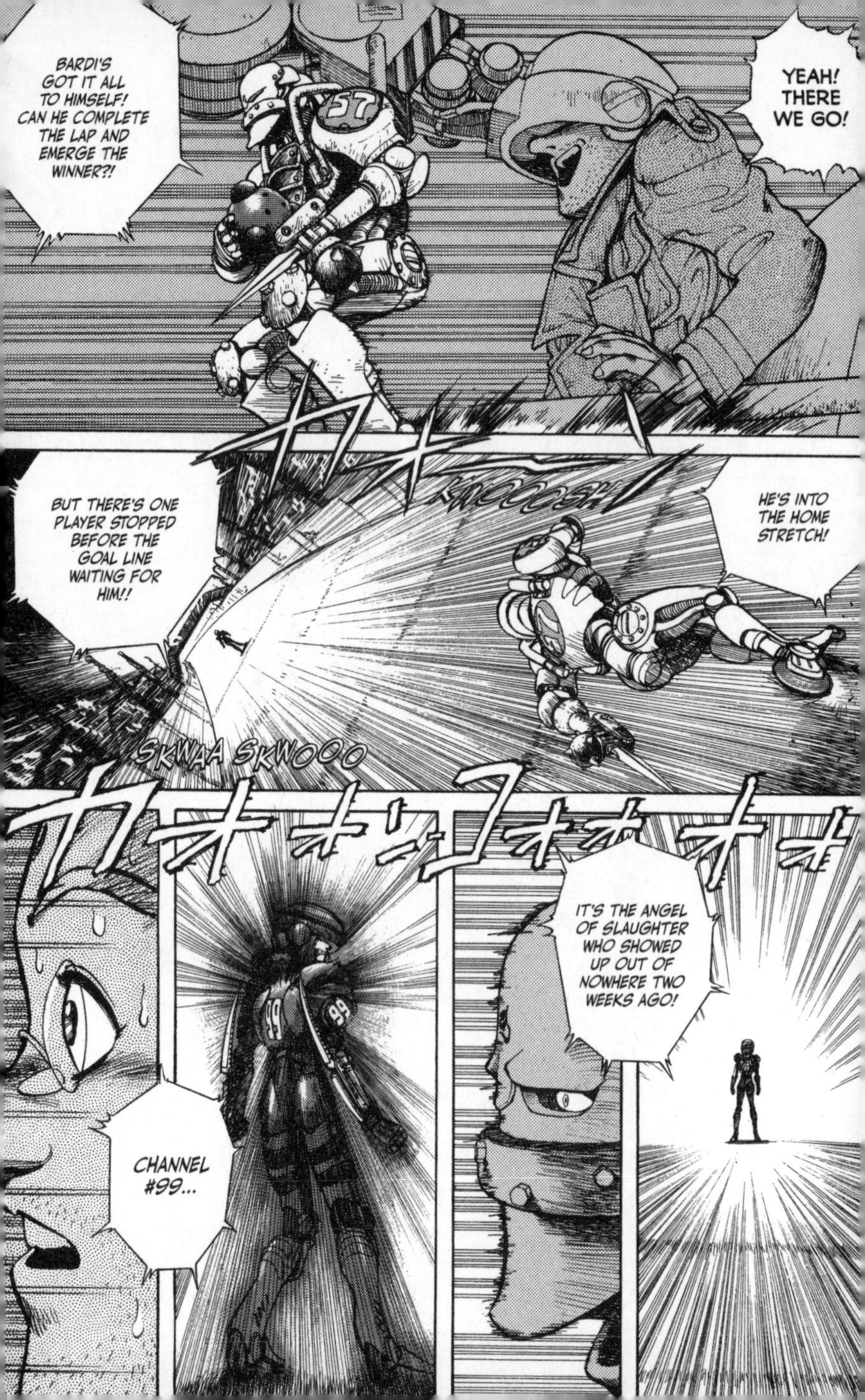
YEAH! THERE WE GO!
BARDI'S GOT IT ALL TO HIMSELF! CAN HE COMPLETE THE LAP AND EMERGE THE WINNER?!
HE'S INTO THE HOME STRETCH!
KWOOOSH!!
BUT THERE'S ONE PLAYER STOPPED BEFORE THE GOAL LINE WAITING FOR HIM!!
SKWAA SKWOOO
IT'S THE ANGEL OF SLAUGHTER WHO SHOWED UP OUT OF NOWHERE TWO WEEKS AGO!
CHANNEL #99...

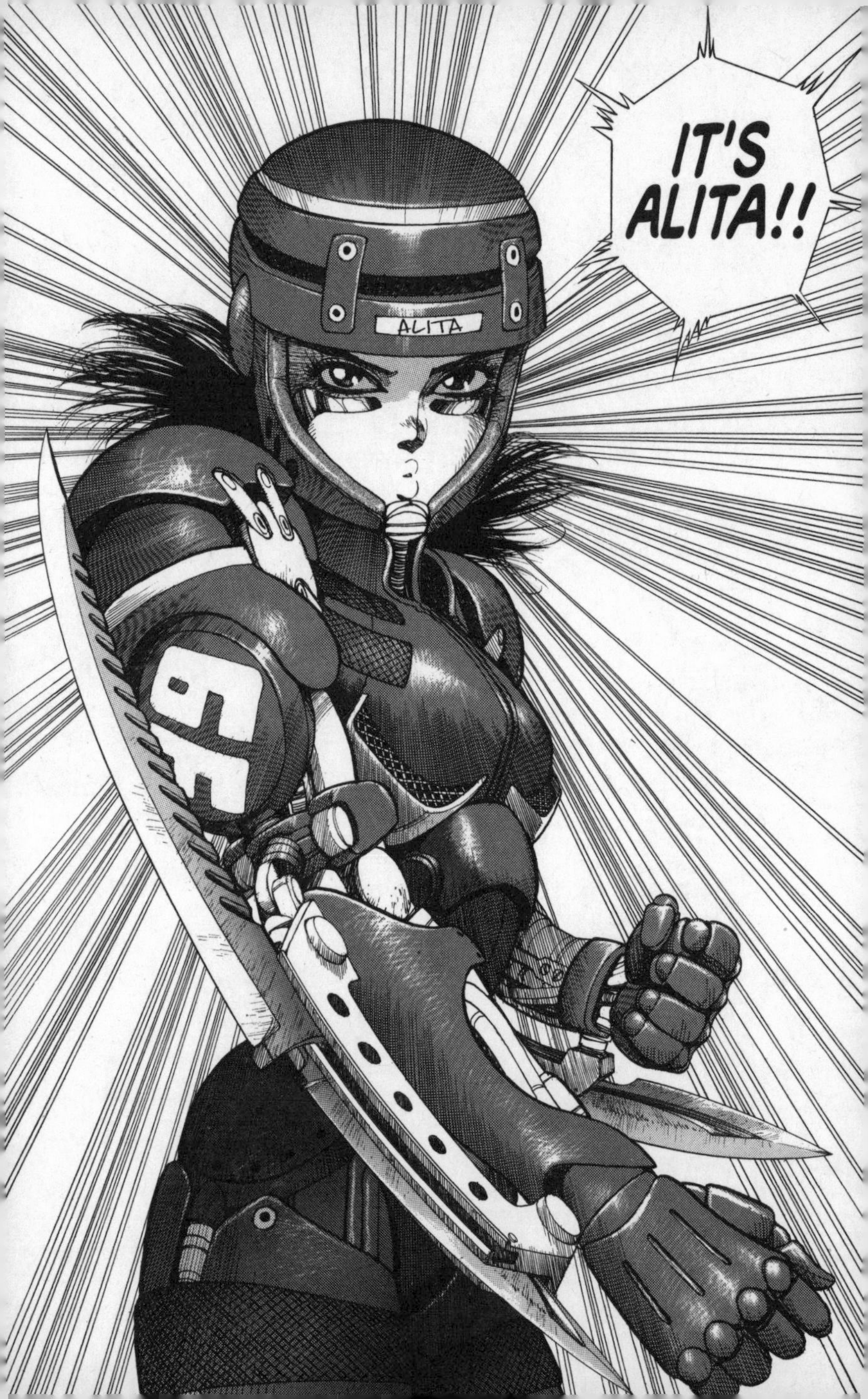
IT'S ALITA!!
ALITA
99

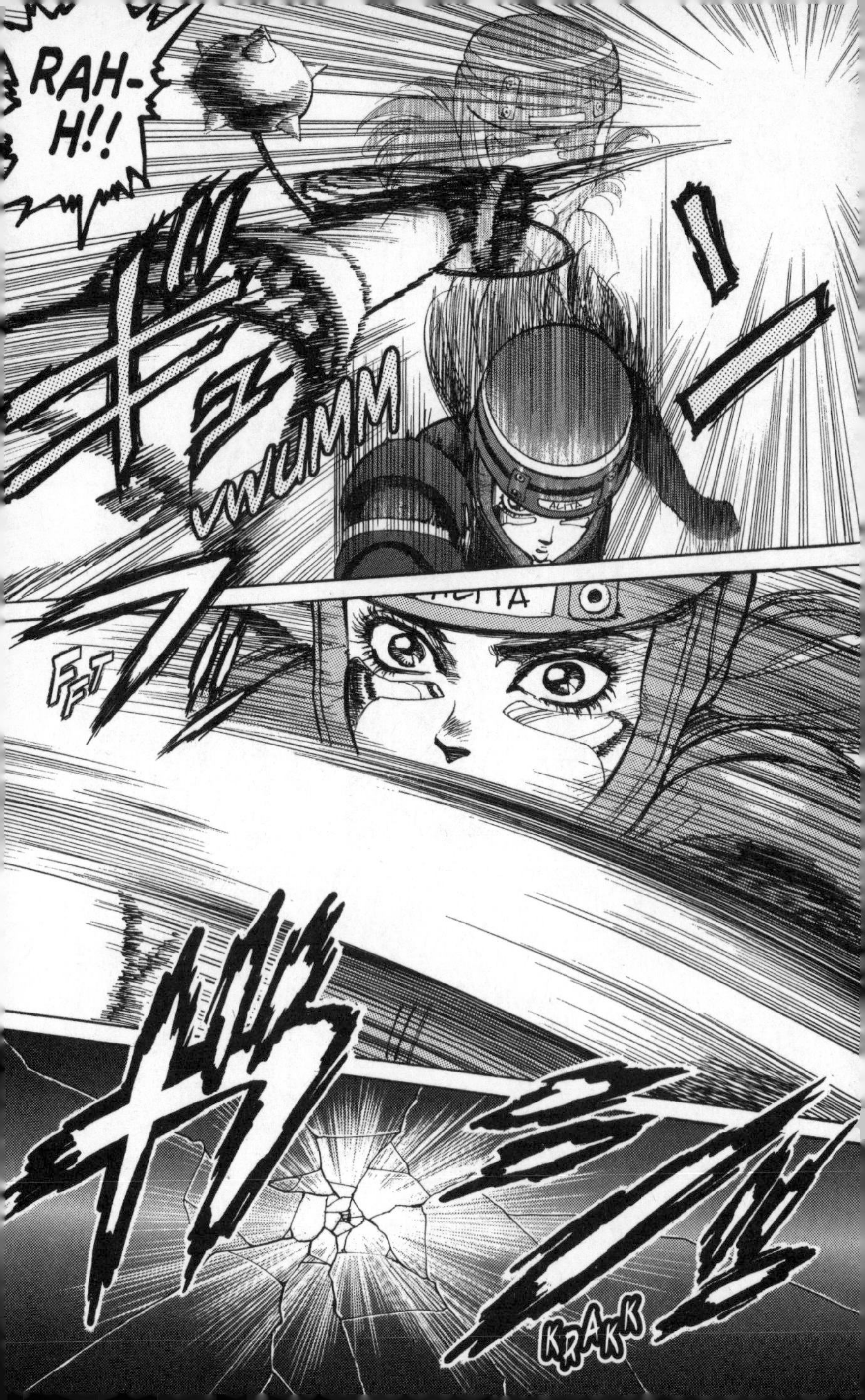
RAH-H!!
VWUMM
FFT
KRAKK

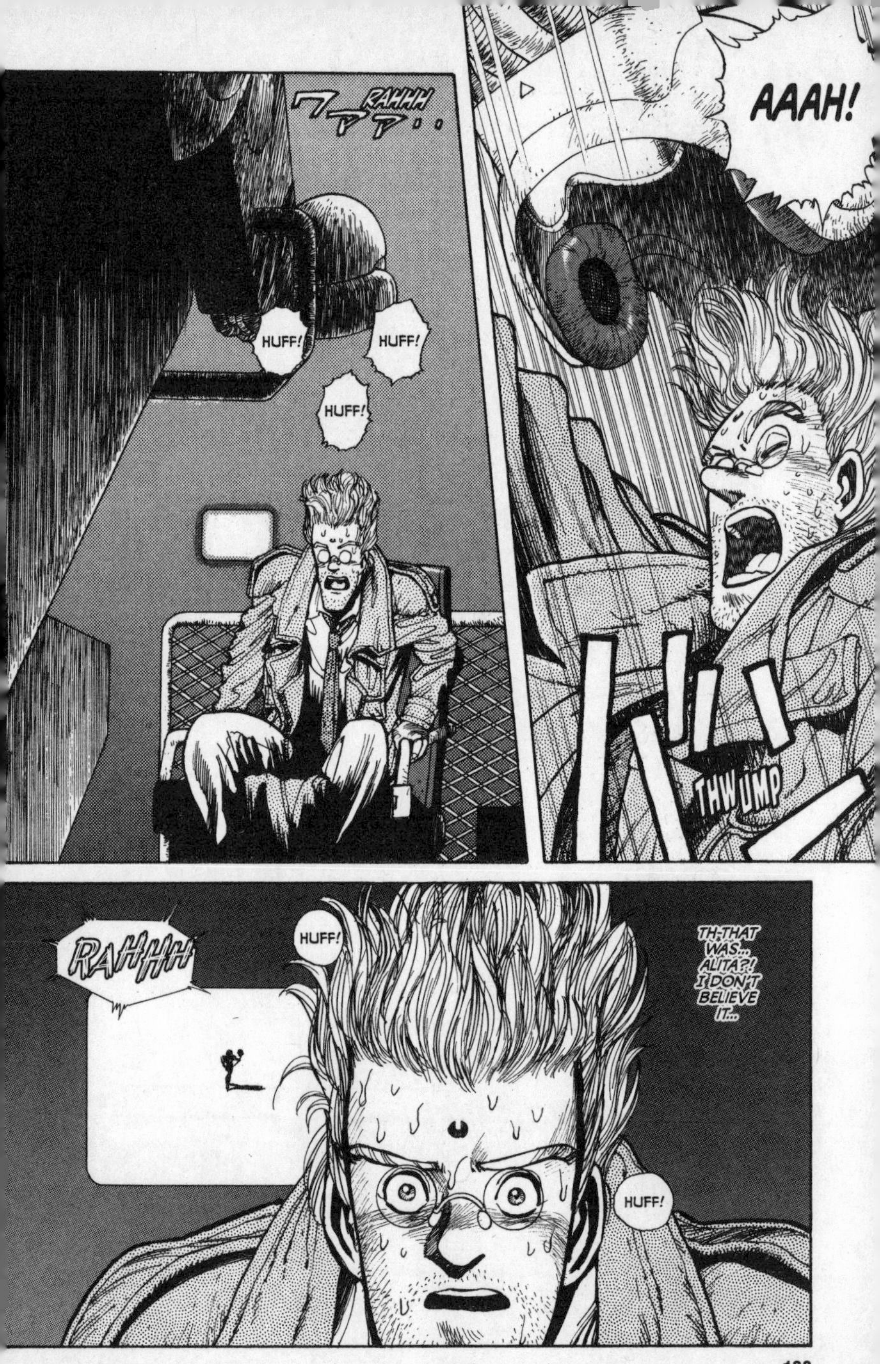
AAAH!
THWUMP
ワァア・・ RAHHH
HUFF!
HUFF!
HUFF!
TH-THAT WAS... ALITA?! I DON'T BELIEVE IT...
HUFF!
RAHHH
HUFF!

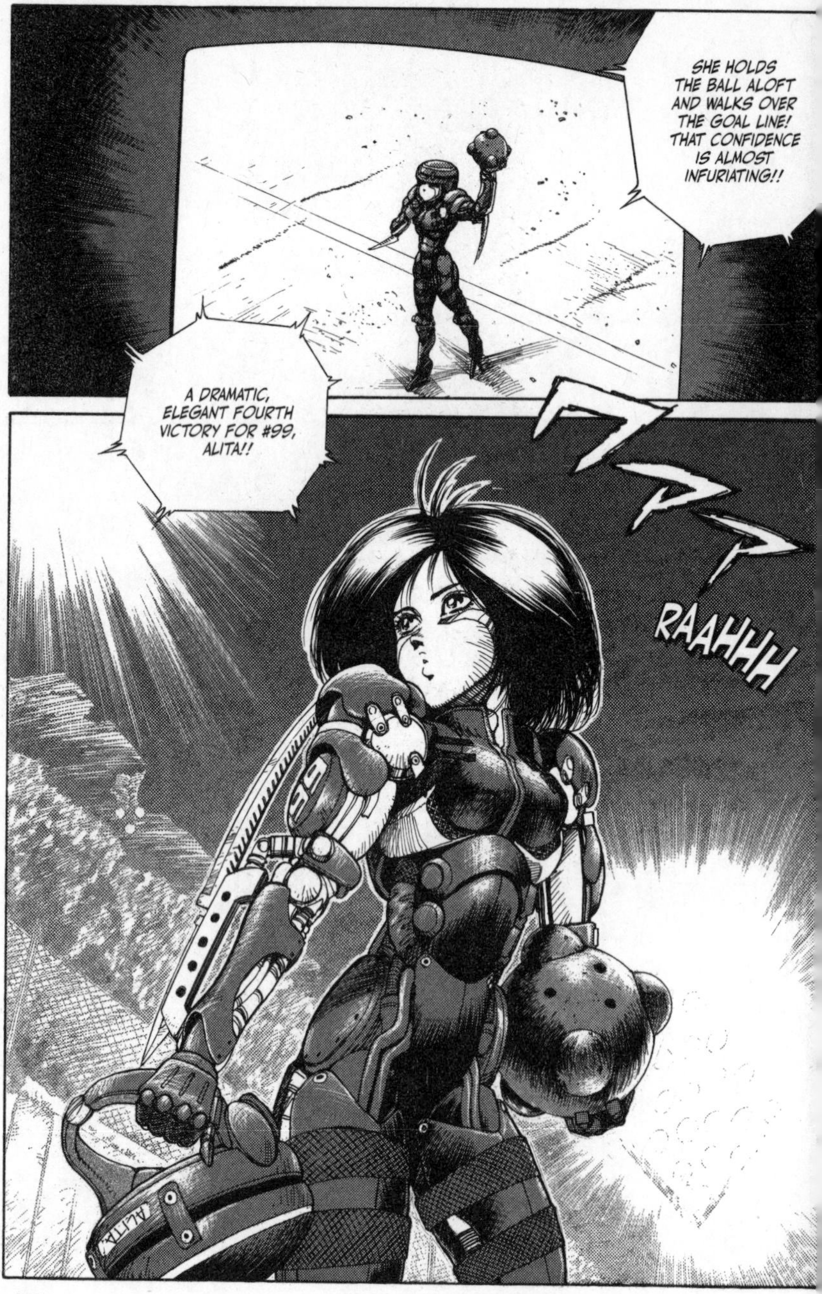
SHE HOLDS THE BALL ALOFT AND WALKS OVER THE GOAL LINE! THAT CONFIDENCE IS ALMOST INFURIATING!!
A DRAMATIC, ELEGANT FOURTH VICTORY FOR #99, ALITA!!
RAAHHH

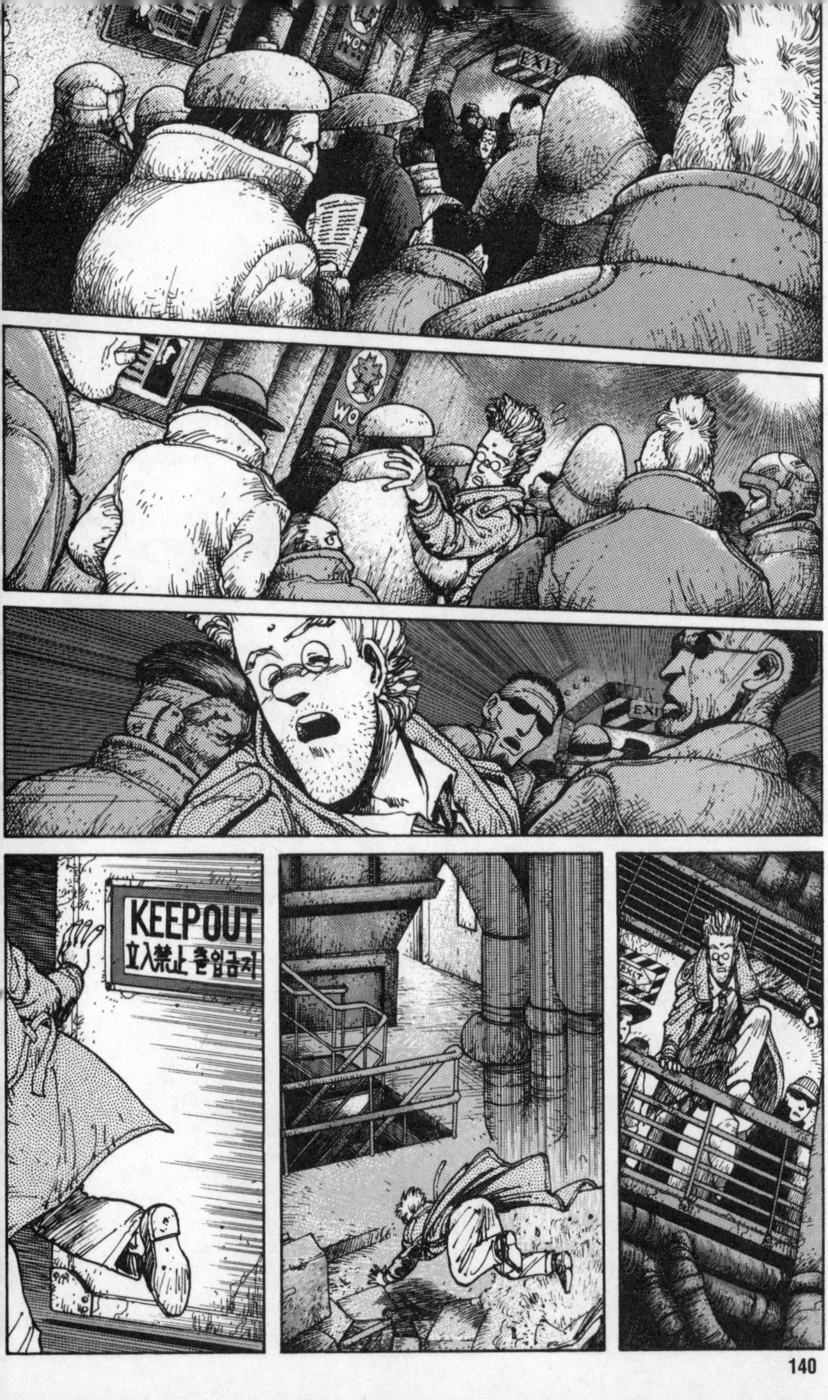
EXIT
WO
WO
EXIT
EXIT
KEEP OUT
立入禁止 출입금지

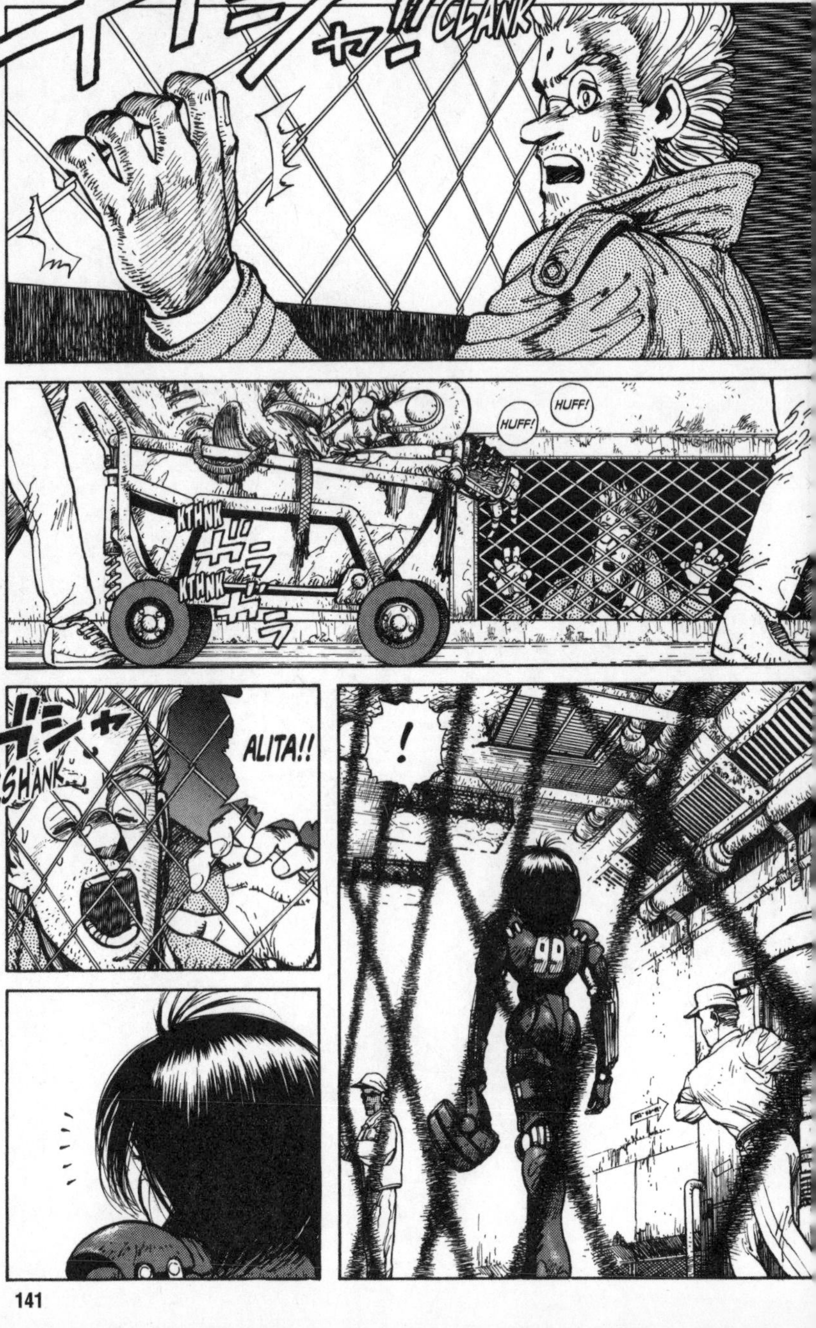
ガシャ!! CLANK
HUFF!
HUFF!
ガラ KTHNK
ガラ KTHNK
!
ガシャ KSHANK
ALITA!!

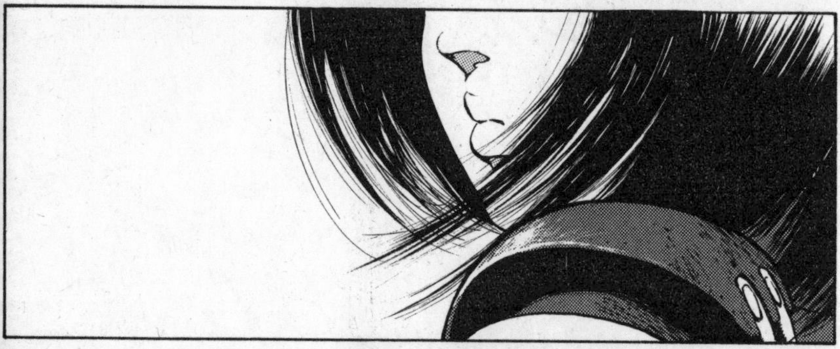
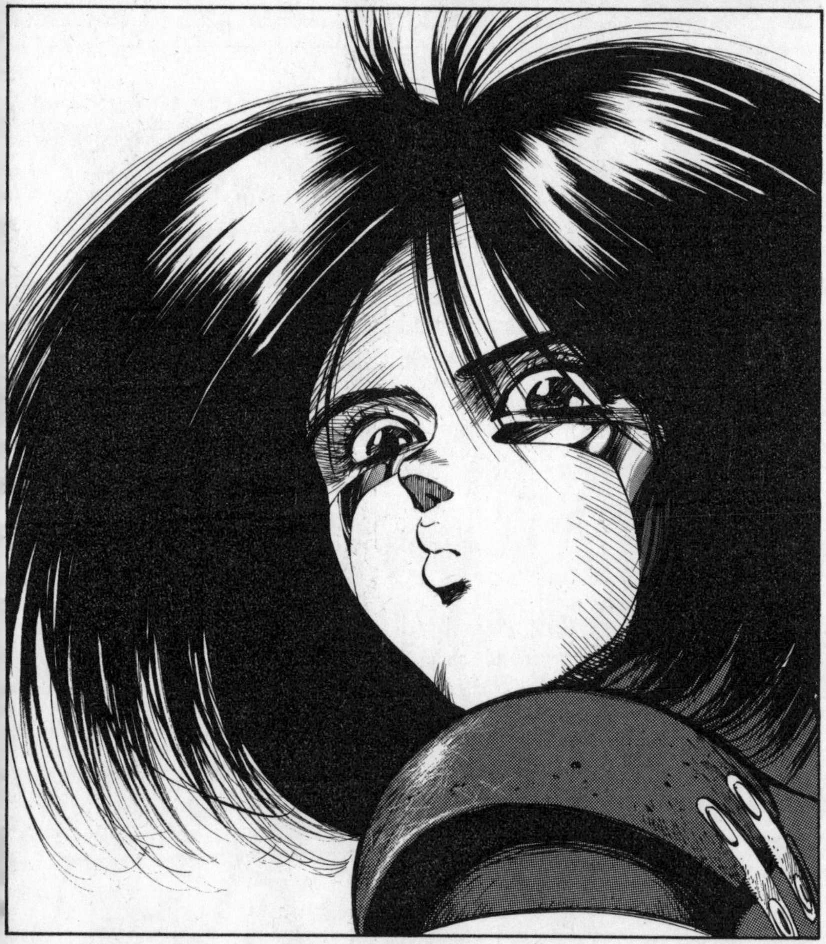

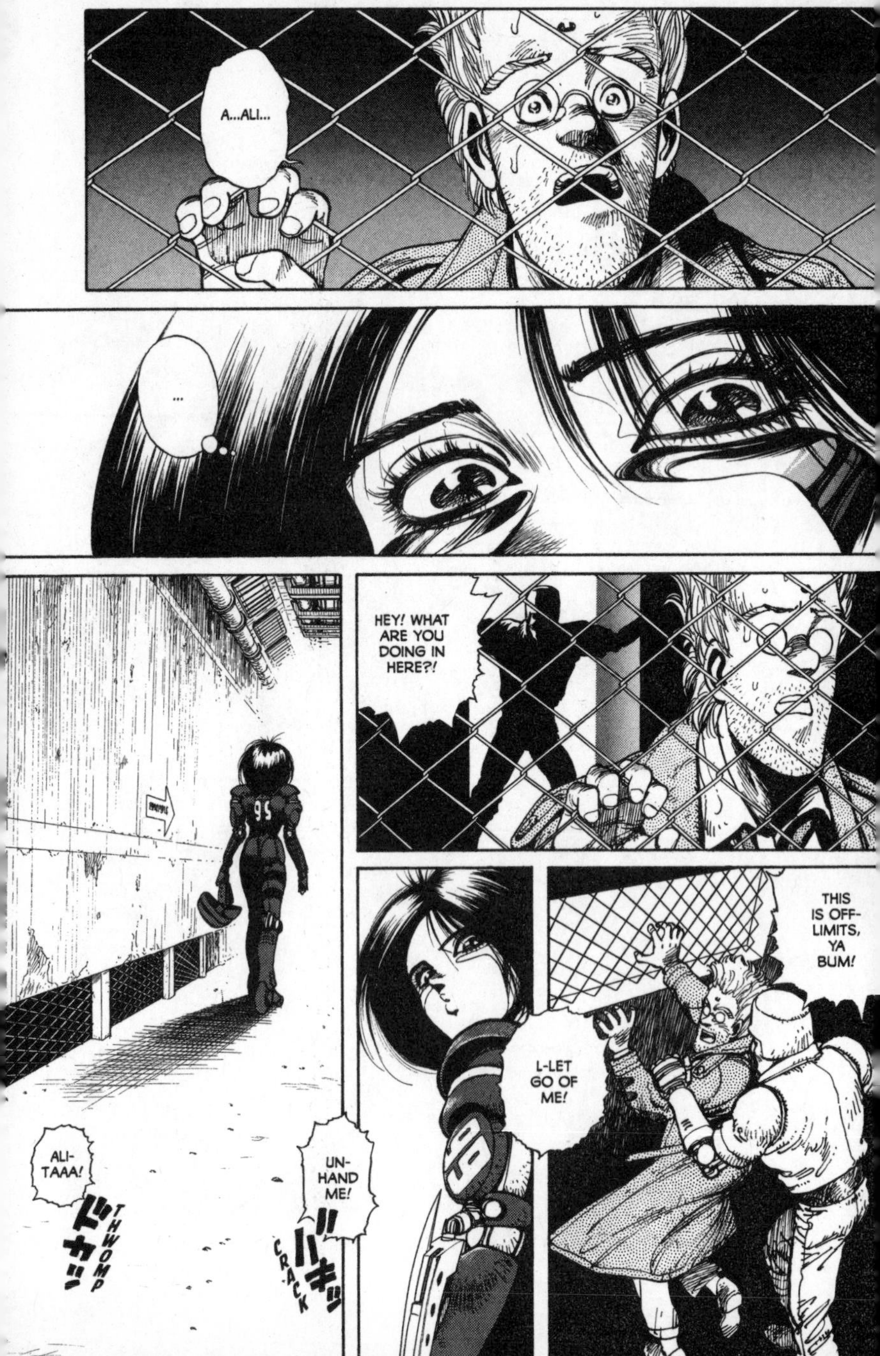
A...ALI...
...
HEY! WHAT ARE YOU DOING IN HERE?!
THIS IS OFF-LIMITS, YA BUM!
L-LET GO OF ME!
UN-HAND ME!
バキッ
CRACK
ALI-TAAA!
ドカッ!!
THWOMP

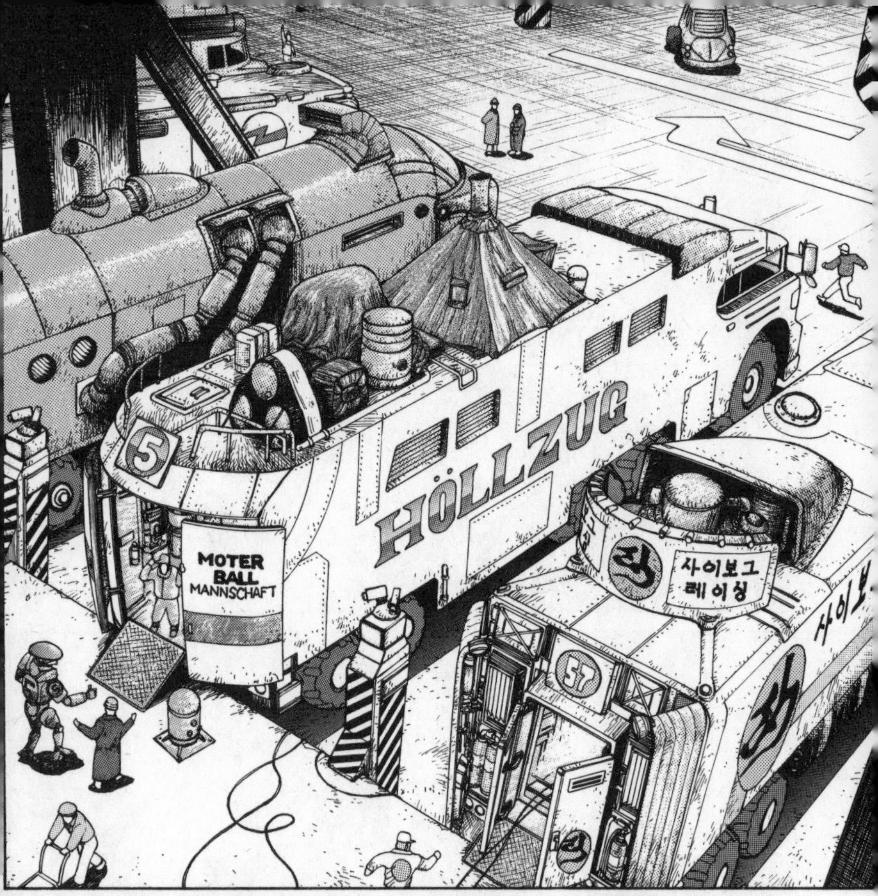
HÖLLZUG
MOTER BALL MANNSCHAFT
5
사이보그 레이싱
57

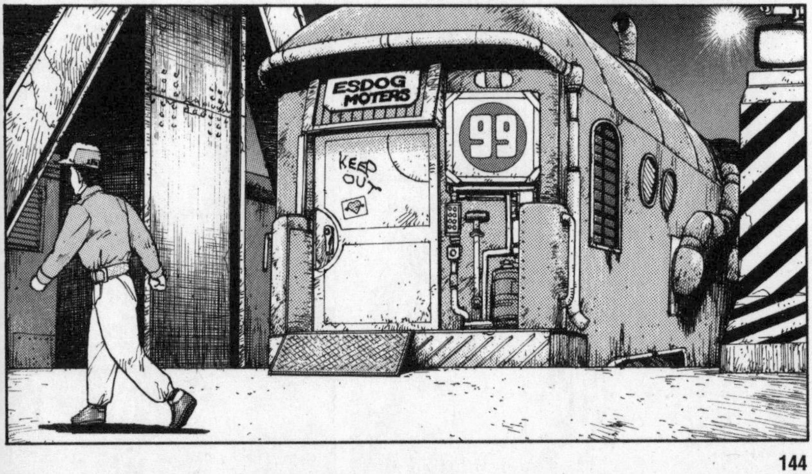
ESDOG MOTERS
99
KEEP OUT

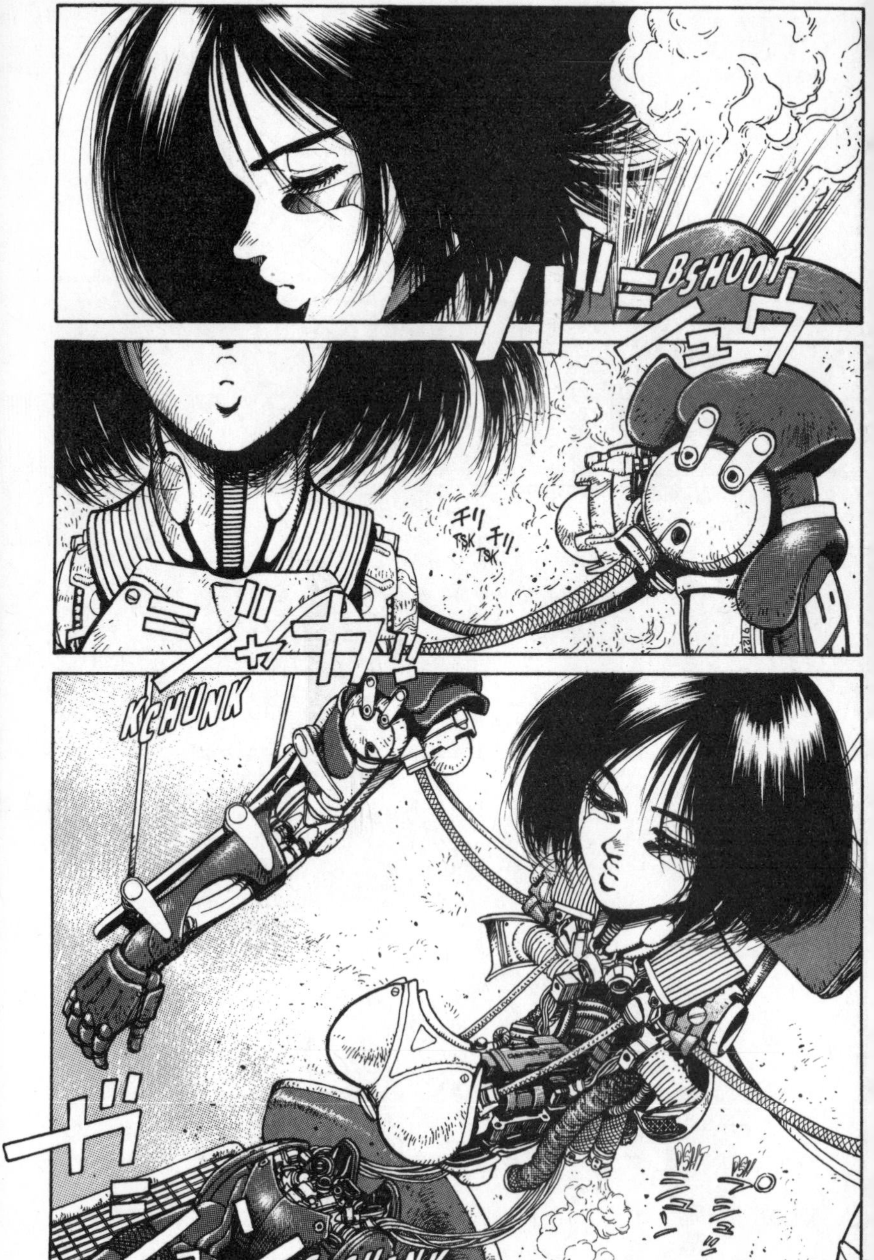
バシュウ
BSHOOT
チリ チリ
TSK TSK
ジャカッ
KCHUNK
ガシュー
GASHANK
プシュー
PSHT
プシュ
PSH

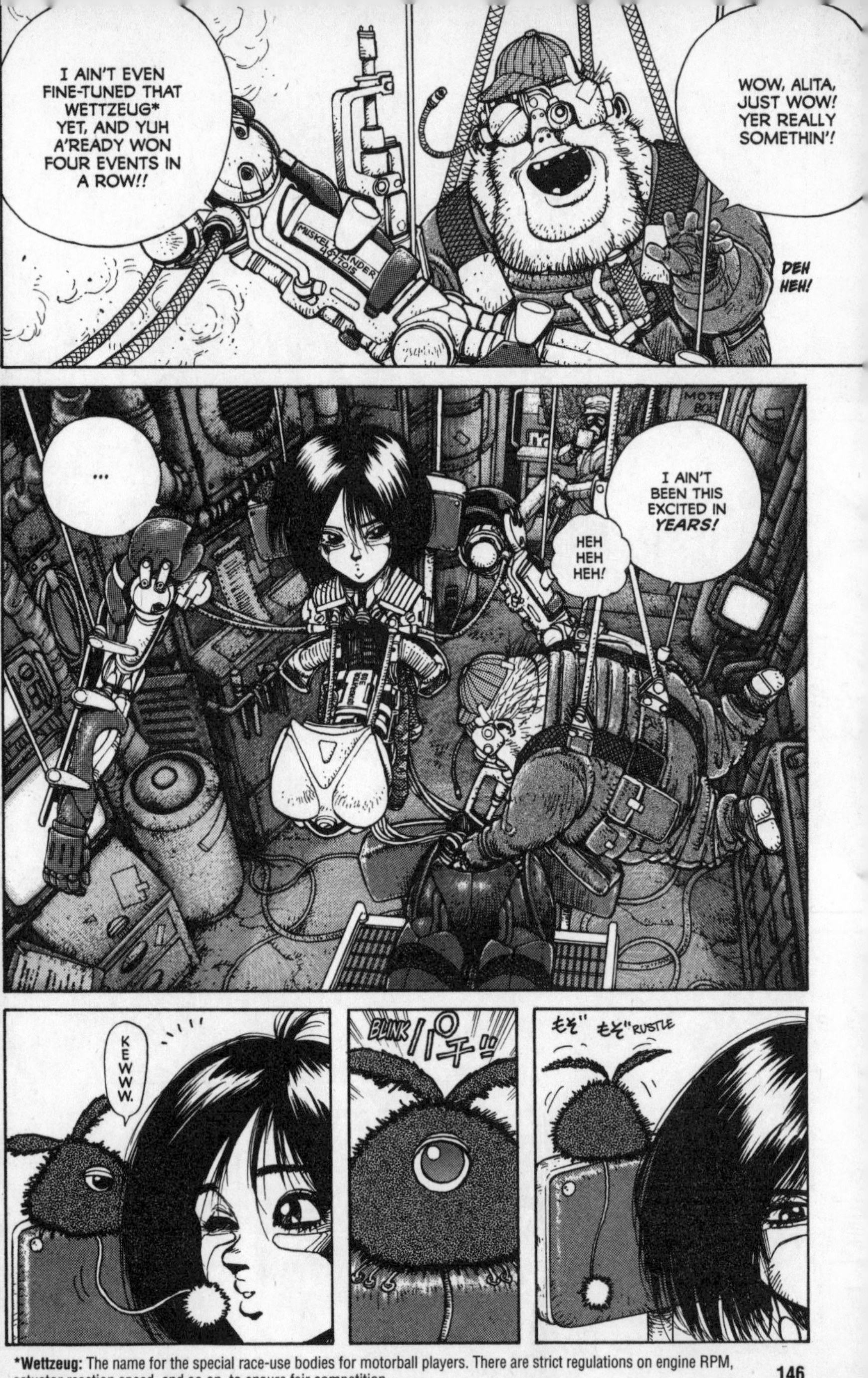
WOW, ALITA, JUST WOW! YER REALLY SOMETHIN'!
DEH HEH!
I AIN'T EVEN FINE-TUNED THAT WETTZEUG* YET, AND YUH A'READY WON FOUR EVENTS IN A ROW!!
MUSKEL ZYLINDER
I AIN'T BEEN THIS EXCITED IN YEARS!
HEH HEH HEH!
...
もぞ もぞ RUSTLE
BLINK パチ
KEWWW.

*Wettzeug: The name for the special race-use bodies for motorball players. There are strict regulations on engine RPM, actuator reaction speed, and so on, to ensure fair competition.

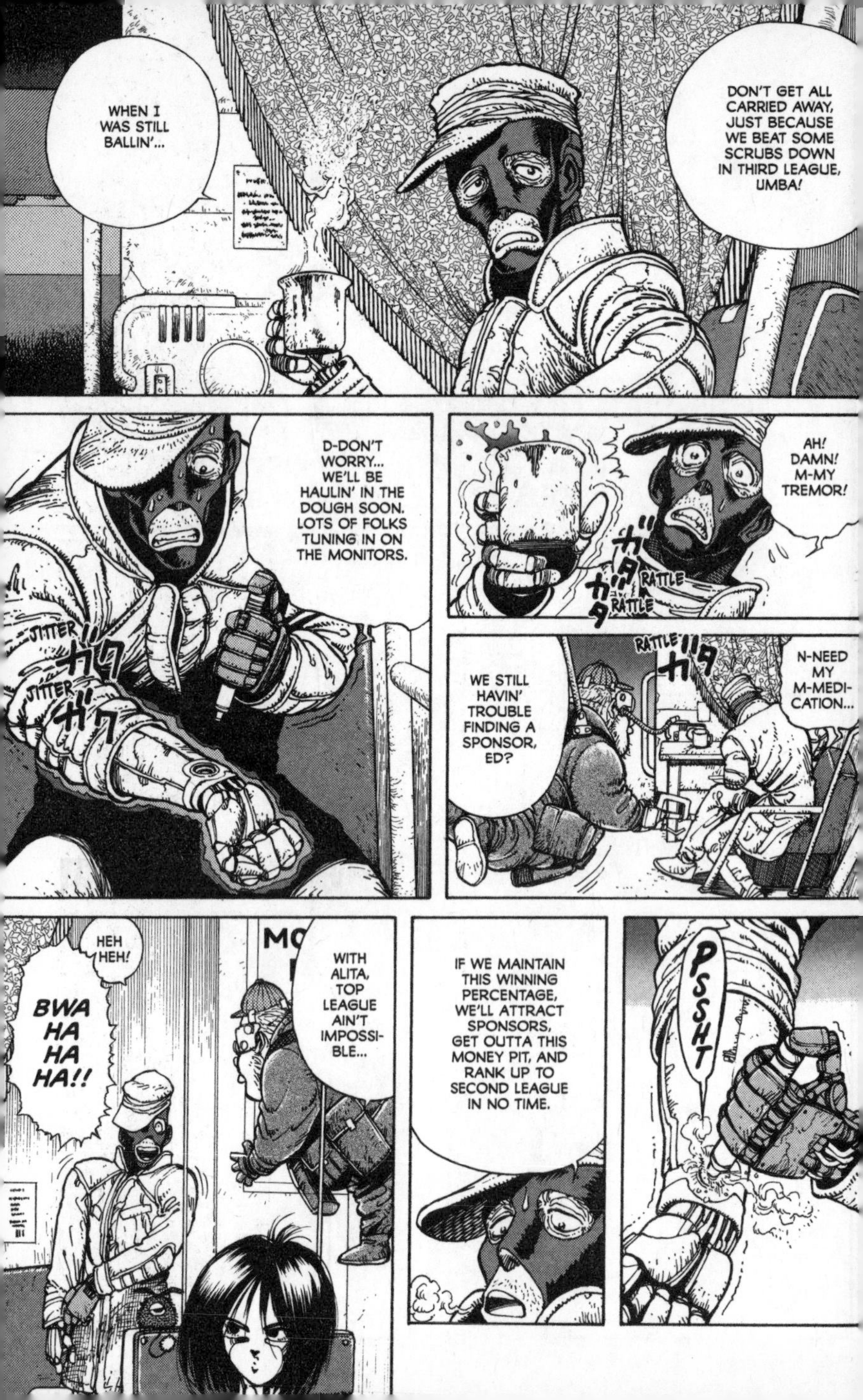
DON'T GET ALL CARRIED AWAY, JUST BECAUSE WE BEAT SOME SCRUBS DOWN IN THIRD LEAGUE, UMBA!
WHEN I WAS STILL BALLIN'...
AH! DAMN! M-MY TREMOR!
RATTLE
RATTLE
D-DON'T WORRY... WE'LL BE HAULIN' IN THE DOUGH SOON. LOTS OF FOLKS TUNING IN ON THE MONITORS.
JITTER
JITTER
N-NEED MY M-MEDICATION...
RATTLE
WE STILL HAVIN' TROUBLE FINDING A SPONSOR, ED?
PSSHT
IF WE MAINTAIN THIS WINNING PERCENTAGE, WE'LL ATTRACT SPONSORS, GET OUTTA THIS MONEY PIT, AND RANK UP TO SECOND LEAGUE IN NO TIME.
WITH ALITA, TOP LEAGUE AIN'T IMPOSSIBLE...
HEH HEH!
BWA HA HA HA!!

YOU NEVER KNOW WHAT'LL HAPPEN IN LIFE, EH?
TO THINK THIS GIRL WAS BAWLIN' HER EYES OUT AT JOE'S PUB JUST A MONTH AGO...
!
ED!
WHOOPS... FORGOT, I PROMISED NOT TO BRING THAT UP.
UMBA.
WHUT ?
WHY DID YOU CREATE THIS PLAYER BODY TO HAVE FEMALE PROPOR-TIONS?
W-WELL, BECUZ YUH A WIMMIN, O' COURSE.
IT MAKES SENSE FOR THE HIGH-SPEED, LIGHTWEIGHT HUMANOID ARCHITEC-TURE.
AN' THE CROWDS LOVE IT!

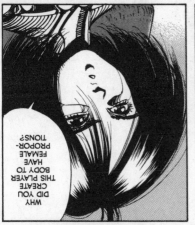

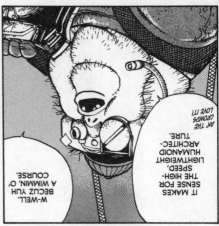

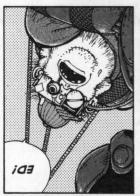

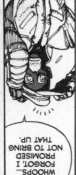

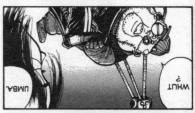

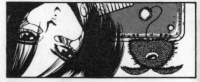

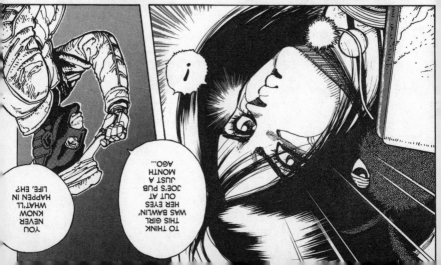

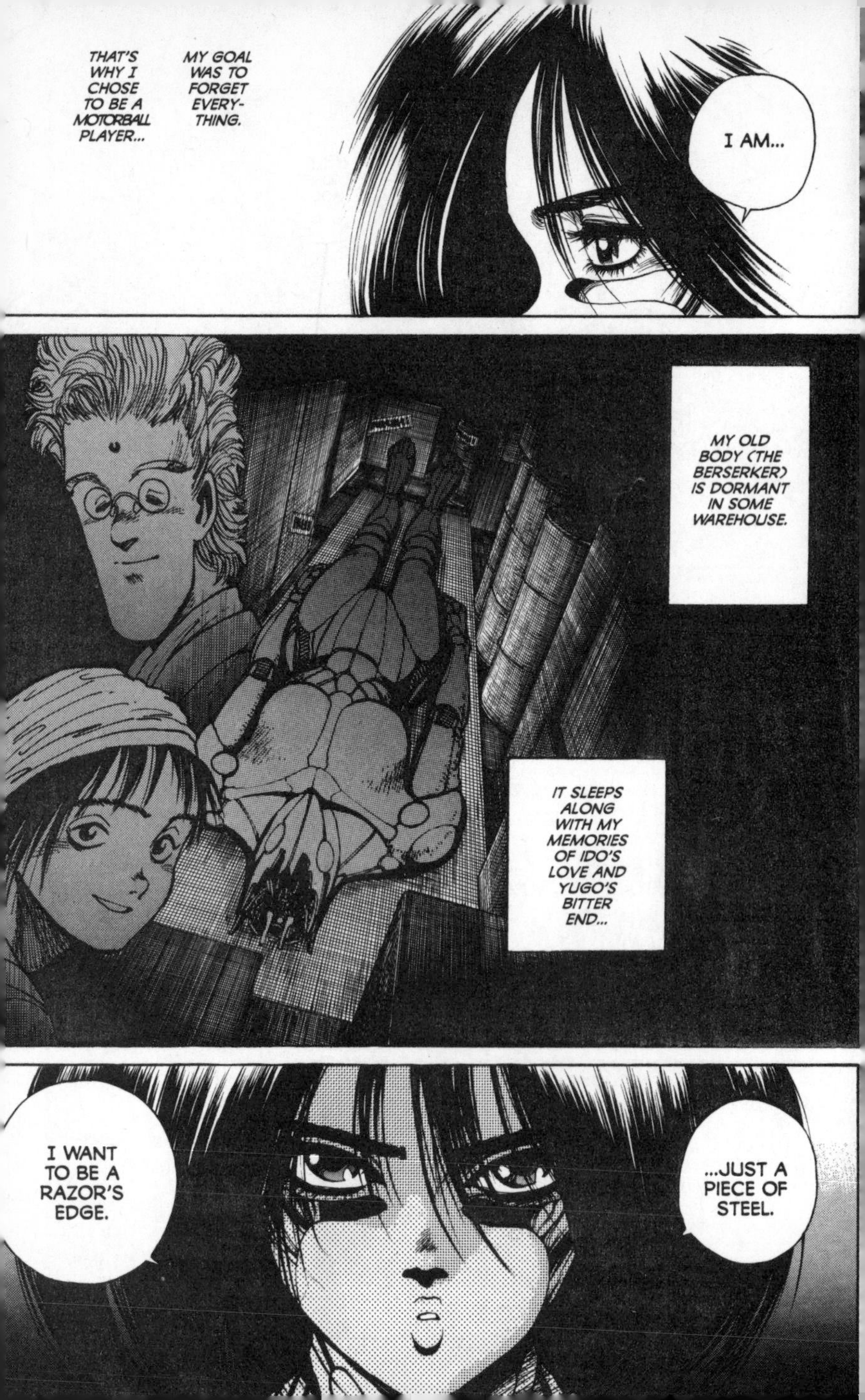
I AM...
MY GOAL WAS TO FORGET EVERY-THING.
THAT'S WHY I CHOSE TO BE A MOTORBALL PLAYER...
MY OLD BODY (THE BERSERKER) IS DORMANT IN SOME WAREHOUSE.
IT SLEEPS ALONG WITH MY MEMORIES OF IDO'S LOVE AND YUGO'S BITTER END...
...JUST A PIECE OF STEEL.
I WANT TO BE A RAZOR'S EDGE.

I'VE HAD ENOUGH OF YOU!
GET LOST, BUM!
THWOMP
SLAM
UGH...
!
PWUN
...
FWIP
ARGH!

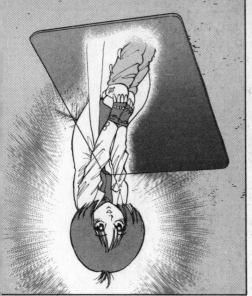

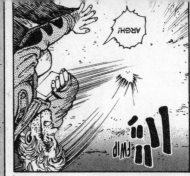

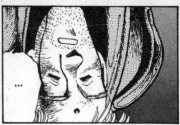

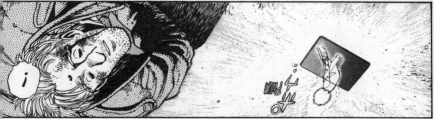

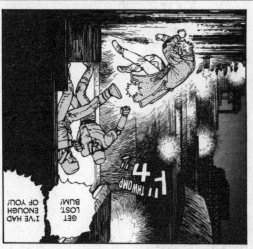

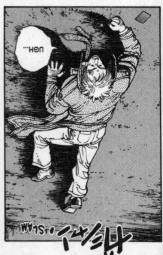

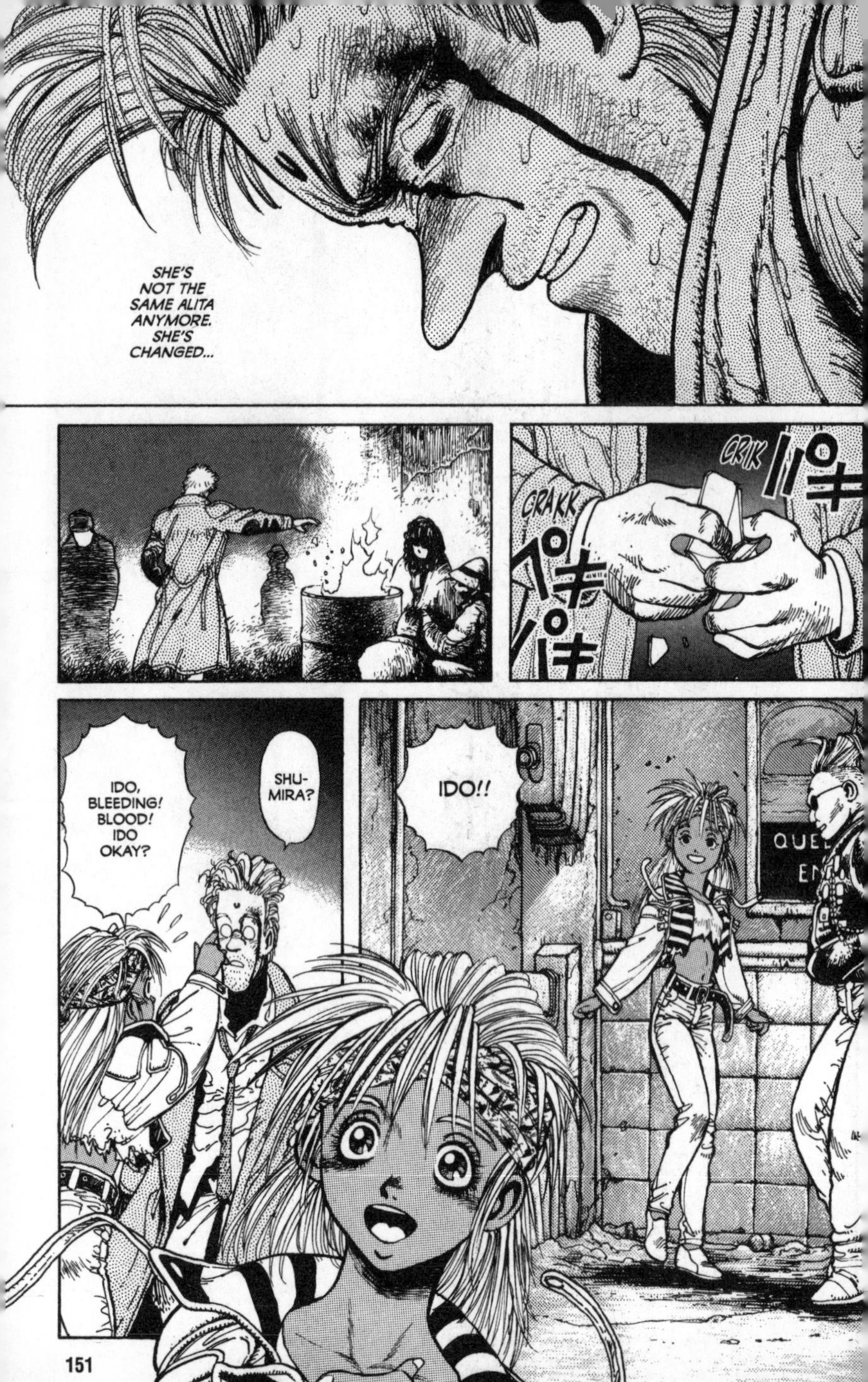
SHE'S NOT THE SAME ALITA ANYMORE. SHE'S CHANGED...
パキ
CRIK
ペキ パキ
CRAKK
IDO!!
SHU-MIRA?
IDO, BLEEDING! BLOOD! IDO OKAY?

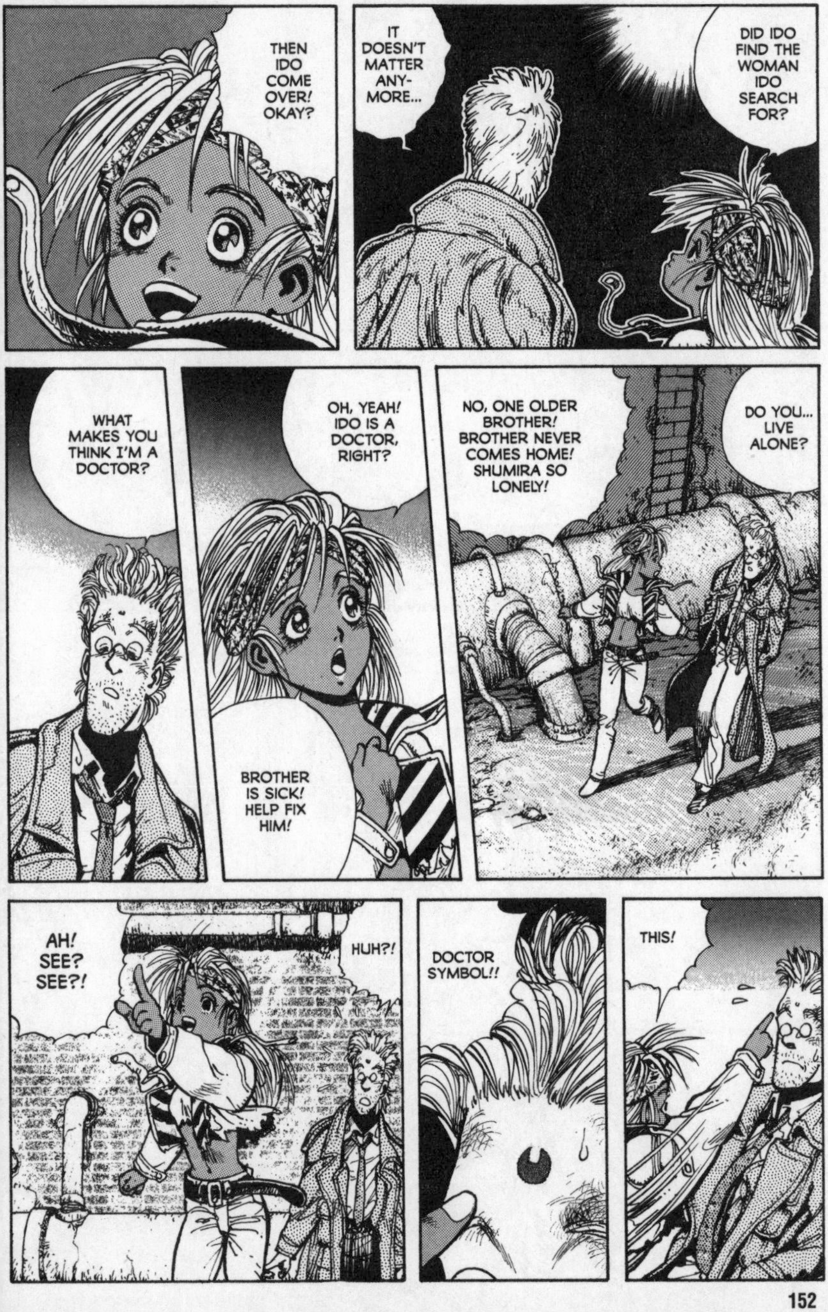
DID IDO FIND THE WOMAN IDO SEARCH FOR?
IT DOESN'T MATTER ANY-MORE...
THEN IDO COME OVER! OKAY?
DO YOU... LIVE ALONE?
NO, ONE OLDER BROTHER! BROTHER NEVER COMES HOME! SHUMIRA SO LONELY!
OH, YEAH! IDO IS A DOCTOR, RIGHT?
BROTHER IS SICK! HELP FIX HIM!
WHAT MAKES YOU THINK I'M A DOCTOR?
THIS!
DOCTOR SYMBOL!!
AH! SEE? SEE?!
HUH?!

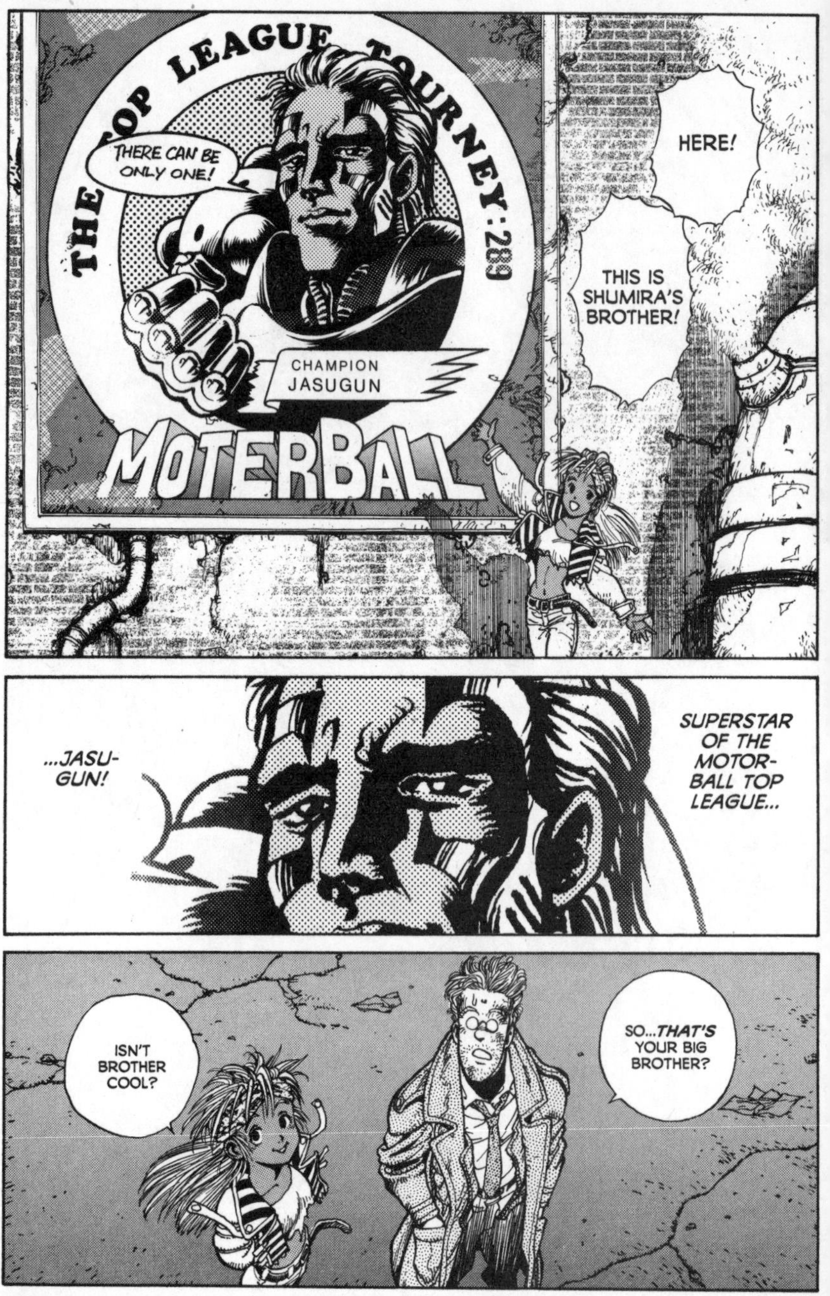
HERE!
THIS IS SHUMIRA'S BROTHER!
THE
OP LEAGUE
OURNEY:289
THERE CAN BE ONLY ONE!
CHAMPION JASUGUN
MOTERBALL
SUPERSTAR OF THE MOTOR-BALL TOP LEAGUE...
...JASU-GUN!
SO...*THAT'S* YOUR BIG BROTHER?
ISN'T BROTHER COOL?

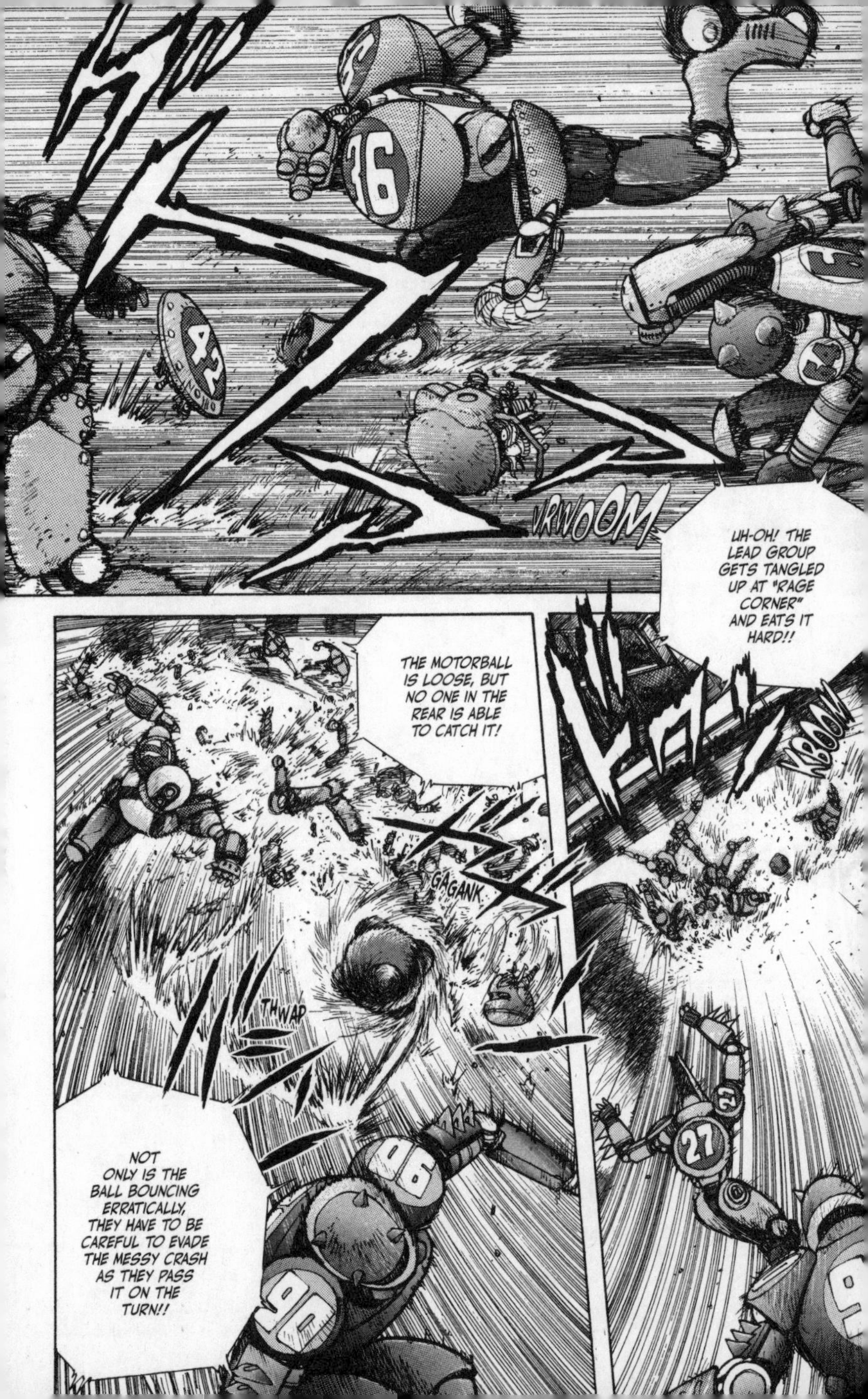
VRWOOM
UH-OH! THE LEAD GROUP GETS TANGLED UP AT "RAGE CORNER" AND EATS IT HARD!!
KBOOM
THE MOTORBALL IS LOOSE, BUT NO ONE IN THE REAR IS ABLE TO CATCH IT!
GAGANK
THWAP
NOT ONLY IS THE BALL BOUNCING ERRATICALLY, THEY HAVE TO BE CAREFUL TO EVADE THE MESSY CRASH AS THEY PASS IT ON THE TURN!!

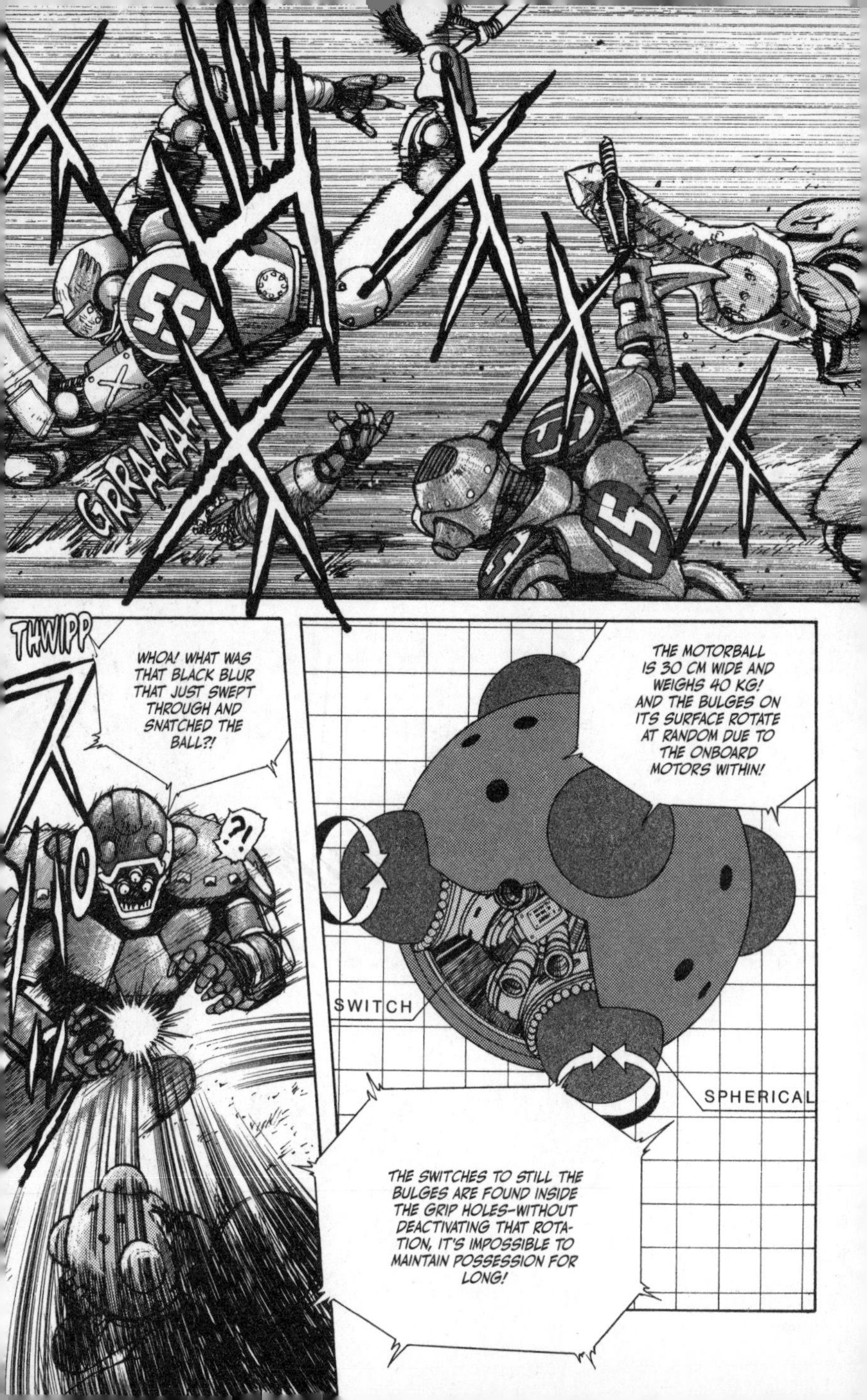
GRAAAH
THE MOTORBALL IS 30 CM WIDE AND WEIGHS 40 KG! AND THE BULGES ON ITS SURFACE ROTATE AT RANDOM DUE TO THE ONBOARD MOTORS WITHIN!
SPHERICAL
SWITCH
THE SWITCHES TO STILL THE BULGES ARE FOUND INSIDE THE GRIP HOLES—WITHOUT DEACTIVATING THAT ROTATION, IT'S IMPOSSIBLE TO MAINTAIN POSSESSION FOR LONG!
THWIPP
WHOA! WHAT WAS THAT BLACK BLUR THAT JUST SWEPT THROUGH AND SNATCHED THE BALL?!
?!

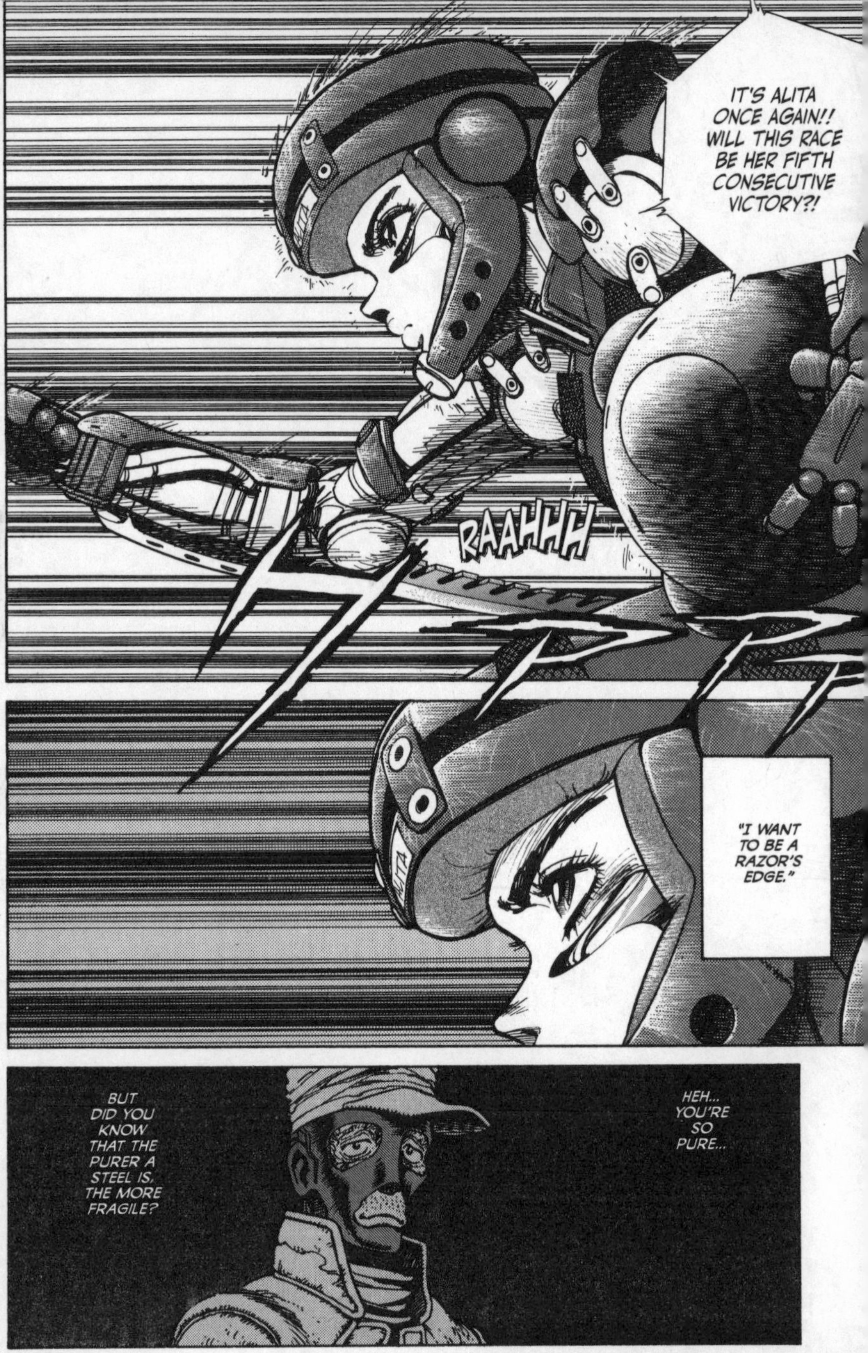
IT'S ALITA ONCE AGAIN!! WILL THIS RACE BE HER FIFTH CONSECUTIVE VICTORY?!
RAAHHH
"I WANT TO BE A RAZOR'S EDGE."
HEH... YOU'RE SO PURE...
BUT DID YOU KNOW THAT THE PURER A STEEL IS, THE MORE FRAGILE?

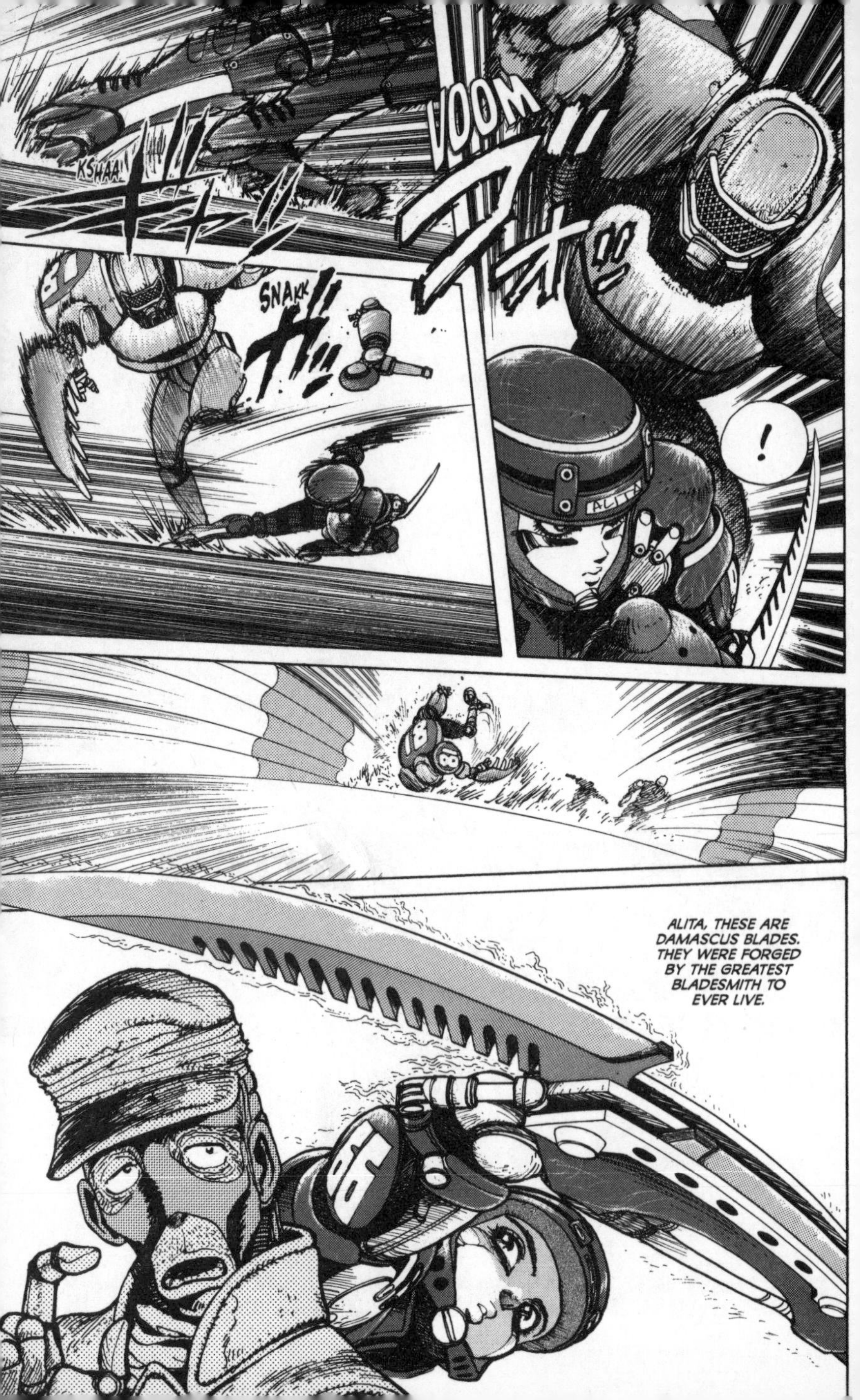
VOOM
KSHAA
!
SNAKK
ALITA
ALITA, THESE ARE DAMASCUS BLADES. THEY WERE FORGED BY THE GREATEST BLADESMITH TO EVER LIVE.

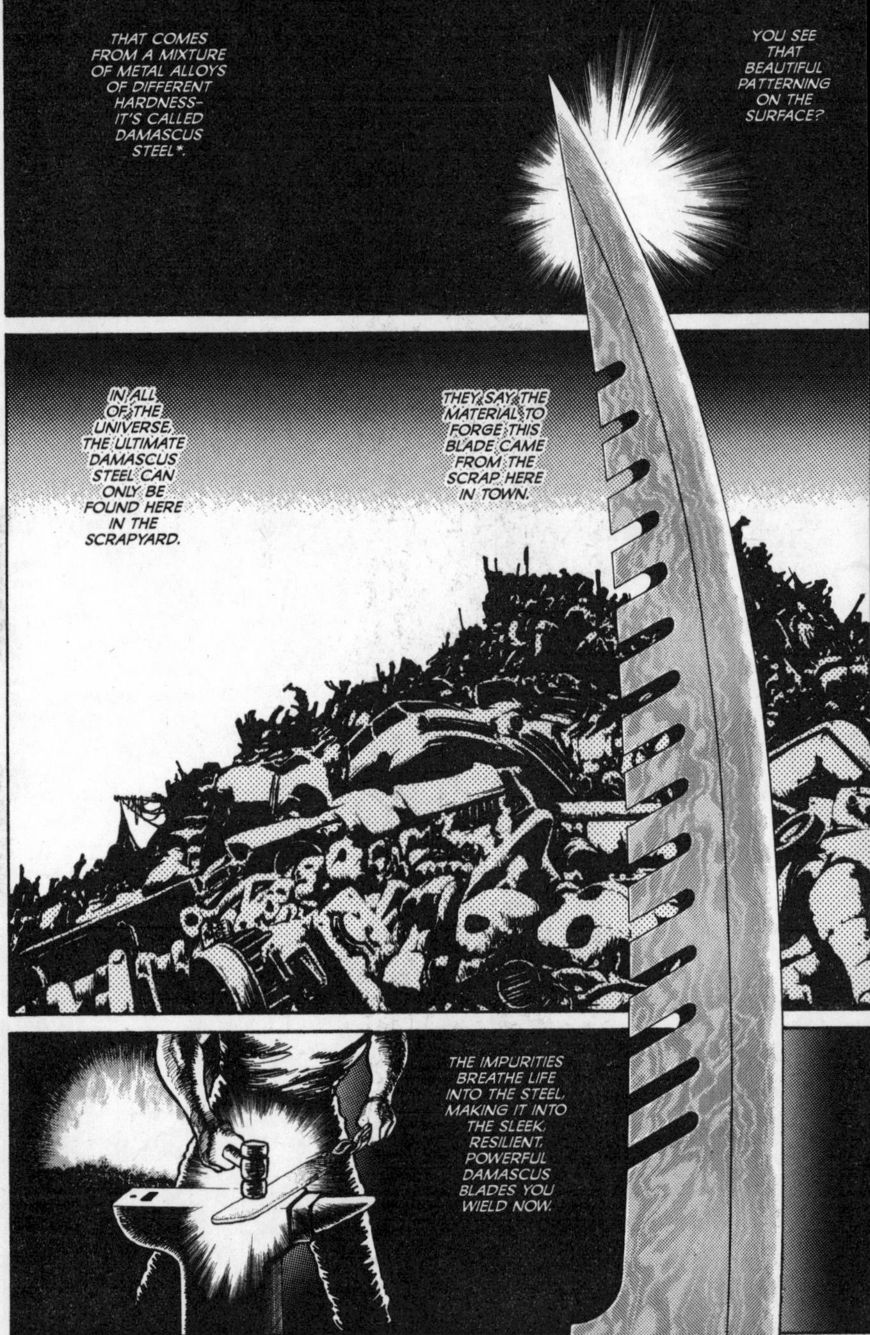
YOU SEE THAT BEAUTIFUL PATTERNING ON THE SURFACE?
THAT COMES FROM A MIXTURE OF METAL ALLOYS OF DIFFERENT HARDNESS- IT'S CALLED DAMASCUS STEEL*.
THEY SAY THE MATERIAL TO FORGE THIS BLADE CAME FROM THE SCRAP HERE IN TOWN.
IN ALL OF THE UNIVERSE, THE ULTIMATE DAMASCUS STEEL CAN ONLY BE FOUND HERE IN THE SCRAPYARD.
THE IMPURITIES BREATHE LIFE INTO THE STEEL, MAKING IT INTO THE SLEEK, RESILIENT, POWERFUL DAMASCUS BLADES YOU WIELD NOW.

***Damascus steel:** Steel made using a unique production method, thought to originate from the city of Damascus in Syria.

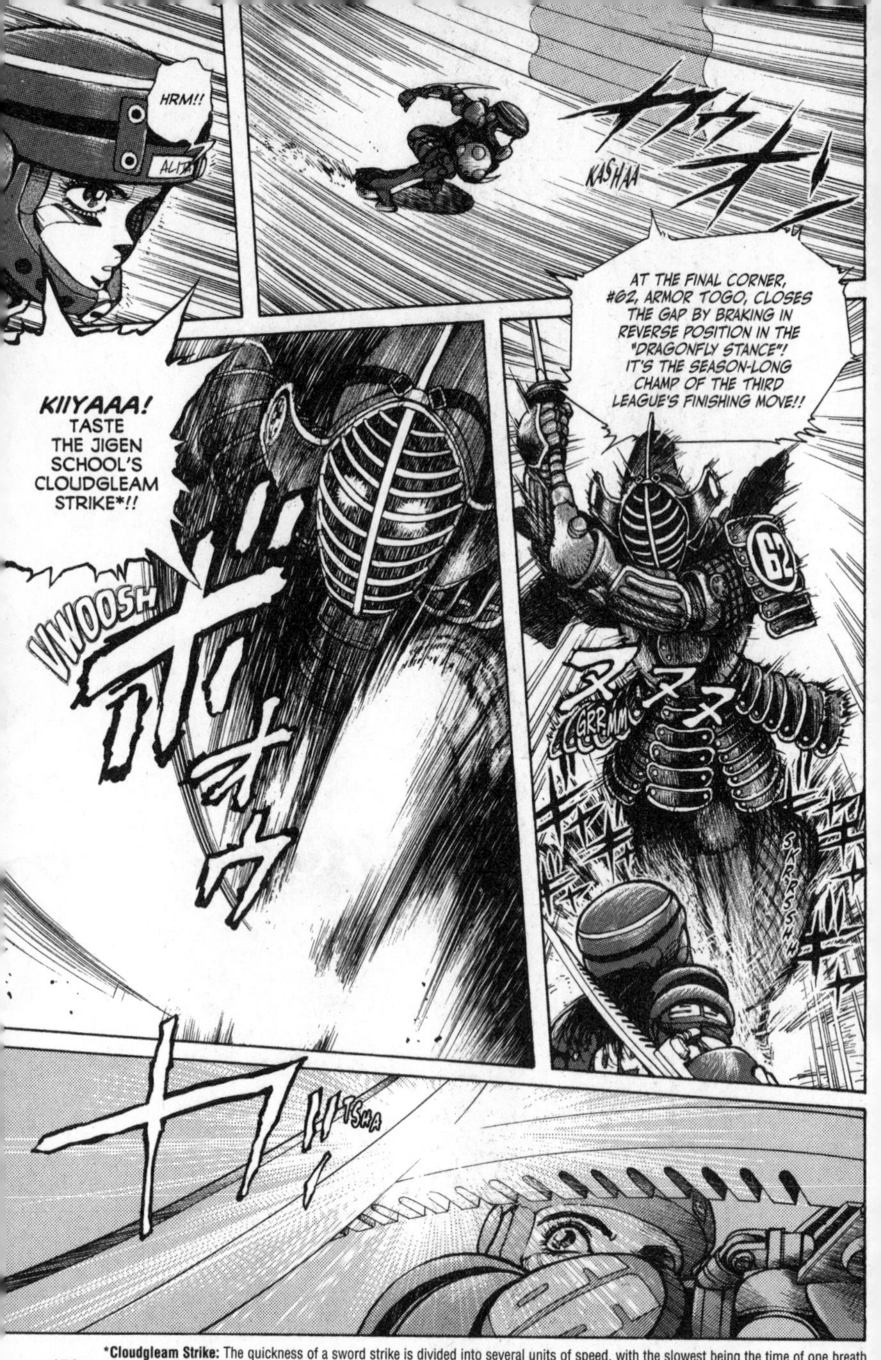
KASHAA
HRM!!
AT THE FINAL CORNER, #62, ARMOR TOGO, CLOSES THE GAP BY BRAKING IN REVERSE POSITION IN THE "DRAGONFLY STANCE"! IT'S THE SEASON-LONG CHAMP OF THE THIRD LEAGUE'S FINISHING MOVE!!
62
GRRMM
SKRRSSHH
KIIYAAA! TASTE THE JIGEN SCHOOL'S CLOUDGLEAM STRIKE*!!
VWOOSH
HITSHA

***Cloudgleam Strike:** The quickness of a sword strike is divided into several units of speed, with the slowest being the time of one breath or heartbeat (called *bun*). In increasing speed, this is followed by *byô* (1/8 *bun*), *shi* (1/10 *byô*), *kotsu* (1/10 *shi*), *gô* (1/10 *kotsu*), and *unyô* (1/10 *gô*). The fastest unit, *unyô*, or "cloud gleam," is 1/8000 of one breath. It is a poetic metaphor for the speed of lightning.

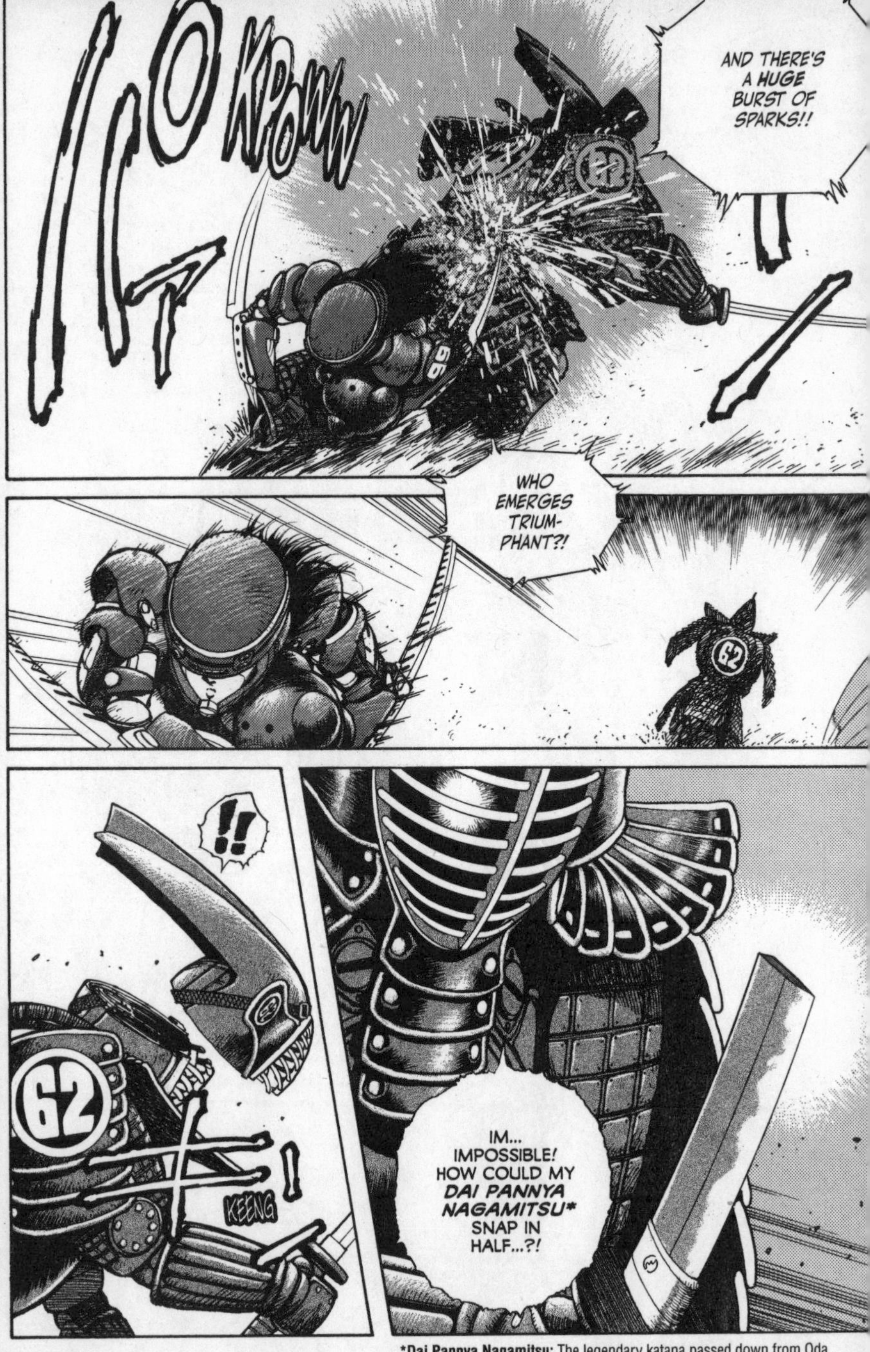
AND THERE'S A **HUGE** BURST OF SPARKS!!
KPOWW
WHO EMERGES TRIUM-PHANT?!
IM... IMPOSSIBLE! HOW COULD MY ***DAI PANNYA NAGAMITSU**** SNAP IN HALF...?!
!!
KEENG

***Dai Pannya Nagamitsu:** The legendary katana passed down from Oda Nobunaga to Tokugawa Ieyasu, "Dai Hannya Nagamitsu," is not this sword.

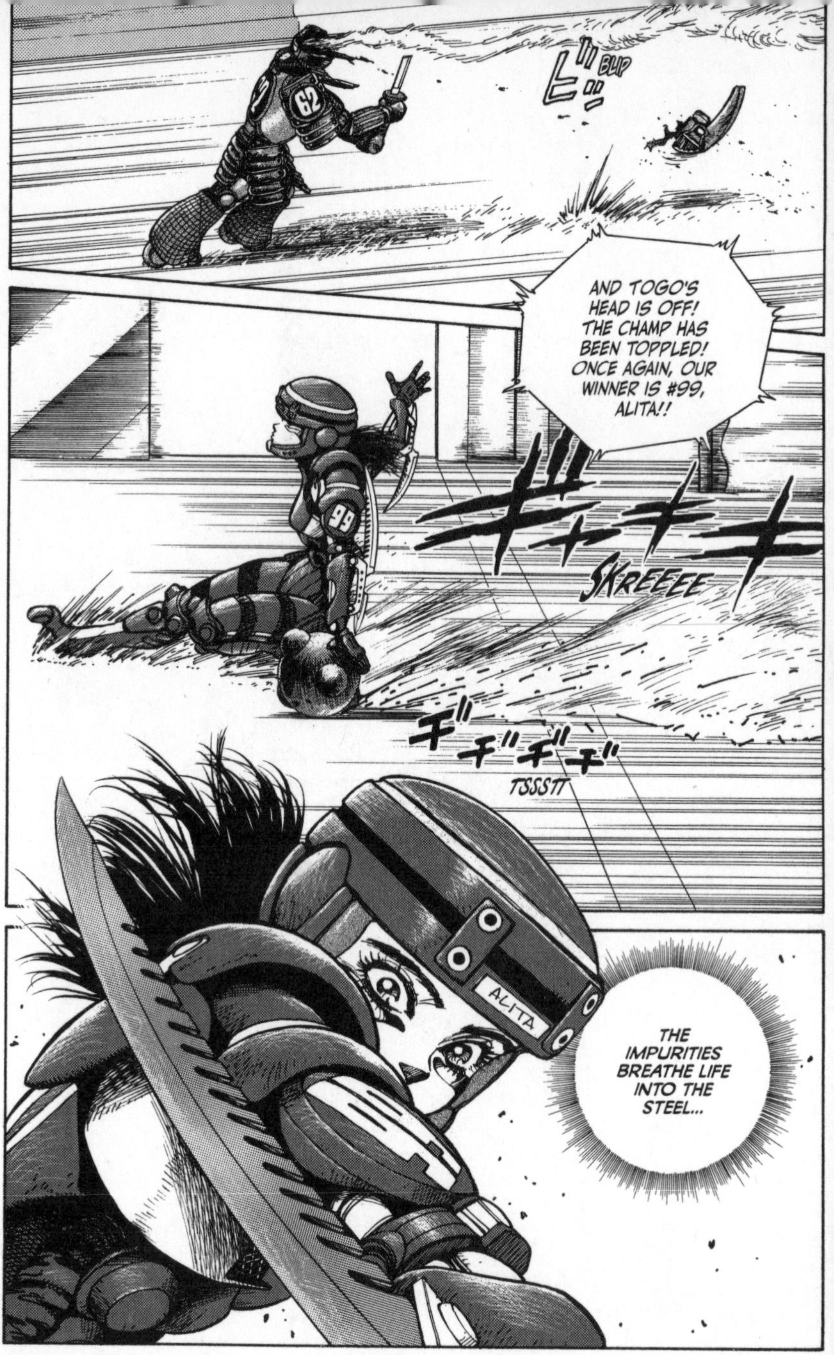
BUP
AND TOGO'S HEAD IS OFF! THE CHAMP HAS BEEN TOPPLED! ONCE AGAIN, OUR WINNER IS #99, ALITA!!
SKREEEEE
TSSSTT
ALITA
THE IMPURITIES BREATHE LIFE INTO THE STEEL...

FIGHT_014 Audience with the King of Kings

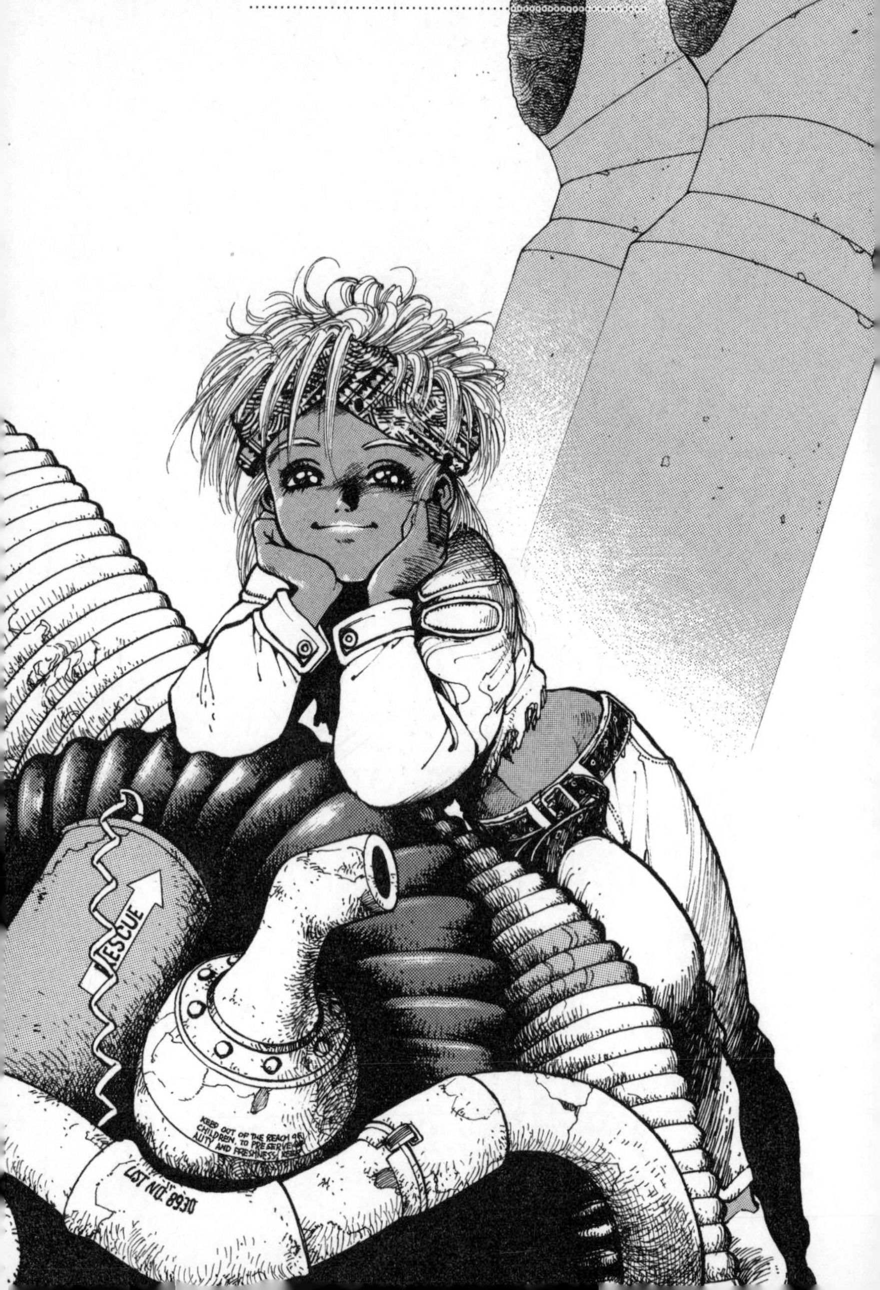
RESCUE
KEEP OUT OF THE REACH OF
CHILDREN, TO PRESERVE
LOT NO. 8930

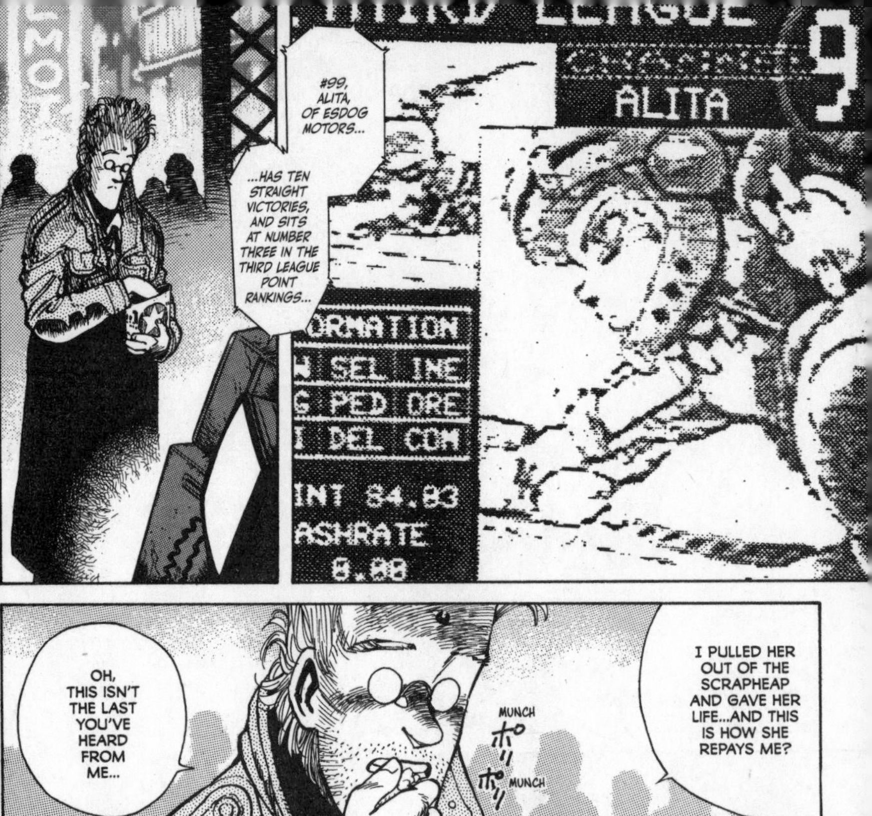

THIRD LEAGUE
ALITA
ORMATION
N SEL INE
G PED ORE
I DEL COM
INT 84.83
ASHRATE
8.88
#99, ALITA, OF ESDOG MOTORS...
...HAS TEN STRAIGHT VICTORIES, AND SITS AT NUMBER THREE IN THE THIRD LEAGUE POINT RANKINGS...
I PULLED HER OUT OF THE SCRAPHEAP AND GAVE HER LIFE...AND THIS IS HOW SHE REPAYS ME?
ポリ MUNCH
ポリ MUNCH
OH, THIS ISN'T THE LAST YOU'VE HEARD FROM ME...
IDO, COME ON! NO STANDING AROUND!!
YANK
BIG BROTHER'S GAME IS ABOUT TO START!!

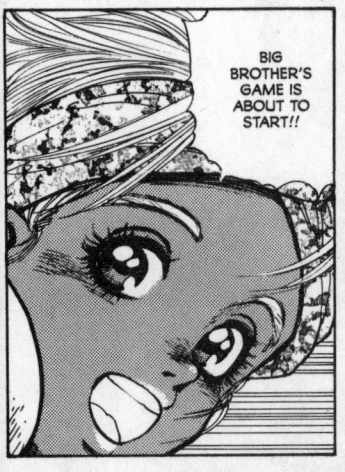

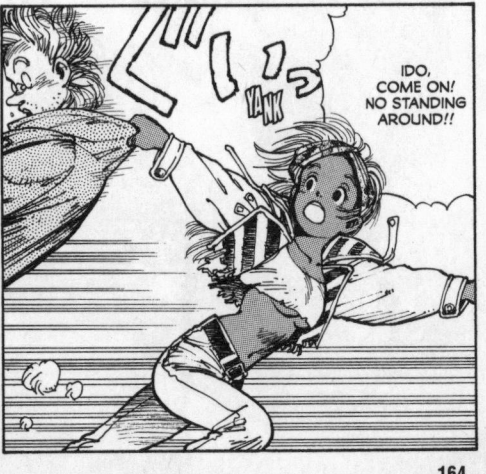

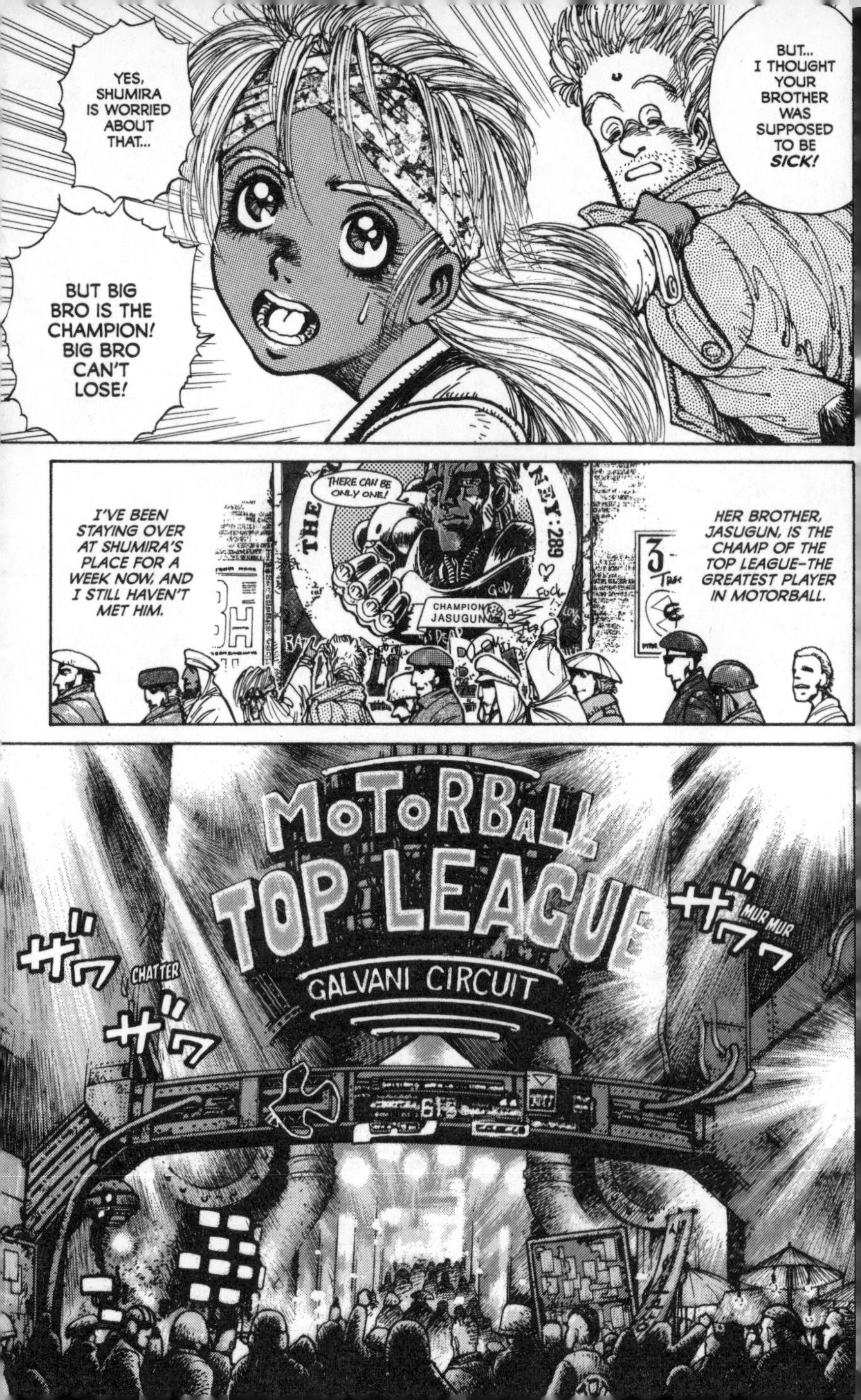
BUT... I THOUGHT YOUR BROTHER WAS SUPPOSED TO BE SICK!
YES, SHUMIRA IS WORRIED ABOUT THAT...
BUT BIG BRO IS THE CHAMPION! BIG BRO CAN'T LOSE!
HER BROTHER, JASUGUN, IS THE CHAMP OF THE TOP LEAGUE–THE GREATEST PLAYER IN MOTORBALL.
THERE CAN BE ONLY ONE!
CHAMPION JASUGUN
I'VE BEEN STAYING OVER AT SHUMIRA'S PLACE FOR A WEEK NOW, AND I STILL HAVEN'T MET HIM.
MOTORBALL
TOP LEAGUE
GALVANI CIRCUIT
ザワ
MUR MUR
ザワ
CHATTER
ザワ

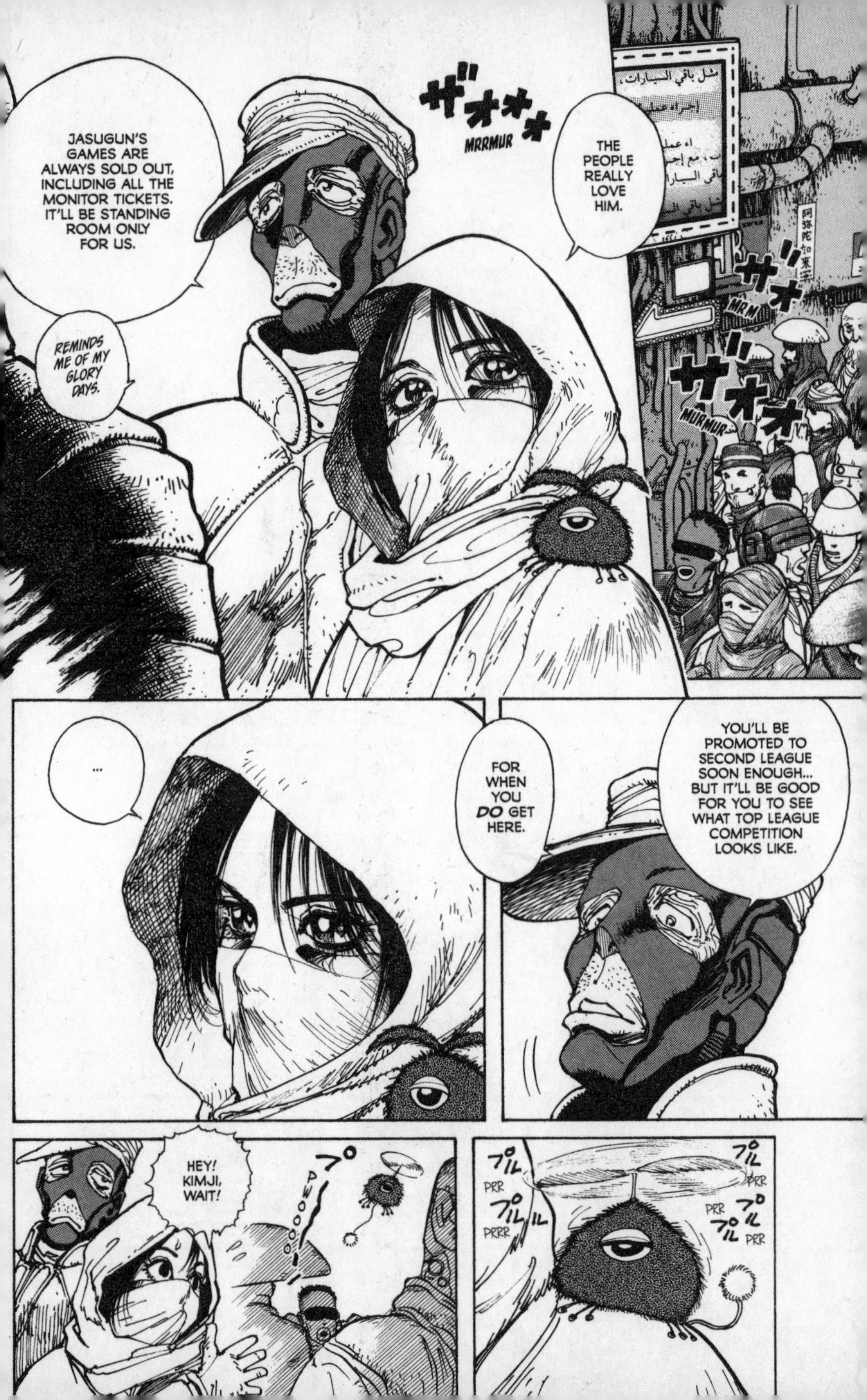

サオオ
MRM
サオオ
MURMUR
ザオオオ
MRRMUR
THE PEOPLE REALLY LOVE HIM.
JASUGUN'S GAMES ARE ALWAYS SOLD OUT, INCLUDING ALL THE MONITOR TICKETS. IT'LL BE STANDING ROOM ONLY FOR US.
REMINDS ME OF MY GLORY DAYS.
YOU'LL BE PROMOTED TO SECOND LEAGUE SOON ENOUGH... BUT IT'LL BE GOOD FOR YOU TO SEE WHAT TOP LEAGUE COMPETITION LOOKS LIKE.
FOR WHEN YOU *DO* GET HERE.
...
プル PRR
プル PRR
プルル PRRR
プル PRR
PWOOOO—!
HEY! KIMJI, WAIT!

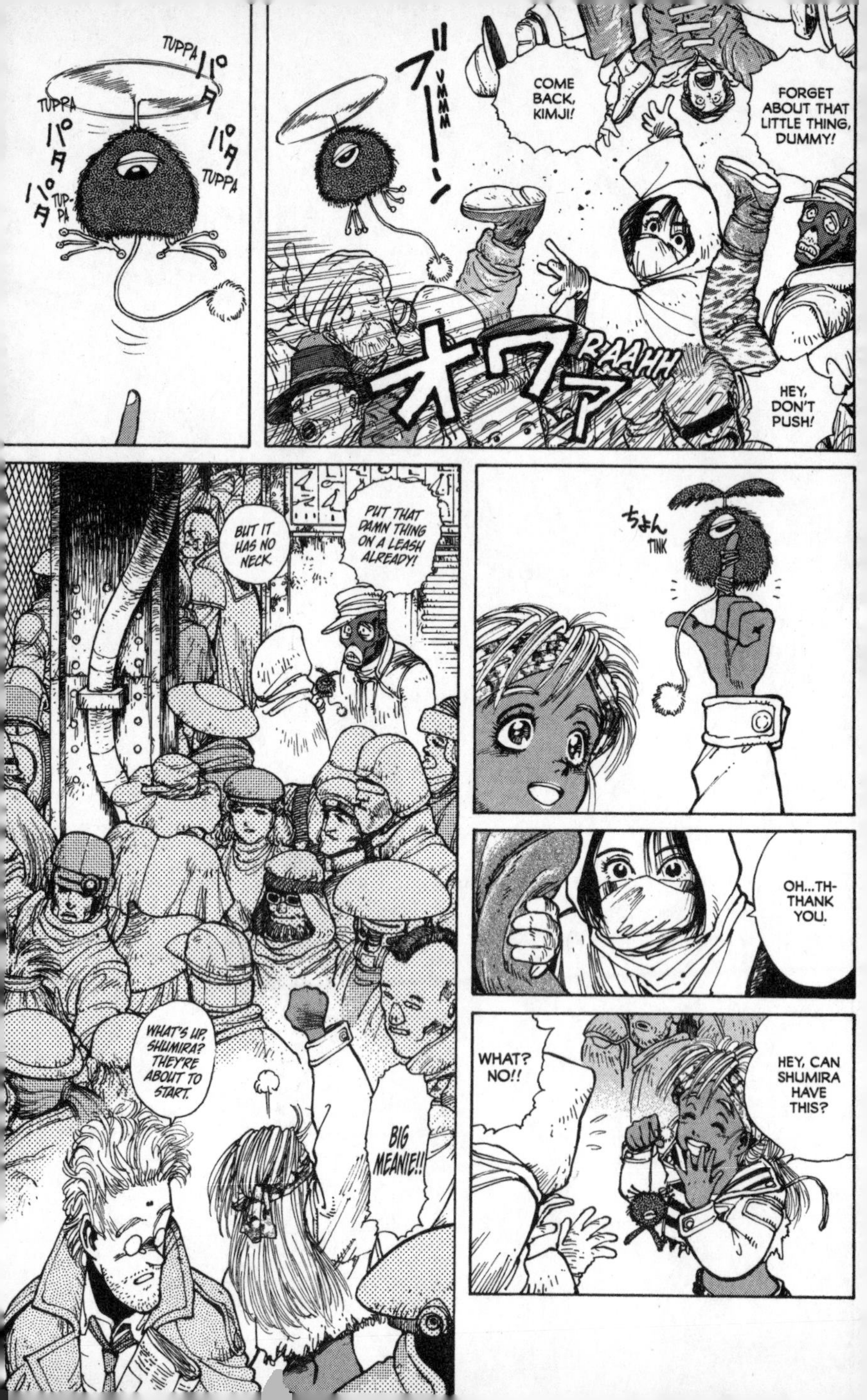
FORGET ABOUT THAT LITTLE THING, DUMMY!
COME BACK, KIMJI!
HEY, DON'T PUSH!
ブーン VMMM
オワァ RAAHH
パタ TUPPA
パタ TUPPA
パタ TUP-PA
パタ TUPPA
ちょん TINK
OH...TH-THANK YOU.
HEY, CAN SHUMIRA HAVE THIS?
WHAT? NO!!
PUT THAT DAMN THING ON A LEASH ALREADY!
BUT IT HAS NO NECK.
WHAT'S UP, SHUMIRA? THEY'RE ABOUT TO START.
BIG MEANIE!!

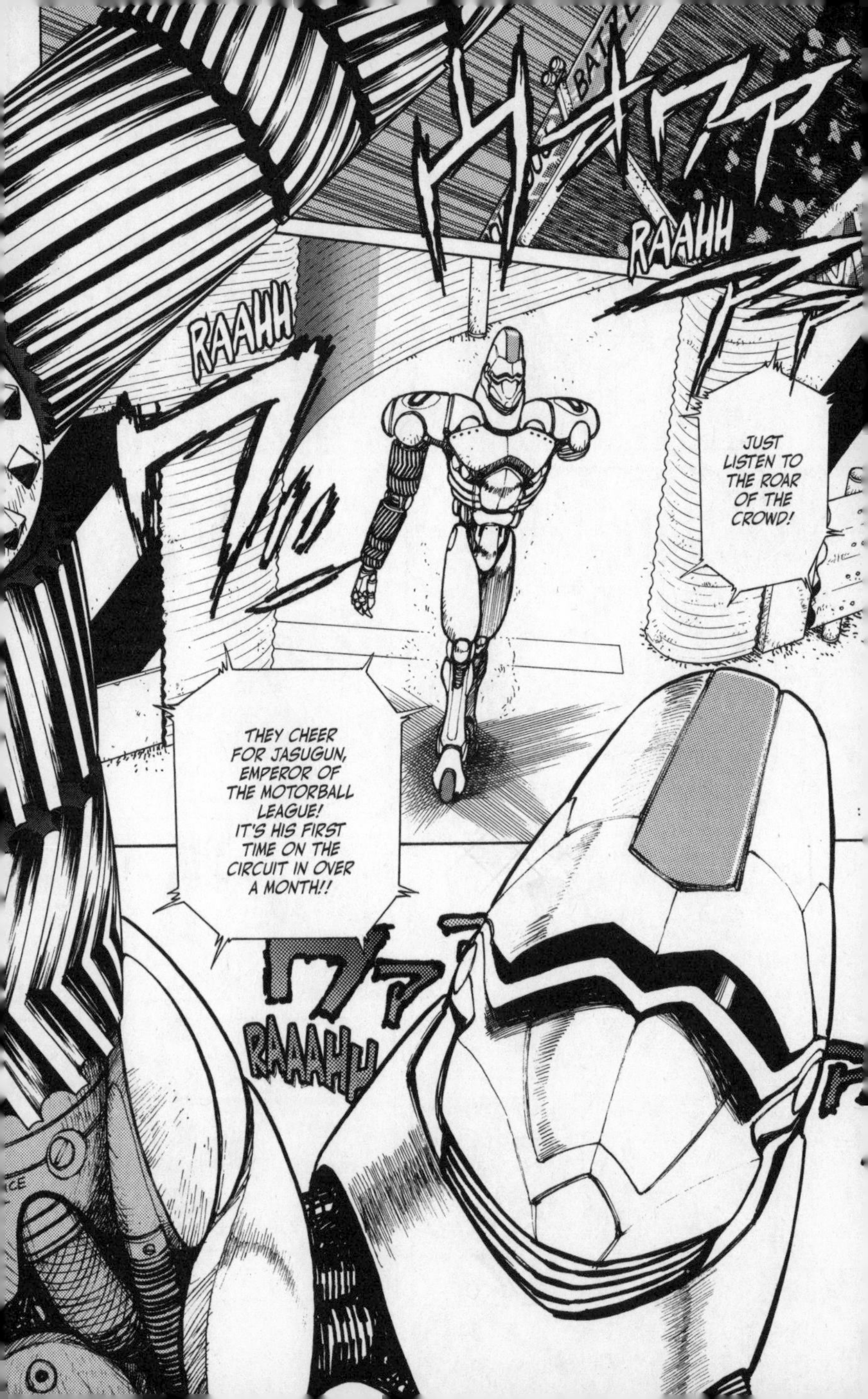
RAAHH
RAAHH
JUST LISTEN TO THE ROAR OF THE CROWD!
THEY CHEER FOR JASUGUN, EMPEROR OF THE MOTORBALL LEAGUE! IT'S HIS FIRST TIME ON THE CIRCUIT IN OVER A MONTH!!
RAAAHH

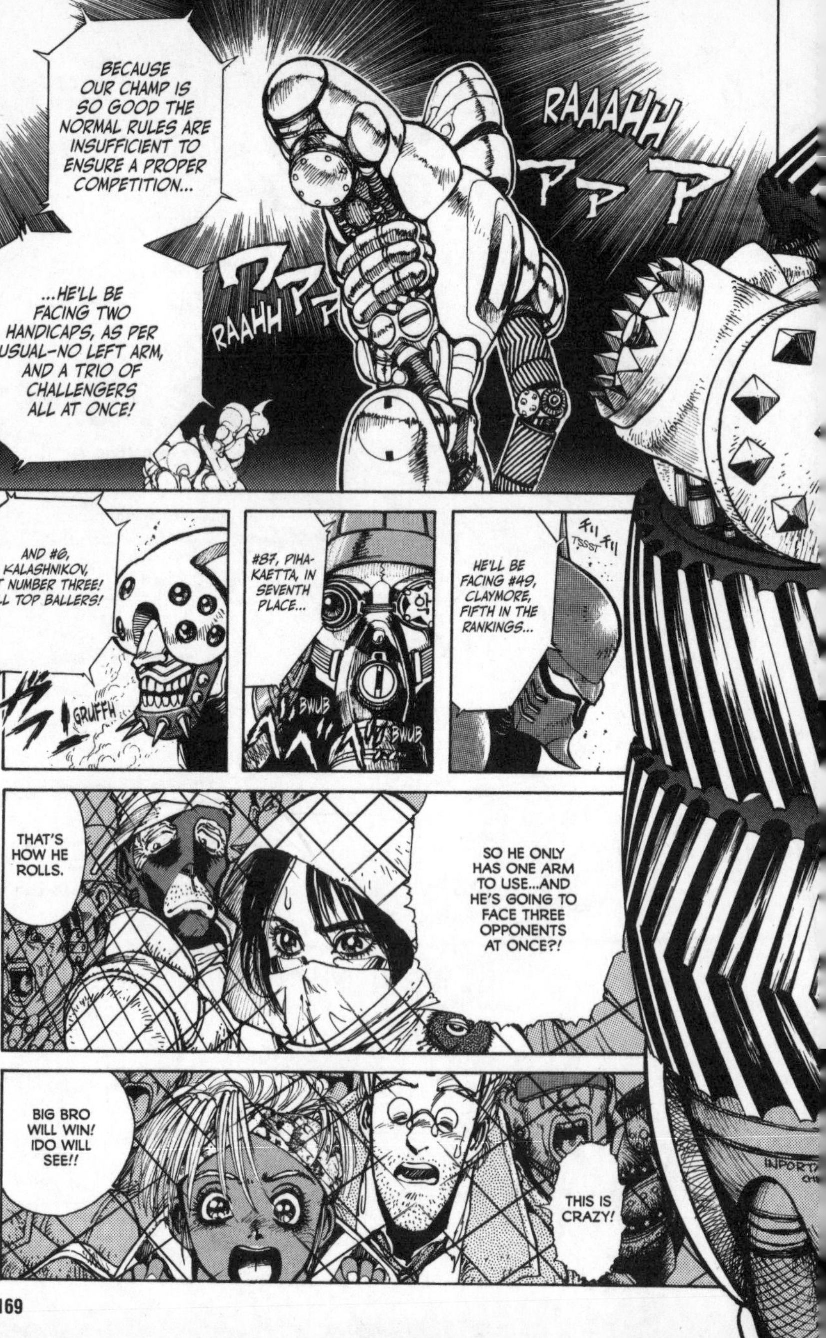
BECAUSE OUR CHAMP IS SO GOOD THE NORMAL RULES ARE INSUFFICIENT TO ENSURE A PROPER COMPETITION...
RAAAHH
...HE'LL BE FACING TWO HANDICAPS, AS PER USUAL—NO LEFT ARM, AND A TRIO OF CHALLENGERS ALL AT ONCE!
RAAHH
TSSST
HE'LL BE FACING #49, CLAYMORE, FIFTH IN THE RANKINGS...
#87, PIHA-KAETTA, IN SEVENTH PLACE...
BWUB
BWUB
AND #6, KALASHNIKOV, AT NUMBER THREE! ALL TOP BALLERS!
GRUFFH
SO HE ONLY HAS ONE ARM TO USE...AND HE'S GOING TO FACE THREE OPPONENTS AT ONCE?!
THAT'S HOW HE ROLLS.
THIS IS CRAZY!
BIG BRO WILL WIN! IDO WILL SEE!!

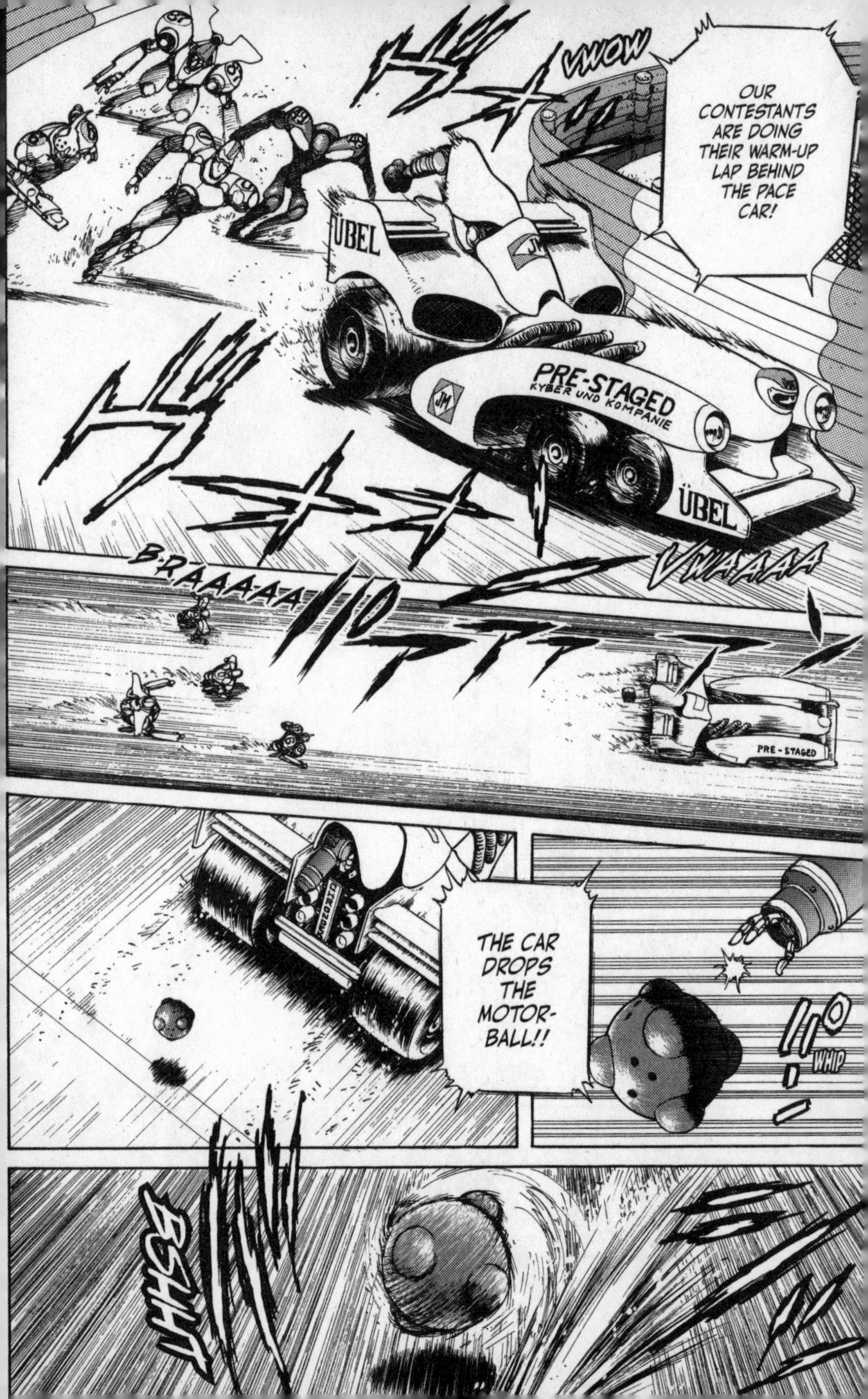
OUR CONTESTANTS ARE DOING THEIR WARM-UP LAP BEHIND THE PACE CAR!
VWOW
ÜBEL
PRE-STAGED
KYBER UND KOMPANIE
ÜBEL
B-RAAAAAA
VWAAAAA
PRE-STAGED
THE CAR DROPS THE MOTOR-BALL!!
WHIP
BSHHT

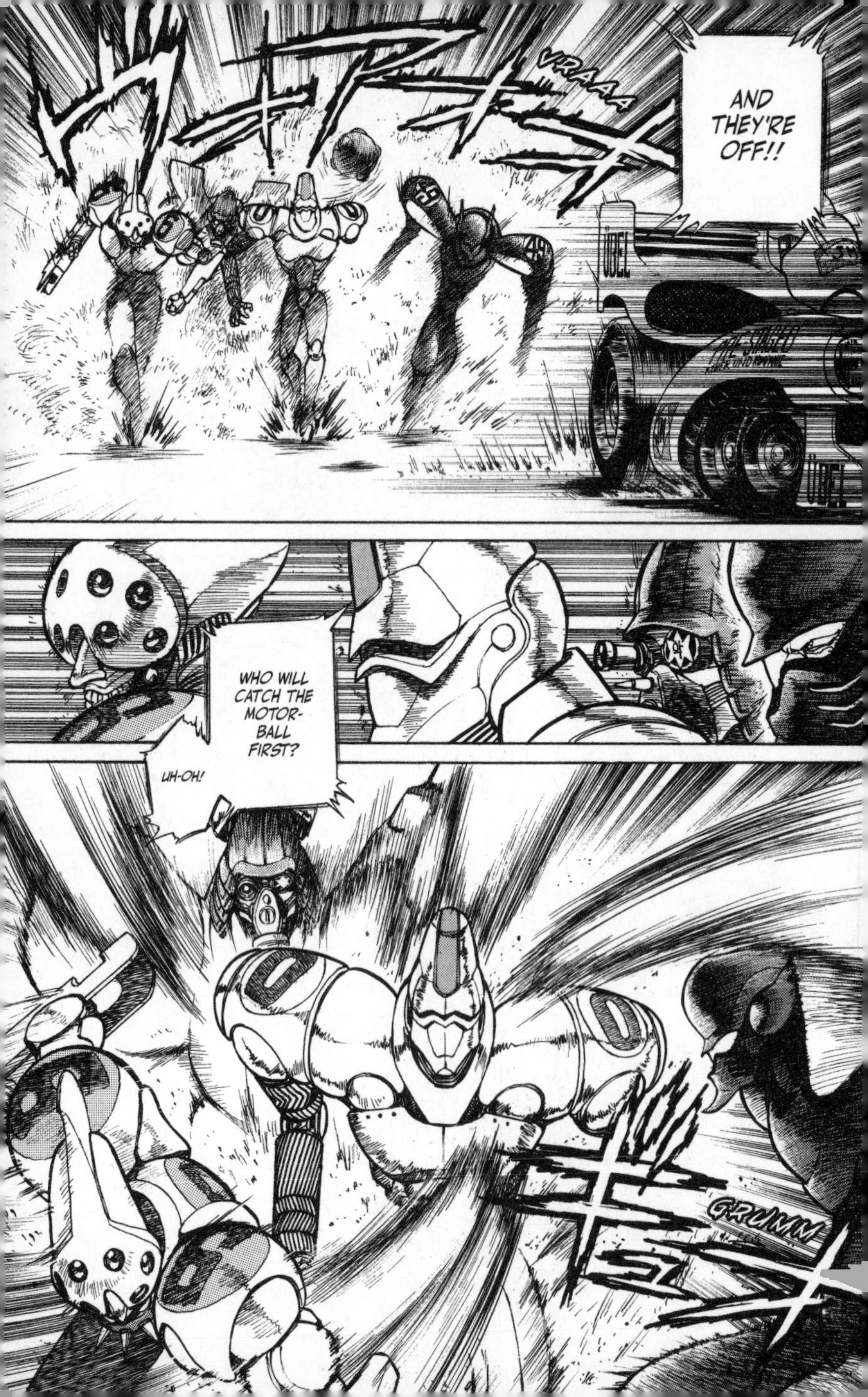
AND THEY'RE OFF!!
VRAAA
ÜBEL
ÜBEL
WHO WILL CATCH THE MOTOR-BALL FIRST?
UH-OH!
GRUMM

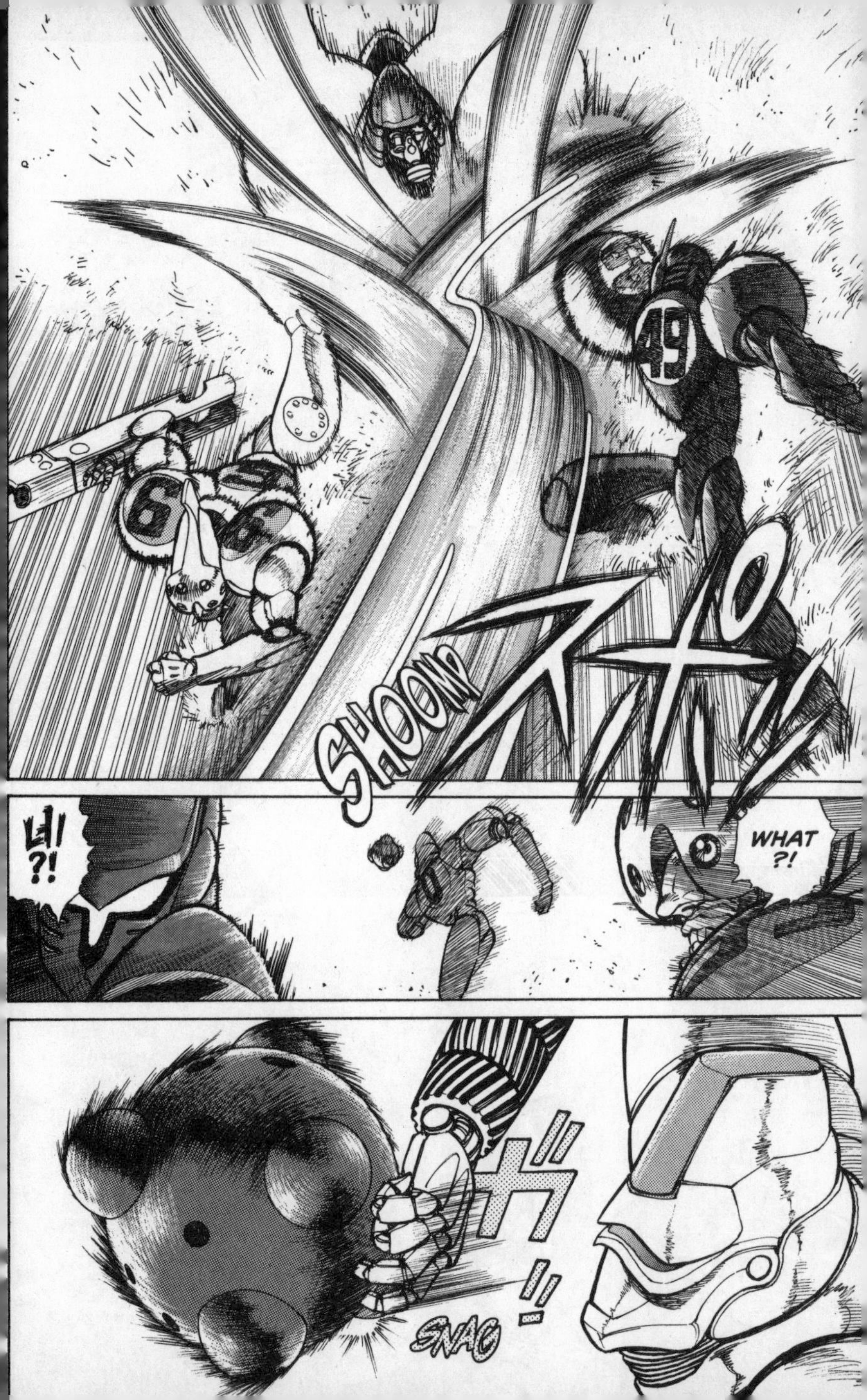
SHOOMP
WHAT ?!
SNAG

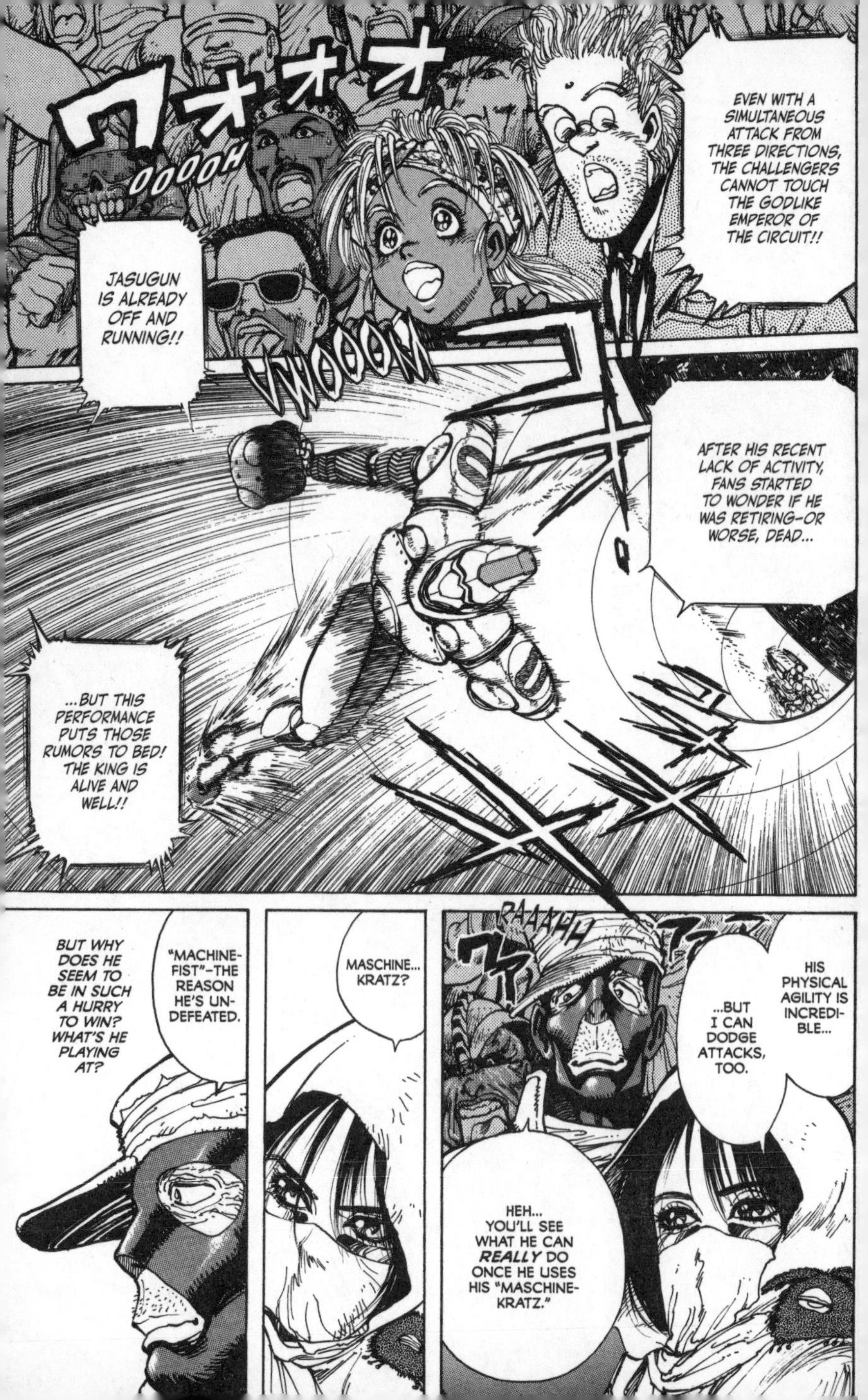
EVEN WITH A SIMULTANEOUS ATTACK FROM THREE DIRECTIONS, THE CHALLENGERS CANNOT TOUCH THE GODLIKE EMPEROR OF THE CIRCUIT!!
OOOOH
JASUGUN IS ALREADY OFF AND RUNNING!!
AFTER HIS RECENT LACK OF ACTIVITY, FANS STARTED TO WONDER IF HE WAS RETIRING—OR WORSE, DEAD...
VWOOOM
...BUT THIS PERFORMANCE PUTS THOSE RUMORS TO BED! THE KING IS ALIVE AND WELL!!
RAAAHH
HIS PHYSICAL AGILITY IS INCREDI-BLE...
...BUT I CAN DODGE ATTACKS, TOO.
HEH... YOU'LL SEE WHAT HE CAN REALLY DO ONCE HE USES HIS "MASCHINE-KRATZ."
MASCHINE... KRATZ?
"MACHINE-FIST"—THE REASON HE'S UN-DEFEATED.
BUT WHY DOES HE SEEM TO BE IN SUCH A HURRY TO WIN? WHAT'S HE PLAYING AT?

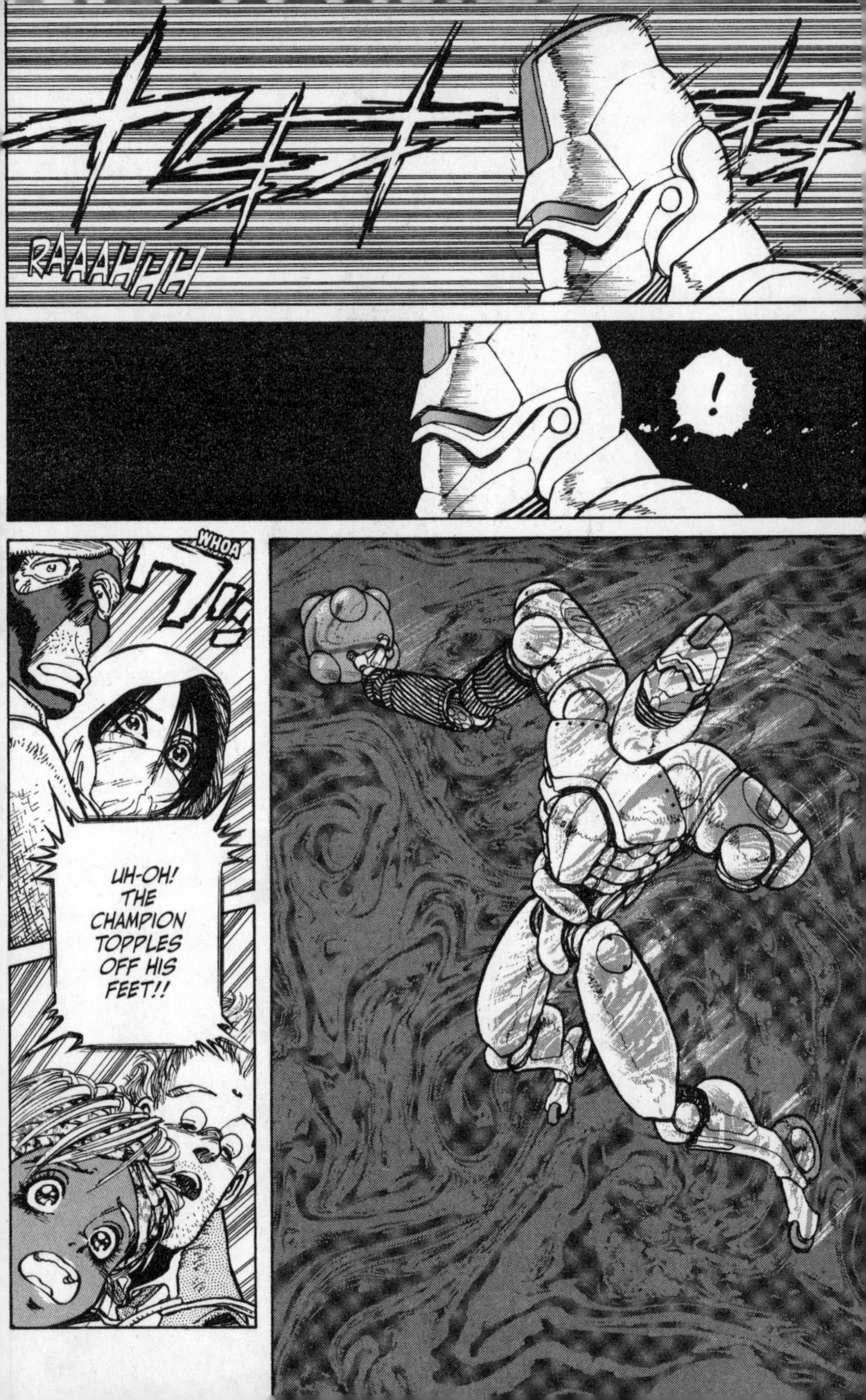
RAAAHHHH
!
WHOA
UH-OH! THE CHAMPION TOPPLES OFF HIS FEET!!

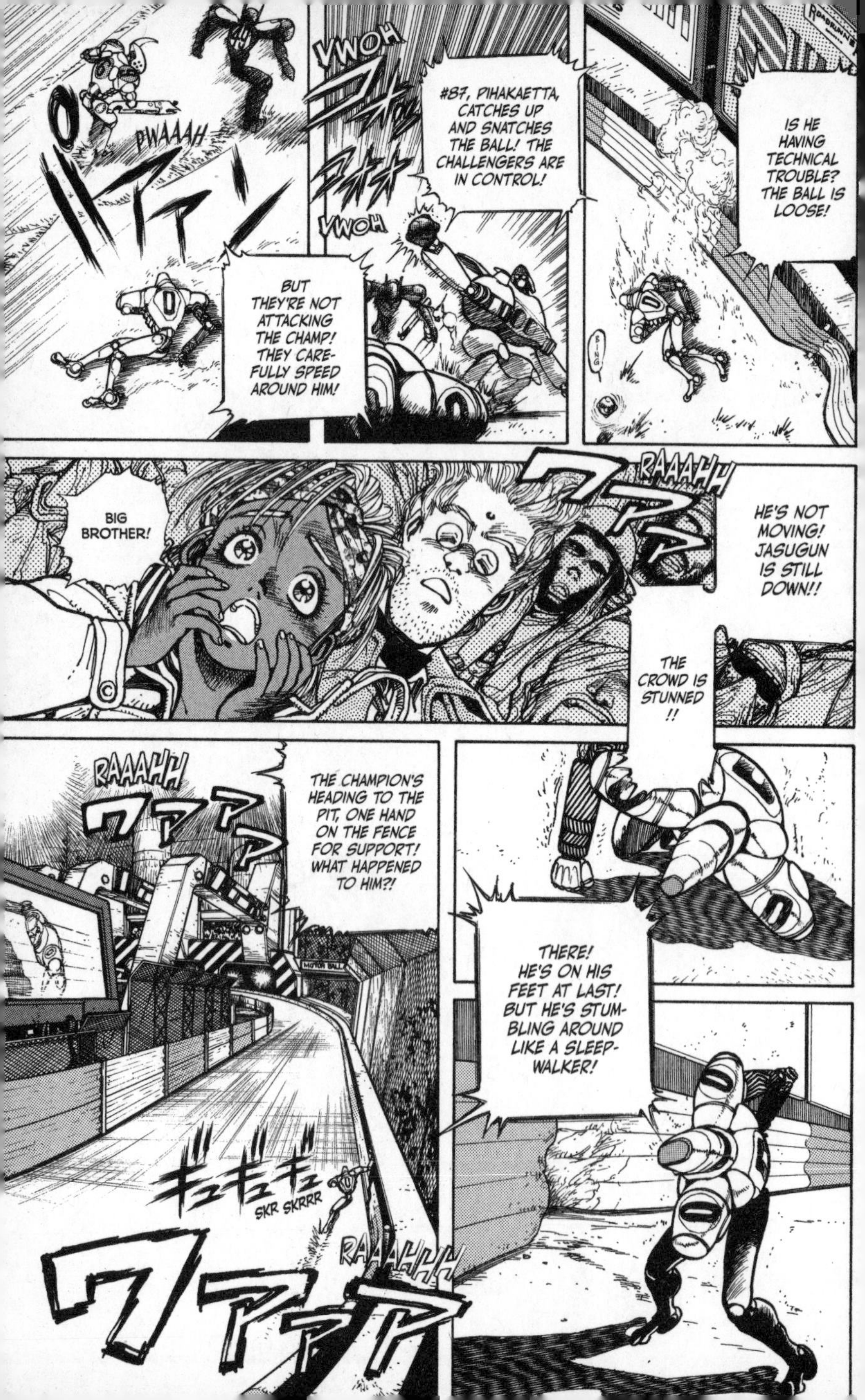
IS HE HAVING TECHNICAL TROUBLE? THE BALL IS LOOSE!
BING
VWOH
#87, PIHAKAETTA, CATCHES UP AND SNATCHES THE BALL! THE CHALLENGERS ARE IN CONTROL!
VWOH
PWAAAH
BUT THEY'RE NOT ATTACKING THE CHAMP! THEY CAREFULLY SPEED AROUND HIM!
RAAAHH
HE'S NOT MOVING! JASUGUN IS STILL DOWN!!
THE CROWD IS STUNNED !!
BIG BROTHER!
THERE! HE'S ON HIS FEET AT LAST! BUT HE'S STUMBLING AROUND LIKE A SLEEPWALKER!
RAAAHH
THE CHAMPION'S HEADING TO THE PIT, ONE HAND ON THE FENCE FOR SUPPORT! WHAT HAPPENED TO HIM?!
MOTOR BALL
SKR SKRRR
RAAAHH

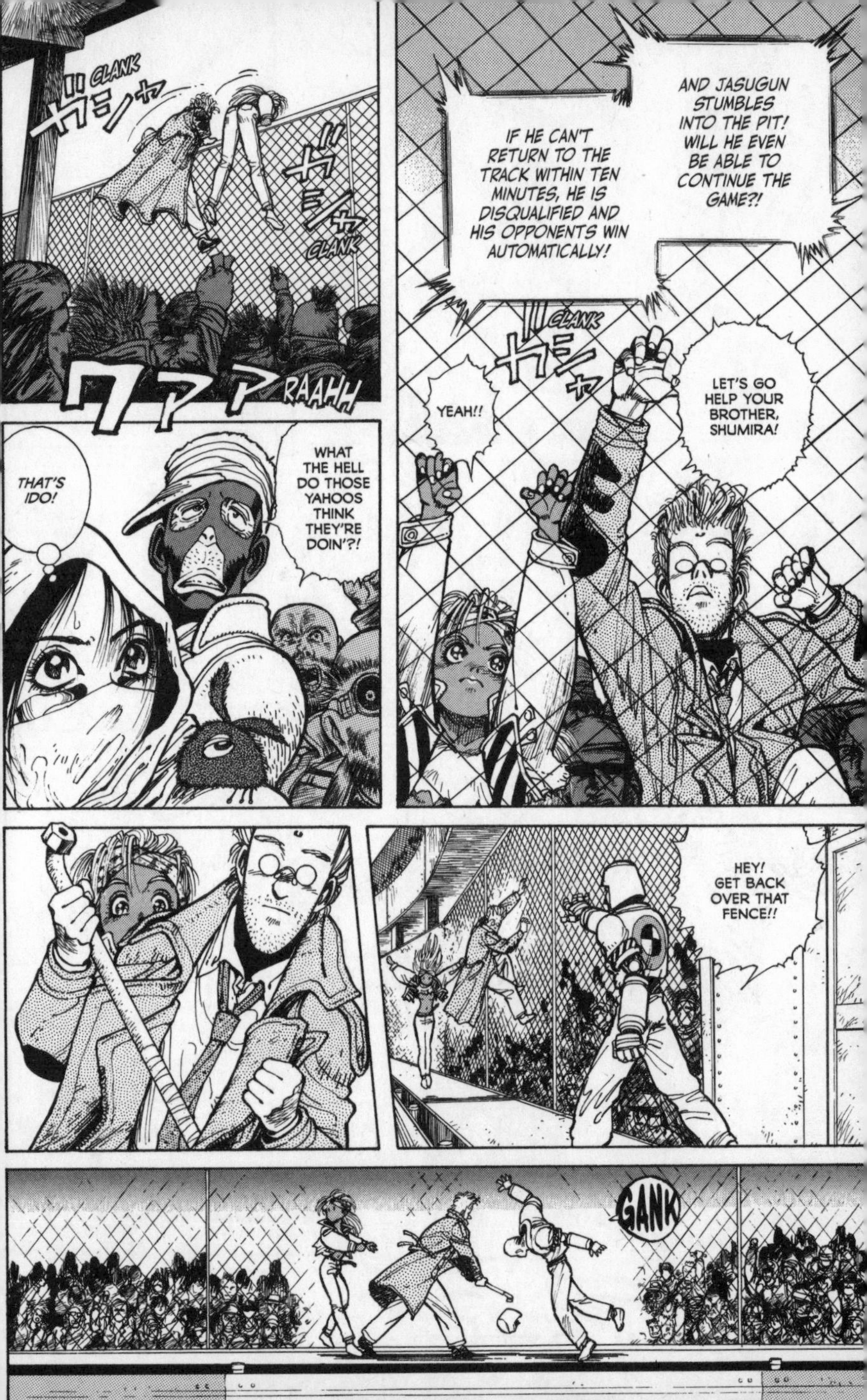
AND JASUGUN STUMBLES INTO THE PIT! WILL HE EVEN BE ABLE TO CONTINUE THE GAME?!
IF HE CAN'T RETURN TO THE TRACK WITHIN TEN MINUTES, HE IS DISQUALIFIED AND HIS OPPONENTS WIN AUTOMATICALLY!
LET'S GO HELP YOUR BROTHER, SHUMIRA!
ガシャ CLANK
YEAH!!
ガシャ CLANK
ガシャ CLANK
ワァァ RAAHH
WHAT THE HELL DO THOSE YAHOOS THINK THEY'RE DOIN'?!
THAT'S IDO!
HEY! GET BACK OVER THAT FENCE!!
GANK

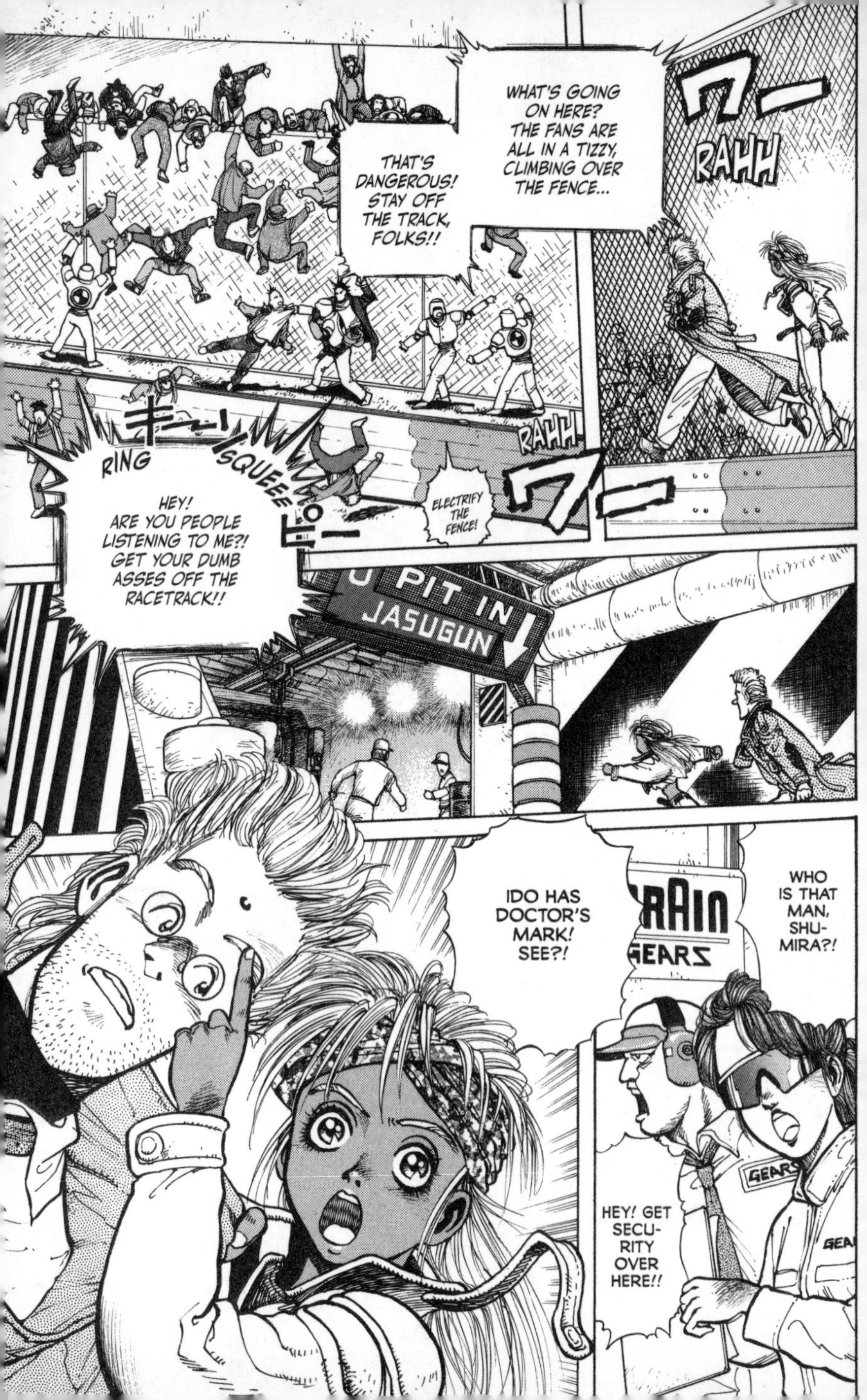
ワー
RAHH
WHAT'S GOING ON HERE? THE FANS ARE ALL IN A TIZZY, CLIMBING OVER THE FENCE...
THAT'S DANGEROUS! STAY OFF THE TRACK, FOLKS!!
RAHH
ワー
ELECTRIFY THE FENCE!
ピー
SQUEEEE
キーン
RING
HEY! ARE YOU PEOPLE LISTENING TO ME?! GET YOUR DUMB ASSES OFF THE RACETRACK!!
PIT IN
JASUGUN
WHO IS THAT MAN, SHU-MIRA?!
HEY! GET SECU-RITY OVER HERE!!
IDO HAS DOCTOR'S MARK! SEE?!

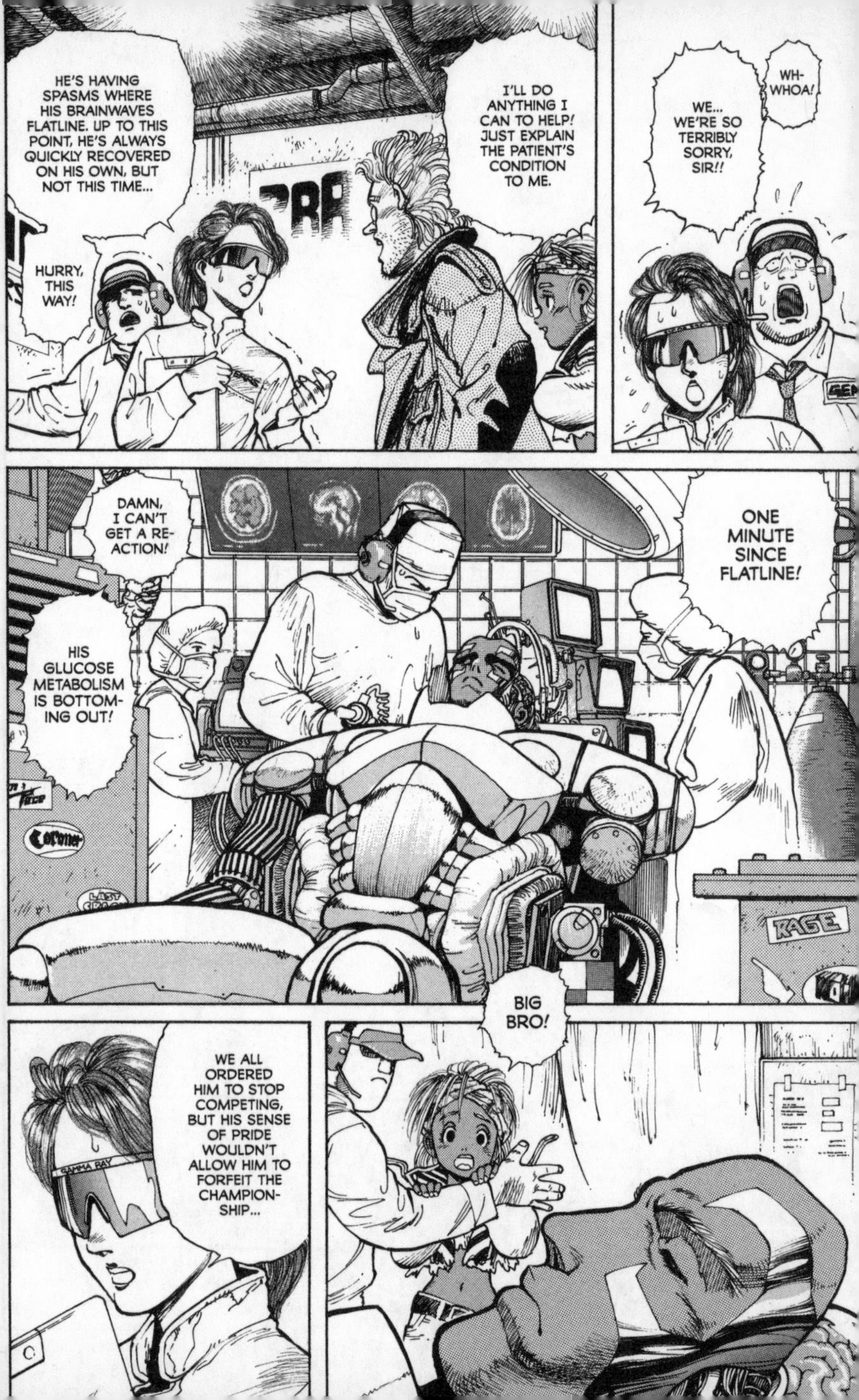
WH-WHOA!
WE... WE'RE SO TERRIBLY SORRY, SIR!!
I'LL DO ANYTHING I CAN TO HELP! JUST EXPLAIN THE PATIENT'S CONDITION TO ME.
HE'S HAVING SPASMS WHERE HIS BRAINWAVES FLATLINE. UP TO THIS POINT, HE'S ALWAYS QUICKLY RECOVERED ON HIS OWN, BUT NOT THIS TIME...
HURRY, THIS WAY!
ONE MINUTE SINCE FLATLINE!
DAMN, I CAN'T GET A RE-ACTION!
HIS GLUCOSE METABOLISM IS BOTTOM-ING OUT!
BIG BRO!
WE ALL ORDERED HIM TO STOP COMPETING, BUT HIS SENSE OF PRIDE WOULDN'T ALLOW HIM TO FORFEIT THE CHAMPION-SHIP...

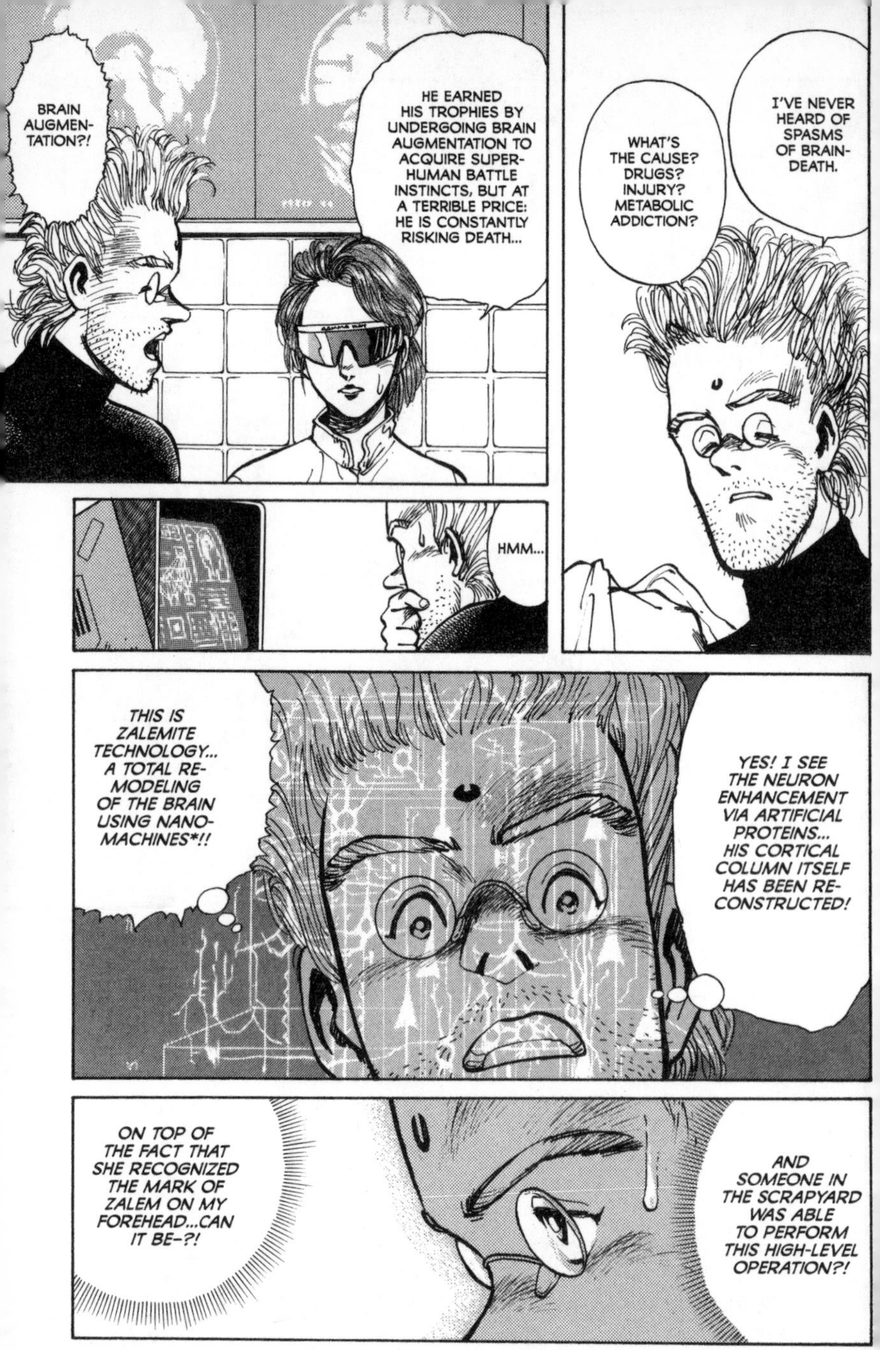

I'VE NEVER HEARD OF SPASMS OF BRAIN-DEATH.
WHAT'S THE CAUSE? DRUGS? INJURY? METABOLIC ADDICTION?
HE EARNED HIS TROPHIES BY UNDERGOING BRAIN AUGMENTATION TO ACQUIRE SUPER-HUMAN BATTLE INSTINCTS, BUT AT A TERRIBLE PRICE: HE IS CONSTANTLY RISKING DEATH...
BRAIN AUGMEN-TATION?!
HMM...
YES! I SEE THE NEURON ENHANCEMENT VIA ARTIFICIAL PROTEINS... HIS CORTICAL COLUMN ITSELF HAS BEEN RE-CONSTRUCTED!
THIS IS ZALEMITE TECHNOLOGY... A TOTAL RE-MODELING OF THE BRAIN USING NANO-MACHINES*!!
AND SOMEONE IN THE SCRAPYARD WAS ABLE TO PERFORM THIS HIGH-LEVEL OPERATION?!
ON TOP OF THE FACT THAT SHE RECOGNIZED THE MARK OF ZALEM ON MY FOREHEAD...CAN IT BE–?!

*Nanomachines: Microscopic robots, measured in nanometers (one millionth of a millimeter), that are constructed on a molecular level.

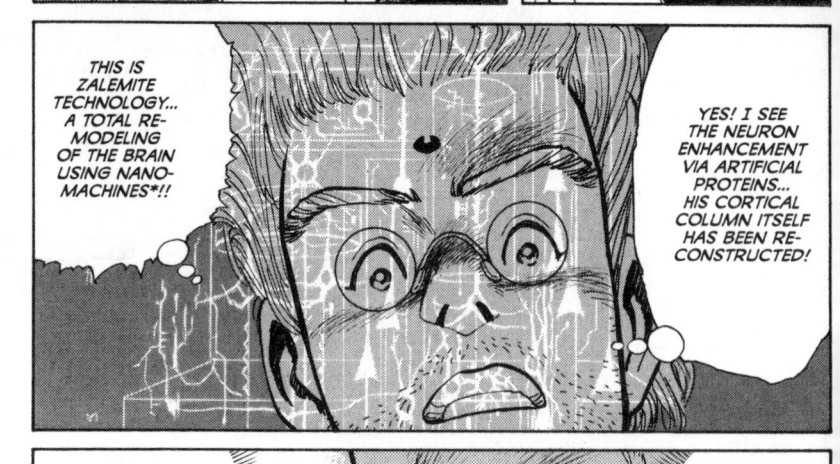

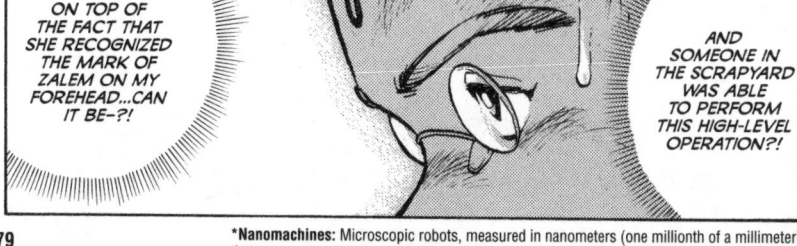

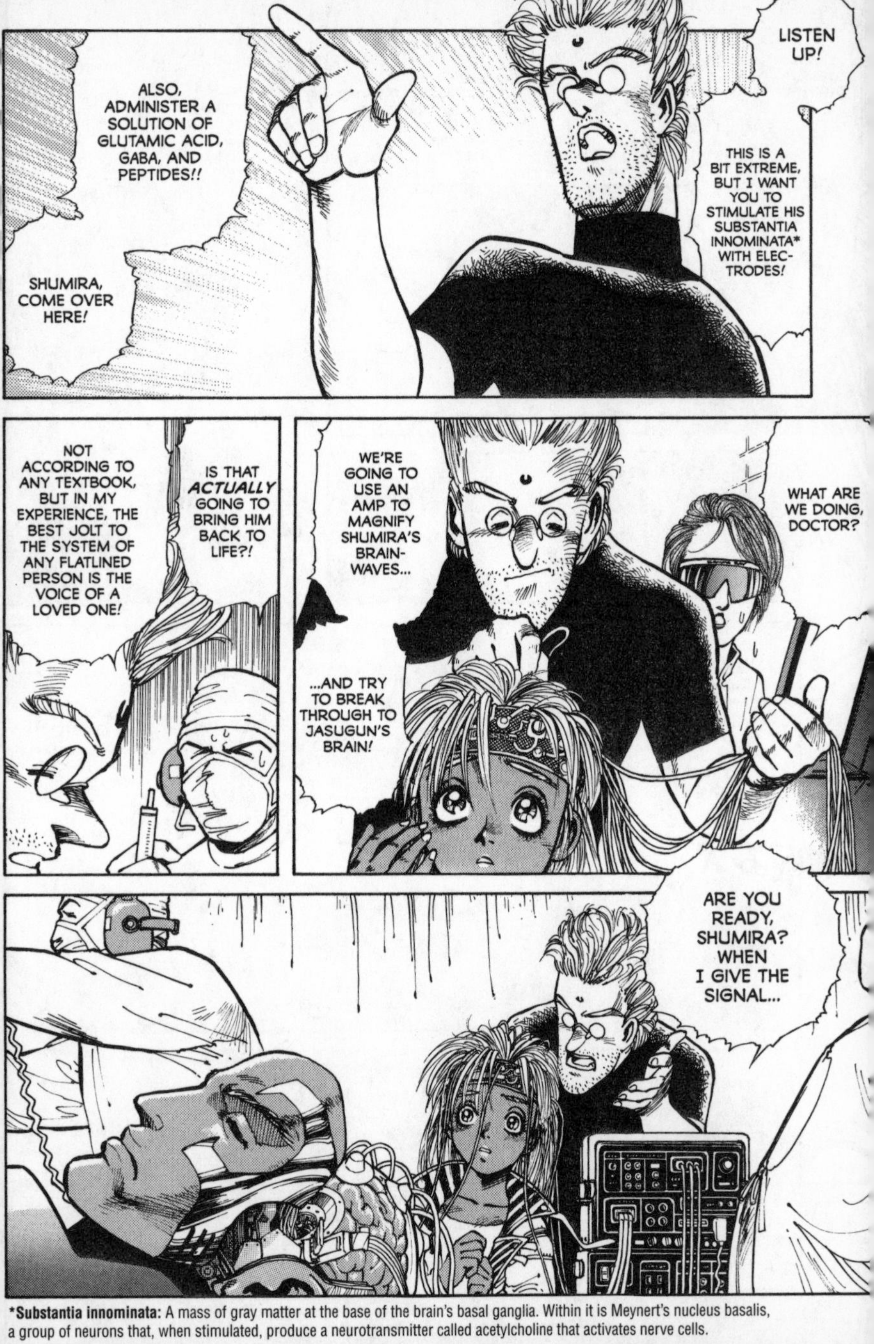
LISTEN UP!
THIS IS A BIT EXTREME, BUT I WANT YOU TO STIMULATE HIS SUBSTANTIA INNOMINATA* WITH ELEC-TRODES!
ALSO, ADMINISTER A SOLUTION OF GLUTAMIC ACID, GABA, AND PEPTIDES!!
SHUMIRA, COME OVER HERE!
WHAT ARE WE DOING, DOCTOR?
WE'RE GOING TO USE AN AMP TO MAGNIFY SHUMIRA'S BRAIN-WAVES...
...AND TRY TO BREAK THROUGH TO JASUGUN'S BRAIN!
IS THAT *ACTUALLY* GOING TO BRING HIM BACK TO LIFE?!
NOT ACCORDING TO ANY TEXTBOOK, BUT IN MY EXPERIENCE, THE BEST JOLT TO THE SYSTEM OF ANY FLATLINED PERSON IS THE VOICE OF A LOVED ONE!
ARE YOU READY, SHUMIRA? WHEN I GIVE THE SIGNAL...

***Substantia innominata:** A mass of gray matter at the base of the brain's basal ganglia. Within it is Meynert's nucleus basalis, a group of neurons that, when stimulated, produce a neurotransmitter called acetylcholine that activates nerve cells.

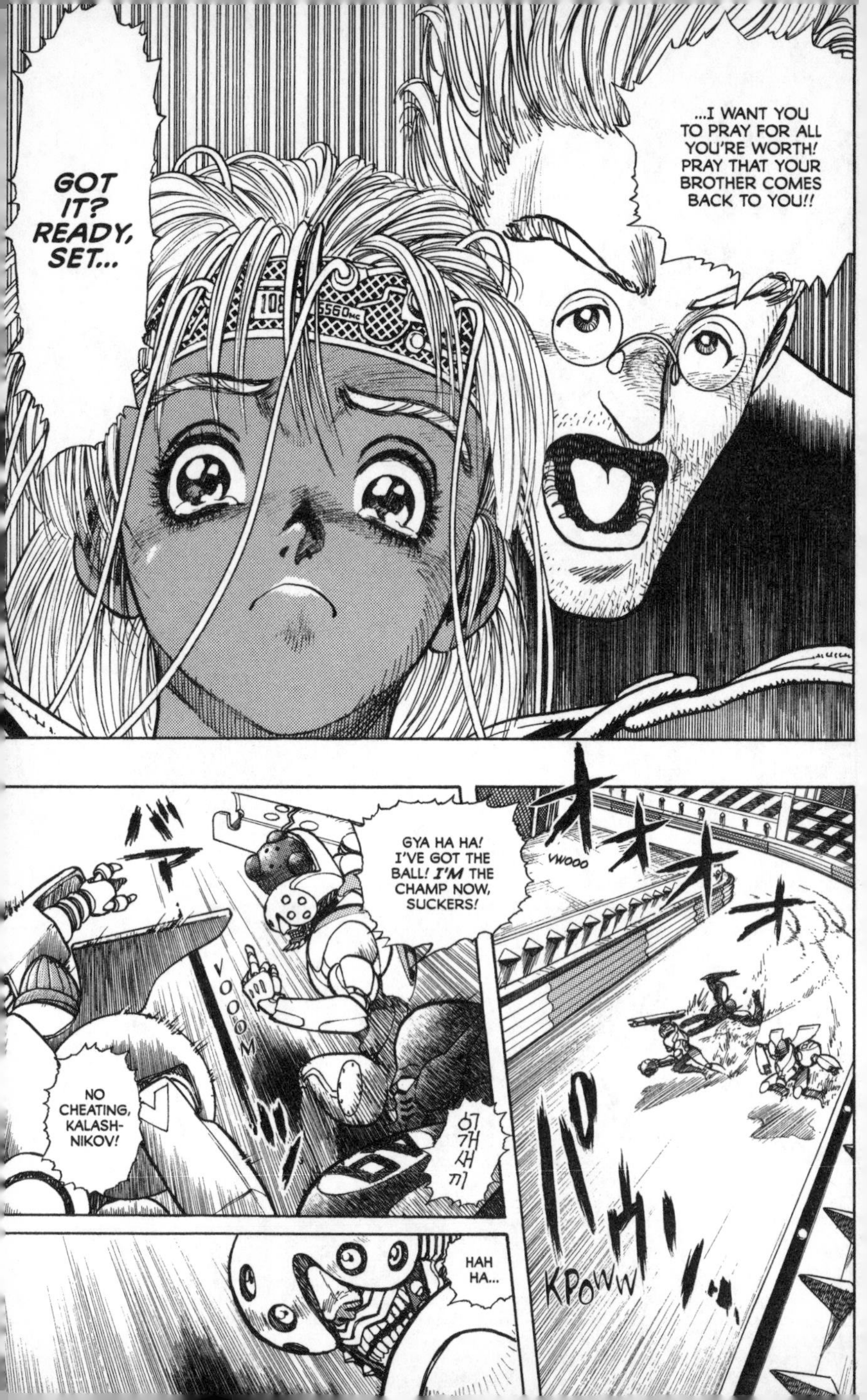
...I WANT YOU TO PRAY FOR ALL YOU'RE WORTH! PRAY THAT YOUR BROTHER COMES BACK TO YOU!!
GOT IT? READY, SET...
VWOOO
KPOWW
GYA HA HA! I'VE GOT THE BALL! I'M THE CHAMP NOW, SUCKERS!
VOOOOM
NO CHEATING, KALASH-NIKOV!
이개새끼
HAH HA...

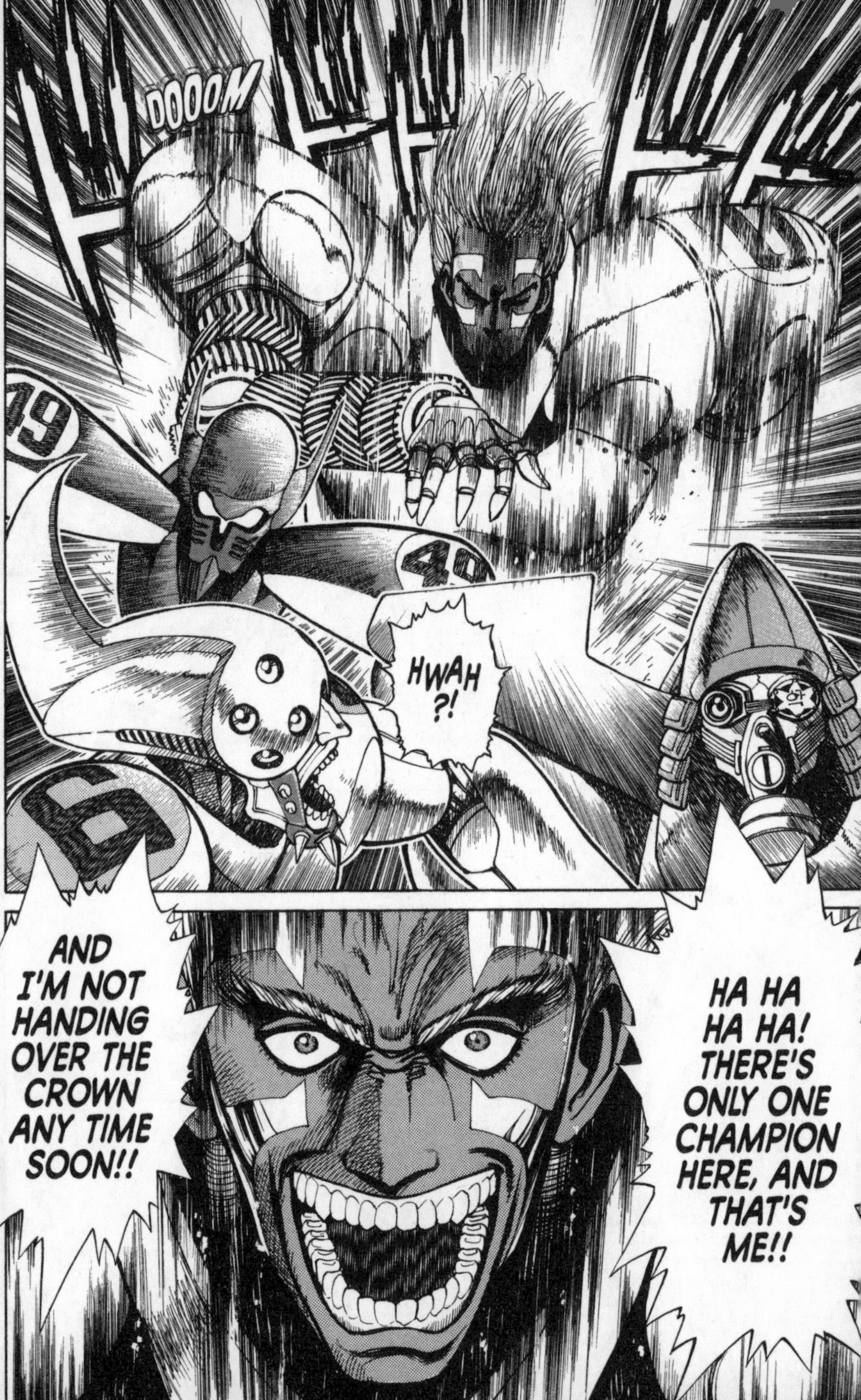
DOOOM
HWAH ?!
HA HA HA HA! THERE'S ONLY ONE CHAMPION HERE, AND THAT'S ME!!
AND I'M NOT HANDING OVER THE CROWN ANY TIME SOON!!

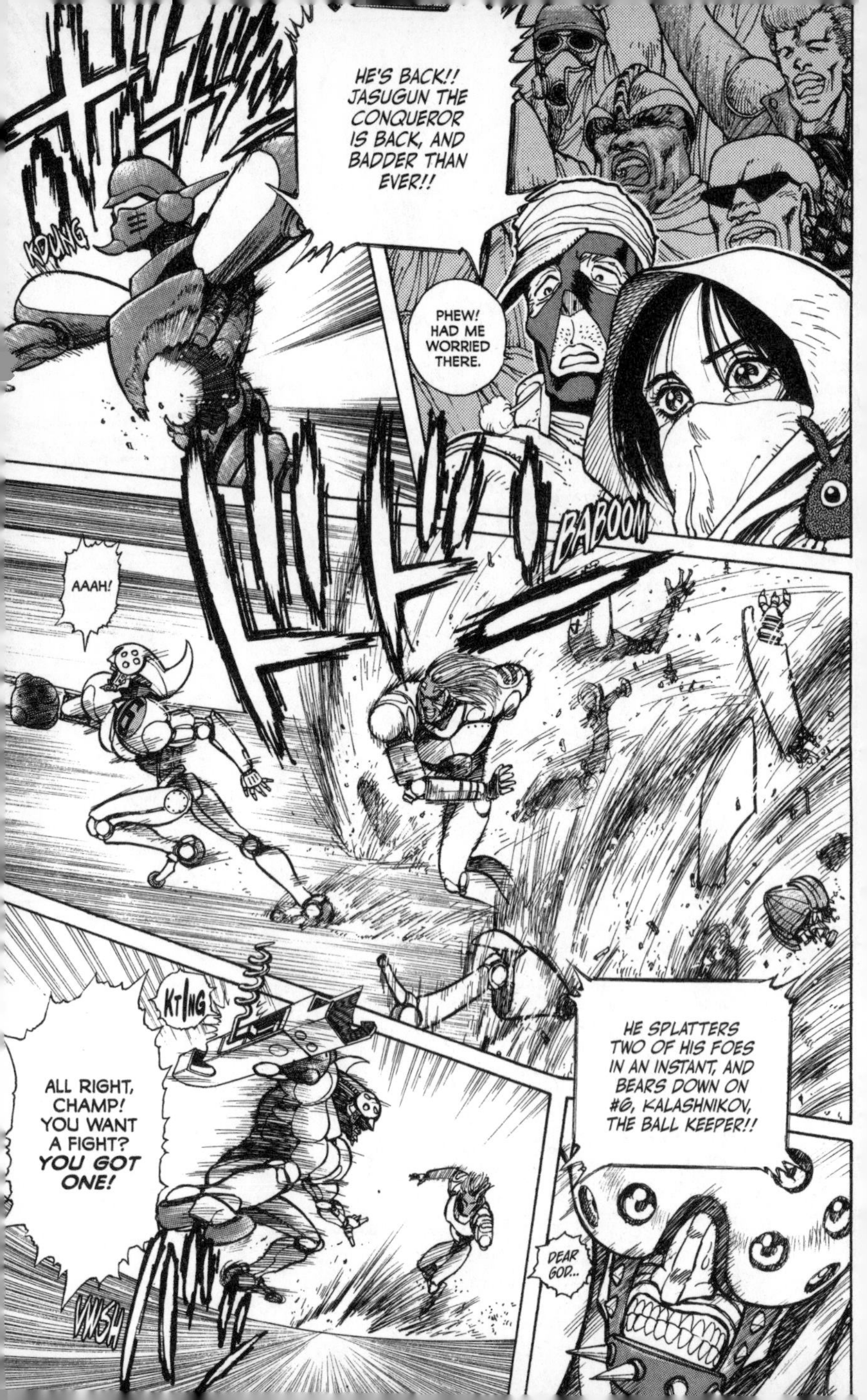
HE'S BACK!! JASUGUN THE CONQUEROR IS BACK, AND BADDER THAN EVER!!
KDUNG
PHEW! HAD ME WORRIED THERE.
BABOOM
AAAH!
HE SPLATTERS TWO OF HIS FOES IN AN INSTANT, AND BEARS DOWN ON #6, KALASHNIKOV, THE BALL KEEPER!!
DEAR GOD...
KTING
ALL RIGHT, CHAMP! YOU WANT A FIGHT? YOU GOT ONE!
VWSH

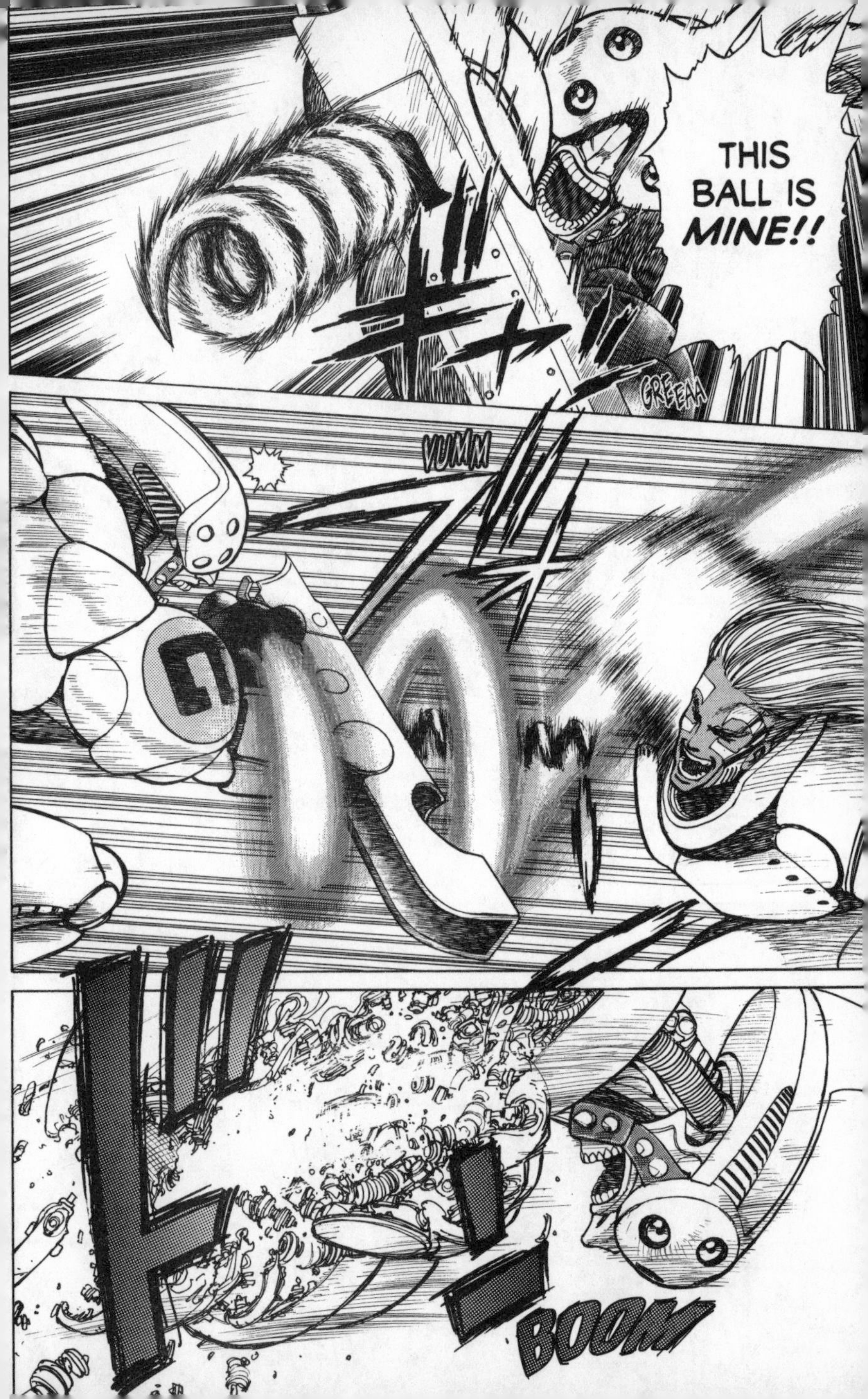
THIS BALL IS MINE!!
GREEAA
VUMM
BOOM

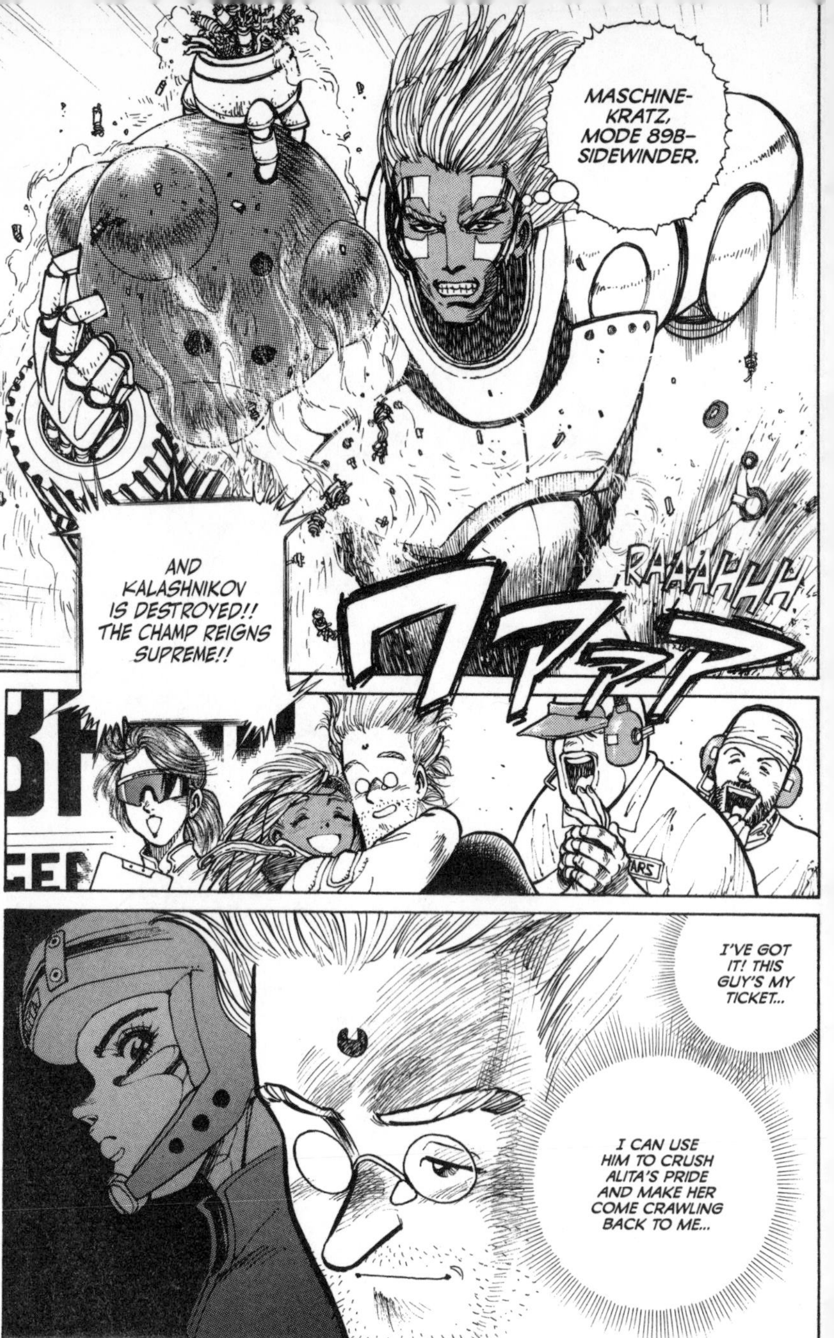
MASCHINE-KRATZ, MODE 89B-SIDEWINDER.
RAAAHHH
AND KALASHNIKOV IS DESTROYED!! THE CHAMP REIGNS SUPREME!!
I'VE GOT IT! THIS GUY'S MY TICKET...
I CAN USE HIM TO CRUSH ALITA'S PRIDE AND MAKE HER COME CRAWLING BACK TO ME...

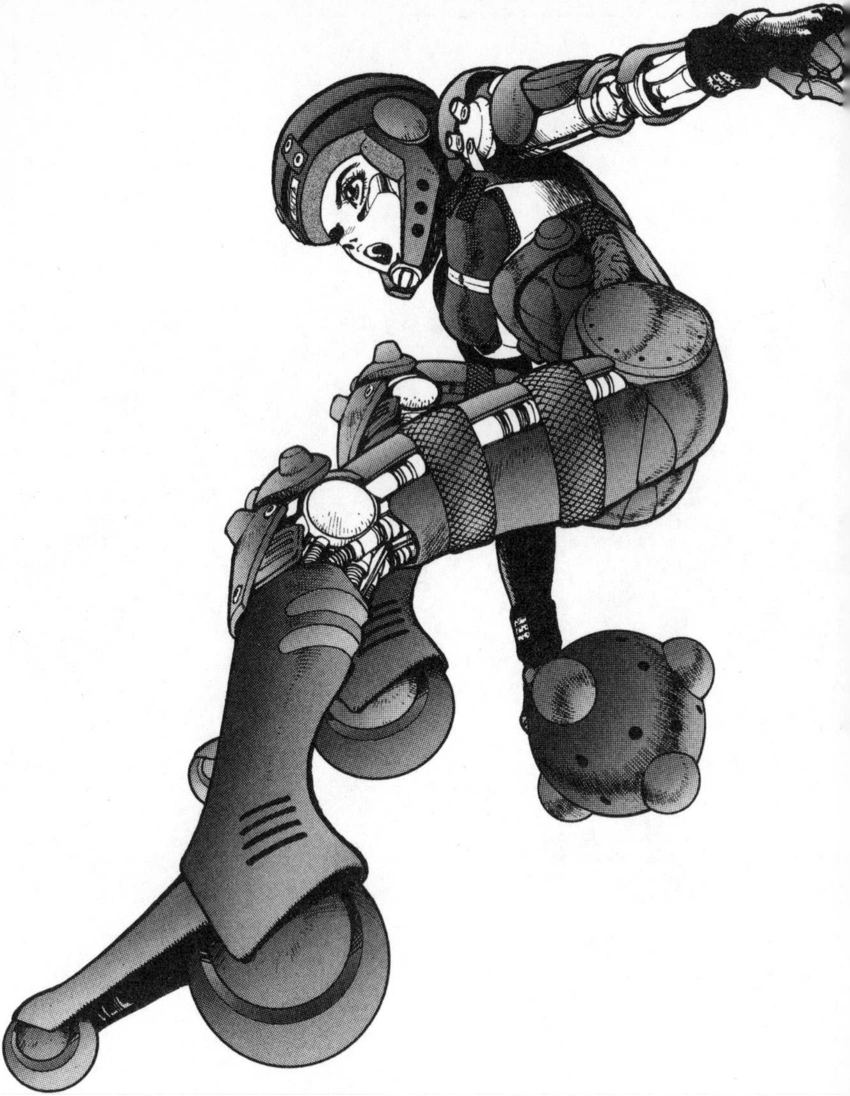

FIGHT_015 Skull Sport

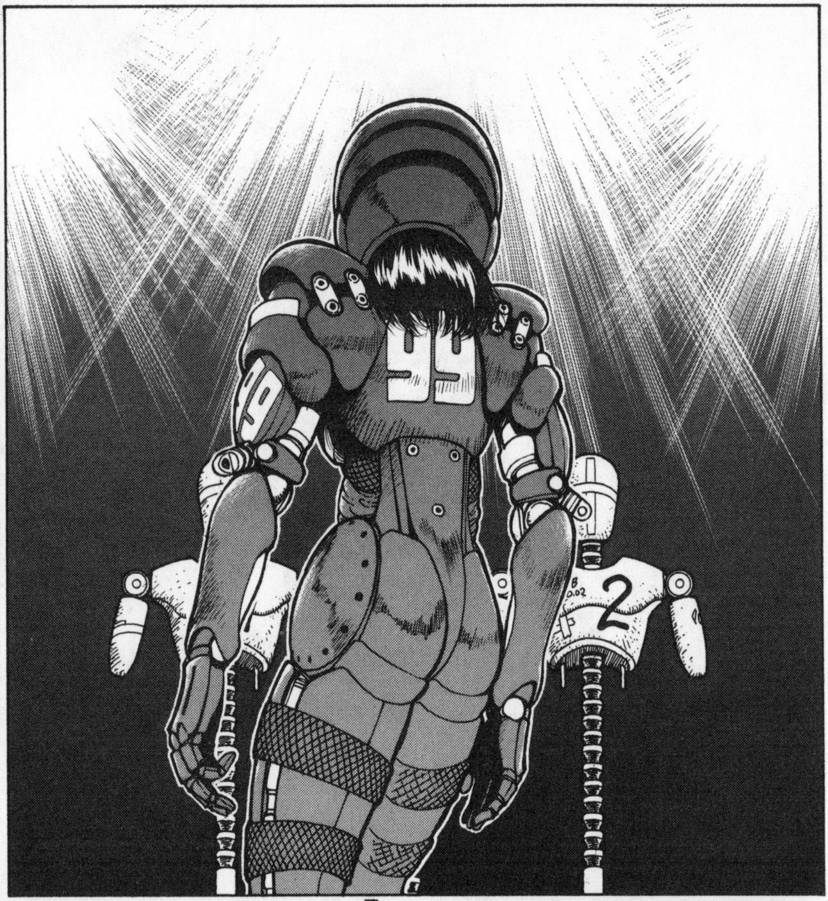
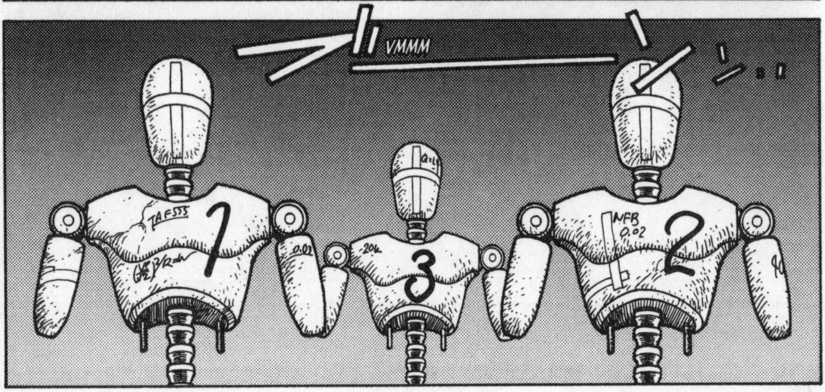
VMMM

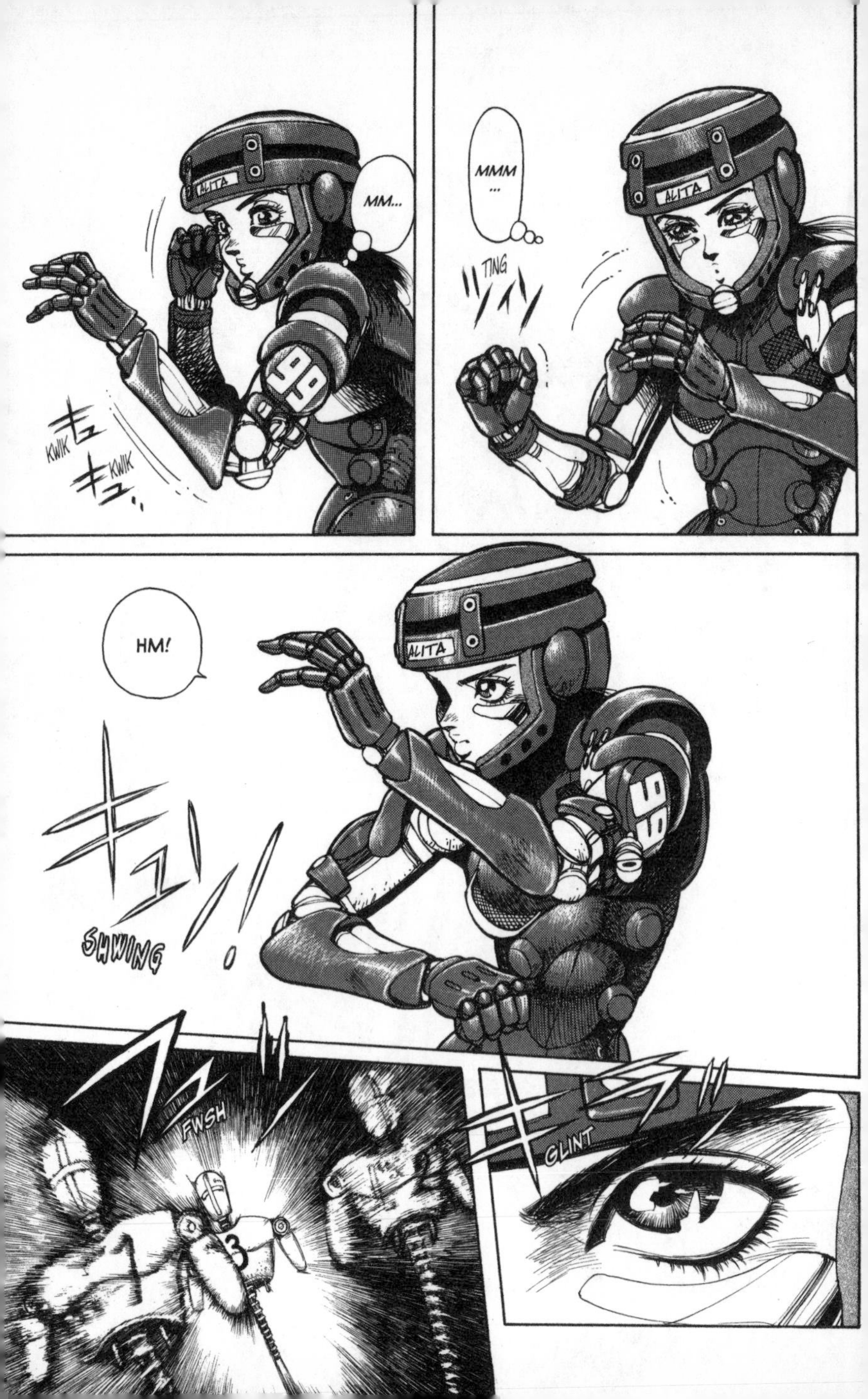
MMM ...
TING
ALITA
MM...
KWIK
KWIK
ALITA
HM!
SHWING
ALITA
GLINT
FWSH

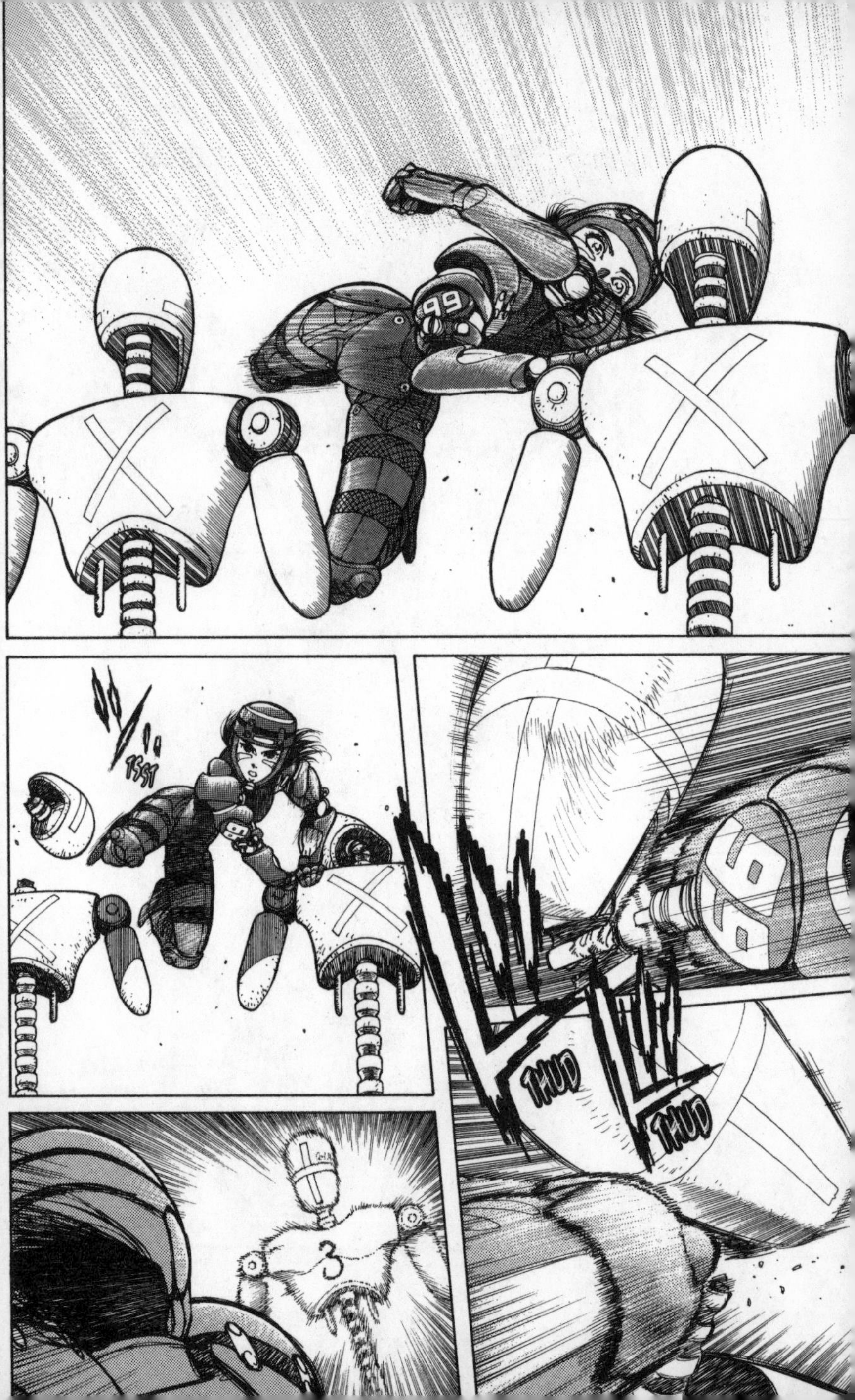
FSSST
THUD
THUD

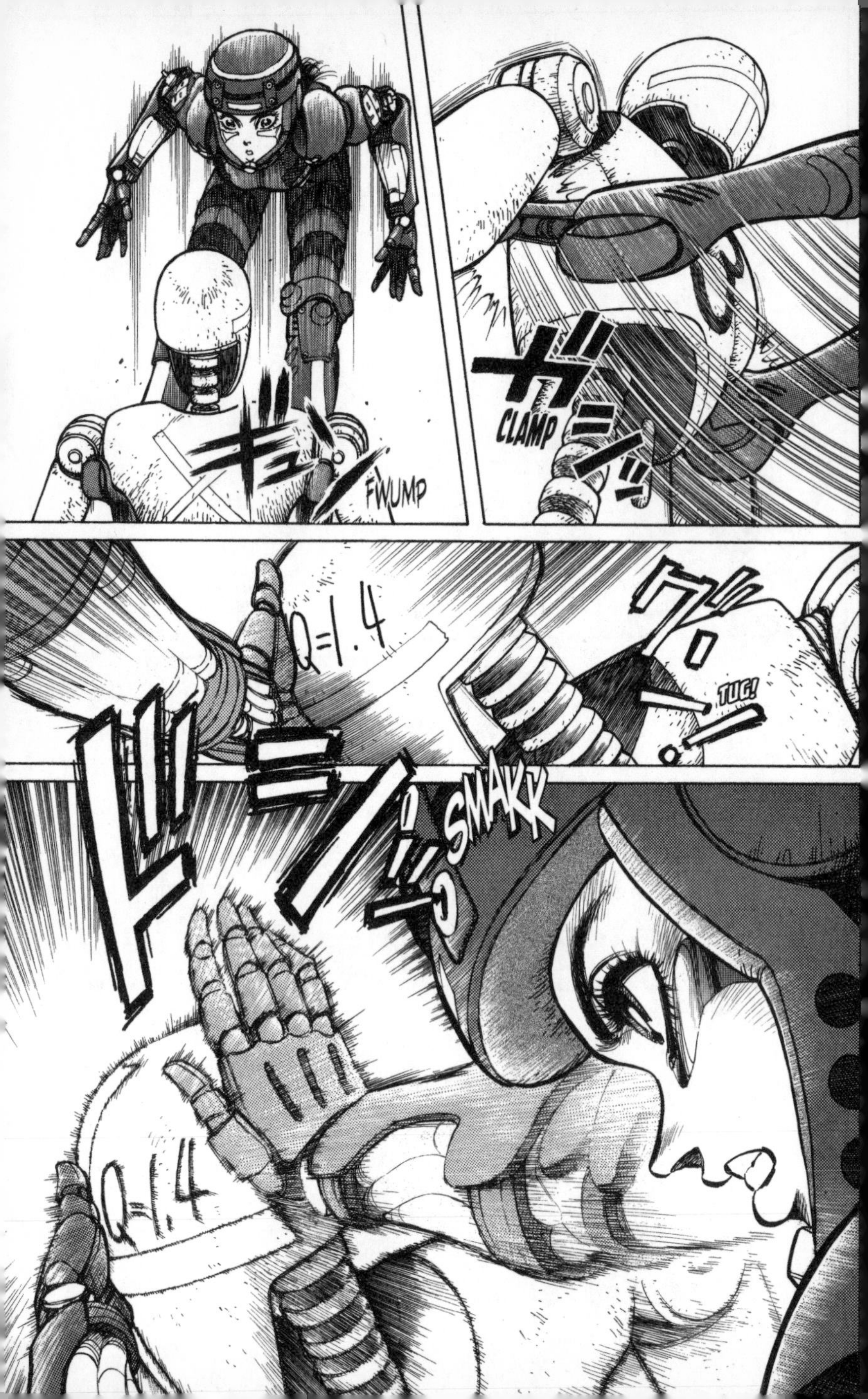
CLAMP
FWUMP
Q=1.4
TUG!
SMAKK
Q=1.4

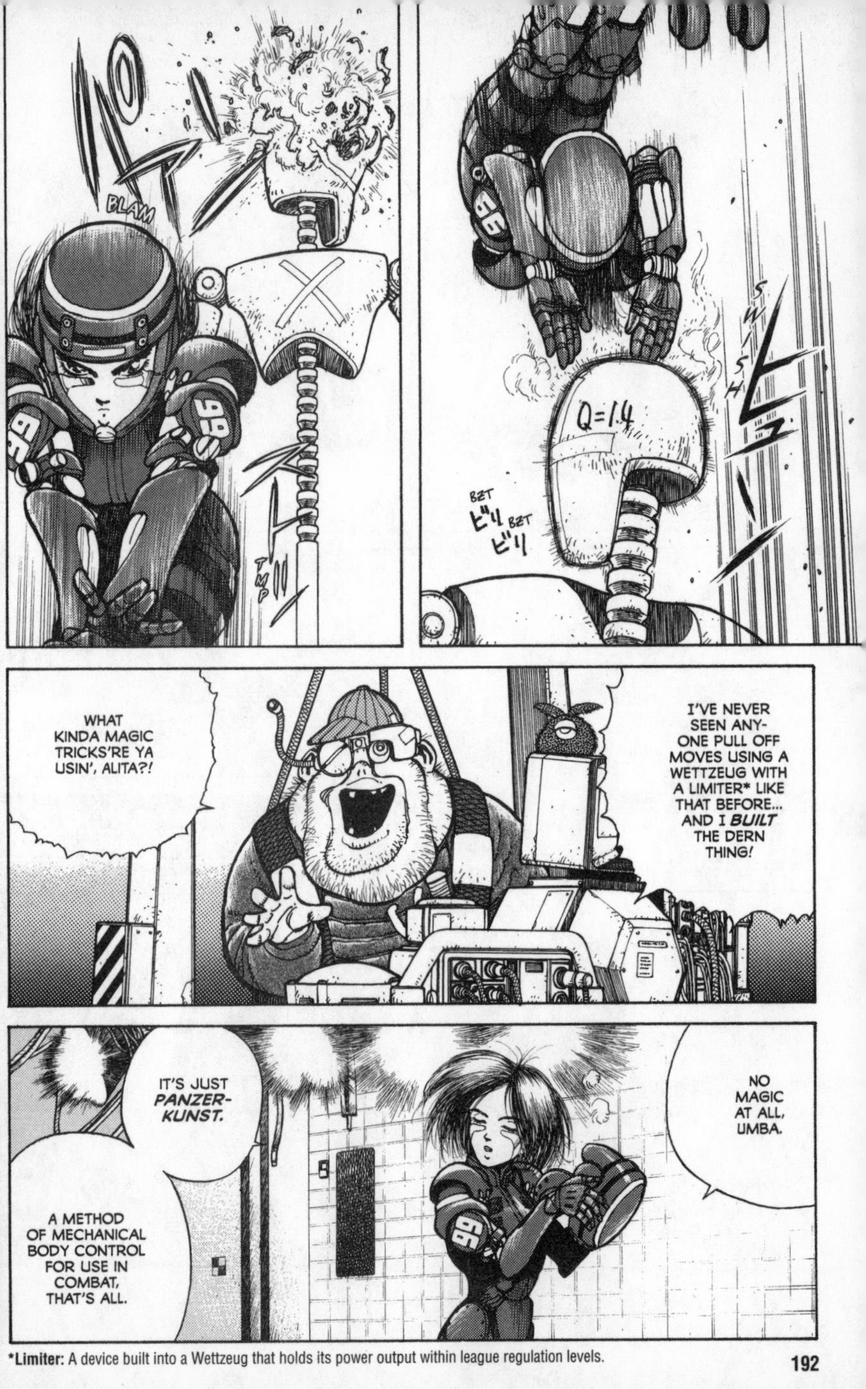
SWISH
BZT
ビリ
BZT
ビリ
BLAM
TMP
I'VE NEVER SEEN ANY-ONE PULL OFF MOVES USING A WETTZEUG WITH A LIMITER* LIKE THAT BEFORE... AND I *BUILT* THE DERN THING!
WHAT KINDA MAGIC TRICKS'RE YA USIN', ALITA?!
NO MAGIC AT ALL, UMBA.
IT'S JUST *PANZER-KUNST.*
A METHOD OF MECHANICAL BODY CONTROL FOR USE IN COMBAT, THAT'S ALL.

***Limiter:** A device built into a Wettzeug that holds its power output within league regulation levels.

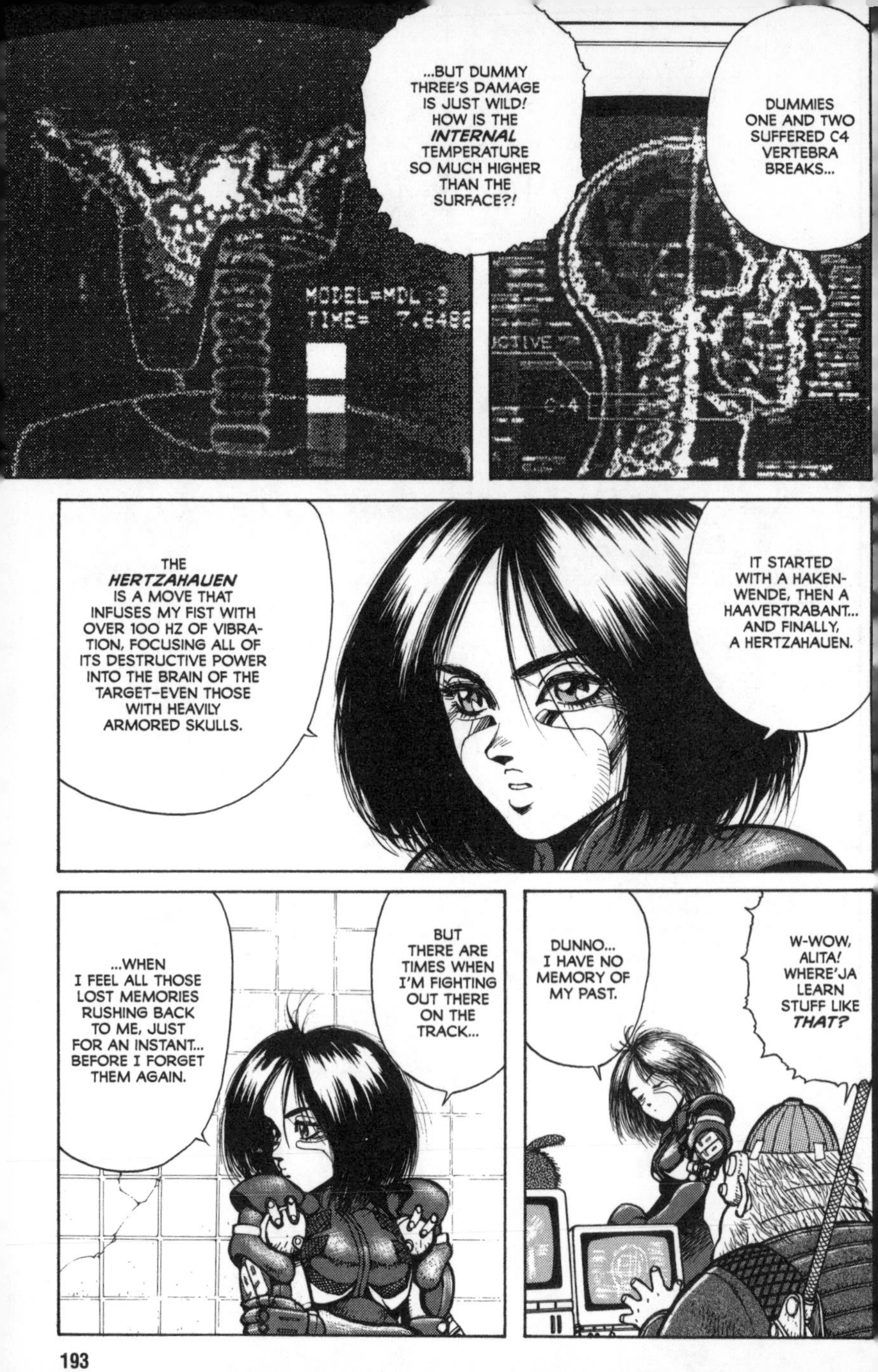
DUMMIES ONE AND TWO SUFFERED C4 VERTEBRA BREAKS...
...BUT DUMMY THREE'S DAMAGE IS JUST WILD! HOW IS THE ***INTERNAL*** TEMPERATURE SO MUCH HIGHER THAN THE SURFACE?!
IT STARTED WITH A HAKEN-WENDE, THEN A HAAVERTRABANT... AND FINALLY, A HERTZAHAUEN.
THE ***HERTZAHAUEN*** IS A MOVE THAT INFUSES MY FIST WITH OVER 100 HZ OF VIBRA-TION, FOCUSING ALL OF ITS DESTRUCTIVE POWER INTO THE BRAIN OF THE TARGET–EVEN THOSE WITH HEAVILY ARMORED SKULLS.
W-WOW, ALITA! WHERE'JA LEARN STUFF LIKE ***THAT?***
DUNNO... I HAVE NO MEMORY OF MY PAST.
BUT THERE ARE TIMES WHEN I'M FIGHTING OUT THERE ON THE TRACK...
...WHEN I FEEL ALL THOSE LOST MEMORIES RUSHING BACK TO ME, JUST FOR AN INSTANT... BEFORE I FORGET THEM AGAIN.

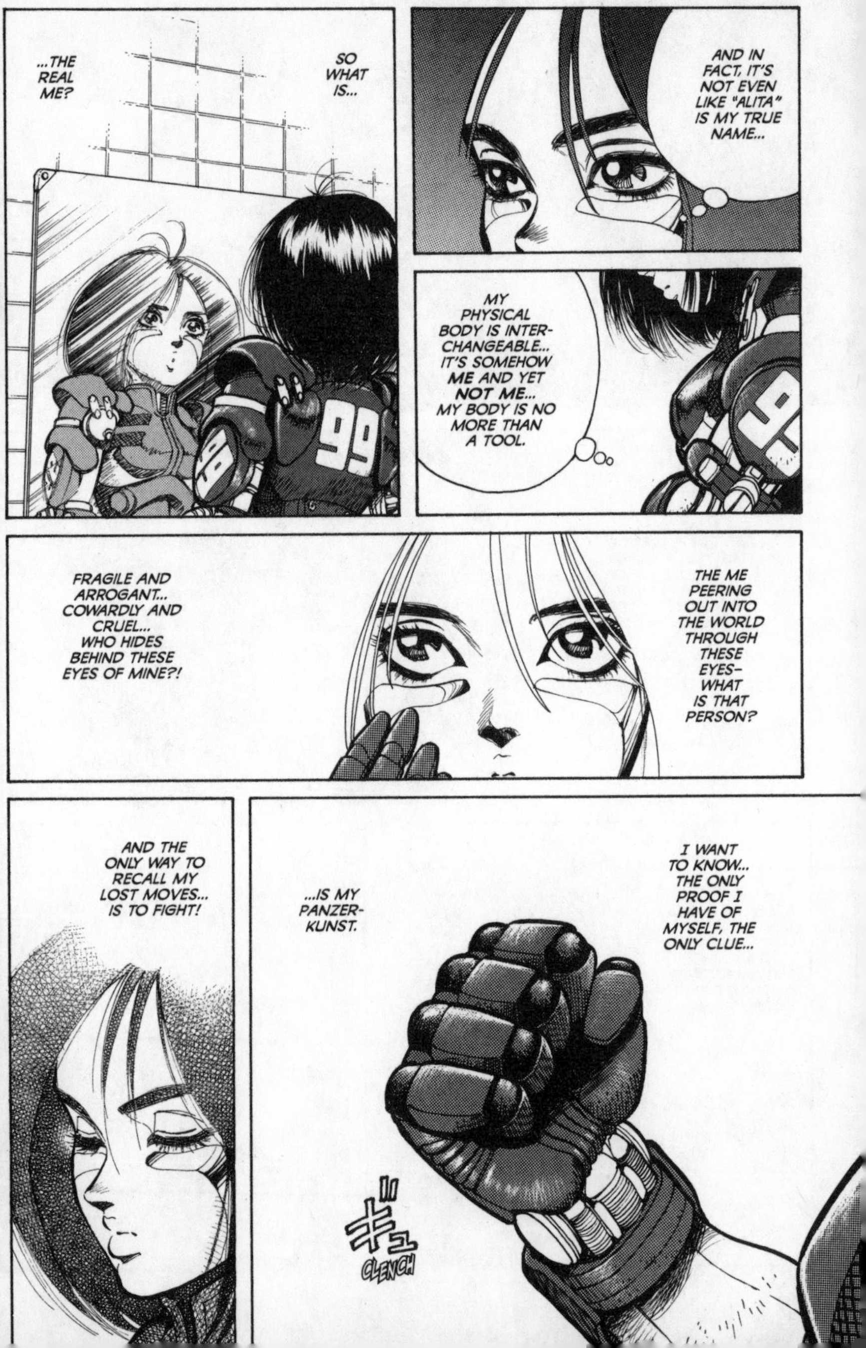
AND IN FACT, IT'S NOT EVEN LIKE "ALITA" IS MY TRUE NAME...
MY PHYSICAL BODY IS INTER-CHANGEABLE... IT'S SOMEHOW ME AND YET NOT ME... MY BODY IS NO MORE THAN A TOOL.
SO WHAT IS...
...THE REAL ME?
THE ME PEERING OUT INTO THE WORLD THROUGH THESE EYES– WHAT IS THAT PERSON?
FRAGILE AND ARROGANT... COWARDLY AND CRUEL... WHO HIDES BEHIND THESE EYES OF MINE?!
I WANT TO KNOW... THE ONLY PROOF I HAVE OF MYSELF, THE ONLY CLUE...
...IS MY PANZER-KUNST.
ギュ
CLENCH
AND THE ONLY WAY TO RECALL MY LOST MOVES... IS TO FIGHT!

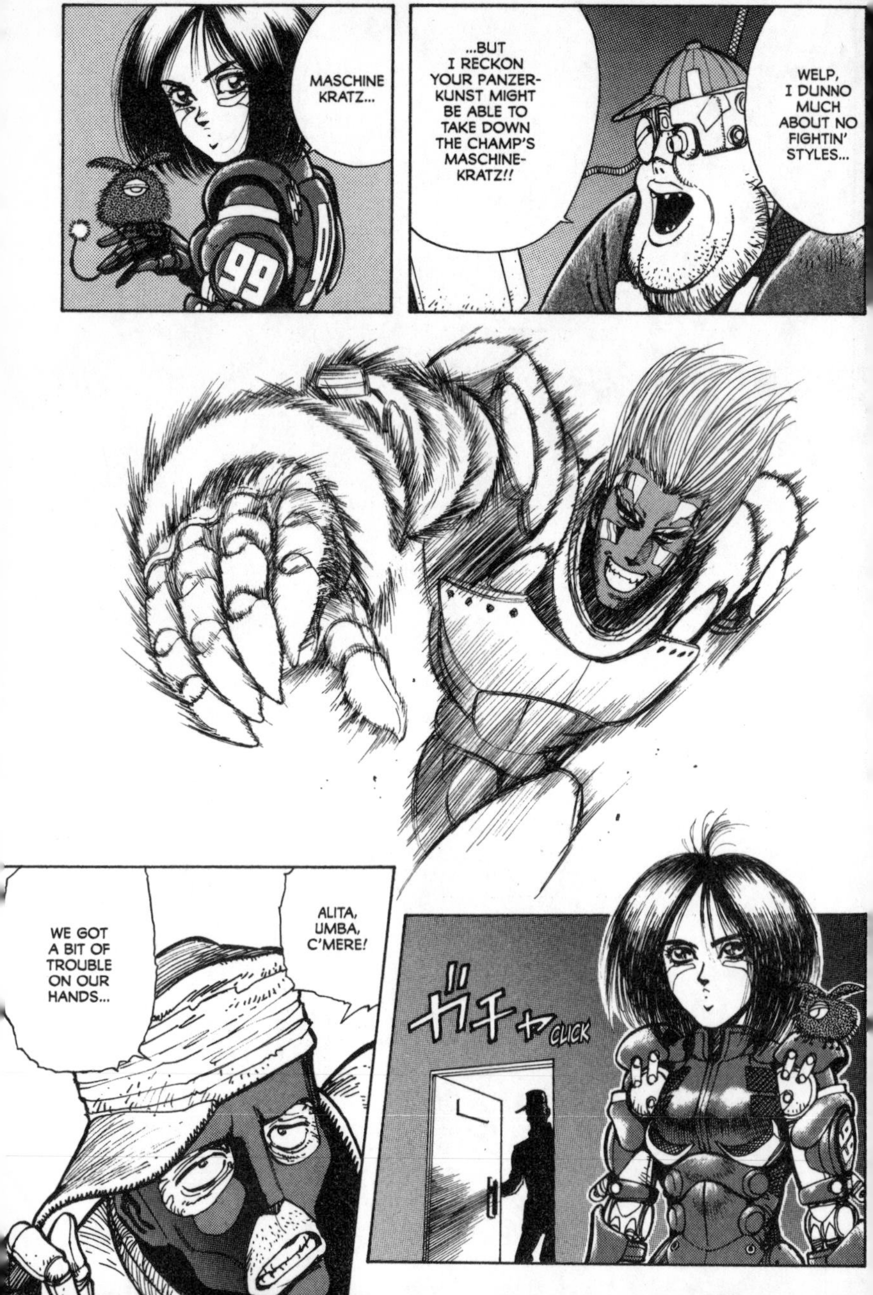
WELP, I DUNNO MUCH ABOUT NO FIGHTIN' STYLES...
...BUT I RECKON YOUR PANZER-KUNST MIGHT BE ABLE TO TAKE DOWN THE CHAMP'S MASCHINE-KRATZ!!
MASCHINE KRATZ...
ガチャ CLICK
ALITA, UMBA, C'MERE!
WE GOT A BIT OF TROUBLE ON OUR HANDS...

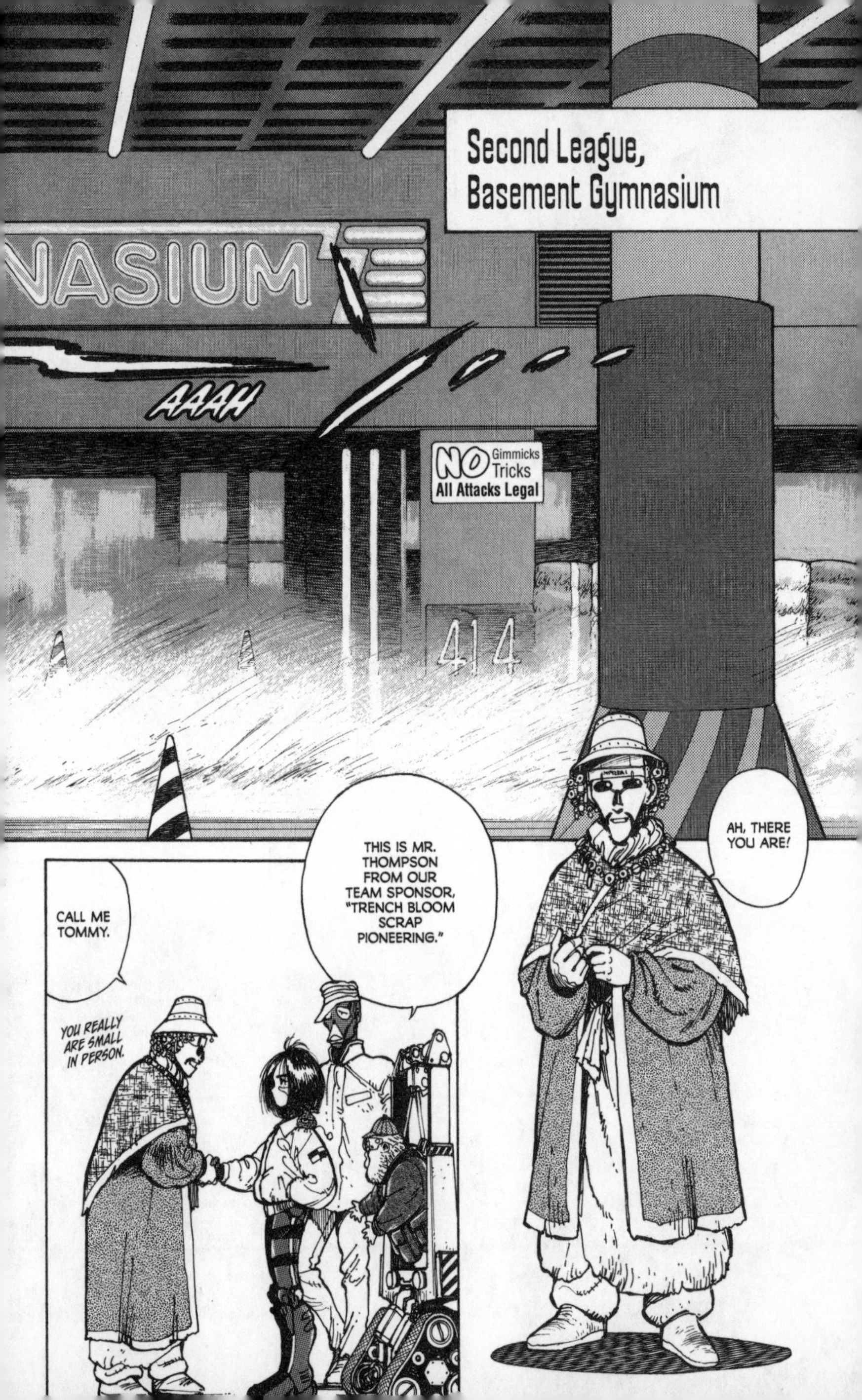
Second League,
Basement Gymnasium
NASIUM
AAAH
NO Gimmicks Tricks
All Attacks Legal
414
AH, THERE YOU ARE!
THIS IS MR. THOMPSON FROM OUR TEAM SPONSOR, "TRENCH BLOOM SCRAP PIONEERING."
CALL ME TOMMY.
YOU REALLY ARE SMALL IN PERSON.

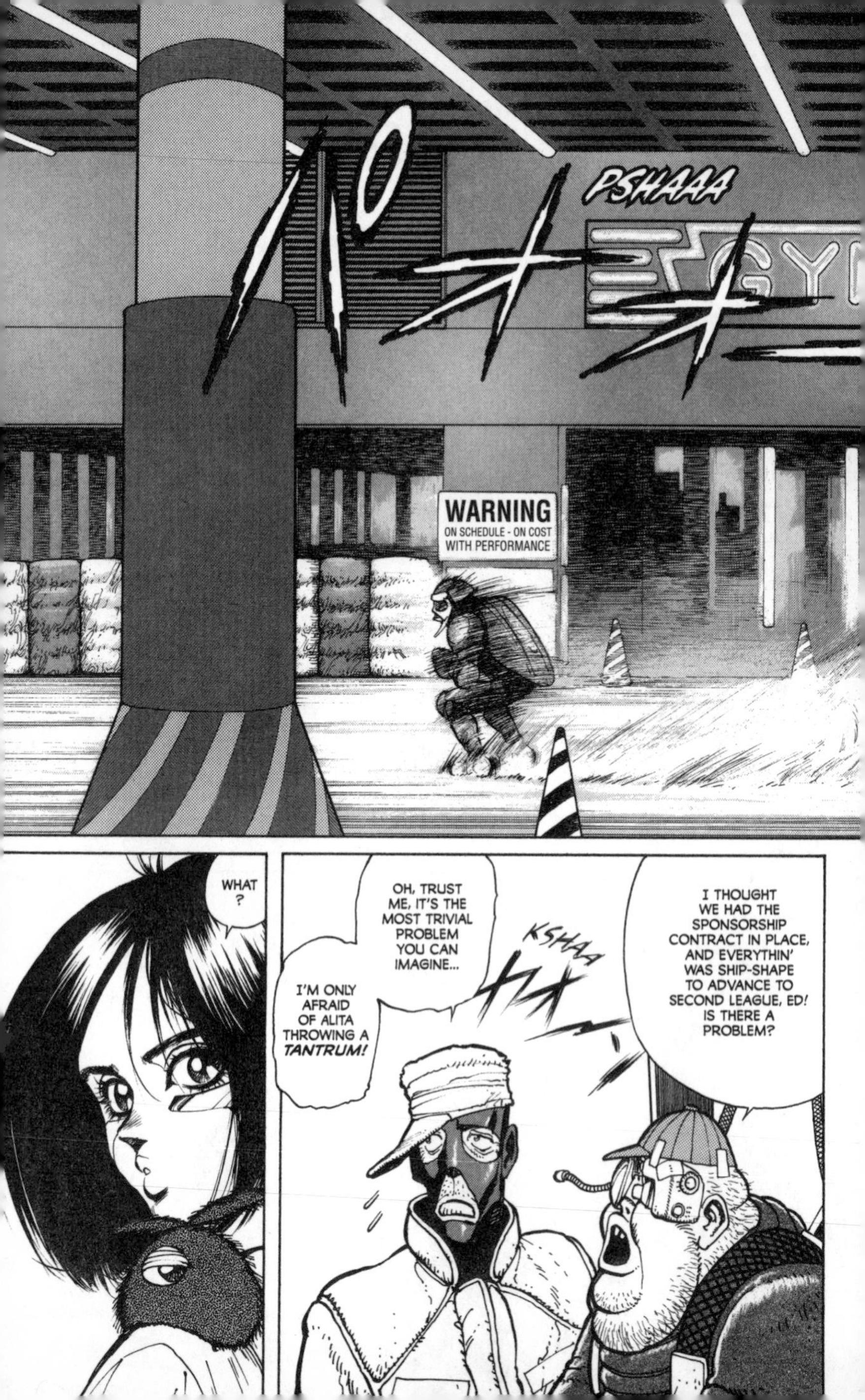
PSHAAA
WARNING
ON SCHEDULE - ON COST
WITH PERFORMANCE
I THOUGHT WE HAD THE SPONSORSHIP CONTRACT IN PLACE, AND EVERYTHIN' WAS SHIP-SHAPE TO ADVANCE TO SECOND LEAGUE, ED! IS THERE A PROBLEM?
KSHAA
OH, TRUST ME, IT'S THE MOST TRIVIAL PROBLEM YOU CAN IMAGINE...
I'M ONLY AFRAID OF ALITA THROWING A *TANTRUM!*
WHAT ?

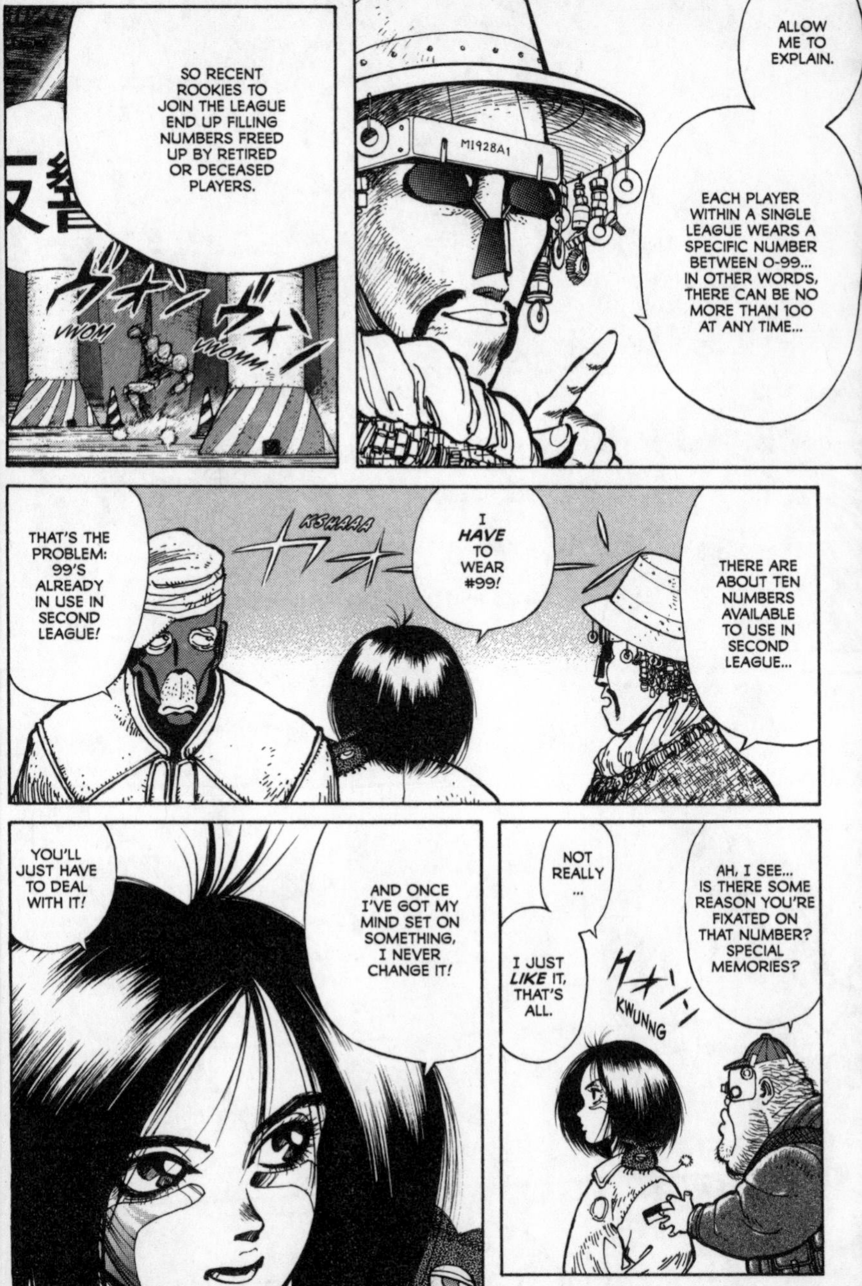
ALLOW ME TO EXPLAIN.
EACH PLAYER WITHIN A SINGLE LEAGUE WEARS A SPECIFIC NUMBER BETWEEN 0-99... IN OTHER WORDS, THERE CAN BE NO MORE THAN 100 AT ANY TIME...
M1928A1
SO RECENT ROOKIES TO JOIN THE LEAGUE END UP FILLING NUMBERS FREED UP BY RETIRED OR DECEASED PLAYERS.
VWOM
VWOMM
THERE ARE ABOUT TEN NUMBERS AVAILABLE TO USE IN SECOND LEAGUE...
I ***HAVE*** TO WEAR #99!
KSHAAA
THAT'S THE PROBLEM: 99'S ALREADY IN USE IN SECOND LEAGUE!
AH, I SEE... IS THERE SOME REASON YOU'RE FIXATED ON THAT NUMBER? SPECIAL MEMORIES?
NOT REALLY ...
KWUNNG
I JUST ***LIKE*** IT, THAT'S ALL.
AND ONCE I'VE GOT MY MIND SET ON SOMETHING, I NEVER CHANGE IT!
YOU'LL JUST HAVE TO DEAL WITH IT!

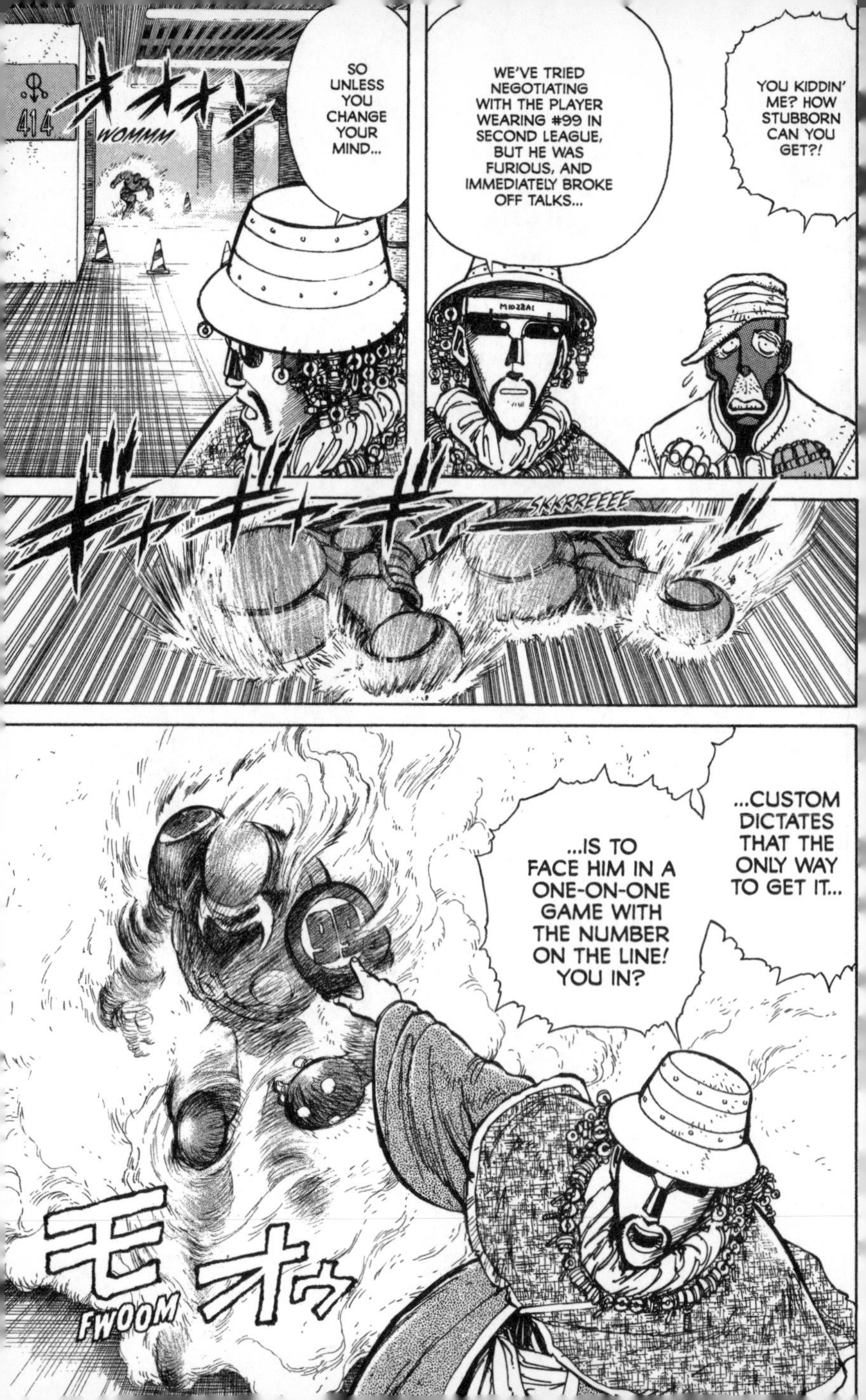
YOU KIDDIN' ME? HOW STUBBORN CAN YOU GET?!
WE'VE TRIED NEGOTIATING WITH THE PLAYER WEARING #99 IN SECOND LEAGUE, BUT HE WAS FURIOUS, AND IMMEDIATELY BROKE OFF TALKS...
SO UNLESS YOU CHANGE YOUR MIND...
414
WOMMM
SKKRREEEE
...CUSTOM DICTATES THAT THE ONLY WAY TO GET IT...
...IS TO FACE HIM IN A ONE-ON-ONE GAME WITH THE NUMBER ON THE LINE! YOU IN?
FWOOM

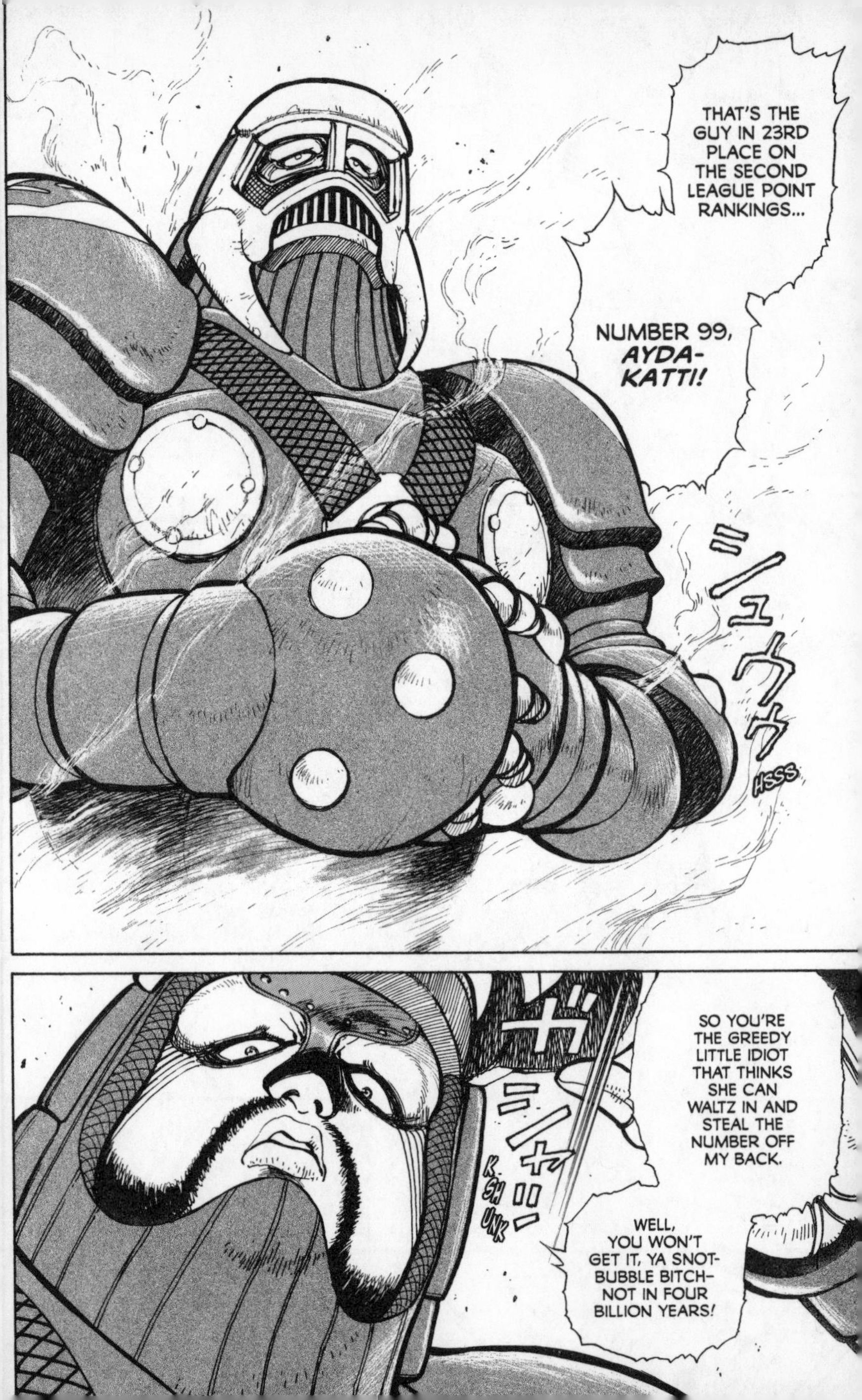
THAT'S THE GUY IN 23RD PLACE ON THE SECOND LEAGUE POINT RANKINGS...
NUMBER 99, AYDA-KATTI!
シュウウ
HSSS
SO YOU'RE THE GREEDY LITTLE IDIOT THAT THINKS SHE CAN WALTZ IN AND STEAL THE NUMBER OFF MY BACK.
ガシャ
K-SHUNK
WELL, YOU WON'T GET IT, YA SNOT-BUBBLE BITCH— NOT IN FOUR BILLION YEARS!

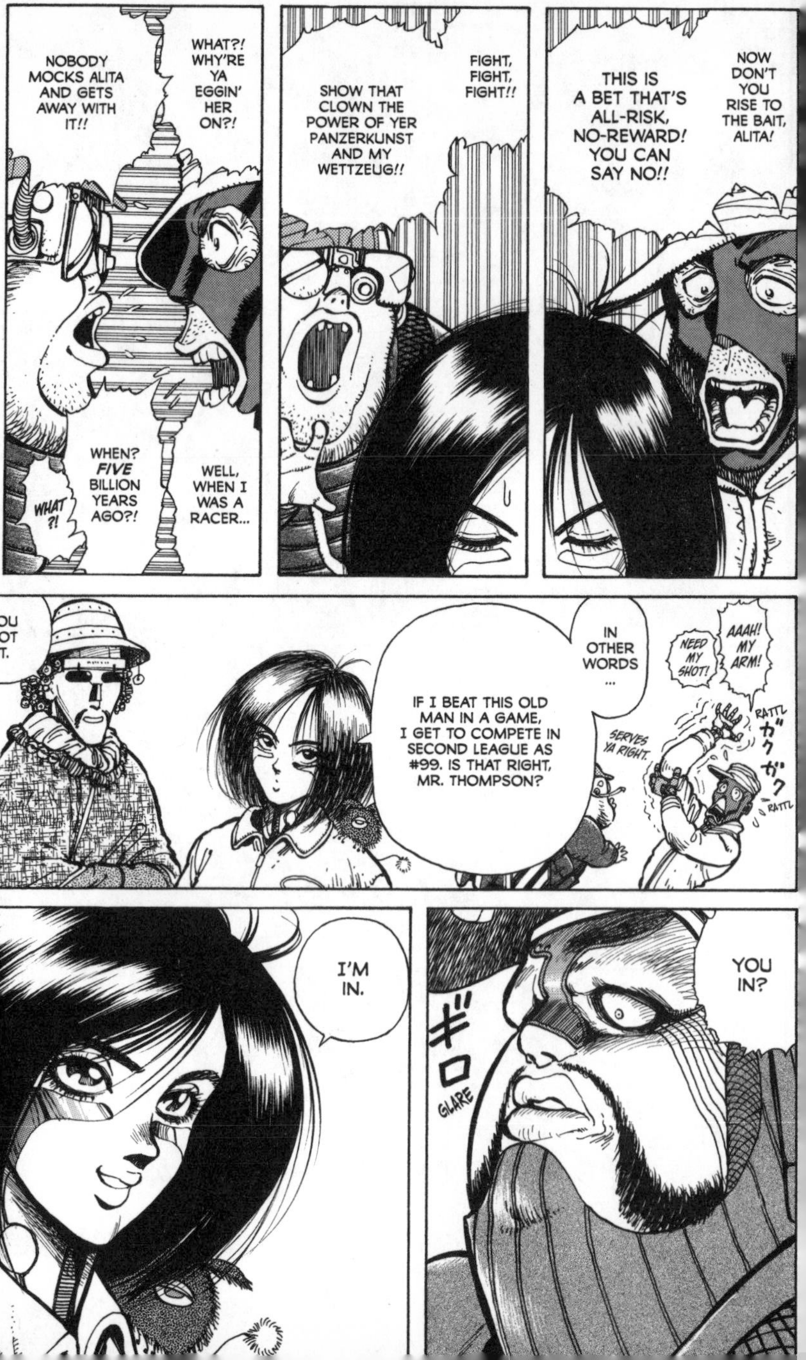
NOW DON'T YOU RISE TO THE BAIT, ALITA!
THIS IS A BET THAT'S ALL-RISK, NO-REWARD! YOU CAN SAY NO!!
FIGHT, FIGHT, FIGHT!!
SHOW THAT CLOWN THE POWER OF YER PANZERKUNST AND MY WETTZEUG!!
WHAT?! WHY'RE YA EGGIN' HER ON?!
NOBODY MOCKS ALITA AND GETS AWAY WITH IT!!
WELL, WHEN I WAS A RACER...
WHEN? FIVE BILLION YEARS AGO?!
WHAT?!
AAAH! MY ARM!
NEED MY SHOT!
RATTL
RATTL
SERVES YA RIGHT.
IN OTHER WORDS ...
IF I BEAT THIS OLD MAN IN A GAME, I GET TO COMPETE IN SECOND LEAGUE AS #99. IS THAT RIGHT, MR. THOMPSON?
YOU GOT IT.
CALL ME TOMMY.
YOU IN?
GLARE
I'M IN.

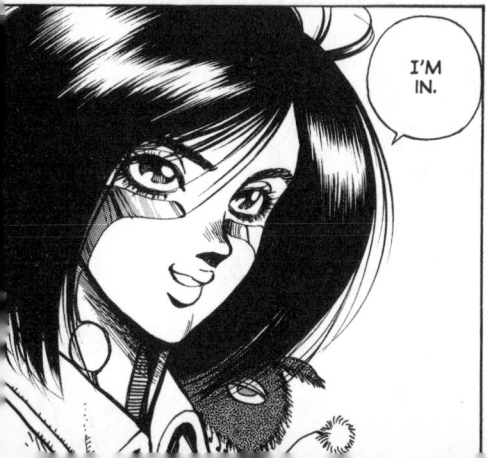

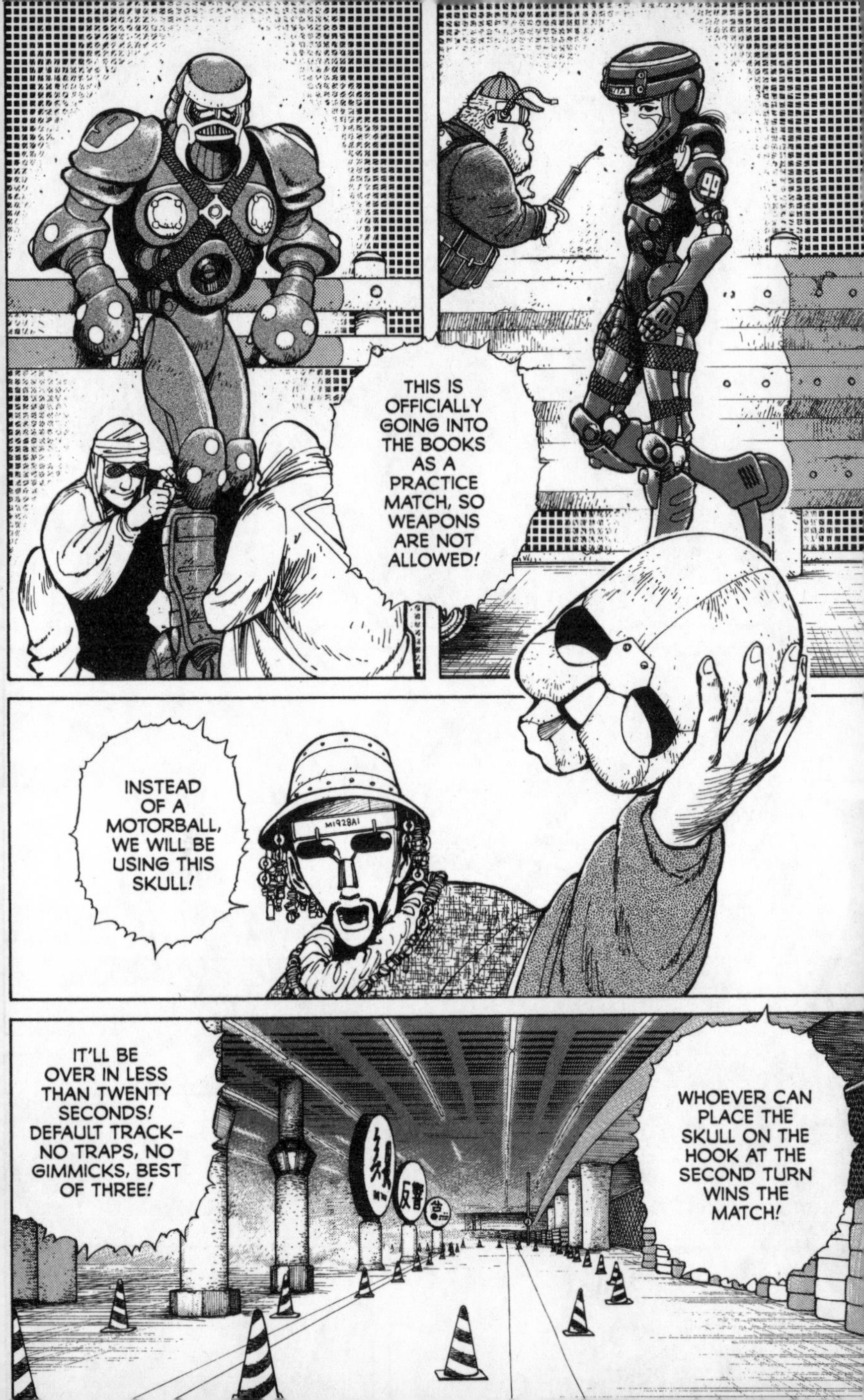
THIS IS OFFICIALLY GOING INTO THE BOOKS AS A PRACTICE MATCH, SO WEAPONS ARE NOT ALLOWED!
INSTEAD OF A MOTORBALL, WE WILL BE USING THIS SKULL!
M1928A1
WHOEVER CAN PLACE THE SKULL ON THE HOOK AT THE SECOND TURN WINS THE MATCH!
IT'LL BE OVER IN LESS THAN TWENTY SECONDS! DEFAULT TRACK-NO TRAPS, NO GIMMICKS, BEST OF THREE!

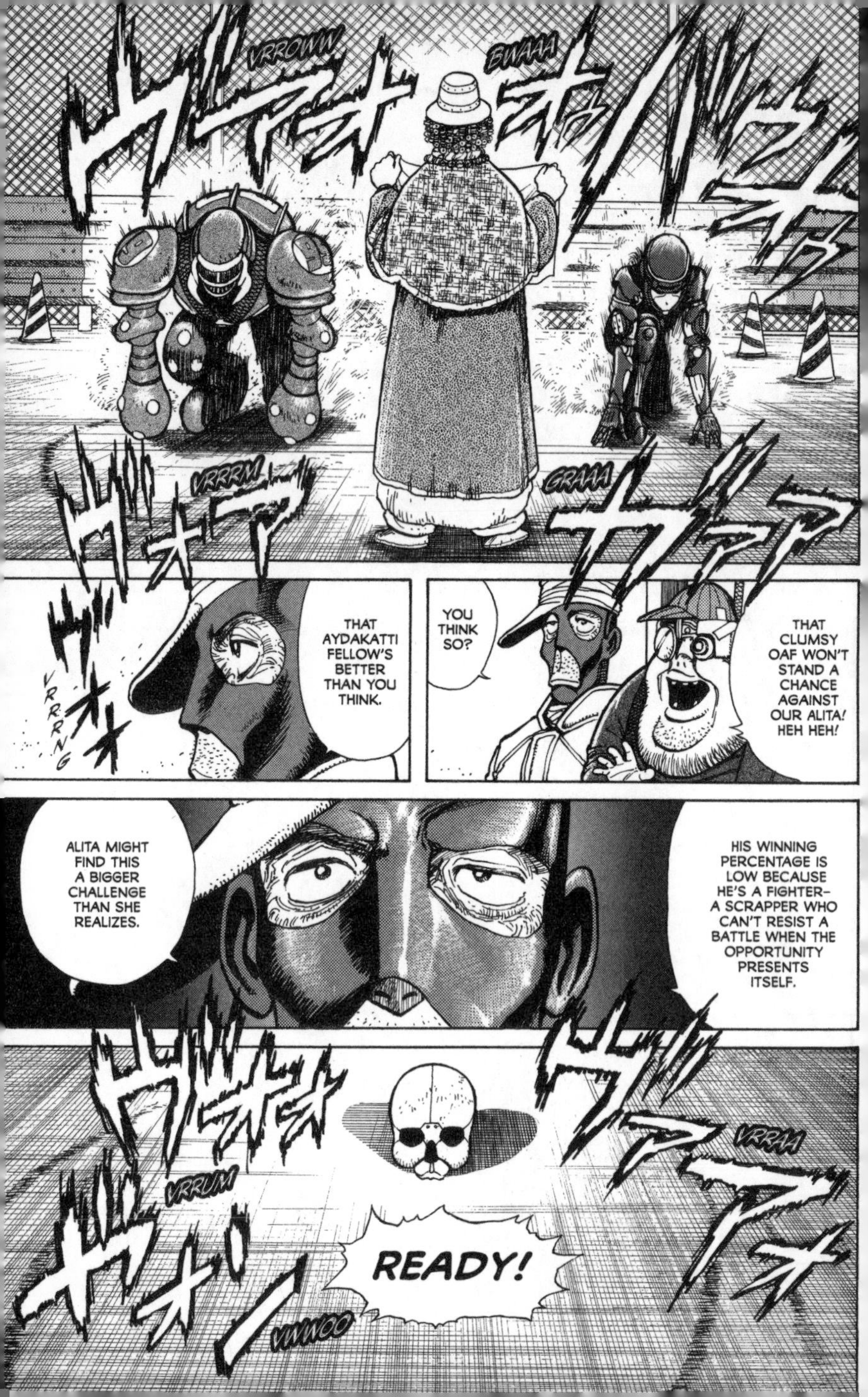
BWAAA
VRROWW
GRAAA
VRRRM
THAT CLUMSY OAF WON'T STAND A CHANCE AGAINST OUR ALITA! HEH HEH!
YOU THINK SO?
THAT AYDAKATTI FELLOW'S BETTER THAN YOU THINK.
VRRRNG
HIS WINNING PERCENTAGE IS LOW BECAUSE HE'S A FIGHTER– A SCRAPPER WHO CAN'T RESIST A BATTLE WHEN THE OPPORTUNITY PRESENTS ITSELF.
ALITA MIGHT FIND THIS A BIGGER CHALLENGE THAN SHE REALIZES.
VRRAA
READY!
VRRUM
VWWOO

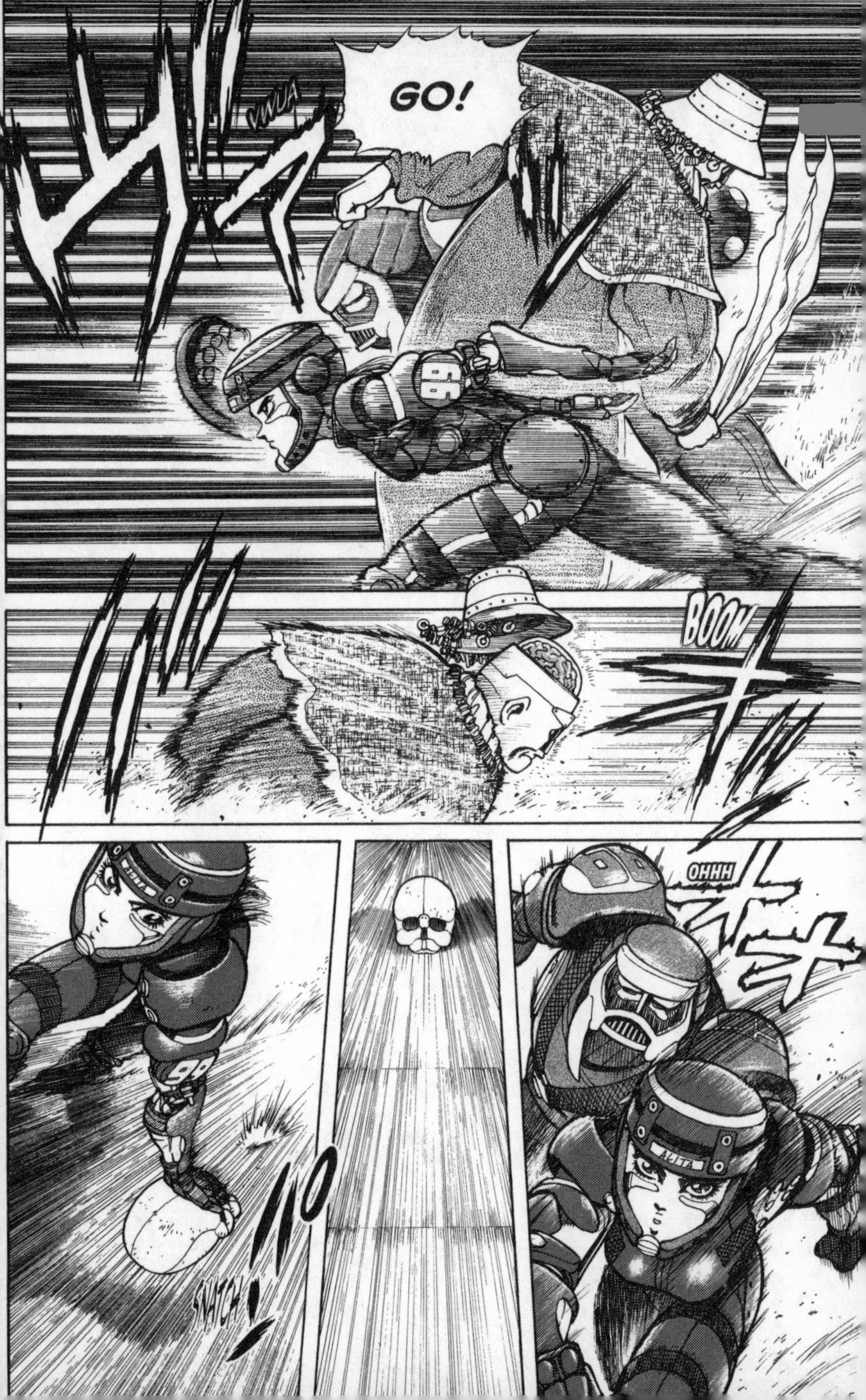
GO!
VWUA
BOOM
OHHH
SNATCH

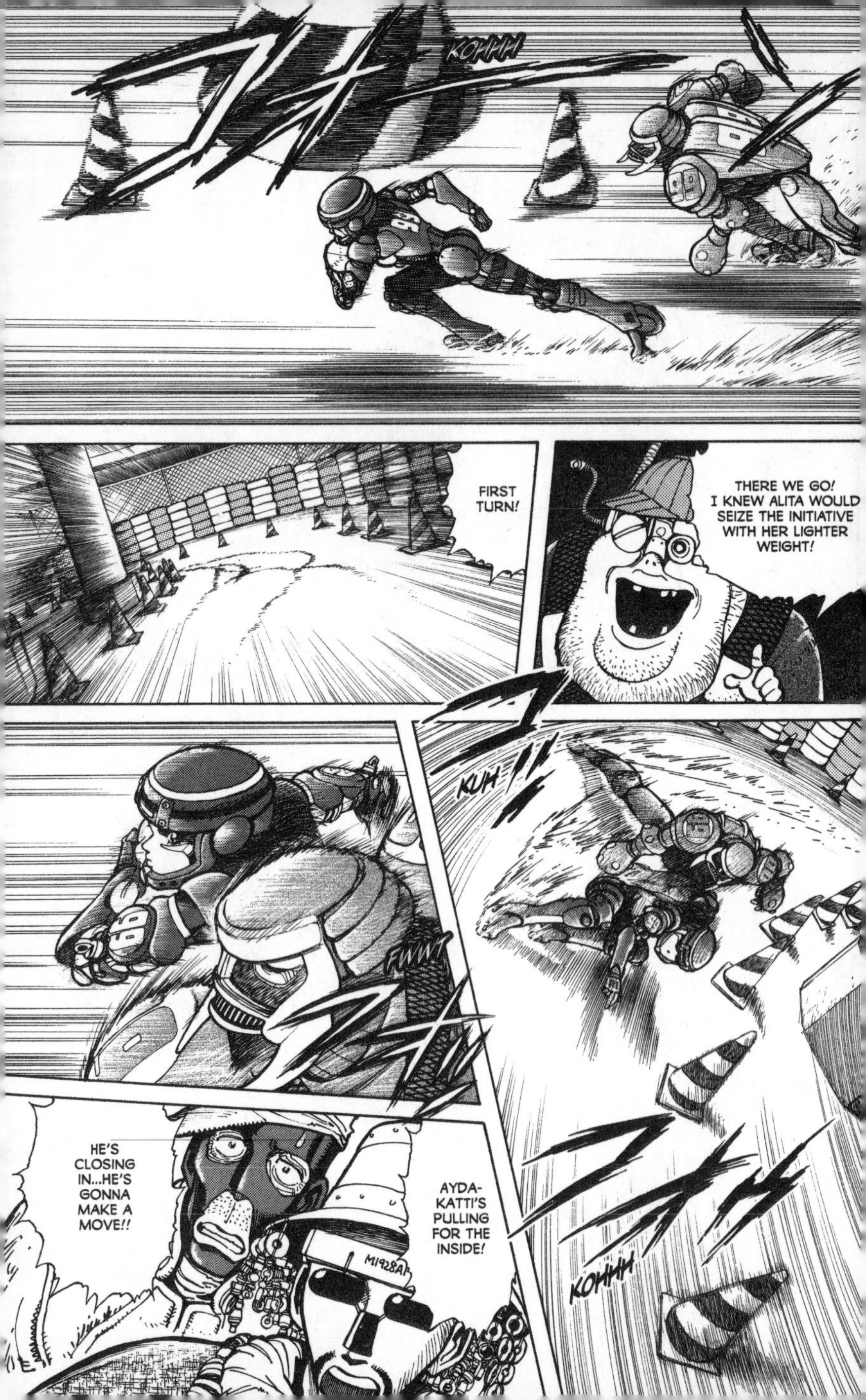
KOHHH
THERE WE GO! I KNEW ALITA WOULD SEIZE THE INITIATIVE WITH HER LIGHTER WEIGHT!
FIRST TURN!
KUH
KOHHH
FWWT
AYDA-KATTI'S PULLING FOR THE INSIDE!
HE'S CLOSING IN...HE'S GONNA MAKE A MOVE!!
M1928AP

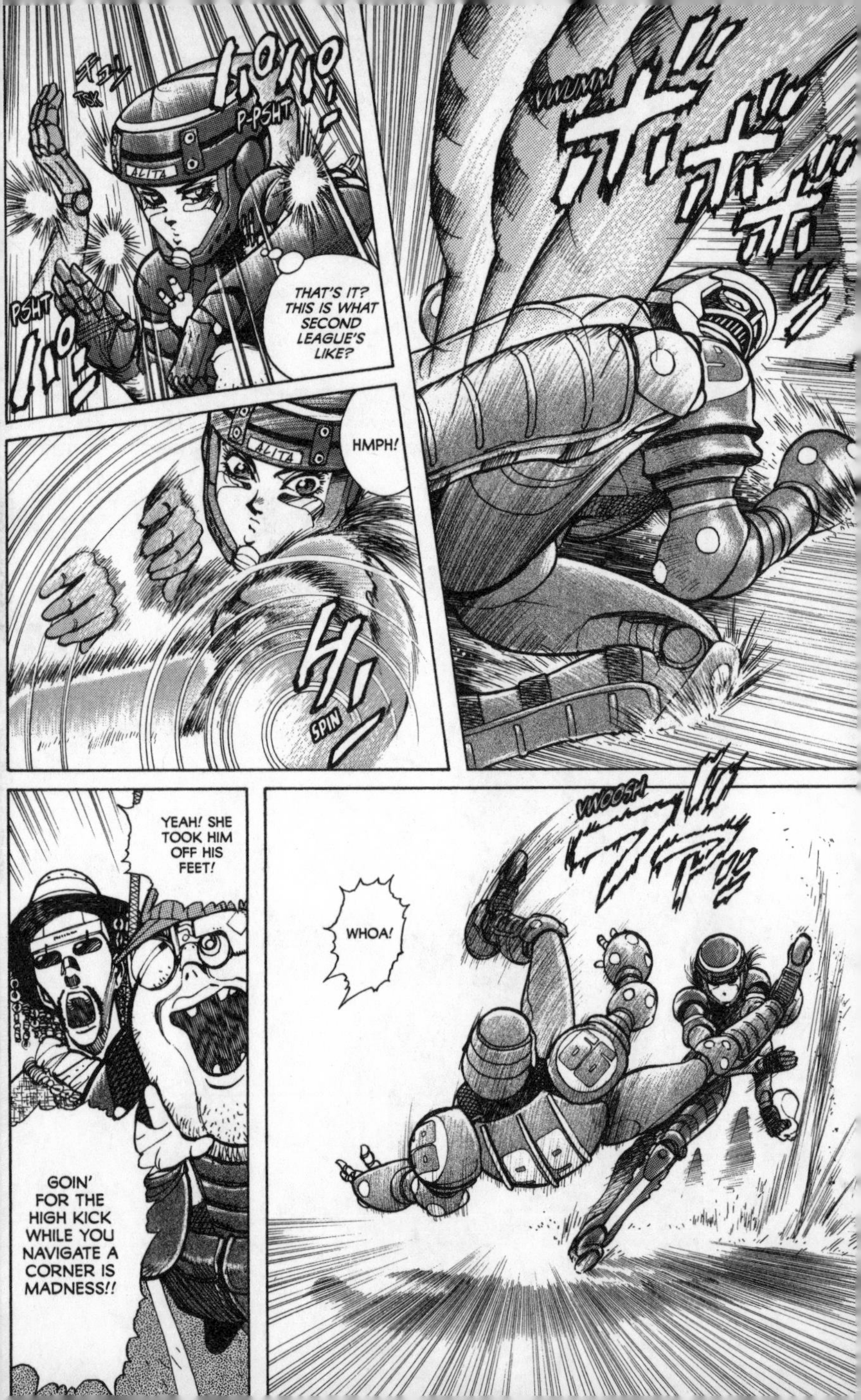
VWUMM
TSK
P-PSHT
PSHT
THAT'S IT? THIS IS WHAT SECOND LEAGUE'S LIKE?
HMPH!
SPIN
VWOOSH
WHOA!
YEAH! SHE TOOK HIM OFF HIS FEET!
GOIN' FOR THE HIGH KICK WHILE YOU NAVIGATE A CORNER IS MADNESS!!

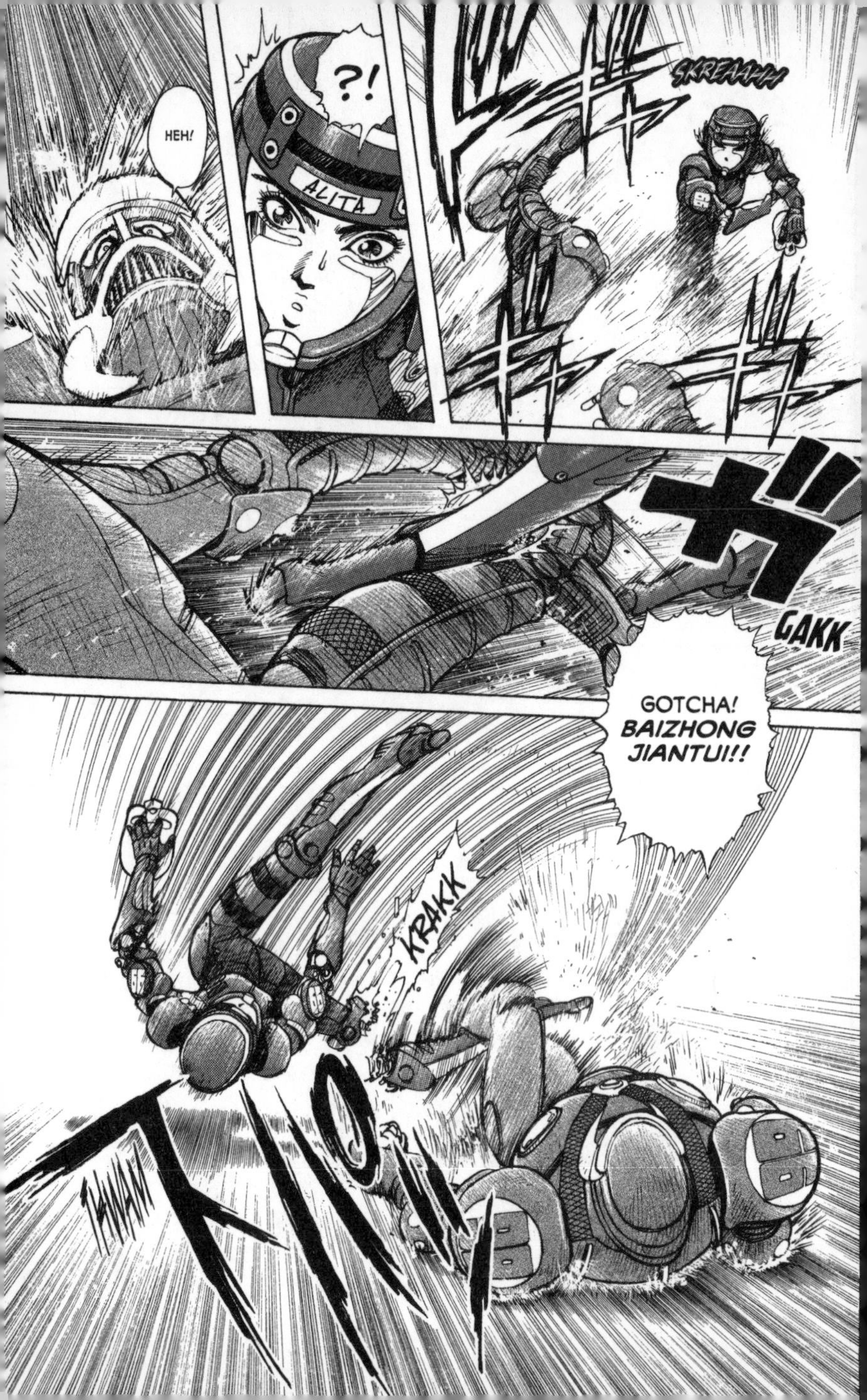
SKREAAHH
?!
ALITA
HEH!
GAKK
GOTCHA! BAIZHONG JIANTUI!!
KRAKK
THWAM

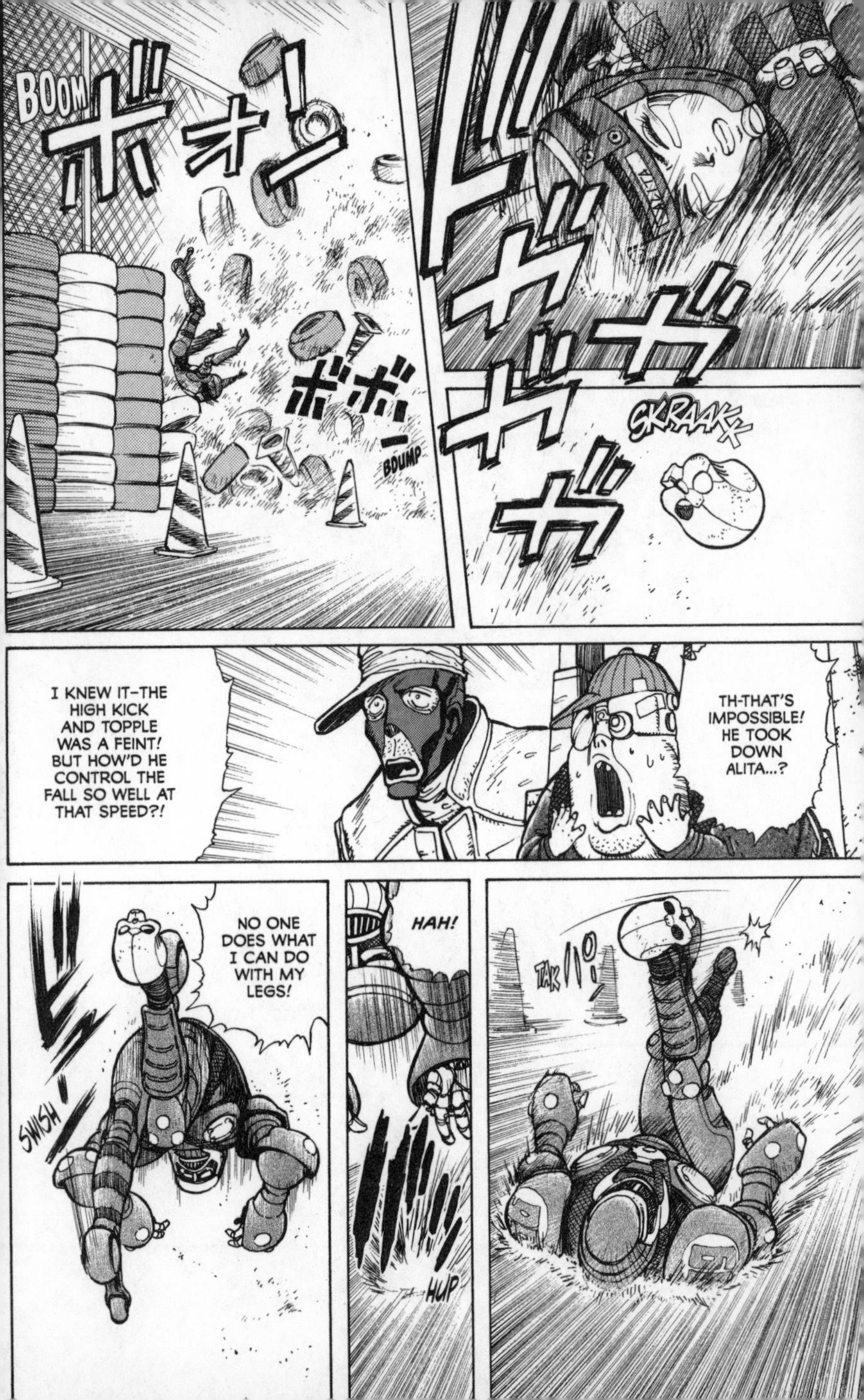
SKRAAKK
BOOM
BDUMP
TH-THAT'S IMPOSSIBLE! HE TOOK DOWN ALITA...?
I KNEW IT–THE HIGH KICK AND TOPPLE WAS A FEINT! BUT HOW'D HE CONTROL THE FALL SO WELL AT THAT SPEED?!
TAK
HAH!
HUP
NO ONE DOES WHAT I CAN DO WITH MY LEGS!
SWISH

THESE ARE THE *ASIAN ARTS!*

YOU GOT THAT, YOU LITTLE HUSSY ?!

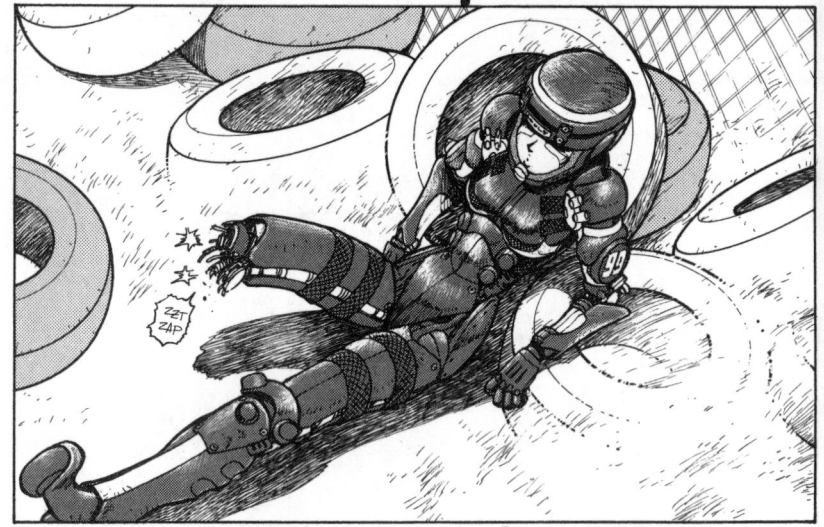

ZZT ZAP

NOW THAT'S A LITTLE MORE LIKE IT...

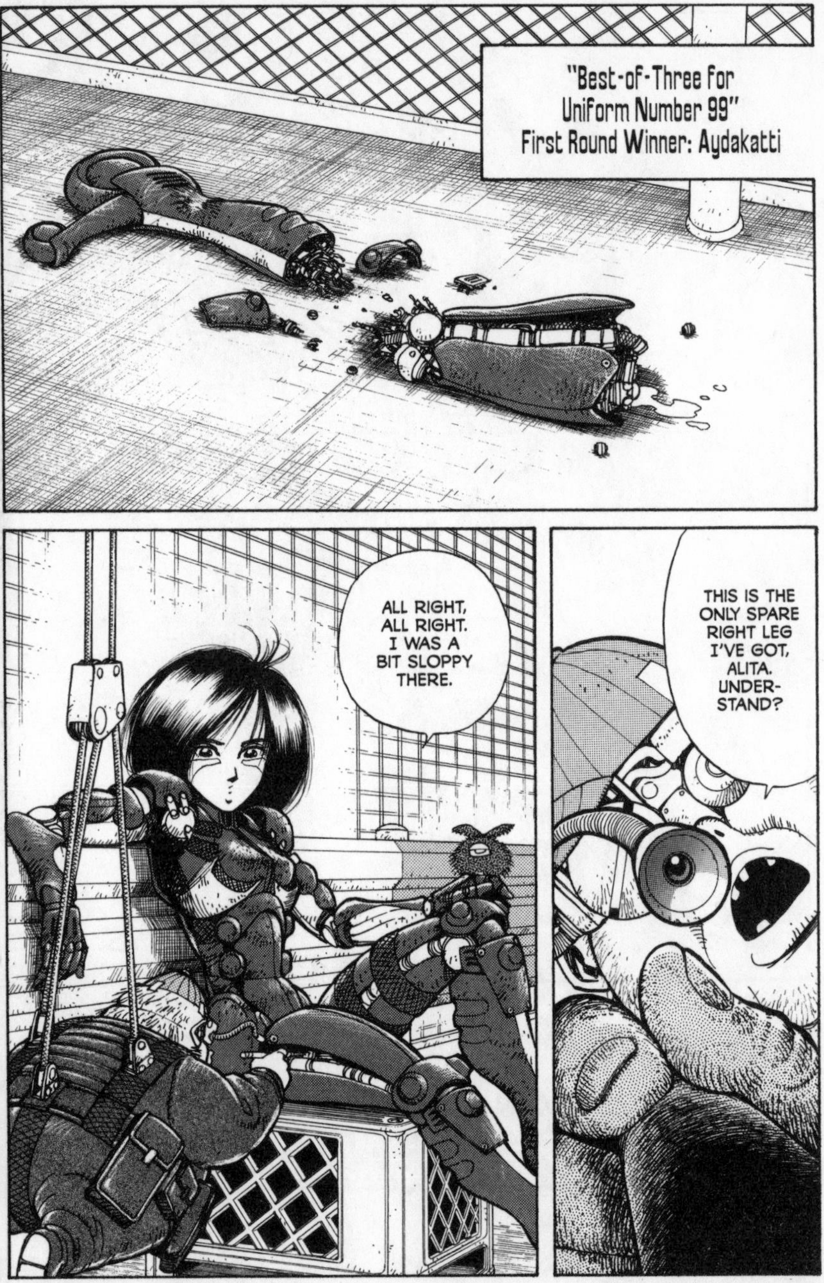
"Best-of-Three for Uniform Number 99" First Round Winner: Aydakatti
THIS IS THE ONLY SPARE RIGHT LEG I'VE GOT, ALITA. UNDER-STAND?
ALL RIGHT, ALL RIGHT. I WAS A BIT SLOPPY THERE.

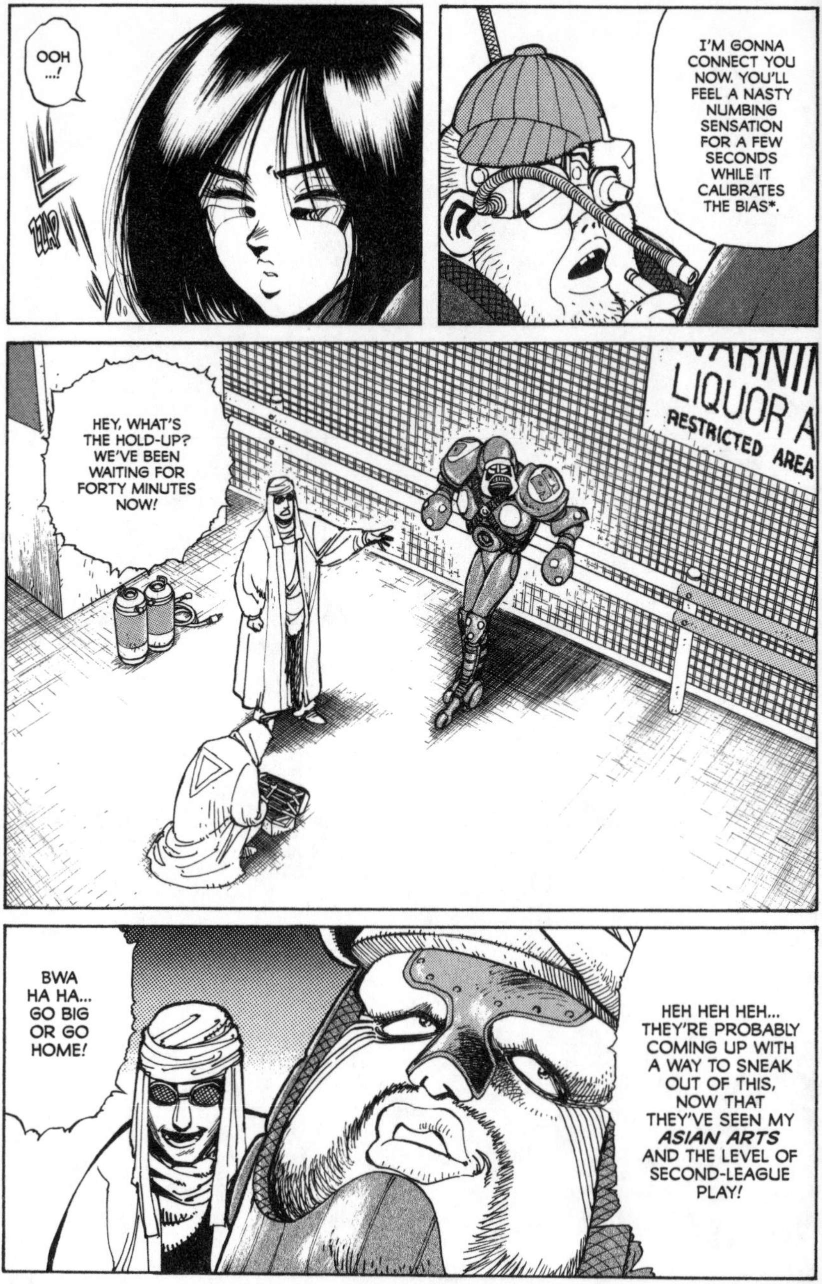
I'M GONNA CONNECT YOU NOW. YOU'LL FEEL A NASTY NUMBING SENSATION FOR A FEW SECONDS WHILE IT CALIBRATES THE BIAS*.
OOH ...!
HEY, WHAT'S THE HOLD-UP? WE'VE BEEN WAITING FOR FORTY MINUTES NOW!
WARNI
LIQUOR A
RESTRICTED AREA
HEH HEH HEH... THEY'RE PROBABLY COMING UP WITH A WAY TO SNEAK OUT OF THIS, NOW THAT THEY'VE SEEN MY *ASIAN ARTS* AND THE LEVEL OF SECOND-LEAGUE PLAY!
BWA HA HA... GO BIG OR GO HOME!

*Bias: The voltage level that sets the operating point of an electrical signal or system.

THE GAME'S BACK ON.
IT JUST TOOK US A LITTLE TIME TO LOAD UP ALL OUR TOOLS AND SUPPLIES. SORRY ABOUT THE DELAY.
HEY, ESDOG...
WHAT IS IT, MR. THOMP-SON?
CALL ME ED.
ALITA'S AN EXCELLENT PLAYER WITH AMPLE PROMISE... BUT I THINK WE MAY HAVE PICKED THE WRONG OPPONENT.
I SUGGEST WE FORFEIT NOW AND CUT OUR LOSSES BEFORE SOMETHING BAD HAPPENS.
AYDAKATTI MAY ONLY BE 23RD IN THE POINT RANKINGS, BUT HE'S DESTROYED OVER 145 OPPONENTS ON THE TRACK.
HE'S KNOWN AMONG FANS AS "THE CRUSHER" AND "THE KING WITHOUT A CROWN"!

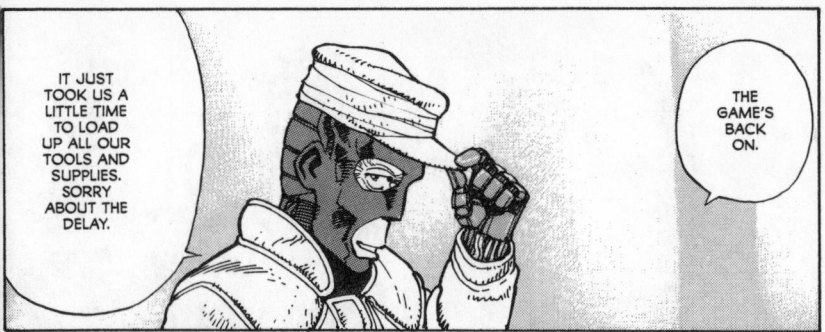

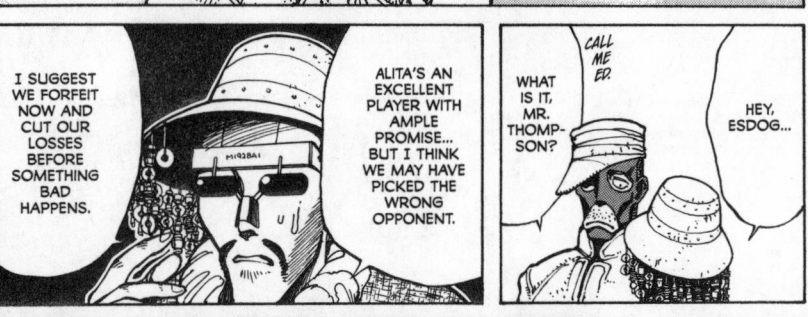

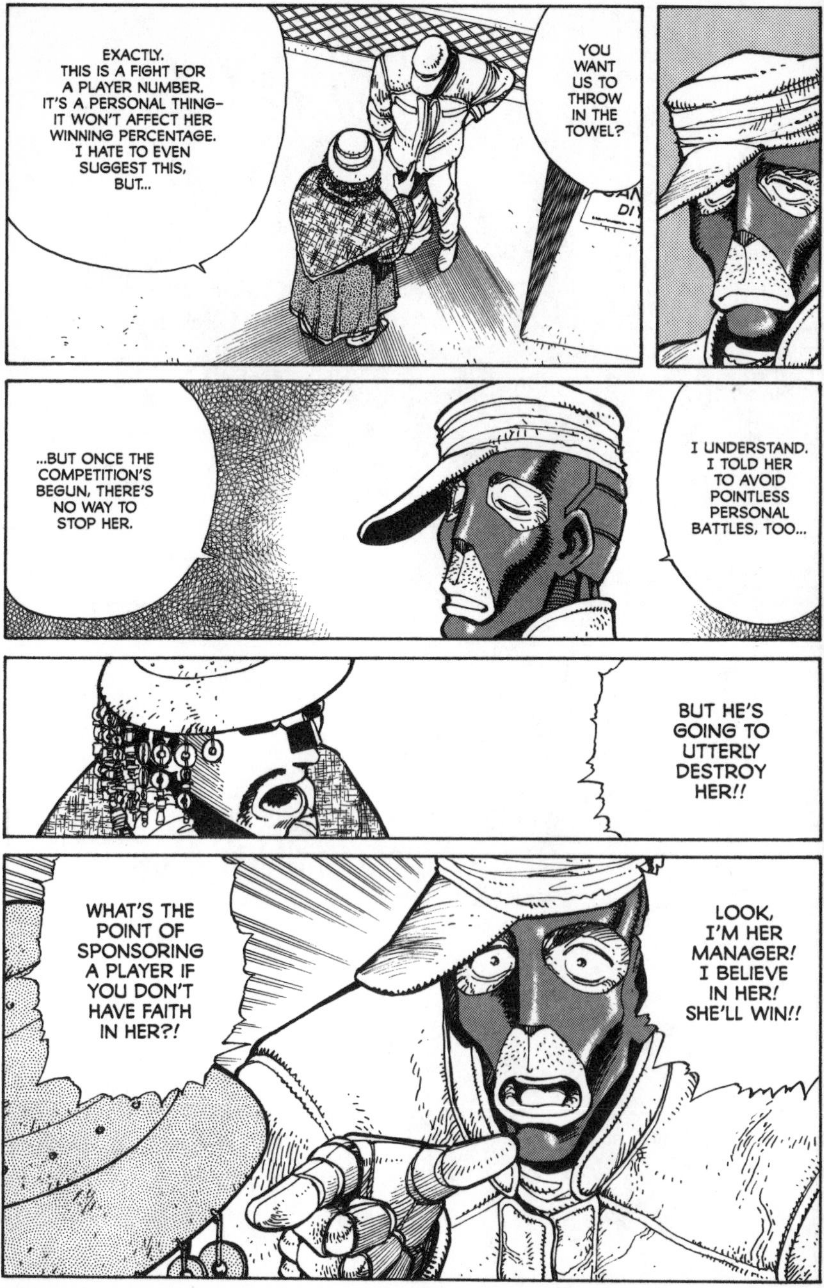
YOU WANT US TO THROW IN THE TOWEL?
EXACTLY. THIS IS A FIGHT FOR A PLAYER NUMBER. IT'S A PERSONAL THING– IT WON'T AFFECT HER WINNING PERCENTAGE. I HATE TO EVEN SUGGEST THIS, BUT...
I UNDERSTAND. I TOLD HER TO AVOID POINTLESS PERSONAL BATTLES, TOO...
...BUT ONCE THE COMPETITION'S BEGUN, THERE'S NO WAY TO STOP HER.
BUT HE'S GOING TO UTTERLY DESTROY HER!!
LOOK, I'M HER MANAGER! I BELIEVE IN HER! SHE'LL WIN!!
WHAT'S THE POINT OF SPONSORING A PLAYER IF YOU DON'T HAVE FAITH IN HER?!

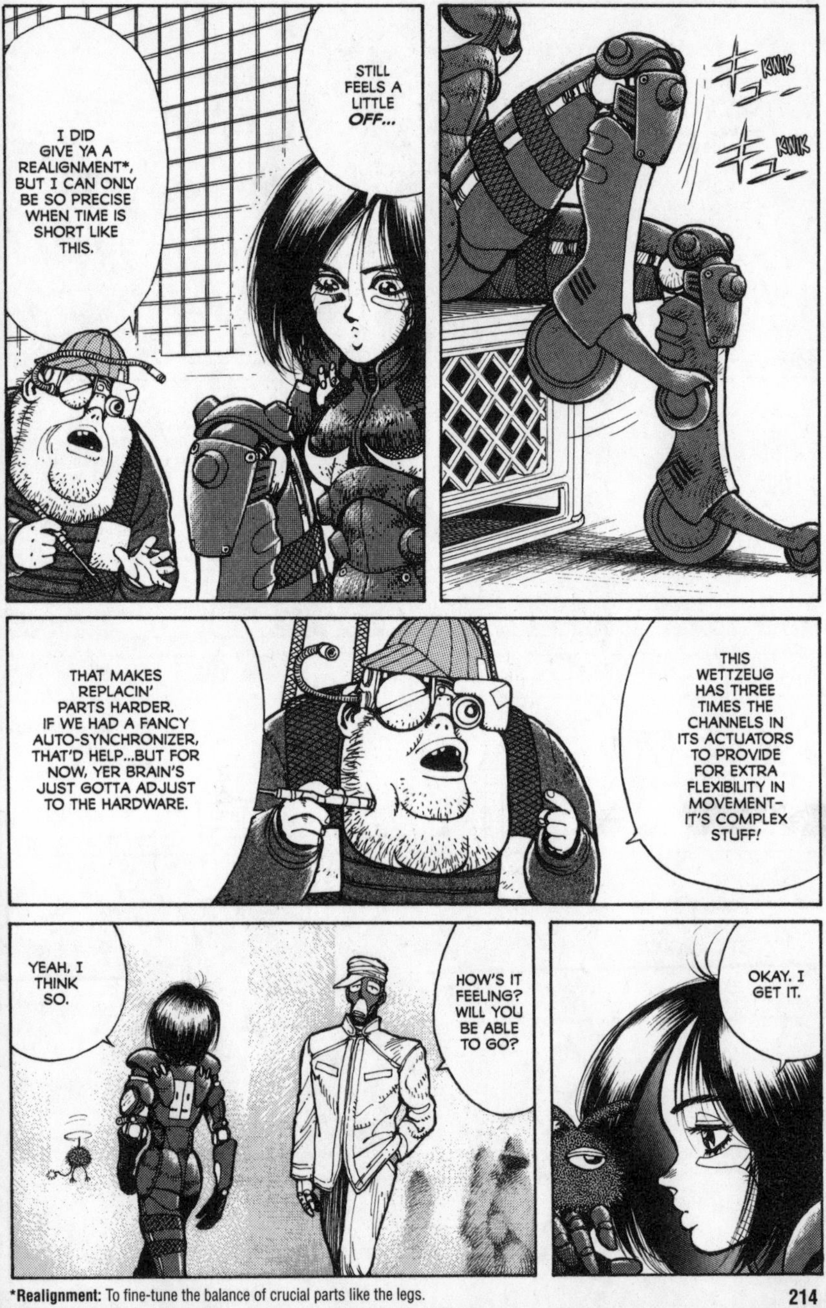
KWIK
KWIK
STILL FEELS A LITTLE *OFF...*
I DID GIVE YA A REALIGNMENT*, BUT I CAN ONLY BE SO PRECISE WHEN TIME IS SHORT LIKE THIS.
THIS WETTZEUG HAS THREE TIMES THE CHANNELS IN ITS ACTUATORS TO PROVIDE FOR EXTRA FLEXIBILITY IN MOVEMENT–IT'S COMPLEX STUFF!
THAT MAKES REPLACIN' PARTS HARDER. IF WE HAD A FANCY AUTO-SYNCHRONIZER, THAT'D HELP...BUT FOR NOW, YER BRAIN'S JUST GOTTA ADJUST TO THE HARDWARE.
OKAY. I GET IT.
HOW'S IT FEELING? WILL YOU BE ABLE TO GO?
YEAH, I THINK SO.

***Realignment:** To fine-tune the balance of crucial parts like the legs.

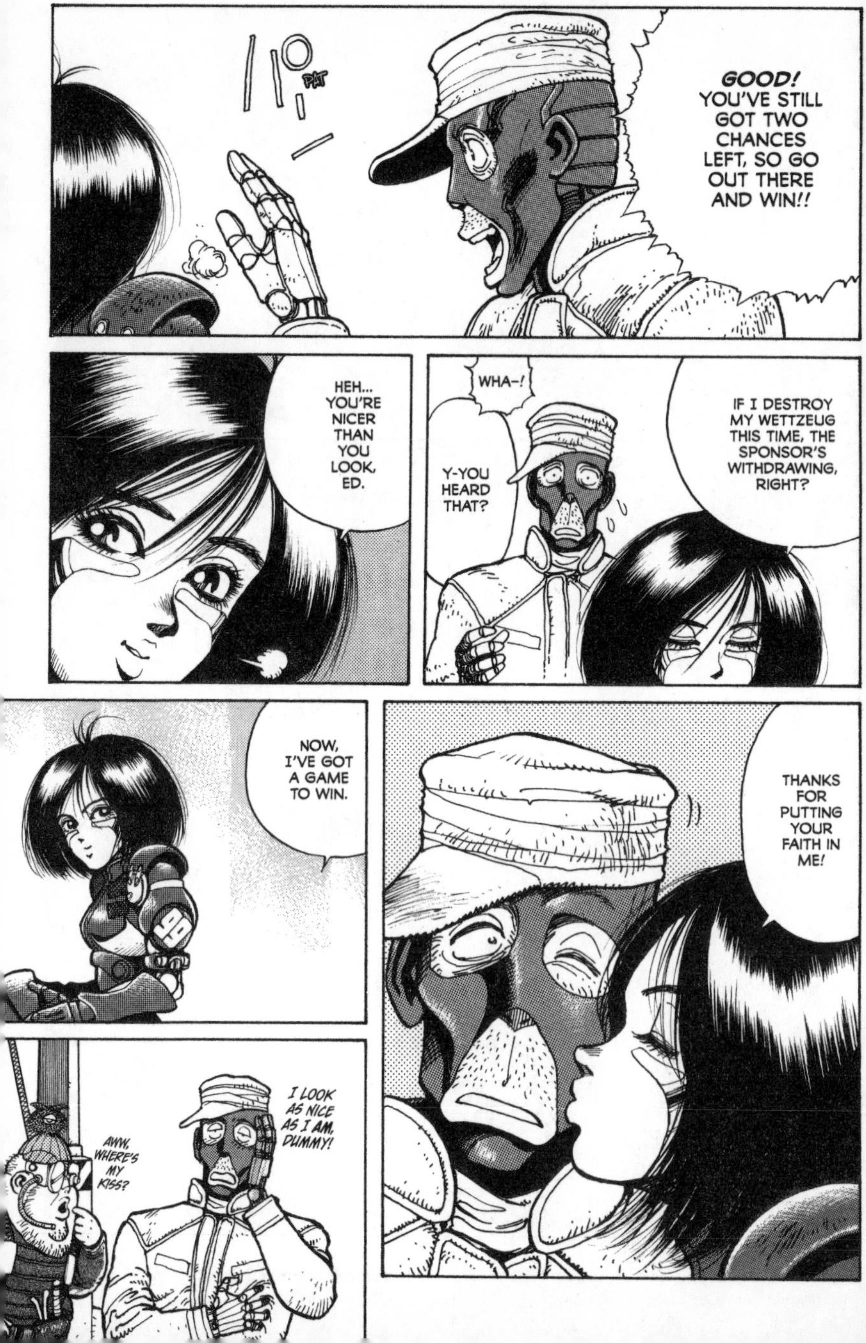
PAT
GOOD! YOU'VE STILL GOT TWO CHANCES LEFT, SO GO OUT THERE AND WIN!!
IF I DESTROY MY WETTZEUG THIS TIME, THE SPONSOR'S WITHDRAWING, RIGHT?
WHA-!
Y-YOU HEARD THAT?
HEH... YOU'RE NICER THAN YOU LOOK, ED.
THANKS FOR PUTTING YOUR FAITH IN ME!
NOW, I'VE GOT A GAME TO WIN.
I LOOK AS NICE AS I AM, DUMMY!
AWW, WHERE'S MY KISS?

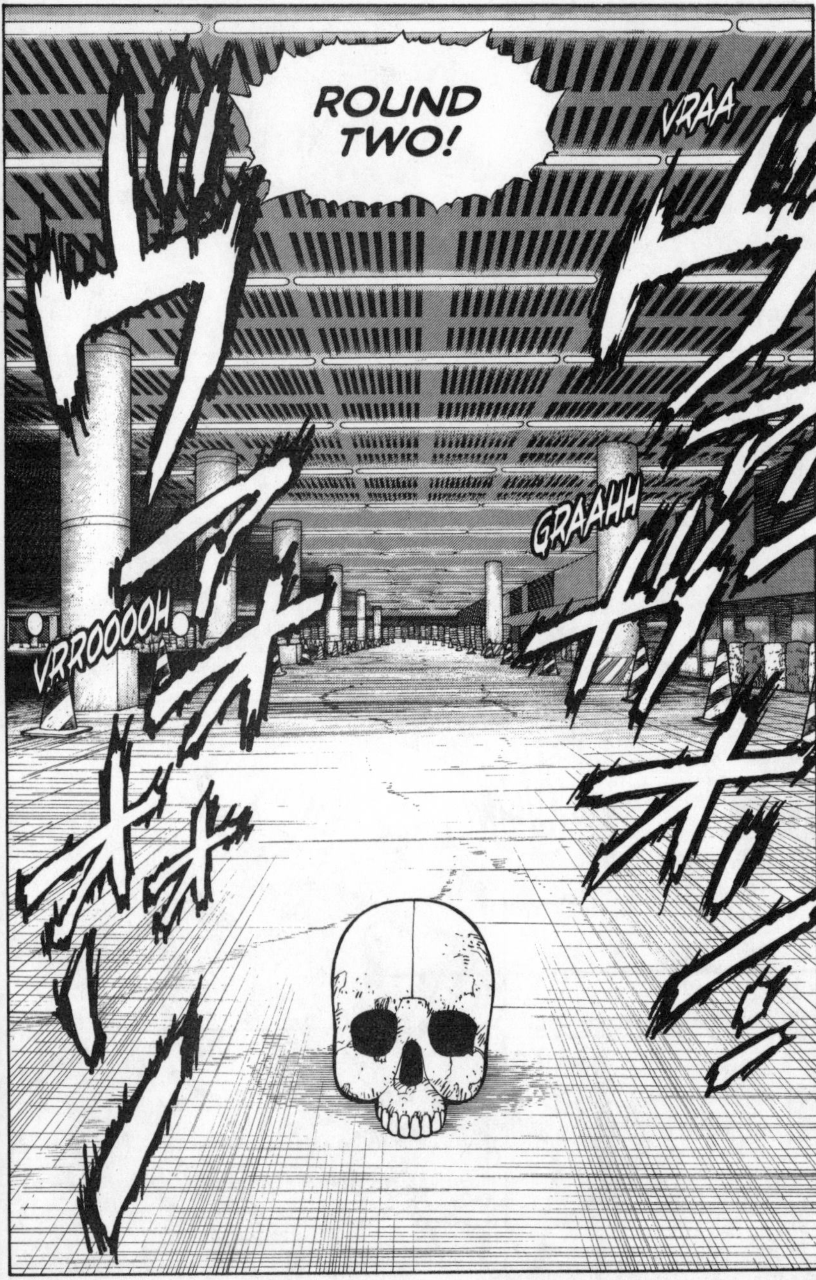
VRAA
ROUND TWO!
GRAAHH
VRROOOOH

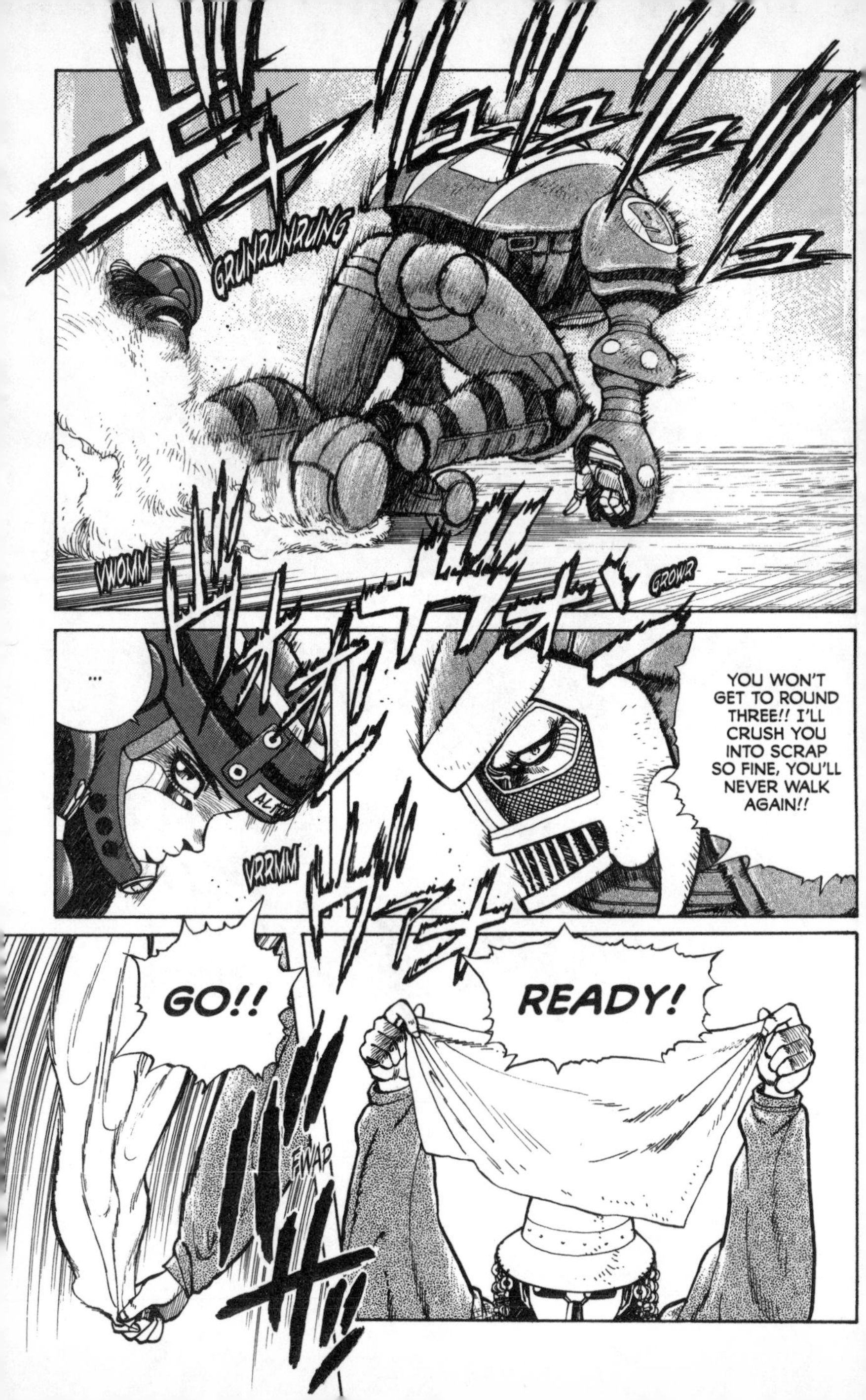
GRUNRUNRUNG
VWOMM
GROWR
YOU WON'T GET TO ROUND THREE!! I'LL CRUSH YOU INTO SCRAP SO FINE, YOU'LL NEVER WALK AGAIN!!
VRRMM
...
READY!
GO!!
FWAP

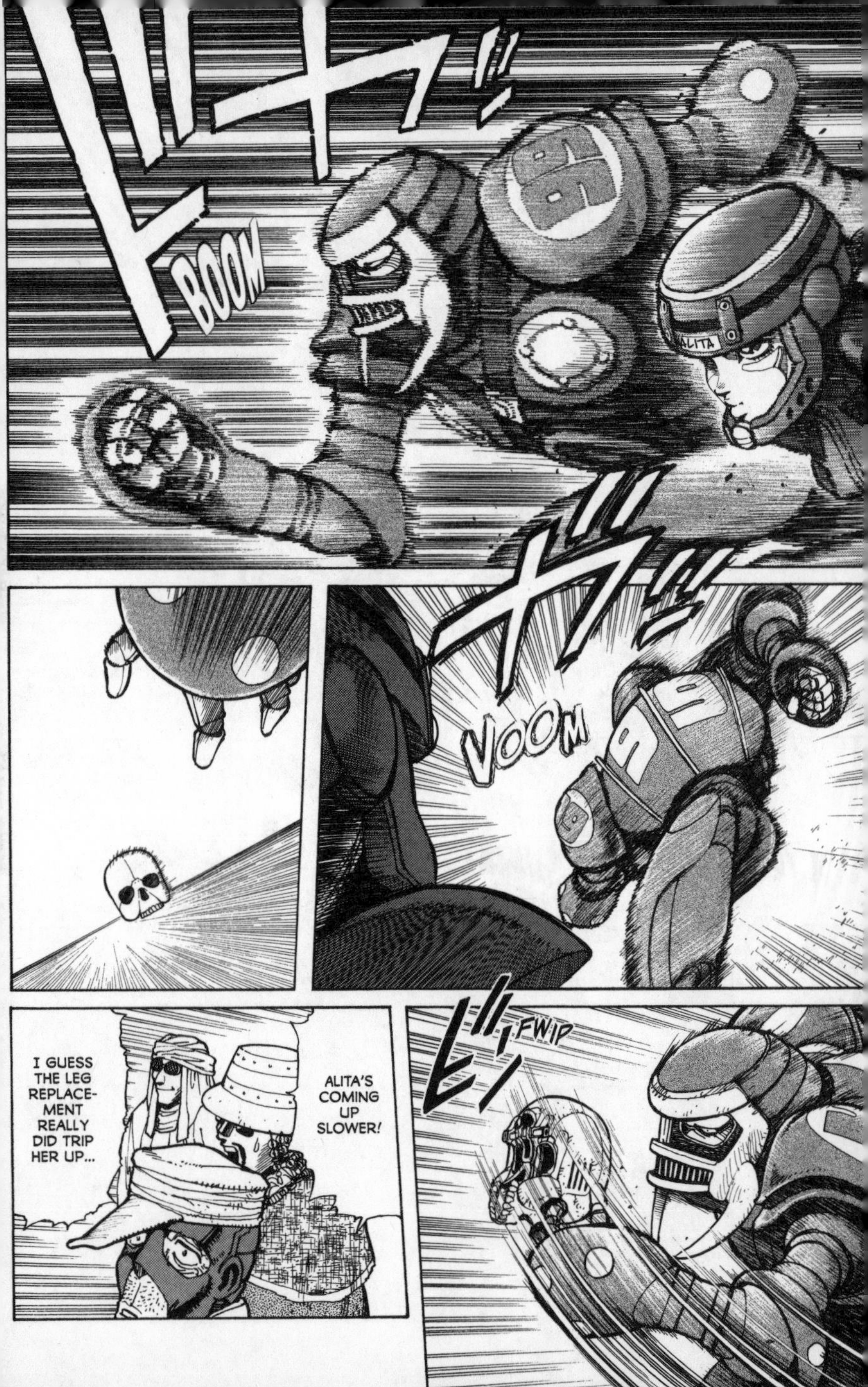
BOOM
ALITA
VOOM
FWIP
ALITA'S COMING UP SLOWER!
I GUESS THE LEG REPLACE-MENT REALLY DID TRIP HER UP...

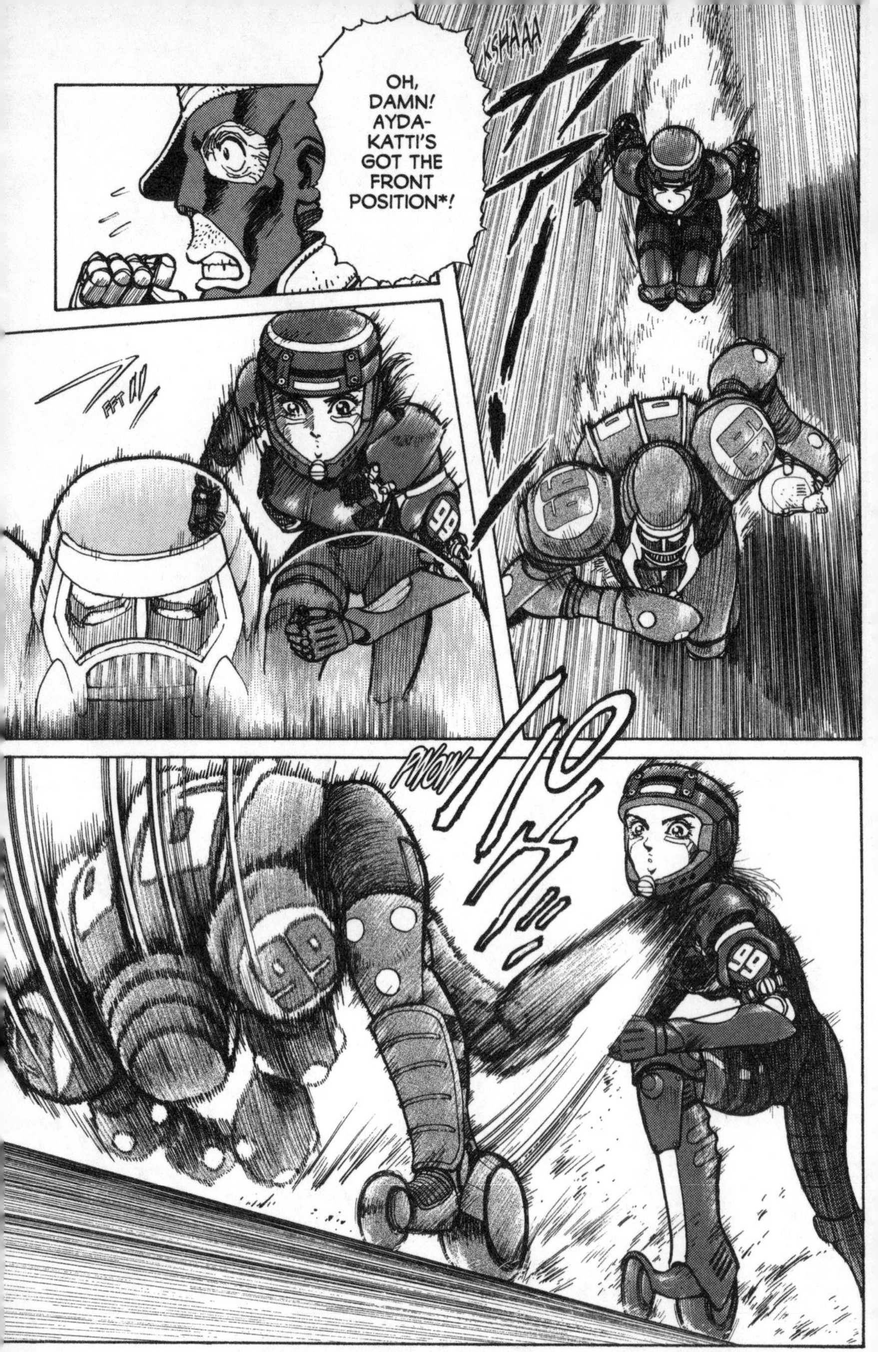
KSHAAA
OH, DAMN! AYDA-KATTI'S GOT THE FRONT POSITION*!
FFT
FWOW

*Front position: Unlike in normal martial arts, motorball takes place while moving in the same direction, so unless there is a major difference in strength, the combatant in the lead has the advantage.

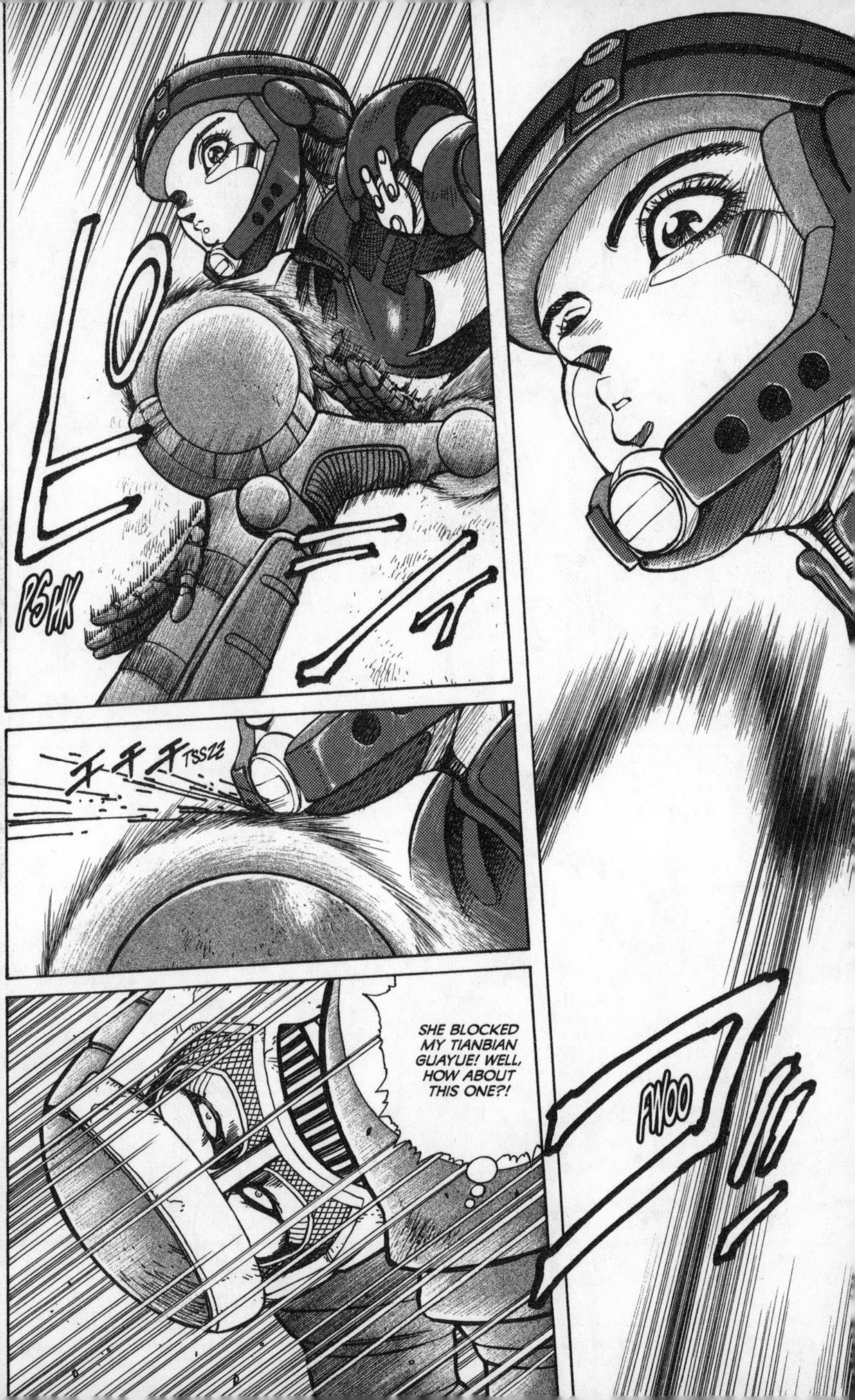
PSHK
TSSZZ
SHE BLOCKED MY TIANBIAN GUAYUE! WELL, HOW ABOUT THIS ONE?!
FWOO

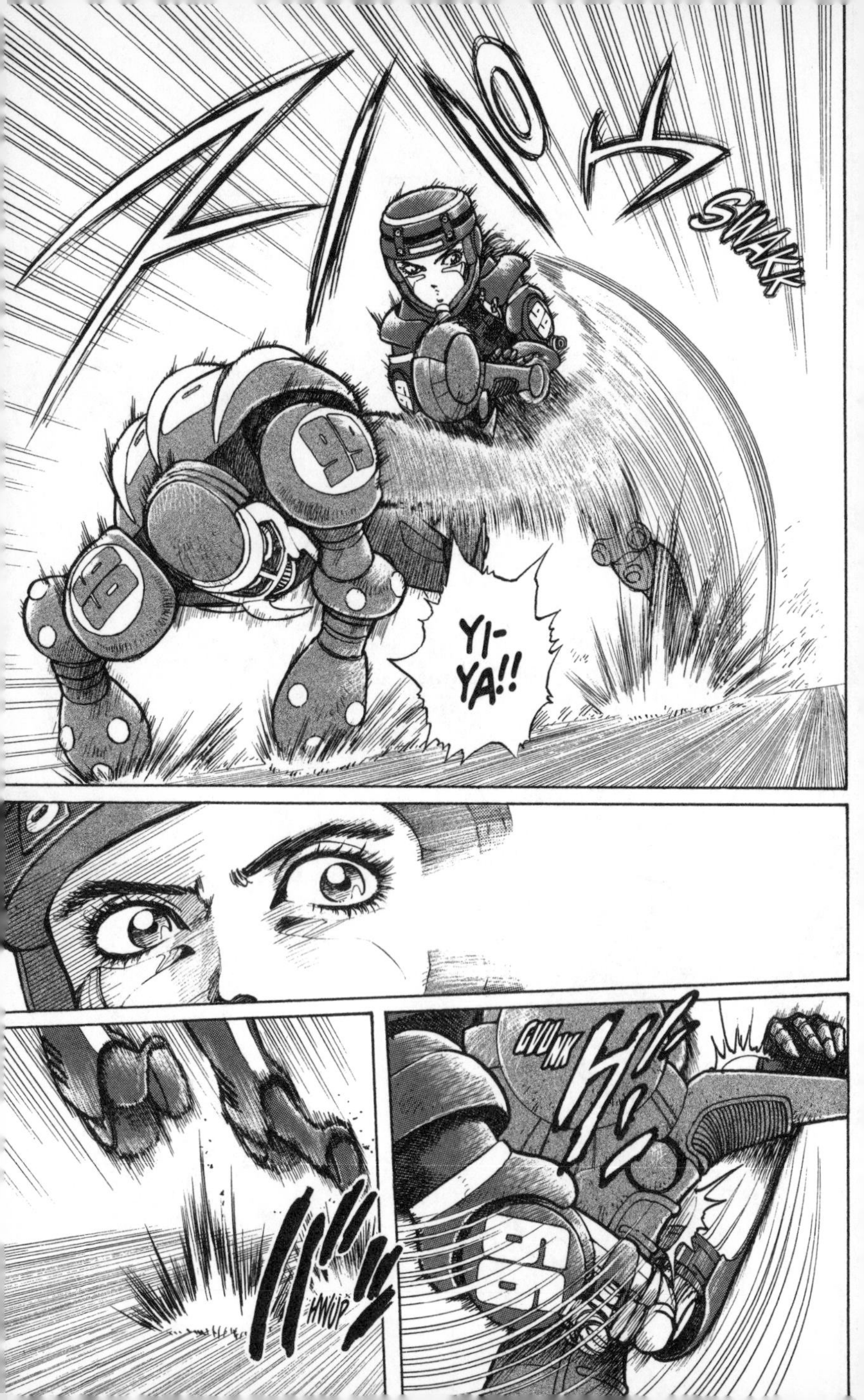
SWAKK
YI-YA!!
GUNK
HWUP

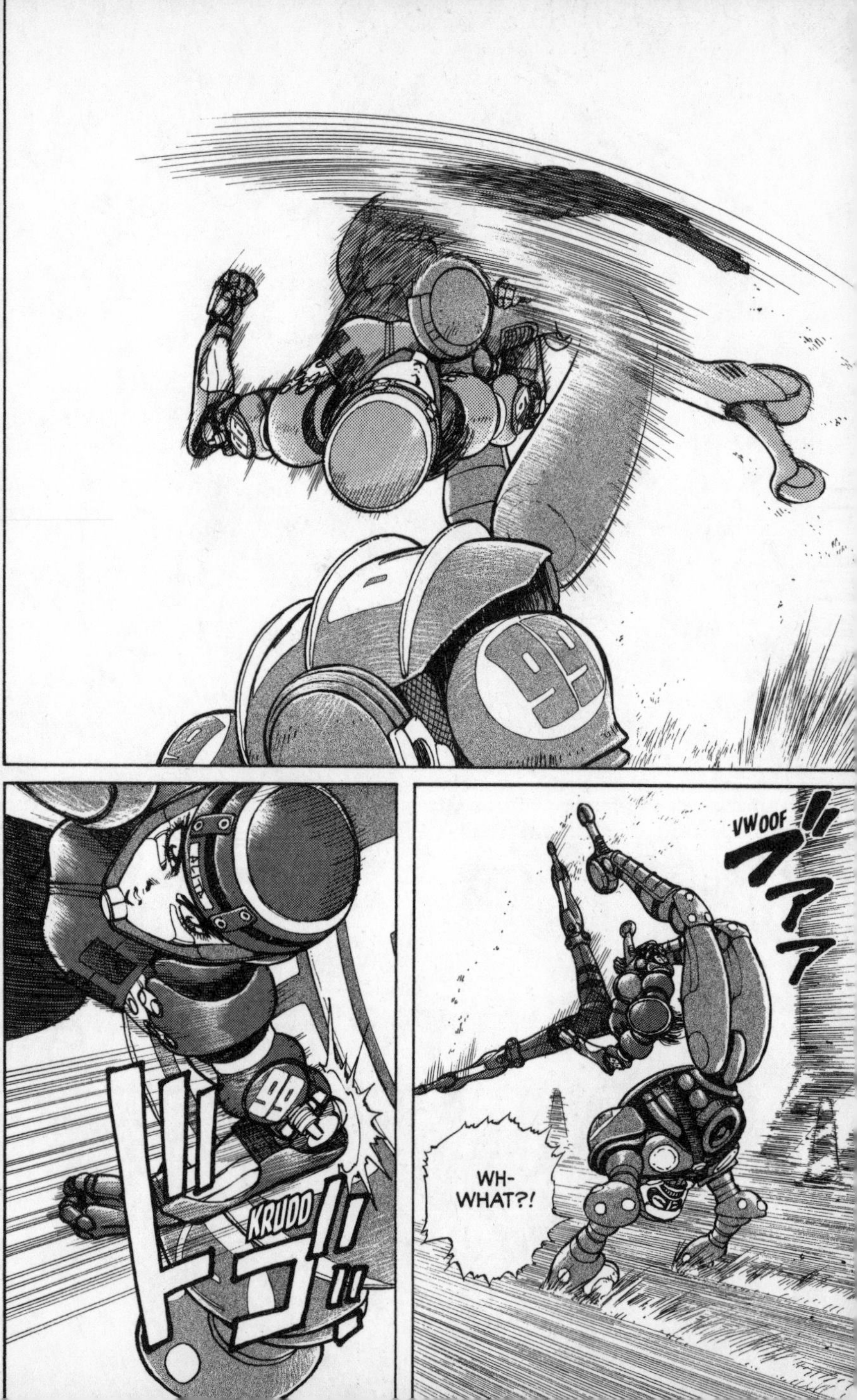
VWOOF
WH-
WHAT?!
KRUDO

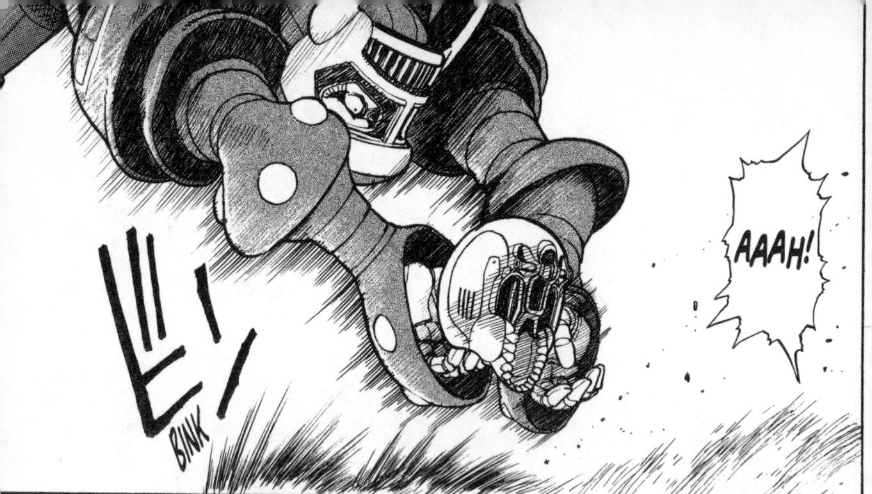
AAAH!
BINK
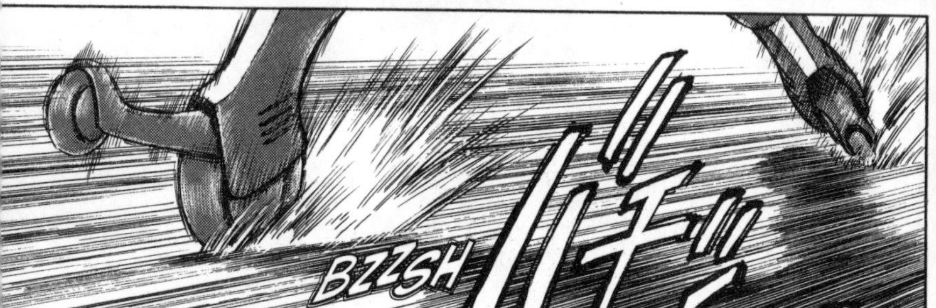
BZZSH
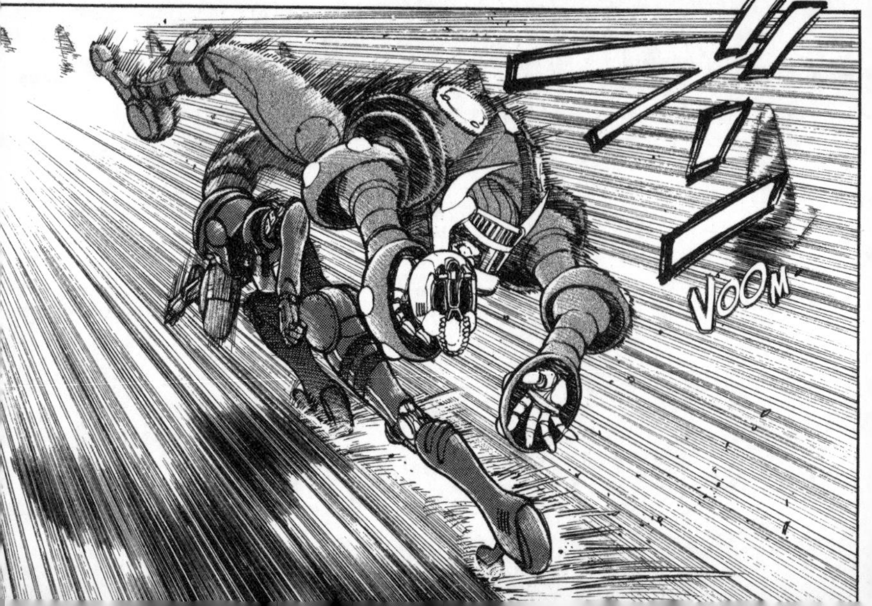
VOOM

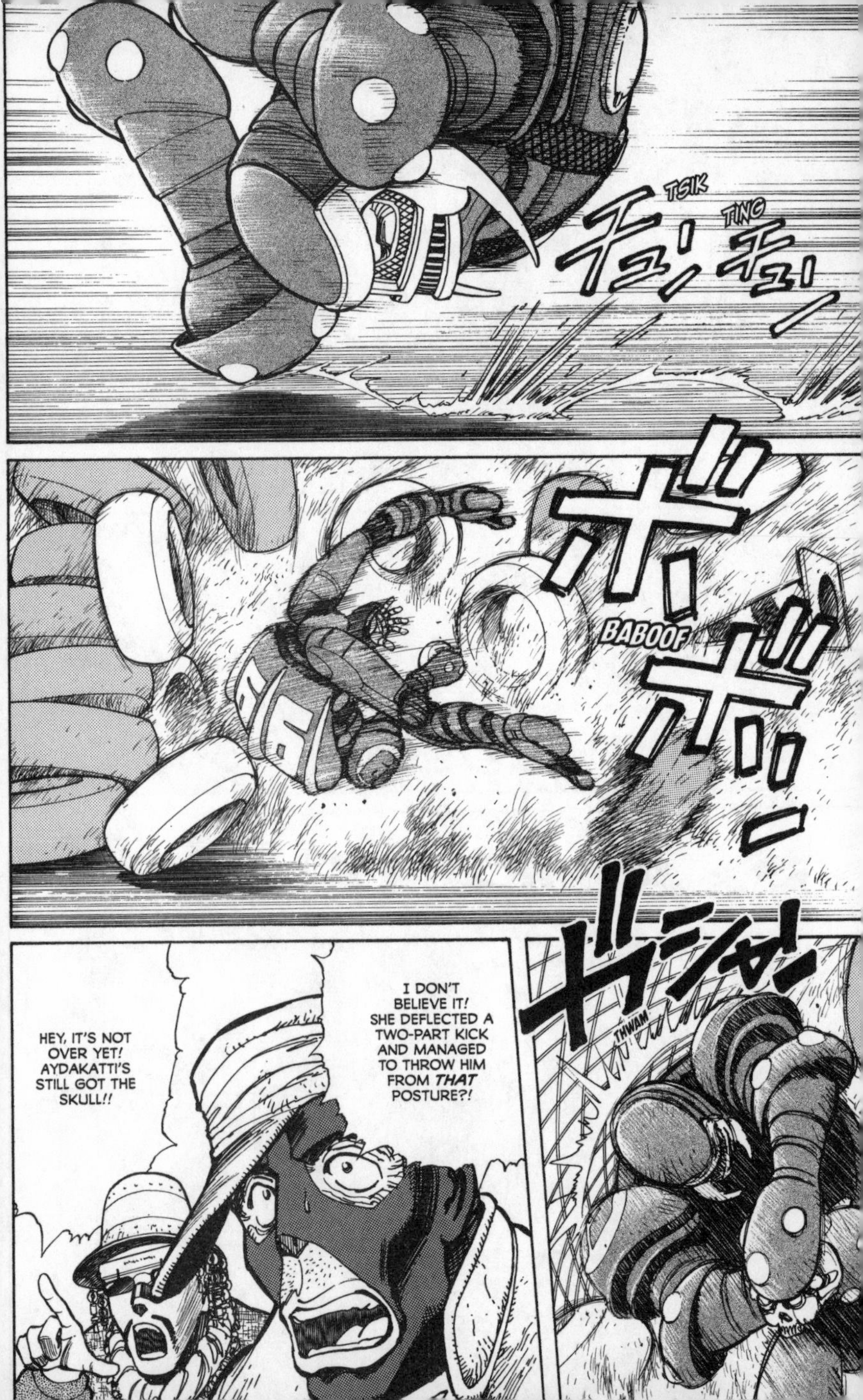
TSIK
TING
BABOOF
THWAM
I DON'T BELIEVE IT! SHE DEFLECTED A TWO-PART KICK AND MANAGED TO THROW HIM FROM *THAT* POSTURE?!
HEY, IT'S NOT OVER YET! AYDAKATTI'S STILL GOT THE SKULL!!

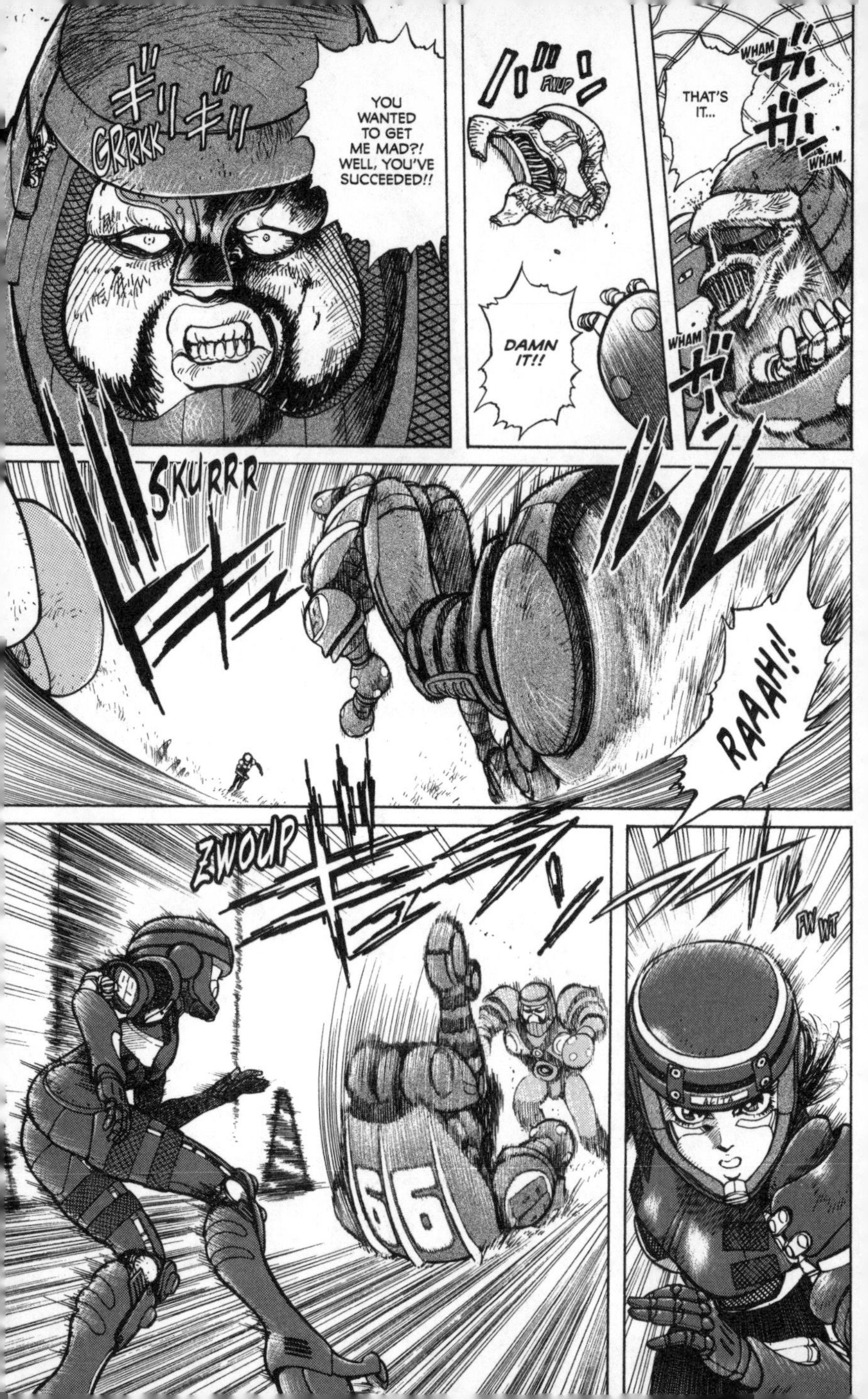
WHAM
THAT'S IT...
WHAM
WHAM
FWUP
DAMN IT!!
GRRKK
YOU WANTED TO GET ME MAD?! WELL, YOU'VE SUCCEEDED!!
RAAAH!!
SKURRR
FW WT
ZWOUP

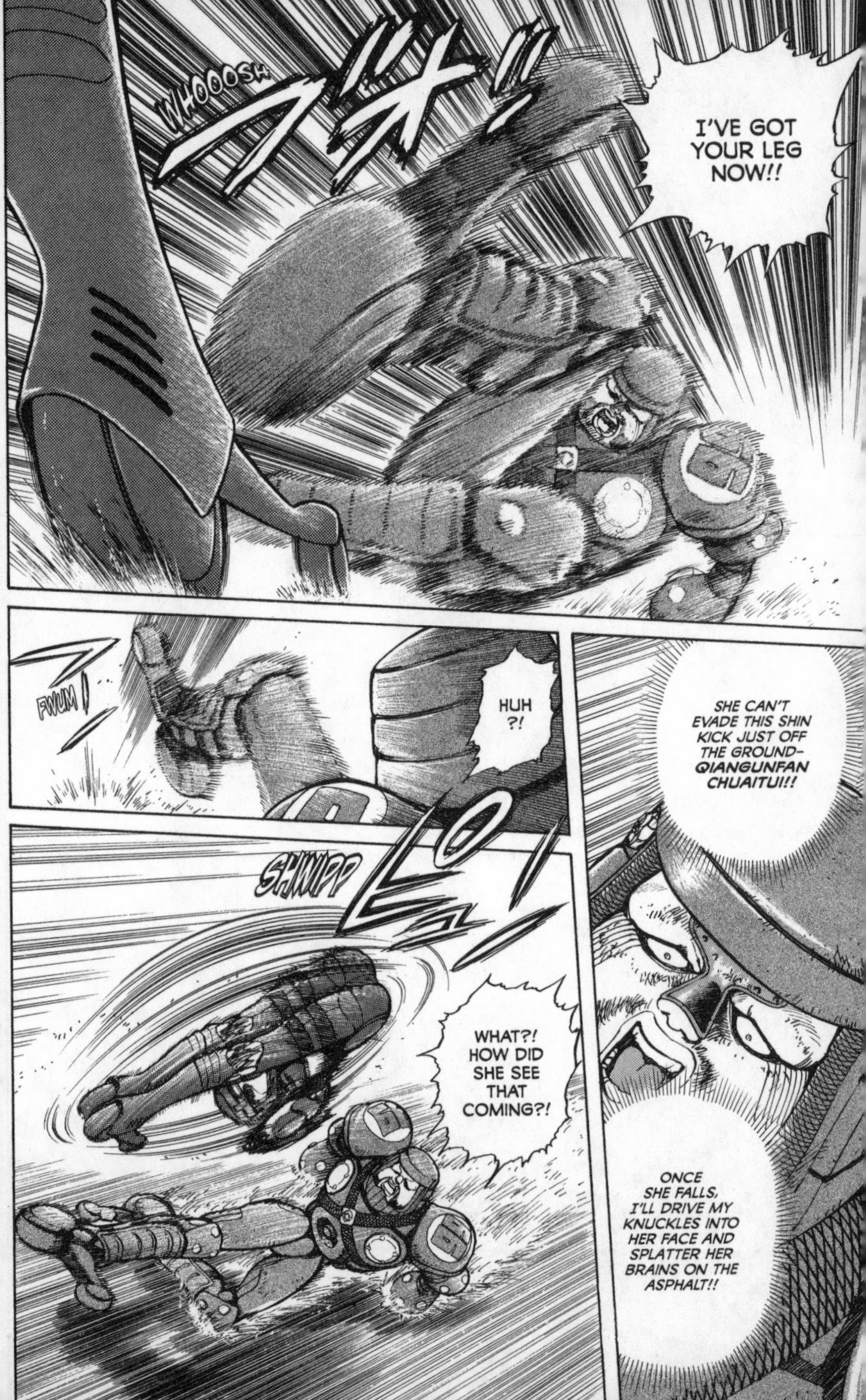
I'VE GOT YOUR LEG NOW!!
WHOOOSH
SHE CAN'T EVADE THIS SHIN KICK JUST OFF THE GROUND-
QIANGUNFAN CHUAITUI!!!
ONCE SHE FALLS, I'LL DRIVE MY KNUCKLES INTO HER FACE AND SPLATTER HER BRAINS ON THE ASPHALT!!
HUH ?!
FWUM
SHWIPP
WHAT?! HOW DID SHE SEE THAT COMING?!

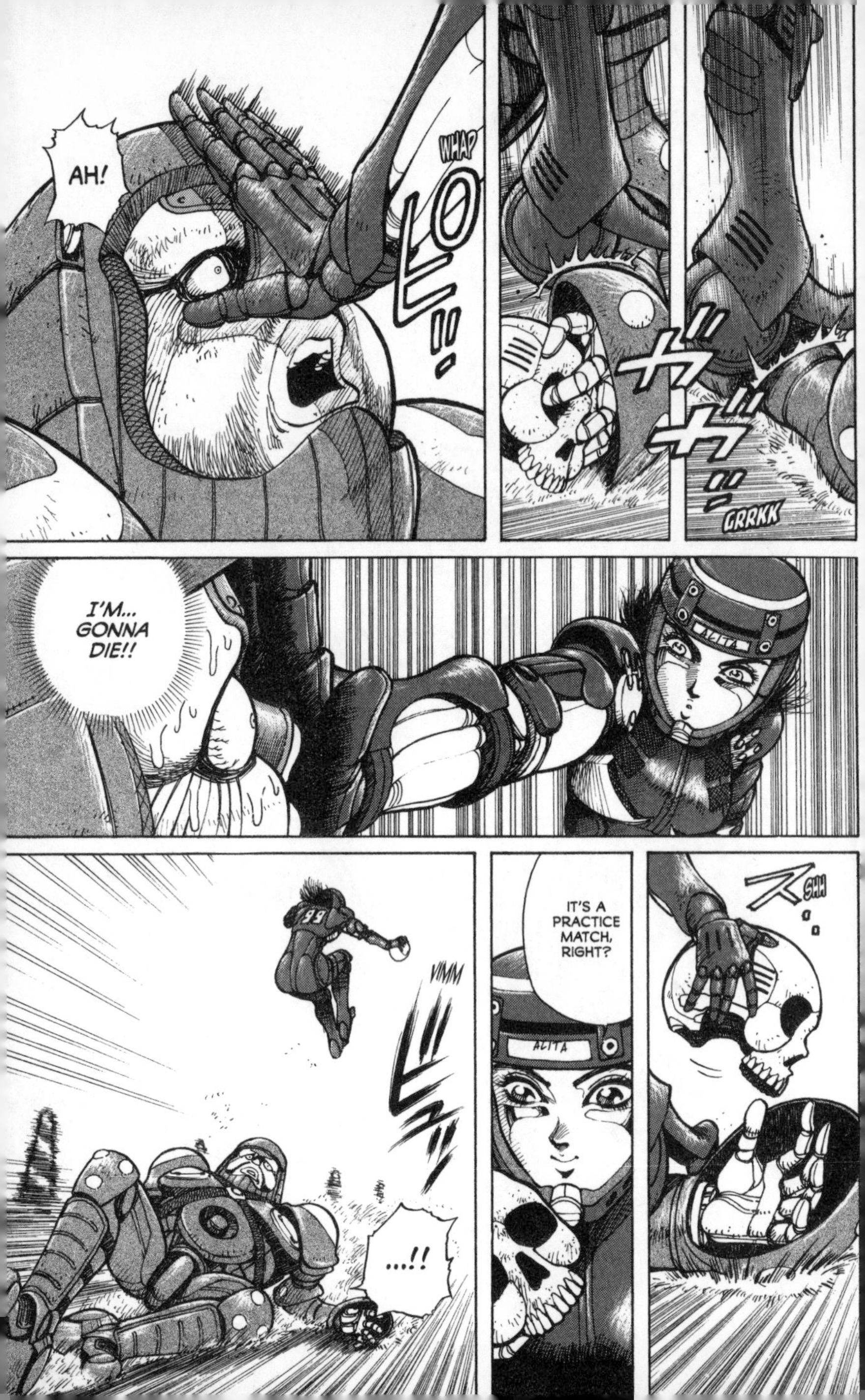
GRRKK
WHAP
AH!
I'M... GONNA DIE!!
SHH
IT'S A PRACTICE MATCH, RIGHT?
VMM
...!!

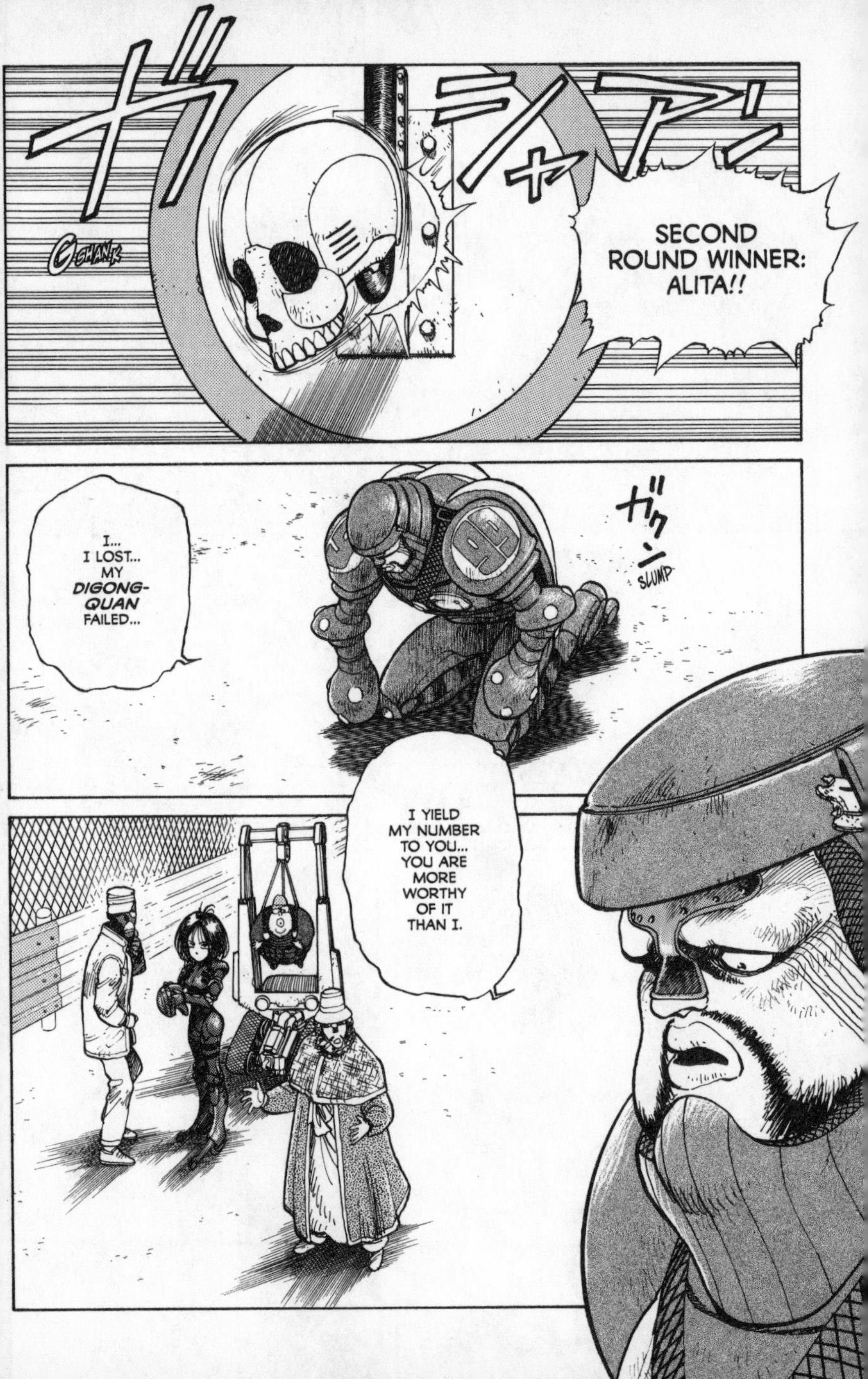
C-SHANK
SECOND ROUND WINNER: ALITA!!
ガクン
SLUMP
I... I LOST... MY *DIGONG-QUAN* FAILED...
I YIELD MY NUMBER TO YOU... YOU ARE MORE WORTHY OF IT THAN I.

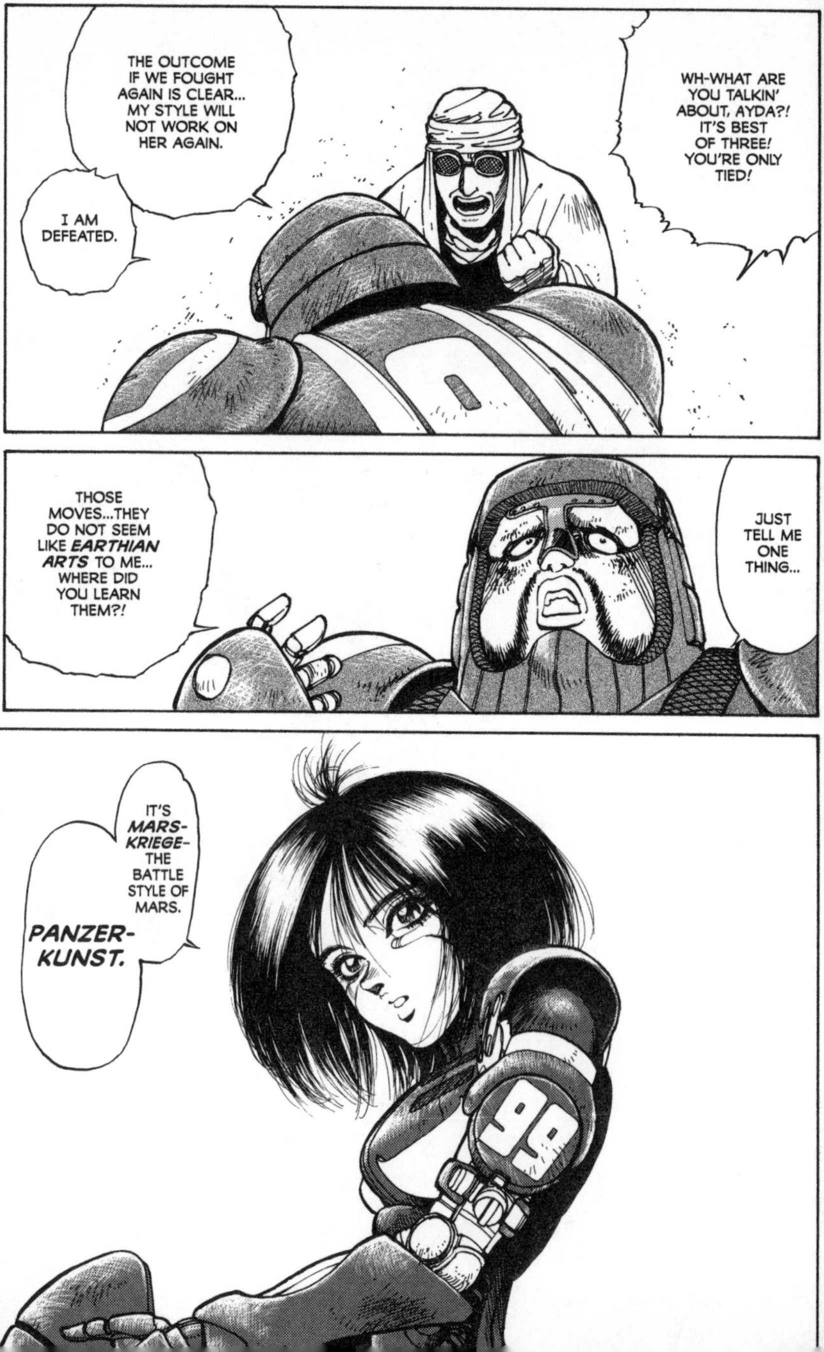
WH-WHAT ARE YOU TALKIN' ABOUT, AYDA?! IT'S BEST OF THREE! YOU'RE ONLY TIED!
THE OUTCOME IF WE FOUGHT AGAIN IS CLEAR... MY STYLE WILL NOT WORK ON HER AGAIN.
I AM DEFEATED.
JUST TELL ME ONE THING...
THOSE MOVES...THEY DO NOT SEEM LIKE *EARTHIAN ARTS* TO ME... WHERE DID YOU LEARN THEM?!
IT'S *MARS-KRIEGE*-THE BATTLE STYLE OF MARS.
PANZER-KUNST.
99

FIGHT_016 Risk One's Heart

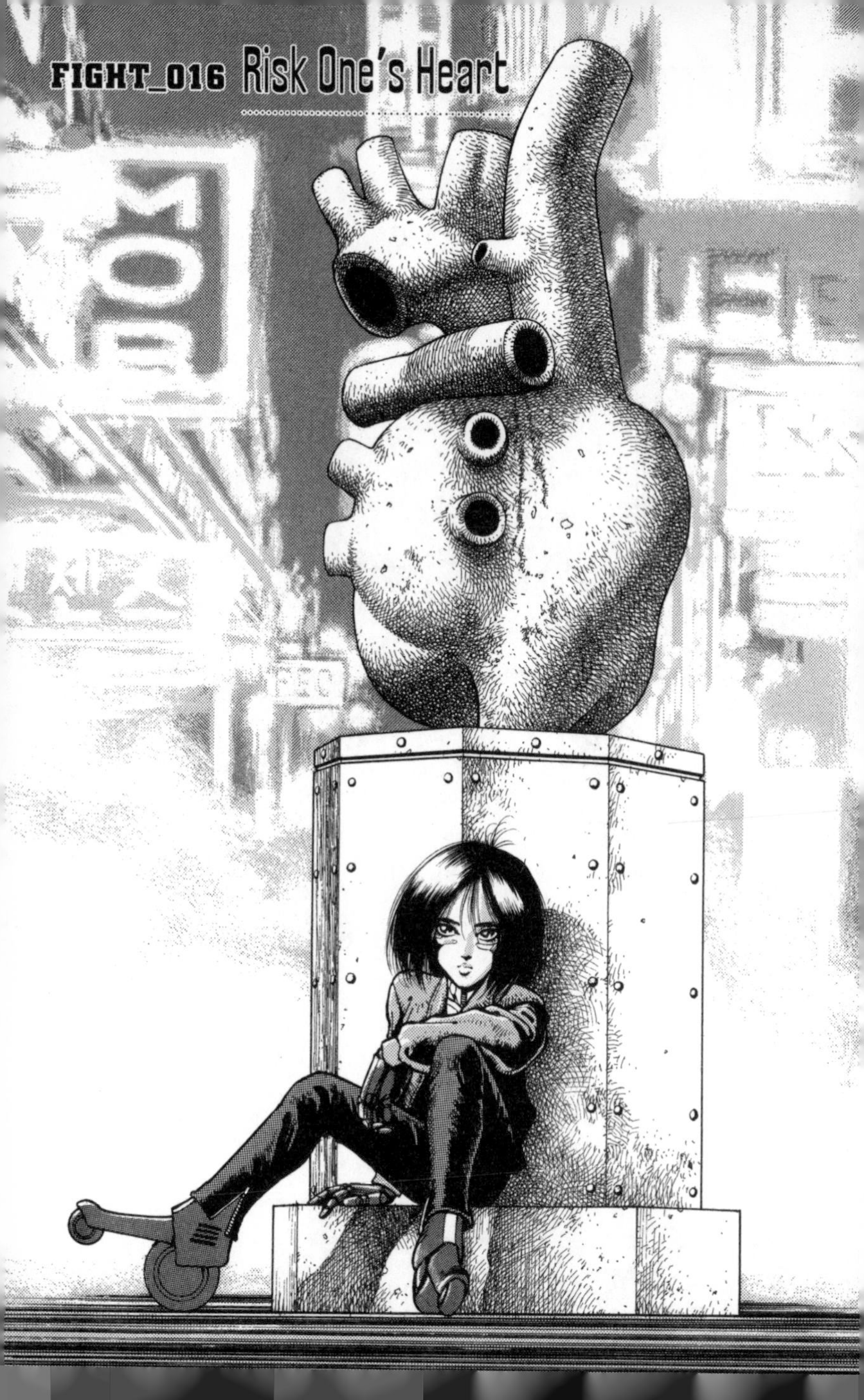

FEO

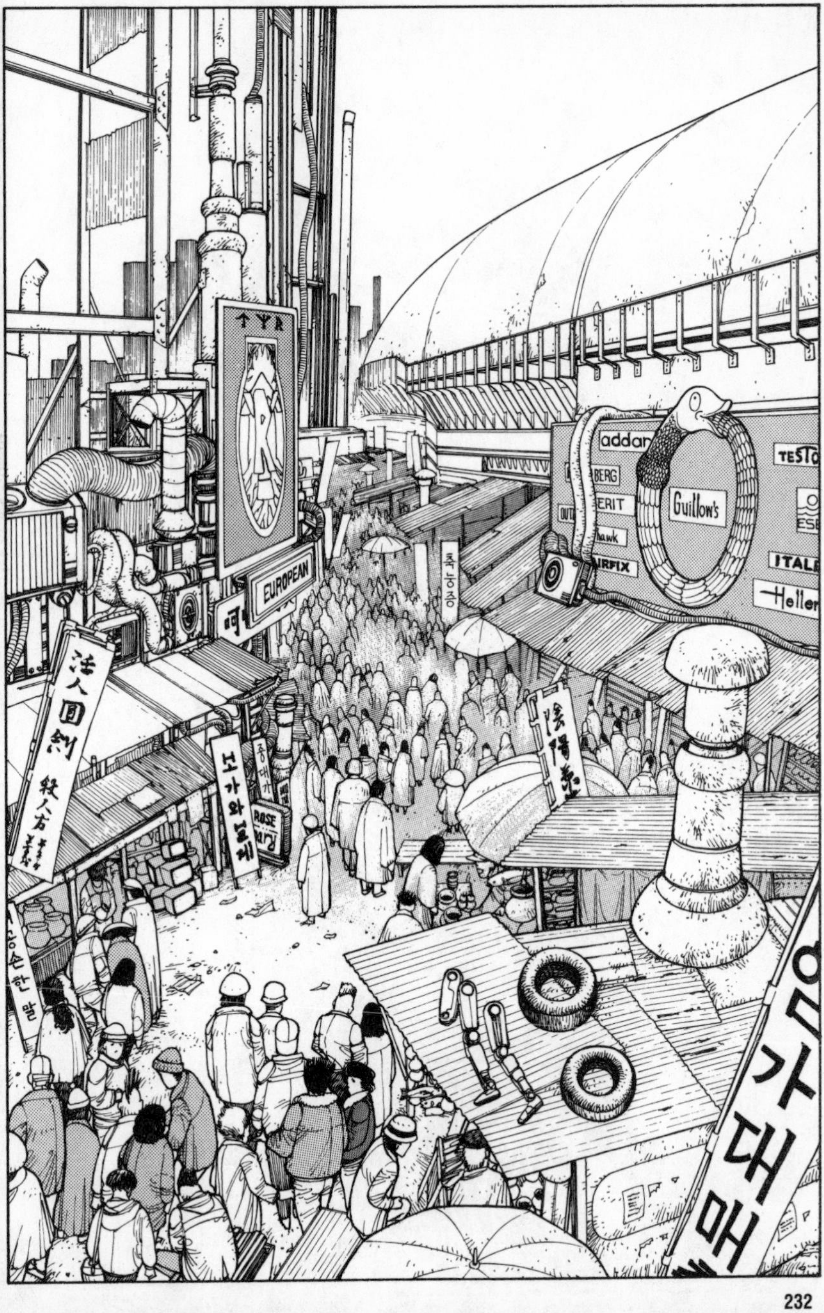
TYR
EUROPEAN
축농증
Guillow's
addan
TESTO
BERG
ERIT
hawk
ITALE
Heller
ROSE
가대매

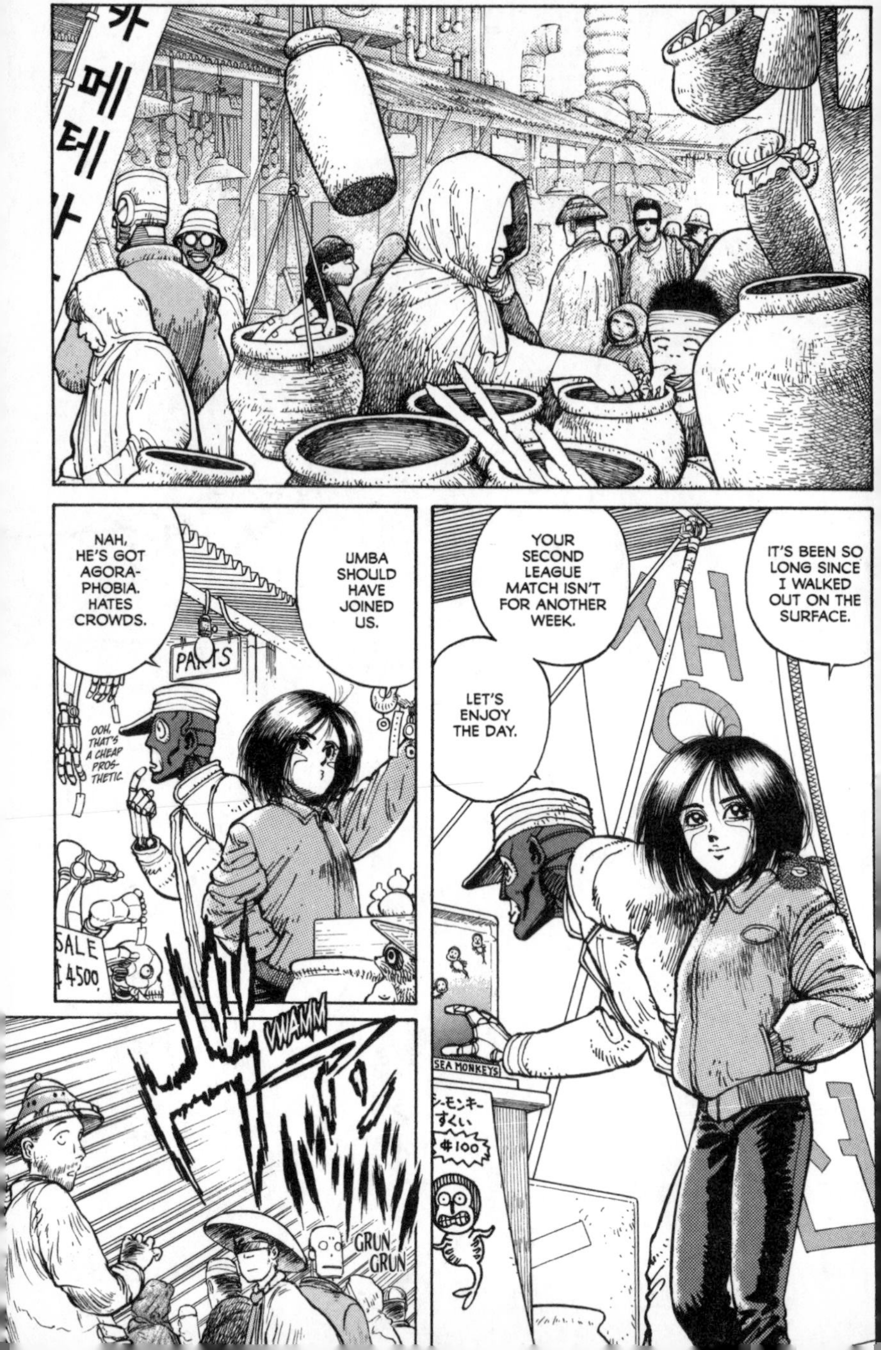
IT'S BEEN SO LONG SINCE I WALKED OUT ON THE SURFACE.
YOUR SECOND LEAGUE MATCH ISN'T FOR ANOTHER WEEK.
LET'S ENJOY THE DAY.
SEA MONKEYS
シーモンキーすくい
UMBA SHOULD HAVE JOINED US.
NAH, HE'S GOT AGORA-PHOBIA. HATES CROWDS.
PARTS
OOH, THAT'S A CHEAP PROS-THETIC.
SALE
VWAMM
GRUN GRUN

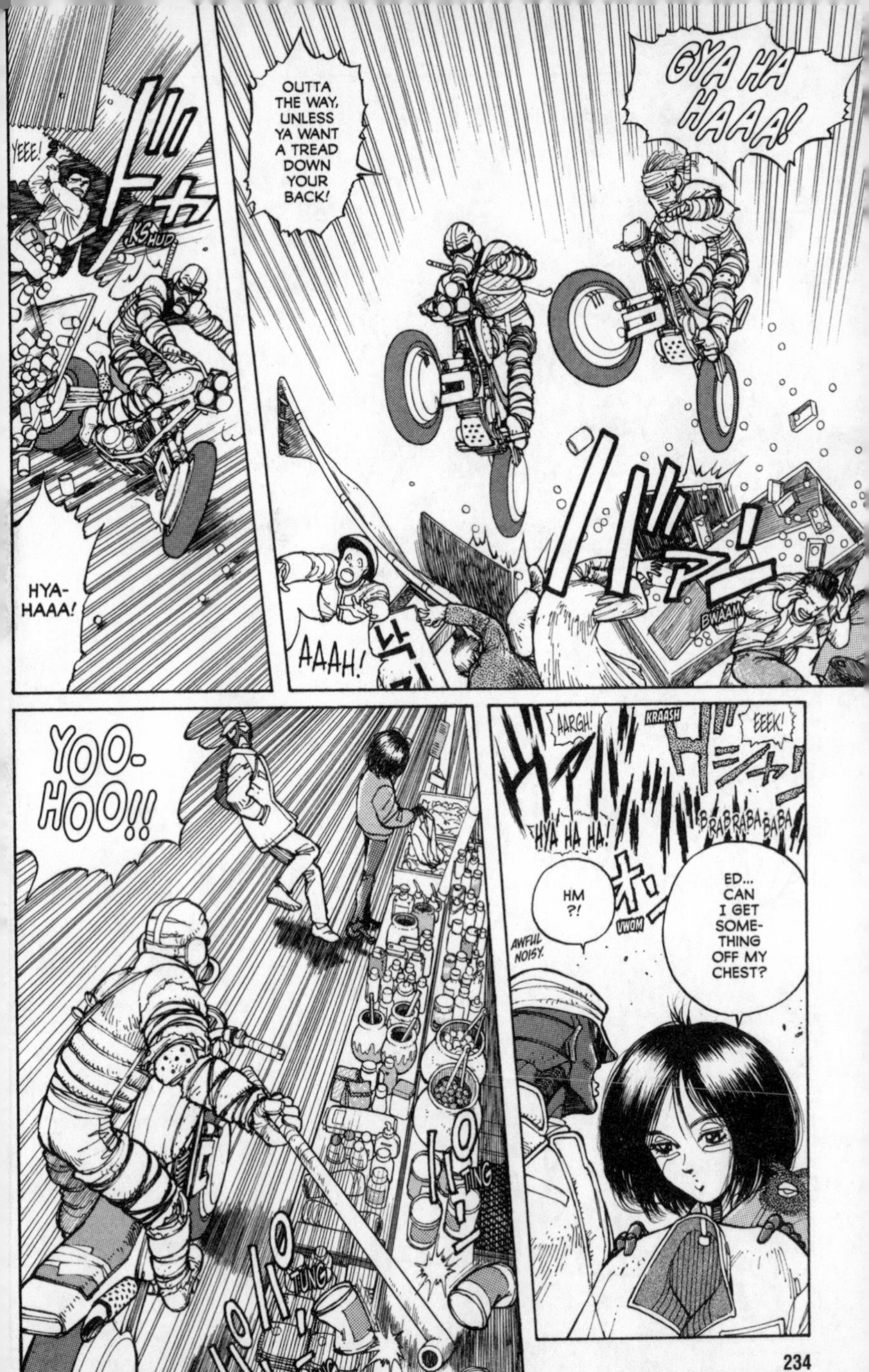
GYA HA HAAA!
OUTTA THE WAY, UNLESS YA WANT A TREAD DOWN YOUR BACK!
AAAH!
BWAAM
YEEE!
KSHUD
HYA-HAAA!
AARGH!
KRAASH
EEEK!
HYA HA HA!
BRABRABA BABA
ED... CAN I GET SOME-THING OFF MY CHEST?
VWOM
HM ?!
AWFUL NOISY.
YOO-HOO!!
TING
TUNG
DANG

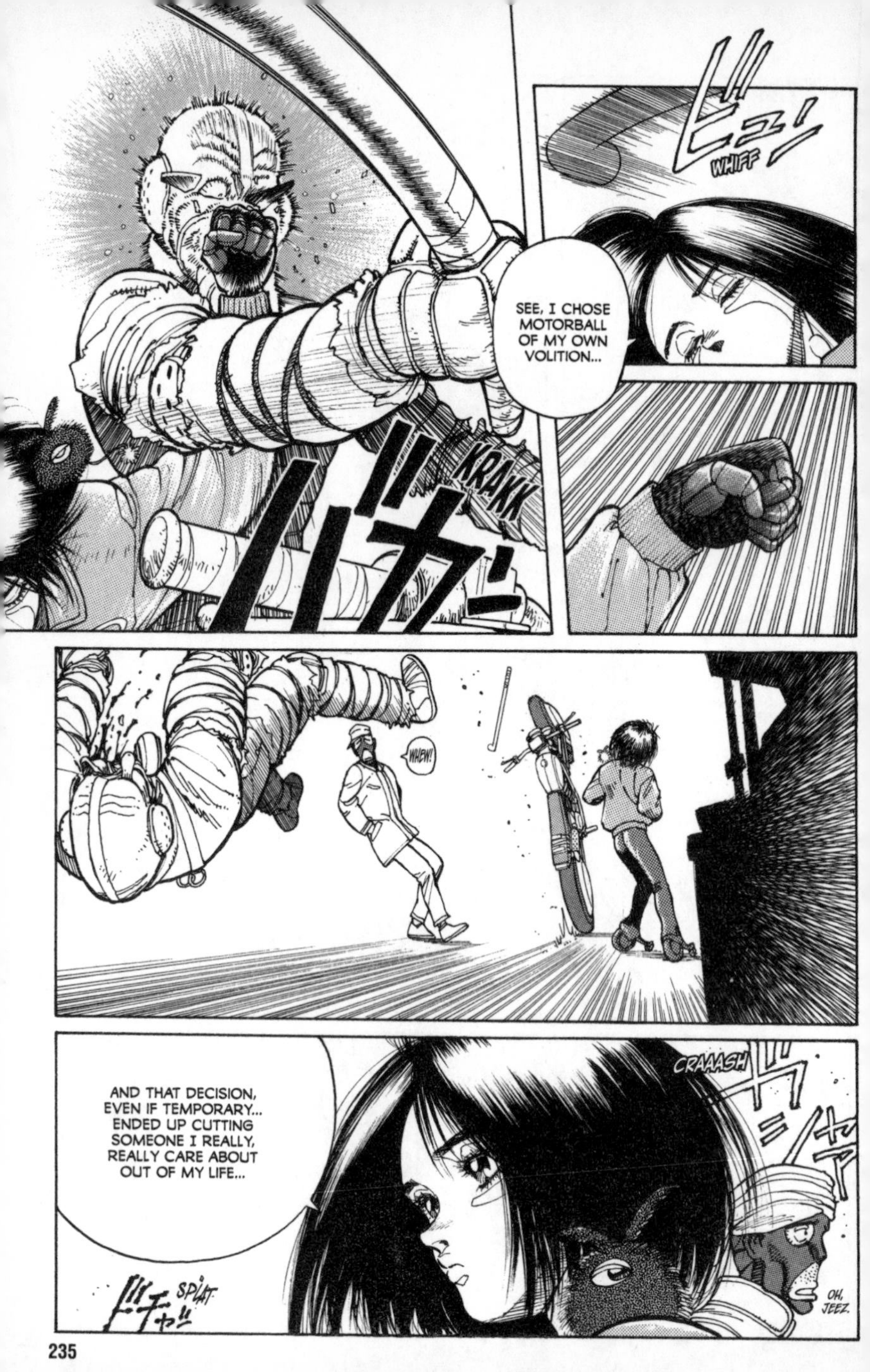
WHIFF
SEE, I CHOSE MOTORBALL OF MY OWN VOLITION...
KRAKK
WHEW!
CRAAASH
AND THAT DECISION, EVEN IF TEMPORARY... ENDED UP CUTTING SOMEONE I REALLY, REALLY CARE ABOUT OUT OF MY LIFE...
OH, JEEZ.
SPLAT

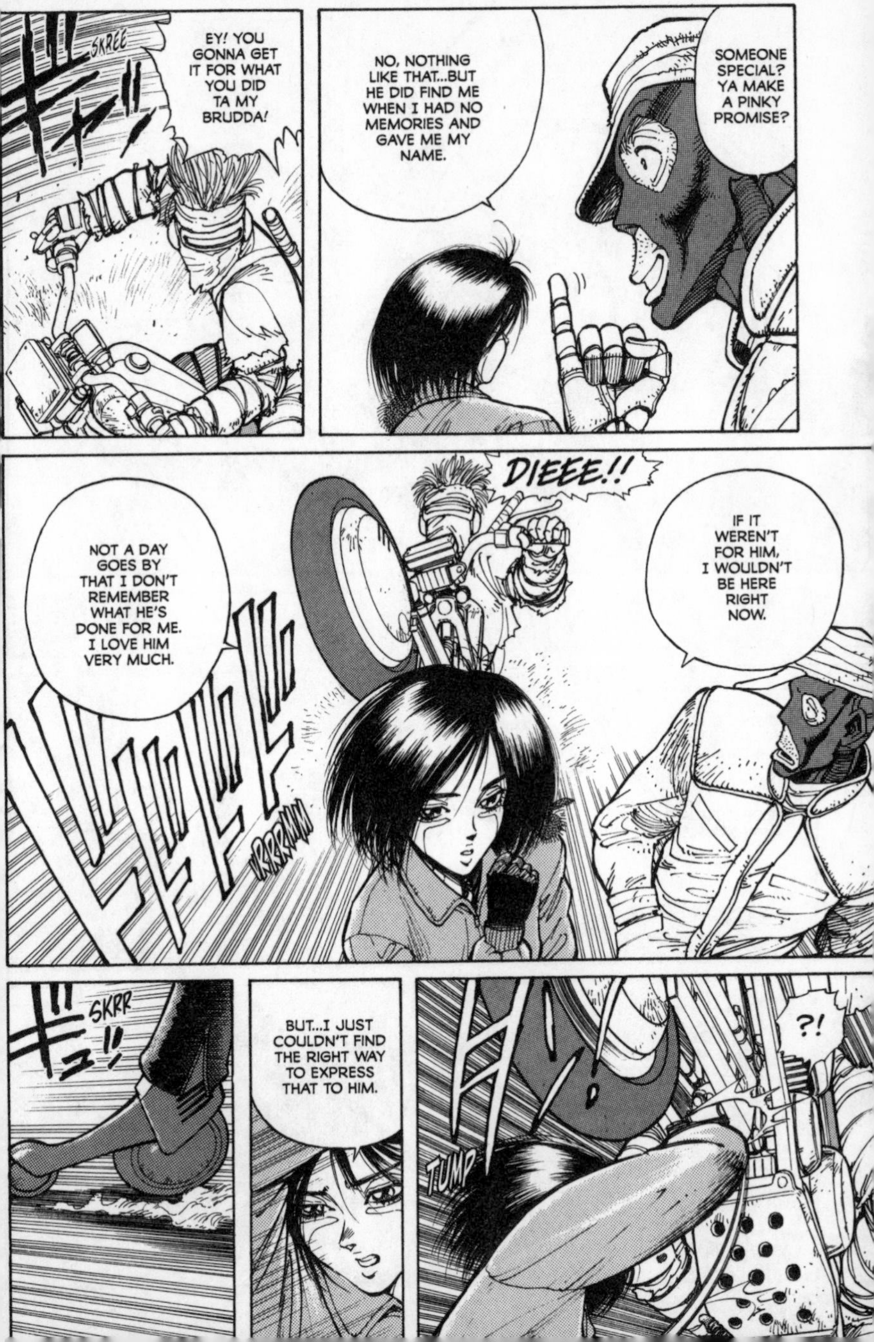
SOMEONE SPECIAL? YA MAKE A PINKY PROMISE?
NO, NOTHING LIKE THAT...BUT HE DID FIND ME WHEN I HAD NO MEMORIES AND GAVE ME MY NAME.
SKREE
EY! YOU GONNA GET IT FOR WHAT YOU DID TA MY BRUDDA!
IF IT WEREN'T FOR HIM, I WOULDN'T BE HERE RIGHT NOW.
DIEEE!!
NOT A DAY GOES BY THAT I DON'T REMEMBER WHAT HE'S DONE FOR ME. I LOVE HIM VERY MUCH.
VRRRMM
?!
TUMP
BUT...I JUST COULDN'T FIND THE RIGHT WAY TO EXPRESS THAT TO HIM.
SKRR

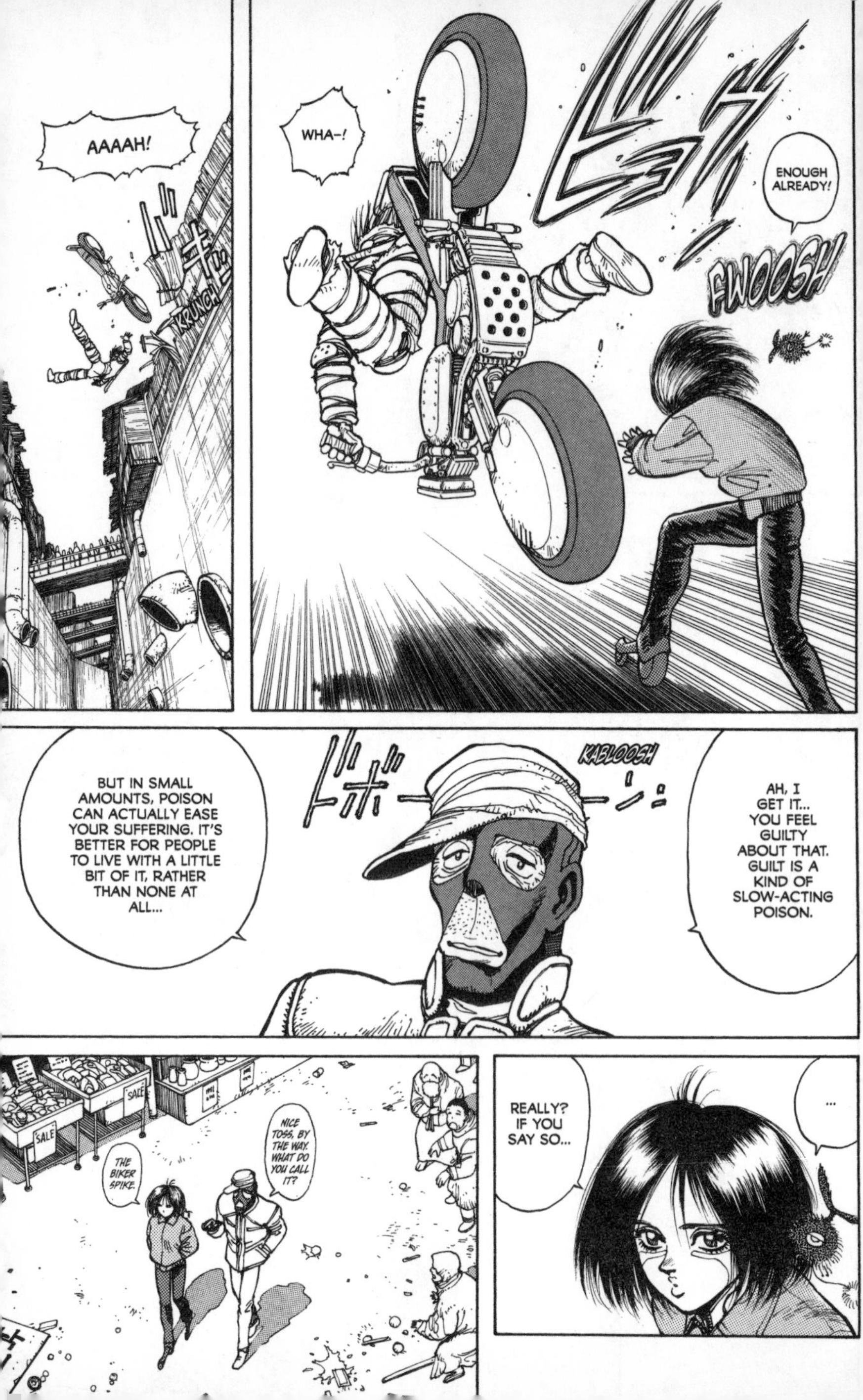
ENOUGH ALREADY!
FWOOSH
WHA-!
AAAAH!
KRUNCH
KABLOOSH
AH, I GET IT... YOU FEEL GUILTY ABOUT THAT. GUILT IS A KIND OF SLOW-ACTING POISON.
BUT IN SMALL AMOUNTS, POISON CAN ACTUALLY EASE YOUR SUFFERING. IT'S BETTER FOR PEOPLE TO LIVE WITH A LITTLE BIT OF IT, RATHER THAN NONE AT ALL...
...
REALLY? IF YOU SAY SO...
NICE TOSS, BY THE WAY. WHAT DO YOU CALL IT?
THE BIKER SPIKE.
SALE
SALE

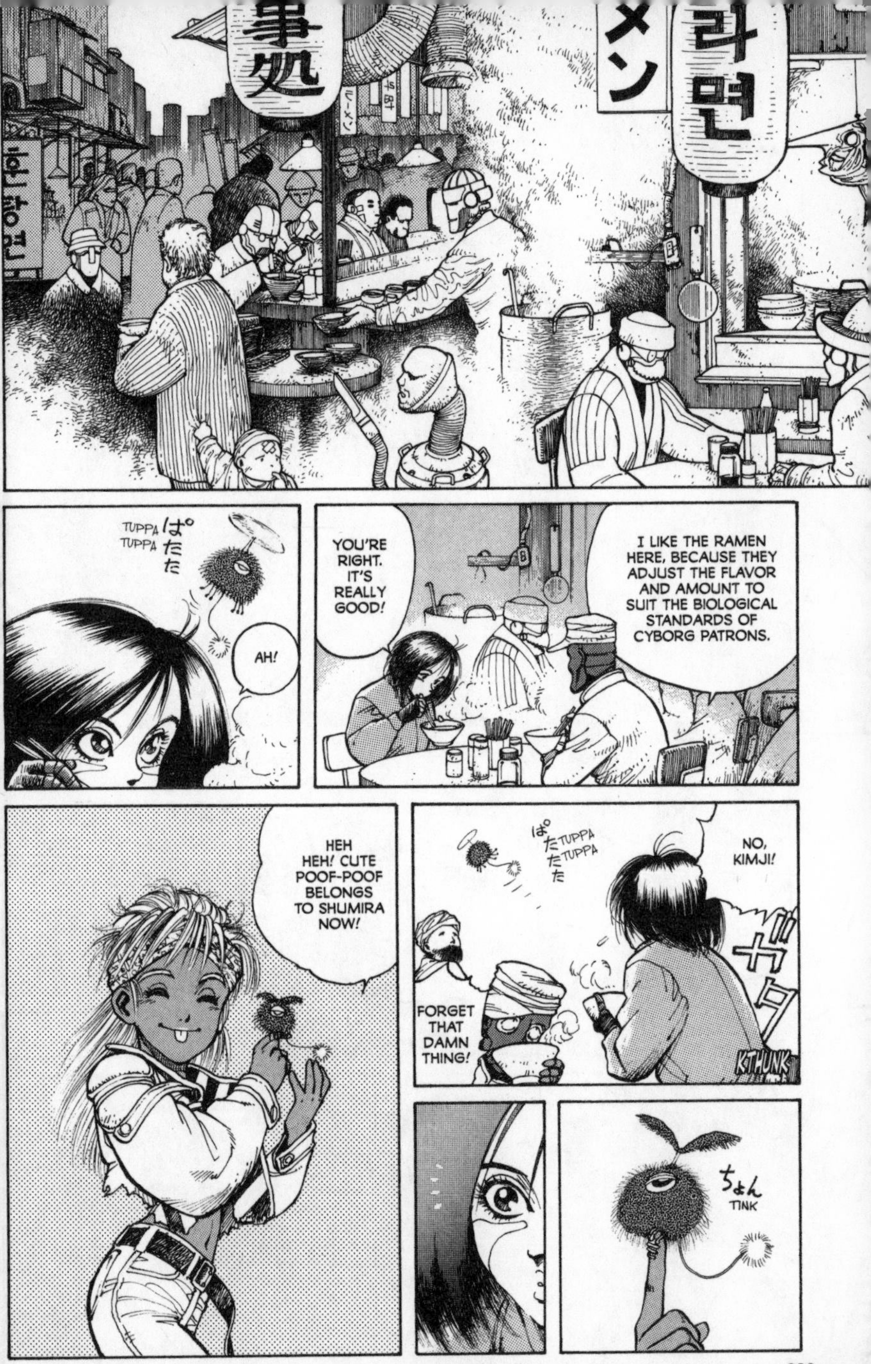

라면
メン
I LIKE THE RAMEN HERE, BECAUSE THEY ADJUST THE FLAVOR AND AMOUNT TO SUIT THE BIOLOGICAL STANDARDS OF CYBORG PATRONS.
YOU'RE RIGHT. IT'S REALLY GOOD!
ぱたた
TUPPA TUPPA
AH!
NO, KIMJI!
ぱたたた
TUPPA TUPPA
ガタ
KTHUNK
FORGET THAT DAMN THING!
ちょん
TINK
HEH HEH! CUTE POOF-POOF BELONGS TO SHUMIRA NOW!

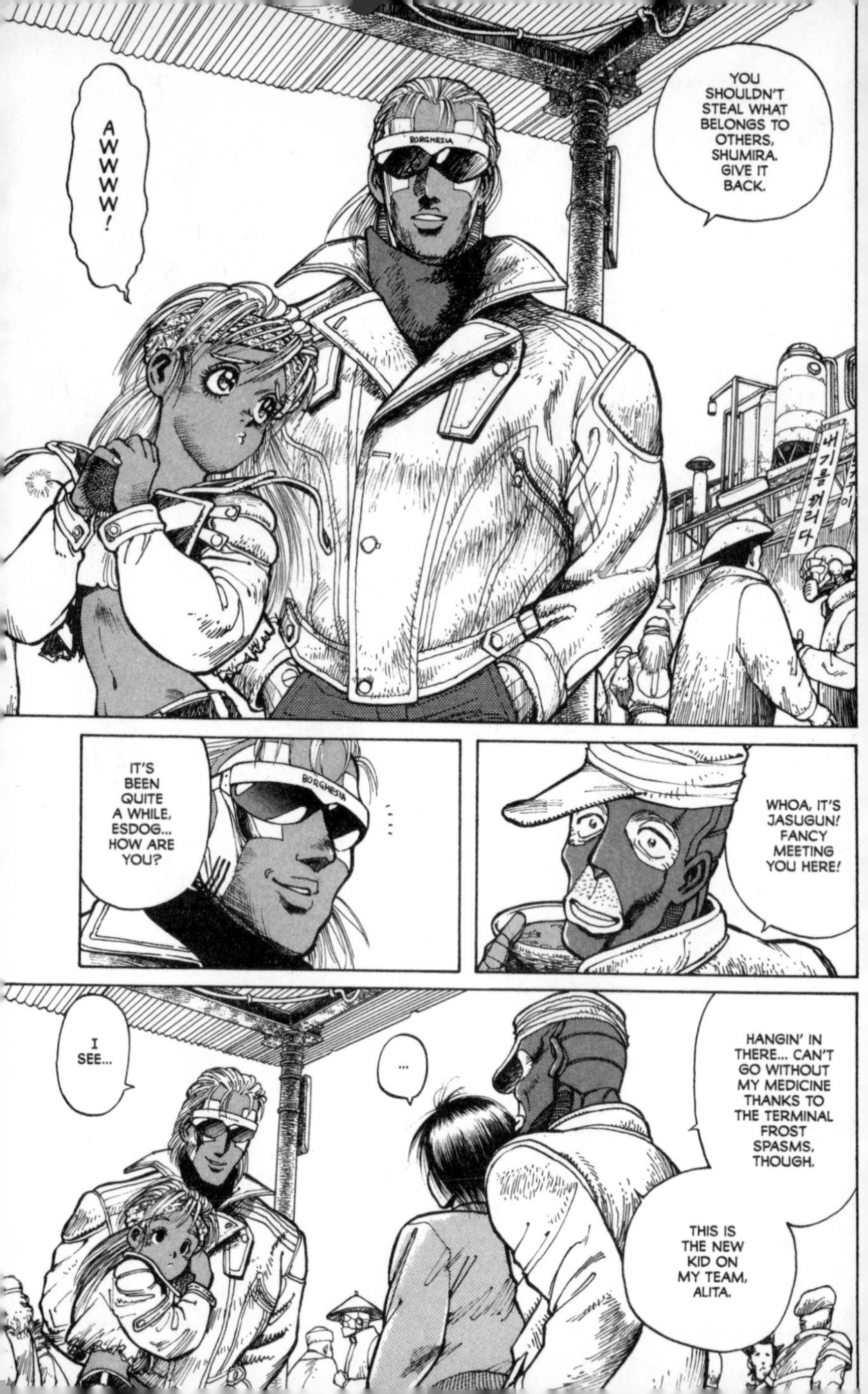
YOU SHOULDN'T STEAL WHAT BELONGS TO OTHERS, SHUMIRA. GIVE IT BACK.
AWWWWW!
BORGHESIA
WHOA, IT'S JASUGUN! FANCY MEETING YOU HERE!
IT'S BEEN QUITE A WHILE, ESDOG... HOW ARE YOU?
HANGIN' IN THERE... CAN'T GO WITHOUT MY MEDICINE THANKS TO THE TERMINAL FROST SPASMS, THOUGH.
THIS IS THE NEW KID ON MY TEAM, ALITA.
...
I SEE...

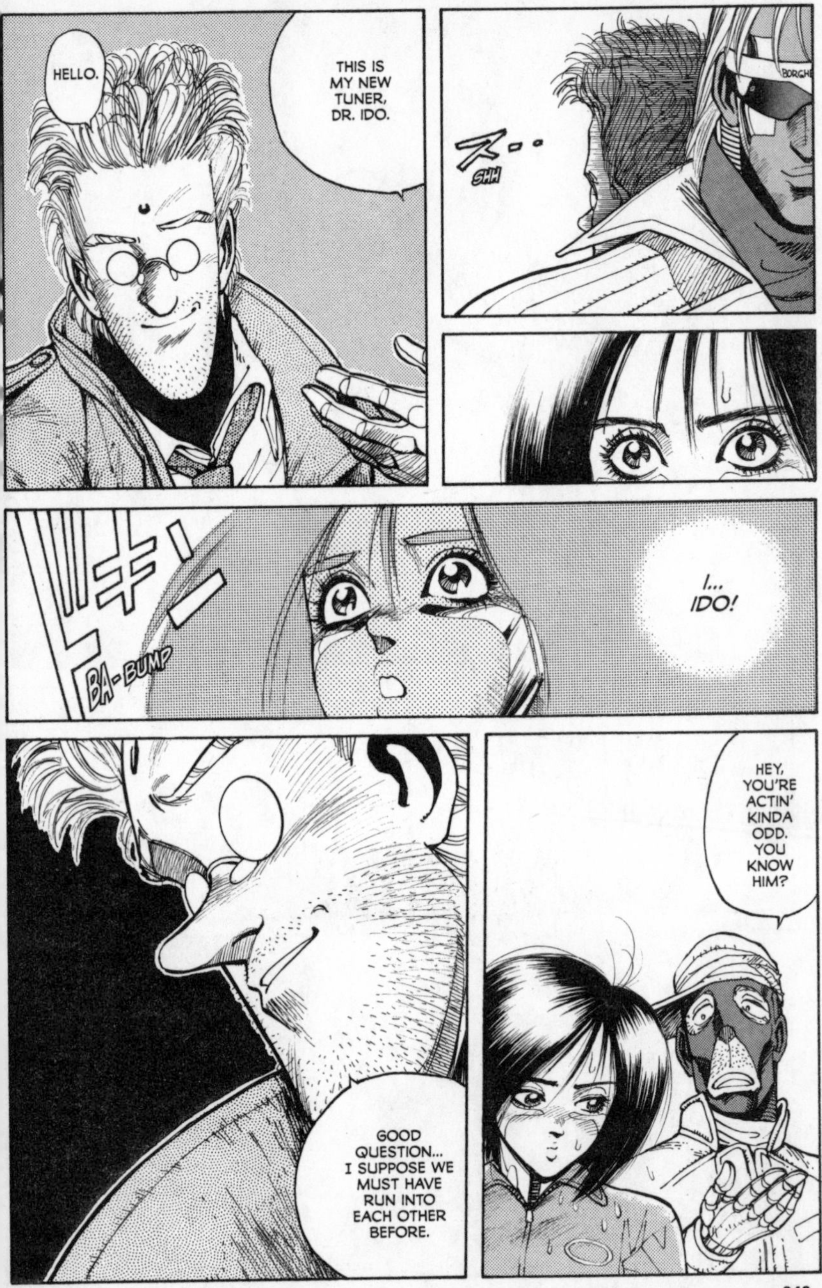
ス・・
SHH
THIS IS MY NEW TUNER, DR. IDO.
HELLO.
ドキッ
BA-BUMP
I... IDO!
HEY, YOU'RE ACTIN' KINDA ODD. YOU KNOW HIM?
GOOD QUESTION... I SUPPOSE WE MUST HAVE RUN INTO EACH OTHER BEFORE.

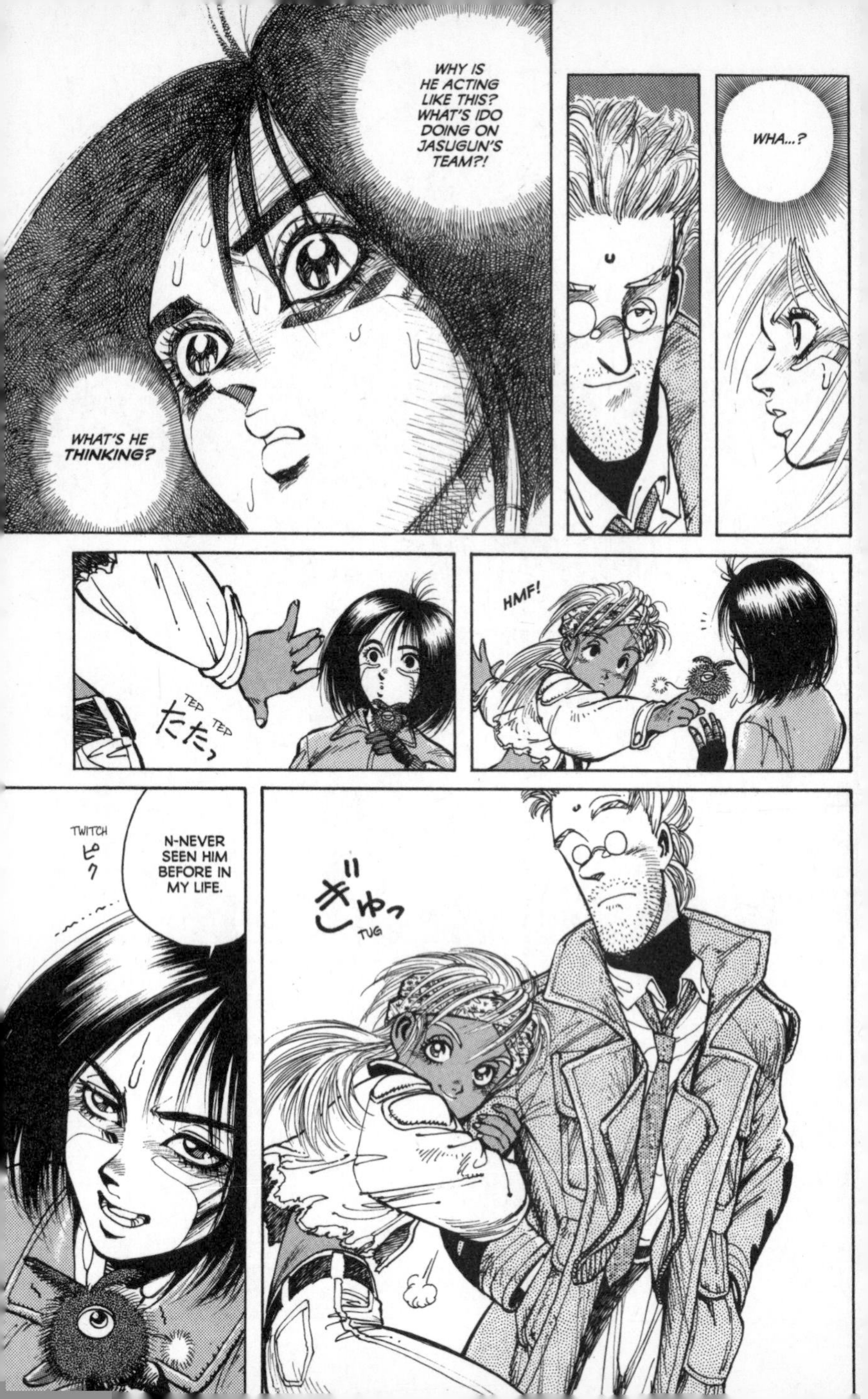
WHA...?
WHY IS HE ACTING LIKE THIS? WHAT'S IDO DOING ON JASUGUN'S TEAM?!
WHAT'S HE THINKING?
HMF!
たたっ
TEP TEP
ぎゅっ
TUG
ピク
TWITCH
N-NEVER SEEN HIM BEFORE IN MY LIFE.

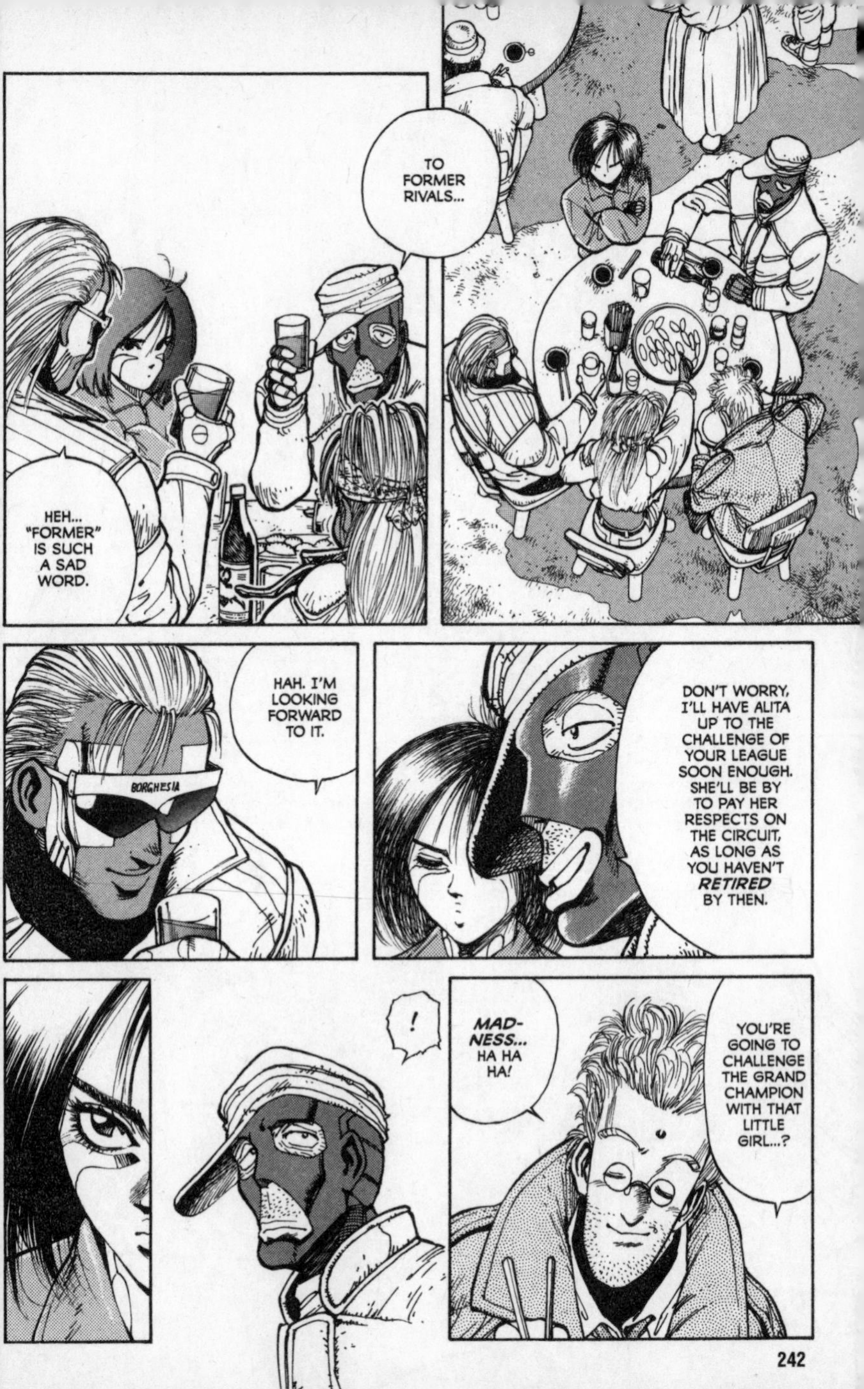
TO FORMER RIVALS...
HEH... "FORMER" IS SUCH A SAD WORD.
DON'T WORRY, I'LL HAVE ALITA UP TO THE CHALLENGE OF YOUR LEAGUE SOON ENOUGH. SHE'LL BE BY TO PAY HER RESPECTS ON THE CIRCUIT, AS LONG AS YOU HAVEN'T *RETIRED* BY THEN.
HAH. I'M LOOKING FORWARD TO IT.
BORGHESIA
YOU'RE GOING TO CHALLENGE THE GRAND CHAMPION WITH THAT LITTLE GIRL...?
MAD-NESS... HA HA HA!
!

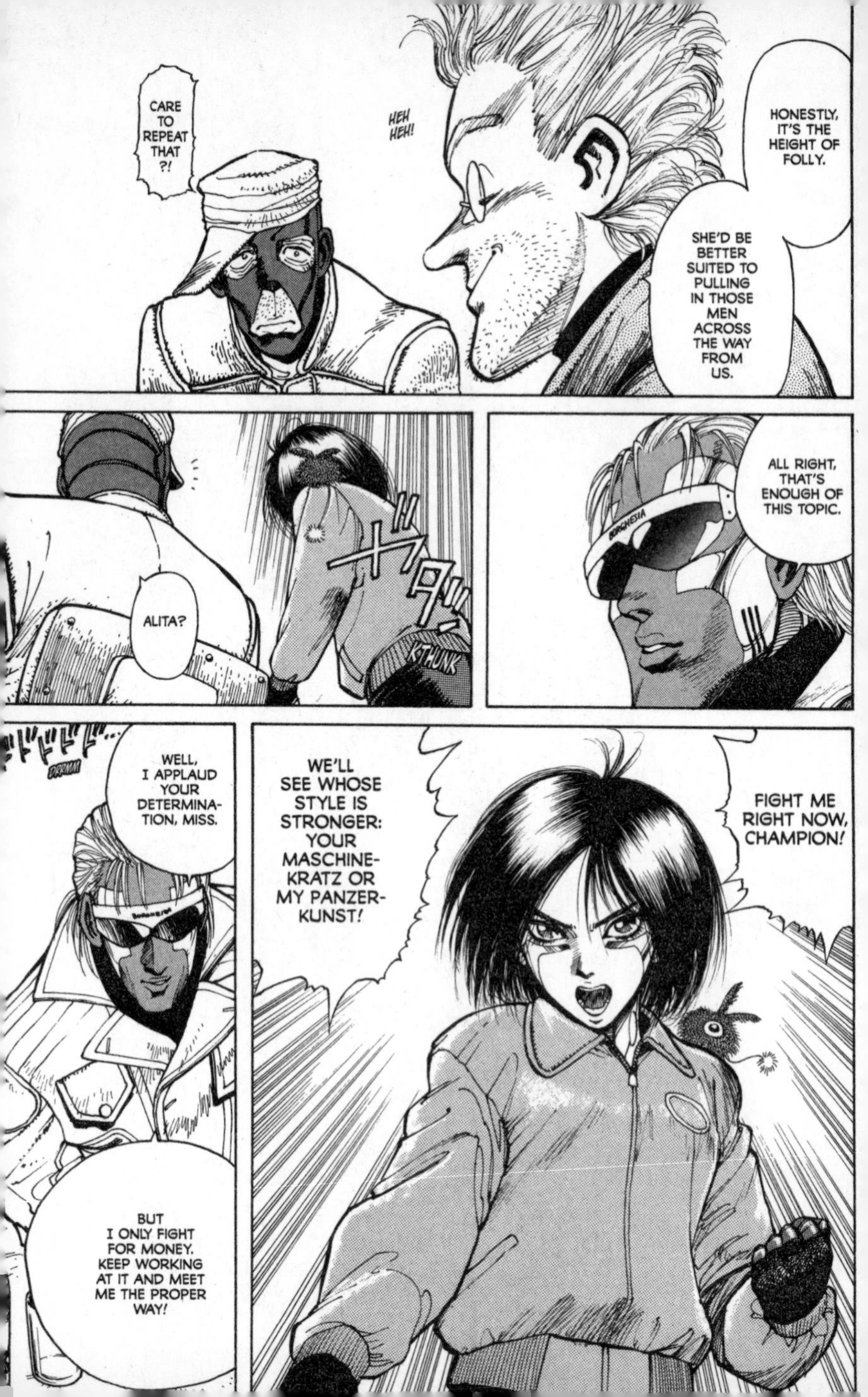
HONESTLY, IT'S THE HEIGHT OF FOLLY.
SHE'D BE BETTER SUITED TO PULLING IN THOSE MEN ACROSS THE WAY FROM US.
HEH HEH!
CARE TO REPEAT THAT ?!
ALL RIGHT, THAT'S ENOUGH OF THIS TOPIC.
K-THUNK
ALITA?
FIGHT ME RIGHT NOW, CHAMPION!
WE'LL SEE WHOSE STYLE IS STRONGER: YOUR MASCHINE-KRATZ OR MY PANZER-KUNST!
DRMM
WELL, I APPLAUD YOUR DETERMINA-TION, MISS.
BUT I ONLY FIGHT FOR MONEY. KEEP WORKING AT IT AND MEET ME THE PROPER WAY!

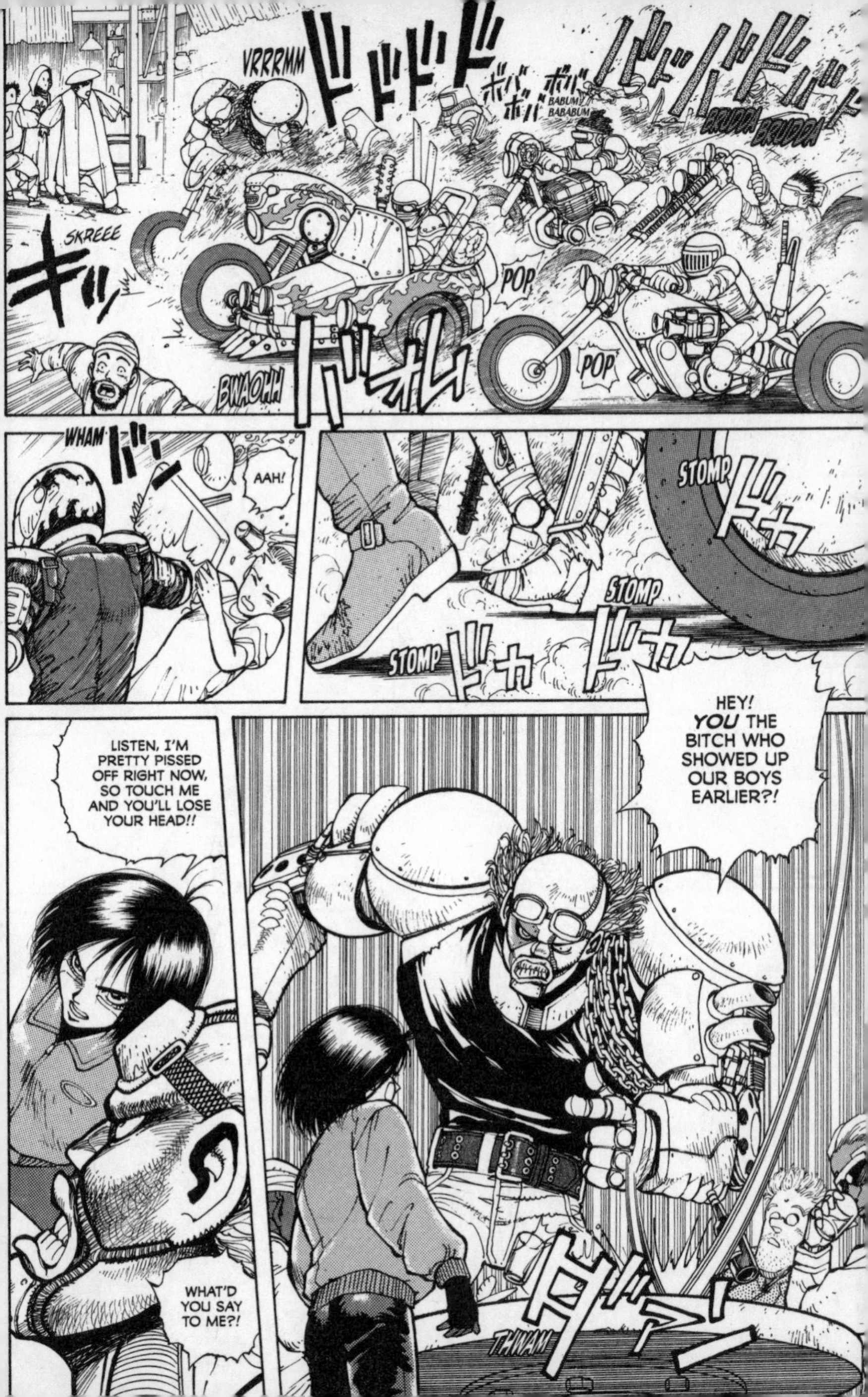
BRUDA BRUDA
BABUM BABABUM
VRRRMM
POP
POP
BWAOHH
SKREEE
STOMP
STOMP
STOMP
WHAM
AAH!
HEY! *YOU* THE BITCH WHO SHOWED UP OUR BOYS EARLIER?!
THWAM
LISTEN, I'M PRETTY PISSED OFF RIGHT NOW, SO TOUCH ME AND YOU'LL LOSE YOUR HEAD!!
WHAT'D YOU SAY TO ME?!

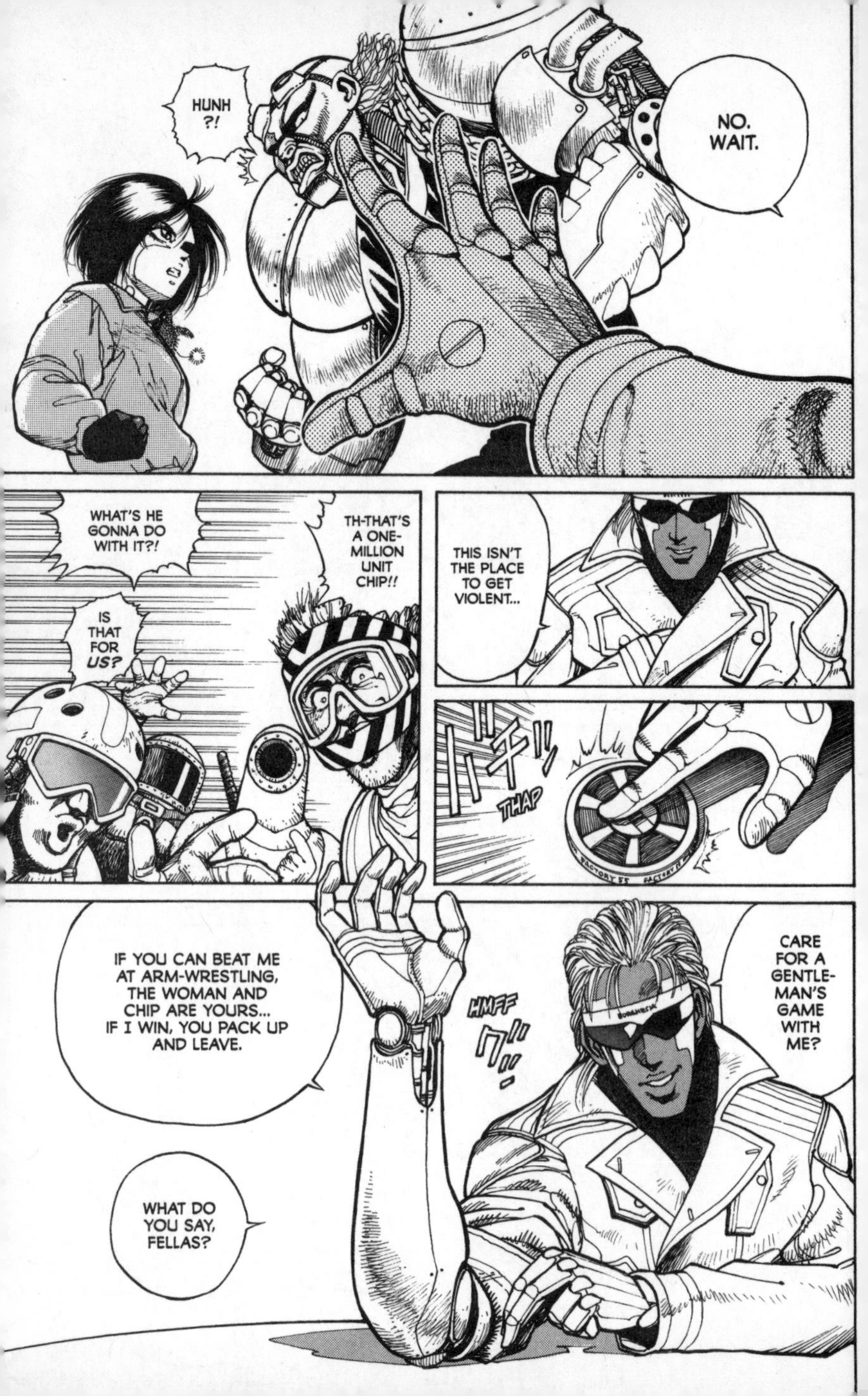
NO. WAIT.
HUNH ?!
THIS ISN'T THE PLACE TO GET VIOLENT...
TH-THAT'S A ONE-MILLION UNIT CHIP!!
WHAT'S HE GONNA DO WITH IT?!
IS THAT FOR US?
THAP
CARE FOR A GENTLE-MAN'S GAME WITH ME?
HMFF
IF YOU CAN BEAT ME AT ARM-WRESTLING, THE WOMAN AND CHIP ARE YOURS... IF I WIN, YOU PACK UP AND LEAVE.
WHAT DO YOU SAY, FELLAS?

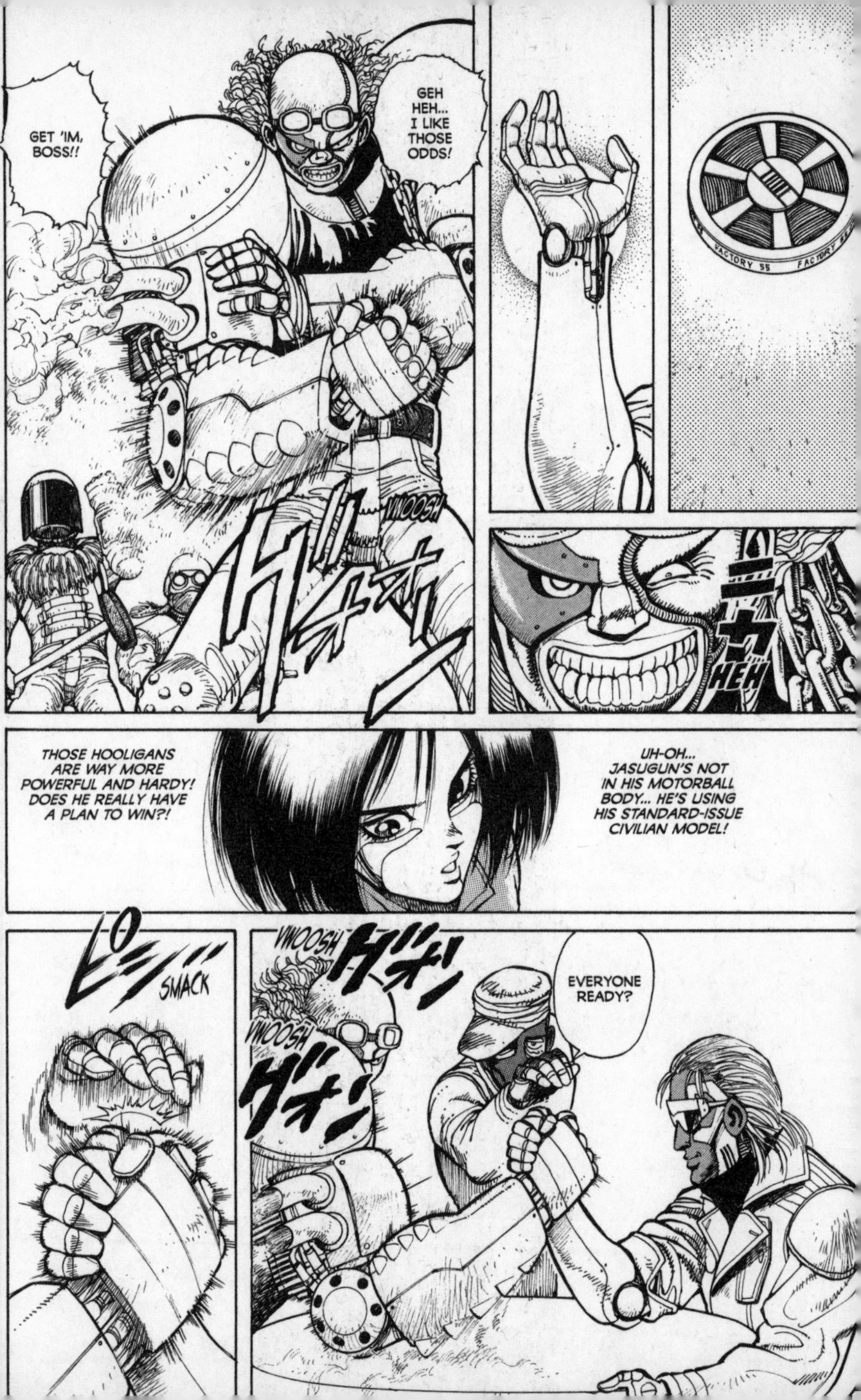
FACTORY 55
HEH
GEH HEH... I LIKE THOSE ODDS!
VWOOSH
GET 'IM, BOSS!!
UH-OH... JASUGUN'S NOT IN HIS MOTORBALL BODY... HE'S USING HIS STANDARD-ISSUE CIVILIAN MODEL!
THOSE HOOLIGANS ARE WAY MORE POWERFUL AND HARDY! DOES HE REALLY HAVE A PLAN TO WIN?!
EVERYONE READY?
VWOOSH
VWOOSH
SMACK

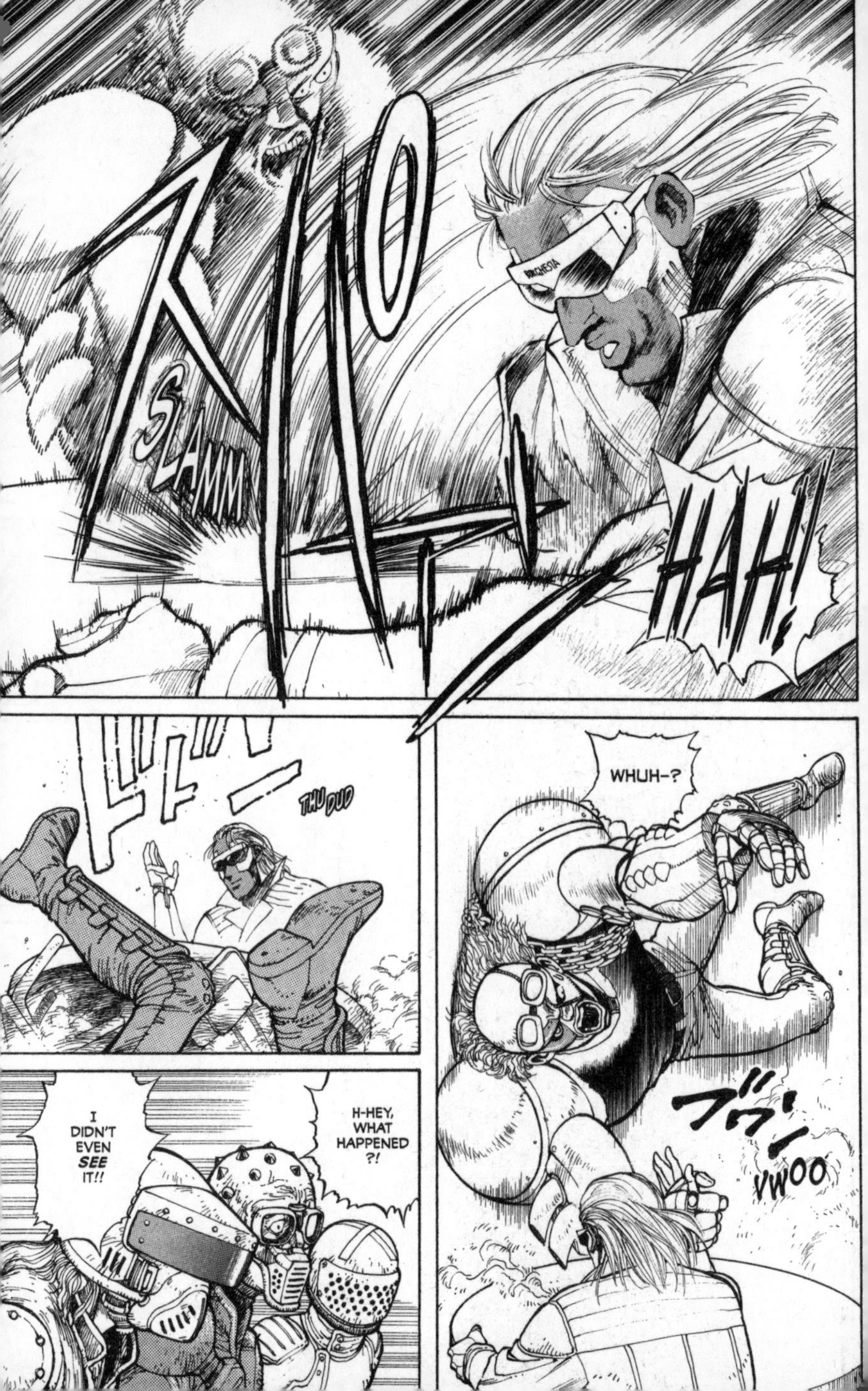
HAH!
SLAMM
WHUH-?
VWOO
THUDUD
H-HEY, WHAT HAPPENED ?!
I DIDN'T EVEN SEE IT!!

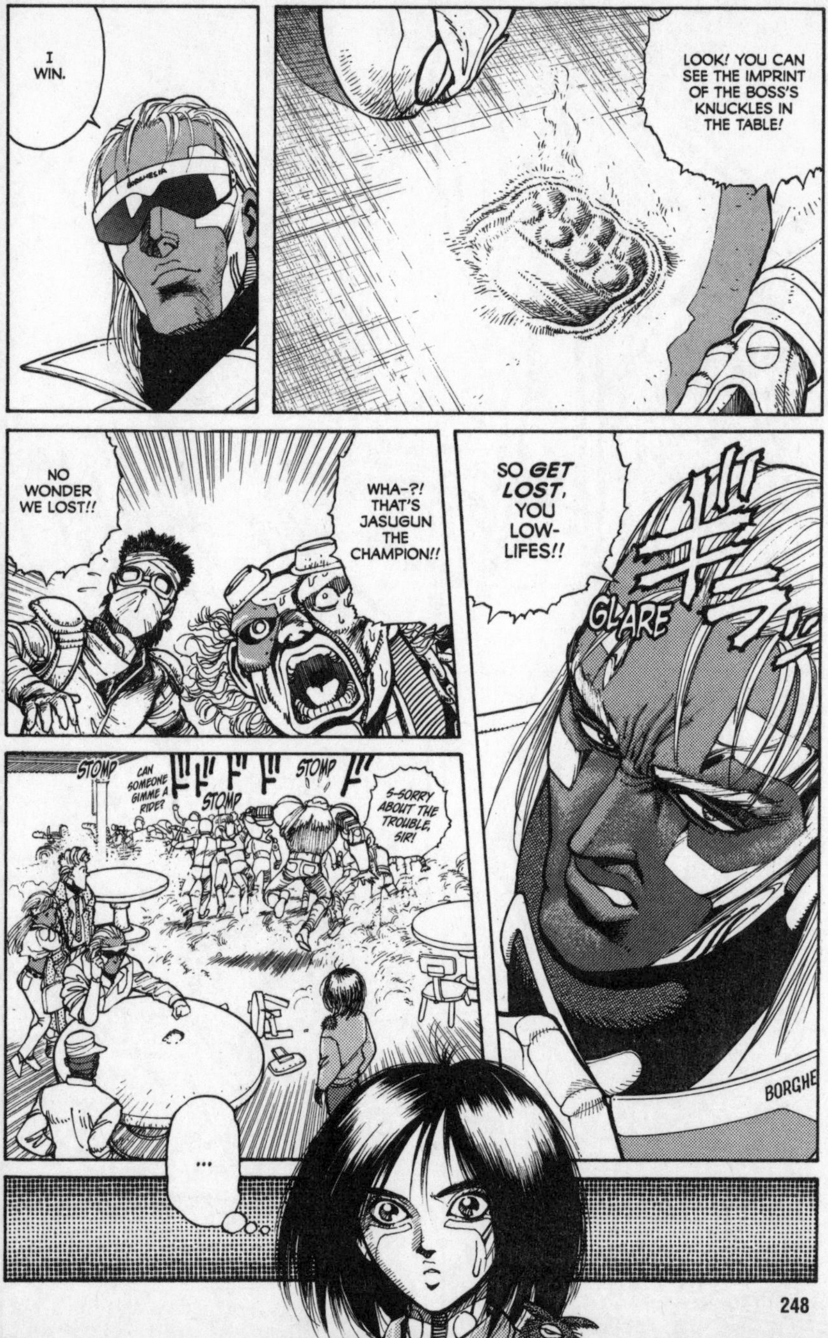
LOOK! YOU CAN SEE THE IMPRINT OF THE BOSS'S KNUCKLES IN THE TABLE!
I WIN.
SO GET LOST, YOU LOW-LIFES!!
GLARE
WHA-?! THAT'S JASUGUN THE CHAMPION!!
NO WONDER WE LOST!!
S-SORRY ABOUT THE TROUBLE, SIR!
STOMP
STOMP
CAN SOMEONE GIMME A RIDE?
STOMP
BORGHE
...

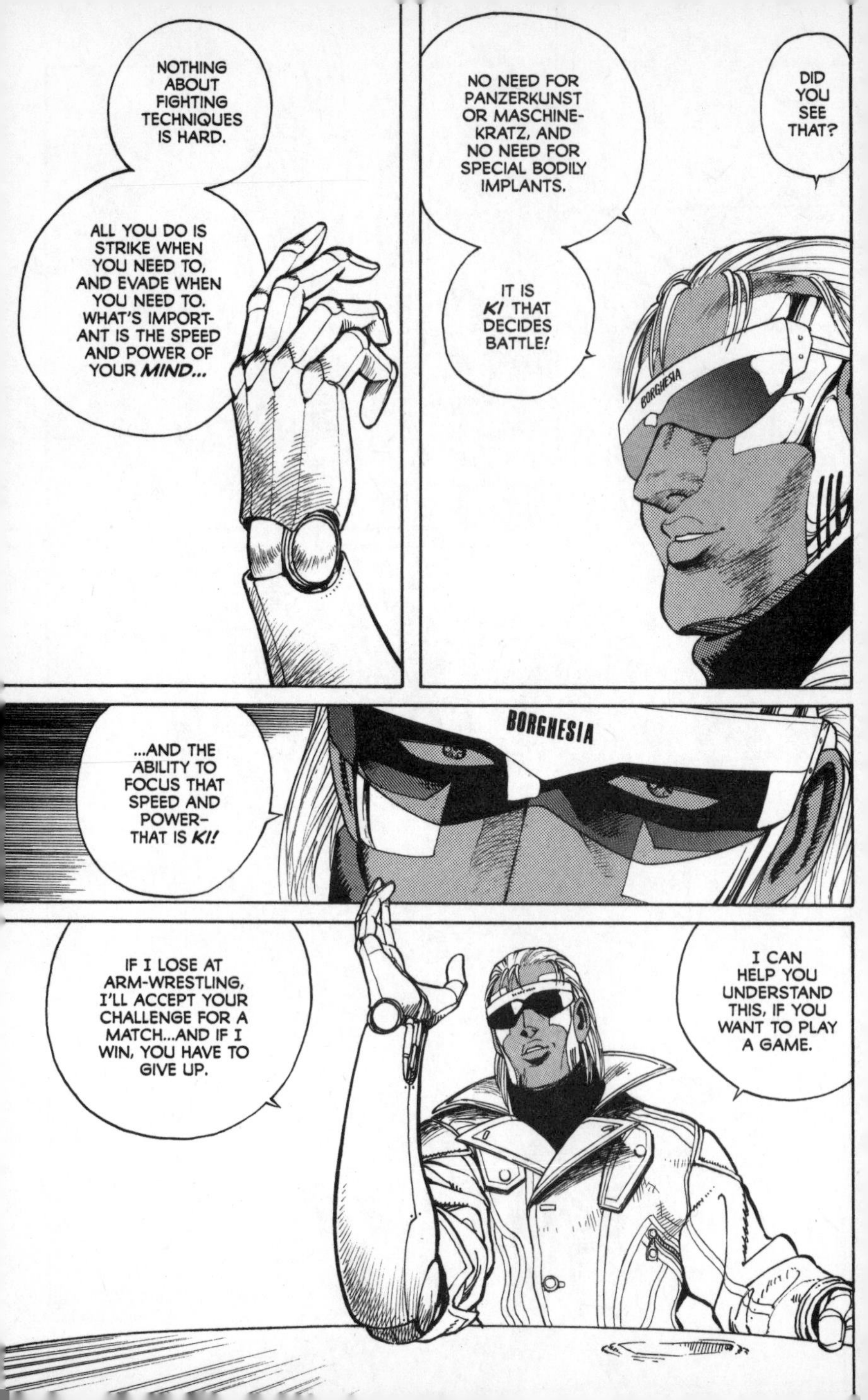
DID YOU SEE THAT?
NO NEED FOR PANZERKUNST OR MASCHINE-KRATZ, AND NO NEED FOR SPECIAL BODILY IMPLANTS.
IT IS *KI* THAT DECIDES BATTLE!
BORGHESIA
NOTHING ABOUT FIGHTING TECHNIQUES IS HARD.
ALL YOU DO IS STRIKE WHEN YOU NEED TO, AND EVADE WHEN YOU NEED TO. WHAT'S IMPORT-ANT IS THE SPEED AND POWER OF YOUR ***MIND...***
BORGHESIA
...AND THE ABILITY TO FOCUS THAT SPEED AND POWER– THAT IS ***KI!***
I CAN HELP YOU UNDERSTAND THIS, IF YOU WANT TO PLAY A GAME.
IF I LOSE AT ARM-WRESTLING, I'LL ACCEPT YOUR CHALLENGE FOR A MATCH...AND IF I WIN, YOU HAVE TO GIVE UP.

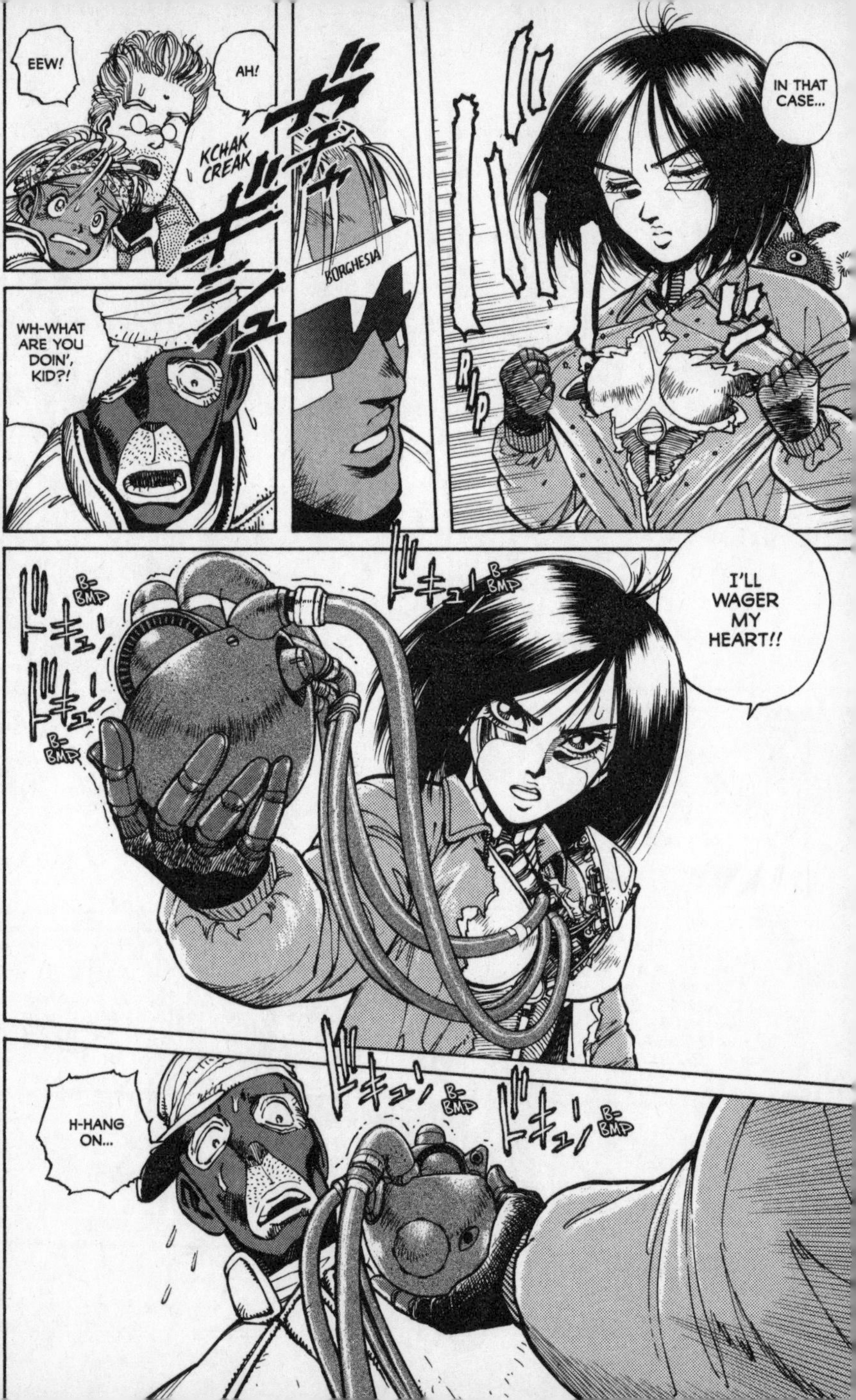
IN THAT CASE...
RIP
BORGHESIA
KCHAK CREAK
AH!
EEW!
WH-WHAT ARE YOU DOIN', KID?!
I'LL WAGER MY HEART!!
B-BMP
B-BMP
B-BMP
B-BMP
B-BMP
H-HANG ON...

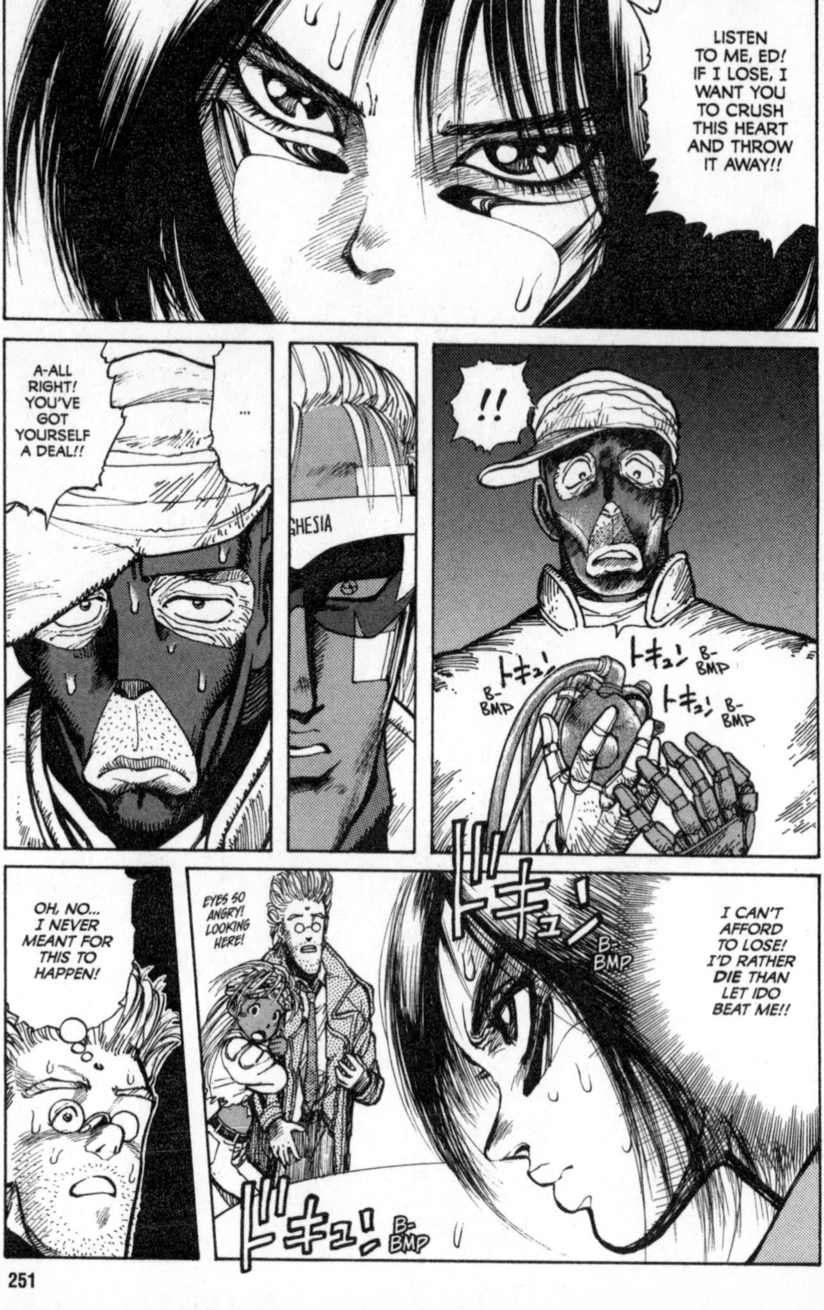
LISTEN TO ME, ED! IF I LOSE, I WANT YOU TO CRUSH THIS HEART AND THROW IT AWAY!!
!!
トキュン B-BMP
トキュン B-BMP
トキュン B-BMP
GHESIA
...
A-ALL RIGHT! YOU'VE GOT YOURSELF A DEAL!!
ドキュン B-BMP
I CAN'T AFFORD TO LOSE! I'D RATHER DIE THAN LET IDO BEAT ME!!
ドキュン B-BMP
EYES SO ANGRY! LOOKING HERE!
OH, NO... I NEVER MEANT FOR THIS TO HAPPEN!

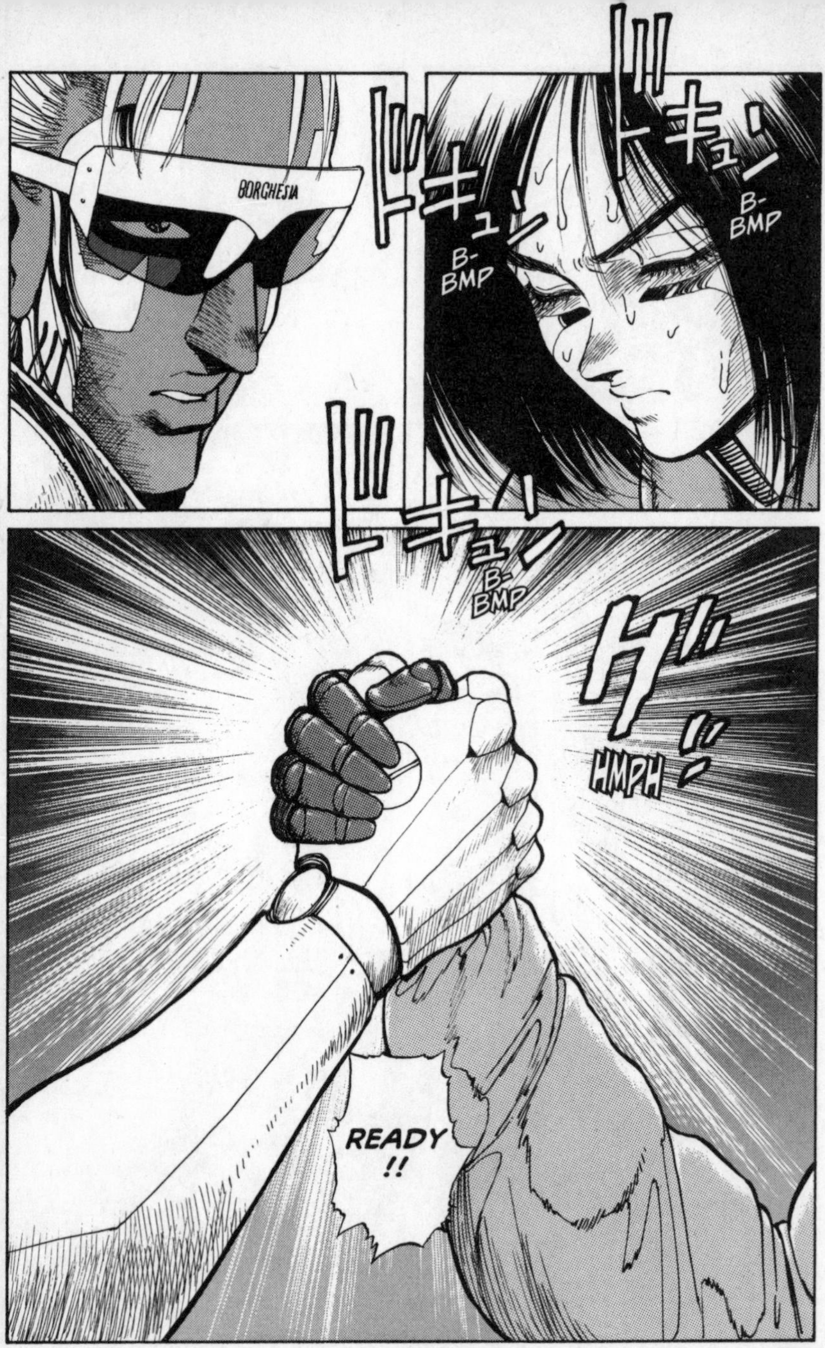
ドキュン
B-BMP
ドキュン
B-BMP
BORGHESIA
ドキュン
B-BMP
グッ
HMPH
READY !!

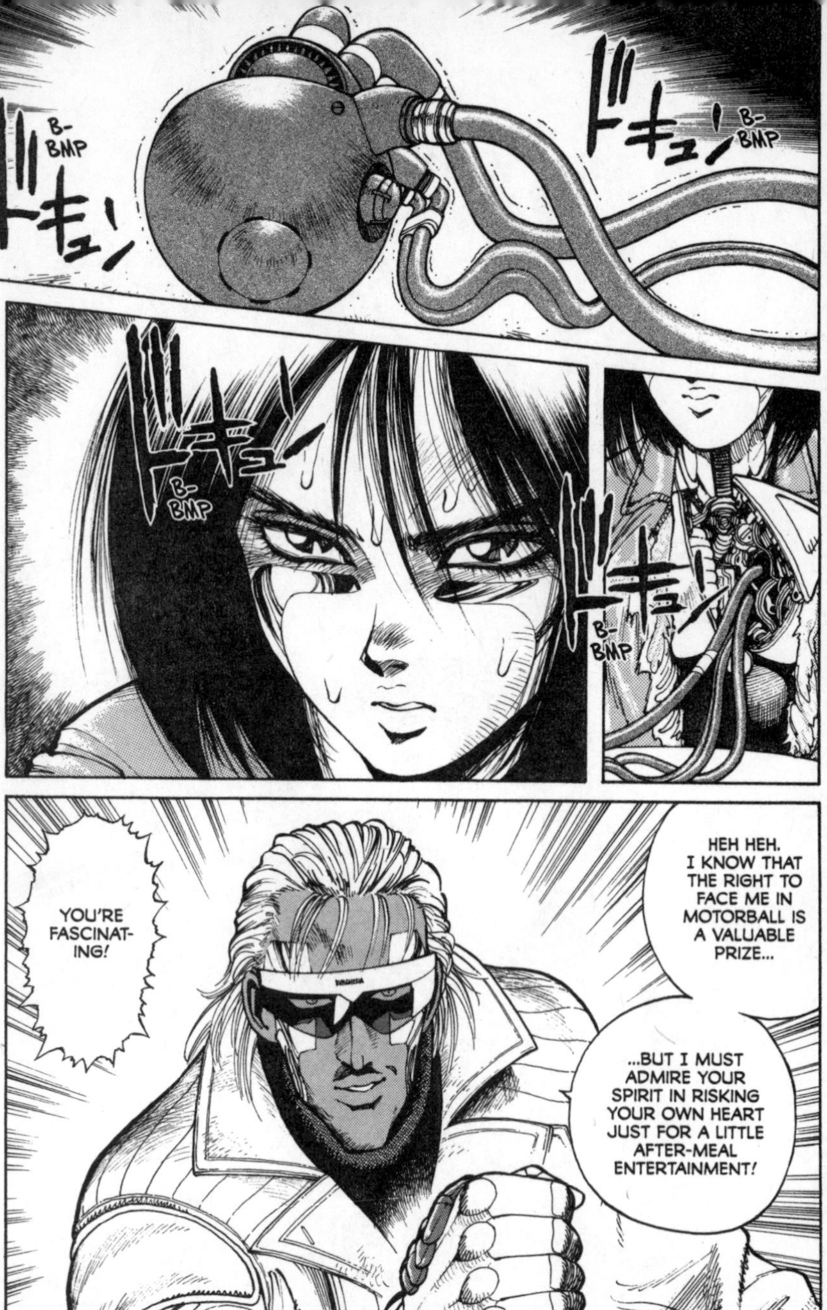
B-BMP
B-BMP
B-BMP
B-BMP
HEH HEH. I KNOW THAT THE RIGHT TO FACE ME IN MOTORBALL IS A VALUABLE PRIZE...
...BUT I MUST ADMIRE YOUR SPIRIT IN RISKING YOUR OWN HEART JUST FOR A LITTLE AFTER-MEAL ENTERTAINMENT!
YOU'RE FASCINAT-ING!

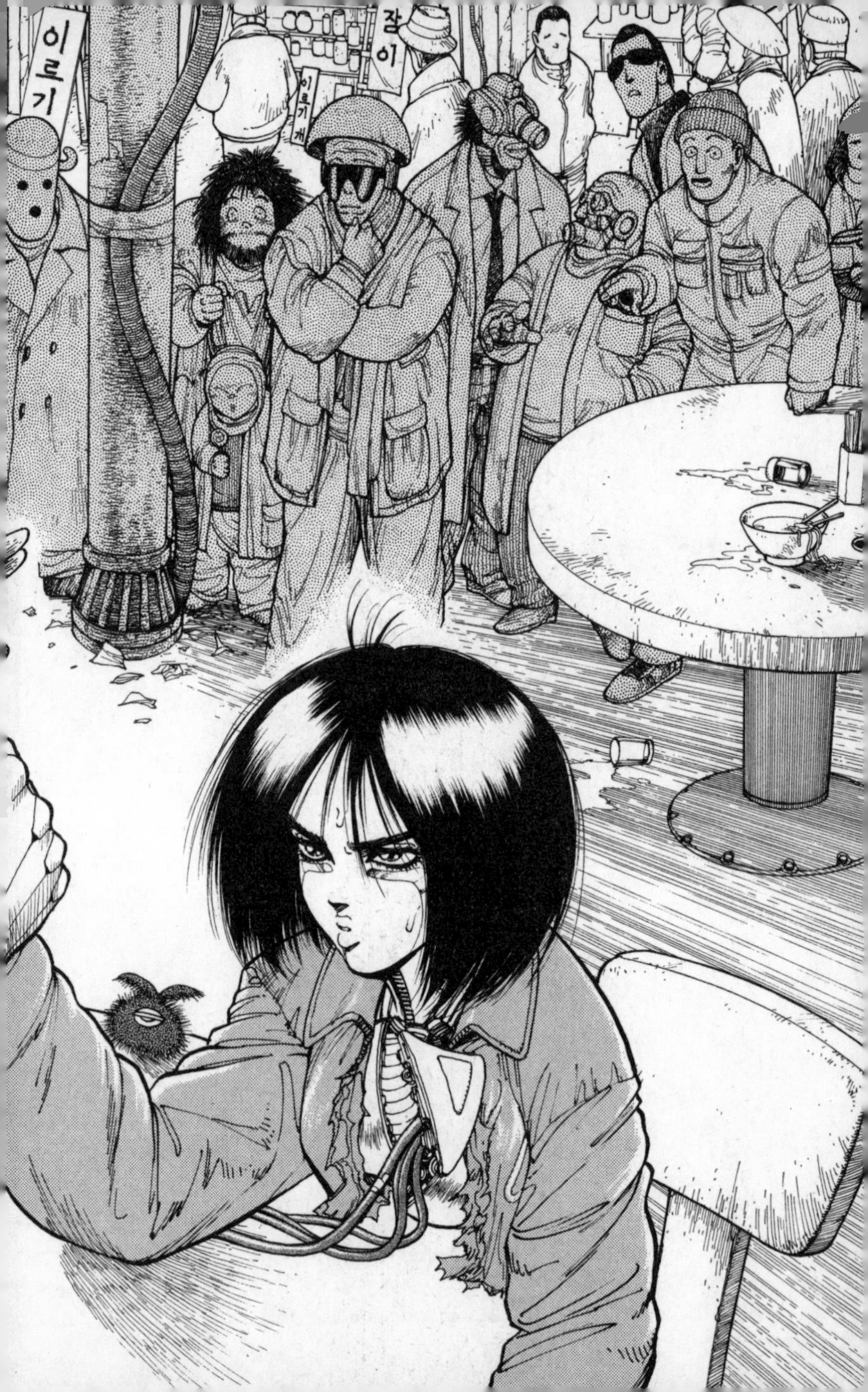
장이
이르기게
이르기

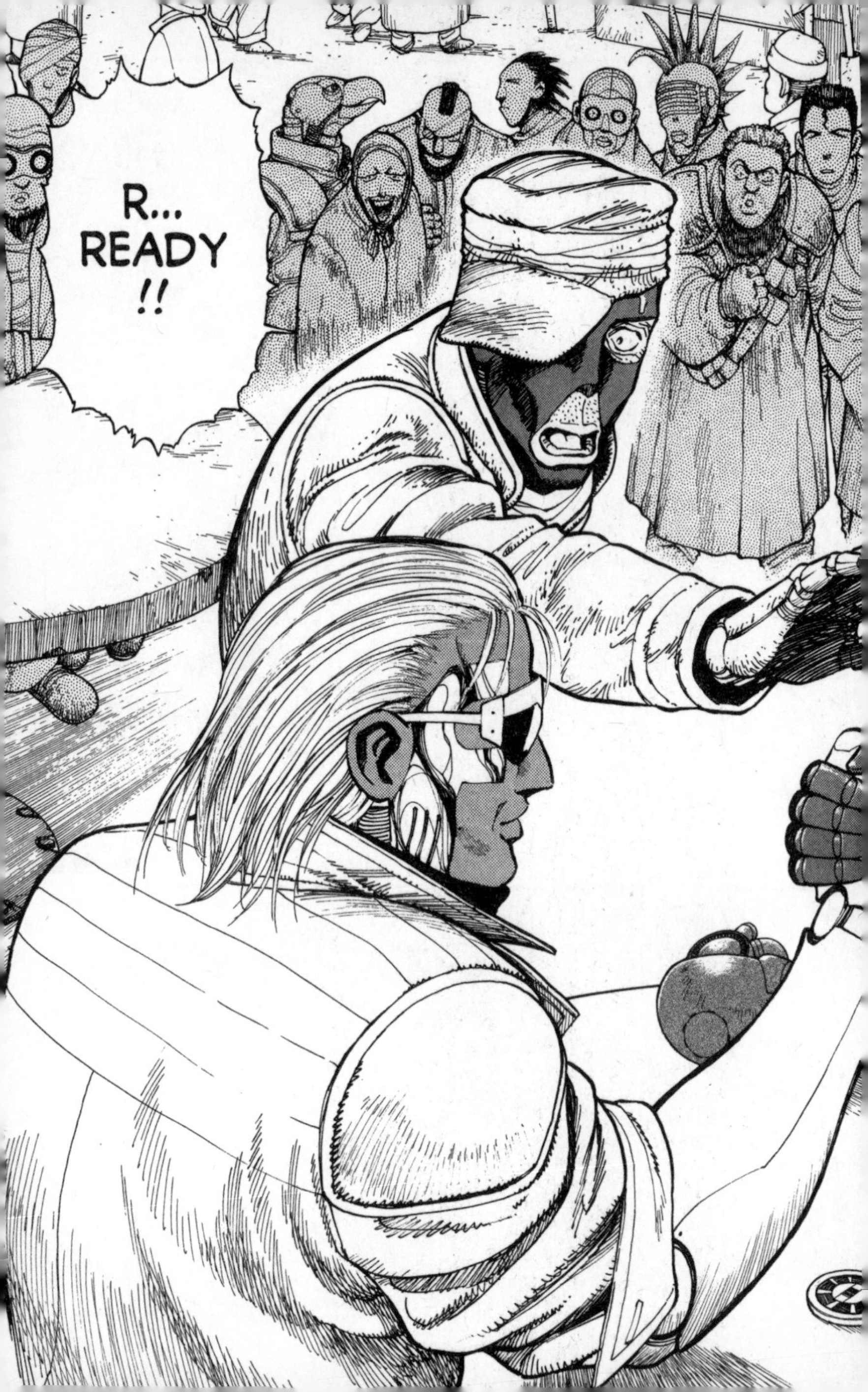
R... READY !!

ALITA...

GULP

YOU SHOULDN'T TENSE UP SO MUCH BEFORE THE START.

HANG ON.

MY ARM ISN'T LIKE YOURS— I'M IN MY DAILY-USE BODY RIGHT NOW.

HRRGG

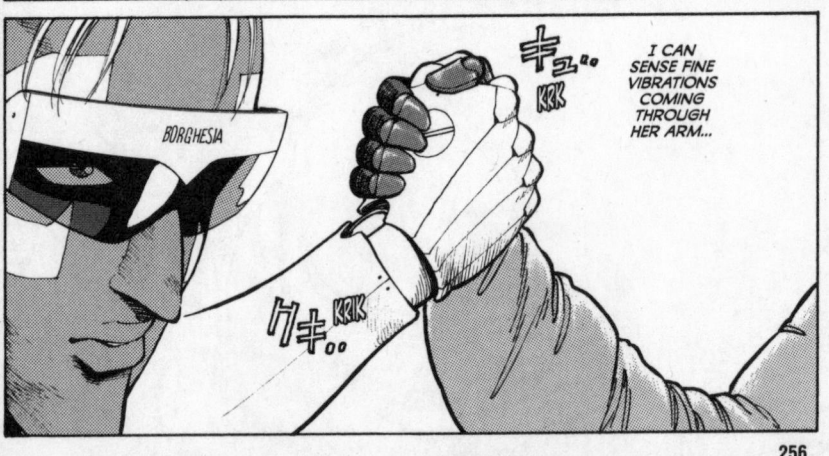

BORGHESIA

I CAN SENSE FINE VIBRATIONS COMING THROUGH HER ARM...

KRK

KRIK

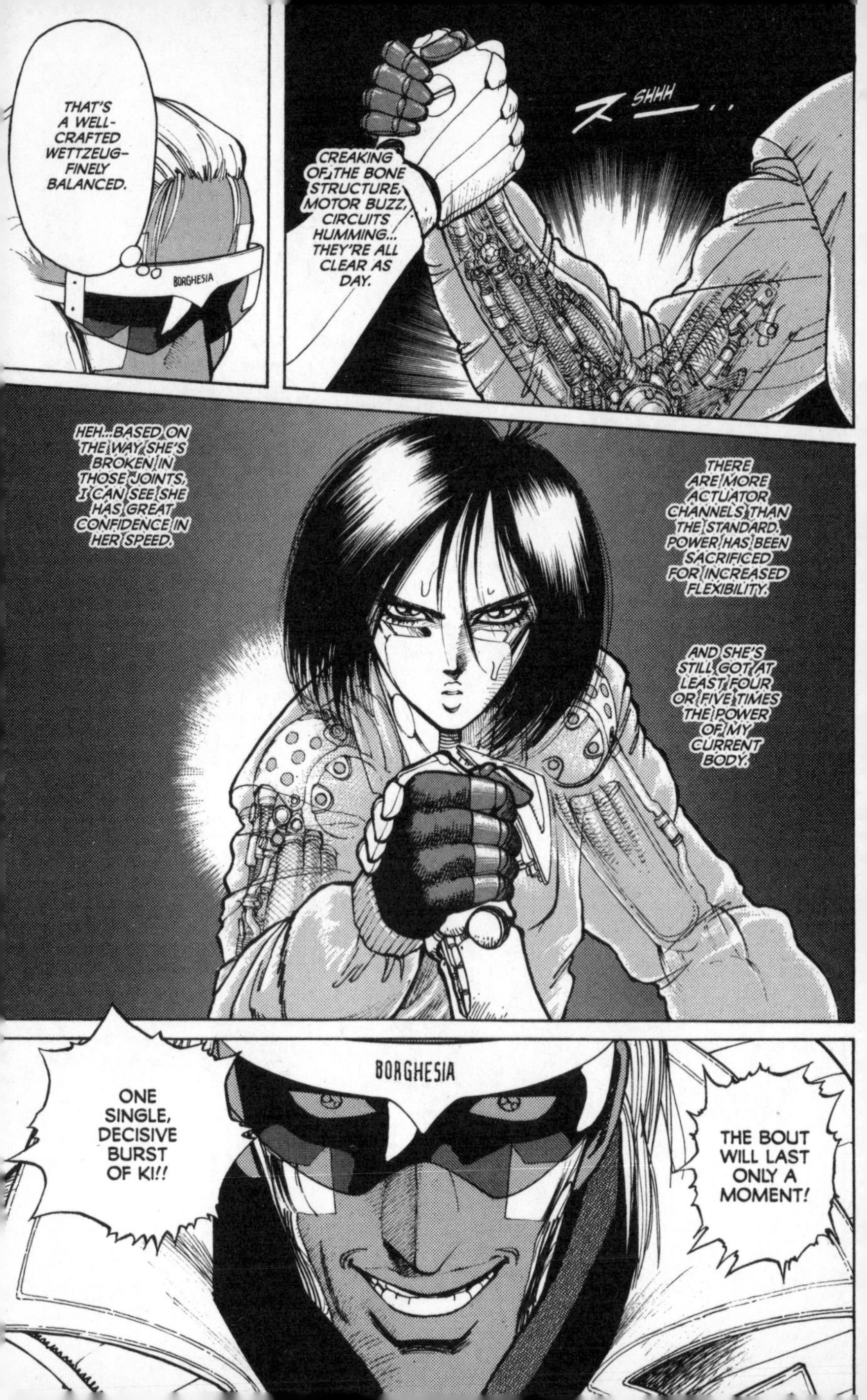

ス SHHH ー. .
CREAKING OF THE BONE STRUCTURE, MOTOR BUZZ, CIRCUITS HUMMING... THEY'RE ALL CLEAR AS DAY.
THAT'S A WELL-CRAFTED WETTZEUG-FINELY BALANCED.
BORGHESIA
THERE ARE MORE ACTUATOR CHANNELS THAN THE STANDARD. POWER HAS BEEN SACRIFICED FOR INCREASED FLEXIBILITY.
AND SHE'S STILL GOT AT LEAST FOUR OR FIVE TIMES THE POWER OF MY CURRENT BODY.
HEH...BASED ON THE WAY SHE'S BROKEN IN THOSE JOINTS, I CAN SEE SHE HAS GREAT CONFIDENCE IN HER SPEED.
BORGHESIA
THE BOUT WILL LAST ONLY A MOMENT!
ONE SINGLE, DECISIVE BURST OF KI!!

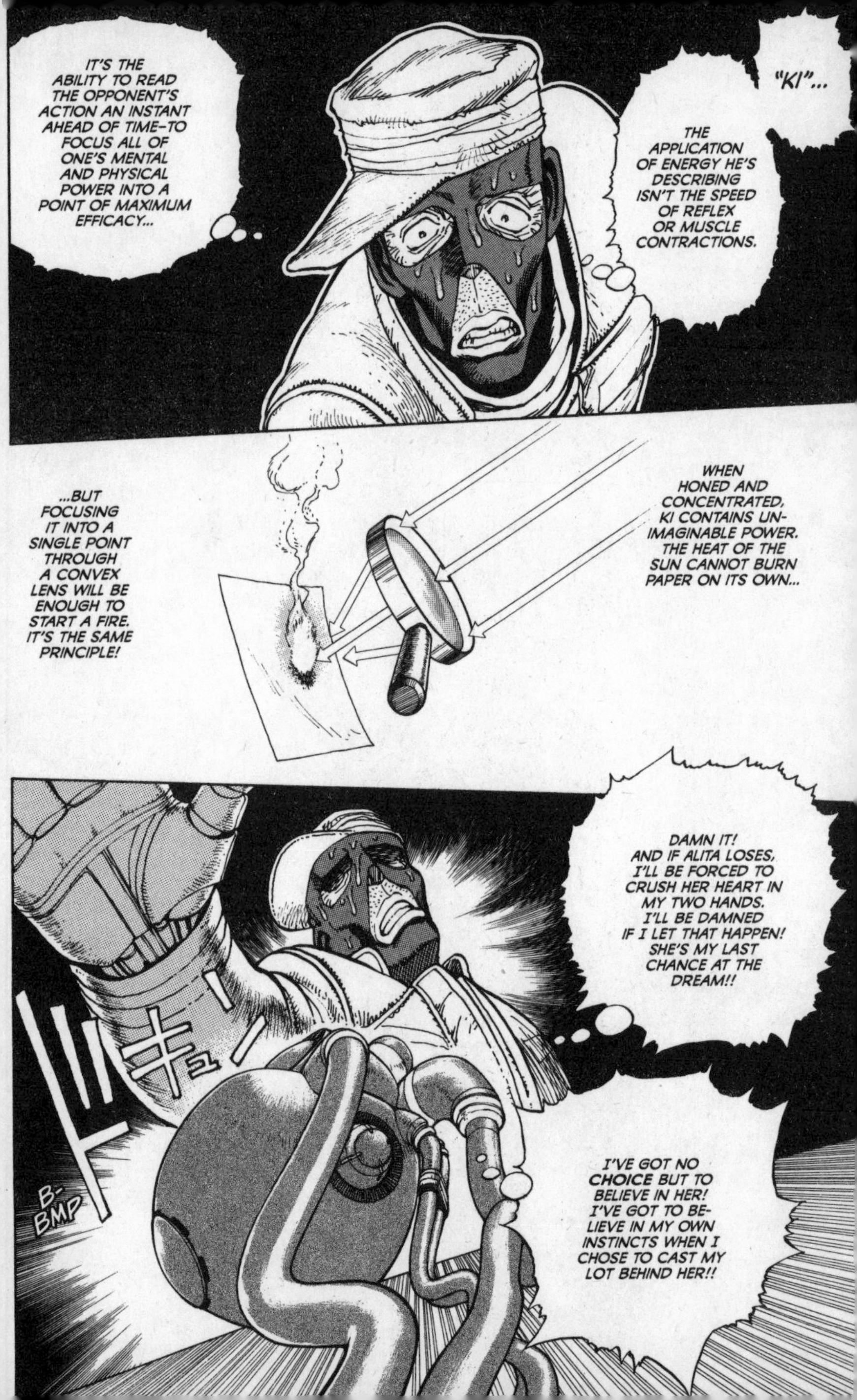
"KI"...
THE APPLICATION OF ENERGY HE'S DESCRIBING ISN'T THE SPEED OF REFLEX OR MUSCLE CONTRACTIONS.
IT'S THE ABILITY TO READ THE OPPONENT'S ACTION AN INSTANT AHEAD OF TIME–TO FOCUS ALL OF ONE'S MENTAL AND PHYSICAL POWER INTO A POINT OF MAXIMUM EFFICACY...
WHEN HONED AND CONCENTRATED, KI CONTAINS UN-IMAGINABLE POWER. THE HEAT OF THE SUN CANNOT BURN PAPER ON ITS OWN...
...BUT FOCUSING IT INTO A SINGLE POINT THROUGH A CONVEX LENS WILL BE ENOUGH TO START A FIRE. IT'S THE SAME PRINCIPLE!
DAMN IT! AND IF ALITA LOSES, I'LL BE FORCED TO CRUSH HER HEART IN MY TWO HANDS. I'LL BE DAMNED IF I LET THAT HAPPEN! SHE'S MY LAST CHANCE AT THE DREAM!!
I'VE GOT NO **CHOICE** BUT TO BELIEVE IN HER! I'VE GOT TO BE-LIEVE IN MY OWN INSTINCTS WHEN I CHOSE TO CAST MY LOT BEHIND HER!!
ドキュー
B-BMP

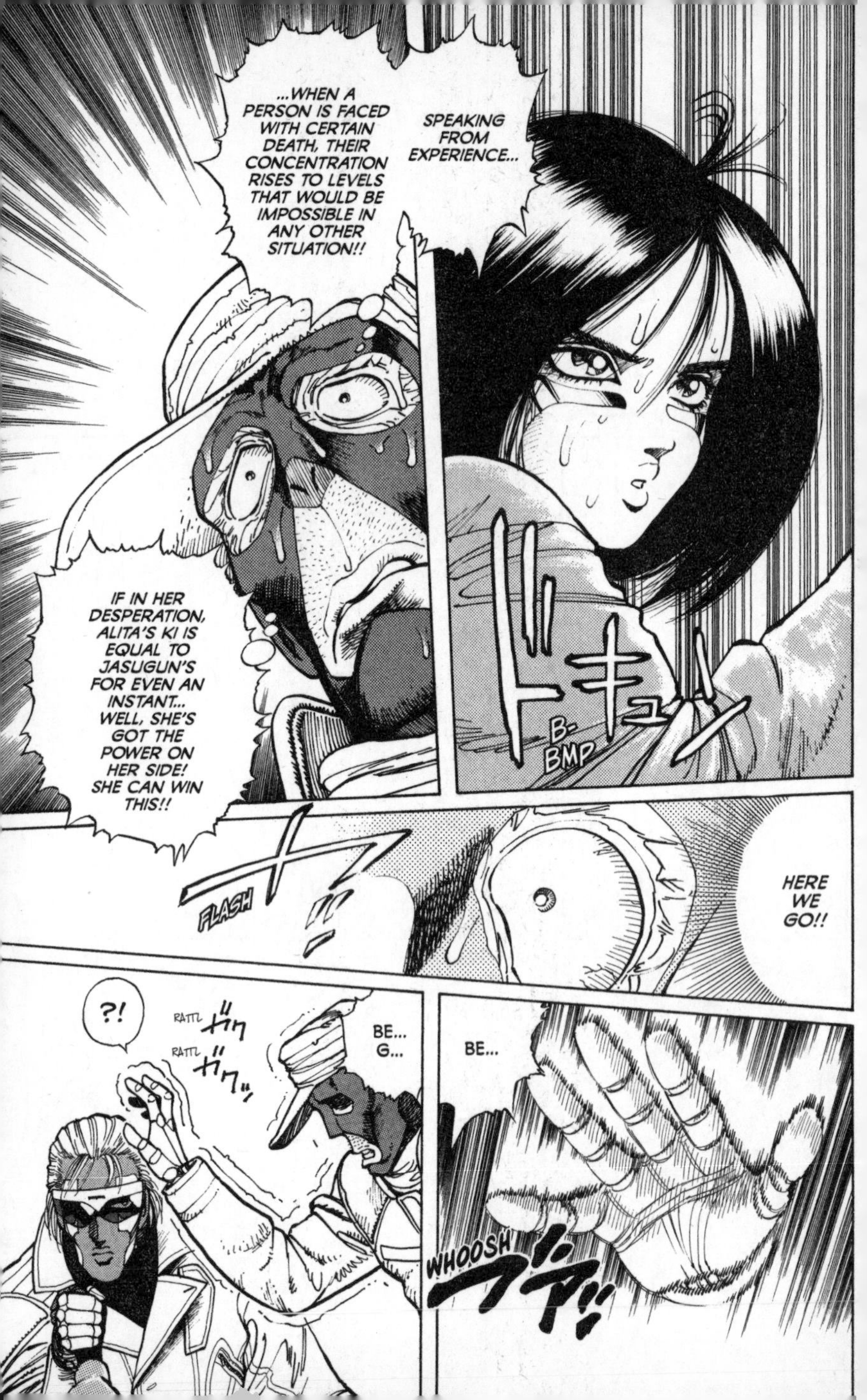
SPEAKING FROM EXPERIENCE...
B-BMP
...WHEN A PERSON IS FACED WITH CERTAIN DEATH, THEIR CONCENTRATION RISES TO LEVELS THAT WOULD BE IMPOSSIBLE IN ANY OTHER SITUATION!!
IF IN HER DESPERATION, ALITA'S KI IS EQUAL TO JASUGUN'S FOR EVEN AN INSTANT... WELL, SHE'S GOT THE POWER ON HER SIDE! SHE CAN WIN THIS!!
HERE WE GO!!
FLASH
BE...
WHOOSH
BE... G...
?!
RATTL
RATTL

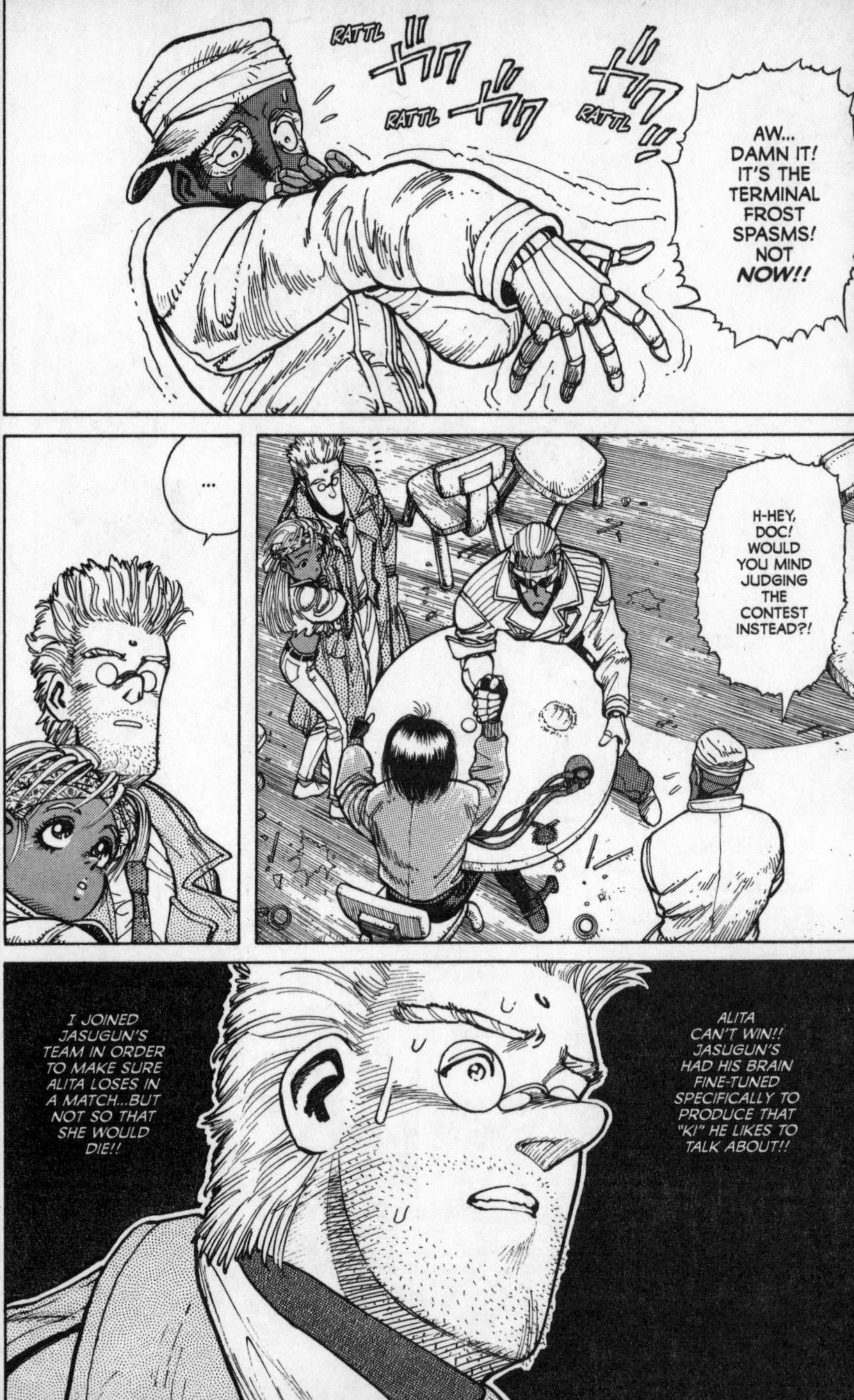
RATTL
RATTL
RATTL
AW... DAMN IT! IT'S THE TERMINAL FROST SPASMS! NOT **NOW!!**
H-HEY, DOC! WOULD YOU MIND JUDGING THE CONTEST INSTEAD?!
...
ALITA CAN'T WIN!! JASUGUN'S HAD HIS BRAIN FINE-TUNED SPECIFICALLY TO PRODUCE THAT "KI" HE LIKES TO TALK ABOUT!!
I JOINED JASUGUN'S TEAM IN ORDER TO MAKE SURE ALITA LOSES IN A MATCH...BUT NOT SO THAT SHE WOULD DIE!!

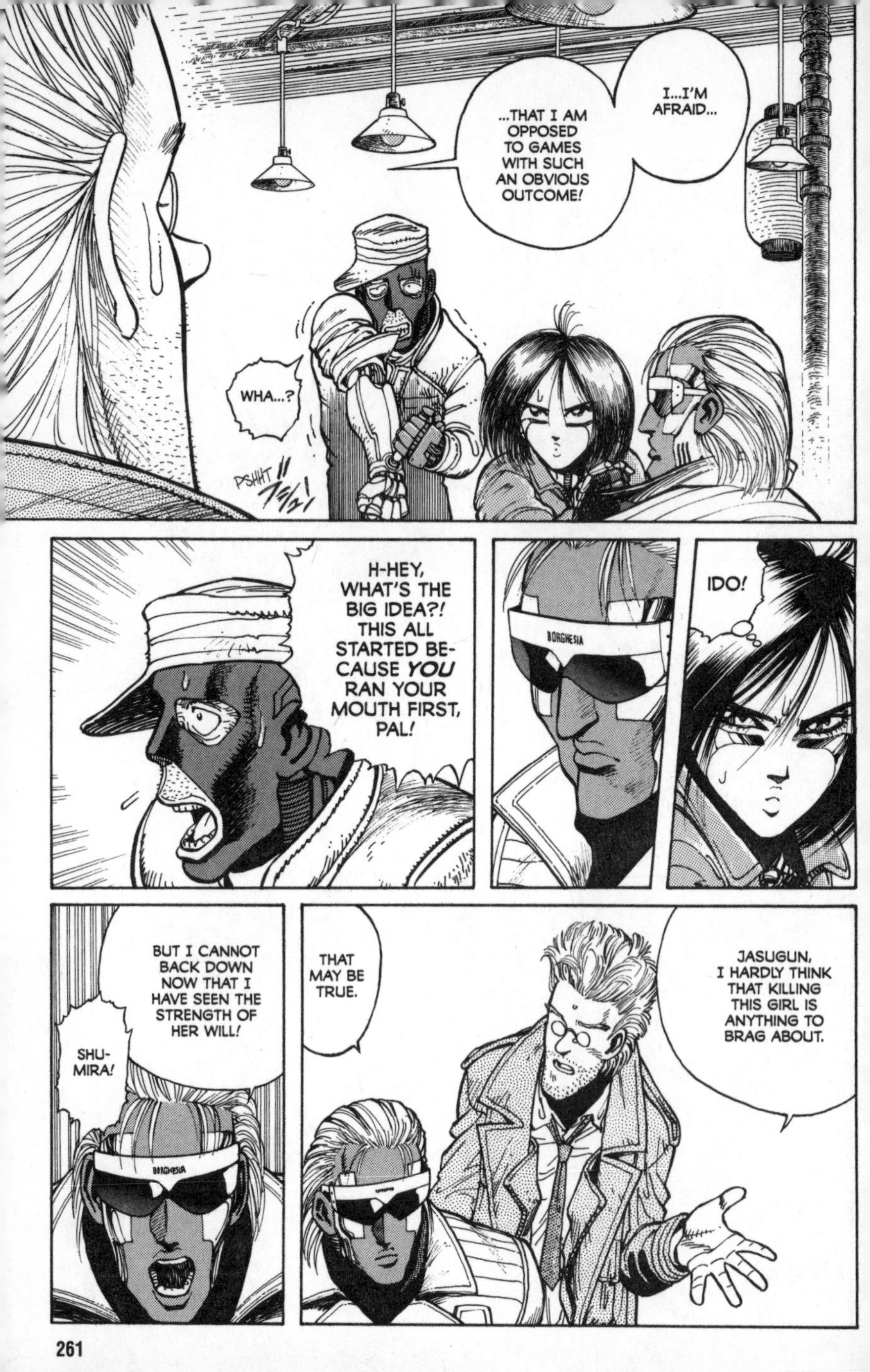
I...I'M AFRAID...
...THAT I AM OPPOSED TO GAMES WITH SUCH AN OBVIOUS OUTCOME!
WHA...?
PSHHT!!
IDO!
H-HEY, WHAT'S THE BIG IDEA?! THIS ALL STARTED BE-CAUSE *YOU* RAN YOUR MOUTH FIRST, PAL!
JASUGUN, I HARDLY THINK THAT KILLING THIS GIRL IS ANYTHING TO BRAG ABOUT.
THAT MAY BE TRUE.
BUT I CANNOT BACK DOWN NOW THAT I HAVE SEEN THE STRENGTH OF HER WILL!
SHU-MIRA!

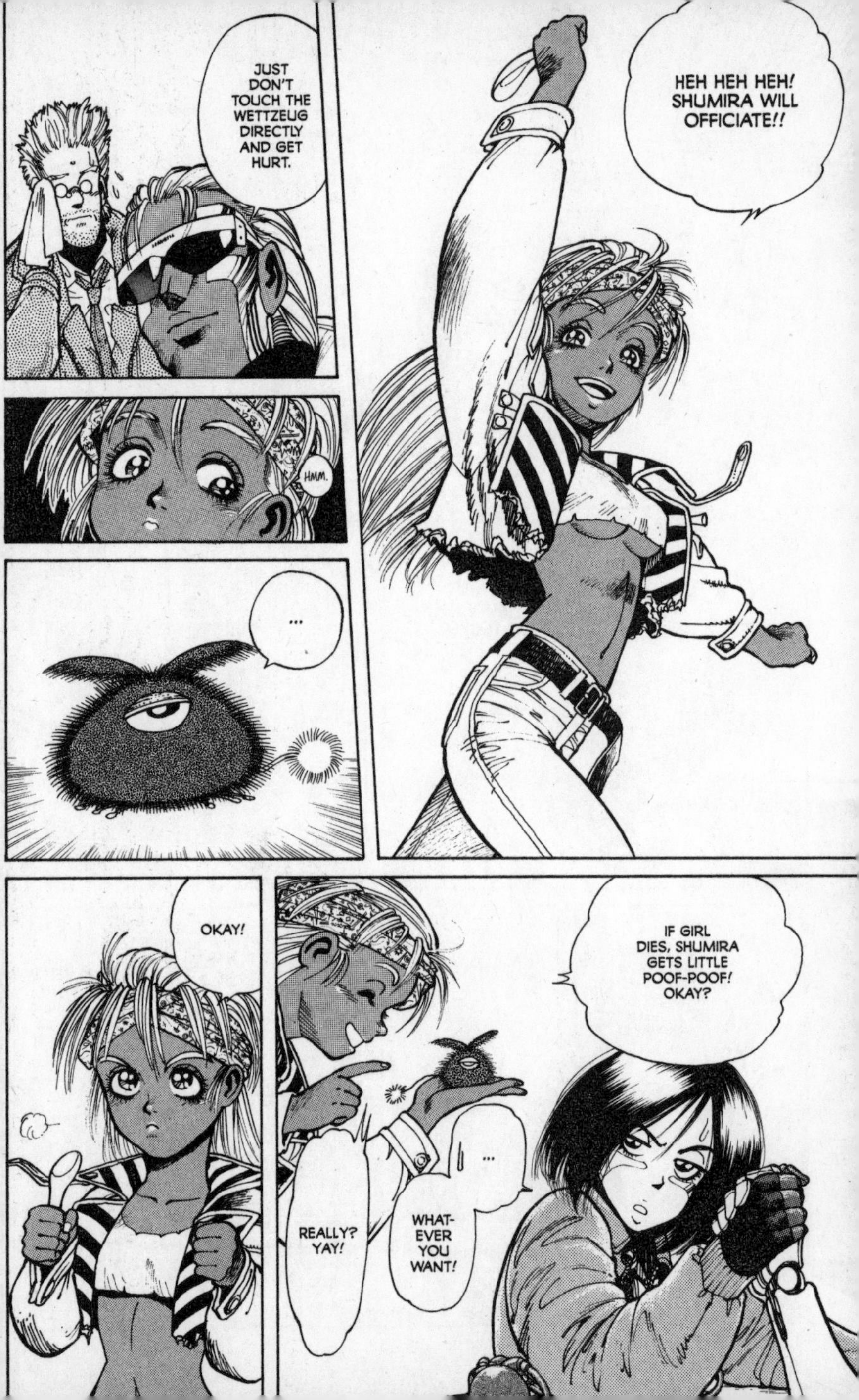
HEH HEH HEH! SHUMIRA WILL OFFICIATE!!
JUST DON'T TOUCH THE WETTZEUG DIRECTLY AND GET HURT.
HMM.
...
IF GIRL DIES, SHUMIRA GETS LITTLE POOF-POOF! OKAY?
...
WHAT-EVER YOU WANT!
REALLY? YAY!
OKAY!

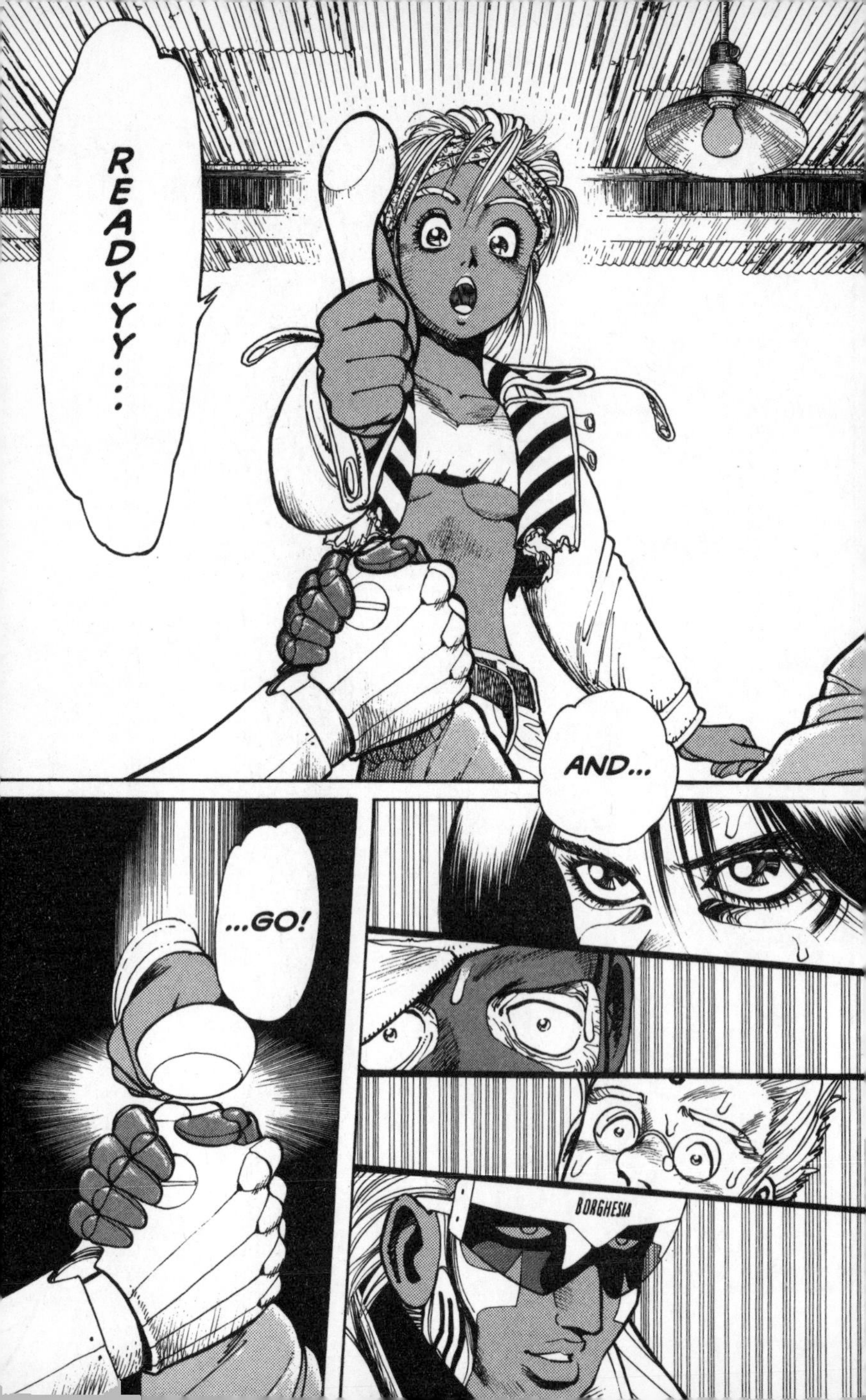
READYYYY...
AND...
BORGHESIA
...GO!

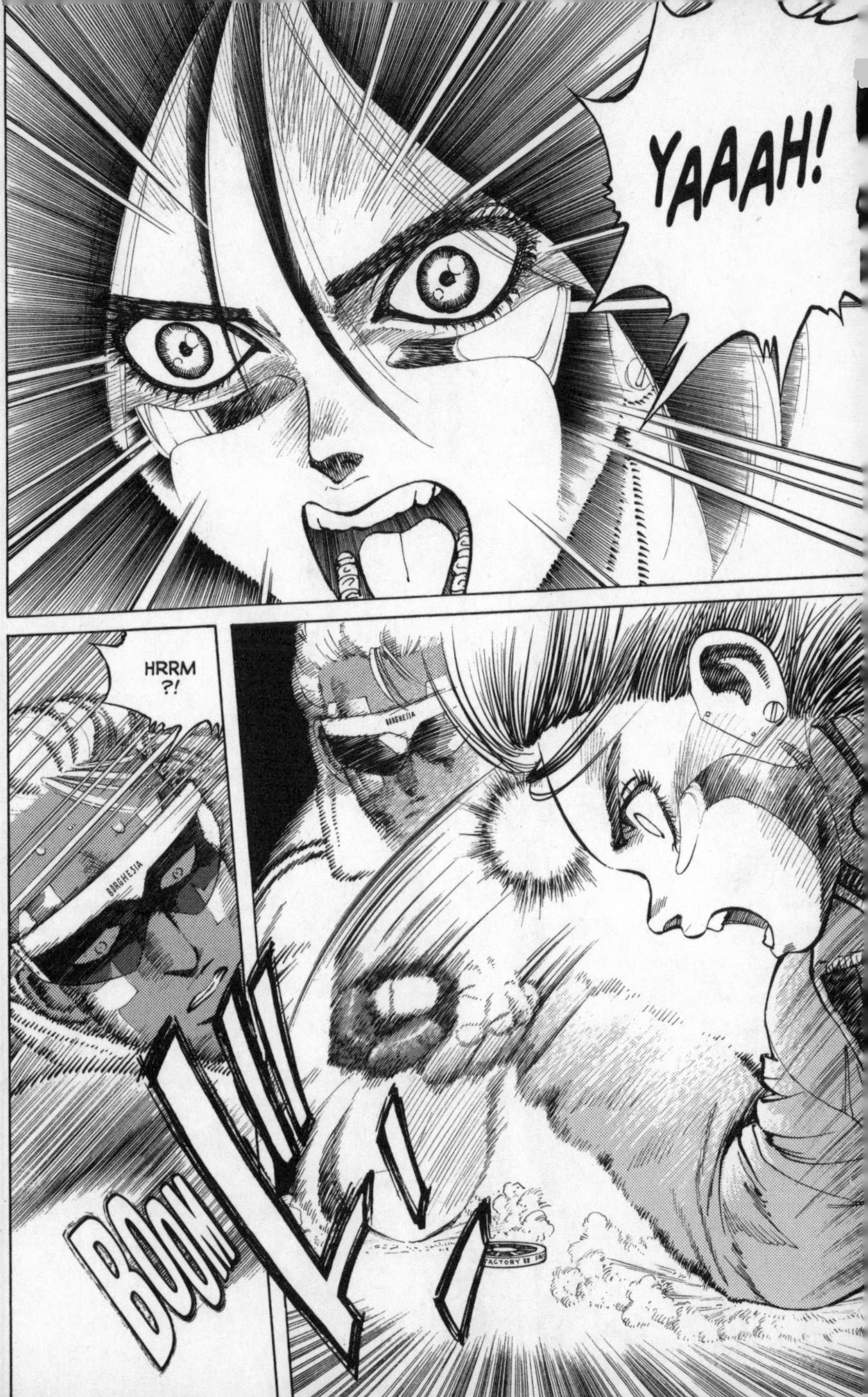
YAAAH!
BOOM
HRRM ?!

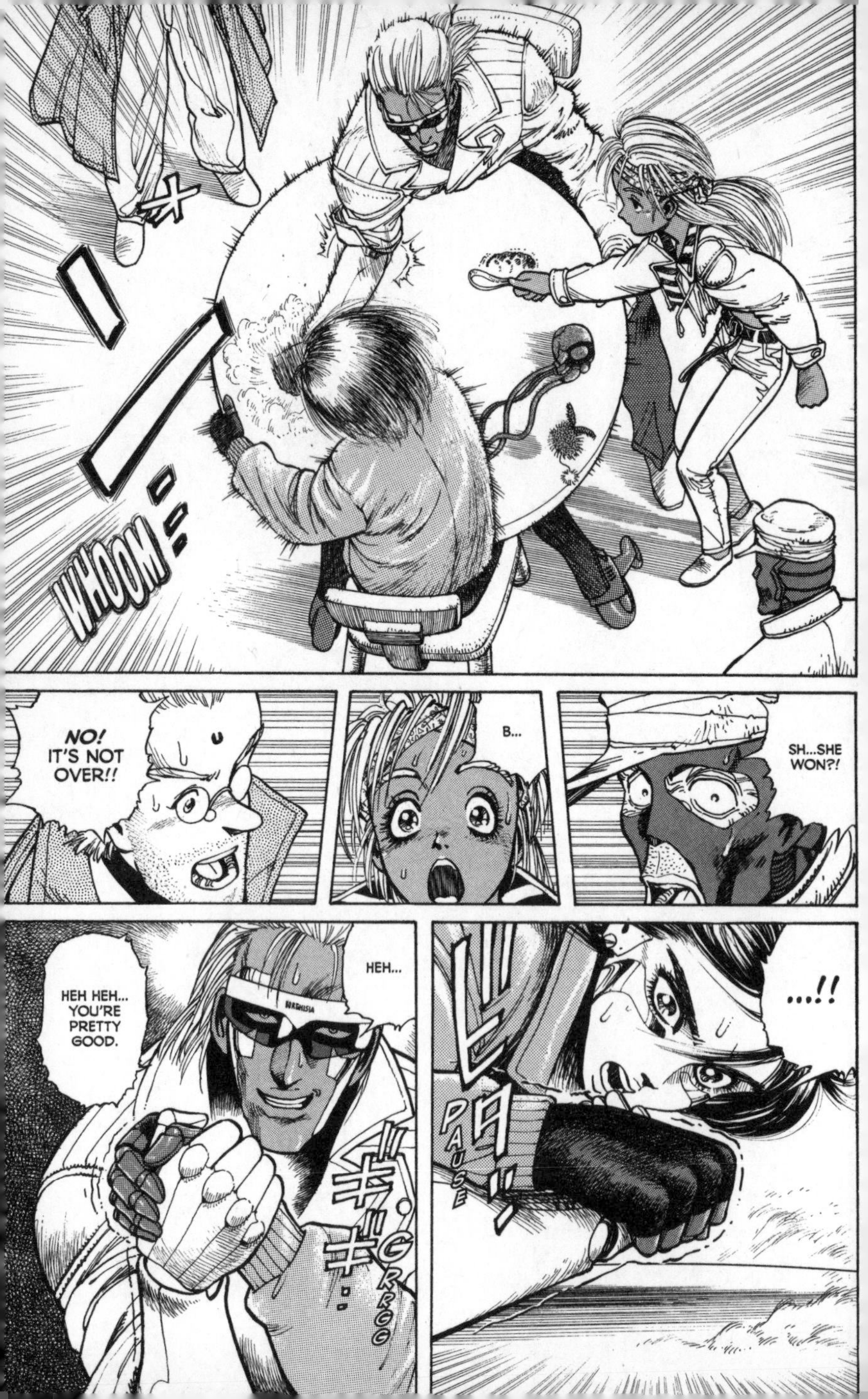
WHOOM
SH...SHE WON?!
B...
NO! IT'S NOT OVER!!
...!!
PAUSE
HEH...
HEH HEH... YOU'RE PRETTY GOOD.
GRRGG

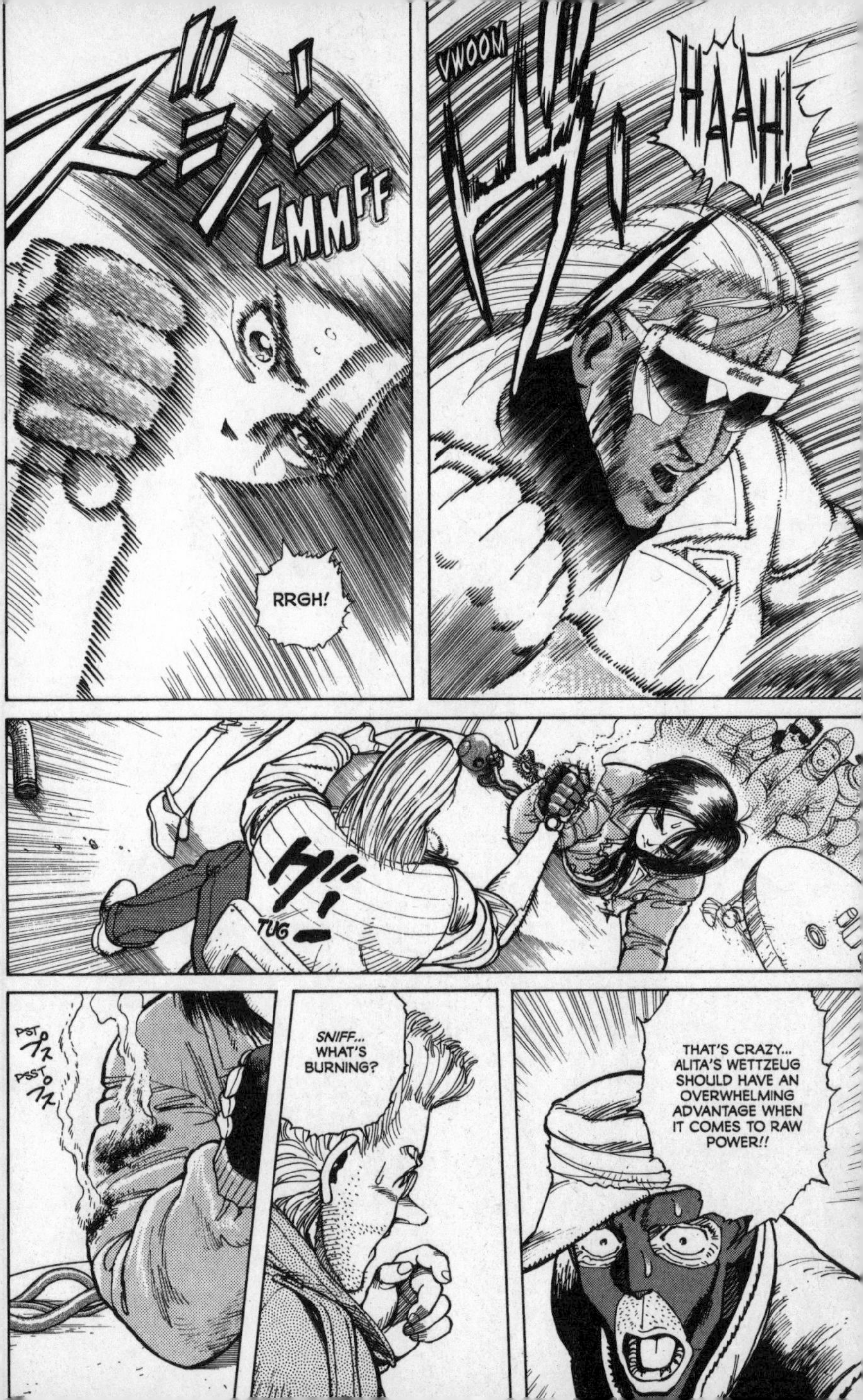
VWOOM
HAAH!
ZMMFF
RRGH!
TUG
THAT'S CRAZY... ALITA'S WETTZEUG SHOULD HAVE AN OVERWHELMING ADVANTAGE WHEN IT COMES TO RAW POWER!!
SNIFF... WHAT'S BURNING?
PST
PSST

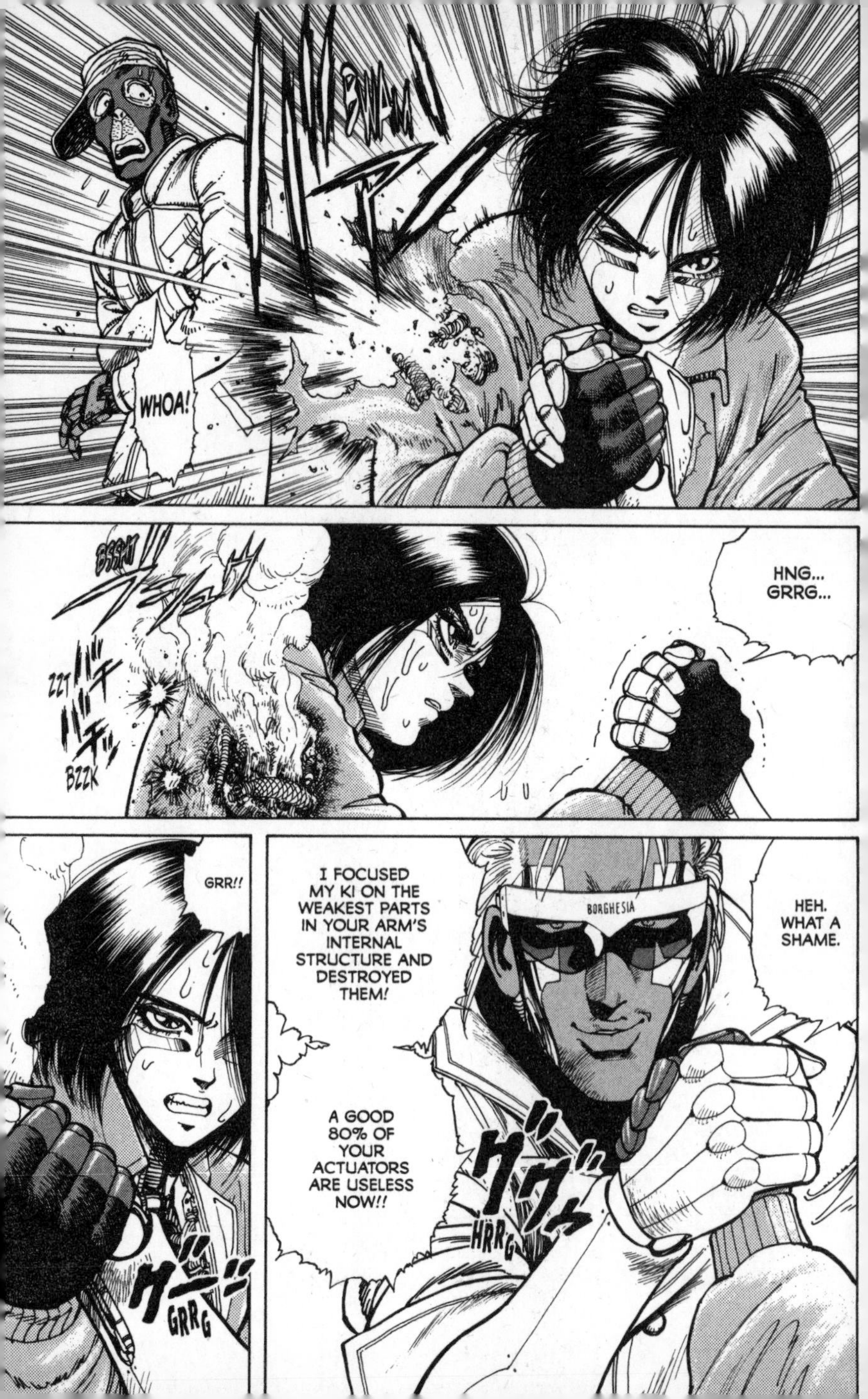
WHOA!
BSSHT
ZZT
BZZK
HNG... GRRG...
HEH. WHAT A SHAME.
BORGHESIA
I FOCUSED MY KI ON THE WEAKEST PARTS IN YOUR ARM'S INTERNAL STRUCTURE AND DESTROYED THEM!
A GOOD 80% OF YOUR ACTUATORS ARE USELESS NOW!!
HRRG
GRR!!
GRRG

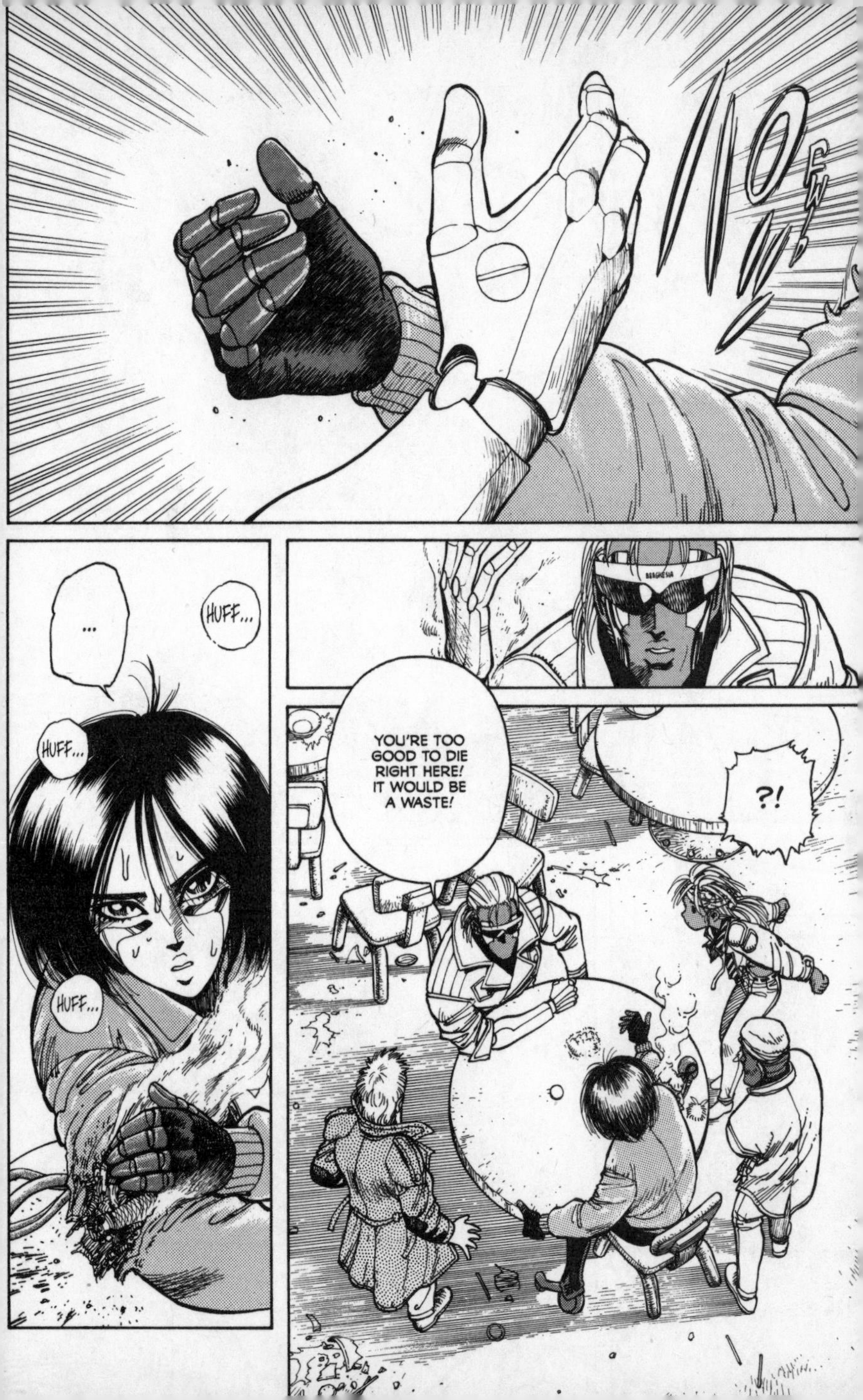
YOU'RE TOO GOOD TO DIE RIGHT HERE! IT WOULD BE A WASTE!
?!
HUFF...
...
HUFF...
HUFF...

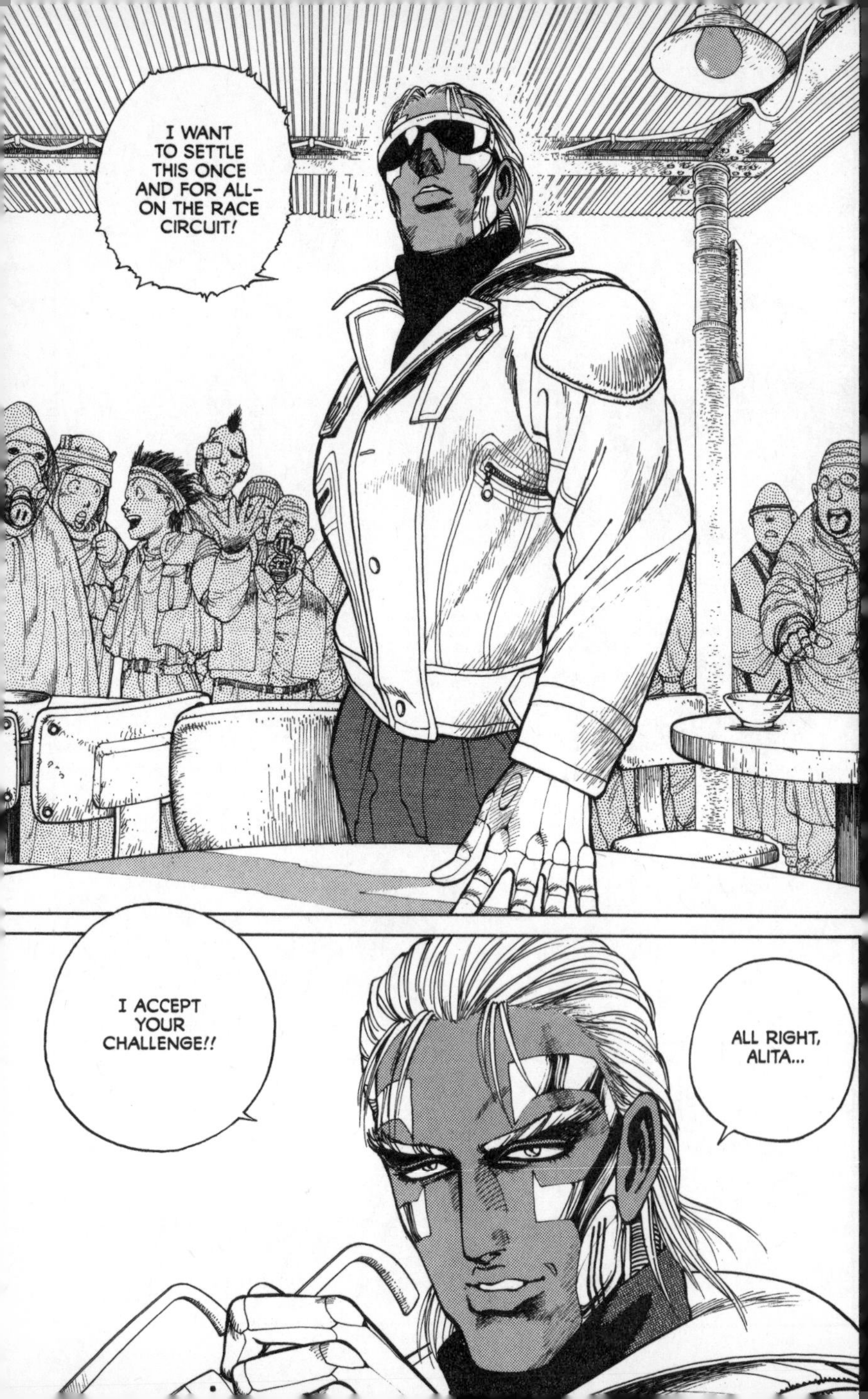
I WANT TO SETTLE THIS ONCE AND FOR ALL— ON THE RACE CIRCUIT!
ALL RIGHT, ALITA...
I ACCEPT YOUR CHALLENGE!!

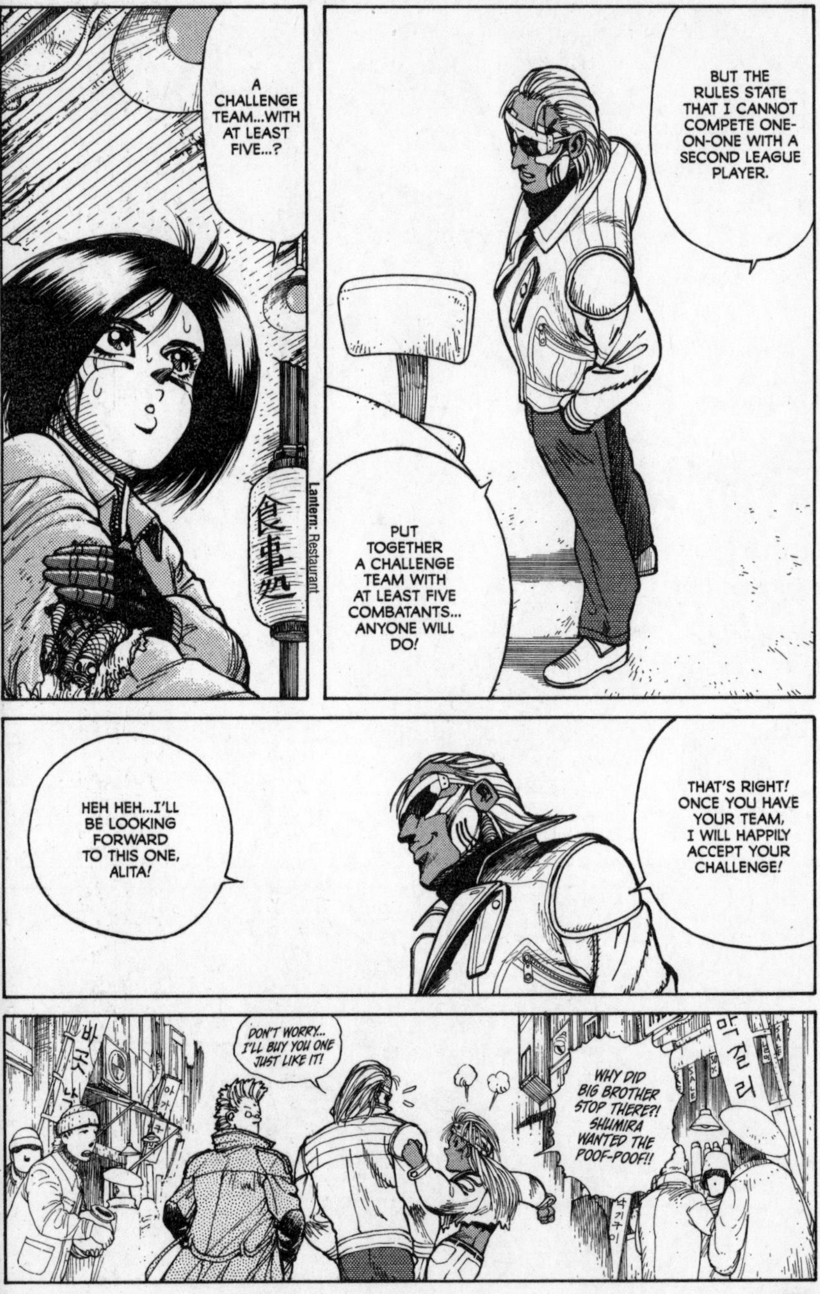
BUT THE RULES STATE THAT I CANNOT COMPETE ONE-ON-ONE WITH A SECOND LEAGUE PLAYER.
PUT TOGETHER A CHALLENGE TEAM WITH AT LEAST FIVE COMBATANTS... ANYONE WILL DO!
A CHALLENGE TEAM...WITH AT LEAST FIVE...?
食事処
Lantern: Restaurant
THAT'S RIGHT! ONCE YOU HAVE YOUR TEAM, I WILL HAPPILY ACCEPT YOUR CHALLENGE!
HEH HEH...I'LL BE LOOKING FORWARD TO THIS ONE, ALITA!
WHY DID BIG BROTHER STOP THERE?! SHUMIRA WANTED THE POOF-POOF!!
DON'T WORRY... I'LL BUY YOU ONE JUST LIKE IT!

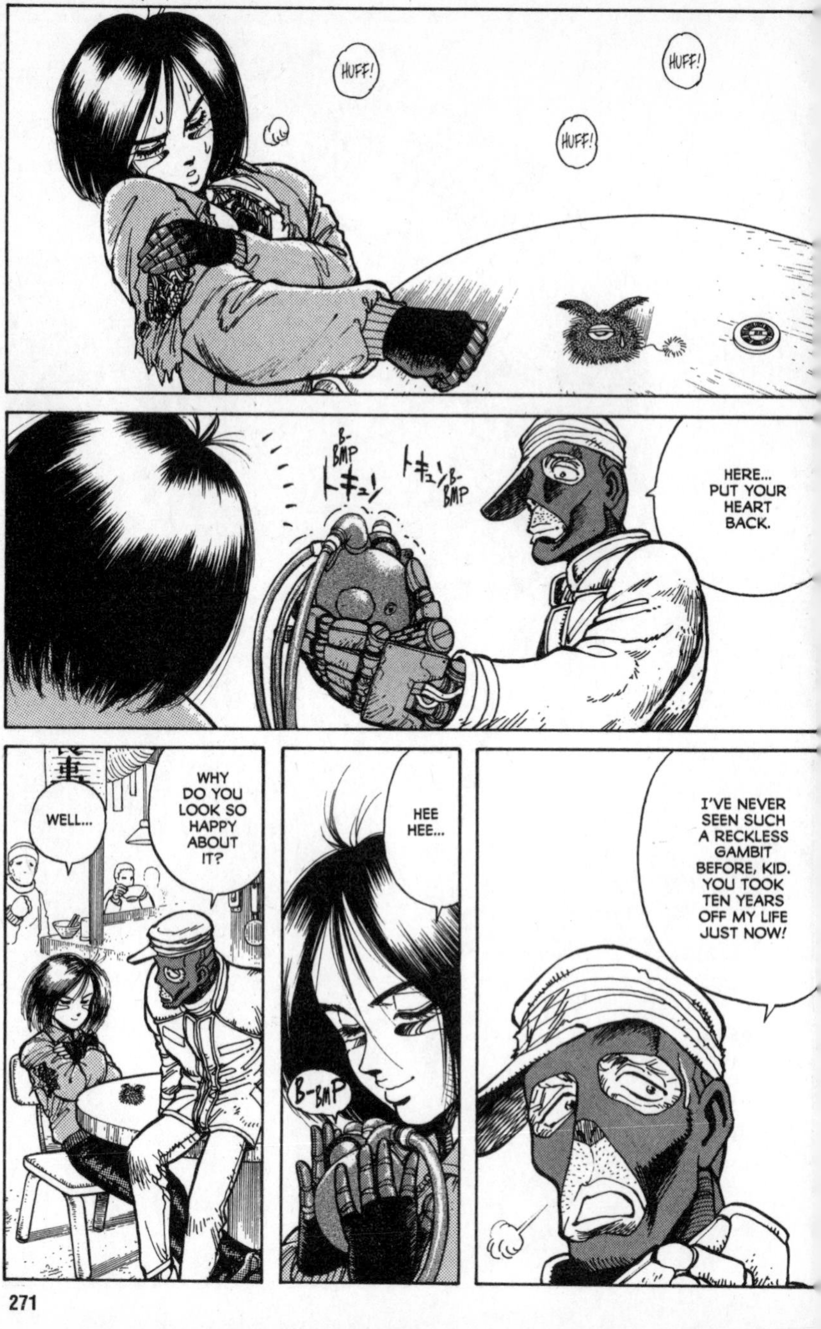
HUFF!
HUFF!
HUFF!
HERE... PUT YOUR HEART BACK.
トキュン B-BMP
トキュン B-BMP
I'VE NEVER SEEN SUCH A RECKLESS GAMBIT BEFORE, KID. YOU TOOK TEN YEARS OFF MY LIFE JUST NOW!
HEE HEE...
B-BMP
WHY DO YOU LOOK SO HAPPY ABOUT IT?
WELL...

I'M JUST GLAD TO LEARN THAT THERE ARE PEOPLE AS INCREDIBLE AS HIM OUT THERE IN THE WORLD.

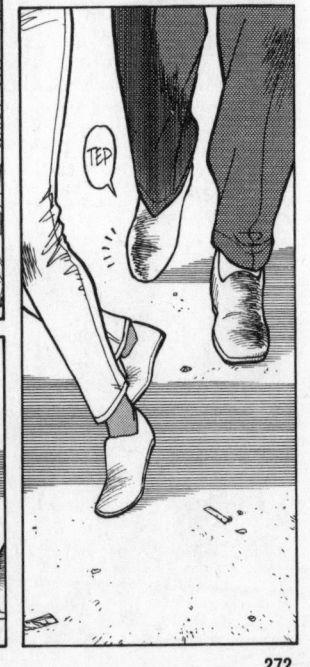

TEP

?!

MMF...

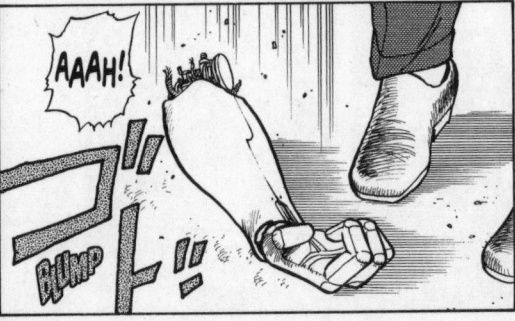

AAAH!

GUMP

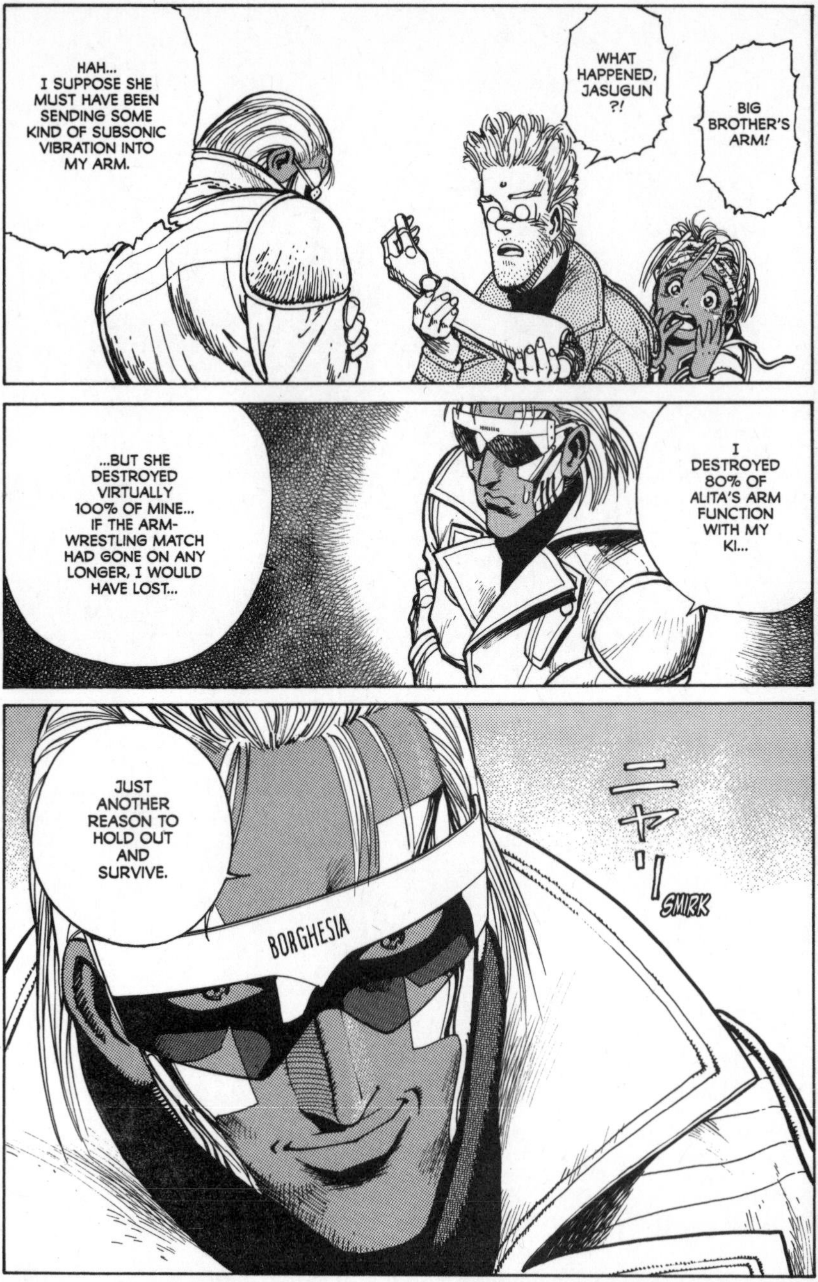
BIG BROTHER'S ARM!
WHAT HAPPENED, JASUGUN ?!
HAH... I SUPPOSE SHE MUST HAVE BEEN SENDING SOME KIND OF SUBSONIC VIBRATION INTO MY ARM.
I DESTROYED 80% OF ALITA'S ARM FUNCTION WITH MY KI...
...BUT SHE DESTROYED VIRTUALLY 100% OF MINE... IF THE ARM-WRESTLING MATCH HAD GONE ON ANY LONGER, I WOULD HAVE LOST...
ニヤー
SMIRK
JUST ANOTHER REASON TO HOLD OUT AND SURVIVE.
BORGHESIA

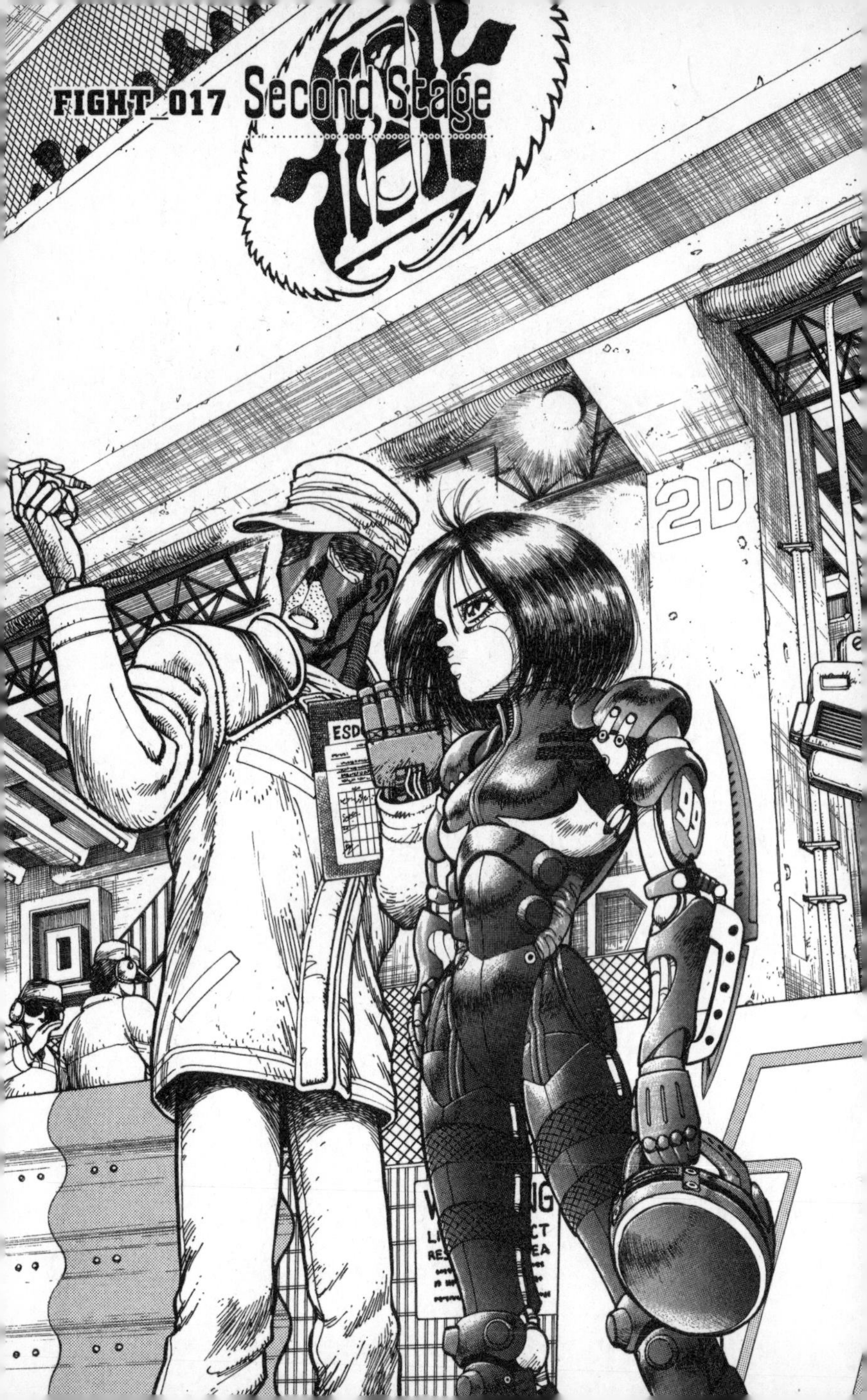
FIGHT_017 Second Stage
2D
ESD
99

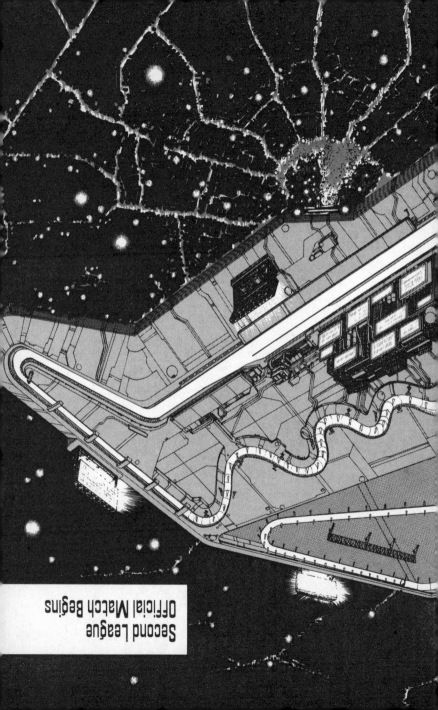

Second League
Official Match Begins

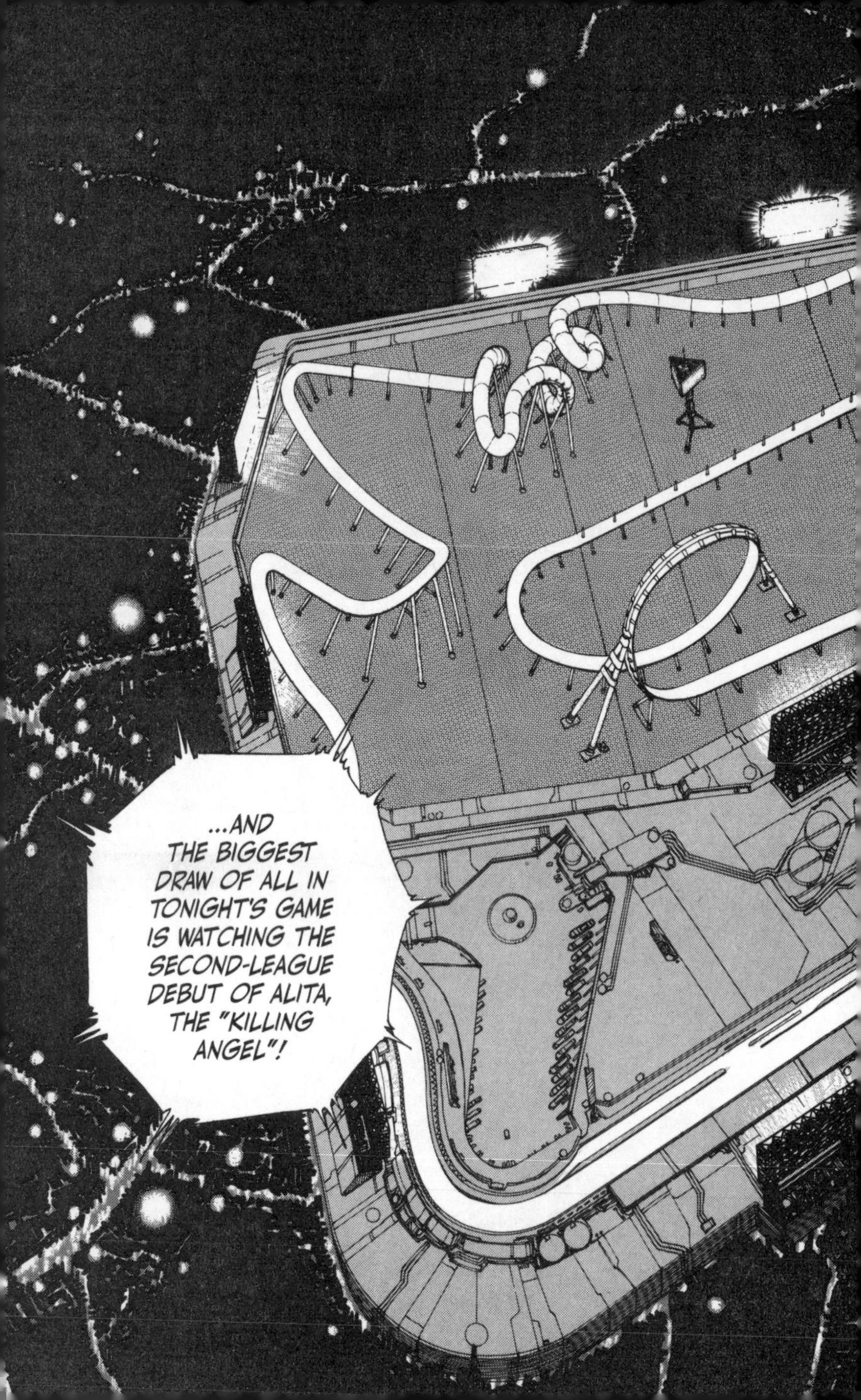
...AND THE BIGGEST DRAW OF ALL IN TONIGHT'S GAME IS WATCHING THE SECOND-LEAGUE DEBUT OF ALITA, THE "KILLING ANGEL"!

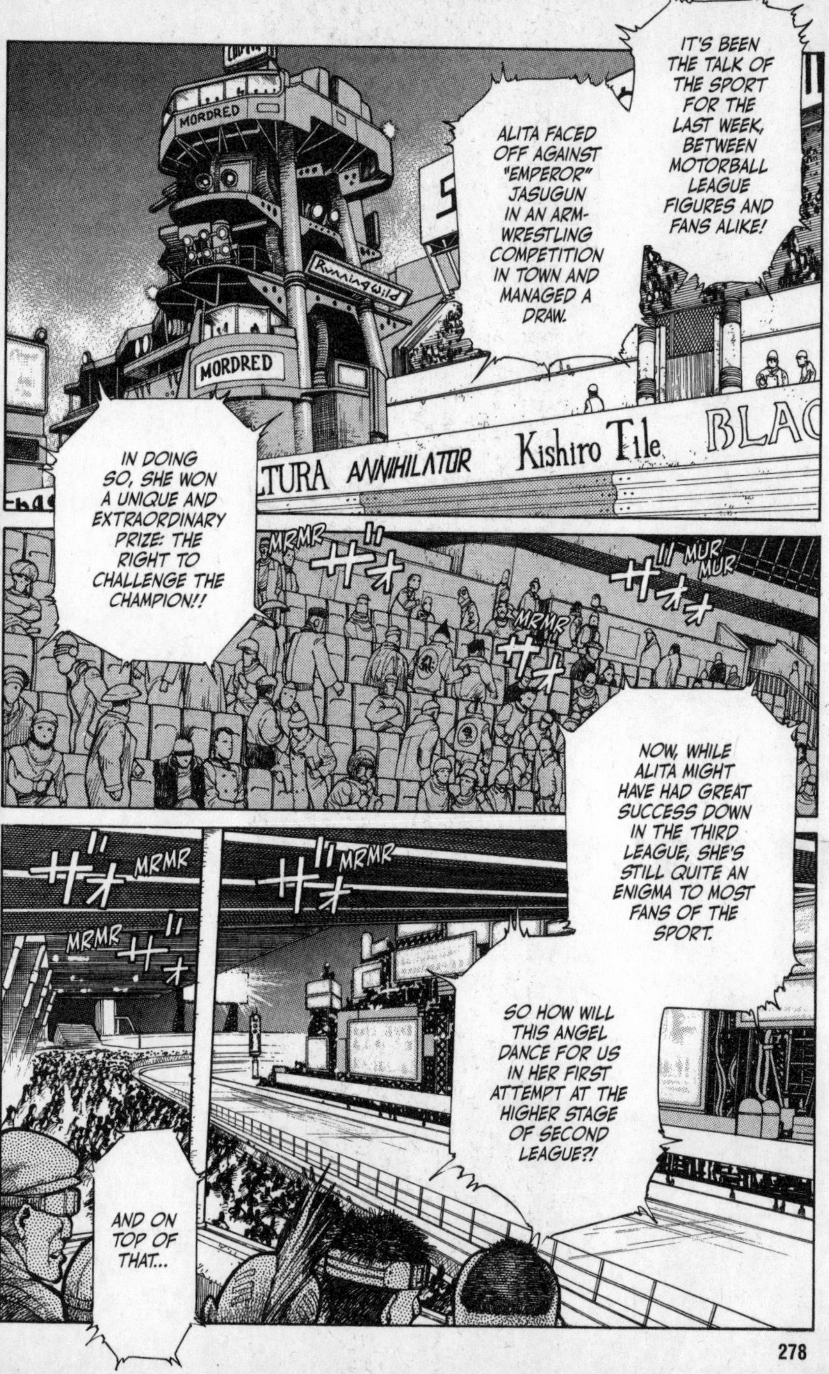
IT'S BEEN THE TALK OF THE SPORT FOR THE LAST WEEK, BETWEEN MOTORBALL LEAGUE FIGURES AND FANS ALIKE!
ALITA FACED OFF AGAINST "EMPEROR" JASUGUN IN AN ARM-WRESTLING COMPETITION IN TOWN AND MANAGED A DRAW.
MORDRED
Running wild
MORDRED
BLAC
Kishiro Tile
ANNIHILATOR
LTURA
IN DOING SO, SHE WON A UNIQUE AND EXTRAORDINARY PRIZE: THE RIGHT TO CHALLENGE THE CHAMPION!!
MUR MUR
MRMR
MRMR
NOW, WHILE ALITA MIGHT HAVE HAD GREAT SUCCESS DOWN IN THE THIRD LEAGUE, SHE'S STILL QUITE AN ENIGMA TO MOST FANS OF THE SPORT.
MRMR
MRMR
MRMR
SO HOW WILL THIS ANGEL DANCE FOR US IN HER FIRST ATTEMPT AT THE HIGHER STAGE OF SECOND LEAGUE?!
AND ON TOP OF THAT...

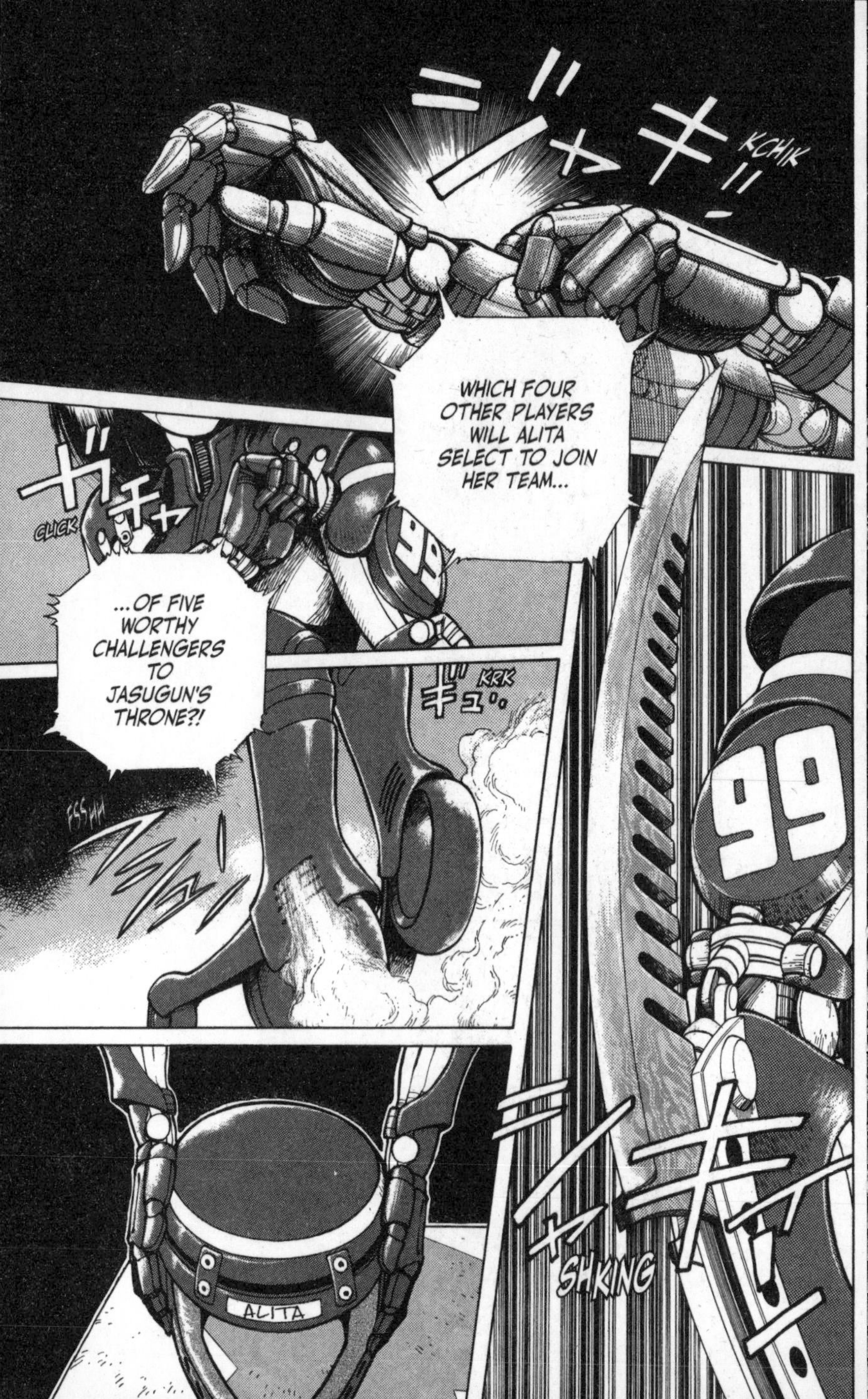
KCHIK
WHICH FOUR OTHER PLAYERS WILL ALITA SELECT TO JOIN HER TEAM...
SHKING
CLICK
...OF FIVE WORTHY CHALLENGERS TO JASUGUN'S THRONE?!
KRK
FSSHH
ALITA

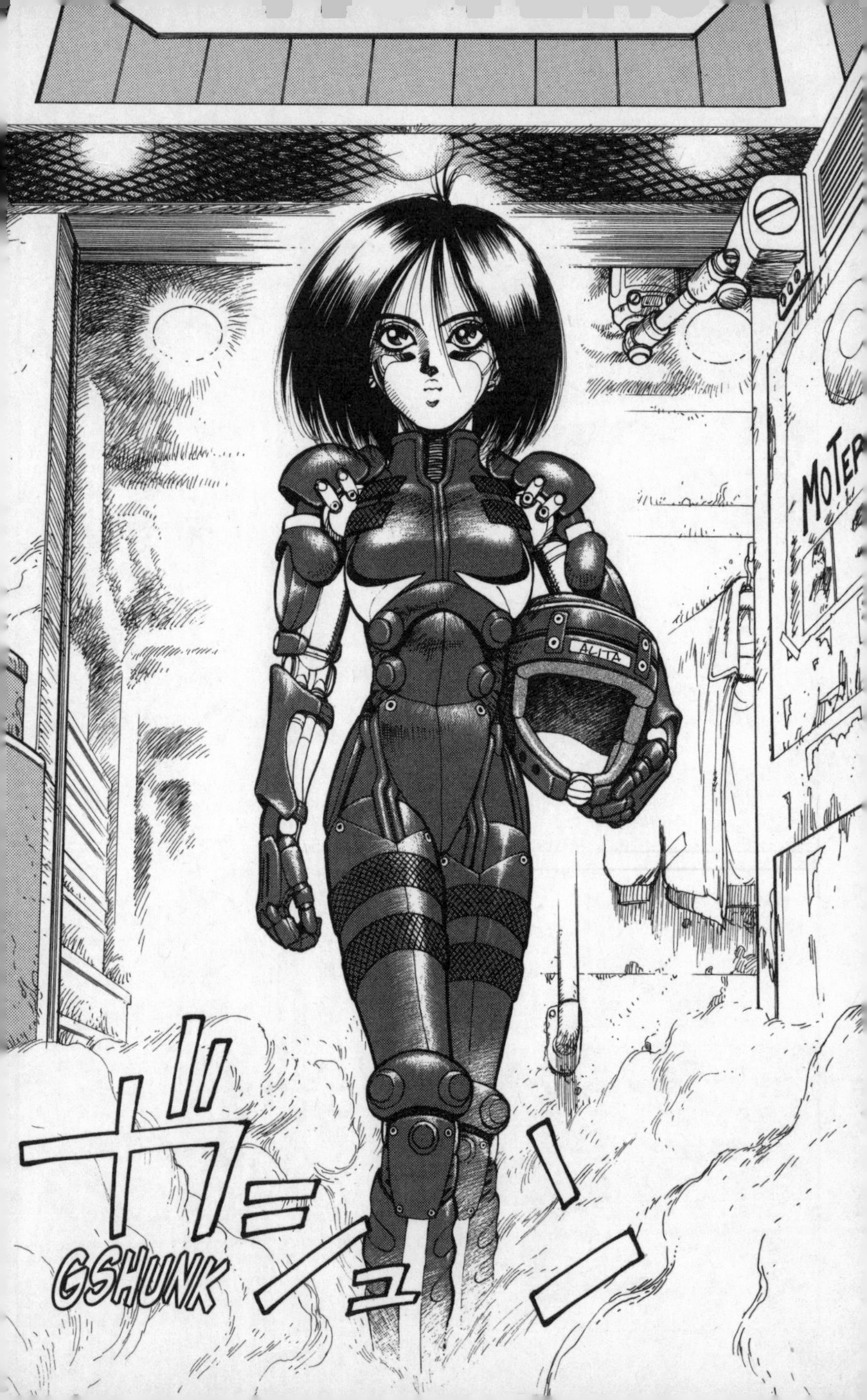
ALITA
MOTER
ヴィシュイン
GSHUNK

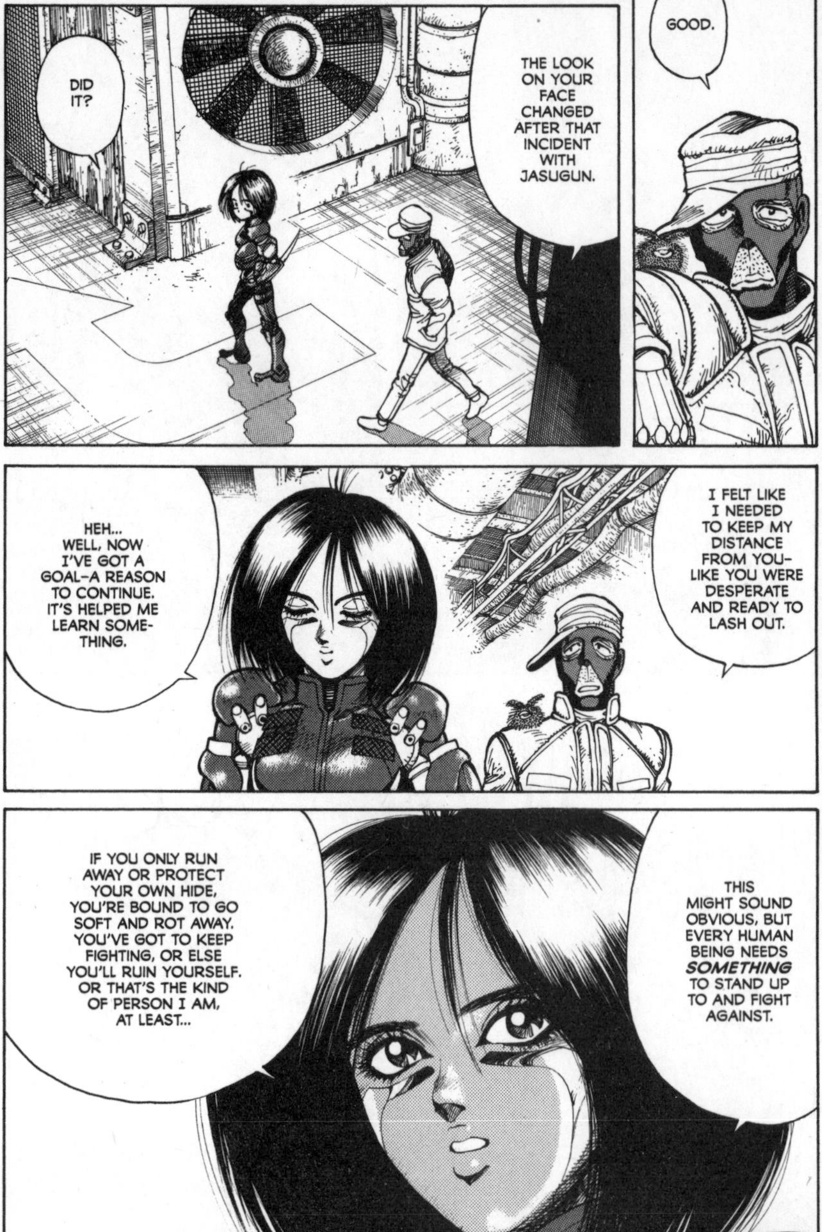
GOOD.
THE LOOK ON YOUR FACE CHANGED AFTER THAT INCIDENT WITH JASUGUN.
DID IT?
I FELT LIKE I NEEDED TO KEEP MY DISTANCE FROM YOU–LIKE YOU WERE DESPERATE AND READY TO LASH OUT.
HEH... WELL, NOW I'VE GOT A GOAL–A REASON TO CONTINUE. IT'S HELPED ME LEARN SOME-THING.
THIS MIGHT SOUND OBVIOUS, BUT EVERY HUMAN BEING NEEDS SOMETHING TO STAND UP TO AND FIGHT AGAINST.
IF YOU ONLY RUN AWAY OR PROTECT YOUR OWN HIDE, YOU'RE BOUND TO GO SOFT AND ROT AWAY. YOU'VE GOT TO KEEP FIGHTING, OR ELSE YOU'LL RUIN YOURSELF. OR THAT'S THE KIND OF PERSON I AM, AT LEAST...

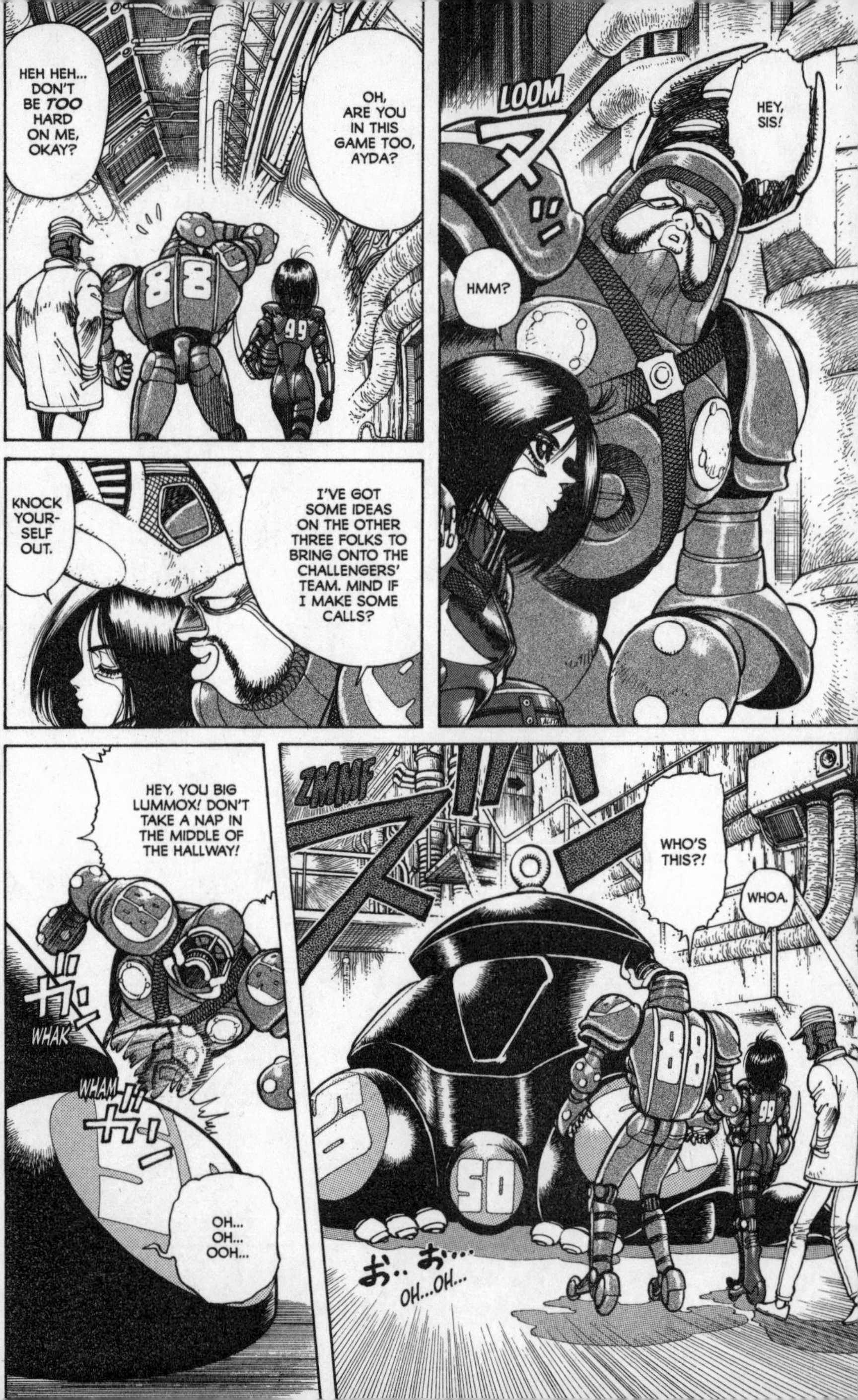
HEY, SIS!
LOOM
HMM?
OH, ARE YOU IN THIS GAME TOO, AYDA?
HEH HEH... DON'T BE *TOO* HARD ON ME, OKAY?
I'VE GOT SOME IDEAS ON THE OTHER THREE FOLKS TO BRING ONTO THE CHALLENGERS' TEAM. MIND IF I MAKE SOME CALLS?
KNOCK YOURSELF OUT.
WHO'S THIS?!
WHOA.
ZMMF
お.. お...
OH...OH...
HEY, YOU BIG LUMMOX! DON'T TAKE A NAP IN THE MIDDLE OF THE HALLWAY!
WHAK
WHAM
OH... OH... OOH...

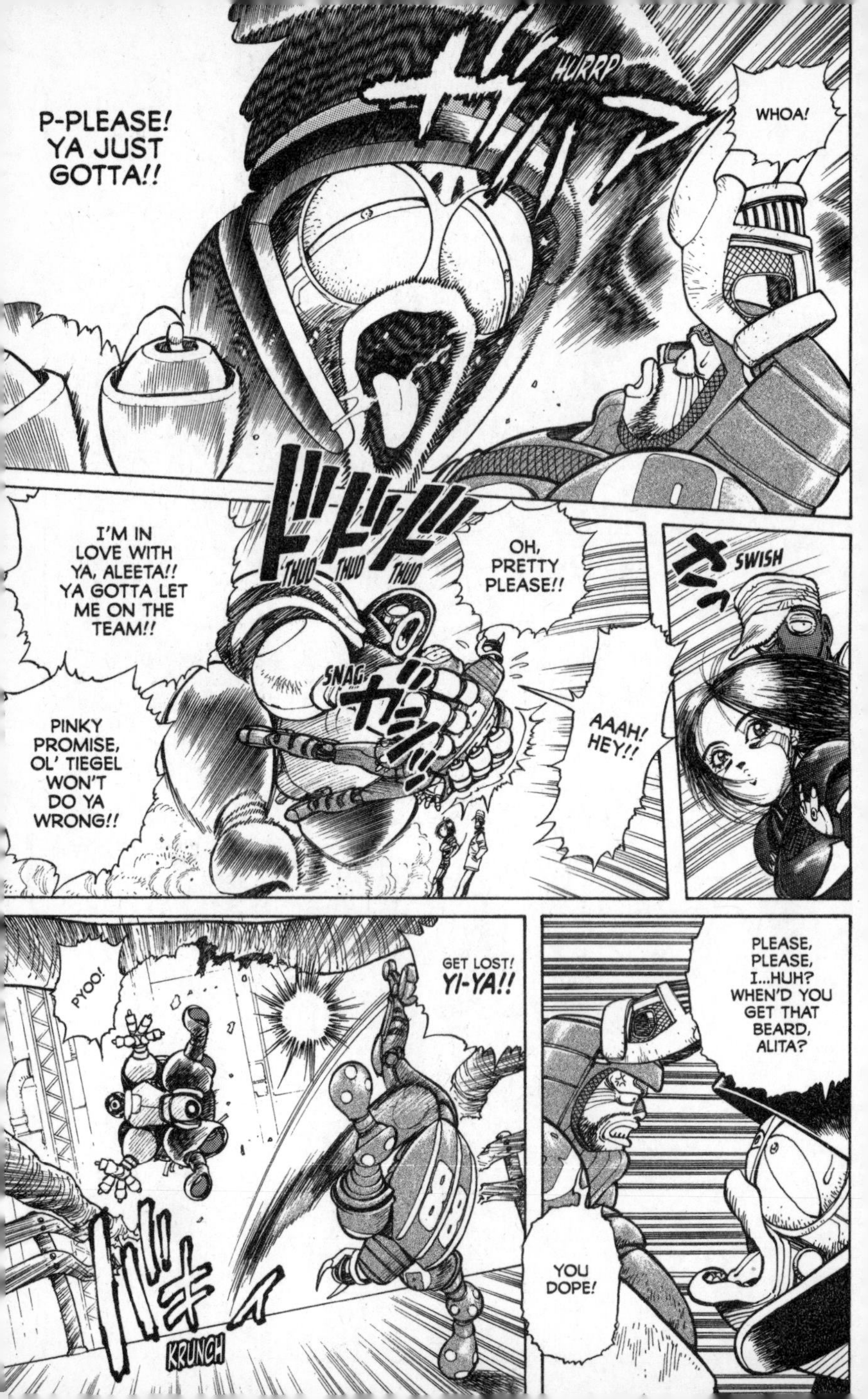
WHOA!
HURRP
P-PLEASE! YA JUST GOTTA!!
SWISH
THUD THUD THUD
OH, PRETTY PLEASE!!
I'M IN LOVE WITH YA, ALEETA!! YA GOTTA LET ME ON THE TEAM!!
AAAH! HEY!!
SNAG
PINKY PROMISE, OL' TIEGEL WON'T DO YA WRONG!!
PLEASE, PLEASE, I...HUH? WHEN'D YOU GET THAT BEARD, ALITA?
YOU DOPE!
GET LOST! YI-YA!!
PYOO!
KRUNCH

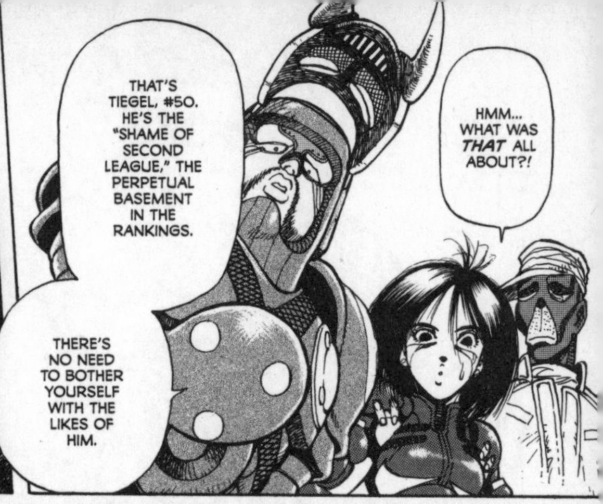
HMM... WHAT WAS *THAT* ALL ABOUT?!
THAT'S TIEGEL, #50. HE'S THE "SHAME OF SECOND LEAGUE," THE PERPETUAL BASEMENT IN THE RANKINGS.
THERE'S NO NEED TO BOTHER YOURSELF WITH THE LIKES OF HIM.
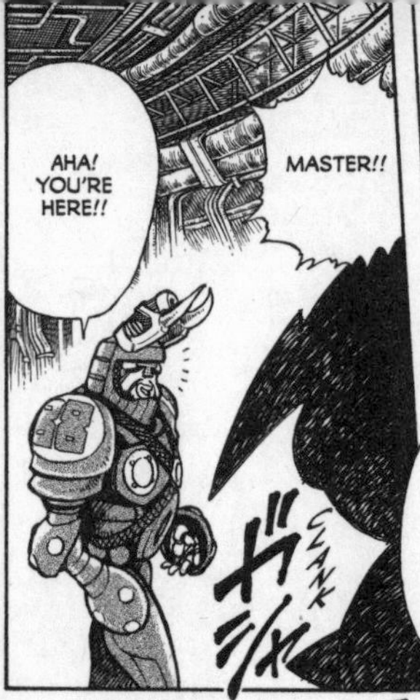
MASTER!!
AHA! YOU'RE HERE!!
CLANK
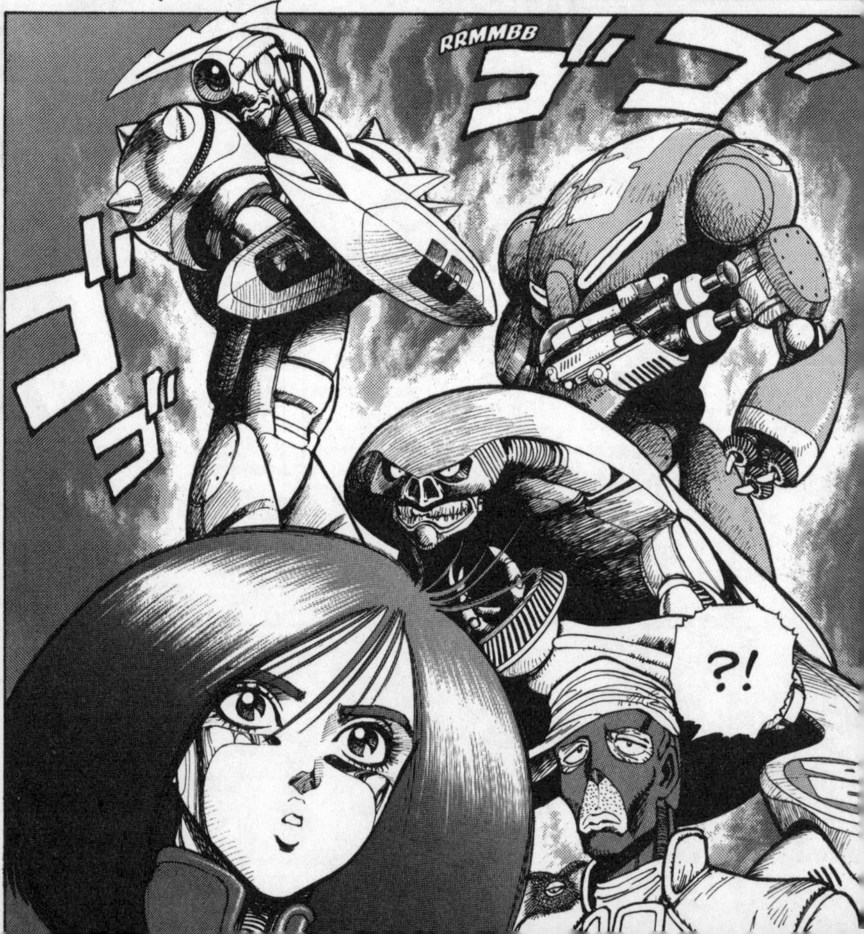
RRMMBB
?!

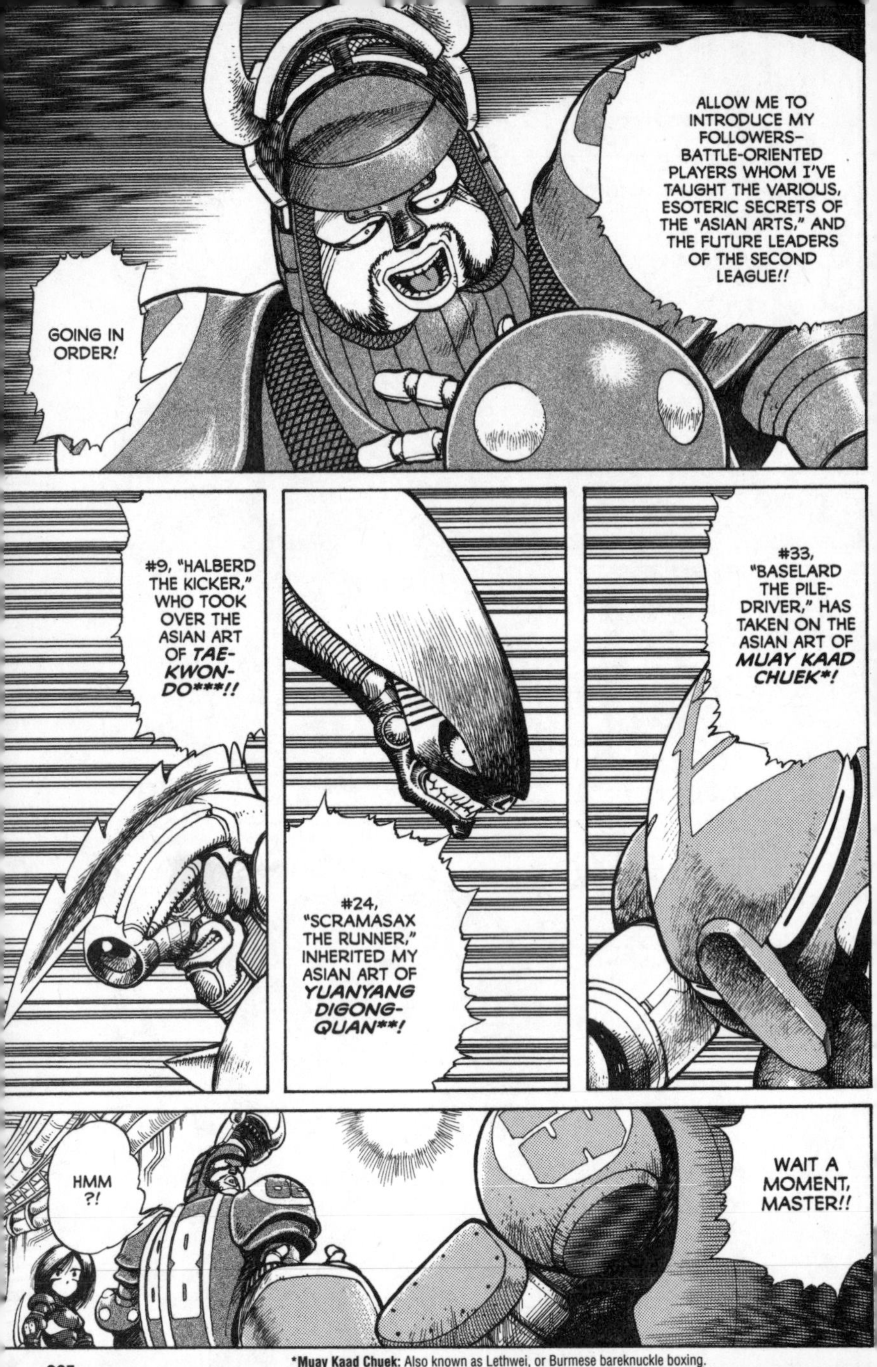
ALLOW ME TO INTRODUCE MY FOLLOWERS– BATTLE-ORIENTED PLAYERS WHOM I'VE TAUGHT THE VARIOUS, ESOTERIC SECRETS OF THE "ASIAN ARTS," AND THE FUTURE LEADERS OF THE SECOND LEAGUE!!
GOING IN ORDER!
#33, "BASELARD THE PILE-DRIVER," HAS TAKEN ON THE ASIAN ART OF *MUAY KAAD CHUEK**!
#24, "SCRAMASAX THE RUNNER," INHERITED MY ASIAN ART OF *YUANYANG DIGONG-QUAN***!
#9, "HALBERD THE KICKER," WHO TOOK OVER THE ASIAN ART OF *TAE-KWON-DO****!!
WAIT A MOMENT, MASTER!!
HMM ?!

***Muay Kaad Chuek:** Also known as Lethwei, or Burmese bareknuckle boxing.
****Yuanyang Digongquan:** A type of Chinese martial arts. Aydakatti used this in his earlier fight against Alita.
*****Taekwondo:** The traditional fighting style of Korea.

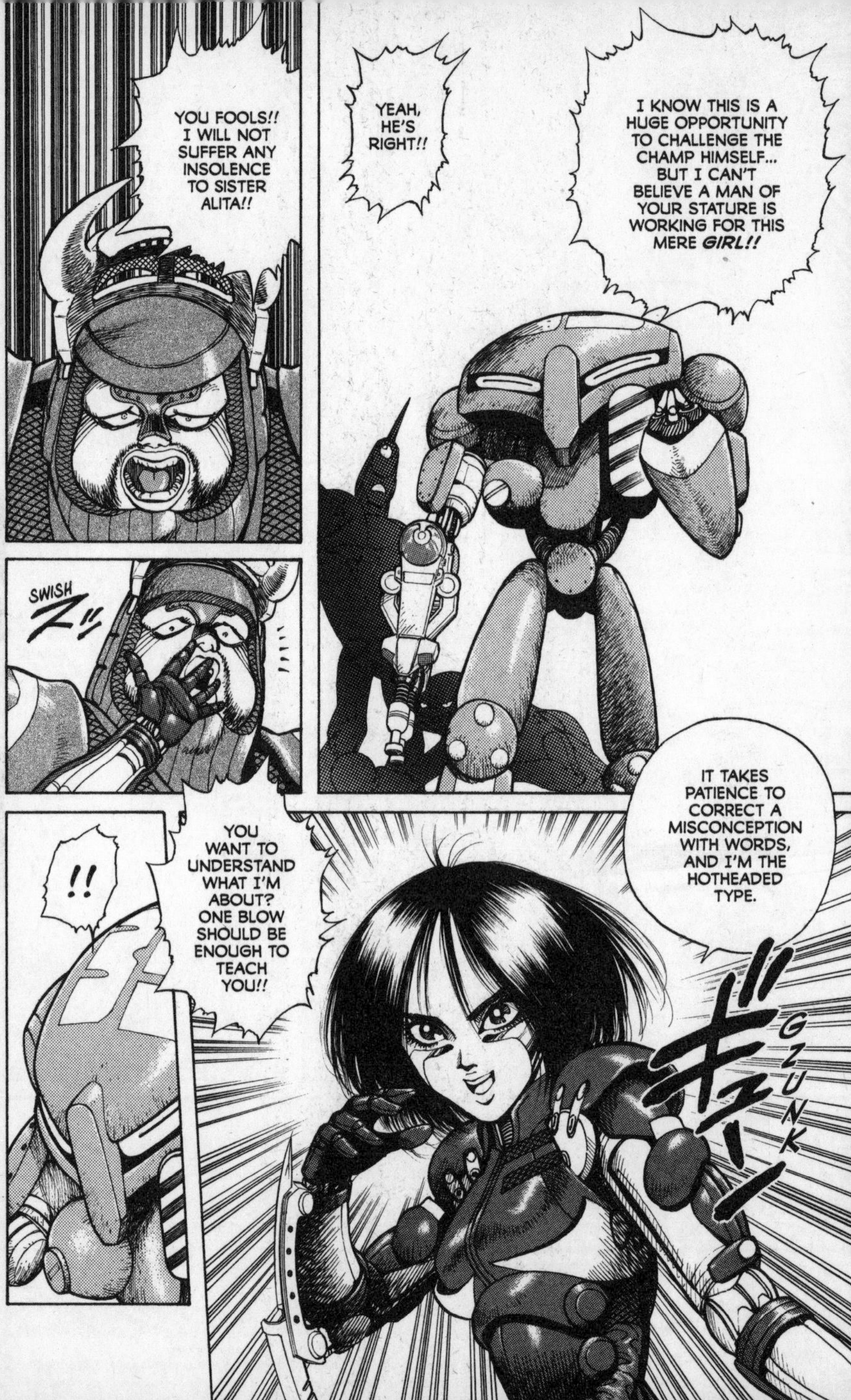
I KNOW THIS IS A HUGE OPPORTUNITY TO CHALLENGE THE CHAMP HIMSELF... BUT I CAN'T BELIEVE A MAN OF YOUR STATURE IS WORKING FOR THIS MERE *GIRL!!*
YEAH, HE'S RIGHT!!
YOU FOOLS!! I WILL NOT SUFFER ANY INSOLENCE TO SISTER ALITA!!
SWISH
IT TAKES PATIENCE TO CORRECT A MISCONCEPTION WITH WORDS, AND I'M THE HOTHEADED TYPE.
GZUNK
YOU WANT TO UNDERSTAND WHAT I'M ABOUT? ONE BLOW SHOULD BE ENOUGH TO TEACH YOU!!
!!

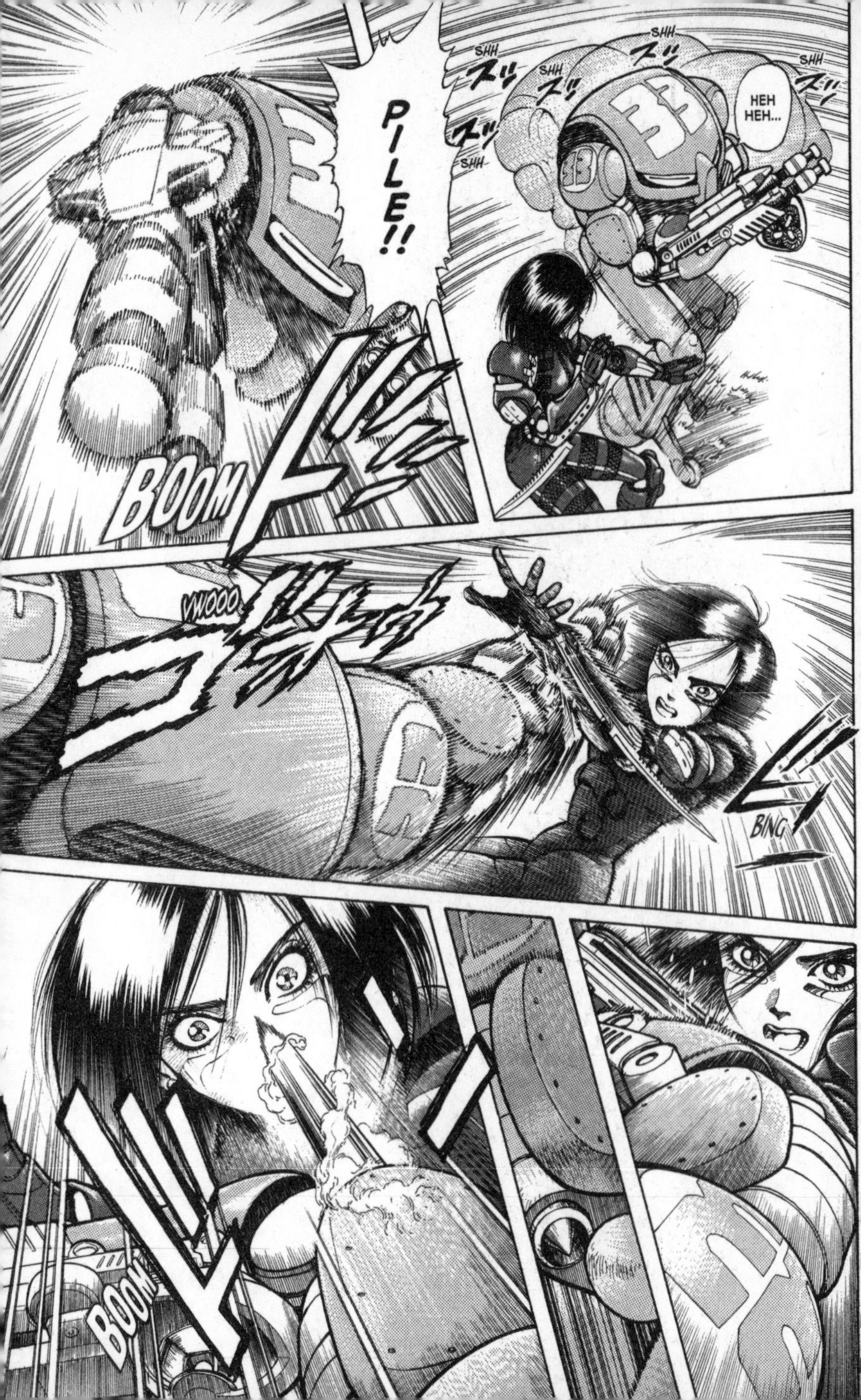
HEH HEH...
SHH
SHH
SHH
SHH
PILE!!
BOOM
BING
VWOOO
BOOM

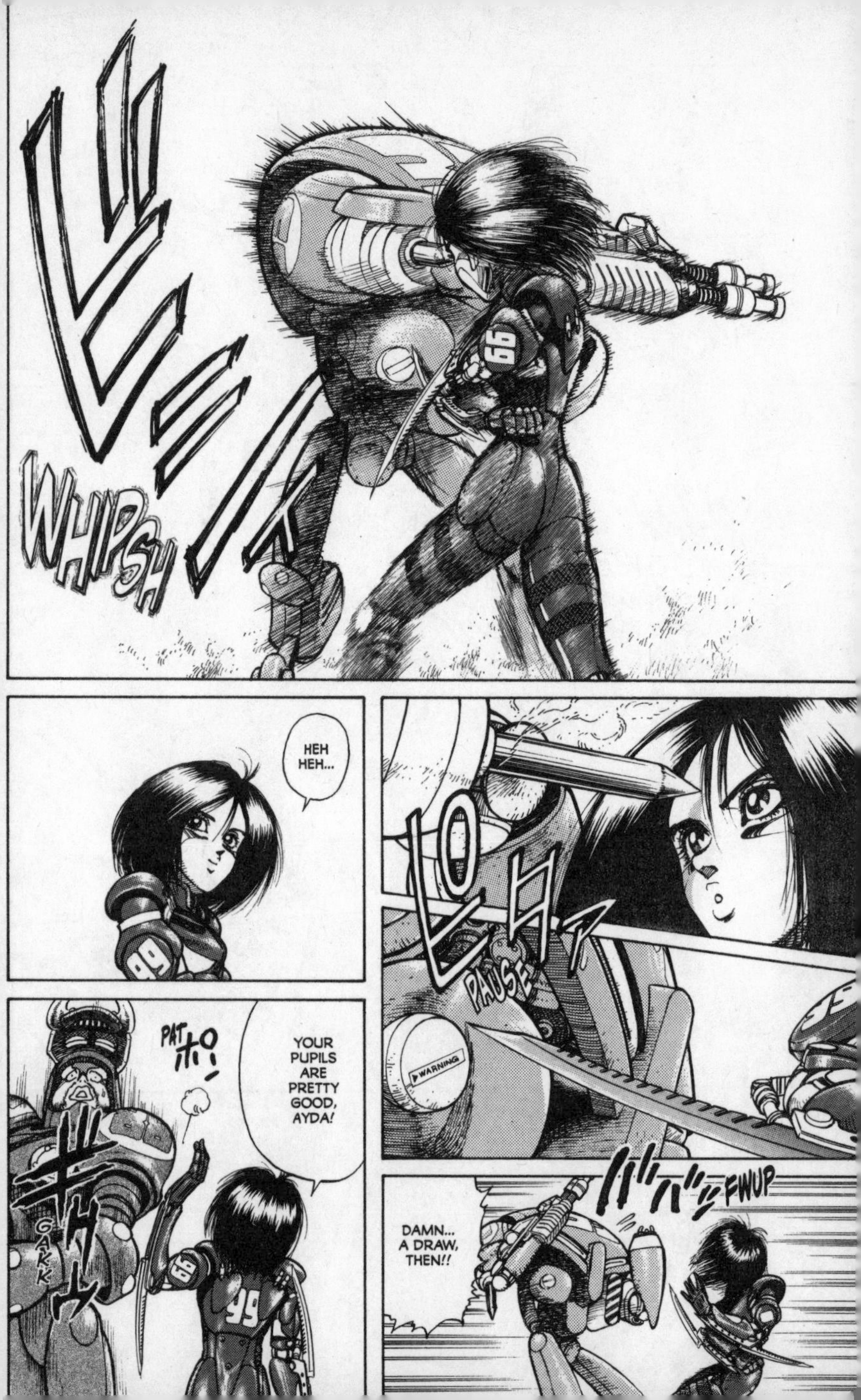
WHIPSH
PAUSE
▶WARNING
FWUP
DAMN... A DRAW, THEN!!
HEH HEH...
PAT
YOUR PUPILS ARE PRETTY GOOD, AYDA!
GAKK

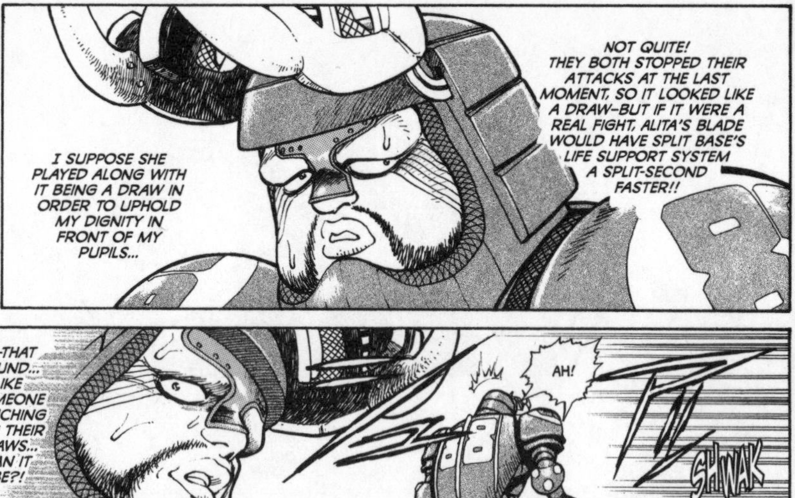
NOT QUITE! THEY BOTH STOPPED THEIR ATTACKS AT THE LAST MOMENT, SO IT LOOKED LIKE A DRAW–BUT IF IT WERE A REAL FIGHT, ALITA'S BLADE WOULD HAVE SPLIT BASE'S LIFE SUPPORT SYSTEM A SPLIT-SECOND FASTER!!
I SUPPOSE SHE PLAYED ALONG WITH IT BEING A DRAW IN ORDER TO UPHOLD MY DIGNITY IN FRONT OF MY PUPILS...
SHWAK
AH!
TH-THAT SOUND... LIKE SOMEONE TOUCHING UP* THEIR CLAWS... CAN IT BE?!

***Touching up:** To sharpen a blade.

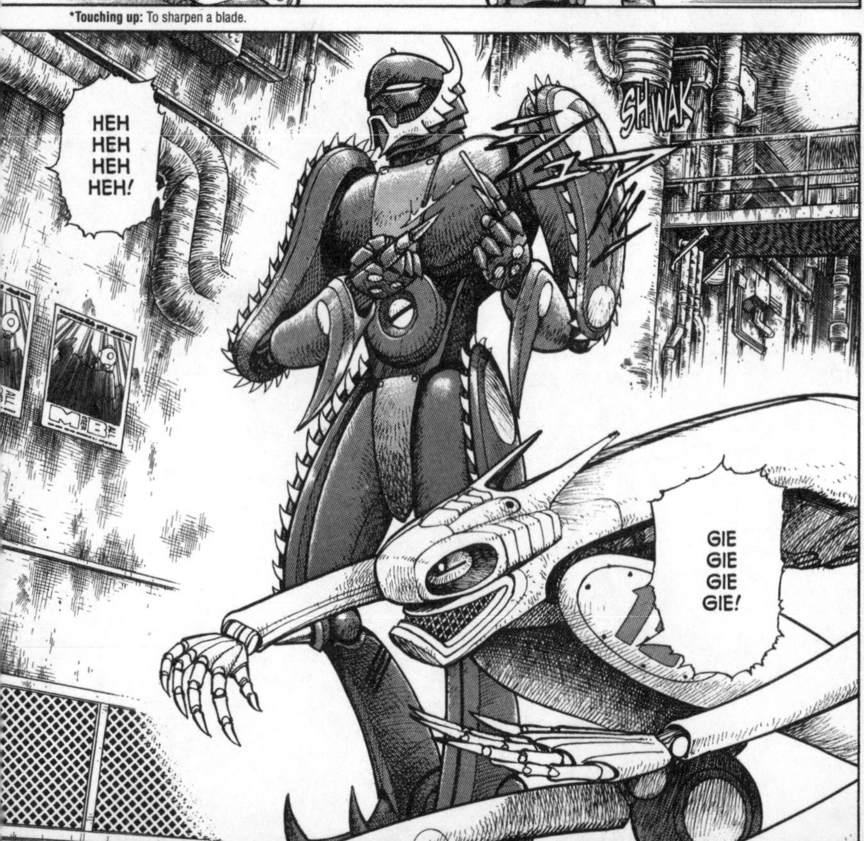
SHWAK
HEH HEH HEH HEH!
GIE GIE GIE GIE!

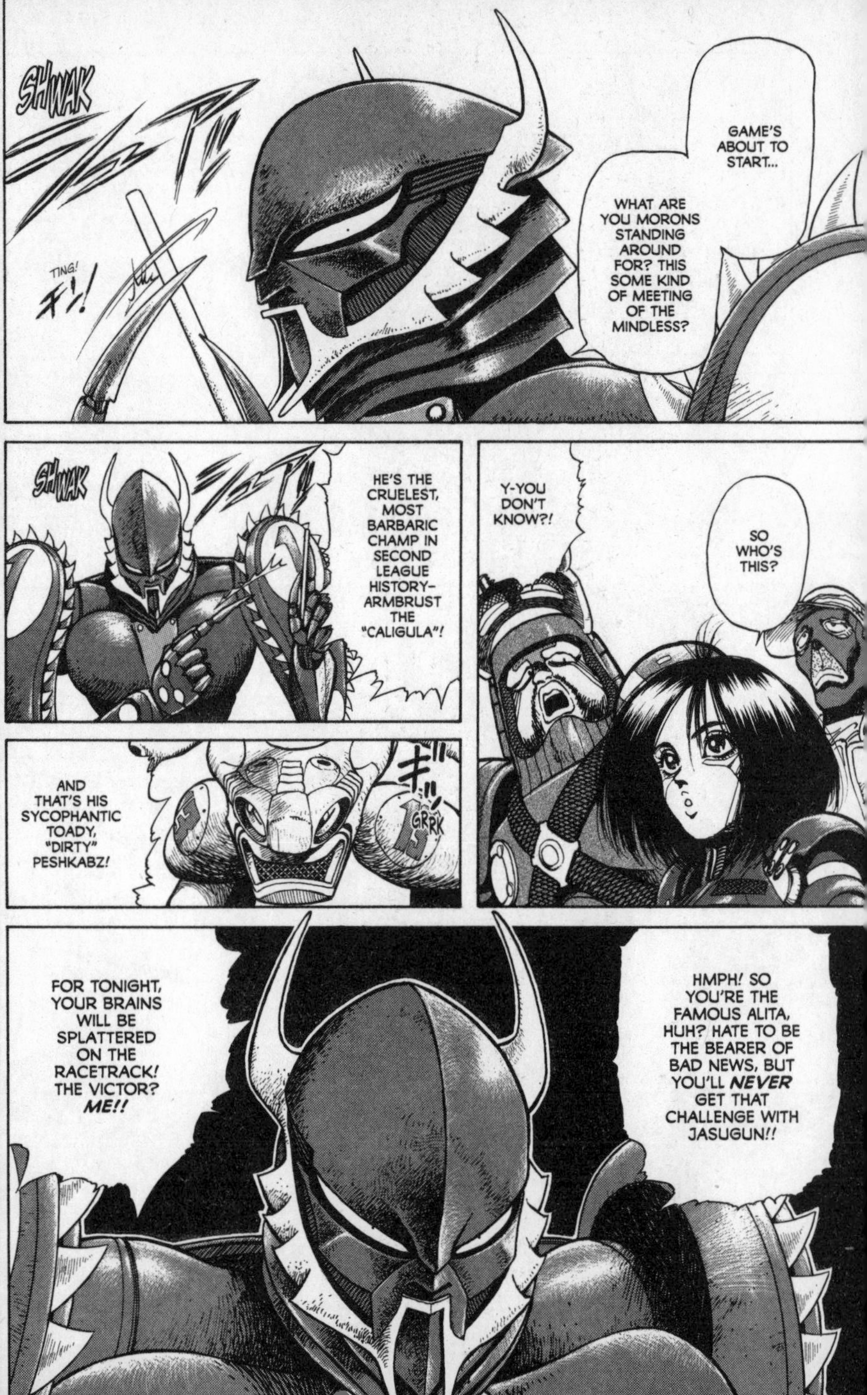
GAME'S ABOUT TO START...
WHAT ARE YOU MORONS STANDING AROUND FOR? THIS SOME KIND OF MEETING OF THE MINDLESS?
TING!
SHWAK
SO WHO'S THIS?
Y-YOU DON'T KNOW?!
HE'S THE CRUELEST, MOST BARBARIC CHAMP IN SECOND LEAGUE HISTORY– ARMBRUST THE "CALIGULA"!
SHWAK
AND THAT'S HIS SYCOPHANTIC TOADY, "DIRTY" PESHKABZ!
GRRK
HMPH! SO YOU'RE THE FAMOUS ALITA, HUH? HATE TO BE THE BEARER OF BAD NEWS, BUT YOU'LL ***NEVER*** GET THAT CHALLENGE WITH JASUGUN!!
FOR TONIGHT, YOUR BRAINS WILL BE SPLATTERED ON THE RACETRACK! THE VICTOR? ***ME!!***

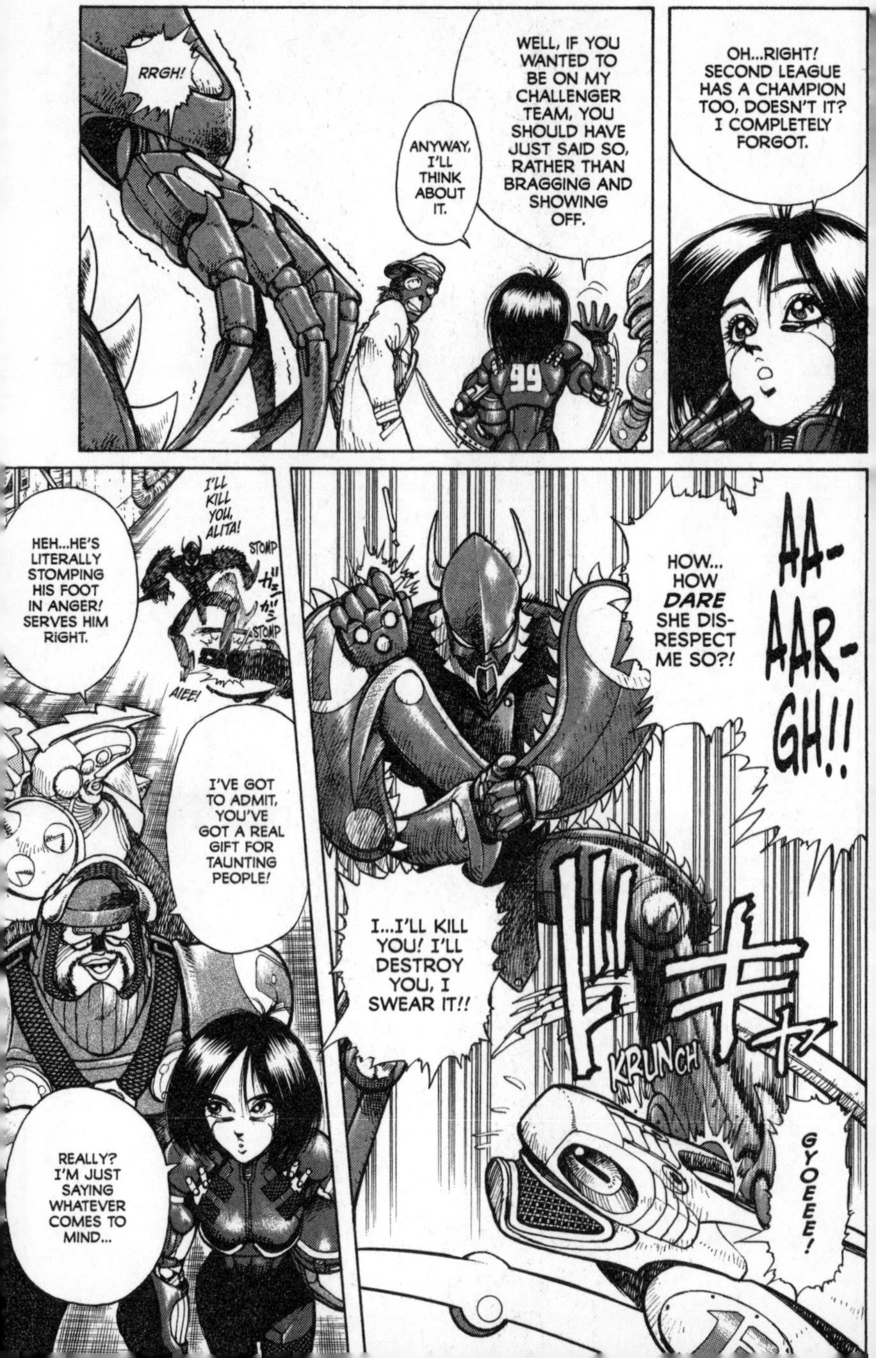
OH...RIGHT! SECOND LEAGUE HAS A CHAMPION TOO, DOESN'T IT? I COMPLETELY FORGOT.
WELL, IF YOU WANTED TO BE ON MY CHALLENGER TEAM, YOU SHOULD HAVE JUST SAID SO, RATHER THAN BRAGGING AND SHOWING OFF.
ANYWAY, I'LL THINK ABOUT IT.
RRGH!
AA-AAR-GH!!
HOW... HOW DARE SHE DIS-RESPECT ME SO?!
I...I'LL KILL YOU! I'LL DESTROY YOU, I SWEAR IT!!
KRUNCH
GYOEEE!
I'LL KILL YOU, ALITA!
STOMP
STOMP
AIEE!
HEH...HE'S LITERALLY STOMPING HIS FOOT IN ANGER! SERVES HIM RIGHT.
I'VE GOT TO ADMIT, YOU'VE GOT A REAL GIFT FOR TAUNTING PEOPLE!
REALLY? I'M JUST SAYING WHATEVER COMES TO MIND...

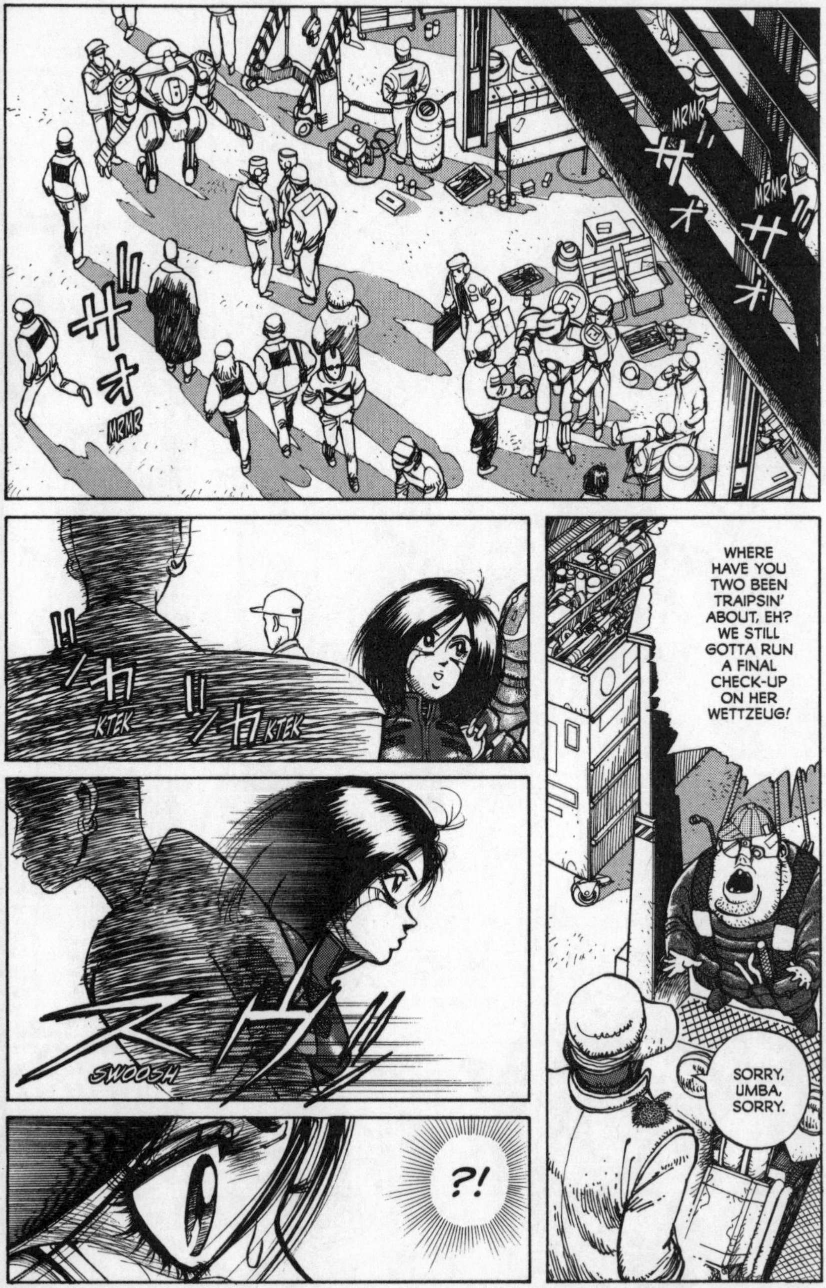
MRMR
MRMR
MRMR
WHERE HAVE YOU TWO BEEN TRAIPSIN' ABOUT, EH? WE STILL GOTTA RUN A FINAL CHECK-UP ON HER WETTZEUG!
SORRY, UMBA, SORRY.
KTEK
KTEK
SWOOSH
?!

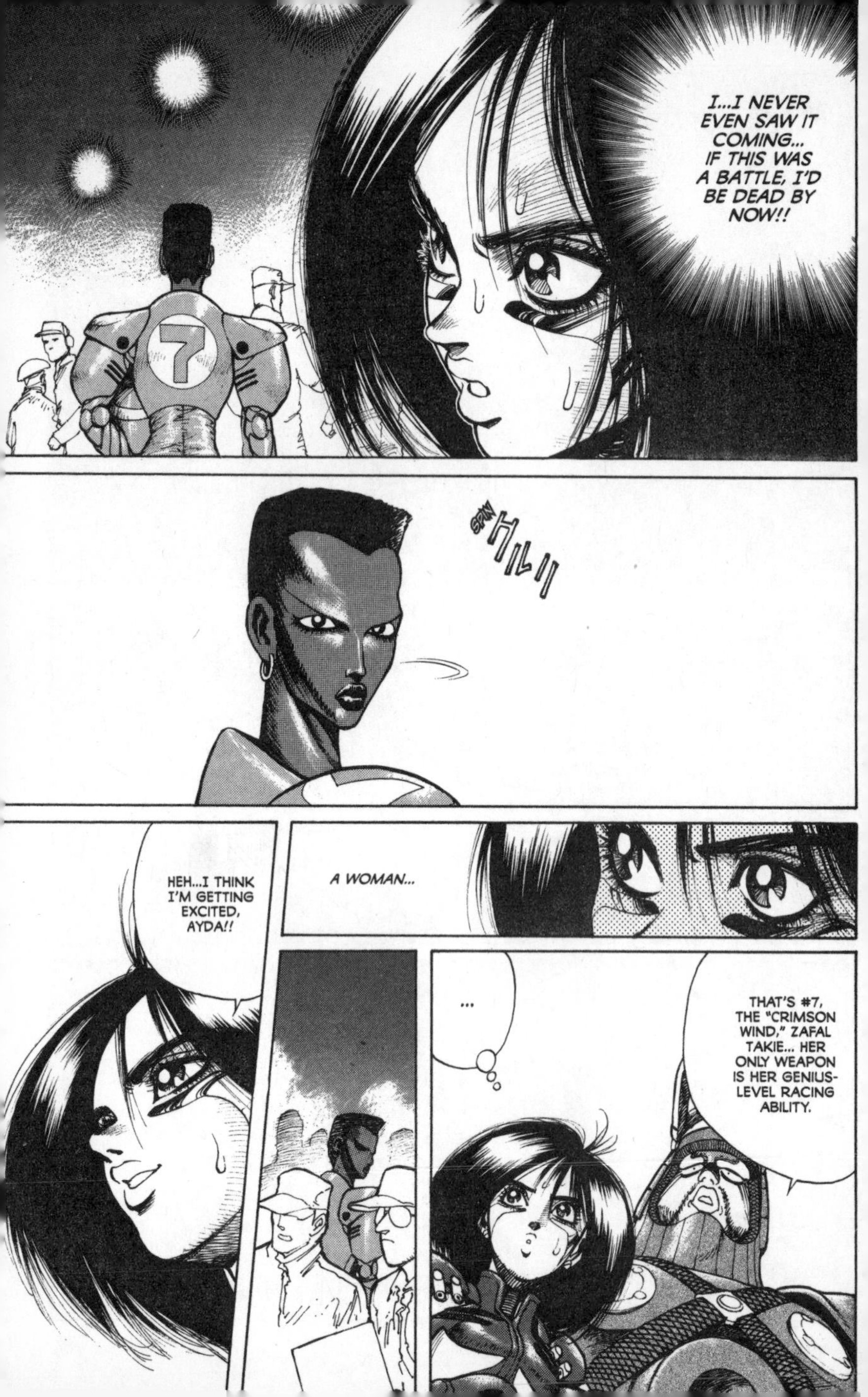
I...I NEVER EVEN SAW IT COMING... IF THIS WAS A BATTLE, I'D BE DEAD BY NOW!!
SPIN
A WOMAN...
THAT'S #7, THE "CRIMSON WIND," ZAFAL TAKIE... HER ONLY WEAPON IS HER GENIUS-LEVEL RACING ABILITY.
...
HEH...I THINK I'M GETTING EXCITED, AYDA!!

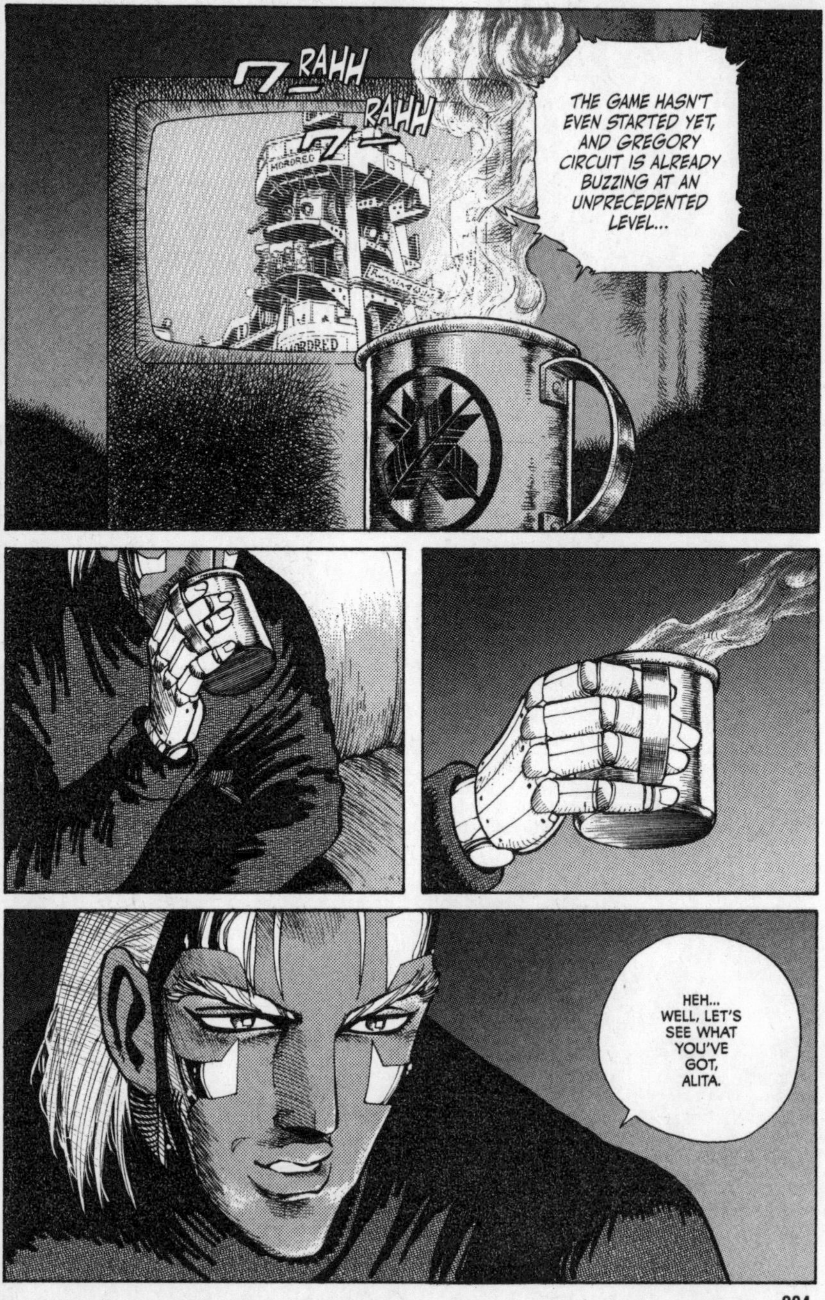
RAHH
RAHH
THE GAME HASN'T EVEN STARTED YET, AND GREGORY CIRCUIT IS ALREADY BUZZING AT AN UNPRECEDENTED LEVEL...
HEH... WELL, LET'S SEE WHAT YOU'VE GOT, ALITA.

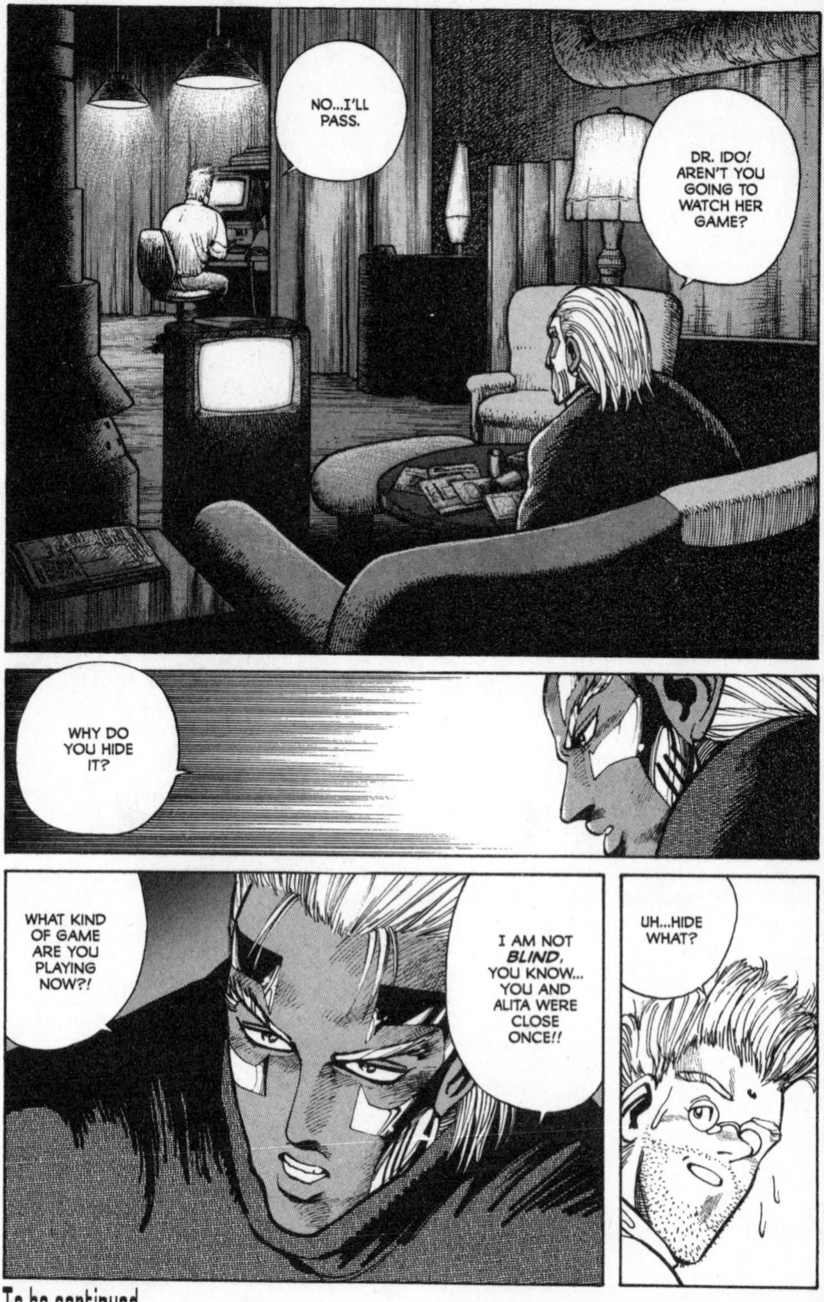
DR. IDO! AREN'T YOU GOING TO WATCH HER GAME?
NO...I'LL PASS.
WHY DO YOU HIDE IT?
UH...HIDE WHAT?
I AM NOT *BLIND*, YOU KNOW... YOU AND ALITA WERE CLOSE ONCE!!
WHAT KIND OF GAME ARE YOU PLAYING NOW?!

To be continued...

The Scrapyard and Motorball

EXPLAINED!

THE TWO BIG SOURCES OF ENTERTAINMENT TO THE DENIZENS OF THE SCRAPYARD ARE THE COLISEUM IN THE EASTERN SECTOR AND MOTORBALL IN THE WESTERN SECTOR (BY THE WAY, IDO'S BUSINESS IS ON TEMPEST STREET IN THE EASTERN SECTOR).

THE UNDERGROUND COLISEUM IS A FLASHY, SHOWY FIGHTING EVENT THAT FEATURES POWERFUL BATTLES BETWEEN GIANT CYBORGS OVER FIVE METERS TALL. IT HAS A SIMILAR APPEAL TO PRO WRESTLING IN MODERN TIMES.

UNDERGROUND
COLISEUM

MEANWHILE, MOTORBALL IS A MUCH LARGER AND MORE ELABORATE, VARIED EVENT. IT'S AKIN TO BASEBALL OR MOTOR SPORTS LIKE F1 RACING.

SEVEN BASIC RULES OF MOTORBALL

1. WHOEVER MAINTAINS POSSESSION OF THE MOTORBALL OVER A SET NUMBER OF LAPS AND REACHES THE FINISH, WINS.
2. THE TRACK IS ONE-WAY ONLY. INTENTIONAL REVERSING OF MORE THAN THREE METERS IS SUBJECT TO PENALTY.
3. STOPPING ON THE TRACK FOR MORE THAN A MINUTE IS AN AUTOMATIC DISQUALIFICATION.
4. IF THE MOTORBALL GOES OFF THE TRACK OR LOSES FUNCTIONALITY, PLAY IS TEMPORARILY HALTED UNTIL A NEW BALL IS INTRODUCED.
5. HANDHELD WEAPONS, FLYING/SHOOTING WEAPONS, SPRAYING/ RADIATING WEAPONS, AND EXPLODING WEAPONS ARE PROHIBITED.
6. FIGHTING IN THE PIT IS INSTANT DISQUALIFICATION.
7. THE BALL KEEPER CANNOT ENTER THE PIT.

*SPECIAL RULE: IF THERE ARE ONLY TWO PLAYERS IN AN ACTIVE STATE ON THE TRACK, THIS PROMPTS A "SHOWDOWN" TO ACCENTUATE THE ONE-ON-ONE COMPETITION. IN A SHOWDOWN, RULES 1 TO 4 NO LONGER APPLY.

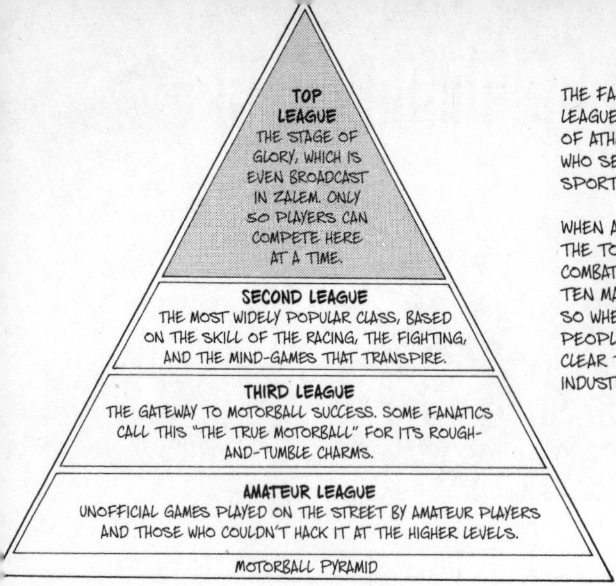
TOP LEAGUE
THE STAGE OF GLORY, WHICH IS EVEN BROADCAST IN ZALEM. ONLY 50 PLAYERS CAN COMPETE HERE AT A TIME.
SECOND LEAGUE
THE MOST WIDELY POPULAR CLASS, BASED ON THE SKILL OF THE RACING, THE FIGHTING, AND THE MIND-GAMES THAT TRANSPIRE.
THIRD LEAGUE
THE GATEWAY TO MOTORBALL SUCCESS. SOME FANATICS CALL THIS "THE TRUE MOTORBALL" FOR ITS ROUGH-AND-TUMBLE CHARMS.
AMATEUR LEAGUE
UNOFFICIAL GAMES PLAYED ON THE STREET BY AMATEUR PLAYERS AND THOSE WHO COULDN'T HACK IT AT THE HIGHER LEVELS.
MOTORBALL PYRAMID

THE FACTORY RUNS THE MOTORBALL LEAGUES, WHICH DRAW THE ATTENTION OF ATHLETES FROM FAR AND WIDE WHO SEEK GLORY UNDER THE SPORT'S BRIGHT LIGHTS.

WHEN AMATEURS ARE INCLUDED, THE TOTAL NUMBER OF MOTORBALL COMBATANTS IS VAST. THERE ARE TEN MAJOR MOTORBALL CIRCUITS, SO WHEN CONSIDERING THE VARIOUS PEOPLE WORKING AT THEM, IT'S CLEAR THAT THE SPORT IS A MAJOR INDUSTRY WITHIN THE SCRAPYARD.

THERE IS AN OFFICIAL BETTING WINDOW AT ALL THE RACE CIRCUITS. IN ADDITION TO THAT, THERE ARE MONITOR ROOMS WHERE FANS CAN CHOOSE TO EXPERIENCE THE SIGHTS COMING FROM THEIR FAVORITE PLAYER'S SENSES.

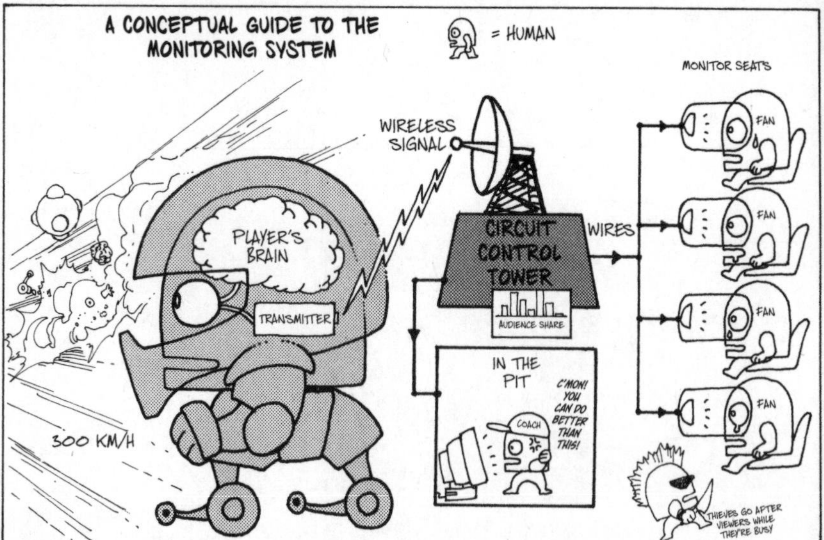
A CONCEPTUAL GUIDE TO THE MONITORING SYSTEM
= HUMAN
MONITOR SEATS
WIRELESS SIGNAL
PLAYER'S BRAIN
TRANSMITTER
CIRCUIT CONTROL TOWER
WIRES
AUDIENCE SHARE
FAN
FAN
FAN
FAN
IN THE PIT
C'MON! YOU CAN DO BETTER THAN THIS!
COACH
300 KM/H
THIEVES GO AFTER VIEWERS WHILE THEY'RE BUSY

BECAUSE THE NUMBER OF AUDIENCE MEMBERS WATCHING VIA MONITORS ACTUALLY HAS A LARGE INFLUENCE ON THE SCORING SYSTEM, PLAYERS ARE ENCOURAGED NOT JUST TO WIN RACES, BUT TO PUT ON A SHOW TO ATTRACT FANS.

YUKITO.
1992.6.8.

Substantist Thought, page 47

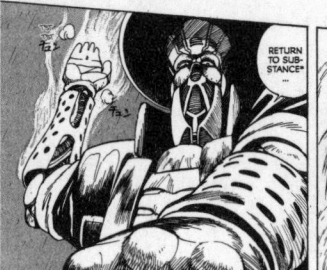

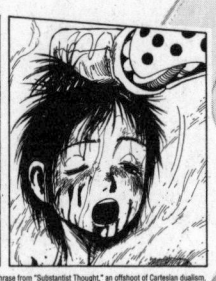

RETURN TO SUB-STANCE* ...

*Return to substance: To pass beyond the troubles of the world and return to matter. A phrase from "Substantist Thought," an offshoot of Cartesian dualism.

An in-story creation. The line of dialogue the cyborg says is a homophone of the Buddhist term *jôbutsu*, which means to become a Buddha, pass into Nirvana, or in most cases: to die. When said in this context, it would be akin to saying "Prepare to meet your maker," or "Ashes to ashes." However, Kishiro-sensei altered the *butsu* character in the word (meaning Buddha) to a different *butsu* that means "matter," or in other words, "to become matter." Cartesian dualism is the philosophy that the mind and body are separate things; when the body decays, the mind or soul remains. In short, it sounds like something a person might ordinarily say in this situation, except that the underpinning philosophy has been created specifically for the futuristic setting described in *Battle Angel Alita*.

Motorball players, page 169

TSSST
HE'LL BE FACING #49, CLAYMORE, FIFTH IN THE RANKINGS...
#87, PIHA-KAETTA, IN SEVENTH PLACE...
BWUB
BWUB
AND #6, KALASHNIKOV, AT NUMBER THREE! ALL TOP BALLERS!
GRUFFH

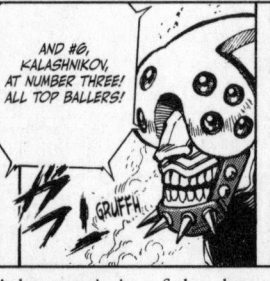

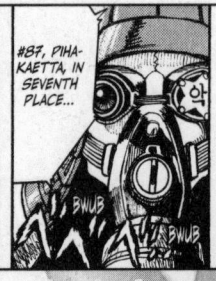

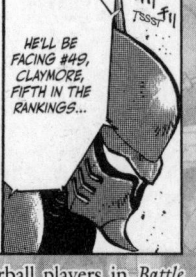

A large majority of the characters introduced as motorball players in *Battle Angel Alita* are named after weapons—either traditional bladed arms or modern guns. For instance, in this scene we meet several such characters; Claymore is a Scottish two-handed sword, Piha-kaetta is a type of Sri Lankan knife, and Kalashnikov is the name of a Russian automatic rifle maker. A little while later, Aydakatti refers to the traditional sword of the Kodava people of western India.

Maschinekratz, page 185

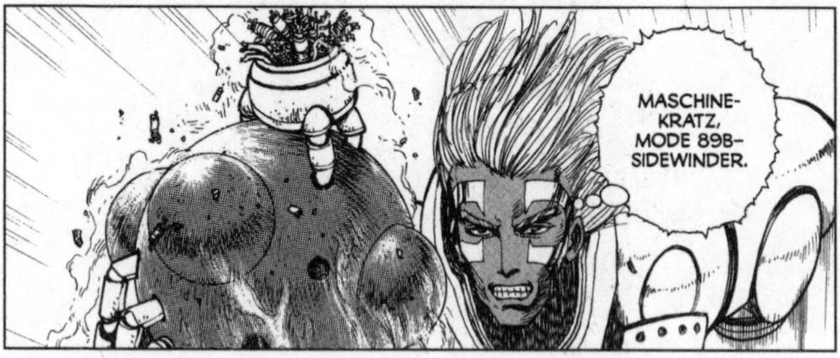
MASCHINE-KRATZ, MODE 898–SIDEWINDER.

While the story defines the name of this type of martial arts as "Machine Fist," the original German means more like "machine claw."

Hertzahauen, page 193

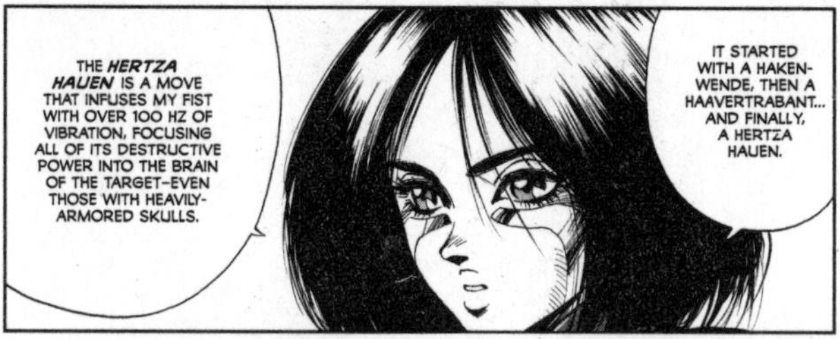
IT STARTED WITH A HAKEN-WENDE, THEN A HAAVERTRABANT... AND FINALLY, A HERTZA HAUEN.
THE ***HERTZA HAUEN*** IS A MOVE THAT INFUSES MY FIST WITH OVER 100 HZ OF VIBRATION, FOCUSING ALL OF ITS DESTRUCTIVE POWER INTO THE BRAIN OF THE TARGET–EVEN THOSE WITH HEAVILY-ARMORED SKULLS.

Many of the Panzerkunst abilities take their names from German terms, or at least, inspiration from them. They are given both descriptive kanji that describe the action, as well as the creative (phonetic) names, which might be literal in nature, or more abstract. Hakenwende means "hook turn," while Haavertrabant is intended to mean "satellite spin smash" or perhaps "orbital smash." Lastly, the kanji for Hertzahauen suggest something like "frequency splitting fist," while the given German name contains "hauen" (to beat or punch) and a resemblance to Hertz, the standard unit of frequency.

GOTCHA! ***BAIZHONG JIANTUI!!***

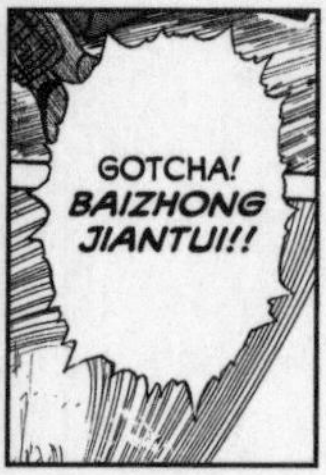

Baizhong Jiantui
page 207

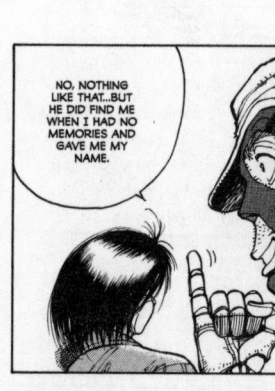

This attack's name comes from Chinese and means something like "scissor kick to reverse defeat."

SHE BLOCKED MY TIANBIAN GUAYUE! WELL, HOW ABOUT THIS ONE?!

Tianbian Guayue
page 220

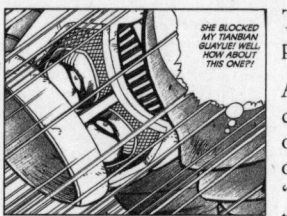

Another Chinese-derived attack name of Aydakatti's, this one sounds like "hanging moon in the heavens."

SHE CAN'T EVADE THIS SHIN KICK JUST OFF THE GROUND- QIANGUNFAN CHUAITUI!!

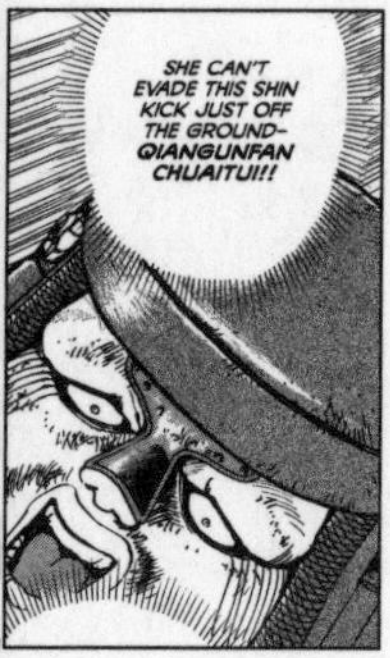

Qiangunfan Chuaitui
page 226

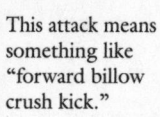

This attack means something like "forward billow crush kick."

I... I LOST... MY ***DIGONG-QUAN*** FAILED...

Digongquan
page 228

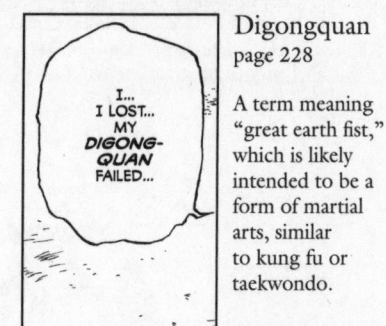

A term meaning "great earth fist," which is likely intended to be a form of martial arts, similar to kung fu or taekwondo.

SOMEONE SPECIAL? YA MAKE A PINKY PROMISE?
NO, NOTHING LIKE THAT...BUT HE DID FIND ME WHEN I HAD NO MEMORIES AND GAVE ME MY NAME.

Pinky, page 236

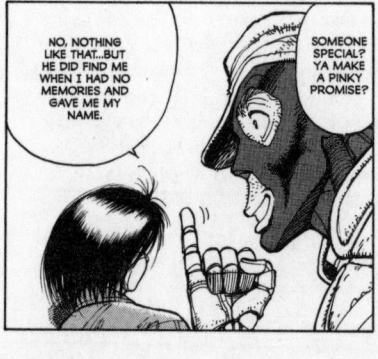

The text is adapted to get the concept across in English, but in the original Japanese, Ed just says "Is he this?" referring to his pinky finger. This is a commonly understood gesture that refers to a lover.

Ki, page 257

BORGHESIA
THE BOUT WILL LAST ONLY A MOMENT!
ONE SINGLE, DECISIVE BURST OF KI!!

A common concept in East Asian cultures. Ki (also romanized as chi or qi from Chinese) is sometimes described as spirit, breath, life force, or energy flow. It forms a vital part of many Eastern martial arts, and often appears in more fanciful, supernatural form in anime and manga as a kind of magical power. Interestingly, for his futuristic setting, Yukito Kishiro chose to replace the typical ki character (気) with a homonym ki (機) that is used in many "machine" and "mechanical" words. In a sense, it's presenting the concept of martial arts ki as it would be understood by cyborgs.

Motorball players, page 285, 290

#33, "BASELARD THE PILE-DRIVER," HAS TAKEN ON THE ASIAN ART OF *MUAY KAAD CHUEK*!*
#24, "SCRAMASAX THE RUNNER," INHERITED MY ASIAN ART OF *YUANYANG DIGONG-QUAN*!**
#9, "HALBERD THE KICKER," WHO TOOK OVER THE ASIAN ART OF *TAE-KWON-DO*!!***

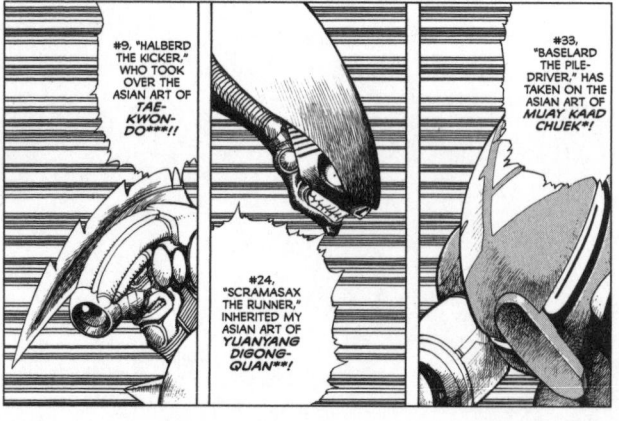

Many of the motorball competitors introduced here are named after medieval weapons. Baselard, Scramasax, and Halberd are all named after European bladed weapons, while Armbrust is the German word for the arbalest (crossbow) and Peshkabz is a kind of Persian dagger. In addition, while it's not a weapon (this is perhaps appropriate, given his character), Tiegel is the German word for a pot or crucible.